Be a Fodor's Correspondent

Share your trip with Fodor's.

Our latest guidebook to Egypt—now in full color—owes its success to travelers like you. Throughout, you'll find photographs submitted by members of Fodors.com to our "Show Us Your . . . Egypt" photo contest. On page 120 you'll find the grand prize–winning photograph by Fodors.com member Bryan Snider, who captured a perfect portrait of a camel near the Great Pyramids of Giza.

We are especially proud of this color edition. No other guide to Egypt is as up to date or has as much practical planning information, along with hundreds of color photographs and illustrated maps. We've also included "Word of Mouth" quotes from travelers who shared their experiences with others on our forums. If you're inspired and can plan a better trip because of this guide, we've done our job.

We invite you to join the travel conversation: Your opinion matters to us and to your fellow travelers. Come to Fodors.com to plan your trip, share an experience, ask a question, submit a photograph, post a review, or write a trip report. Tell our editors about your trip. They want to know what went well and how we can make this guide even better. Share your opinions at our feedback center at fodors.com/feedback, or e-mail us at editors@fodors.com with the subject line "Egypt Editor." You might find your comments published in a future Fodor's guide. We look forward to hearing from you.

Happy traveling!

Tim Jarrell, Publisher

FODOR'S EGYPT

Editor: Doug Stallings

Writers: Lindsay and Pete Bennett, Andrew Bossone, Sara Lafleur-Vetter, Cam McGrath, Chip Rosetti, Toni Salama

Production Editor: Evangelos Vasilakis
Maps & Illustrations: David Lindroth, *cartographer;* Bob Blake, Rebecca Baer, *map editors;* William Wu, *information graphics*
Design: Fabrizio La Rocca, *creative director*; Guido Caroti, Siobhan O'Hare, *art directors*; Tina Malaney, Nora Rosansky, Chie Ushio, Jessica Walsh, Ann McBride, *designers*; Melanie Marin, *senior picture editor*
Cover Photo: (Felucca sailboats, Nile River, Aswan): MIVA Stock/eStock Photo
Production Manager: Angela L. McLean

4th Edition

ISBN 978-1-4000-0519-2

ISSN 0147-8176

SPECIAL SALES

This book is available at special discounts for bulk purchases for sales promotions or premiums. Special editions, including personalized covers, excerpts of existing books, and corporate imprints, can be created in large quantities for special needs. For more information, write to Special Markets/Premium Sales, 1745 Broadway, MD 6-2, New York, New York 10019, or e-mail specialmarkets@randomhouse.com.

AN IMPORTANT TIP & AN INVITATION

Although all prices, opening times, and other details in this book are based on information supplied to us at press time, changes occur all the time in the travel world, and Fodor's cannot accept responsibility for facts that become outdated or for inadvertent errors or omissions. So **always confirm information when it matters,** especially if you're making a detour to visit a specific place. Your experiences—positive and negative—matter to us. If we have missed or misstated something, **please write to us.** We follow up on all suggestions. Contact the Egypt editor at editors@fodors.com or c/o Fodor's at 1745 Broadway, New York, NY 10019.

PRINTED IN SINGAPORE

10 9 8 7 6 5 4 3 2 1

Fodor's

EGYPT

4th Edition

Fodor's Travel Publications   New York, Toronto, London, Sydney, Auckland

www.fodors.com

CONTENTS

Fodor's Features

MAPS

ABOUT
THIS BOOK

Our Ratings

Sometimes you find terrific travel experiences and sometimes they just find you. But usually the burden is on you to select the right combination of experiences. That's where our ratings come in.

As travelers we've all discovered a place so wonderful that its worthiness is obvious. And sometimes that place is so experiential that superlatives don't do it justice: you just have to be there to know. These sights, properties, and experiences get our highest rating, **Fodor's Choice**, indicated by orange stars throughout this book.

Black stars highlight sights and properties we deem **Highly Recommended**, places that our writers, editors, and readers praise again and again for consistency and excellence.

By default, there's another category: any place we include in this book is by definition worth your time, unless we say otherwise. And we will.

Disagree with any of our choices? Care to nominate a place or suggest that we rate one more highly? Visit our feedback center at www.fodors.com/feedback.

Budget Well

Hotel and restaurant price categories from ¢ to $$$$ are defined in the opening pages of each chapter. For attractions, we always give standard adult admission fees; reductions are usually available for children, students, and senior citizens. Want to pay with plastic? **AE, D, DC, MC, V** after restaurant and hotel listings indicate if American Express, Discover, Diners Club, MasterCard, and Visa are accepted.

Restaurants

Unless we state otherwise, restaurants are open for lunch and dinner daily. We mention dress only when there's a specific requirement and reservations only when they're essential or not accepted—it's always best to book ahead.

Hotels

Hotels have private bath, phone, TV, and air-conditioning and operate on the European Plan (aka EP, meaning without meals), unless we specify that they use the Continental Plan (CP, with a Continental breakfast), Breakfast Plan (BP, with a full breakfast), or Modified American Plan (MAP, with breakfast and dinner) or are all-inclusive (including all meals and most activities). We always list facilities but not whether you'll be charged an extra fee to use them, so when pricing accommodations, find out what's included.

Listings	
★	Fodor's Choice
★	Highly recommended
⊠	Physical address
⊕	Directions or Map coordinates
⬠	Mailing address
☎	Telephone
🖷	Fax
⊕	On the Web
✑	E-mail
☜	Admission fee
☉	Open/closed times
Ⓜ	Metro stations
⊟	Credit cards

Hotels & Restaurants	
🏨	Hotel
⮡	Number of rooms
☖	Facilities
⫟⦿⫟	Meal plans
✕	Restaurant
⤬	Reservations
⚏	Dress code
⤳	Smoking
🕮	BYOB

Outdoors	
🏌	Golf
⛺	Camping

Other	
☾	Family-friendly
⇨	See also
⊠	Branch address
☞	Take note

Experience
Egypt

1

WHAT'S NEW IN EGYPT

Egyptian Museum Gets a Children's Wing

The Egyptian Museum in Cairo opened the Children's Museum with LEGO models beside original artifacts. The LEGO monuments, which previously toured the world, form a permanent collection in the museum. Explanations are simplified for children and are arguably more organized than the rest of the museum. The exhibit depicts scenes of ancient Egyptian life, such as workers chiseling stone as well as monuments like a sphinx, a colossal statue, a god, and a treasure chest. Children can sit in a workshop area to construct their own LEGO creations. The government of Denmark donated the LEGO monuments, and the collection is free.

White Taxis Hit the Streets

Clunky and dirty taxis used to be the bane of visitors and residents of Cairo. The rickety vehicles dating to the 1960s and '70s often smelled of gasoline and didn't have air-conditioning in Cairo's sweltering summers. Many of the taxis did not have doorknobs or levers to roll down the windows, and they often rattled so loudly they sounded as if they were about to fall to pieces. Moreover, they caused traffic jams when they broke down. But what was more frustrating was that the taxis had no meters, so prices ranged greatly depending on the rider. Drivers frequently argued and shouted, demanding unfair prices, particularly for foreigners. All this is disappearing with new white taxis under a plan from the government. Tens of thousands of taxi owners have turned in their old clunkers for new vehicles with metered fares. Just make sure to ask the driver to turn on the meter, and negotiate a price if you take one from the airport.

Third Airport Terminal Opens

The Cairo Airport doubled its yearly capacity of passengers to 22 million with the opening of the state-of-the-art Terminal 3. The new terminal handles all domestic flights and all international flights with state carrier EgyptAir as well as a handful of other airlines. Terminal 3 is composed of 211,000 square meters of floor area with nearly 4,000 square meters of retail space. The wings are linked together with skywalk bridges; a light-rail system is slated for construction to link it to Terminals 1 and 2. The older terminals have also received renovations, including new coffee shops and a mall. The construction of a 9-km (5½-mi) airport access road from the Cairo Ring Road has significantly reduced traffic to the area.

Luxor Monuments Saved from Water Damage

The greatest monuments in Luxor were facing severe damage from water and salt invading their structures. In a process known as capillary action, porous stones suck up underground water. The salt within the water is then attracted to the humidity in the air, forming salt crystals on the stone's surface. The salt was not only damaging the inscriptions on the faces of the stones, but also threatening to destroy the foundations of the monuments themselves. Archaeologists have been removing the salt by applying acid-free paper and clay to the stones, but the condition worsened. A series of underground pipelines were installed around the monuments on the East and West Banks, through funding by USAID, to drain ground water and save several temples from disintegration.

Sites Added to Endangered List

UNESCO's World Heritage Fund (WHF) added two sites in Egypt to its list of endangered sites: the Old Mosque of Shali Fortress in Siwa and the New Gourna Village in Luxor, raising the number of Egyptian sites to 14. The white fortress, which stands in the town center of the lush oasis in the Western Desert, is the oldest mosque in the world built of calcified soil. It was constructed in the 13th century by using an ancient technique of naturally hardening earth with salt. The New Gourna Village, also called the Hassan Fathy Village after its architect/social scientist creator, was a pioneering experiment of sustainably developed communities. In the late 1940s and early 1950s Fathy built an eco-friendly village constructed of mud brick by Aswan carpenters skilled in an ancient technique of vaulted roofs. He envisioned a village based on values of community, culture, and environment. Although the village broke ground for anthropologists and sociologists, envious government officials and the villagers themselves, who were unable to sustain the project, stifled his dreams. The village is now mixed between new concrete buildings and the crumbling remains of the original mud-brick buildings.

Temples and Tombs in Saqarra Uncovered

It's been estimated that some 80% of the world's antiquities are located in Egypt, while only 20% of Egypt's objects have been removed from the sand. The perfect example of these astounding figures can be found in the vast cemetery of Saqarra on the Giza Plateau. Temples and tombs have been discovered with regularity in the last few years as the Egyptian Supreme Council of Antiquities (SCA) has led a number of missions in the area. Discoveries include the 4,300-year-old Pyramid of Queen Sesheshet, the mother of Pharaoh Teti, the founder of ancient Egypt's 6th dynasty; a 3,000-year-old noblewoman's tomb complex; and the Pyramid of King Menkauhor, who ruled in the mid-2400s BC.

DNA Studied on Tut and Family

Archaeologists are determined to find out the story of the boy king Tutankhamun. Using what the SCA describes as the only DNA lab in the world dedicated exclusively to the study of mummies, scientists have been examining Tut and his family to figure out his origins. They discovered that, unlike previous hypotheses that the boy died on a chariot while hunting or fighting, he was likely beset by malaria and a bone disorder caused by incestuous parents. It is unknown, however, just who the parents of this frail pharaoh were. The boy reigned almost 3,350 years ago and is thought by some to be the son of the Pharaoah Akhenaton and his wife Kiya, but others say he was the son of Queen Nefertiti, whose power facilitated the ascendency of Tut. The DNA lab has studied three mummies—two female and one male—as well as two mummified fetuses found in Tut's tomb. These and another "mystery mummy" seem to be raising more questions than answers about Tut's origin.

FAQS

How expensive is Egypt?

Egypt is a poor nation, but even though inflation has driven up the cost of basic essentials, the cost of living is still significantly lower than in a Western country. Tourists and foreigners will be expected to pay more than Egyptians for many items where there are no fixed prices. In upscale establishments, alcoholic drinks are as expensive in Egypt as in big cities like New York or Paris.

Should I get a mobile phone while I'm there?

If you are traveling independently, having a local phone number will make your trip in Egypt much easier to coordinate. Most people in Cairo simply accept that half an hour is an acceptable amount of time to be late for any appointment as long as you call to let the person know you're running late. Egypt has three mobile phone providers, and making local phone calls is relatively inexpensive; you can buy an inexpensive mobile phone for about £E200. When you sign up, you simply need to fill out an application and show your passport. Your own quad-band GSM phone will probably work in Egypt as well, but unless your provider will unlock it for use with other providers, you'll pay a hefty surcharge to make calls.

Will it be hard to find an alcoholic beverage in a Muslim country?

Although Egypt is a religiously conservative society, alcohol is readily available, if you know where to look. Most free-standing bars will be filled exclusively with men; rooftop bars of modest hotels are a bit more comfortable for women. Many upscale cafés do not serve alcohol, but most restaurants do. However, drinking on the street is unacceptable. Local alcohol stores sell liquor, beer, and wine, and some locals wines are reasonably palatable. Stay away from any of the very cheap, local hard alcohol. Two liquor store chains, Drinkies and Cheers, also deliver.

Is the food safe to eat?

Food poisoning is a frequent complaint of visitors to Egypt. The origin is often from food that has not been stored and refrigerated properly. It's generally safer to stick with cooked food and fresh fruits and vegetables that can be peeled by you. If you want to try street food, chicken is a safer bet than red meat because much chicken is imported frozen while red meat is local. If you order grilled meat, make sure it is cooked thoroughly. A lot of Egyptian food is fried, so although it not a healthy option, it does increase the likelihood that you won't get sick. Western fast-food chains are abundant in Cairo and tourist spots and are a good bet. For raw vegetables and salads, if it looks like it was not cut fresh, avoid it.

Will Ramadan affect my visit?

The Muslim holy month of Ramadan, which occurs anywhere from late summer to the middle of autumn, completely changes a visit to Egypt but does not necessarily hinder visitors that much. Muslims fast from sunrise to sunset, though food service in tourist hotels continues. Many shops are closed during the day. At the breaking of the fast, or *iftar*, the streets are nearly empty of cars, a rare sight in Cairo. An Egyptian iftar starts with eating a single date and drinking lots of liquids, and is followed by a huge feast. A typical Ramadan night has loud music, bright lights, water pipes of flavored tobacco (*sheesha*), lots of tea and coffee, and late conversations with friends and family. Right before sunrise is another

feast, *sohour*, to keep the belly full while fasting. During the day, some people are more on edge from not having caffeine and cigarettes, so arguments occur with more frequency.

How conservatively should I dress?

Egypt has become increasingly conservative, particularly when it comes to women's attire. The majority of Muslim females wear the headscarf, or *higab*. That being said, outside mosques women do not have to cover their hair. Sexual harassment and staring occurs with regularity, irrespective of a woman's attire. In public, women should cover their legs and shoulders. Wear long pants, preferably light cotton to deal with the heat. Many women wear short-sleeved shirts but cover their shoulders and upper arms with a thin scarf, which can be bought on the street and in bazaar markets. Egyptian men typically wear long pants, but shorts are acceptable on the street. On beaches geared for tourists, men and women can dress how they please, but women should wear a T-shirt and shorts at public beaches.

Are the people friendly?

Egyptians are well known in the Arab world—mostly through cinema and television—for having a wonderful sense of humor. They love to joke around, and children are extremely playful. Egyptians are generally sensitive and affectionate. For an Egyptian, a smile or a kind word is greatly appreciated. You may find yourself quickly receiving an invitation to someone's home for a family meal, where you will be stuffed with more food than you can handle. Eating a large quantity in someone else's home is a sign that you enjoyed the food, which is considered a high compliment. The guest is treated like a king in Egypt. Women, however, should be wary of private invitations to men's apartments without members of his family around.

What if I don't speak Arabic?

Arabic is the first language of Egypt, but most Egyptians speak at the very least basic English and are more than happy to show off the words they know. Street signs are in both languages. Knowing a few basic phrases of Arabic can be helpful.

Is Egypt a safe country?

The Egyptian government is particularly sensitive to the global problem of terrorism. Tourist areas and groups are heavily guarded. Travelers who venture off the beaten track must have their names registered with local police, who will often accompany them to sites and villages. Violent crime, even at night, is very low in Egypt. Cairo and Alexandria are safer than just about any big city in the world. Street arguments may be common, but an actual exchange of punches is rare. For women, sexual harassment is an ongoing problem.

What do I need to know about tipping?

Tip everywhere and often. In fact, even though most people expect only a modest tip, the whole tipping issue may start to wear on your nerves as you travel around the country. It's very unusual to find an unattended public restroom, so be sure to find and keep myriad smaller £E1 notes for this purpose; these can be surprisingly difficult to find. If you're on a tour, your guide should help to supply you with smaller change.

WHAT'S WHERE

The following numbers refer to chapters.

2 Cairo. One of the world's great cosmopolitan cities for well over 1,000 years, Egypt's capital is infinite and inexhaustible. Just don't expect a city frozen in time: Cairo's current vitality is as seductive as its rich past.

3 Alexandria. Alexandria still embodies the Mediterranean side of Egypt's character: breezy, relaxed, oriented toward the sea. It is a city of cafés and late-night dinners, of horse-drawn carriages and long strolls along the Corniche. Since its founding by Alexander the Great in the 4th century BC, the city has constantly reinvented itself and remains vibrant.

4 The Nile Valley and Luxor. From the implacable nobility of its pharaonic monuments at Karnak to the towering stone walls of the Valley of the Kings, Luxor never fails to impress. Stark desert borders verdant fields and silvery palm groves, and the diamond gleam of the late-afternoon sun plays on the mighty river. Prepare yourself for a dose of pure iconography.

5 Aswan and Lake Nasser. Aswan, the gateway to Nubia, is much less hectic than either Luxor or Cairo, so it offers a chance to slow down and relax. To the south is the expansive Lake Nasser, where a cruise here is even more laid-back than one on the busier stretch of the Nile. But most people are happy with a day trip to visit the magnificent temple of Ramses II at Abu Simbel.

6 The Sinai and the Red Sea Coast. The Sinai Peninsula and the Red Sea Coast make up Egypt's holiday land, where great beaches and year-round sunshine attract thousands of vacationers. Visitors here worship at the temple of pleasure—the exceptional diving and water sports, plus great golf courses—while others seek spiritual strength at Christian monasteries hidden in the hills.

7 The Western Desert Oases. Far to the west of the Nile Valley, at the edge of the Great Sand Sea before Egypt gives way to Libya, lie a series of remote oases—refuges from an inhospitable desert landscape and fertile enclaves historically famed for their dates and olives. In the past, these oases were isolated, many days' caravan journey from civilization; today they are hot spots for desert adventures and expeditions that push us beyond the boundaries created by our modern lives.

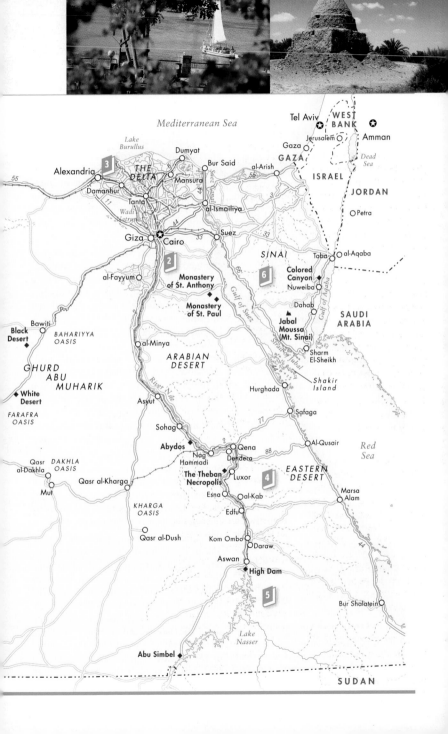

EGYPT TODAY

Politics

For almost 30 years Egypt has been steered by the strong hand of President Hosni Mubarak. Elected in 1981 in the aftermath of the assassination of Anwar El Sadat, Mubarak positioned Egypt at the heart of mainstream Middle Eastern politics, although the country's position in the region has been in decline. Egypt serves as a geographical venue for international congresses and diplomatic meetings, is the home of the Arab League, and also acts as an active intermediary in the thorny Israeli–Palestinian situation.

Mubarak has had his own domestic problems, particularly workers' protests, which have at times turned into clashes with security forces. The Muslim Brotherhood, which has branches across North Africa and the region, has been linked in its history to violent acts and presents a different kind of problem for the government. Although founded in Egypt in 1928, it is officially banned as a political party because the Constitution does not allow parties based on religion; nevertheless, its members hold a number of seats in Parliament as independents. The group has a wide footprint in the country, acting as the benefactor of social services to the poor where the state fails. Its members are also active in professional organizations. The government repeatedly cracks down on the group through arrests and raids of members' homes, though the Muslim Brotherhood still enjoys popular support, as the country has become increasingly religiously conservative and the public more disillusioned with corruption.

Regardless, Egyptians tend to have pride in their country and support President Mubarak because the country has not been in a war during his reign. His son Gamal is widely considered the next president. Gamal's aging father has groomed him as such for several years by installing him into powerful positions at the head of the ruling party. The passing of the current president leaves a number of question marks for the country's future, but Egypt will likely remain stable as long as the military retains its power.

Economics

Since the 1990s, the government has changed its former socialist policies toward free-market capitalism, selling off many of the state's assets. This has increased since 2004 under the cabinet of Prime Minister Ahmed Nazif, who has helped guide the country's strong economic growth and weather the global financial crisis. The government's policies, however, have failed to trickle down to the poor. Slums are swelling, inflation has hit staple goods and meager wages—some of the lowest in the world—have only increased in a handful of sectors.

The economy is supported by a handful of sectors: revenue from shipping on the Suez Canal, tourism, agriculture, steel, cement, and remittances from expatriate workers. Egyptian oil production has declined, but this has been balanced by the discovery of rich natural gas fields.

Four and a half million Egyptians (around 5% of the population) still work on the land and are dependent on crops like sugar cane, corn, and cotton for their livelihoods. Civil servants still earn low salaries of little more than $50 per month. The minimum wage has not been raised since the 1980s and is rarely enforced because employment rights are flaunted in the private sector. Large sections of the population are living in poverty, with some 20 million people receiving direct

subsidies for staple items. Rises in the price of such staples as bread and rice led to riots in spring 2008. While rising food prices should be helping farmers, the rising costs of fertilizer and fuel are currently eating into or surpassing increased profits.

Technology and Science

Egypt is one of the strongest countries in technology in Africa, and the government has invested heavily in the Information Communications Technology (ICT) sector. Mobile penetration is reaching complete saturation, while Internet usage has steadily risen at the same time. Egypt has become a popular destination for outsourcing, with large call centers by international firms such as Microsoft and Oracle.

The country's infrastructure, however, is in need of an update. Cairo has only two subway lines, with a third near completion, for a greater metropolitan area of about 20 million people. Farming with flood irrigation and overuse by consumers wastes the water resources. This will likely have to change, however, as the countries that share the Nile have recently signed a new agreement about the distribution of its resources.

Eight million acres of Egyptian soil are currently under agricultural production, but the country needs to keep producing more, so efficient irrigation is vital. The fertile Delta area is under threat by increased salinity, and wastewater is not cleaned properly—if at all—when used to irrigate plants. Although the Aswan High Dam still supplies electricity to the national grid, the maximum output is declining as a percentage of total needs in this energy-hungry country. In 2007, Egypt resurrected plans for a nuclear power program, and four new nuclear power plants are planned. Sustainable energy sources have been employed only slightly, with wind farms west of the Red Sea. The government heavily subsidizes oil and gas, and each time it has tried to decrease its subsidies, inflation has pushed up prices in general, while industries have lobbied hard to retain below-market prices.

Sports

Egypt boasts some of the top-ranked squash players in the world, but soccer is by far the most popular sport in Egypt, and the national team—nicknamed The Pharaohs—is currently riding the crest of popularity after winning the African Cup of Nations in 2006 and 2008. Fans were extremely disappointed when the team failed to qualify for the World Cup after a heated contest with Algeria. Domestic clubs have won several other pan-African championships, including the African Champions League Cup (12 times). Egypt's Premier League (the highest level) is composed of 16 teams with Ahly and Zamalek of Cairo as the most powerful and heated rivals, as well as Ismaily of Ismailiya, Itihad of Alexandria, and Masry of Bur Said among the most successful. Egyptian players also play in big-league European teams in England, Germany, and Holland.

For tourists, water sports and golf have become increasingly popular. The Red Sea has some of the best air in the world for kite- and windsurfing. Egypt is also a world-class destination for diving; Sharm El-Shiekh and Dahab have excellent reefs.

EGYPT
TOP ATTRACTIONS

The Great Pyramids of Giza

(A) The only one of the Seven Wonders of the Ancient World to have made it into modern times, the Great Pyramids are truly worthy of the over-abused adjective *awesome*. Everyone's got a theory as to their true purpose, but whatever you believe, your first glimpse will be truly breathtaking.

Saint Catherine's Monastery

(B) Protector of the biblical burning bush and the approach to mystical Mount Sinai, Saint Catherine's has been constantly inhabited for more than 1,600 years. Christians, Jews, and Muslims revere the pilgrimage site. The resident monks still live the simple life, but the monastery is an important reliquary for priceless art and rare ecumenical documents.

Cairo's Khan al-Khalili Bazaar

(C) The best souvenir-hunting spot in Egypt—if not the whole Middle East—this sprawling Cairo bazaar has been hawking since the late 14th century. Known locally as the Khan, Bloomingdale's it ain't. Haggling is compulsory, so go armed with a supply of cash and your sense of humor. When you're all shopped out, retreat to the El Fishawy café for a soothing glass of sweet tea.

The Karnak Temple

(D) The largest religious complex in Egypt—a kind of Vatican City meets Salt Lake City—Karnak gives up the secrets of the gods that sustained the ancient world and the human dynasties that built the ancient empire. Whether you can understand the hieroglyphs or not, you'll marvel at the sheer scale and beauty of the temple here. Stroll around aimlessly to find a less busy corner for quiet reflection.

The Valley of the Kings

(E) You may feel a little Howard Carter-ish when you enter this arid cleft on the Nile's West Bank. You'll be bowled over by the sheer beauty of the decoration and scale in some of the burial chambers of the pharaohs—true subterranean palaces, these were in effect waiting rooms for the start of the journey to the afterlife. New secrets are still giving themselves up.

The Red Sea Reefs

(F) Hundreds of miles of coral, a wealth of sea life, and crystal-clear waters put Egypt's Red Sea Coast near the top spot on the list of the planet's best dive destinations. Whether you're a novice or you want to upgrade your diving skills, you'll find excellent instructors here.

The River Nile

(G) A serene journey along the Nile in Upper Egypt drops you on the doorstep of many of the country's finest temples and monuments—though you'll also pass equally fascinating glimpses of traditional rural life along the way. Your boat is your home for the duration, at once mode of transport, hotel, restaurant, and entertainment venue. Sitting on deck watching the ruby-red sunset across the river will be one of the magical moments of your trip.

The Egyptian Antiquities Museum

(H) Nowhere else on earth brings you so close to ancient Egypt in its multifarious guises—from the mundane chores punctuating daily life to the elaborate rituals surrounding death, from the smallest item of jewelry to monumental public statuary. Bask in the glow of Tutankhamun's golden funerary mask until it moves to its fancy new digs, or come face-to-face with the mummified remains of the great Pharaoh Ramses II.

QUINTESSENTIAL EGYPT

If you want to get a sense of Egyptian culture and indulge in some of its pleasures, start by familiarizing yourself with the rituals of daily life. These are a few highlights—things you can take part in with relative ease.

Insha'Allah

Literally translated as "if Allah wills it," the phrase *Insha'Allah* invites a blessing on whatever arrangements are being made for the future—from the crops a farmer hopes to harvest when he plants in the spring to the bus ride you booked for next week. But the phrase also indicates that you're in a part of the world where arrangements can and do come unraveled, where time isn't counted to the exact second, and where life isn't as regimented as it is at home. Adapting your mindset to expect and accept the occasional delay or change in schedule will allow minor frustrations to flow over you and will certainly add to your enjoyment of the trip.

Tea

Tea oils the wheels of daily life at all levels of Egyptian society. It's served during business negotiations in executive office suites, and it warms the Bedouins as they sit around their campfires in the chill of the desert night. Egyptian tea is served strong and black; in glasses, not cups. Egyptians love it sweet. If the standard brew is not to your liking, then you may find hibiscus, mint, or apple tea to your taste. Do spend some quality time at a traditional café such as El Fishawy in Cairo's Khan al-Khalili bazaar, where sipping a glass or two over a newspaper or a game of backgammon is as authentic an experience as you can get.

Haggling

There's no such thing as a fixed price in Egyptian souks; haggling or bartering is a reality of daily life. So if you want to head home with a souvenir or two, you'll need to get with the program. First, remember that haggling isn't a battle; it's a time-honored method used to achieve a mutually suitable price. Negotiations should always be polite and good-humored. Express surprise at the vendor's first price. Smile and even chuckle. Then counter with a much lower offer. The vendor will certainly reject your bid, but he will also lower his own first offer, upon which you raise your first offer. This process continues until a compromise is reached. Tactics include acting nonchalant. Tell the vendor you've seen bigger or better at a shop around the corner—then throw in a lower counter offer. Keep smiling, and if the price isn't suitable, simply walk away. You'll live to haggle another day.

Shisha

When Egyptians get together to relax and while away a few hours with friends, they often do so over a *shisha*. This ornate, glass water pipe is ubiquitous everywhere from local street-corner joints to chic hangouts. Young and old alike enjoy it. You simply suck on the shisha's mouthpiece. This pressure draws smoke from the tobacco burning on the small bowl at the top of the pipe through a water-filled vessel and into the smoker's mouth. The regular sucking and consequent blowing of smoke out the mouth over a period of an hour or so is meant to induce a state of relaxation. Shisha tobacco is sweeter than the cigarette variety and can be flavored with fruit or molasses, but that doesn't mean it's better for your health!

IF YOU LIKE

Ancient Monuments

Egypt's long and illustrious history has left a rich legacy in sandstone and granite. Nowhere else on earth is there such a wealth of fine ancient architecture. The major monuments listed here are simply the tip of a huge iceberg.

The Great Pyramids, Giza. Tomb of the Pharaoh Khufu (Cheops), this iconic monument constituted a design and engineering revolution and was the largest manmade structure on the planet for almost 4,000 years.

The Temple Complex of Ramses II, Abu Simbel. The colossal statues of the pharaoh dominating the facade represent a high point in New Kingdom art and architecture. The relocation of the temple in the 1970s to save it from the rising waters of Lake Nasser was a triumph of engineering and of international cooperation.

Deir al-Bahri, Luxor. She didn't manage to get a tomb plot in the Valley of the Kings, but the facade of Deir el-Bahri, the mortuary temple of Queen Hatshepsut, is one of the most graceful and elegant buildings in Egypt.

Valley of the Kings, Luxor. Burial ground of Egypt's ancient rulers, the tombs of the Middle and New Kingdom pharaohs are vividly decorated, and one—that of Tutankhamun—held a vast cache of treasures interred alongside the dead king for use in the afterlife.

Religious Edifices

Faith always has played an important role in daily life in Egypt, from the temples dedicated to the earliest ancient deities to the churches of Christianity and mosques of Islam still in use today.

Karnak Temple, Luxor. For centuries the most important place of worship in Egypt was Karnak, cult temple of Amun, which is really three temples in one. It charts the development of religion and power in this ancient realm.

Philae Temple, Aswan. Dedicated to Isis, the Queen of the Gods—or at least the leading Egyptian female deity—Philae's island setting helps make it the most romantic temple in Egypt. It was also in use most recently; offerings were still being made here in the 6th century AD.

Saint Catherine's Monastery, Sinai. This 6th-century monastery at the foot of holy Mount Sinai was built to protect the site of the biblical burning bush. The site is considered holy by Christians, Jews, and Muslims, while the monastery guards a wealth of religious treasures and documents.

The Hanging Church, Cairo. Testament to the strength of the Coptic community even after the arrival of Islam, this 9th-century church is the most famous Christian place of worship in Cairo.

Mosque of Ibn Tulun, Cairo. Cairo's first mosque complex was completed in the late 9th century and is still the largest in the city. The center is also a fine example of early Islamic architecture.

The Natural World

The waters of the Nile and the sands of the desert are the two major natural combatants in the story of Egypt, but the country displays tremendous variety of topography both above and below the water.

The White Desert, the Western Desert. It seems as if icebergs have somehow been transported from the north here in Egypt's own Big Sky Country. Forests of white chalk towers fill the landscape, formed over many millennia by the action of the winds and the sand.

The Black Desert, the Western Desert. Scores of black-tipped conical hills rise from the desert floor in this uninhabited corner of the country.

Ras Mohammed National Park, Sinai. An arid cape at the top of the Sinai Peninsula on land, Ras Mohammed is one of the world's richest submarine environments and one of its top dive spots.

The Nile, the Nile Valley. The ancient Greek researcher and traveler Herodotus—the man who invented the notion of writing history—put it succinctly when he said, "Egypt is a gift of the Nile." This most mighty of rivers brings fertility and beauty to the land and was a conduit for trade and information from the dawn of civilization.

The Era of Grand Touring

The ancient history of Egypt fascinated the world in the years after the great temples were rediscovered and Champollion deciphered the hieroglyphs on the Rosetta Stone in the 1820s. This interest spawned Egypt's first tourist development—new museums, hotels, and restaurants, some of which have become tourist attractions in their own right.

Mena House Hotel, Giza. Originally the Khedive Ismail's hunting lodge in the shadow of the Great Pyramids, this mansion was built in 1869 and became a hotel early in the following century. Guests have included Franklin Roosevelt, Richard Nixon, Cecil B. DeMille, Randolph Hearst, and William Faulkner.

The Old Cataract Hotel, Aswan. Built in 1899 by Thomas Cook, the man who invented tourism in Egypt, the Cataract was *the* place to stay when the genteel arrived in Aswan on the new rail line. The setting, overlooking the boulder-strewn whitewater narrows that gives the hotel its name, couldn't be more dramatic.

Grand Trianon Café, Alexandria. The Grand Trianon has been a place to meet for afternoon tea since it opened in the 1920s. From the literary glitterati of that era to the academics of the present day, the period interior has been a party to many conversations.

The Old Winter Palace Hotel, Luxor. Completed in 1886 as a place for the royal family to spend the cooler months, the Winter Palace adds an understated elegance to Luxor waterfront.

GREAT ITINERARIES

IN THE FOOTSTEPS OF THE PHARAOHS: THE CLASSIC TOUR OF EGYPT

7 Days

This weeklong itinerary will give you the opportunity to see the most important locations relating to ancient Egypt in a limited period of time. If you are coming from the United States, remember to figure in the travel time (more than 10 hours from New York), so this tour actually requires nine full days away from home.

Cairo

1 Day. Hit the ground running with an action-packed day. In the morning visit the Egyptian Museum, whose hallowed halls have the largest collection of artifacts of the Pharaonic era. The signage in this museum is abysmal, so you'll be at an advantage if you bring along a guide (or hire one once you arrive at the museum). Have lunch, either around the museum or in Giza, on the outskirts of the city. Then, in the afternoon, explore the mysteries of the Great Pyramids and the Sphinx. (⇨ *Chapter 2, Cairo*)

Memphis, Dahshur, and Saqqara

1 Day. Take a day to see these three Old and Middle Kingdom sites from your base in Cairo. Memphis was the first capital of Egypt, but there's little grandeur left on the ground. Saqqara is famous as the site of the first pyramid ever built, while Dahshur has five pyramids, including the Red Pyramid and the Bent Pyramid. Of the three areas, Dahshur is the less visited, and if you time your visit well, you may not encounter large crowds. (⇨ *Chapter 2, Cairo*)

Abu Simbel and Aswan

1 Day. In the early morning, fly south from Cairo to Abu Simbel, site of two monumental temples commissioned by Ramses II. As you head south along the Nile, you'll be able to see Lake Nasser as it snakes through the desert south of Aswan. A round-trip shuttle bus to the Temple of Ramses II is included in the price of your airline ticket; flights are carefully timed (they leave Cairo very early, arriving at Aswan around 9:30 AM) and will allow you just a couple of hours to view the temple. The colossal statues fronting the Great Temple are among the most photographed sites in the world, and rightly so, having been rescued through a heroic effort from the rising waters of Lake Nasser in the 1970s. Then fly to Aswan, which will get you to your hotel or cruise ship around lunchtime. In the afternoon tour the unfinished obelisk, Aswan High Dam, and Philae. Return to Philae in the evening for the Sound & Light show (depending on day and languages broadcast). (⇨ *Chapter 5, Aswan and Lake Nasser*)

Kom Ombo

½ Day. The Ptolemaic Temple of Haroeris and Sobek combines the worship of two gods: the crocodile-headed Sobek, protector of the earth, and Haroeris, a hawk-headed manifestation of Horus and god of medicine. The temple was also an ancient center for medicine and healing. If you are on a cruise, you'll probably arrive at the temple around sunset; if you are visiting on a day trip from Aswan, try to go in the morning to avoid the crowds disembarking from the dozens of ships in the afternoon. (⇨ *Chapter 4, The Nile Valley and Luxor*)

Edfu

½ **Day.** The Temple of Horus was built in the Ptolemaic era and completed in only 180 years; this is the best-preserved temple on the Nile. On a cruise, you'll arrive in Edfu in the morning. You must take some kind of transportation from the cruise docks to the temple. The traditional method is by horse and carriage, but you can also take a taxi. (⇨ *Chapter 4, The Nile Valley and Luxor*)

Luxor

2 Days. You have much to see in Luxor, on both sides of the river. Split your two days into a West-Bank day and an East-Bank day. Devote Day 1 to the West Bank, spending the morning at the Valley of the Kings; have lunch, then tour Madinat Habu, the Valley of the Nobles, the Ramesseum, and the Colossi of Memnon. Tour the East Bank on Day 2, hitting the sprawling Karnak Temple in the morning, then after lunch visit Luxor Temple, returning to Karnak for the Sound & Light show in the evening. (⇨ *Chapter 4, The Nile Valley and Luxor*)

Dendera and Luxor

1 Day. One significant temple is on few one-week itineraries (and almost no cruise itineraries), but if you want to get a little off the beaten path, then book a tour to

TIPS

The least stressful way to see Upper Egypt is on a Nile cruise, which always includes shore excursions to the major temples. Allow an extra day in Luxor to visit Dendera; add a pre- or post-cruise half-day in Aswan visit to Abu Simbel.

■ Fly from Cairo to Upper Egypt and back.

■ If you choose not to do a cruise, take advantage of the many organized guided tours that allow you to make more of your time on the ground.

■ The cruise you choose will dictate the order in which you see these sights.

visit the Temple of Hathor at Dendera, 40 km (25 mi) north of Luxor, especially noted for its Greco-Roman depictions of Queen Cleopatra presenting her son and heir Caesarion to the Egyptian gods. Return to Luxor, and shop in the *souk* for souvenirs on your final afternoon. (⇨ *Chapter 4, The Nile Valley and Luxor*)

GREAT ITINERARIES

THE BEST OF EGYPT

14 to 16 Days

No visit to Egypt is complete without taking in some or all of the ancient sites in itinerary one, but you can certainly add a few important attractions to those already listed should you have a few more days in the country. More important, you can linger in each major destination for another day and experience some of the secondary sights and still have time to make a swing through the Sinai Peninsula.

Cairo

3 Days. After spending your first two days exploring ancient Cairo (as described on the 7-day itinerary), it's time to immerse yourself in the post-Pharaonic era. On Day 3 explore the Islamic city and the attractions leading off Shar'a al-Mu'iz; the streets and alleys all still brim with life. Browse in Khan al-Khalili or the Tent Maker's bazaar for souvenirs, and stop for some tea or even lunch at El Fishawy or the Naguib Mahfouz Café. Later, take a taxi to the Citadel to explore the mosques and museums here, and for wonderful views over the city. One night, have dinner in one of Cairo's floating restaurants or in one of the top hotels along the Nile. (⇨ *Chapter 2, Cairo*)

Alexandria (optional)

2 Days. If you have the time, take a side-trip to Egypt's second city, Alexandria. The Turbini or Espani trains from Cairo's main station are the fastest, taking 2½ hours to get to Alex. If you take a morning train, you can spend your first afternoon visiting the picture-perfect Fort Qait Bay in the Eastern Harbor, followed by a delicious fish dinner. The following morning, visit the Bibliotheca Alexandrina, and in the afternoon head out to Pompey's Pillar and descend into the eerie Kom al-Shoqafa catacombs, and you can fly directly to your next destination, Aswan. (⇨ *Chapter 3, Alexandria*)

Aswan and Abu Simbel

2 Days. A visit to Abu Simbel requires a half day, assuming you fly; spend the afternoon of Day 1 visiting the Philae Temple, and, if you have the time and energy, stop by the Nubian Museum for at least an hour or two either before or after your visit to Philae. On Day 2, cross to the West Bank for the Tombs of the Nobles and the Tomb of the Aga Khan. If you still have time after your tour of the major sights, make for Kitchener's Island in the center of the river to explore the Botanical Gardens, then take a felucca ride in the late afternoon to enjoy the boulder-strewn cataracts of the Nile. Don't forget to leave some time for shopping; the souks of Aswan are less frenetic than those in Luxor or Cairo. (⇨ *Chapter 5, Aswan and Lake Nasser*)

Edfu and Kom Ombo

2 Days. Don't forget these important temples between Aswan and Luxor. If you don't take a cruise, then Edfu is more easily seen on a full-day excursion from Luxor, and Kom Ombo on a half-day excursion from Aswan. (⇨ *Chapter 4, The Nile Valley and Luxor*)

Luxor, Dendera, and Abydos

4 Days. Spend two days seeing the highlights of Luxor, as outlined above. Spend a third day visiting Dendera. On your fourth day, book a trip to the Temple of Seti I at Abydos (150 km [93 mi] north of Luxor), which is dedicated to the god Osiris. Cruises rarely stop here, and relatively few tourists make this trip, but the carvings on this temple are magnificent. After visiting the Osiris Temple, you can walk over to the Temple of Ramses;

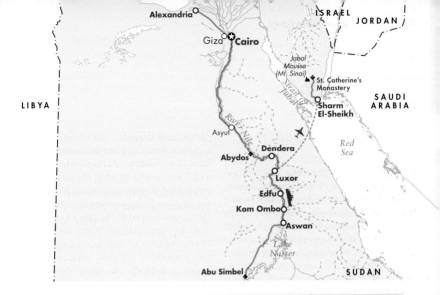

though not as well preserved as Seti I's temple, the remaining walls still have some of their vibrant color. If you are traveling by land, because of the convoy system, you'll be allowed two hours at the site before you return to Luxor for an evening stroll or carriage ride along the riverside Corniche. (⇨ Chapter 4, The Nile Valley and Luxor)

Sharm El-Sheikh

2 Days. Early on Day 1, fly into Sharm El-Sheikh. Take an afternoon tour into the Sinai by camel or quad and then cool off in your hotel's pool or at the beach. Spend Day 2 at Ras Mohammed National Park. Divers should book a dive on one of the famed sites offshore—perhaps *Thistlegorm*—while nondivers can take a snorkeling trip or glass-bottom boat ride. Nonswimmers can enjoy an overland tour of the terrestrial elements of the park with some beach time. If you plan to spend the night at the base of Mount Sinai, head there in the afternoon so you arrive before dark. (⇨ Chapter 6, The Sinai and Red Sea Coast)

Saint Catherine's Monastery and Jabal Moussa

1 Day. Stay overnight close to Saint Catherine's Monastery, which is deep in the Sinai Mountains. Wake before dawn

TIPS

■ If you are taking the classic tour and adding these extra elements into the schedule, you'll save time by flying directly to Sharm El-Sheikh from Luxor.

■ Tour companies can arrange your trip to Saint Catherine's Monastery, or you can rent a car in Sharm El-Sheikh and make your own way.

■ If you have *more* than two weeks to spend in Egypt, you may wish to add three or four days in Siwa in the Western Desert region, or perhaps visit the White Desert, Black Desert, and Farafra, a trip of four or five days (for Siwa and Farafra, see ⇨ Chapter 7, The Western Desert).

■ Return flights from Egypt to the United States generally leave in the morning.

to climb Jabal Moussa (Mount Sinai), reaching the summit just as dawn breaks. Retrace your steps and explore the monastery in the early morning. After returning to Sharm, you can fly back to Cairo that evening. (⇨ Chapter 6, The Sinai and Red Sea Coast)

GREAT ITINERARIES

THE DESERT IN DEPTH

10 Days (or 2 Months)

For the ancient Egyptians, the Western Desert was a land of mystery and dread. It was the land of the dead, which is why they built all their pyramids west of the Nile. But for many visitors, Egypt is inseparable from the desert, and a trip to these remote oases is an awe-inspiring experience. Although no longer as isolated as they once were, thanks to modern roads connecting them to Cairo and Luxor, they make a stunning contrast to the hustle and bustle of life on the Nile.

Siwa

4 Days. Close to the Libyan border, Siwa has always been only tangentially linked to Egypt: its people belong to the easternmost branch of the Amazigh (Berber) peoples who can be found across North Africa, and speak their own language, Siwi. A visit involves a 9-hour bus ride from Alexandria, or a slightly longer car ride from Cairo. On Day 2, your first full day in Siwa, stroll around Siwa town, and check out the tombs on nearby Gebel al-Mawta. That afternoon, drive out (or better yet, hire a local horse-and-cart) to Aghurmi, the ruins of the ancient Oracle of Amun, where the priests declared Alexander the Great's divinity. On Day 3, take a swim in Cleopatra's Bath and hire a guide to see the desert outside town, such as Bir Wahed spring, some Roman-era tombs, and Siwa's massive salt lake. Return to Cairo (or take the desert road to Bahariyya Oasis) on Day 4. (⇨ *Chapter 7, The Western Desert*)

Bahariyya Oasis

1 or 2 Days. Most people start their tour of the Western Desert oases in Bahariyya, about a five-hour drive from Cairo. Although its main city, Bawiti, is not particularly beautiful, it is home to a local museum showing some of the mummies from the "Valley of the Golden Mummies" uncovered nearby. There are a few other 26th-Dynasty tombs in town, and the pleasant El Beshmo spring nearby. On Day 2, you'll head to the area's real attraction, though, the Black Desert on the way to Farafra Oasis. Stark black-stoned hills cluster one after the other beside the main highway: a guide with an off-road vehicle is the best way to see them up close; you'll either spend the night in the desert or return to Bahariyya. (⇨ *Chapter 7, The Western Desert*)

Farafra Oasis

1 or 2 Days. Trips to the Black Desert often include a visit to the even more impressive White Desert as well, usually including an overnight stay among the moonscape rock formations—the nighttime stars and the breath-taking experience of sunrise in the desert alone make it worth the trip. If you are not returning the next morning to Bahariyya, you can arrange to continue ahead to Farafra Oasis, the smallest and most remote of the four oases, where you can take a look around and spend the day (and perhaps the night) before moving on. Check out the Badr Museum, in fact a gallery owned by a local sculptor, and enjoy the greenery in town, before continuing on to Dakhla. (⇨ *Chapter 7, The Western Desert*)

Dakhla Oasis

1 Day. About 260 km (160 mi) southeast of Qasr al-Farafra is the medieval town-complex of Qasr al-Dakhla, worth visiting for its Ayyubid-era mosque and carved-wood doors. Nearby is the well-preserved Roman temple Deir al-Haggar. For hotel and restaurant options, continue on another 32 km (20 mi) to Mut,

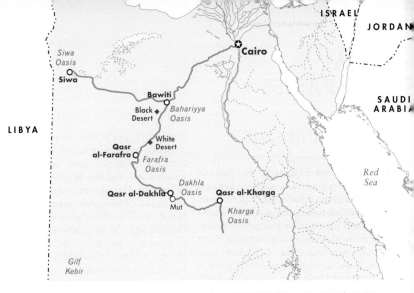

the largest town in this sprawling oasis. (⇨ *Chapter 7, The Western Desert*)

Kharga Oasis

2 Days. Although Qasr al-Kharga is the most modernized (and least interesting) of the oasis cities you'll likely be staying in, it does have some excellent ruins outside of town that may make it worth a two-night stay. Start with a visit to the New Valley Museum outside of town, and continue with a visit to al-Bagawat, possibly the oldest Christian cemetery in existence, with some painted tombs. Also within easy driving distance is the majestic Persian-built Temple of Hibis. Farther afield are the evocative ruined Roman forts Qasr al-Labeka and Ain Om al-Dabadib, as well as the fortress Deir al-Muneira. South of Kharga, in the almost separate oasis of Baris, is Qasr al-Dush, a remote Roman way-station guarding the 40 Days Road trade route. (⇨ *Chapter 7, The Western Desert*)

Gilf Kebir

12–28 Days. For true desert explorers, a safari across the Great Sand Sea to the remote Gilf Kebir plateau is the trip of a lifetime. The existence of this remote oasis was only confirmed in the early 20th century, and later hardy visitors like Ralph Bagnold and Laszlo Almasy

TIPS

Most people take organized tours of the Western Desert, and since air travel (except by chartered plane) isn't an option, most people make this trip by road.

■ Many tour companies put together trips that link Bahariyya, Farafra, Dakhla, and Kharga.

■ It's possible to do this itinerary, in reverse order, by starting out in Luxor, which is connected to Kharga Oasis by road.

■ If you travel independently, you will need to hire local guides with 4x4s for off-road desert travel; it's dangerous if you don't know the terrain.

■ Siwa Oasis is better taken as a separate trip, as is the truly remote Gilf Kebir.

(of *The English Patient* fame) frequented it. Because of the heat, travel companies generally only run trips between September and March. Because of security clearances and the limited travel window, you will need to make arrangements for this trip three to six months before you arrive in Egypt.

GREAT ITINERARIES

RED SEA AND SAND

9 Days

If diving, snorkeling, and other aquatic sports are your passion, then Egypt's Red Sea Coast and Sinai are hard to beat. Tourism development has mushroomed in the last 20 years in places like Sharm El-Sheikh and Hurghada: although they are no longer as isolated as they once were, dive sites like Giftun Island and Ras Muhammad National Park are justifiably famous and are considered some of the top dive sites in the world. There are some impressive sites on dry land as well up and down the Red Sea Coast. Depending on your own inclination and the amount of time you have, your Red Sea vacation could be the focus of your trip to Egypt, or it could be an addition to the standard Cairo–Luxor–Aswan tour.

Saint Anthony and Saint Paul Monasteries

1 Day. If you leave Cairo in the morning, take the new highway east to Ain Sukhna and head south when you hit the coast. Continue another 113 km (70 mi) to visit these two historic Coptic monasteries, which are named for the two first hermit saints. Both walled monasteries are off the main highway, in the Red Sea Mountains, and can be viewed in one afternoon. El Gouna and Hurghada are another three hours' drive south, but you'll find accommodations in Zafarana if it is too late in the day to continue. (⇨ *Chapter 6, The Sinai and Red Sea Coast*)

Hurghada

4 Days. If you didn't continue to Hurghada at the end of Day 1, then leave Zafarana in the morning and head down the coast, perhaps stopping for lunch en route in the upscale Egyptian resort town of El Gouna. If you're diving, you'll want to arrange your next day's dive that afternoon, either through your hotel's dive shop or through one of the many diving companies in town. The rest of your days can be devoted to diving, snorkeling, kite surfing, or any other activity on offer. You can break up your time diving with a day in the Red Sea Mountains: from Hurghada you can do a half day or overnight camel trip (usually accompanied by local Bedouins) into the desert, or hire a guide with a 4x4 to visit the Roman mining mountains of Mons Porphyrites (known in Arabic as Gebel Abu Dukhan) and Mons Claudianus. Spend Day 3 in the water again. On Day 4, you can take the two-hour high-speed ferry to Sharm El-Sheikh and visit Sinai, or you can continue down the coast road toward Quseir. (⇨ *Chapter 6, The Sinai and Red Sea Coast*)

Option 1: Sharm El-Sheikh and Beyond

4 Days. While the best diving in Egypt is generally along the Red Sea Coast near Hurghada and El Gouna, the best beaches are in the Sinai around Sharm. This is a place to relax and refresh at one of the big, modern resorts. But if you get tired of the beach, there are several other options. Some travelers will want to do a long day trip (or even an overnight trip) to visit Saint Catherine's Monastery at the base of Mount Sinai. Divers may want to take the drive up to ramshackle Dahab to view some different reefs. Others may want to go even further to Nuweiba or Taba and take a very long day trip to see the fabled city of Petra in Jordan. (⇨ *Chapter 6, The Sinai and Red Sea Coast*)

Option 2: Quseir and Beyond

1 Day. Once an important city for trade and transport—it was a way station for pilgrims from the Nile Valley making

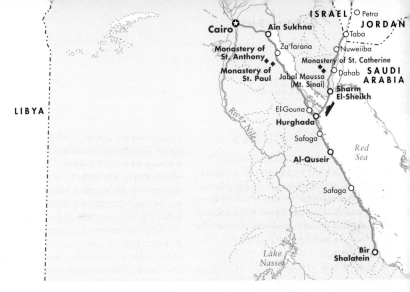

the hajj across the Red Sea to Mecca—Quseir is now a quiet city known for its recently restored fort, which provides good views of the coast. Spend the night in the architecturally sumptuous Mövenpick al-Quseir Sirena Beach, a few miles north of the town, or take a room at the more basic Quseir Hotel, a restored Ottoman-era coffee merchant's house on the waterfront. From Quseir there is a daily bus that makes the four-hour trip to Bir Shalatein. (⇨ *Chapter 6, The Sinai and Red Sea Coast*)

Option 1: Points South

3 Days. To really get away from it all, continue south from Quseir, where the coast becomes more scenic, and the feeling of isolation more tangible. You will occasionally come across the striking sight of camels owned by local Bedouins wandering among the mangroves on the beach. Mersa Alam is a favorite of Italian diving-tour companies, who fly directly to the international airport there. Another 290 km (180 mi) past Mersa Alam down the coast road, you come to Bir Shalatein, a windswept town known for its vast camel market. The town is inhabited by the Bishari, the ethnic group that inhabit the border region between Egypt and Sudan. Bir Shalatein is the farthest point on the

TIPS

This itinerary can be done leaving either from Luxor or Cairo, but if leaving from Luxor, start in Hurghada.

■ If you are short of time, you can fly directly from Cairo to Hurghada, where you can rent a car for the rest of the itinerary.

■ If you have time, you can rent a car in Cairo for the full trip; once outside the capital, traffic jams are almost nonexistent, and the coastal h ighway is in good condition.

■ If you want to begin in Sharm, then it's better to fly from Cairo; it's possible to drive, but it's a very long and difficult trip.

■ Ferries connect Hurghada with Sharm El-Sheikh if you don't want the expense of flying to Sinai.

coast accessible to non-Egyptians. Turning around, it's 563 km (350 mi) north back to Hurghada, where you can catch a plane back to Cairo. Or you can break up your trip by staying the night at Bur Safaga or Mersa Alam, or at one of the diving resorts that are popping up all along the coast. (⇨ *Chapter 6, The Sinai and Red Sea Coast*)

GREAT ITINERARIES

OTHER POSSIBILITIES

If you have more than two weeks in Egypt, you have more options to choose from and may wish to get a bit farther off the beaten path. If you base your trip on the 14-day "Best of Egypt" itinerary, you can expand it with various side trips from Cairo, Alexandria, and Aswan.

Alexandria

3 Days. If you arrive in Alex by midday, check into your hotel, and visit Fort Qayt Bay that sits out on the Eastern Harbor (on the site of the old Lighthouse of Alexandria), you can have a fish dinner in El Anfushi and return to Maydan Sa'd Zaghlul for pastries at Athineos or Trianon. The next day, take a tram or taxi out to the park at Pompey's Pillar, site of the ancient Serapeum, and then walk a few hundred yards away to the catacombs of Kom al-Shoqafa. That afternoon, you can stroll along Sharia Nabi Danyal (in ancient times, a glittering marble-paved street) and visit the Cavafy Museum, once the home of Alexandria's most famous modern poet. Stop in the historic Cecil Hotel, famous for its role in Lawrence Durrell's *Alexandria Quartet.* The next day, tour the Bibliotheca Alexandrina, including its manuscript and antiquities exhibits, perhaps with a stop at the Greco-Roman Museum and the Roman excavations at Kom al-Dikka, near the train station before returning to Cairo or moving onward. (⇨ *Chapter 3, Alexandria*)

Rosetta

1 Day. Best known as the site where the famous Rosetta Stone was found by Napoleon's soldiers, this pretty seaside town (known as Al-Rashid in Arabic) makes for a very easy half-day trip from Alexandria. It has a pleasant Corniche and plenty of fishing boats and greenery.

Its greatest attraction, however, is its cluster of handsome Ottoman-era buildings, a group of redbrick homes with wooden *mashrabiyya* windows in Rosetta's small downtown. From the Corniche, you can see the Nile—at the end of its long journey from Uganda and Ethiopia—merge into the Mediterranean. You can hire a long-distance taxi to take you the 64 km (40 mi) and back from Alex, or take a service taxi or minibus leaving from Midan al-Gomhurriya in Alexandria, across from the train station.

Port Said and Ismailiya

2 Days. Reminders of Egypt's 19th-century heyday, these two cities on the Suez Canal make a great side trip from Cairo or Alexandria. Ismailiya, the smaller of the two, is about 2½ hours by bus from Cairo, and is home to plenty of 19th-century French-style buildings, as well as the home of canal builder Ferdinand de Lesseps, and the Ismailiya Museum with its impressive Roman mosaic. For a treat, stay at the Mercure Forsan Island Ismailiya or continue on to Port Said and watch the massive cargo ships make their way through the canal. Like Ismailiya, Port Said has a colonial-era feel to it. Take the free ferry across the canal to stroll around the equally European sister city of Port Fouad. It is three hours by bus back to Cairo. (⇨ *Chapter 6, The Sinai and Red Sea Coast*)

Fayyum

2 Days. A little more than an hour away by car from the Giza Pyramids, visitors often overlook the green semioasis of Fayyum, although it's a refreshing change of pace from Cairo. Join a tour from Cairo or hire a car with a driver—you will need a car to get around. Skip the fairly unattractive modern city of Medinet Fayyum and go

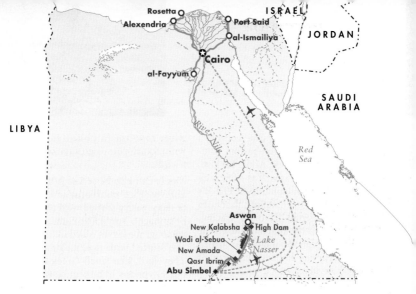

right to the Birket Qarun, which is particularly beautiful around sunset. Visit ancient sites like Kom Aushim and the Al-Hawara and Al-Lahun pyramids, and stay in the scenic village of Tunis—now known as an artists' colony and a haven for expats living in Cairo. (⇨ *Chapter 2, Cairo*)

Lake Nasser Cruise

4 Days. Traveling across the man-made Lake Nasser, south of the High Dam, is an unforgettable experience and one that few visitors make: at this writing, only four cruise ships traverse the lake. Compared with the crowds and the swarms of cruise ships plying the Luxor–Aswan route, Lake Nasser is isolated and pristine. Cruises leave from a dock south of Aswan and stop at three sites where pharaonic temples that were rescued when the lake was created were grouped together: at New Kalabsha (just south of the High Dam), at Wadi al-Sebua, and at New Amada. You'll also pass the site of Qasr Ibrim, a structure that once sat on a high cliff over the Nile, but which now sits above the much-closer waters of Lake Nasser. The sites are usually empty, the cruise ships are elegant, and the waters of the lake are a gorgeous azure color. The tour ends with Abu Simbel, approached dramatically from a distance. Arriving by

TIPS

■ From Cairo, Alexandria is most easily reached by train, a trip of only two to three hours.

■ A stop in Alexandria can also be added either before or after a trip to the Western Desert.

■ You can rent a car to drive to Ismailiya and Port Said, but a bus is usually cheaper and more convenient.

■ Overnight trips to Fayyum should be done on a tour. If you go for a day trip, a taxi will do nicely.

■ If you have done a Nile cruise before, the Lake Nasser cruise will show you new temples and allow you to skip Aswan; you may still want to return to Luxor to explore the temples of Dendera and Abydos.

boat, you can also appreciate Abu Simbel without facing the crowds that arrive with the daily convoy from Aswan. Cruises starting from Abu Simbel do the same journey in reverse in only three days. In either case, you can fly into or out of the small airport at Abu Simbel, with onward flights to Aswan or Cairo. (⇨ *Chapter 8, Nile and Lake Nasser Cruises*)

FLAVORS OF EGYPT

Egyptian cuisine reflects the country's long history of foreign occupation, combining elements of Greek, Arab, Turkish, and French cuisines—as well as a few recipes dating back to the pharaonic era. It's wholesome and tasty cooking that uses seasonal ingredients, flavorful spicing, and perhaps a bit too much oil. With the majority of Egyptians unable to afford meat, the national diet revolves around vegetable-based recipes.

Egyptian Breakfast

Fuul medammes (stewed fava beans) is a morning staple, cooked overnight and served in a bowl or on a piece of flatbread. It's packed with carbs and sits heavy in the stomach, but it will keep you charged for hours.

Bread

Bread is a staple of the Egyptian diet and served with every meal. The most common variety, *aysh baladi*, is a round flatbread made of coarse whole-wheat flour that tastes great fresh but hardens like rock within a day. *Aysh shami* is a higher-quality white-flour version. In southern Egypt, you'll also come across *aysh shamsi*, a delicious, pitalike bread made at home by allowing the dough to rise in the sun.

Appetizers

Egyptians often begin their meals with a selection of small salads and dips called *mezze*. It's a Mediterranean tradition reflected in the food, which puts a local spin on recipes shared from Morocco to Greece to Lebanon.

Cold mezze include the distinctively Middle Eastern flavors of *hummus* (a puree of chickpeas) and *tahina* (a sauce made from sesame paste). *Baba ghanoug* (a creamy dip made from a puree of smoked eggplant, tahina, and garlic) is also popular,

while *toumiya* (a potent garlic spread) will require you to go easy or lose a few friends.

Mezze can also be served hot. Watch for *kobeba* (fried meatballs) and *sambousak* (a flaky pastry stuffed with cheese, meat, or spinach). You'll also come across *wara einab* (grape leaves rolled like small cigars and stuffed with rice, meat, and spices). They look like small Greek dolmathes, but Egyptians like them served hot and drizzled with lemon juice.

Meat

Meat is a luxury for most Egyptians, but they'll gladly tuck into beef, lamb, goat, poultry, and even camel if given the chance. Pork is prohibited in Islam, so it's extremely unlikely you'll see it served anywhere.

Grill houses build their reputation on *kofta* (spiced, minced meat) and *kebab* (grilled chunks of meat), which are barbequed on skewers and served with salads and dips. The most-tender meats are those served in a slow-cooked stew known as a *tagen*, which is prepared in an earthenware pot with onions, tomatoes, and rice.

Poultry is the most affordable meat, and in even the smallest village you'll find some hole-in-the-wall serving roasted chicken. Stuffed pigeon is also popular, and quail sometimes find their way onto the menu.

Seafood

Egyptians fortunate enough to live by the sea make the most of its bounty. Alexandria is rightfully famous for its seafood, but you'll also find it on the menu in upscale Cairo restaurants and at those in the Red Sea resorts. Seafood restaurants usually price fish by weight. Pick your selection from the ice box, and it will be weighed and cooked to order. Fish can be

fried, baked, or grilled—charcoal grilling being a favorite with coastal folks. Prawns, calamari, and clams are often served with lemon, oil, and spices, or in a zesty tomato sauce.

Vegetarian Options

While vegetable-based dishes form the bulk of the average Egyptian diet, vegetarianism is not a concept they are familiar with. Meat or chicken is added to dishes whenever it can be afforded. That being said, Egypt's streets are saturated with small eateries offering cheap fuul and taamiya, and spicy eggplant sandwiches. Other safe vegetarian bets with sustenance include your basic salads: *taboula* (made from bulgar wheat, mint, parsley, tomato, an onion), *fatoush* (with pita slices), baba ghanoug, hummus, *koshary* (a stew of rice, brown lentils, macaroni, and chickpeas in a tomato sauce), and *molokhiya* (a thick garlicky soup made from corchorus leaves, popularly known as Jew's mallow).

If you are a vegetarian, be careful when choosing your dishes since not everything is as it appears to be. Beef or chicken stock creeps into the preparation of many soups and sauces. And while *bamia* (okra stew) and *mahshi* (stuffed vegetables) may appear to be vegetarian, Egyptians often prepare these dishes with meat.

Desserts

Egyptians usually end their meal with seasonal fruit, but occasions call for more tantalizing treats. Local specialties include *ruz bi-laban* (a creamy rice pudding) and *mahalabia* (cream thickened by cornstarch and topped with chopped pistachios). More elaborate still is *umm ali*, a delicious bread pudding with coconut, raisins, nuts, and cream, served hot.

Sweet, sticky pastries are served at social gatherings instead of dessert. A selection will usually include *baklawa* (filo pastry soaked in honey and nuts), *basbousa* (semolina cake with syrup and nuts), and *konafa* (angel hair filled with thick cream or chopped nuts and syrup). It's no wonder dentistry is such a popular profession here.

Tea, Coffee, and Herbal Drinks

Tea is the national beverage, served strong and sugary, with the grounds at the bottom of the glass. Order coffee, and you'll probably receive it Turkish-style—thick, black, and sweet, and served in a tiny cup. The pharaohs preferred *karkaday*, a crimson infusion made from crushed hibiscus flowers and served hot or cold. Other traditional herbal drinks still popular today include *helba* (fenugreek), *yansoon* (anise), *irfa* (cinnamon), *ganzabeel* (ginger), *nanaa* (mint), *tamr hindi* (tamarind), *kharoob* (lotus bean), *doum* (palm), and *ersous* (licorice). Many of them have proven therapeutic properties.

Alcohol

You'll find beer and wine in many tourist establishments, while upscale nightspots keep well-stocked bars. Stella is the national beer and is refreshing when served cold; Sakkara, Meister, and Heineken are also available in many places.

Egyptian wines have greatly improved in recent years. Grand Marquis and Château du Rêves are decent local reds, while Cru des Ptolémées is a passable white. Steer clear of local spirits, which are mostly cheap and potentially dangerous; one exception is *zibeeb*, which resembles ouzo and is usually drunk neat.

ISLAM IN EGYPT

Islam and Muhammad

Islam is one of the three largest (and somewhat interrelated) monotheistic religions in the world. The prophet Muhammad is believed to be descended from Ishmael, son of Abraham. Abraham also sired Isaac, who was one of the patriarchs of Judaism and Christianity. Thus, many of the prominent figures in Judaism and Christianity—Adam, Moses, and Jesus— are also revered as prophets in Islam.

Muhammad was born in Mecca on the Arabian Peninsula (near the Red Sea in present day Saudi Arabia). He became a religious figure in 610 AD when, according to Islamic tradition, while meditating in solitude he began to receive visions from the angel Gabriel. The words of these visitations became the *ayats* (verses) that were later organized into the *suras*, or chapters, of the Qur'an, the holy book of Islam. When Muhammad first began preaching the new religion he was met with hostility by pagan tribesmen, and he and his followers were forced to flee to Medina (also in Saudi Arabia).

After converting the majority of the people of Medina to Islam, Muhammad returned to Mecca and converted his hometown, and by the end of the 6th century, Islam had become the dominant religion in Arabia. In the subsequent centuries, Muslim armies swept across North Africa and into Spain, throughout the Levant and eastward into Central Asia and Persia.

Islam Today

Egypt is a predominately Muslim country. Egyptians are overwhelmingly Sunnis, with less than 1% of the population practicing Shia Islam.

In order to walk in God's grace, Muslims adhere to the Five Pillars of Islam: First, they declare that there is no God except for Allah and that Muhammad is his Prophet. Second, Muslims pray five times a day towards Mecca; visitors to Egypt will hear the commanding sound of the call to prayer—called the *azaan*— radiating from the loudspeakers of local mosques. Third, is *zakat,* or "alms giving," which means providing for the poor and less fortunate. Fourth, is fasting; Muslims fast from dusk to dawn during the holy month of Ramadan (*see below*). Fifth, all able Muslims should make the *hajj,* or the pilgrimage to Mecca, the birthplace of Muhammad at least once during their lifetime.

Visitors will encounter a range of conservative and liberal Muslims in Egypt. While mainstream Islam forbids drinking alcohol and smoking is generally frowned upon, don't be surprised when you see some cosmopolitan Egyptians enjoying a beer or a cigarette in one of Cairo's back-alley bars. Egyptian Muslims do not, however, eat pork. Although the Qur'an expressly forbids eating carnivores, pigs are held with particular disregard. Some Coptic Christians, on the other hand, have historically relied on pigs for their livelihood. In the slums of Cairo, the *Zabaleen,* or "garbage people," once used pigs to dispose of the city's waste and slaughtered the animals for food. However, during the 2009 hysteria of so-called swine flu, practically all the pigs in Egypt were killed. Most Shia Muslims consider fish, however, to be *halal,* or lawful, and it is therefore much more common.

Most Egyptian Muslim women wear the *hijab,* a head covering that conceals the hair, and a smaller number wear the *niqab,* a veil that completely covers the face except for the eyes. During the 1950s, '60s, and '70s, very few Egyptian women

wore any head covering. The hijab became increasingly popular during the 1980s when an influx of Egyptian women traveled to Saudi Arabia to work and adopted Saudi ideas and practices concerning the purification of Islam. Upon their return, Egyptian women brought these practices home, including the hijab. Veiling is also popularized by various societal factors, including the way Islam is communicated over the TV and radio. Amr Khaled, who *Time* recently called one of the world's most influential people and *New York Times Magazine* describes as the world's most influential Muslim television preacher, has been particularly influential. His sermons have contributed to the decision to take the veil for many young, educated, more-upper-class women.

Ramadan

Ramadan represents the month in which the Qur'an was revealed to the Prophet Muhammad. This celebration of the transmission of Allah's message lasts 30 days and is an especially pious time, during which Muslims abstain from eating, drinking, smoking, and sexual relations from dawn to sunset; this self-denial teaches restraint and humility and is meant to bring one closer to God. Although most people fast during this time, the elderly, sick, travelers, and children are allowed to abstain. Even some Christians take part in the fast as a sign of national unity. Those who are fasting start each day with a predawn meal called *sohour.* At sundown, the fast is broken with a meal called *iftar. This is the main meal of the day.* Many restaurants offer special iftar fixed menus during Ramadan.

In small towns, many restaurants will be closed during the day, but in most cities and tourist areas this is not an issue. Though it's understood that non-Muslims are not fasting, it's respectful to avoid eating in public (e.g., on the street or on public transportation) during Ramadan. Alcoholic beverages may not be served in some restaurants during this time. Most hotels, however, run as usual, including their bars. Traditionally, men known as *mesaharaty* used to wake people up for *sohour* singing and drumming in the streets at dawn. Although this profession no longer exists, tourists can expect a musical awakening from local amateurs trying to keep this tradition alive. The end of Ramadan is marked by a new moon and celebrated with a feast called *eid,* meaning celebration in Arabic. This is the start of *Eid-al-Fitr,* or festival of the breaking of the fast, a three-day holiday during which Muslims enjoy plentiful feasts and gift giving with their families.

Ramadan is a great time to visit Egypt. You'll usually start your days a little earlier, and some museums and tourist attractions may close an hour early, though most restaurants, parks, zoos, and cinemas remain open. Take a walk after iftar, when the streets are nearly empty and soak in the festive lights. The last week of Ramadan is an especially busy time to travel, comparable to Thanksgiving in the United States, so be sure to plan ahead if you want to travel during this time. One can also expect heightened traffic the hour before iftar as everyone is trying to reach their families. Projected dates are as follows. In 2011: Ramadan, August 1 to 30; Eid al Fitr, begins August 30. In 2012: Ramadan, July 20 to August 19; Eid al Fitr, begins August 19.

READING EGYPT

There is no shortage of books on Egypt's history, culture, and people, both by outsiders and by Egyptians themselves, so consider the following a partial list of recommended titles to read ahead of (and during) your visit. Egypt has a vibrant modern literature, and the works of many of its best writers are now available in English, including the fiction listed below.

Ancient Egypt

Alexander's Tomb: The Two-Thousand Year Obsession to Find the Lost Conqueror, by Nicholas Saunders

An investigation into the disappearance of one of the biggest tourist attractions in the ancient world: the body of Alexander the Great.

Ancient Egyptian Hieroglyphs: A Practical Guide, by Janice Kamrin

With this full-color handbook, you'll be able to decipher ancient inscriptions wherever you go, and perhaps write them yourself.

Egyptian Mythology: A Guide to the Gods, Goddesses, and Traditions of Ancient Egypt, by Geraldine Pinch

A who's who of every figure you'll encounter on temple walls and in museums.

Mountains of the Pharaohs, by Zahi Hawass.

Hawass, Egypt's top archaeologist, writes a narrative history of the 3rd- through 5th-Dynasty pharaohs who built the iconic Pyramids of Giza and Saqqara.

Red Land, Black Land: Daily Life in Ancient Egypt, by Barbara Mertz

An Egyptologist's highly readable account of the everyday existence of both pharaohs and commoners.

General History

A History of Egypt: From Earliest Times to the Present, by Jason Thompson

Historian Thompson manages to pack seven millennia of Egyptian history into one concise, very readable volume.

Cairo, The City Victorious, by Max Rodenbeck

A popular history of "the Mother of the World," from its founding as the Fatimid capital to its current status as a global megacity.

Egypt's Belle Epoque: Cairo and the Age of the Hedonists, by Trevor Mostyn

The heady years of Khedive Ismail and the building of the Suez Canal.

Two Thousand Years of Coptic Christianity, by Otto F. A. Meinardus

A comprehensive account of Egypt's Coptic heritage, its traditions, and its evolution over the centuries.

Traveler's Tales and Memoirs

Down the Nile: Alone in a Fisherman's Skiff, by Rosemary Mahoney

Peppered with historical and cultural details, Mahoney's account of rowing her way down the Nile is a fascinating narrative of a woman traveling solo in Upper Egypt.

Flaubert in Egypt: A Sensibility on Tour, by Gustave Flaubert

Translated by Francis Steegmuller. Flaubert's sometimes racy account of his 1849 sojourn in Egypt—from desert treks to his encounters with prostitutes—reconstructed from diaries and letters.

The Lost Oases, by Ahmed Hassanein Bey

A wonderful 1924 memoir by an Oxford-educated Egyptian diplomat, whose treks in the Sahara confirmed the existence of the "lost oases" of the Gilf Kebir and Jebel Uweinat—later made famous by the "English Patient" Laszlo Almasy.

The Names of Things, by Susan Brind Morrow

A lyrical memoir by an American woman about language and Egypt's natural world, including her travels to the Red Sea desert and to Sudan.

Traveling Through Egypt, by Deborah Manley and Sahar Abdel Hakim

A collection of narratives by wanderers, pilgrims, explorers, and others, across 2000 years of Egypt's history.

Out of Egypt, by Andre Aciman

Though it reveals little of life in Alexandria, the story of Aciman's Alexandrian Jewish family and their exodus from Egypt is exquisitely written.

Fiction

The Cairo Trilogy, Midaq Alley, The Thief and the Dogs, Adrift on the Nile, Karnak Café, by Naguib Mahfouz

The Nobel-winning Mahfouz is the towering figure of modern Egyptian literature, a chronicler of Cairo's back alleys and Egypt's encounter with modernity in the last century. Published in the 1950s, *The Cairo Trilogy* is a family saga that parallels the story of Egypt in the 20th century. *Midaq Alley,* another early work, offers a slice of life in a Cairo neighborhood. Three later novels—*The Thief and the Dogs, Adrift on the Nile,* and *Karnak Café*—all offer a critical look at Egypt after the 1952 Revolution.

The Map of Love, by Ahdaf Soueif

The tale of an American woman whose discovery of her great-grandmother's love letters leads her to modern Egypt, and to encounter her family's secret history.

In the Eye of the Sun, by Ahdaf Soueif

The first half of this lengthy novel gives an excellent feel for Nasser's Cairo.

The Yacoubian Building, by Alaa Al-Aswany

A phenomenal bestseller in the Arab, Al-Aswany's novel offers a cross-section of modern Egyptian life through the lives of various characters who all live in one Downtown Cairo building.

Zayni Barakat, by Gamal Al-Ghitani

Set in Mamluk Cairo just before the Ottoman invasion, this is a classic novel of political intrigue, official hypocrisy and betrayal

The Open Door, by Latifa Al-Zayyat

Originally published in 1960, this autobiographical novel about a young woman's education marks an early example of Arabic feminist fiction.

Being Abbas el Abd, by Ahmed Alaidy

A funny, mordant, *Fight Club*–inspired novel—and a snapshot of Cairo's cell-phone-addicted, distracted younger generation.

Beer in the Snooker Club, by Waguih Ghali

This quirky, hard-to-find, semi-autobiographical novel subtly mocks all the sacred cows of the revolution.

The Alexandria Quartet, by Lawrence Durrell

A classic of 20th-century literature, these four interlocking novels—*Justine, Balthazar, Mountolive,* and *Clea*—evoke the decadent, cosmopolitan world of pre-war Alexandria.

EGYPTIAN CINEMA

Imagine Egypt. All right, now try to do it without your mind's eye calling up Angela Lansbury ogling Karnak Temple's ram-headed sphinxes in *Death on the Nile*, without Elizabeth Taylor enthroned with crook and flail in *Cleopatra*, without Brendan Fraser fending off a host of slimy foes—not to mention bugs—in *The Mummy*. It's OK if you can't. Those images have been around long enough to be part of our modern mythology of the place. But to really embrace a trip to Egypt, it's good to expand your cinematic horizons. Here's a cross-section of Egyptian movies that will help you better understand how Egyptians imagine themselves.

Destiny (Massir): This anti-fundamentalist musical historical drama—if you can imagine such a thing—by the late Youssef Chahine, one of Egypt's best-known directors, was one reason he was given a lifetime achievement award at Cannes, though the DVD from France is hard to find. Better still is *Cairo Station (Bab al-Hadid)* from 1958, an affecting story about people who sell drinks and newspapers on the platform of the main train station.

The Genie Lady (Afrita Hanem): Poor crooner Asfour (Farid al-Atrash) has just about given up hope of marrying the girl of his dreams; she's the boss's daughter at the theater where he sings. He thinks all his problems are solved when he finds a magic lamp. But the lamp's beautiful genie (Samia Gamal) has romantic ideas of her own. This lighthearted 1949 classic is a showpiece for Atrash's renowned musical talents—he was one of the most respected singers and oud players in the Arabic-speaking world—and Gamal's graceful mastery of dance. And, like so many Egyptian films of its era, it delivers a feel-good moral to the story.

Hassan and Marcus: Unbeknownst to each other, a Coptic priest (Adel Imam) and an Islamic shopkeeper (Omar Sharif) must assume new identities in a witness-protection program. Each man, along with his family, is obliged to hide under the guise of the other religion. When the son of one man asks to marry the daughter of the other, their cover is blown, threatening the lives of both families and, judging from the ensuing neighborhood uproar, Egyptian society at large. Directed by Ramy Imam, this 2008 film drew fire from religious quarters for blasphemy.

Hello America ('Alo Amreeka): Down on his luck, Egyptian everyman Bekheet (Adel Imam) wins the immigration lottery and is off to New York City, where everything that can go wrong, does. This 1998 comedy suffers from poor production quality; but its insightful, often poignant, contrasts between Egyptian and American moral values make it a must-see.

The Yacoubian Building (Omaret Yakobean): Half a century after the military coup that ousted the Egyptian monarchy, Cairo is mired in corruption and decline. Based on the novel by Alaa Al Aswany, the 2006 film tackles greed, deceit, economic prejudice, sexual hypocrisy, religious extremism, the illegal drug trade, and government corruption all at once, through the lives of those who reside in a single Cairo apartment building. Marwan Hamed directed the all-star cast in what is said to be Egypt's highest-budgeted film, and one of its most controversial.

WHEN TO GO

It's best to visit Egypt in the cooler season, which begins in November and ends in March. Summers can be oppressive, especially in Cairo, Luxor, and Aswan. And forget about going to the desert oases in summer.

Generally speaking, it doesn't rain in Egypt. In cooler months, Alexandria and the Mediterranean coast can get cloudy, and a few wet days aren't uncommon. Considering how arid and relentlessly sunny the rest of the country is, these brief wet conditions can be a welcome relief.

Weather along the Mediterranean or Red Sea coasts remains temperate throughout the year. The water does get a bit cold between December and March, but never frigid.

Climate

Egypt's climate is characterized by hot and dry summers in most of the country. The areas that are most humid are the Delta and along the Mediterranean coast. Summer lasts from the end of April until the beginning of October. Spring is very short, if not nonexistent. Winter is mild, but nights do get cool.

The most important time of year to keep in mind is the 50 days of the *khamaseen*. Between the end of March and mid-May, dust storms whip up occasionally and blot out the sky.

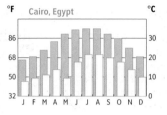

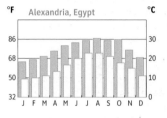

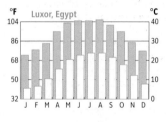

CULTURE WRITTEN ON THE TEMPLE WALLS

EGYPTIAN MYTHOLOGY AND HIEROGLYPHICS

By Andrew Bossone

Religion and mythology played a central role in all facets and institutions of society in ancient Egypt, guiding the lives of the pharaohs as well as their subjects. But Egyptian religion was certainly not monolithic; and the beliefs and practices of the state and those of the people often differed.

Belief in life after death was central to Egyptian religion, and most Egyptians believed that an honorable life was the key to a rewarding afterlife. Egyptians placed considerable weight on cardinal virtues such as self-control and restraint. Day-to-day life emphasized family solidarity and the community. Egyptians believed in taking care of those less fortunate in their society. Good deeds would be rewarded, and as long as an Egyptian took the proper measures at burial and passed a final judgment, he or she would live on in eternity. However, at times Egyptians complained of the injustice of an untimely death or helplessness at death, leading to a conviction that humans should make the most of life when possible.

The gods were primarily viewed as the keepers of cosmic order, and the kings were the preservers of Maat, or harmony. This order could not be changed, giving the gods the power to affect circumstances with their will, just as one might describe a fateful event. Egyptians determined that will through communications from the gods, often in the form of dreams. They examined the divine order by looking to the past and studying ancient texts.

Egyptians honored the gods frequently through festivals. They celebrated local patron deities, the state gods, as well as the god of one's particular cult. They retold many stories such as creation myths and had a complicated set of rituals and beliefs attached to the afterlife. Private citizens practiced at home and in small community shrines as well, making requests such as fertility and protection, employing any number of magic spells and incantations, although these would not have been considered distinct from religion at-large.

Mural of Anubis in the Tomb of Horemheb, Valley of the Kings

IMPORTANT EGYPTIAN GODS AND GODDESSES

The Egyptian state religion taught that the gods communicated with Egyptians through the king, who was bound to maintain the cults of the gods and keep their support. Temple decorations always showed the king performing daily rituals, although priests actually performed this duty. Egyptian religion had a large number of deities and demons and was sometimes contradictory. The gods were responsible for maintaining the divine, cosmic order of the universe.

Statue of Horus in Edfu Temple

RA

The Sun, the cycle of death, and rebirth

Arguably the most important deity, his cult center dates back to the 2nd Dynasty.

Ra was the supreme god, and beginning in the 4th Dynasty pharaohs took the title "son of Ra." Through syncretism (combining deities), Ra took on many forms. The important myths of solar cycle and daily rebirth were identified with Ra, displayed frequently in the Valley of the Kings.

AMUN

Kingship, creation

Linked with sun god Ra, as Amun-Ra, the King of the Gods, Lord of the Thrones of the Two Lands, often shown seated at a throne.

Originally a Theban god, Amun eventually became the state god of Egypt. He was usually depicted as a human with a tall crown, or as Amun-Ra with a falcon head and the disc of the sun above his head, holding an ankh. Amun–Ra was worshipped at Karnak Temple.

MUT

Queenship

The wife of Amun, a goddess of queens and associated with the white vulture, the hieroglyph that signified her name.

She holds an ankh and a papyrus sceptre, usually wearing a vulture headdress with the double crown of Upper and Lower Egypt. Mut was also the king's divine mother, as well as the daughter and eye of Ra, sent to terrorize the earth.

KHONSU

The moon

The son of Amun and Mut was the moon god, often depicted as a hawk with a crescent inside the full disc of the moon.

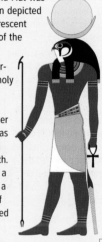

Khonsu, with his parents, make up the holy family of Egyptian mythology. Khonsu was linked with other child deities, and was often depicted with the sidelock of youth. The Egyptians used a lunar calendar, and a strict observation of the moon determined religious festivals.

OSIRIS

Death, rebirth, and fertility

The god of the dead and ruler of the underworld. He usually appears with green, black, or white skin, holding the royal regalia of the crook and the flail.

Osiris was killed by his brother Set, who scattered his remains around Egypt. His wife Isis put the pieces back together and was impregnated by him with Horus, who avenged his father's death by killing Set. His annual festival at Abydos drew pilgrims from all over Egypt.

ISIS

Wifehood, motherhood, magic, protection

This very powerful goddess was often linked to the cow goddess Hathor, and later depicted with a sun disc between cattle horns

Isis was often shown as a mother nursing her infant son Horus. Her temple at Philae was a place of pilgrimage not only for Egyptians, but also later by Greeks and Romans, particularly for members of female goddess cults.

HORUS

Kingship, the sky, and heavens

The god most closely associated with the king, Horus usually appeared as a falcon or a man with the head of one.

In predynastic times, rulers were called the Followers of Horus. Later Horus merged with Ra, becoming the god of the rising sun, or Ra-Horakhty. Another name for this dual god was Horemakhet. His four sons protected the mummified internal organs of the dead stored in canopic jars.

ANUBIS

Burial, the afterlife, mummification

Typically shown as a black jackal, he may have also had attributes of dogs and foxes, who often scavenged on the edge of the desert at cemeteries in Egypt.

Priests conducting the mummification process may have worn a mask of Anubis for part of the ceremony. Anubis frequently appeared in the Pyramid Texts of pharaohs dating back to the Old Kingdom and First Intermediate period.

MAAT

Truth, justice, and cosmic order

She personified the three most important values in Egyptian morality and religion.

At death, the "Weighing of the Heart" ceremony judged a person against the ideal of Maat. The king's vizier was expected to dispense balanced justice without favor as her priest. The king was the protector of the order as her supreme guardian. She usually sits with a scepter and ankh in her head and with an ostrich feather on her head, or she may appear just as a feather.

HATHOR

The heavens, music, sexuality, and joyfulness

Hathor was originally mother of Horus (later usurped by Isis), and was thus the king's divine mother.

Hathor usually appeared with cow horns. She was invoked to protect newborn children and Egyptians outside of the Nile Valley, with her cult reaching as far as Byblos, in modern Lebanon. Her principle cult center from the New Kingdom was in the well-preserved temple in Dendera.

PTAH

Craftsmen, creation

The Memphite god is usually depicted in mummified form with green skin wearing a skullcap exposing his ears and a beard.

He was a creator god, described by the priests of Memphis in the Creation Myth. He also became associated through syncretism with the underworld gods Sokar and Osiris. The name of one of the temples at Memphis, Hut-ka-Ptah (mansion of the life force of Ptah) is thought to be the origin of the Greek name for Egypt, Aigyptos.

THOTH

Writing, knowledge, and the moon

He was usually depicted with the head of an ibis, holding a scribal palette, wearing a headdress combining the full and crescent moon.

The patron deity of scribes, the literate ruling class of ancient Egypt was a guardian of the dead in the afterlife, wrote down the names of kings on the leaves of the sacred Ished Tree, and took note of the outcome of the "Weighing of the Heart" ceremony. He also acted as intermediary between Horus and Set.

HAPY

Fertility and the inundation

He was most often depicted as a man with blue skin, a large belly, and pendulous breasts.

The Egyptians did not have a god identified exclusively with the Nile, but Hapy was associated with its floods. He carried papyrus and lotus plants of the Nile, often with a clump of papyrus on his head. He later appeared beside the hieroglyphic sign for unity, emphasizing the Nile as the geographic unifier of the country.

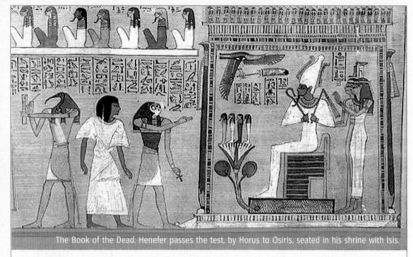

The Book of the Dead. Henefer passes the test, by Horus to Osiris, seated in his shrine with Isis.

OSIRIS AND HIS DOMAIN

THE STORY OF OSIRIS

One of the most popular creation myths is about **Osiris**, the god of the dead and the underworld. The story remained popular in all the dynasties starting in the Old Kingdom, and was even written about by the Greek historian Plutarch. Osiris was murdered by his brother **Set**, another of the nine deities of the creation story of Heliopolis, known as the **Ennead of Heliopolis** (*ennead* comes from the Greek word for nine). Set, the god of confusion and disorder, scattered the pieces of Osiris's body throughout Egypt, from where they were then gathered by his widow, the goddess **Isis**. She put Osiris back together to form the first mummy, and then was impregnated by him. Their son, the god **Horus**, avenged his father's death and won the kingship.

Osiris thus became the god of resurrection. Deceased people wanted to associate themselves with him. The supposed spots of his scattered remains became cemeteries, and his cult center at Abydos became an important place of pilgrimage and offerings. His brother Set fell out of favor with most Egyptians, who regarded him as the incarnate of evil, a strange beast too dangerous to depict on walls. Through the Osiris myth, each ruler legitimized his succession by association with Horus, son of Osiris, associated with the previous ruler.

AFTERLIFE

For the Egyptians, eternal life was more or less a continuation of earthly existence. The Osiris myth gave the deceased king an important role in the sun's cycle, as it passed through the underworld joined with the god of the dead. The king had a dangerous journey, aided by the sun god Ra, to defeat the serpent Apophis each night. This scene is depicted in several places, including the tombs in the **Valley of the Kings**. Eventually private citizens could also meet Osiris after death, as long as they passed the Weighing of the Heart ceremony. The earliest explanations of the afterlife come from the Pyramid Texts, which normal Egyptians eventually added to their own burials.

HIEROGLYPHICS

Hieroglyphics form a complex system of writing for monumental purposes. The average visitor probably does not need to spend much time learning all its symbols. Rely on a guide if you have one, although books are available to teach reading and writing it if you want to learn about it in depth.

The word *hieroglyph* comes from the Greek for "sacred carvings." Egyptians employed hieroglyphics mostly for the walls of temples and mortuary monuments. The ancient Egyptians also had their own form of cursive script, known as hieratic by Egyptologists. This appears on papyrus or *ostraca*—best written with ink—and was used for legal, administrative, and literary purposes. Only a small number of Egyptians could read or write, about 10% of the population. These people, almost entirely males, came from the literate ruling class known as scribes. The ability to read and write would have been very prestigious in Egypt, and the ability conferred access to the highest positions in the country. The first known instance of the word *sheshat*, meaning "female scribe," comes from the 26th Dynasty (664–525 BC).

Hieroglyphs only convey consonants and comprise three basic types of symbols: phonetic, logographic, and determinative. Phonetic symbols convey sounds or combinations of sounds; logographic symbols convey meaning; and determinative symbols convey the general concept of the word that precedes it. The hieroglyphic writing system does not have any punctuation or spacing between words. Hieroglyphs could be written in horizontal lines from either left to right or vice versa, or in vertical columns. Individual signs representing dangerous beings or animals would be mutilated or left out entirely to prevent them from causing harm.

The earliest known hieroglyphs were found in Abydos on some 150 labels of a tomb dating to the Predynastic Period, circa 3150 BC. The excavator, Günter Dreyer, discovered traces of a royal burial such as an ivory scepter, possibly belonging to King Scorpion, although he might have reigned in the following century. In the Old Kingdom hieroglyphic writing became a completely developed system for decorating monuments. Unlike the spoken language of ancient Egypt, hieroglyphs remained largely unchanged throughout the pharaonic period, until the Greek and Roman period, when it expanded from about 1,000 symbols to more than 6,000 as different temples developed their own systems.

Hieroglyphics at Edfu temple

THE ROSETTA STONE

The Hieroglyphic writing system baffled the earliest modern Egyptologists until Jean-François Champollion deciphered the Rosetta Stone in Paris in 1822. This opened the window to understanding ancient Egyptian life. Housed in the British Museum in London, it is one of the important ancient objects confiscated during colonial rule and, controversially, was never returned to Egypt.

Napoléon's first great foreign expedition was to Egypt in 1799. In his first year there, his expedition found a black granite *stela* now known as the Rosetta Stone. Inscribed with Hieroglyphic, Demotic, and Greek, the Rosetta Stone is the most important artifact used to decipher the Hieroglyphic writing system. Napoléon's scientists found the stone reused in the walls of a medieval fort near the town of Rosetta, now known as el-Rashid, on Egypt's Mediterranean coast.

Although Napoléon eventually had to flee the country, beaten back by British and local forces, he returned home a hero and set the stage for his empire. Long after his empire crumbled, however, the world's fascination with ancient

Experts inspecting the Rosetta Stone during the Second International Congress of Orientalists, 1874

Egypt remained. He brought teams of civilian scientists with him, and they eventually created the most comprehensive explanation of Egypt ever written, *La Description de l'Egypte*. But the scientists could only describe what they saw and understood, and given they had yet to decipher hieroglyphs, they were still missing a large part of ancient Egypt until Jean-François Champollion deciphered the Rosetta Stone 23 years after they landed in Egypt. Napoléon's scientists only fully released *La Description* six years later in 1829, taking the world by storm.

The Rosetta Stone has an inscription with a royal decree issued at Memphis on the 27th of March, 196 BC. It celebrated the anniversary of the coronation of Ptolemy V Epiphanes, who was ruling Egypt at the time (during the Ptolemaic period, also known as the Greek period). Since the same inscription appeared in three languages, it allowed archaeologists to understand both the written language of religion found on tombs, Heiroglyphic, as well as the written cursive used for most other purposes, Demotic, which had supplanted its precursor hieratic.

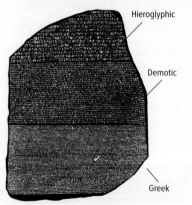
Hieroglyphic

Demotic

Greek

Cairo

INCLUDING MEMPHIS, SAQQARA, THE
FAYYUM, AND WADI NATRUN MONASTERIES

WORD OF MOUTH

"Overall I really liked Cairo. I had heard that it can be scary, especially for American women traveling without a male, but I never felt
threatened or in danger. It's a big city with a big city vibe. Yes it's
dirtier than many American cities, but anyone who has traveled to
developing countries shouldn't be shocked by Cairo."

—memejs

WELCOME TO CAIRO

TOP REASONS TO GO

★ **The First View of the Great Pyramids.** Stand at the viewing platform on the Pyramids' plateau and gaze out over the only remaining wonder of the ancient world.

★ **King Tut.** Come face to face with Tutankhamun's golden funerary mask—and other treasures from his tomb—at the Egyptian Antiquities Museum.

★ **The Call to Prayer.** Stand in Islamic Cairo at sunset and enjoy the muezzins calling from hundreds of minarets in the district.

★ **Bettering Your Bargaining Skills.** Never pay the first asking price for that must-have treasure at Cairo's famous Khan al-Khalili bazaar.

★ **The Nightlife.** Enjoy a cocktail while chilling out to cool vibes at Buddha Bar, one of Cairo's trendiest night spots in the Sofitel El Gezirah Hotel.

1 Islamic Cairo North. The Khan al-Khalili bazaar is the heart of this district, surrounded by exceptional Islamic architecture.

2 Islamic Cairo South. Historic mosques, madrasas, and mansions lie in this tightly knit district, where the Museum of Islamic Arts has an excellent collection reflecting Islamic traditions.

3 The Citadel. For several centuries Egypt was ruled from this fortress on a rocky boss overlooking the city. Several important mosques lie within or around its sturdy walls.

4 Mari Girgis. The Christian heartbeat of the city emanates from the Coptic churches and monasteries here. The Coptic Museum reveals the long history of Christianity in Egypt.

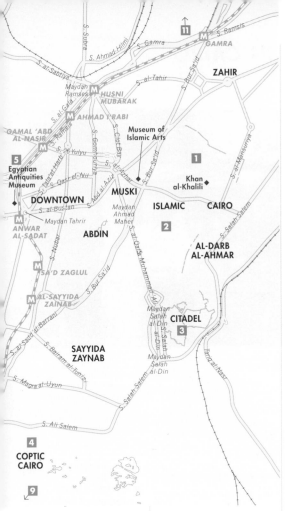

2

GETTING ORIENTED

Cairo is a large, sprawling city of some 15 million people. The oldest parts of the city are the Coptic quarter (Mari Girgis), the Islamic quarter, and the Citadel. The Downtown area along the river dates from the mid-19th century. Newer-planned areas such as Heliopolis and Mohandiseen are more European in feel and scope. Giza is really a relatively new development, having been built between the pyramids and modern-day Cairo, so that there is scarcely a gap now.

5 **Downtown Cairo and Bulaq.** The epicenter of the city, with major hotels, shopping malls, and the not-to-be-missed Egyptian Antiquities Museum.

6 **Rodah Island and Garden City.** Home to a thriving expat community in the 19th and early 20th centuries, these districts now have period mansions and a selection of upmarket hotels.

7 **Zamalek and Gezira.** Occupying the Nile's largest island, these two districts are relatively quiet enclaves in the heart of the city, home to elegant apartment blocks, independent boutiques, and neighborhood restaurants.

8 **Mohandiseen.** This modern commercial district is buzzing with offices, shops, and eateries for every budget.

9 **Ma'adi.** A preplanned district laid out in the early 20th century, this is the least densely populated part of Cairo.

10 **Giza.** Location of the Pyramids and the Sphinx, the Giza plateau was once isolated from Cairo but is now caught in the embrace of its growing suburbs.

11 **Heliopolis.** A planned expansion northeast of the city center has modern shopping malls and hotels as well as the airport.

STREET FOOD IN CAIRO

Cairo's impatient masses demand tasty, cheap food—and they want it now. The capital's myriad of take-away outlets, stand-up diners, and snack stalls cater to 18 million inhabitants who are always on the move.

(above) Fresh baked pita bread on the streets of Cairo. (opposite left) Fuul beans and pita bread: a typical meal in Cairo. (opposite right) The king of Egyptian street food: koshary.

Wherever, whenever a craving hits, you can find something to satisfy it. An army of food vendors occupies busy streets and sidewalks, dishing out quick meals and tasty nosh to diners in a hurry. It's all there: grilled meats, felafel, spicy sandwiches, and even a carb-fest in a bowl known as *koshary*. For a feast of choices, follow the crowds and discarded paper wraps to the hole-in-the wall eateries that line the pedestrianized streets of Ezbekiya, the streets near Maydan Tala'at Harb, and the far end of Shar'a Gameat al-Dowal al-Arabiya in Mohandiseen. Most places stay open obscenely late, and there's always something to hit the spot. Pushcart vendors also ply the capital's streets, peddling seeds, sweets, and other tasty snacks. They congregate near busy squares and transport hubs, gravitating at night to the Nile Corniche, where a carnivalesque atmosphere prevails until the wee hours.

JUICY DRINKS

Cairo's brightly colored juice bars attract thirsty customers and press whatever is in season into delicious juices. Order a chilled glass of orange, mango, guava, banana, strawberry, lemon, carrot, pomegranate, tamarind, cantaloupe, or watermelon juice—or a combination. Most juice bars also stock a forest of sugarcane for making *aseer asab* (sugarcane juice).

2

FUUL

Fuul is the staple of low-income, strong-stomached Egyptians who eat it for breakfast and often for lunch and dinner as well. It's a slow-cooked stew of whole and mashed fava beans and spices served in a bowl, or tucked inside a piece of flatbread. Packed with protein and carbohydrates, it's filling and nutritious, provided you go easy on the oil. You'll find fuul served at most restaurants, but locals swear the best is dished up at some of the capital's 25,000 street carts. Look for tasty variations: *fuul iskanderani* (with chopped tomatoes, onions, and coriander) or *fuul bi zeit al-harr* (with hot, spicy oil). And keep an eye open for *fuul naabit* (marinated fava beans ready to sprout, often served as a bar snack). Eat the bean, toss the outer skin—you'll never go back to peanuts.

TAAMIYA

If Egypt had an equivalent to the fast-food hamburger, this would be it. *Taamiya* are balls of ground fava beans, spiced with coriander and garlic, and fried to greasy perfection. It's like felafel, only greener. Street food vendors pack taamiya patties into pitalike bread and garnish them with lettuce.

SHAWARMA

A Middle Eastern favorite, *shawarma* is marinated lamb or chicken grilled on a slowly rotating vertical spit. Slices are shaved off and stuffed with lettuce and

tahina (sesame seed paste) into flatbread or small buns. The better shawarma stands elaborate on the formula, adding in grilled tomatoes, onions, parsley, and spices.

KOSHARY

The king of Egyptian street food, *koshary* is a fusion of macaroni, rice, noodles, lentils, chickpeas, and dry-fried onions with a crown of spicy tomato sauce. It's cheap and delicious, and it will keep you fueled for hours. You'll find koshary in specialized tile-floored diners around the city. You can't miss them—just look for the heaping piles of cooked rice and macaroni in the window.

FITEER

Fiteer is made of flaky filo pastry with a light coating of *ghee* (clarified butter) and your choice of fillings and toppings. It's often described as "Egyptian pizza," but the comparison isn't particularly apt. Fiteer has a unique taste, and can be eaten plain or topped with sweet or savory ingredients. You order fiteer at a specialized bakery known as a *fatatri*—consisting of little more than a brick oven, rolling board, and a few tables. Choose from savory toppings such as white cheese, ground meat, tuna, egg, onions, peppers, and olives; or load it up with raisins, coconut flakes, pistachios, honey, jam, custard, or a dusting of icing sugar to create a sweet dessert.

Updated by
Lindsay and
Pete Bennett

On first impression, there is hardly a superlative too extreme to capture the epic scale of this city of some 15 million—or 14, or 16; no one really knows for sure—that sprawls in all directions. The traffic, the people, the chaotic rhythm of Cairo will all reinforce this impression, threatening to overwhelm you. So take your time, relax over a mint tea in a café, or wander the quiet back alleys, and a different world will be revealed to you. In many ways Cairo is the proverbial overgrown village, full of little districts and communities that feel much smaller and more intimate than the city of which they're part.

Like so much else in Egypt, Cairo's charm is a product of its history, its network of districts and communities the physical remains of a thousand years of being conquered and reconquered by different groups. The city didn't really begin, as you might expect, with the pharaohs; they quartered themselves in nearby Memphis and Heliopolis, areas only recently overtaken by Cairo's outward urban spread. The Pyramids at Giza, on the west bank of the Nile, mislead the eye in search of Cairo's origins because this has always been an east-bank city. It's only since the 1960s that the city has moved faster than the river, leaping the banks and drawing in the endless modern suburbs on the west bank.

No, Cairo's history begins with a Roman trading outpost called Babylon—now referred to as Old or Coptic Cairo—at the mouth of an ancient canal that once connected the Nile to the Red Sea. But it was the 7th-century AD Arab invaders who can be said to have founded the city we know today with their encampment at Fustat, just north of Old Cairo. Under their great leader 'Amr Ibn al-As, the Arabs took over a land that had already been occupied by the Greeks, the Persians, and the Romans. And in the millennium that followed 'Amr's conquest, the city was ruled by the Fatimids (969–1171), the Ayyubids (1171–1250), the

Mamluks (1250–1517), the Ottomans (1517–1798), and then experienced 150 years of French and British colonial administration until the revolution of 1952 finally returned power to Egyptian hands.

But what makes Cairo unique is that each new set of rulers, rather than destroying what they had conquered, chose to build a new city upwind from the old one. Thus, from a bird's-eye view above the Nile, you can follow the progression of the historic center of Cairo cutting a question-mark-shaped path from Old Cairo in the south, curving north through Fustat, east to Islamic Cairo, and then west to the colonial Downtown district until you reach Maydan Tahrir (Liberation Square), where it has settled for the moment. But as the city continues to expand, the heart threatens to relocate again, perhaps to Maydan Sphinx, or Bulaq, or somewhere in Giza.

Cairo's districts have changed, of course, since the time they were founded. Still, each district retains a distinct identity, not only in its buildings, but also among its residents and their way of life. Pre-Islamic Babylon is, to this day, a disproportionately Christian area, with more crosses visible than crescents. And the medieval precinct of Islamic Cairo is still where families traditionally go during Ramadan to spend the night eating and smoking after a day of abstinence. Indeed, one of the joys of Cairo is that its historic areas are still vibrant living spaces and not open-air museums. The past here is more a state of mind than a historical fact—and that, ultimately, is the way in which the city is truly overwhelming.

PLANNING

WHEN TO GO

Cairo is only uncomfortable for a couple of months a year. Spring and autumn are both gorgeous, with warm days and cool nights, though spring brings the *khamaseen* dust storms that can turn the air yellow for a couple of days. Summer is *very* hot, but relatively dry. Winter is brief, eight weeks at most, and chillier than you might expect, though never truly cold. Cairo gets about 10 rainy days a year, mostly in winter. Ramadan, the holy month of fasting, brings both rewards and inconveniences for visitors.

GETTING HERE AND AROUND

BY AIR

Cairo is the main entry point for international flights and has the most international arrivals of any other destination in Egypt. The airport is divided into three terminals: Terminal 1 for domestic flights only, Terminal 2 for most international flights, and Terminal 3 for EgyptAir and its Star Alliance partners.

AIRPORT TRANSFERS

If you are traveling independently, taxis and limousines are the best option for getting to and from the airport. The minute you exit the arrivals hall, you will be inundated with offers from taxi drivers. This will be your first opportunity to test out your bargaining skills—you should be able to bring the price down to around £E60. Keep in mind that most taxis will not use their meters. If you are too tired to go through the hassle, opt for one of the limousine companies located in the arrivals hall for a flat fee of £E80 to £E100 for central Cairo hotels, £E140 for Giza hotels. Cairo taxis are black and white or black and yellow; limousines are black, usually old-model Mercedes sedans. Getting to the airport from the city is much easier, because you can have your hotel arrange your transportation.

The airport also has a fleet of modern shuttle buses that travel to and from the airport to Downtown, Giza, Heliopolis, Mohandiseen, Ma'adi, Nasr City, and Zamalek. Buses depart every 30 minutes, and single tickets cost £E25 to Heliopolis and £E35 to Downtown.

BY BUS

TO AND FROM CAIRO

Buses are an inexpensive means of traveling between cities. Generally they are safe, if not always relaxing. Most companies have installed videos to play Arabic and Indian movies at top volume, even on night buses. If this counts as local color rather than an annoyance, take a bus. It's wise to buy your ticket a day in advance, especially when traveling during peak periods. However, be aware that currently the security authorities do not encourage independent bus travel on routes down the Nile Valley, preferring visitors to travel by train or by plane, modes of travel that can more easily be kept under surveillance by relatively small numbers of officers.

Popular bus companies include the East Delta Bus Company, El Gouna Bus Company, Super Jet, and Upper Egyptian Bus Company. Buses in Cairo depart from Turgoman Station (now officially called Cairo Gateway Station) off Gala' Street, Downtown. *For more specific information about bus lines and bus travel in Egypt, see ⇨ By Bus, under Transportation in Egypt Essentials.*

WITHIN CAIRO

Most visitors to Cairo aren't likely to use the local city buses, but they are far and away the cheapest mode of transportation in the city, with tickets costing a mere 25pt to £E2. Buses arrive at and depart from stations at Maydan Tahrir, Maydan Ataba, Opera Square, Pyramids Road, Ramses Station, and the Citadel. Route numbers are sometimes missing from the buses, so it is always best to ask where a bus is going before it lurches off with you onboard.

Much less of an experience, and more reliable, are the orange-trimmed minibuses. They charge slightly more than the larger buses (£E2) and are usually much less crowded. ⚠ **If you decide to use either type of bus service, be very cautious. Especially on large buses, pickpockets are known to look for potential victims.**

The Cairo Transport Authority operates a fleet of comfortable air-conditioned buses that are surprisingly convenient and affordable. Marked with a large CTA logo on the side, for £E2 the bus will take you from the airport, through the city's northeastern suburbs and Downtown, eventually passing through Giza to deposit you at the foot of the Pyramids. Route 356 stops at Abdel Meneim Riyadh Station in Maydan Tahrir, and route 799 runs via Shubra to Maydan Ramses, but you can flag them down or ask the driver to let you off at any point along the routes.

MAJOR BUS ROUTES

To and from Maydan Tahrir: No. 400 for Heliopolis and Cairo International Airport (all terminals) and 27 to the airport via Maydan Roxi; 268, 63, and 66 for the Khan al-Khalili; 951 and 154 for Ibn Tulun Mosque and the Citadel; 800, 900, and 997 for the Pyramids in Giza; all lines except 154, 951, and 268 for Ramses Station.

To and from Maydan Ataba and Opera Square: 948 for Cairo International Airport; 950 and 80 for Khan al-Khalili; 104, 17, and 202 for Maydan Tahrir and Mohandiseen; 94 for Fustat and the Mosque of 'Amr; 50 and 150 for the Shrine of Imam Sahfe'i; 48 for Zamalek; 57 and 951 for the Citadel.

To and from the Pyramids: 804 for Ramses Square and the Citadel; 905 for Maydan Tahrir and the Citadel.

To and from Ramses Station: 971 for the airport, 65 for Khan al-Khalili, 174 for the Citadel, 83 to Fustat.

To and from the Citadel: 840 for Maydan Ataba and Maydan Tahrir; 905 for Rodah Island, Shar'a al-Haram, and the Pyramids.

Another option is the microbus, or service taxis. These privately owned 12-seaters, painted blue and white, cost 60 pt to £E1 and go from all the major terminals to just about anywhere you want to go. They are unnumbered, however, so ask the driver where he's headed.

BY CAR

Attempting to rent a car and drive oneself around Cairo is something we would discourage in the strongest terms. If you manage to find (and fend) your way driving through the aggressive streets of Cairo, parking will prove to be an even greater challenge. Either you will spend half your day looking for a parking place or you will be ripped off by a *monadi* (one of the self-employed valet parking boys). Just do yourself a favor and forget about driving.

If you simply must rent a car and drive it yourself, you must be at least 25 years old, possess an international license, and have nerves of steel. *For more information, see ⇨ By Car, under Transportation in Egypt Essentials.*

Major car-rental agencies have offices in Cairo; cars come with or without chauffeurs.

Car Rentals Budget Rent-a-Car (✉ *Shar'a Ring, Mirage City* ☏ *012/235–5290* ⊕ *www.budget.com* ✉ *Cairo International Airport* ☏ *02/2265–2395*). **Europcar** (✉ *Cairo International Airport* ☏ *016/661–1027* ⊕ *www.europcar.com*). **Hertz** (✉ *Ramses Hilton, 1115 Corniche al-Nil* ☏ *02/2575–8914, 02/347–2238 for central reservations office* ⊕ *www.hertz.com* ✉ *Cairo International Airport*

☎ *02/2265–2430* ✉ *Le Méridien Pyramids Hotel, Giza* ☎ *02/3377–3388* ✉ *Giza Pyramids Park Hotel & Resort, Giza* ☎ *02/3838–8300*).

BY SUBWAY

By far the most efficient mode of public transportation in Cairo, the Metro is clean, reliable, and cheap. Tickets cost from £E1; there are no multiday passes. Trains run from South Cairo (Helwan) to North Cairo (Heliopolis), with sublines to Shubra, Ataba, and Abdin. One of the most useful lines is the cross-Nile line from Giza to Shubra. The Metro runs from 5:30 AM to midnight in winter (to 1 AM in summer), with trains arriving every 5 to 10 minutes. Each train has cars in the middle reserved for women and children. Women traveling alone are advised to sit here, especially during rush-hour travel, to avoid being hassled or groped.

BY TAXI

The fact that Cairo taxi drivers rarely use meters makes life a bit more difficult for visitors, who are considered to be the best prey for the exorbitant fares that some drivers try to charge. The first rule is that you should not take any taxi parked in front of a hotel unless you bargain the price down before getting in. It is always cheaper to hail a taxi off the street after walking a few meters away from the hotel.

Fares vary according to the time you are in the taxi and the distance you cover. Early in the morning and very late at night, fares are about 40% to 50% higher than during daylight. During normal daylight hours and in the evening, a 20-minute cab ride from Maydan Tahrir to the Pyramids should cost about £E60 one way; a 5- to 10-minute ride should cost no more than £E10. If you are going a long distance, such as all the way to Saqqara, the ride should be about £E100 one way, and you should have the driver wait—it is extremely difficult to get a cab back to the city from there. With waiting this may push the price up to around £E230 to £E250.

Some drivers are extremely stubborn, so you must set a price before embarking on your ride to avoid unpleasant scenes once you arrive at your destination. When giving directions, name a major landmark near your destination (rather than a street address), such as Maydan Tahrir, or al-Azhar University. As you get closer to the destination, give more specifics; this will avoid confusion.

Most taxis are independently operated—the blue-and-white fleet—so they can't be called. Just go hail one on the street. There are always taxis in the streets of Cairo; however, the condition of some of these taxis is dire, with mechanical defects and poor conditions inside. City Cabs operates a fleet of better-serviced vehicles with a distinctive yellow livery. Though City Cabs is more expensive than the blue-and-white taxi fleet, the cabs should have working meters, and they run on natural gas, so they're better for the environment. City Cab drivers are not allowed to smoke in the vehicles.

Contacts City Cabs (☎ *16516 or 19195*).

2

BY TRAIN

All railway lines from Cairo depart from and arrive at Ramses Station, 3 km (2 mi) northeast of Maydan Tahrir. Trains traveling to and from Alexandria, the Nile Delta towns, and Suez Canal cities use tracks 1–7 in the station's main hall. Trains to Al Minya, Luxor, and Aswan depart from platforms 8, 9, 10, and 11 outside the main hall.

Cairo and Alexandria have several convenient daily connections, with a travel time of 2 to 3¼ hours depending on the type of service. Tickets cost between £E19 and £E50, depending on the class of service.

Abela Egypt operates the long-distance and sleeper trains that connect Cairo, Luxor, and Aswan. Tickets for these trains should be purchased at least 10 days in advance, either in person at the station or from a travel agent or tour company.

For more information, see ⇨ Train Travel under Transportation in Egypt Essentials.

Contacts Abela Egypt (☎ *02/2574–9474 for reservations* ⊕ *www. sleepingtrains.com*).

MONEY MATTERS

Banking hours are Sunday through Thursday, from 8 AM to 2 PM. The travel offices of American Express and Thomas Cook offer currency exchange, and there are numerous commercial exchange offices. Commercial exchange offices open later into the evening than banks and are, therefore, more convenient. Many larger hotels have bank branches within. Your hotel will also change currency directly, but may offer a poor rate of exchange.

You'll find lots of ATMs across the city, at bank branches, in shopping malls, and in hotel lobbies. You can rely on getting access to Egyptian pounds from ATMs in Cairo—though not so much in the rest of the country as machines are not filled up as regularly outside the capital.

Keep any receipts from currency exchange of ATM withdrawals, as you may need to show these to customs officials.

INTERNET

The number of Wi-Fi hotspots have exploded in the city over the last couple of years. Look for café chains like Starbucks, Costa, Cilantro, and Beano's, as well as fast food outlets such as Pizza Hut and McDonalds, which usually have free access. Internet cafés are usually dusty back-street affairs, but they stay open until around midnight, and access is cheap—around £E4 to £E10 per hour. Cafés open and close with great regularity. Your hotel will also probably offer Internet service, but at a higher price.

VISITOR INFORMATION

Contacts **Egyptian Tourist Authority** (☎ *126 for Tourist Information Hotline* ✉ *Misr Travel Tower, Abbasia Square, Abbasia* ☎ *02/2285–4509* ✉ *Ramses Station, Maydan Ramses, Downtown* ☎ *02/2579–0767* ✉ *Shar'a al-Adli 5, Downtown* ☎ *02/2391–3454* ✉ *Manyal Palace, Rodah Island* ☎ *02/2363–3006* ✉ *Pyramids Village, Pyramids Rd., Giza* ☎ *02/3385–0259*).

EXPLORING CAIRO

Cairo is big: just how big you'll see on the drive in from the airport, which sometimes takes so long you'll think you're driving to Aswan. And what you see on the way into town, amazingly, is only half of it—Cairo's west-bank sister city, Giza, stretches to the Pyramids, miles from Downtown. But if you are the sort of person who instinctively navigates by compass points, exploring Cairo will be a breeze because the Nile works like a giant north–south needle running through the center of the city. If not, you might find the city bewildering at first.

Taxi drivers generally know only major streets and landmarks, and often pedestrians are unsure of the name of the street they stand on—when they do know, it's as often by the old names as the postindependence ones—but they'll gladly steer you in the wrong direction in an effort to be helpful. Just go with the flow and try to think of every wrong turn as a chance for discovery.

Thankfully, too, you don't have to conquer all of Cairo to get the most out of it. Much of the city was built in the 1960s, and the new areas hold relatively little historical or cultural interest. The older districts, with the exception of Giza's pyramids, are all on the east bank and easily accessible by taxi or Metro. These districts become relatively straightforward targets for a day's exploration on foot.

Old Cairo, on the east bank a couple miles south of most of current-day Cairo, was the city's first district. Just north of it is Fustat, the site of the 7th-century Arab settlement. East of that is the Citadel. North of the Citadel is the medieval walled district of al-Qahira that gave the city its name. It is better known as Islamic Cairo. West of that is the colonial district. Known as Downtown, it is one of several—including Ma'adi, Garden City, Heliopolis, and Zamalek—laid out by Europeans in the 19th and 20th centuries. (The west-bank districts of Mohandiseen and Doqqi, by comparison, have only sprouted up since the revolution in 1952.) The most interesting sights are in the older districts; the newer ones have the highest concentrations of hotels, restaurants, and shops.

PLANNING YOUR TIME

Although the Pyramids are usually at the top of everyone's itinerary, it is more interesting to work your way back through the city's history and end with its pharaonic origins. So start with **Khan al-Khalili,** the great medieval marketplace, and wander the narrow alleys of nearby **Islamic Cairo** to get a feel for the texture of life in the city. In a full day you can explore the surface of Old Cairo, seeing both its Islamic and Coptic core. The **Great Pyramids** and **Sphinx** can be seen in a half day, but also

Young women in Cairo

spend a half day at Memphis and Saqqara or at the less-visited sights such as Abu Sir or Dahshur. Another day can be spent in either Fayyum or on a trip to the monasteries in Wadi Natrun.

ISLAMIC CAIRO NORTH: AL-HUSAYN MOSQUE TO BAB AL-FUTUH

If the Mamluks hadn't stopped the Mongols' furious advance at Ain Djalout (Palestine) in AD 1260, Cairo, like Baghdad and scores of other towns, might have been left in rubble. As it is, Misr al Mahrousa—a popular appellation that translates as "Egypt the Protected"—offers one of the richest troves of Islamic architecture in the world. This is also because Cairo has been the capital of Islamic Egypt since its founding. Today the areas between Bab al-Futuh and Bab al-Nasr in the north and the Mosque of Amr in the south are still home to a rare concentration of buildings that represents a continuous, evolving architectural tradition.

Unfortunately, Islamic monuments don't attract as many visitors as pharaonic ones, and government funds for restoration haven't been so generous. A great many buildings were seriously damaged in the 1992 earthquake (some areas still lie in ruins), but much of the al-Azhar area has undergone a facelift since the start of the new millennium, and a visit to these historic neighborhoods should figure prominently on your agenda. A walk along these time-warped streets studded with monuments from different eras offers a rare taste of the extravagant beauty that once characterized the heart of the city. It is a visit to the past, light years away from the behemoth that modern Cairo has become.

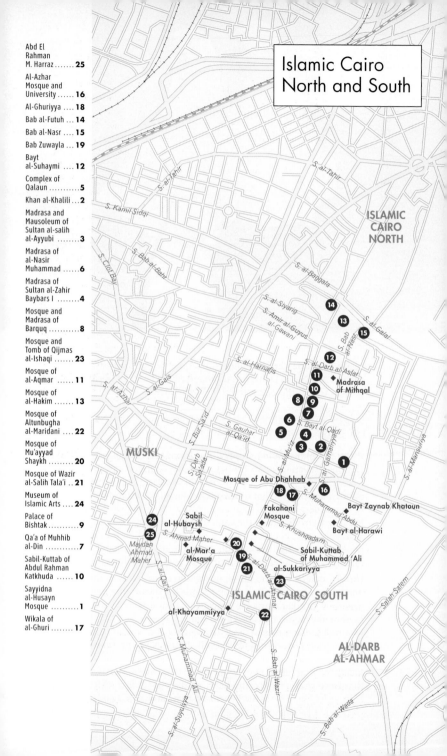

Islamic Cairo North and South

You can get a very good feel for this area in a half day, depending on how long you spend at each of the attractions. Leave enough time for a break and shopping afterward, if you wish. You can spend hours in the Khan al-Khalili, depending on how much browsing and haggling interests you. Keep in mind that most of the shops are closed on Sunday. Friday before noon is also a quieter time in the neighborhood.

TOP ATTRACTIONS

⓬ **Bayt al-Suhaymi.** Considered the best example of domestic Islamic architecture in Cairo, this coolly luxurious 16th-century merchant's house is huge (more than 6,000 square feet), and with its gardens, well, and flour mill, it resembles a self-sufficient hamlet. As is the case with Islamic houses, the entrance passageway leads to a lush courtyard that is totally unexpected from the outside. On the ground floor are the *salamlik* (public reception rooms), and upstairs are the *haramlik* (private rooms). The house and adjacent alley have been restored, making this a charmingly evocative little corner of Cairo. ⊠ *19 Shar'a al-Darb al-Asfar, Islamic Cairo North* ☎ *No phone* 💰 *£E30* ⊙ *Daily 9–5.*

❷ **Khan al-Khalili.** The Khan has been a marketplace since the end of the
★ 14th century; commercial activity is its lifeblood. A maze of small streets and narrow alleys charts its way around the bazaar, and these passages are filled with scores of vendors hawking their wares and attempting to draw customers into their small shops. It is a chaotic mixture of Egyptians and tourists, smells of perfume and incense, fragments of age-old buildings next to modern amenities—and always noise and confusion. With a little determination, you can find just about anything you want to take home as proof of your trip to Cairo. Carpets, gold, silver, clothing, belly-dancing outfits, spices, perfumes, water pipes, woodwork, books, pottery, blown glass, leather, papyrus, pharaonic replicas—you name it, it's here. There are hundreds of little stores that will attract or repel.

A few words of advice: never take something at the first price; bargaining is the modus operandi in the Khan, and if you do not show interest, the price is likely to drop. In the case of a silver- or goldsmith, for example, while a fixed price for the weight of the piece exists, you can bargain on the quality of the workmanship. If a shopkeeper offers you tea or coffee and you take it, you are in no way obligated to buy something from his shop; it's just Middle Eastern hospitality. If someone offers to take you to his workshop on the second floor, accept if you have time; most of these crafts are fascinating to see in progress. If you pay by credit card, there may be a service charge of 3% to 6%;

Continued on page 74

THE ISLAMIC DAY

Islamic sights are open from about 9 AM until 4 or 5 PM, depending on the custodian's whims. Muslims pray five times a day, and prayers usually last 15 minutes or so. Prayer times vary according to the season. The first of these is just before dawn (the *al-Fagr* prayer); the others are at noon or 1 PM (*al-Duhr*), mid afternoon around 3 or 4 (*al-'Asr*), sunset (*al-Maghrib*), and evening (*al-'Esha*) at about 8 or 9 PM. If you happen to be visiting a mosque during prayer time, you may be asked to wait outside the main hall until prayers are completed.

2

SHOPPING IN CAIRO By Lindsay Bennett

From the mid-1300s Cairo was the center of the world trade in spices controlled by the Mamluks, and the Khan el-Khalili was the major marketplace where these spices were bought and sold. From this staple trade the Khan developed to serve the expensive and sophisticated tastes of the ruling classes from around medieval Arabia, Europe, and North Africa who came to buy gold and the best in hand-crafted decorative goods. It was one of the world's first shopping-malls.

In many ways not much has changed. In the bustling alleyways Cairenes jostle with visitors from around the world, and hundreds of in-your-face vendors play out their well-honed sales pitches: it's a hot and intense experience, but one not to be missed.

(opposite) Night at Khan al-Khalili Market (top) a typical street in the bazaar (right) Dried herbs for sale in the spice stalls.

SHOPPING IN THE KHAN

A tourist stall in the Khan El Khahili

Opened in 1382 and named after the Khan (an Islamic rest house for travelers and their pack animals) of Emir Djaharks el-Khalili that still stands nearby, Khan El-Khalili is a hodgepodge of lanes and alleyways packed with thousands of small, family-owned stores.

The Khan sits in the heart of historic Islamic Cairo. Shar'a Gawr al-Qayid forms the southern edge with Sayyidna al-Husayn, marked by al-Husayn Mosque, to the east. On the western edge, Shar'a el-Mu'izz with its medieval palaces forms the historical boundary between the Khan el-Khalili and Muski Bazaar, a place where local Cairenes shop for their daily needs, buying everything from clay cooking pots to buttons. In practice the two markets run seamlessly into one another, extending your possibilities for exploration.

GET READY TO SHIMMY

If you are a fan of the exotic Egypt of the Arabic era, it might be worth checking out **Al Wikala** (✉ *73 Gawr al-Qayid, Old Cairo* ☎ *02/589–7443*). Here Mahmoud el-Ghaffar sells genuine belly dancing costumes and accessories, not the poor quality mass-produced tourist ensembles you'll find hanging in the souvenir stalls. All the best artistes in the city come here to buy their veils and jewel encrusted bustiers.

Bags of beans and corn for sale

In-laid mother of pearl boxes

A golden array of perfume bottles

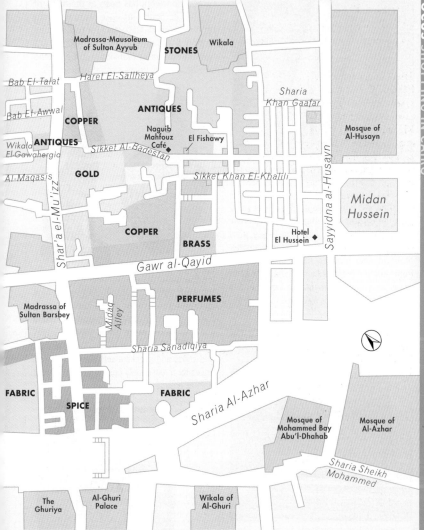

Madrassa-Mausoleum of Sultan Ayyub

Wikala

STONES

Bab El-Talat

Haret El-Sallheya

Sharia Khan Gaafar

Bab El-Awwal

ANTIQUES

COPPER

Naguib Mahfouz Café

El Fishawy

Mosque of Al-Husayn

Wikala El-Gawahergia

ANTIQUES

Sikket Al-Badestan

Al-Maqasis

GOLD

Sikket Khan El-Khalili

Sayyidna al-Husayn

Midan Hussein

COPPER

BRASS

Hotel El Hussein

Gawr al-Qayid

Madrassa of Sultan Barsbey

Midaq Alley

PERFUMES

Sharia Sanadiqiya

FABRIC

FABRIC

Sharia Al-Azhar

SPICE

Mosque of Mohammed Bay Abu'l-Dhahab

Mosque of Al-Azhar

Sharia Sheikh Mohammed

The Ghuriya

Al-Ghuri Palace

Wikala of Al-Ghuri

WHAT TO BUY

With a little determination, you can find just about anything you might want to take home as a souvenir of your trip to Egypt. You name it, and you can probably find it in the Khan, from the best in artisan crafts to the kitsch, the fake, and the mass-produced wares shipped from factories thousands of miles from Egypt. Here's a guide to what's traditional and local.

CARPETS AND TEXTILES

The Khan was a major center for carpet sales from the earliest days. The finest come from around the Arab world including Turkey, Iran, and Afganistan; however, the nomadic peoples of Egypt also produce hand-made carpets from sheep and camel hair, as well as cotton kilims woven on narrow, mobile looms. Prices start at around $40 for a runner.

ALABASTER AND STONEWORK

Carved stonework has been at the heart of Egyptian decorative art since Khufu furnished his first pyramid. Alabaster is a native stone fashioned into many different objects. You'll find exquisite vases that would cost a fortune on Fifth Avenue. Prices start at around $25.

MARQUETRY

The workmanship of artisans is extremely high and can be seen in the varied items showing inlaid patterns of different woods, or wood and mother of pearl. Small jewelry boxes are the most portable items, but you can find chess and checkers sets and side tables. Prices for a reasonably good-quality chess set start at around $150.

GOLD AND SILVER

Gold and silver are sold by the day's market rate with only a small amount for workmanship, so weight for weight compared to prices in the United States it represents a relatively good value. ■TIP➜ Find out the current price of gold before heading out to shop.

PERFUMES AND PERFUME BOTTLES

The use of sweet-smelling oils and unguents was well developed in the ancient world and later became a central part of Arabic society. High-quality natural oil–based perfumes are concentrated and heady with scent. Delicate, ornate perfume bottles make the ideal storage vessels, their prettiness designed to highlight the high-value liquids inside. Prices depend on the type of oil but start at around $5 for half an ounce.

POTTERY AND CERAMICS

Plain terracotta cookware on sale is used in millions of Egyptian homes every day but needs to be sealed before use. Or take home a ceramic plate, bowl, or vase hand-painted with the traditional Arabic pattern. These come in all shapes and sizes. If someone offers to take you to his workshop on the second floor, accept if you have time; most of these crafts are fascinating to see in progress.

METALWARE

Egypt has a long tradition of work in various metals, and you have the choice of a whole range of brass and copper decorative items from tables to samovars and pitchers or ornate light fittings incorporating hand-blown glass. The finest of this decoration is still done by hand. Expect to pay around $60 for a small hand-carved serving tray.

SOUVENIRS

Phaoronic-era replicas are always popular souvenirs

It's hard to escape the shadow of the Pharaohs in Egypt even when you are shopping. "Tut-mania" can be seen in thousands of imported mass-produced items, from refrigerator magnets to key rings to coffee mugs, that form the ever-expanding kitsch end of the market.

But it's worth remembering that even the most humble souvenir can resonate to the heart of Egypt's ancient history. Tiny alabaster scarab beetles were placed in the linen wrappings as the bodies of the pharoahs were being mummified to ensure the body passed into the next world, and the simple ankh was an important symbol for the ancient Egyptians—literally the breath of life. Modern versions of both these items are easily available and inexpensive souvenirs today, with prices of less than $10.

One of the most popular souvenirs of a trip to Egypt is to buy a cartouche (an oblong tablet) of your given name in hieroglyphics, either in gold or silver. Usually a cartouche takes a day or so to make.

HAGGLING

Haggling is a way of life in Egypt—it's not a system only used to confuse visitors—and you'll notice Egyptians haggling over every type of purchase as you stroll around the Khan. Put simply, purchasers use every opportunity to minimize the price they pay, while vendors want the best price possible for their goods. The idea is to arrive at a price that makes both buyer and seller happy. Shop owners will expect you to bargain, so here are a few tips:

■ Show interest in and ask the price of several items before you begin haggling over the item you like. This gives you an idea of the store's prices in general and masks your intentions.

■ When the store owner quotes a price, make a counter-offer which is around half (or less) of that amount. The merchant will lower his original offer and you raise your offer until you meet somewhere in the middle.

■ Use reasons to counter why the merchant's price is too much (they don't need to be true). These could include the color/size not being quite right, or questions about the quality of the material or workmanship. It's not uncommon to say that you prefer an item at another stall but are prepared to take his goods for a lower price.

■ If you are offered refreshment (tea, soda, water) as you haggle, do accept. It is a custom of the vendors, a nicety that doesn't happen in the United States, and it doesn't obligate you to buy anything.

■ If you can't reach an agreement, walking away often results in the merchant lowering his offer price.

■ Shopping early in the morning or later in the evening can mean lower prices. An early sale is considered a sign of a lucky day ahead, while a late sale is a bonus.

SPICES

(above) Spices for sale in the Khan

Many of the most important herbs and spices sold in Cairo are native of this part of the world. Several were important in the Pharaonic era, including during the mummification process, but on a more mundane level herbs and spices were used to scent the air, to flavor many dishes, and for the homeopathic treatment of a range of illnesses and conditions from stomach cramps to diarrhea, from breath fresheners to diuretics. The spice stalls are certainly among the most colorful and fragrant in the Khan. Cooking back home with the spices you buy will bring back great memories of your trip.

WHAT TO BUY

Some of the more common herbs and spices you'll find in the bazaar include anise, caraway seeds, cardamom, chili, cloves, cinnamon, coriander, cumin, fennel, fenugreek, mace, mustard seed, nutmeg, pepper, star anise, sumac, and tamarind. Various curry powders are also sold premixed. The king of all the herbs and spices is saffron. The best saffron will not be cheap, but it's less expensive than in the United States.

You'll also see various items—from powders to dried roots—sold as "Egyp-

tian Viagra." Since it's certain that these haven't been tested under laboratory conditions, treat any claims with healthy skepticism.

KARKADAY

The dried flowers of the hibiscus bush are the major ingredient in one of Egypt's staple drinks. The sweet, deep-red infusion is very refreshing served chilled but is also delicious hot. The health benefits of karkaday are said to be a lowering of blood pressure and cholesterol.

Pass on the long strings of sampler packs of spices that many stalls sell. You'll be buying many spices you'll never use, and you can't be sure how fresh many of these items are, as this packaging is only for the tourists and may have been hanging in the sunlight for several days or weeks.

Karkaday and other spices on display

ask before handing over the plastic. The Khan has ATMs where you can take out Egyptian pounds. Finally, if someone offers to sell you marijuana or hashish, *do not* accept; you're likely to get oregano, compressed henna, or a stay in a dreadful local jail.

The Khan has plenty of places to eat, including the grilled-meat restaurants on the corner of Maydan al-Husayn and Shar'a Muski and places that serve *fiteer,* Egyptian pancakes filled with everything from feta cheese to raisins. They form a row just outside the Khan, between Shar'a Muski and Shar'a al-Azhar. Most stores are closed on Sundays and during Friday prayers (the hour around noon, 1 PM from April through October, during daylight saving time). ⊠ *Main entrance on Shar'a al-Ahzar, near Sikkat Khan al-Khalili, Islamic Cairo North* ⊗ *Stores generally open Mon.–Sat., 10–9.*

NEED A BREAK?

El Fishawy. Just past the Hotel el Hussein is this famous café in the Khan al-Khalili bazaar. The area has dozens of cafés, but this is the oldest, best known, and most frequented by Egyptians and visitors alike. Here you can sip a Turkish coffee or mint tea; a *karkadeh,* a hibiscus drink served hot or cold; and *sahleb,* a warm milk-based drink sprinkled with coconut and nuts. You can also have your shoes shined or smoke a *shisha* (water pipe). ⊠ *5 Sikkit Khan al-Khalili, Islamic Cairo North* ☎ *02/2590–6755.*

Naguib Mahfouz Café. This air-conditioned, upscale coffee shop is the perfect refuge from the clamor of the Khan. Have a drink, a light lunch, or—at the adjoining restaurant—a proper meal. To get here, face the Sayyidna al-Husayn Mosque and turn left into the passage that begins at the level of the minaret. Follow this through a couple of archways; the café is on the right. ⊠ *5 al-Badestan La., Islamic Cairo North* ☎ *02/2590–3788.*

⓮ Bab al-Futuh *(the Futuh Gate).* To the left, inside the entrance to the ⇨ *Mosque of al-Hakim* is a small passageway that leads to a stairway up to the roof of the mosque. From here, you can get access to the Bab al-Futuh, one of the main gates of the Islamic city. Built in 1087 by Badr al-Gamali al-Gayushi, it was designed to protect al-Qahira from the Seljuk Turks who held Syria and were threatening Egypt. But the gate was never put to the test. ⊠ *Shar'a al-Mu'iz, Islamic Cairo North.*

NEED A BREAK?

If you feel a little hungry during your tour of the Islamic architectural treasures, make a short detour to Zizo's (⊠ *1 Midan Bab al-Futah, Islamic Cairo North*), which has made excellent inexpensive *sogoq* (spicy sausage) sandwiches served with piquant pickled vegetables. The little hole-in-the-wall café has been run by the same family since the 1960s.

⓯ Bab al-Nasr *(the Nasr Gate).* This gate is similar to Bab al-Futuh, except that two square towers flank it. On one of the towers is the inscription: TOUR CORBIN, a memento of the Napoleonic expedition, which renamed all the gates after French army officers during its occupation. (Bab al-Futuh also has TOUR JUNOT and TOUR PERRAULT carved into its two rounded towers.) The wall between the two gates is fun to explore. Tunnels with slit windows to provide light once connected the entire wall and its 60 gates with rooms and storehouses within the girth of the wall, making it possible for an army to defend the city without ever having to leave the wall. ⊠ *Shar'a Bab al-Nasr, Islamic Cairo North.*

❺ Complex of Qalaun. One of the early Mamluk rulers of Egypt, Mansur Qalaun was originally a Tartar (Mongol) brought to Egypt as a slave. Mamluks (literally, "those owned") were first imported from the Volga to Egypt by al-Salih Ayyubi, the man buried in the tomb across the street, who used them as his personal bodyguards. Aybak, the first Mamluk ruler, and his successor, Baybars al-Bunduqdari, both had been al-Salih's slaves. Qalaun was acquired by Baybars. In short, one's lot in life could be worse than being a slave to the Sultan in medieval Cairo.

Qalaun died at the ripe old age of 70, on his way to attack the Crusader fortress of Acre in 1290. The complex that he had built (it was begun in 1284) is noteworthy for its workmanship and the diverse styles that it displays.

A *bimaristan* (hospital and psychiatric ward) has existed on the site since Qalaun first saw the need for one. Only fragments of the original hospital remain, having been replaced by a modern (not necessarily better) one. In its heyday, Qalaun's bimaristan was famous for its care of the physically and mentally ill, and its staff was said to include musicians and storytellers as well as surgeons capable of performing delicate eye surgery.

The madrasa and mausoleum present the complex's impressive street facade, a series of pointed-arch recesses, almost Gothic in their proportions, each one pierced with groups of three windows, a much-seen feature of Islamic architecture. Look up at the 194-foot minaret with its horseshoe-shaped arched recesses and its corniced overhang, a device used since pharaonic times. The entrance is set slightly forward up a set of steps; its semicircular arch was the first of its kind in Egypt. Beyond the entrance is a long, tall corridor with the madrasa to the left and the tomb to the right. A door at the end of the corridor used to lead to the bimaristan but has been sealed off.

The gem of the complex, however, is the mausoleum, the burial place of Qalaun and his son al-Nasir Muhammad. The chamber is dark, cool, and mammoth. In its center is a wooden grille that encloses the tombs. There is much here to suggest that Qalaun was deeply influenced by what he saw on his exploits in Palestine. The plan of the mausoleum is similar to that of the Dome of the Rock in Jerusalem in that it contains an octagon fit within a square. The stained glass and tall proportions have a Gothic quality that are reminiscent of Crusader churches that he saw in the Levant. ⊠ *Shar'a al-Mu'iz, Islamic Cairo North* ☎ *No phone* 💴 *Free* ⊙ *Daily 9–4.*

❶ Sayyidna al-Husayn Mosque. One of the holiest sites in Egypt, the mosque was originally built by the Fatimids in the 12th century as a shrine and is said to contain the head of Husayn, the Prophet's grandson. Al-Husayn is the spiritual heart of the Islamic city. It is here that the president and his ministers come to pray on important religious occasions. Many of the Sufi orders in the neighborhood perform Friday prayers at al-Husayn. During the *mulid* (celebration) of al-Husayn, held during the

DID YOU KNOW?

The Sayyidna al-Husayn Mosque is one of the holiest sites in Cairo and is believed to house the oldest complete manuscript of the Koran.

Muslim month of Rabi'a al-Akhiri (the fourth month in the Muslim calendar), the square in front of the mosque becomes a carnival. During Ramadan, the area is packed with people from sunset to dawn.

Not only was Husayn the grandson of the Prophet, but he was also the son of 'Ali, the fourth caliph and cousin of the Prophet. A group of followers who believed that 'Ali and his descendants should lead the faithful broke ranks with the majority (known as the Sunnis) when the Ummayads took control of the *umma* (the Islamic nation). This group became known as "the group of 'Ali" or Shi'a 'Ali, later Shi'a for short. Husayn is greatly revered by the Shi'a for his role as a martyr to the cause when, in 680, he and a band of his followers were massacred at the battle of Kerbala in Iraq.

If it seems strange that the head of a Shi'a martyr be given such importance in a country that is overwhelmingly Sunni, it should be noted that the Fatimids, the original builders of al-Qahira, were Shi'a. The 200 years in which they ruled the city left an impact on the traditions of the people. Not only did the Shi'a found the most prestigious Islamic university, al-Azhar, but they also were responsible for inculcating in the populace a veneration for saints, holy men, or relatives of the Prophet—a practice not at all in keeping with a strict interpretation of Sunni Islam. Thus, although the head of Husayn was brought to Cairo for safekeeping by a ruling minority, the Sunni majority quickly accepted the shrine as part of its heritage.

The mosque itself is a 19th-century stone building heavily influenced by the Gothic Revival; only elements of older structures remain. On the south end of the southeast facade stands a partial wall with a gate, known as Bab al-Akhdar (the Green Gate), which probably dates from the Fatimid dynasty. Inside the mosque, past the main prayer hall, is the Tomb of Husayn, a domed chamber built by 'Abd al-Rahman Katkhuda in the 1760s. The grave is enclosed with a silver mashrabiyya screen.

The mosque is technically closed to non-Muslims. However, while large tour groups are not allowed to enter, there is more leeway for the individual traveler, provided that you avoid prayer times (the hour around noon; 1 PM between April and October during daylight saving time) and Fridays. ⊠ *Maydan al-Husayn, Islamic Cairo North* ☎ *No phone* ⊠ *Free*.

ALSO WORTH NOTING

❸ **Madrasa and Mausoleum of Sultan al-Salih al-Ayyubi.** Although it does not appear to be very significant from the street, this building occupies an important place in Cairo's history as a point of architectural and political transition. The last descendant of Salah al-Din to rule Egypt, al-Salih Nejm al-Din al-Ayyubi, died in 1249 defending the country against the Crusader attack lead by Louis IX of France. Following his death, his wife, the famous Shagarat al-Dor, ruled for a brief time as queen and then as wife to Aybak, the first Mamluk ruler of Egypt.

This madrasa was the first in Cairo to have a *liwan* (a vaulted area) for more than one legal school. It was also the first to have a tomb attached. These two unique traits became standard features of a Mamluk madrasa. During Mamluk times, the madrasa of al-Salih was used by judges when hearing cases and issuing judgments. The street in front, the Bayn al-Qasrayn section of Shar'a al-Mu'iz, was used for meting out punishments to those deemed guilty. This was the city center for centuries.

Above the madrasa's minaret sits a top in the shape of an incense burner, in Arabic known as a *mabkhara*. It is the only one of its kind remaining from the Ayyubid period (1171–1250). Beneath the minaret, very little remains of this structure—part of an arched liwan in the courtyard, and the fragments of another arch opposite that suggest something of its former scale and importance. Some details, like the keel arch recess on the minaret with shell-like ornamentation and the shallow relieving arch over the doorway, deserve notice. ⊠ *Shar'a al-Mu'iz, Islamic Cairo North* ☎ *No phone* 💲 *Free* ⊗ *Daily 9–4, except mosque during prayers.*

❻ **Madrasa of al-Nasir Muhammad.** Considered the greatest Mamluk sultan, al-Nasir ruled on three different occasions, for a total of 42 years (AD 1293–1340). It was during al-Nasir's reign that Egypt took advantage of its geographical location and gained control of the lucrative maritime trade routes that connected England with China. Al-Nasir built more than 30 mosques, the aqueduct from the Nile to the Citadel, and a canal from Cairo to Alexandria. Eight of his sons ruled Egypt in the 21 years following his death.

If Qalaun's complex has Gothic influences, all the more so his son's madrasa (built in 1304). In fact the entrance was literally lifted from a Crusader church in Acre. The minaret, with its delicate stuccowork, is one of the finest in the city. Little of interest can be found inside. ⊠ *Shar'a al-Mu'iz, Islamic Cairo North* ☎ *No phone* 💲 *Free* ⊗ *Daily 9–4.*

OFF THE BEATEN PATH

Madrasa of Mithqal. This beautifully restored Mamluk madrasa, which is built in a cruciform style, was built by Mithqal, chief eunuch to two Mamluk sultans, in 1361. To get here, start at the Palace of Bishtak and turn right, taking the little road that winds past the small mausoleum of Shaykh Sinan, instead of heading to Shar'a al-Mu'iz. The most interesting part of the complex is the tunnel that passes underneath it. Dare yourself to go through it and try to get to al-Mu'iz this way. (The tunnel takes you out to a small street that leads to the open Maydan Bayt al-Qadi. The last right off the square leads you down Shar'a Bayt al-Qadi to Muhhib al-Din, which in turn feeds onto al-Mu'iz.) ⊠ *Darb al-Qirmiz, Islamic Cairo North* ☎ *No phone* 💲 *Free* ⊗ *Daily 9–4.*

❹ **Madrasa of Sultan al-Zahir Baybars I.** Al-Zahir Baybars' reign (1260–77) marked the real beginning of the Mamluk state, due in large part to his skills as a commander, administrator, and builder. It was he who halted the Mongols' western expansion by defeating them at Ayn Jalout in Palestine (1260), and he staged a series of successful campaigns against the Crusaders. All that survives of this once great madrasa is the restored corner across the street from Qalaun's mausoleum. Check out the leopards above the metal door; they were Baybars' insignia (*baybars* means "leopard lord" in Qipchaq, a Circassian language). ⊠ *Shar'a al-Mu'iz, Islamic Cairo North* ☎ *No phone.*

❽ **Mosque and Madrasa of Barquq.** The first of the Circassian Mamluk Sultans, Barquq assumed power after a series of political intrigues that led to the downfall (and often deaths) of the Bahri (Tartar) Mamluks. Barquq (whose name means "the plum") took power in 1386 and rescued the country from the ravages of the Black Death and related famine and political unrest. His madrasa has an octagonal minaret with marble-inlaid carved stone. Notice the columns attached to the wall in the facade; one of them shows a stylized ram's head in the capital. The cruciform interior is spacious and austere, except for an ornate carved and gilded ceiling in the sanctuary (restored in modern times), and the *qibla* (the direction of Mecca) wall, decorated in marble dado. ⊠ *Shar'a al-Mu'iz, Islamic Cairo North* ☎ *No phone* ✆ *Free* ☉ *Daily 9–4, except mosque at prayer time.*

⓫ **Mosque of al-Aqmar.** The name of the mosque means "the moonlit" and refers to the way the stone catches the moon's reflection at night. Built in 1125, it is one of a few Fatimid buildings that have escaped major alterations. The shell-like recesses in the stone facade, later to become a common decorative element, were used here for the first time. This little mosque was also the first in Cairo to have an ornamented stone facade, and it was the first to alter its plan according to the existing urban structure, as the street existed before the mosque. ⊠ *Shar'a al-Mu'iz, Islamic Cairo North* ☎ *No phone* ✆ *Free* ☉ *Dawn–dusk, except during prayers.*

⓭ **Mosque of al-Hakim.** Originally built in AD 1010 by the Fatimid Khalifa (caliph) al-Hakim bi Amr Allah, this gigantic mosque was restored under the aegis of the Aga Khan, spiritual leader of the Isma'ili Shi'a sect.

Al-Hakim was, to put it nicely, an eccentric character. Some of the strangest edicts were declared during his caliphate, including a ban on *mulokhia*, a favorite Egyptian dish (he didn't care for it), and a ban on women's shoes, to prevent them from going out in public. Rumors began to circulate that he was claiming to be divine, creating extreme unrest among the populace. In order to quell the riots, he sent his main theologian, al-Darazi, to Syria (where he established the Druze religion), and then ordered his troops to attack Fustat, which at the time was the local town outside the royal city of al-Qahira. However, half his troops sided with the people, and the ensuing violence resulted in the burning of Fustat. He was given to riding around town on his donkey to ensure that his orders were being obeyed. One night after riding off into the Muquattam hills, he disappeared, never to be seen again, although the Druze claim that he has vanished only temporarily and will return to lead them to victory.

Built outside the original walls of Cairo (those standing now were constructed in 1087), the mosque has seen varied usage during its lifetime. During the Crusades, it held European prisoners of war who built a chapel inside it. Salah al-Din (1137–93) tore the chapel down when he used it as a stable. For Napoléon's troops it was a storehouse and fortress. Under Muhammad 'Ali in the 1800s, part of it was closed off and used as a *zawya* (small Sufi school). By the end of the 19th century, until the establishment of the **Museum of Islamic Arts** (⇨ *Islamic Cairo South, below*) in 1896, it was a repository for Islamic treasures.

Architecturally, the mosque does not compete among the finest in the city; the most significant element is its minarets, which were restored and reinforced by Baybars II in 1303, giving them that impressive trapezoidal base. Nevertheless, its scale and history are important, and its courtyard is large and breezy, making it a comfortable place to rest or meditate. ⊠ *Shar'a al-Mu'iz, Islamic Cairo North* ☎ *No phone* ✆ *Free* ☉ *Dawn–dusk, except during prayers.*

❾ **Palace of Bishtak.** Bishtak was a wealthy amir who married one of Sultan al-Nasir Muhammad's daughters. The original palace, completed in 1339, was purported to be five stories tall, with running water on each floor. The austere facade gives no hint of the lofty interior space. Only the women's quarters have survived the centuries, and even they are so impressive in scale as to give an idea of what the whole complex must have been like. See the mezzanine level with its *mashrabiyya* (oriel windows) galleries, from which the sequestered ladies of the household watched events in the main hall below without being seen. The coffered wooden ceilings in these galleries are worth the climb, as is the view of the city from the roof. The palace entrance—the building itself fronts Shar'a al-Mu'iz—is around to the left side of the building as you face it. ■ TIP→ Public bathrooms here are reasonably clean. ⊠ *Shar'a al-Mu'iz, Islamic Cairo North* ☎ *No phone* ✆ *Free* ☉ *Daily 9–4.*

❼ **Qa'a of Muhib al-Din.** Halfway up a street called Shar'a Bayt al-Qadi, on the west side of al-Mu'iz, this *qa'a* (great hall) has little to distinguish it save a small plaque (if the door isn't open, knock and the custodian will appear; otherwise, just walk in and find him). Inside is one of the greatest spaces in Islamic Cairo: a hall that towers 50 feet, with exquisite wood and stone carving. Also known as the house of Uthman Kathkhuda, after the 18th-century Ottoman lieutenant who converted the original 14th-century Mamluk qa'a, the hall has superb features from both periods. The marble mosaic around the fountain is remarkable, and if you can get up to the roof, take a look at the *malqaf* (wind catcher) once used to ventilate Cairo houses. ⊠ *Shar'a al-Mu'iz, Islamic Cairo North* ☎ *No phone* ✆ *Free, donation suggested* ☉ *Daily 9–4.*

❿ **Sabil-Kuttab of Abdul Rahman Katkhuda.** *Katkhuda* is a Persian word meaning "master of the house." The powerful gentleman who endowed this building was a patron of the arts and architecture, as befitted his position. Before running water was available to the majority of Cairo's inhabitants, it was customary for wealthy patrons to build a *sabil* (a public fountain) to provide people with potable water. Often attached to a sabil was a *kuttab* (a basic school) for teaching children the Qur'an and other subjects. This 17th-century Ottoman monument is impressive for its ornate facade, tiled interior, and location at the head of a fork in the main road of medieval Cairo. ⊠ *Shar'a al-Mu'iz, Islamic Cairo North* ☎ *No phone* ✆ *£E10* ☉ *Daily 10–6.*

NEED A BREAK?

Hotel el Hussein. On the roof of this hotel on Hussein Square is a restaurant and café with a great view of the area—not to mention clean restrooms. The hotel is on the top floor of the large building on the left side of the square facing al-Sayyidna al-Husayn. To enter, take the arched passage (the hotel's name is written above it) on Shar'a al-Muski, just off the square. The hotel foyer is on the right side of the passage. Take the elevator up.

✉ *Hussein Square, Khan al-Khalili, Islamic Cairo North* ☏ *02/2591–8479.*

ISLAMIC CAIRO SOUTH: AL-AZHAR TO BAB ZUWAYLA

Here is a teeming, commercial area, more typically Egyptian and less geared toward tourism than the Khan area. But if you feel like shopping, you can find all sorts of postmodern "1,001 Nights" gear here, from pierced brass lanterns to Asian spices and teapots to pigeon-feather fans.

Anecdotes abound with regard to Bab Zuwayla, the southern gate of Fatimid Cairo: the severed heads of criminals were displayed there, warning of the perils of breaking the sultan's law; a troll was said to live behind the massive door; and the surrounding area was the center of activity for crafty ladies of the night who sometimes held their customers for ransom. On the way to Bab Zuwayla and beyond is a wealth of monuments. As in Islamic Cairo North, many buildings here are being restored, but there are a few gems that you shouldn't miss, culminating at the Museum of Islamic Arts, at the end of the walk.

There is much to capture the attention in this area, but relatively few monuments are open for visiting. Depending on how long you spend along the way and in the tent-makers' bazaar, this area is worth three or four hours, excluding lunch and the visit to the Museum of Islamic Arts; set aside about an hour for the latter. *For Islamic sights' hours and prayer times, see* ⇨ *The Islamic Day in Islamic Cairo North, above.*

TOP ATTRACTIONS

⑯ Al-Azhar Mosque and University. Originally built in AD 970 by the conquering Fatimid caliph al-Mu'iz, al-Azhar is the oldest university in the world. Although the Fatimids were Shi'ite, the Sunni Mamluks who ousted them recognized the importance of the institution and replaced the Shi'ite doctrine with the Sunni orthodoxy. Today the university has faculties of medicine and engineering in addition to religion, and it has auxiliary campuses across the city.

Al-Azhar's primary significance remains as a school of religious learning. All Egyptian clerics must go through the program here before they are certified—a process that can take up to 15 years. Young men from all over the Islamic world come to study here, learning in the traditional Socratic method where students sit with a tutor until both agree that the student is ready to go on. The Shaykh of al-Azhar is not just the director of the university, but also the nation's supreme religious authority.

Built in pieces throughout the ages, al-Azhar is a mixture of architectural styles. The stucco ornamentation and the open courtyard represent early Islamic tastes; the solid stone madrasas and the ornate minarets are Mamluk; additions in the main sanctuary and its walls are Ottoman. The enclosure now measures just under 3 acres.

After you enter through the **Gates of the Barbers,** an Ottoman addition constructed under the auspices of Abd al-Rahman Katkhuda in 1752, remove your shoes. Then turn left to the **Madrasa and Tomb of Amir**

Atbugha. Check out the recess in the qibla wall; an organic-shaped mosaic pattern rare to Islamic ornamentation can be found near the top.

Return to the ticketing and shoe-removal area and look up at the **Gates of Sultan Qayt Bay,** the second set on the way into the university. Built in 1483, they have a quality of ornamentation that verifies this Mamluk leader's patronage of architecture. The composition as a whole is masterful: from the recessed lintel to the multitier stalactite arch above the doorway, the grilles and medallions above the arch, and, finally, the finely carved minaret placed off center.

To the right of this lobby is the **Madrasa of Taybars.** Once ranked among the most spectacular madrasas in Mamluk Cairo, only its qibla wall remains. It is said that the ceiling was gold-plated and that Taybars, the patron, so wanted to glorify Allah that he specifically asked not to see any bills until it was completed, in 1309.

Sultan Qayt Bay's gateway opens to a spacious courtyard, quite typical of early Islamic design. Originally this court must have appeared similar to that of the Mosque of al-Hakim *(⇨ Islamic Cairo North, above)*, but changes over the centuries have diminished that effect. The keel arches of the arcades and the stucco decoration, however, remain true to that era. The raising of the arch that indicates entrance to the main sanctuary, while a common feature of Persian and Indian Islamic architecture, remains an oddity in Arab buildings.

The main sanctuary, which was traditionally a place to pray, learn, and sleep, is part Fatimid, part Ottoman. The Ottoman extension is distinguished by a set of steps that divides it from the original. Take some time to soak in the atmosphere, and look for the two qibla walls, the painted wooden roof, the old metal gates that used to open for prayer or the poor, and the ornate stuccowork of the Fatimid section. To the right of the Ottoman qibla wall is the **Tomb of 'Abdul Rahman Katkhuda,** the greatest builder of the Ottoman era and the man most responsible for the post-Mamluk extension of al-Azhar. To the extreme left along the Fatimid qibla wall is the small **Madrasa and Mausoleum of the Eunuch Gawhar al-Qunqubay,** treasurer to Sultan Barsbay. Although it is diminutive in size, the quality of the intricately inlaid wooden doors, the stained-glass windows, and the interlacing floral pattern on the dome make it a deserved detour.

Return to the courtyard. To the right of the **minaret of Qayt Bay** is the **minaret of al-Ghuri,** the tallest in the complex. Built in 1510, it is similar to, but not a copy of, Qayt Bay's: it is divided into three sections (the first two are octagonal) like its predecessor, but it is tiled rather than carved. The final section, consisting of two pierced rectangular blocks, is unusual, and not at all like Qayt Bay's plain cylinder.

A restoration project has left the complex shiny and clean and has made the custodians especially sensitive about its upkeep. But the beauty of al-Azhar, unlike many of the other monuments, stems in part from the fact that it is alive and very much in use. ⊠ *Gama' al-Azhar, Shar'a al-Azhar, Islamic Cairo South* ☎ *No phone* ☎ *Free* ☉ *Daily dawn–dusk, except mosque at prayer times.*

⑲ Bab Zuwayla. Built in 1092, this is one of three remaining gates of
Fodor'sChoice Fatimid Cairo. It was named after members of the Fatimid army who
★ hailed from a North African Berber tribe called the Zuwayli.

The gate features a pair of minaret-topped semicircular towers. Notice
the lobed-arch decoration on the inner flanks of the towers in the
entrance. These arches were used earlier in North African architecture
and were introduced here following the Fatimid conquest of Egypt.
They are seen in later Fatimid and Mamluk buildings.

As you pass through the massive doorway, take into account that the ·
street level has risen to such an extent that what you see as you walk
would have been at eye level for a traveler entering the city on a camel.
According to the great architectural historian K.A.C. Creswell, the log-
gia between the two towers on the outside of the wall once housed an
orchestra that announced royal comings and goings.

However, Bab Zuwayla wasn't always such a lighthearted spot. It was
here that public hangings and beheadings took place. The conquering
Turks hanged the last independent Mamluk sultan, Tumanbay II, from
this gate in 1517. The unlucky man's agony was prolonged because the
rope broke three times. Finally, fed up, the Ottomans had him beheaded.

The views from the tower are some of the best in Cairo. Minarets galore
and little glimpses of street life in the alleyways below mean you may
spend more than a few minutes here.

Bab Zuwayla marks the southern end of the Fatimid city, as Bab al-
Futuh marks the north. And al-Mu'iz, the central artery of medieval
Cairo, runs from the latter through the former. Al-Mu'iz continues all
the way to the Southern Cemeteries, but as is common with many older
streets, the name keeps changing along the way, describing the area
it passes through, as when it passes through the tent-makers' bazaar.
⊠ *Shar'a al-Mu'iz, Islamic Cairo South* ⊑ *£E15* ⊙ *Daily 8–5.*

㉔ Museum of Islamic Arts. Too often overlooked, this is one of the finest
★ museums in Cairo, with a rare and extensive collection of Islamic art.
After a major restoration to the fabric of the building, the galleries now
give both a sense of place, with an explanation of the development of
Islamic Cairo, and offer visitors a comprehensive collection of the finest Islamic arts.

Arranged according to medium, there are pieces from every era of development—from Ummayad to Abbasid, Fatimid, Ayyubid, and Mamluk
works. You can see woodwork, stucco, intarsia, ceramics, glass, metalwork, textiles, and carpets.

Particularly notable items include one of the earliest Muslim tomb-
stones, which dates from 652, only 31 years after the Prophet returned
to Mecca victorious; a bronze ewer from the time of the Abbasid caliph
Marwan II that has a spout in the shape of a rooster; a series of Abbasid
stucco panels from both Egypt and Iraq displaying the varied styles of
the time; frescoes from a Fatimid bathhouse; wooden panels from the
Western Palace; carved rock crystal; a wooden piece from the Ayyubid
era covered with exquisite carved inscriptions and foliage; an excellent
brass-plated Mamluk door, which looks at first glance like a standard

The Al-Azhar Mosque

arabesque decoration but is in fact interspersed with tiny animals and foliage; and a series of mosaics from various Mamluk mosques, some made with marble and mother-of-pearl inlay.

The metalwork section contains the doors of the Mosque of al-Salih Tala'i. Metalwork inlaid with silver and gold includes incense burners, candlesticks, and vases, some with Christian symbols. There is also a set of astronomical instruments. The armor and arms hall is still impressive despite the fact that Selim, the conquering Ottoman sultan of 1517, had much of this type of booty carried off to Istanbul, where it is on display at Topkapi Palace. The ceramics display is excellent, particularly pieces from the Fatimid Era and Iran. A hall of glassware merits particular attention, especially the Mamluk mosque lamps. The collection of rare manuscripts and books is also noteworthy. The museum reopened in fall 2010 after a major renovation of its building and galleries. At the time of writing, the renovation was still underway; it's possible that gallery layouts have changed. ⊠ *Shar'a Bur Sa'id at Maydan Ahmad Maher, Islamic Cairo South* ☎ *02/2390–9930* ✉ *£E40* ☉ *Sat.–Thurs. 9–4, Fri. 9–11 and 2–4.*

ALSO WORTH NOTING

㉕ Abd El Rahman M. Harraz Seeds, Medicinal, and Medical Plants. Near the Museum of Islamic Arts is this fantastic shop (with Bab Zuwayla at your back, it's on the right); it has an incredible selection of medicinal herbs, traditional beauty aids, essential oils and cosmetics, and curiosities, including dried lizards. The bizarre window display features a stuffed gazelle. ⊠ *1 Bab el-Kalq Sq., Islamic Cairo South* ☎ *02/2511– 5167* ☉ *Sat.–Thurs. 9 AM–10 PM.*

⑱ Al-Ghuriyya. This medieval landmark stands on either side of Shar'a al-Mu'iz where it crosses Shar'a al-Azhar. The surrounding area was the site of the Silk Bazaar, visible in David Robert's famous 1839 etching of the same name.

Built by Sultan al-Ghuri, who constructed the Wikala al-Ghuri three years later, al-Ghuriyya was the last great Mamluk architectural work before the Ottomans occupied Egypt. On the right side of the street (facing Shar'a al-Azhar) is the madrasa; opposite it stands the mausoleum. The former is a large-scale project, with almost Brutalist proportions (picture large, modern, exposed-concrete buildings). Note the unusual design of the minaret, its square base topped by five chimney pots.

The mausoleum was rebuilt several times during al-Ghuri's reign. After spending a reported 100,000 dinars on the complex, al-Ghuri was not buried here. He died outside Aleppo, and his body was never found. The bodies of a son, a concubine (both victims of a plague outbreak), a daughter, and Tumanbay II (his successor) are interred in the vault. ⊠ *Qasr al-Ghuri, Shar'a al-Mu'iz, Islamic Cairo South* ☏ *02/2735–4234* 🎫 *£E25* ☼ *Daily 9–5.*

OFF THE
BEATEN
PATH

House of Gamal al-Din al Dhahabbi. The second right after al-Ghuriyya along al-Mu'iz leads to a small alley named Shar'a Khushqadam. Fifty yards up on the right, look for the well-preserved, 16th-century, wealthy merchant's house. Enter through the massive wooden doors that feed into the courtyard. Of particular interest are the *mashrabiyya* (wooden latticework screen) and stained-glass windows, the stone Mamluk-style facia panels, the marble floors, and the reception room's wooden ceilings. ⊠ *6 Shar'a Khushqadam, Islamic Cairo South* ☏ *No phone* 🎫 *£E15* ☼ *Daily 9–4.*

㉓ Mosque and Tomb of Qijmas al-Ishaqi. Restored in the early part of the 20th century, this complex was one of the jewels of Mamluk architecture. Its decorated facade reflects the ornate style popular under the reign of Sultan Qayt Bay. Qijmas served in the sultan's court until he took an appointment as viceroy of Damascus, where he died peacefully and was buried in 1487. By the late 15th century, when this mosque was built, space was at a premium in this part of Cairo, and the careful and elegant orientation of the mosque on the small, irregular plot of land demonstrates the architect's creativity.

Despite its irregular footprint, the mosque is a perfect cruciform plan. And the quality of light is excellent, as it filters in through the *shukh-shayhka* (lantern) of the central covered court and through the stained glass of the windows. Notice the prayer niche, with its inlaid white marble. The circle in the middle carries the name of the proud artist, written twice in mirror image—from left to right and vice versa. ⊠ *Shar'a Darb al-Ahmar, Islamic Cairo South* ☏ *No phone* 🎫 *Free* ☼ *Daily 9–4.*

㉒ Mosque of Altunbugha al-Maridani. Built by a son-in-law of Sultan Nasir al-Muhammad who died at the tender age of 25, the mosque was completed under the supervision of the sultan's architect. It features fine examples of virtually every decorative art in vogue in the 14th century. Enter the sanctuary behind the fine mashrabiyya screen and notice the collection of pillars of pharaonic, Christian, and Roman origin. The *mihrab* (prayer niche) is made of marble inlay and mother-of-pearl, and the wooden *minbar* (pulpit) is also beautifully carved and inlaid. Above the mihrab are excellent original stucco carvings, unique in Cairo for their naturalistically rendered tree motif. This wall also features dados of inlaid marble with square Kufic script.

Outside, be sure to admire the first example of a minaret in octagonal form from bottom to top; it is also the earliest extant example of just such a top. It is shaped like a pavilion, with eight columns carrying a pear-shaped bulb crown. Because this mosque is an active community center, its open hours tend to be longer than those of other monuments. ⊠ *Shar'a al-Tabbana, Islamic Cairo South* ☎ *No phone* 💳 *Free* ⊙ *Daily 9–8.*

㉟ Mosque of Mu'ayyad Shaykh. The Sultan Mu'ayyad chose this site because he was once imprisoned at this location. During his captivity, he swore that he would build a mosque here if he was ever freed. He made good on his promise in 1420 and tore down the infamous jails that once occupied the site.

The mosque's facade is remarkable only in that the *ablaq* (the striped wall) is black and white, less common than the usual red and white. The famous entrance of the Sultan Hassan Mosque below the Citadel inspired the high portal. The beautiful bronze-plated door was a little more than inspired; Mu'ayyad had it lifted from the mosque of his better-known predecessor. The two elegant **identical minarets** rest against the towers of Bab Zuwayla, which makes them appear to be a part of the gate and not the mosque.

The interior space is well insulated from the bustle of the surrounding district by high walls blanketed in marble panels. The wood and ivory minbar is flanked by a fine columned mihrab with marble marquetry of an exceptional level of quality. The gilt and blue ceilings are also noteworthy. ⊠ *Gam'a al-Mu'ayyad Shaykh, Shar'a al-Mu'iz at Bab Zuwayla, Islamic Cairo South* ☎ *No phone* 💳 *Free* ⊙ *Daily, dawn–dusk, except during prayers.*

㉑ Mosque of Wazir al-Salih Tala'i. Built in 1160, this is one of the last Fatimid structures constructed outside the city walls. It is also one of the most elegant mosques in Cairo, in part because of its simplicity. Like many mosques in Cairo, the ground floor housed several shops, which allowed the authorities to pay for the upkeep. Today these shops are underground, because the street level has risen considerably over time.

The mosque has a standard, early Islamic, rectangular courtyard plan. The main facade consists of five keel arches on Greco-Roman columns taken from an earlier building that are linked by wooden tie beams. Between each arch, a set of long panels is topped with Fatimid shell niches. The most distinctive architectural feature of this mosque is the porchlike area, underneath the arches of the main facade, that creates an open, airy interior court. Inside, the columns are also taken from elsewhere: no two of their capitals are alike. ⊠ *Gam'a al-Salih Tala'i, Shar'a al-Mu'iz at Bab Zuwayla, Islamic Cairo South* ☎ *No phone* 💳 *Free* ⊙ *Daily, dawn–dusk, except during prayers.*

🔟 **Wikala of al-Ghuri.** This handsome building with its strong, square lines seems almost modern, save for the ablaq masonry, a clear indicator of its Mamluk origin. Built in 1504–05 by Sultan Qansuh al-Ghuri, this classical Mamluk structure was constructed to accommodate visiting merchants. It went up, as fate would have it, at the end of a period of Mamluk prosperity, the result of their control of the spice trade between Asia and Europe. When Vasco da Gama discovered a path around Africa in 1495, the decline in Cairo's importance began. Sadly, although al-Ghuri was a prolific builder and a courageous soldier, he was a decade behind the curve. He died in 1516 staving off the Ottomans in Aleppo, Syria. His successor, Tumanbay II, was destined to last only a year before succumbing to the might of Istanbul.

Nevertheless, the building is in fairly good shape, and it provides an indication of how medieval Cairene commerce operated. Merchants would bring their horses and carts into the main courtyard, where they would be stabled, while the merchants would retire to the upper floors with their goods.

Today the wikala's rooms are used as studios for traditional crafts, including carpet weaving, metalwork, and the making of mashrabiyya that are not so different from the ones that protrude from the upper floors into the courtyard. The restoration also converted the site for cultural events. Traditional musicians, singers, and dancers perform regularly. Sufi chanting music and dancing (the whirling dervishes) takes place every Saturday, Monday, and Wednesday (showtime 8 PM). ✉ *Shar'a Muhammad 'Abdu, Islamic Cairo South* ☎ *02/2735–4234* 💰 *£E15* ⏱ *Daily 9–4, studios Sat.–Wed. 9–4.*

DOWNTOWN AND BULAQ

In the middle of the 19th century, the slavishly Francophile khedive Isma'il laid out this district on a Parisian plan across the old canal from Islamic Cairo, which until then had been the heart of the city. It quickly became the most fashionable commercial and residential district, lined with cafés and jewelers and settled by all the major department stores. In time, as new residential districts such as Garden City and Zamalek opened up, Downtown lost favor as a place to live. But it was, above all else, a colonial city—standing in proximity to traditional Cairo but self-consciously apart from it.

With the rise of Egyptian nationalism in the early 20th century, that could not last. Much of Downtown was systematically torched in anti-foreign riots on Black Saturday in January 1952, in a spasm of violence that demonstrated how closely architecture was associated with colonial rule. The riots marked the beginning of the end for the foreign presence in Egypt: the revolution that overthrew the British-backed monarchy followed Black Saturday within months, and with it all the street names changed to reflect the new heroes. But it was the wave of nationalizations in the early 1960s that finally closed the colonial chapter Downtown, as those foreigners who had stayed on past the revolution lost their businesses, their way of life, and their place in a city that had never really belonged to them.

Downtown—called Wist al-Balad in Arabic—is still loved today, but more for its shoe stores and cinemas than for its architecture and the unique melding of cultures and influences that it once represented. Walking through the district gives you a sense of infinite discovery, of little fragments of a time and place now lost that haven't quite been swept away by the changing politics. Although all the shops at street level have redecorated their own pieces of facade, look higher and the fin-de-siècle city comes alive. Sadly, most of the buildings are in an advanced state of decay, so you have to use a little imagination to re-create the neighborhood's former glory.

Quite apart from the experience of Downtown Cairo, the Egyptian Antiquities Museum is a lens through which to see the ancient world. And it is essential to any trip to Egypt. Its vast stores of treasures from ancient Egypt are as astonishing as they are daunting to take in. Tour the museum in conjunction with a day in Giza, or before you head upriver to Luxor, Aswan, and beyond for the Nile Valley monuments.

TOP ATTRACTIONS

1 ★ Chaar-Hachamaim Synagogue. This unusual concrete block with a subtle art nouveau floral motif is easily overlooked from the outside. Arrive early, passport in hand, act unthreatening—the security guards can be touchy about letting people in—and one of Cairo's great hidden treasures awaits, with an interior of exquisite stained-glass windows and light fixtures rumored to be from Tiffany. Erected in 1899 by the Mosseri family, the synagogue is seldom used because there are too few remaining Jewish men to hold a service. This possible end masks a long and prosperous history for the Jewish community in Egypt. Over the past 500 years, whenever Europe went through its regular waves of persecution and expulsion, Jews sought refuge in Muslim lands such as Egypt, where they were protected as People of the Book. Only in the 20th century, with colonialism and the emergence of Israel, did local sentiment turn against them. Contact the synagogue to organize a visit. ■TIP→ Security is tight, so make sure you carry your passport as proof of identity. ⊠ *Shar'a Adly (opposite Kodak Passage), Downtown* ☎ *02/2482–4613.*

NEED A BREAK? Windsor Hotel. This historic hotel has an atmospheric bar tucked away on its second floor. The Windsor opened in 1901 as the royal baths. Some years later it became an adjunct to the legendary Shepheard's. When Shepheard's burned, the Windsor survived, and the bar still retains a vaguely Anglicized air, with heavy colonial furniture that is ideal for reclining with a cold drink. The place draws a regular clientele that includes many aging members of Cairo's intellectual community. The sense of timelessness infects the staff as well, who appear to have worked here since the 1930s and will never rush you out the door. ⊠ *19 Shar'a Alfi Bey, Downtown* ☎ *02/2591–5277* ⊕ *www.windsorcairo.com.*

7 Fodor'sChoice ★ The Egyptian Antiquities Museum. On the north end of Maydan Tahrir, this huge neoclassical building is home to the world's largest collection of ancient Egyptian artifacts. With more than 100,000 items in

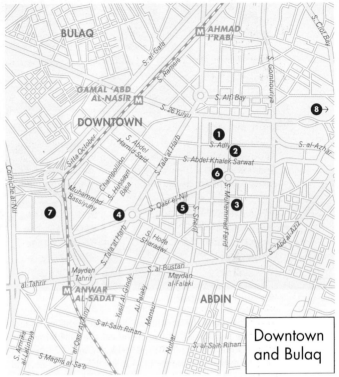

**Downtown
and Bulaq**

total, it is said that if you were to spend just one minute on each item, it would take over nine months to complete the tour. Needless to say, you need to be selective here, and it's a good idea to buy a museum guidebook or hire a museum guide. You can purchase a map of the museum (£E35), helpful in getting your bearings, but it doesn't include much in the way of historical description. *The Egyptian Museum in Cairo: Official Catalogue* (£E100) (available in the museum) is a far more comprehensive and practical guide. Official museum guides are available at £E50 an hour, but if you want a two- or three-hour tour, you can bargain for a lower rate. Five to six hours allow for a fair introduction to the museum.

Some of the museum's finest pieces are in the center of the ground floor, below the atrium and rotunda. The area makes a good place to start, acting as a preview for the rest of the museum. Among the prized possessions here are three colossi of the legendary New Kingdom pharaoh Ramses II (1290–1224 BC); a limestone statue of Djoser (around 2600 BC), the 2nd Dynasty pharaoh who built the Step Pyramid in Saqqara; several sarcophagi; and a floor from the destroyed palace of Akhenaton (1353–1335 BC), the heretic monotheist king. The Narmer Palette, a piece from about 3000 BC, is thought to document the first unification of northern and southern Egypt.

Tutankhamun at the Egyptian Antiquities Museum

Rooms around the atrium are arranged chronologically, clockwise from the left (west) of the entrance: the Old Kingdom (2575–2134 BC) in rooms 31, 32, 36, 37, 41, 42, 46, and 47; the Middle Kingdom (2040–1640 BC) in rooms 11, 12, 16, 17, 21, 22, 26, and 27; the New Kingdom (1550–1070 BC) in rooms 1–10, 14, 15, 19, and 20; Greco-Roman Egypt (332 BC–c. AD 395) in rooms 34, 35, 39, and 40; and Nubian Exhibits in rooms 44 and 45.

Among the most important Old Kingdom items are a superbly crafted statue of Khafre (2551–2528 BC), builder of the second Great Pyramid at Giza (Room 42), and the delightful, lifelike dual statues of Rahotep and Nofret (2500 BC, Room 42). The Middle Kingdom display includes several statues of Senwosret I (1971–1926 BC), responsible for the first major temple to Amun at Karnak (Room 22). The rich collection of New Kingdom artifacts includes an exquisite statue of Thutmose III (1479–1425 BC), Egypt's greatest empire builder, suckling at the teat of the cow-goddess (Room 12); artwork from Akhenaton's reign, the realistic style of which is markedly different from anything that came before or after it (Room 3); and several statues and parts of colossi from the time of Ramses II (Room 20). The works in the Greco-Roman exhibit are not as impressive as those on display in the Greco-Roman Museum in Alexandria, but they are interesting nonetheless in their attempts to weld Hellenistic and pharaonic cultures. Pieces in the Nubian section include saddles, weapons, and a mummified horse skeleton (Room 42)—again, of lesser quality than the Nubian Museum in Aswan but still of interest.

EGYPTIAN MUSEUM TOURING TIPS

■ **Afternoons are quieter.** Visit the museum in the afternoons after the tour groups have left, though be prepared for heat and humidity since most of the museum is not air-conditioned.

■ **Get guidance.** If you are visiting on your own, hire an official guide (at the museum entrance) to help explain the artifacts in more detail.

■ **Take your time.** Full-day Cairo tours give you a small amount of time in the museum, but it's worth

more. In fact, if time permits, visit the museum twice, to allow more time to take in the many thousands of items on view.

■ **Travel light.** Bulky bags and cameras will be confiscated and held at reception during your visit.

■ **Take a guidebook.** Bring your guidebook with you when you visit so that you can relate the artifacts to the geographical sites.

On the museum's upper floor is the famous Tutankhamun collection. Look for its beautiful gold funerary mask and sarcophagus (Room 3), ancient trumpet (Room 30), thrones (rooms 20 and 25), the four huge gilded boxes that fit one inside the other (exhibits 7 and 8, located in the hallway just outside Room 30), and a royal toilet seat to boot (outside Room 30); it is one of the few air-conditioned rooms in the museum. (The collection is scheduled to be relocated to the new Grand Egyptian Museum in Giza as early as 2010.) Also upstairs is the royal Mummy Room, which houses 11 pharaonic dignitaries, including the body of Ramses II (Room 52). If you are discouraged by the Mummy Room's steep entrance fee, don't miss the assortment of mummified animals and birds in the adjacent room (Room 53), which has no additional charge. Also on the upper floor is a series of specialized exhibits, including a collection of papyri and Middle Kingdom wooden models of daily life (rooms 24 and 27).

In 2003, the museum unveiled "Hidden Treasures of the Egyptian Museum," more than 150 of the best objects that form part of the museum's vast stock of artifacts kept in storage. Fittingly, the new galleries sit in the museum basement, where the catalogued items used to lie on dark dusty shelves. In 2009, a permanent Children's Museum was opened and aimed specifically at younger visitors. These galleries combine authentic artifacts with Lego models (donated by the Danish State) to explain aspects of life and customs in ancient Egypt. Children are free to use Lego bricks to construct their own models.

The Egyptian Antiquities Museum is due to close for renovations once the Grand Egyptian Museum on the Giza Plateau—currently slated in late 2012 or early 2013—when the ancient artifacts will be split between this new museum and the Museum of Egyptian Civilization in Fustat in Islamic Cairo. ⊠ *al-Mathaf al-Masri, Maydan Tahrir, Downtown* ☎ *02/2578–2452* ▨ *Museum £80, Mummy Room £E100* ☺ *Daily 9–6:30.*

The Jewish Community in Cairo

The Chaar-Hachamaim Synagogue was paid for with contributions from some of the most powerful men in Cairo—a small coterie of Jewish families (including the Cattaui, Suares, Naggar, and Mosseri families) who owned and controlled many of Egypt's private banks, bus companies, and major department stores. Vita Mosseri was the main energizer behind the campaign for the new place of worship and Maurice Cattaui was the architect who produced the blueprint for the finished building.

The Jewish community lived in peace and security alongside the Muslim Arab and Christian peoples in Egypt for generations, but the founding of the state of Israel and the 1952 revolution in Egypt brought privatization and increased political tension that turned the world upside down for these families within a half decade.

ALSO WORTH NOTING

❸ Banque Misr. Colonial Cairo emulated the French, was run by the British, and was built largely by Italians. Yet for all that colonial layering, its profoundly Middle Eastern cultural origins always won out in the end. Nothing symbolizes this strange synthesis better than the buildings of the Italian architect Antoine Lasciac, who worked in Cairo from 1882 to 1936 and served as the chief architect of the khedivial palaces. Lasciac set out to reflect Egypt's emergent nationalism in a new architectural style by updating the Mamluk decorative work so typical of Islamic Cairo and grafting it onto the technical innovations of his era. The result can be seen in this, his best-preserved building, which dates from 1927. Its mosaics, sculptural work, and decorations all draw on a range of Middle Eastern influences, while the core of the building, in plan and scale, is distinctly Western. ⊠ *Shar'a Muhammad Farid, south of Maydan Mustafa Kamil, Downtown.*

OFF THE BEATEN PATH

Old Red-Light District. Although the area around Shar'a Clot Bey is now rather conservative, at one time in the 20th century it was lined with brothels and bars, and you can still see the arched walkways and hidden nooks that once sheltered unspeakable vices. Prostitution was not made illegal in Cairo until 1949, but the trade had one last great boom period during World War II, when the nearby Shepheard's was commandeered as the British officers' base and the Ezbekiyya teemed with young men less interested in the Pyramids than in more carnal pursuits. To them, this area was known simply as the Birka, after one of the adjoining alleys, and it offered them comforts of all sorts for just 10 piastres. The shuttered second-floor rooms see less traffic these days, reborn as cheap if largely respectable pensions, and the nearby Saint Mark's Cathedral, once a source of succor for guilt-ridden consciences, now serves a more prosaic function for the local Christian community. Every once in a while the local newspapers run interviews with elderly women professing to have been madams in their youth, although few other Egyptians lament the passing of the trade.

❹ Groppi. On the western edge of Maydan Tala'at Harb, recognizable by the gorgeous mosaic decorating the entrance, Groppi was once the chocolatier to royalty. Founded in the 1930s by a Swiss native, this café and dance hall (along with its older branch on nearby Shar'a Adly) was the favorite meeting place for everyone from celebrities and the local aristocracy to political activists and British soldiers. Ravaged by four decades of socialism and several tasteless renovations, Groppi now barely manages a good coffee, although the elaborate metal lights in the rotunda are worth a look. ⊠ *Maydan Tala'at Harb, Downtown* ☎ *02/574–3244* ⊗ *Daily 7* AM*–10* PM.

❻ L'Orientaliste. This small, unostentatious bookstore is one of the world's premier sources for antique maps and out-of-print books with Middle Eastern themes. The store smells appropriately musty, and you might easily while away an afternoon looking through the old postcards, photographs, and assembled treasures. Ask a clerk to show you what Downtown, particularly Opera Square, used to look like—it will aid your imagination as you walk around. Don't leave without seeing the map room, up the stairs in the back. ⊠ *15 Shar'a Qasr al-Nil, Downtown* ☎ *02/575–3418* ⊕ *www.orientalecairo.com* ⊗ *Mon.–Sat. 10–7:30.*

❽ Sednaoui. A spectacular building modeled on a store in Paris, Sednaoui is on a back corner of Ezbekiyya near Ataba Square and is now largely forgotten by most Cairenes. It was built in 1913 as the main branch of a chain owned by a pair of Levantine brothers and has the sort of architectural flourishes rare in Cairo today: a large greenhouse atrium, a swirling central staircase, and two priceless copper elevators that are worth a quick ride. Sadly, since Egypt's department stores were nationalized in the early 1960s, the original owners have long since left and there is little of interest to buy. ⊠ *3 Kazinder Sq., Downtown* ☎ *02/590–3613* ⊗ *Mon.–Sat. 10–8.*

❷ St. David Building. Founded in the 1880s by a Welshman as the Davies Bryan department store—Cairo's largest at the time—this building has an odd, almost witty roofline reminiscent of a fortress. The facade retains the cursive *D* and *B* of its former owner who, patriot that he was, decorated it with Welsh symbols, to which later occupants have added about a hundred little Venus de Milos. The antique, ground-floor **Stephenson Pharmacy**, which is open Monday through Saturday 9:30–9, is not to be missed. It was once one of the best in the city (according to the 1929 Baedeker's guide) and still displays advertisements for ancient cure-alls. Also in the St. David is the beloved **Anglo-Egyptian Bookstore** (☎ *02/2391–4237* ⊕ *www.anglo-egyptian.com*), which has a pleasant search-through-the-stacks ambience. The bookstore is open 9–1:30 and 4:30–8, except for Sunday, when it's closed. ⊠ *Shar'a Muhammad Farid at Shar'a Khalek Sarwat, Downtown.*

❺ Trieste. Designed by the architect of the Banque Misr but even more intriguing, this 1910 building is rich in Islamic sculptural elements. Long neglected, the Trieste was finally renovated as part of the Stock Exchange neighborhood renewal plan and is now disconcertingly tarted up in off-white and salmon. In compensation, the gorgeous mosaic work is easier to see now. ⊠ *South side of Shar'a Qasr al-Nil, 1 block west of Shar'a Sherif, Downtown.*

THE CITADEL AND SAYYIDA ZAYNAB

The view of the huge silver domes and needle-thin minarets of the Muhammad 'Ali Mosque against the stark backdrop of the desert cliffs of the Muquattam is one of Cairo's most striking visual icons. The mosque is just one feature of the Citadel, an immense fortified enclosure that housed the local power brokers from Salah al-Din, its 12th-century founder, to Napoléon in the 18th century and the British colonial governors and troops until their withdrawal in 1946. It served as the base of operations for Mamluk slave kings as well as for a series of sultans and pashas with their colorful retinues, including al-Nasir Muhammad's 1,200-concubine-strong harem.

The Citadel commands wonderful views of the city—smog permitting. From there, you can visit some impressive monuments, including the amazing Mosque and Madrasa of Sultan Hasan, one of the largest such structures in the world, and the remarkably calm, austere Mosque of Ibn Tulun, one of Cairo's oldest buildings.

The areas between these three mosques have been cut through with a series of main roads—including modern attempts to clear paths across the dense medieval urban fabric—and as a result, this part of the city lacks the coherence and charm of, say, Coptic Cairo or the area around Bab Zuwayla. Nevertheless, the scale and quality of these monuments is so impressive that if you have time to see only a few of Cairo's Islamic treasures, the Citadel and the Sultan Hasan and Ibn Tulun mosques should be among them.

For Islamic sights' hours and prayer times, see ⇨ *The Islamic Day in Islamic Cairo North, above.*

TOP ATTRACTIONS

❶ The Citadel. Until Salah al-Din al-Ayyubi arrived in Cairo in 1168, local rulers had overlooked the strategic value of the hill above the city. Within a few years he began making plans for the defense of the city, with **al-Qala'a** (the fortress) the key element. He and his successors built an impenetrable bastion, using the most advanced construction techniques of the age. For the next 700 years, Egypt was ruled from this hill. Nothing remains of the original complex except a part of the walls and Bir Yusuf, the well that supplied the Citadel with water. The Ayyubid walls that circle the northern enclosure are 33 feet tall and 10 feet thick; they and their towers were built with the experience gleaned from the Crusader wars. Bir Yusuf is also an engineering marvel; dug 285 feet straight into solid rock to reach the water table, the well was powered by oxen that would walk in circles all day to draw water up to the level of the Citadel.

During the 1330s al-Nasir Muhammad tore down most of the Ayyubid buildings to make room for his own needs, which included several palaces and a mosque in addition to barracks for his army. These, too, were not to last, for when Muhammad 'Ali assumed power he had all

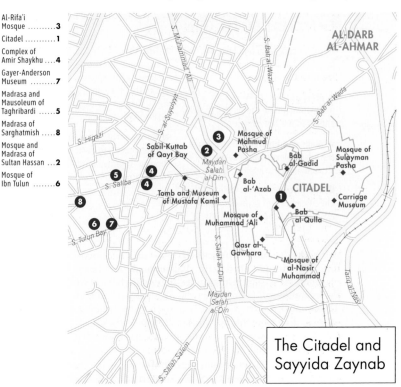

2

The Citadel and
Sayyida Zaynab

the Mamluk buildings razed and the complex entirely rebuilt; only the
green-domed mosque and a fragment of **al-Qasr al-Ablaq** (the striped
palace) remain. The Citadel's appearance today is really the vision of
Muhammad 'Ali, particularly the mosque that bears his name.

The **Muhammad 'Ali Mosque** is the most noticeable in all of Cairo. For
more than 150 years it has dominated the skyline, making it almost the
symbol of the city. This is ironic because it is actually an imitation of
the graceful Ottoman mosques in Istanbul. Notice the alabaster facing
on the outside. The interior reflects a somewhat gaudy attempt to weld
Middle Eastern and French rococo and is finished with ornate lines of
red, green, and gold. Nevertheless, there are interesting aspects to the
place. Ottoman law prohibited anyone but the sultan from building a
mosque with more than one minaret, but this mosque has two. Indeed,
this was one of Muhammad 'Ali's first indications that he did not intend
to remain submissive to Istanbul.

The courtyard within the mosque is spacious and comfortable. It also
has a gilded clock tower given to Muhammad 'Ali by King Louis
Philippe in exchange for the obelisk that stands in the middle of Paris.
It is fair to say that the French got the better end of the bargain: the
clock has never worked.

THE CITADEL TOURING TIPS

The Citadel is large and hilly. Be prepared for a strenuous walk to the top from the entrance.

■ **Start at the top.** Work your way down through the attractions to save energy in the hot climate.

■ **Wear comfortable shoes.** There are many uneven surfaces and a sizeable incline.

■ **Bring your camera.** Views of the old city and Cairo skyline from the walls of the Citadel are exceptional.

■ **Breathe.** This is one of the breeziest and also one of the least crowded parts of Cairo, but don't forget that the sun is still powerful so take all the usual precautions against skin damage.

■ **Come early.** Afternoons are the busiest time here—with many school groups—so arrive in the morning or late afternoon.

Behind Muhammad 'Ali's gilded beast stands a far more elegant creature, the **Mosque of al-Nasir Muhammad.** The beautifully crafted masonry, the elegant proportions, the ornate but controlled work on the minarets—all indicate that the building is a Mamluk work of art. The conquering Ottomans carried much of the original interior decoration off to Istanbul, but the space is nevertheless impressive. The supporting columns around the courtyard were collected from various sources and several are pharaonic.

Directly across from the entrance of al-Nasir is the **National Police Museum.** A prison until 1985, this small structure is hardly worth the five minutes it will take to walk through it. Two things rescue it from complete dismissal: the exhibition on political assassinations in Egypt, and the spectacular view from the courtyard behind it. Directly below is the lower enclosure gated by the Bab al-'Azab, the site where Muhammad 'Ali decisively wrested control from the unruly Mamluk warlords, who, while they had submitted to Ottoman rule for 300 years, had not really accepted it. In his capacity as Ottoman governor, Muhammad 'Ali invited all the powerful Mamluks up to the Citadel where they ate, drank, and were merry. As they were making their way to the gate for their exit, the governor's men ambushed them, eliminating in a single stroke all internal opposition.

To the northwest of al-Nasir's mosque is the **Bab al-Qulla,** which leads to the **Qasr al-Harem** (the Harem Palace), now the site of the **National Military Museum.** The brainchild of King Faruq, the exhibit was intended to chronicle the glories of his family but has been extended by the post-Revolution administrations to include the military glories of presidents Jamal 'Abd al-Nasir (Nasser), Anwar Sadat, and Hosni Mubarak. The display of uniforms and weaponry may be of some interest to historians and military aficionados. For those less taken with martial affairs, the building itself is another example of the eclectic taste appreciated by Muhammad 'Ali and his descendants.

Farther west, the **Carriage Museum** was the dining hall of the British officers stationed at the Citadel in the early 20th century. It now houses eight carriages used by Egypt's last royal dynasty (1805–1952).

In the northwest part of the Citadel is a rarely visited site, the **Mosque of Sulayman Pasha.** Built in 1528 by Egypt's Ottoman governor for his crack Janissary troops, this is a small but graceful mosque. While its plan is entirely a product of Istanbul, the sparse stone decoration shows traces of Mamluk influence. The tomb contains the remains of several prominent Janissary officers, as well as a Fatimid saint.

Before leaving the Citadel, pass by the **Qasr al-Gawhara** (the Jewel Palace), where Muhammad 'Ali received guests. When the khedives moved their residence down to 'Abdin Palace in the city, it was opened to the public, and after the revolution it was turned into a museum displaying the royal family's extravagance. Heavily influenced by the early-19th-century French style, the building is similar in taste to the Harem Palace. The painted murals on the walls and ceiling of the main Meeting Hall are worth the visit, as is the furniture in the model royal bedroom.

There is a small gift shop in the complex that is well stocked with books and CDs. If you stop in, you may want to pick up a copy of *The Citadel of Cairo: A History and Guide,* by William Lyster, a wonderfully detailed book and great companion for your visit, or a copy of the excellent SPARE (Society for the Preservation of the Architectural Resources of Egypt) Map, which covers the area. ⊠ *Al-Qala'a, Shar'a Salih Salem, The Citadel* ☏ *02/2591–3391* ▱ *£E50* ☉ *Daily 8–5.*

❼ ★ Gayer-Anderson Museum. Also known as Bayt al-Kiritliya, the museum consists of two Ottoman houses joined together, restored, and furnished by Major Gayer-Anderson, a British member of the Egyptian civil service in the 1930s and '40s. Gayer-Anderson was a talented collector and a sensitive, artistic gentleman, from the looks of the house's contents, which include lovely pieces of pharaonic, Islamic, and Central Asian art (though there are a few oddities). Spend some time in the reception room, where a mosaic fountain lies at the center of an ornate marble floor. In the courtyard of the east house is the "Well of Bats," the subject of much storytelling in the neighborhood. The house also inspired Gayer-Anderson's grandson, Theo, who illustrated a book on the subject and became an art conservationist, involved in the restoration of Bab Zuwayla. ⊠ *4 Maydan Ibn Tulun, The Citadel* ☏ *02/2364–7822* ▱ *£E35* ☉ *Daily 8–5.*

❷ ★ Mosque and Madrasa of Sultan Hassan. Built between 1356 and 1363 by the Mamluk ruler Sultan Hassan, this is one of the largest Islamic religious buildings in the world. Historians believe that its builders may have used stone from the Pyramids at Giza. The scale of the masterpiece is so colossal that it nearly emptied the vast Mamluk Treasury.

You enter the complex at an angle, through a tall portal that is itself a work of art. Before going in, look at the carving on both sides of the entrance that culminates in a series of stalactites above. A dark and relatively low-ceilinged passageway to the left of the entrance leads to the brightly lit main area, a standard cruciform-plan open court.

What is different about this plan is the fact that between each of the four liwans is a madrasa, one for each of the four Sunni schools of jurisprudence, complete with its own courtyard and four stories of cells for students and teachers. Also unique is the location of the mausoleum behind the qibla liwan, which, in effect, forces people who are praying to bow before the tomb of the dead sultan—a fairly heretical idea to devout Muslims. Nevertheless, the mausoleum, facing the Maydan Salah al-Din, is quite beautiful, particularly in the morning when the rising sun filters through grilled windows.

Only one of the two tall minarets is structurally sound, the one to the left of the qibla liwan. Have the custodian take you up inside of it to get a view of the city, especially of the Citadel. In fact, this roof was used by several armies to shell the mountain fortress, Bonaparte's expedition included. ⊠ *Maydan Salah al-Din, The Citadel* ☎ *No phone* ✏ *£E25* ☉ *Daily 8–5, except during Friday prayers.*

❻ Mosque of Ibn Tulun. This huge congregational mosque was built in 879 by Ahmad Ibn Tulun with the intention of accommodating his entire army during Friday prayers. Ahmad was sent to Egypt by the 'Abbasid caliph in Samarra to serve as its governor, but it seems that he had his own plans. Sensing weakness in Iraq, he declared his independence and began to build a new city, al-Qata'i, northwest of al-Fustat and al-'Askar, the Muslim towns that had grown up north of the Roman fortress of Babylon. Replete with numerous palaces, gardens, and even a hippodrome, al-Qata'i was not destined to survive. When the 'Abbasids conquered Egypt again, in 970, they razed the entire city as a lesson to future rebels, sparing only the great Friday mosque but leaving it to wither on the outskirts.

In 1293, the emir Lagin hid out in the derelict building for several months while a fugitive from the Mamluk sultan, vowing to restore it if he survived. Three years later, after being appointed sultan himself, he kept his word, repairing the minaret and adding a fountain in the courtyard, the mihrab, and the beautiful minbar. All of this background is secondary to the building itself—you can delight in this masterpiece without even the slightest knowledge of history. Its grandeur and simplicity set it apart from any other Islamic monument in Cairo.

The mosque is separated from the streets around it with a *ziyada* (a walled-off space), in which the Friday market was once held and where the famous minaret is located. At the top of the walls a strange crenellation pattern almost resembles the cutout figures that children make with folded paper. Inside, the mosque covers an area of more than 6 acres. Four arcaded aisles surround the vast courtyard. The soffits of the arches are covered in beautifully carved stucco, the first time this medium was used in Cairo. Look for the stucco grilles on the windows, especially those in the qibla wall. The minaret, the only one of its kind in Egypt, is modeled after the minarets of Samarra, with the ziggurat-like stairs spiraling on the outside of the tower. ⊠ *Shar'a Tulun Bay, The Citadel* ☎ *No phone* ✏ *Free* ☉ *Daily, dawn–dusk, except at prayer time.*

ALSO WORTH NOTING

❸ Al-Rifa'i Mosque. Although it appears neo-Mamluk in style, this mosque was not commissioned until 1869, by the mother of Khedive Isma'il, the Princess Khushyar. The project was completed in 1912, but at least from the outside, it seems more timeworn and less modern in style than the 14th-century Sultan Hassan Mosque next to it.

True to the excessive khedivial tastes, the inside is markedly different from the other mosque: where Sultan Hassan is relatively unadorned, al-Rifa'i is lavishly decorated. Inside the mausoleum are the bodies of Khashyar, King Fu'ad (father of Farouk, the last king of Egypt), other members of the royal family, Sufi holy men of the Rifa'i order (hence the establishment's name), and the last shah of Iran. ⊠ *Maydan Salah al-Din, Sayyida Zaynab* ☎ *No phone* 🎫 *£E25* ☉ *Daily 9–4, except at prayer time.*

❹ Complex of Amir Shaykhu. Flanking Shar'a Saliba, this mosque and khan-qah were built by the commander in chief of Sultan Hassan's forces and form a well-integrated whole. The mosque was badly damaged by shelling during the Ottoman takeover because Tumanbay, the last Mamluk sultan, hid here. Nevertheless, the qibla liwan still has the original marble inlay work. Today it is an active mosque frequented by people from the neighborhood.

The khanqah, with its central courtyard surrounded by three floors of 150 rooms, once housed 700 Sufi adherents. As in the mosque, classi-cal pillars support the ground-floor arches. To the left of the qibla wall are the tombs of Shaykhu and the first director of the school. ⊠ *Shar'a Saliba (just east of Shar'a al-Suyuiyya), The Citadel* ☎ *No phone* 🎫 *Free* ☉ *Daily, dawn–dusk, except during prayers.*

❺ Madrasa and Mausoleum of Taghribardi. This small but impressive complex was built in 1440 by the executive secretary to Sultan Jaqmaq. Fitting the standard minaret, entrance portal, sabil-kuttab, and dome into a single ensemble required a talented architect. Much of the top part of the building is an Ottoman reconstruction, including the final tier of the minaret. The work is clearly of a lower standard, demonstrating architecturally the demotion in Cairo's status from the capital of an empire to that of a province within an empire. ⊠ *Saghri Wardi, Shar'a Saliba, The Citadel* ☎ *No phone* 🎫 *£E8* ☉ *Daily 9–4.*

❽ Madrasa of Sarghatmish. Completed in 1356 by the emir who succeeded Shaykhu, Sarghatmish was probably designed by the same architect who designed Sultan Hassan. The layout is a cruciform plan—its inno-vative placement of the madrasa in the corners is identical to that of the great mosque—although smaller in scale. But far from being a diminu-tive copy of a masterpiece, Sarghatmish has several features that make it interesting in its own right, the first being a tall arched entrance that rises slightly above the facade. Most significant are the two domes, which are very unusual for Cairo. One has unfortunately been reno-vated with concrete, the other is sublime. Built in brick, it has a slight bulge reminiscent of the Persian style domes of Iran and central Asia. The interior space is pleasing and replete with Islamic detail in marble and stone. ✉ *Shar'a Saliba, just east of Shar'a Qadry, The Citadel* ☎ *No phone* 🎫 *£E8* 🕙 *Daily 9–4.*

COPTIC CAIRO (MARI GIRGIS)

The area known as Mari Girgis (Saint George) is centuries older than the Islamic city of Cairo. But even calling it Coptic Cairo isn't entirely accurate, because it includes an important synagogue and, nearby, some significant mosques. Known from the ancient historians as the town of Babylon, it was here that the Roman emperor Trajan (AD 88–117) decided to build a fortress around the settlement. At a time when the Nile flowed 1,300 feet east of its current course and was connected by way of canal to the Red Sea, the fortress occupied a strategic location.

Tradition holds that Saint Mark brought Christianity to Egypt in the first century. The Christians of Egypt became the first in Africa to embrace the new faith, and they were persecuted harshly for it. Many fled to the desert or south to the Upper Nile Valley. Later, under the Byzantine emperors, the local Christian population—known as Copts (an Arabic derivative of the Greek word for Egypt)—came out of hiding and began building several churches within and around the town walls.

But harmony within the church was not to last; serious theological disputes about the unity of God (the Coptic view) versus the trinity of God (the Byzantine) arose between the Egyptians and Constantinople, and once again the Copts were threatened with persecution. So when the Arabs arrived across the desert, local Copts initially welcomed them as liberators from the tyranny of Byzantium, despite their religious differences. Fustat, the encampment that the Arabs established just outside the walls of Babylon, quickly grew into a major city, leaving the older town as an enclave for Christians and Jews.

Thus Coptic Cairo encompasses elements from all these eras: portions of the Roman fortress survive; within the walled city stand four churches, a convent, a monastery, and a synagogue that was originally a church; and the oldest mosque in Africa is nearby. The Coptic Museum has a collection of local Christian art that displays pharaonic, Hellenistic, and even Islamic influences. And there is a soothing quality to the neighborhood. In contrast to the big-city feel of Downtown Cairo, or the hustle of the al-Husayn area, Coptic Cairo is relatively quiet and calm.

The sites are generally open to visitors daily from 9 to 4. However, places of worship are not open to tourists during services: no mosque visits during Friday prayers (around noon), no church visits during Sunday services (7–10 AM), and no temple visits Saturday. In churches it is customary to make a small contribution, either near the entrance or beside the votary candle stands.

TOP ATTRACTIONS

❺ **Church of Saint Sergius.** Known in Arabic as *'Abu Serga*, this church is dedicated to two Roman officers, Sergius and Bacchus, who were martyred in Syria in 303. It was a major pilgrimage destination for 19th-century European travelers because it was built over a cave where the Holy Family was said to have stayed the night during their flight from

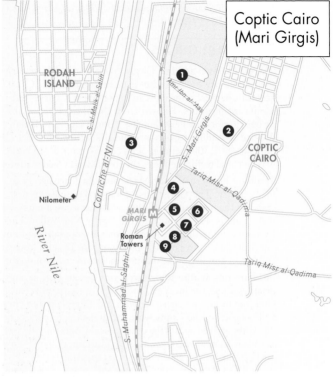

Coptic Cairo
(Mari Girgis)

King Herod—a special ceremony is still held every June 1 to commemorate the event. Originally constructed in the 5th century, the church has been destroyed and rebuilt several times, including a major restoration during the Fatimid era. Reconstructions aside, it is considered to be the oldest church in Cairo and a model of early Coptic church design.

The entrance is down a flight of steps that leads to the side of the narthex, at the end of which is a baptistry. Look up at the ceiling of the nave; 24 marble pillars that were taken from an earlier site, possibly from the Ptolemaic era (304–30 BC), support a series of arched timbers.

Most of the church furnishings are modern replicas of older pieces. The originals can be found in the Coptic Museum, including pieces from a rosewood pulpit and the sanctuary canopy, considered to be one of the museum's prized possessions. To the left of the sanctuary is the crypt in which the Holy Family is believed to have hidden. ⊠ *Hara al-Qadis 'Abu Serga, Mari Girgis* ☏ *No phone* ✉ *Free* ☉ *Daily 9–4 (except during services).*

❹ Convent of Saint George. This convent's namesake holds a special place in the hearts of Copts. The remains of this Roman legionary who was martyred in Asia were brought to Egypt in the 12th century. Images of Saint George abound in Egyptian Christianity, and the most common depicts the saint on a steed crushing a dragon beneath him. So it should

The National Museum of Egyptian Civilization

The Egyptian Department of Culture, in cooperation with UNESCO, has funded the new National Museum of Egyptian Civilization, which is due to open in Fustat (the original district of Islamic Cairo) at the intersection of Shar'a Ain el-Sira and Shar'a Masr al-Qadima sometime in 2011. The museum aims to lead visitors on a chronological journey through the long time frame of the country's history and to host important temporary exhibitions with the same theme. The collection will be divided into eight time eras, namely prehistoric, archaic, pharaonic, Greco-Roman, Coptic, Islamic, modern, and contemporary, and further expanded ideas will fall under the names The Dawn of Civilization, The Nile, State and Society, Material Culture, and Beliefs and Thinking. One of the main draws of the museum will be the collection of Royal Mummies that was still on display at the National Egyptian Museum at this writing.

come as no surprise that within the walls of Babylon are a church, a monastery, and a convent dedicated to the dragon slayer.

The convent, while less impressive in its present-day form than in the past—medieval historians describe a huge complex—is still worth the visit. Enter the courtyard and take the stairway on the left down to a structure that dates from the Fatimid era. Inside is a huge reception hall with a beautiful wooden door about 23 feet tall. Behind the door, a shrine contains the icon of Saint George and a set of chains used for the chain-wrapping ritual (still practiced), said to represent the sufferings of Saint George at the hands of the Romans. ⊠ *Hara al-Qadis Girgis, Mari Girgis* ☎ *No phone* ✆ *Free (donations welcome)* ☉ *Daily 10–4, except during services.*

NEED A BREAK?

Orient Cafe (⊠ *Shar'a Mari Girgis, Mari Girgis* ☎ *No Phone*) is a tiny hole-in-the-wall that sits between a bookshop and an antiques shop. Egyptian mezze-style snacks and kofta are available, but this is more the place for a cold soda, a beer, or a coffee.

⑧ Coptic Museum. Housing the world's largest collection of Coptic Christian artwork, this museum provides a link between ancient and Islamic Egypt. Remember that Christianity was not just a flash in the Egyptian historical pan. Saint Mark made his first convert in Alexandria in AD 61, and the majority of the city's population remained Christian until the 11th century, a half millennium after the Arabs brought Islam to Egypt. This link can be seen stylistically as well, because the collection includes pieces with a late-pharaonic/Greco-Roman feel, as well as items identified as Islamic.

Fodor's Choice
★

The museum is classified by medium, more or less. The first floor has carved stone and stucco, frescoes, and woodwork. The second floor includes textiles, manuscripts, icons, and metalwork. In some cases, chronological divisions are made within each grouping to show the evolution of the art form.

The Coptic Museum

The collection includes many exquisite pieces, but several are noteworthy first for their quirkiness or their syncretism, rather than their beauty. Look, for example, at carvings and paintings that trace the transformations of the ancient key of life, the ankh, to the cross; or Christian scenes with Egyptian gods. The depictions of the baby Jesus suckling at his mother's breast are striking in their resemblance to pharaonic suckling representations, including one at Karnak in which the god Horus is being nursed by Mut. Such characteristics are unique to Egyptian Christianity.

See the 4th-century bronze Roman eagle on the second floor, and a 4th-century hymnal (in the Coptic language) that was found beneath a young girl's head in her shallow grave near Beni Suef. For a detailed guide of the museum, look for Jill Kamil's *Coptic Egypt: History and Guide* (American University in Cairo Press). ⊠ *3 Shar'a Mari Girgis, Mari Girgis, Old Cairo* ☎ *02/2362–8766* ⊠ *£E50* ⊙ *Daily 9–5.*

❾ ★ The Hanging Church. Known in Arabic as *al-Muallaqah* ("the suspended"), the church is consecrated to the Blessed Virgin. Originally built in the 9th century—and sitting on top of a gatehouse of the Roman fortress (hence, its name)—the Hanging Church has been rebuilt several times, like most of Cairo's churches. Only the section to the right of the sanctuary, above the southern bastion, is considered original. Nevertheless, it remains one of the most impressive churches in the city.

The entrance gates lead to a flight of stairs that opens onto a covered courtyard, the narthex, which is partially paved with glazed geometrical tiles that date from the 11th century. Beyond the narthex is the nave, the main section of the church, where services are held. This is divided into a central nave and two side aisles by eight Corinthian columns, a feature that suggests that they were taken from an earlier building. Most columns in Coptic churches were painted with pictures of saints, but few of the paintings survived. Those in the Hanging Church are no exception; only one column still has traces of a figure on it.

Perhaps the most impressive aspect of this space is the marble pulpit. Considered the oldest existing pulpit in the country, it was constructed in the 11th century, with some of its materials coming from earlier furniture. The pulpit is supported by a series of slender columns arranged in pairs of which no two are alike. Some say this represents the sacraments of the Church; others describe it as being symbolic of Christ and his disciples.

The sanctuary screen is also of exceptional quality. It is made of cedar-wood and ivory cut in small segments, then inlaid in wood to form a Coptic cross, which has arms of equal length and three points at the end of each arm. The top of the screen is covered with icons depicting Christ in the center; the Virgin, the archangel Gabriel, and Saint Peter on the right; and Saint John the Baptist, Saint Paul, and the archangel Michael on the left. Behind the screen is the sanctuary dedicated to the Virgin Mary. Two side sanctuaries are dedicated to Saint John the Baptist (right) and Saint George (left), a very popular saint in Egypt.

To the right of Saint George's sanctuary is another beautiful screen dating from the 13th century. Made of wood and mother-of-pearl, it glows dark pink when a candle is held behind it. Behind the screen is a small chapel attached to the Ethiopian Saint Takla Hamanout Church. This chapel is worth visiting for its two wall paintings, one depicting the 24 Elders of the Apocalypse and the other the Virgin and Child. A stairway leads from this chapel to one above it, dedicated to Saint Mark. This area is probably the oldest part of the church, built in the 3rd century, when this was still a bastion of the old Roman fort. ⊠ *Shar'a Mari Girgis, Mari Girgis* ☎ *No phone* 🖅 *Free* ☉ *Daily 9–4, except during services.*

❷ Mosque of 'Amr Ibn al-'Aas. Built in 642 following the conquest of Egypt, this was the first mosque on the African continent. Because the original structure probably had mud-brick walls and a palm-thatch roof, it did not survive for long. It was restored and expanded in 673 and again in 698, 710, 750, and 791. In 827, it was expanded to its current size. It has since been renovated at least five times, most recently in the late 1980s, in an attempt to restore its interior to its 827 appearance. ⊠ *Shar'a Mari Girgis, Mari Girgis* ☎ *No phone* 🖅 *Free* ☉ *Daily 9–4, except during prayer.*

ALSO WORTH NOTING

❼ Ben Ezra Synagogue. Originally the Church of Saint Michael, the synagogue is named after the 12th-century rabbi of Jerusalem who obtained permission to build a temple of worship on this location. According to the local Jewish community, now numbering about 50 families, this was the site of the temple built by the prophet Jeremiah. Some claim that Jeremiah is actually buried here beneath a miracle rock. Another legend associated with the area is that this was the location of a spring where the pharaoh's daughter found the baby Moses.

Little differentiates the synagogue's outside appearance from a church, save, of course, signs like the Star of David on the gate. Inside, a fine 12th-century *bimah* (pulpit in a synagogue), made of wood and mother-of-pearl, remains.

During the last restoration in the 1890s, it was discovered that medieval Jews used the site as a *genizah* (storage) for any documents on which the name of God was written (it is against Jewish law to destroy any such papers). Thus, all contracts, bills of sale, marriage licenses, and the like were placed in the genizah. Needless to say, this find was a treasure trove for medieval Middle Eastern historians. The synagogue is now a museum and is not used for services. ⊠ *Hara al-Qadisa Burbara, Mari Girgis* 🕾 *No phone* 🖃 *Free* ☉ *Daily 9–4, except during services.*

❻ Church of Saint Barbara. Named for a young Nicodemian woman who was killed by her pagan father for converting, the church was originally dedicated to Sts. Cyrus and John (in Arabic, Abu Qir and Yuhanna, respectively), two martyrs from the city of Damanhour. It is said that when they refused to renounce their Christianity, they were shot with arrows, burned, and drawn and quartered, but would not die until they were beheaded.

The church was first built in 684, destroyed in the great fire of Fustat in 750, and then restored in the 11th century. Additions were made when the relics of Saint Barbara were brought here. The church is one of the largest in Cairo. Replete with the standard division of narthex, nave, side aisles, and three sanctuaries, the church is also considered one of the city's finest.

The sanctuary screen currently in place is a 13th-century wooded piece inlaid with ivory—the original screen is in the Coptic Museum. The icons above the church's screen include a newly restored Child Enthroned and a rare icon of Saint Barbara. A domed apse behind the main altar has seven steps decorated in bands of black, red, and white marble. To the left of the sanctuary is the chapel dedicated to Sts. Cyrus and John, a square structure with a nave, transept, two sanctuaries (one for each saint), and a baptistry.

Access to Coptic Cairo's cemetery is through an iron gate to the left of the church. ⊠ *Hara al-Qadisa Burbara, Mari Girgis* 🕾 *No phone* 🖃 *Free* ☉ *Daily 9–4, except during services.*

❶ Church of Saint Mercurius. Yet another Roman legionary, Mercurius, or Abu Sayfayn ("of the two swords"), dreamed one night that an angel gave him a glowing sword and ordered him to use it to fight paganism. He converted to Christianity and was martyred in Palestine. His remains were brought to Cairo in the 15th century.

This site is of great importance to Coptic Christians. It was the cathedral church of Cairo, and when the seat of the Coptic Patriarch moved from Alexandria to Cairo, Saint Mercurius was the chosen location. The complex actually contains a monastery, a convent, and three churches: Abu Sayfayn, Abna Shenouda, and a church of the Virgin. At this

Grand Egyptian Museum

One of the most ambitious architectural designs in the new millennium, the Grand Egyptian Museum will be a fitting home for the mother lode of ancient artifacts excavated in the country in the last 150 years and a world-class showcase for modern Egypt. It will also act as a center of excellence for the study of and research into Egyptology. When open it will be the world's biggest museum dedicated to ancient Egypt, covering 123 acres (50 hectares) on the Giza Plateau less than 3 km (2 mi) from the Pyramids.

Designed by architects Heneghan Peng, the buildings sit low against the Giza Plateau, and several levels flow with the natural contour of the land. The museum's role is to enhance the Pyramid site but sit apart and, thus, not detract from it. This is a 21st-century structure that will afford both the artifacts and the visitors who will flock to see them the optimum temperature and light conditions.

The lowest level will be a lobby. After this, visitors will enter through a piazza and climb via a monumental staircase to the main exhibition galleries, from which there will be clear and dramatic views across the desert to the Pyramids.

The galleries will be divided into themes; transitional sculpture gardens will create a natural flow between the spaces. The vast main facade will be fashioned of translucent stone made up of numerous triangular shapes in a Sierpinski fractal pattern, mimicking the shape of the Pyramids beyond.

Interior floor space will allow for the display of over 100,000 artifacts, from colossal statues to delicate items of jewelry, many of which have never been seen by the public since they've been stored in dusty storage rooms in the basement of the Egyptian Museum in Downtown Cairo. The undoubted highlight will be the collection of Tutankhamun artifacts discovered by Howard Carter in 1922. The gold and turquoise funerary mask is an iconic symbol encapsulating the allure and mystery of Ancient Egypt and Egyptology. These will be moved close to the new museum's opening date.

The foundation stone of the museum was laid in 2002, and at this writing only the research labs of the complex are complete. Current estimates are that the museum will open to the public in 2013.

writing, all three were being restored but remained open to visitors. ⊠ *Shar'a 'Ali Salem, Mari Girgis* ☏ *No phone* 🎟 *Free* ☉ *Daily 9–4, except during services.*

❸ **Tomb of Sulayman al-Faransawi.** Sulayman, a Frenchman, was born Octave de Sèves in Lyons, France. An officer in Napoléon's army, he came to Egypt when Muhammad 'Ali was in need of European trainers for his army. After facing dissent among the ranks, he converted to Islam and took the name Sulayman. Popular with the khedive Ibrahim for his role in victories in Arabia, Crete, Syria, and Anatolia, he died in 1860 a rich man. His tomb was designed by Karl von Diebitsch, the architect responsible for the palace that is now the Marriott Hotel in the suburb of Zamalek. Like the hotel, the cast-iron pavilion manages

Continued on page 119

THE GREAT
PYRAMIDS
OF **GIZA**

By Andrew Bossone

Ascending the throne as a middle-aged man, the Pharaoh Khufu may have personally chosen the plateau in Giza where the largest Egyptian pyramid was built. The only surviving Wonder of the Ancient World remains a majestic site despite the encroachment of modern society. In antiquity it was surely awe-inspiring, rising above the massive necropolis past Saqqara and the city of Memphis.

The oldest and largest monument at the Giza site, **Khufu's Pyramid** (the Great Pyramid) measures 753 feet square and 478 feet high and was finished some 4,500 years ago. The pyramid complex of **Khafre**, son of Khufu, includes a feature not replicated elsewhere, the **Great Sphinx**. Khafre's pyramid is also on higher ground than Khufu's, giving it the appearance that it equals the size of his father. Khafre's son **Menkaure** built the smallest of the three Great Pyramids, which was unfinished at his death and completed by his successor Shepsekaf.

Many others are buried nearby in *mastabas*, from the Arabic word for bench. A few hundred tombs of the workers are to the south of the Sphinx. The pyramids, Sphinx, and some of the mastabas date from the 4th Dynasty, while other mastabas date to the 5th and 6th Dynasties. Next to Khufu's pyramid, a museum holds one of the most interesting objects from antiquity: Khufu's solar boat, modeled after the one that Amun-Ra was said to ride across the sky each day.

Several monuments on the plateau are open to visitors: a combination of pyramids, a mastaba, the Solar Boat Museum, and the Sphinx will give you a taste of the site. Generally, two of the three pyramids can be entered on any given day (this varies depending on restoration and conservation work). If you are able to choose one pyramid to go into, make it the Great Pyramid of Khufu. The sheer mass of it, pierced by the elegant Grand Gallery leading to the burial chamber, is one of the wonders of the world—ancient and modern.

TIMELINE

c. 2613 – Fourth Dynasty
of Egypt begins

c. 2589 to 2556 BC – Khufu reigns,
builds Great Pyramid at Giza

2600 BC   2580   2560

HISTORY OF THE PYRAMIDS

The meaning of the Great Pyramids of Giza has changed through the four-and-a-half millennia they have existed, but their iconic status around the world has survived. At the time of their construction, the pyramids were a great mobilizing force in Egyptian society, becoming the center of civic and religious life. Today few Egyptians actually enter the complex, but at the same time, few tourists ever come to Egypt without visiting them.

When and how the pyramids were built remains a mystery. In 2009, a team of researchers controversially placed an exact date on the start of construction of the **Great Pyramid of Giza** at August 23, 2470 BC. They supposed this would have corresponded with the appearance of the start of the flood season during the first year of the king's reign, when major building projects typically began in pharaonic Egypt. The researchers surmised that if they could determine the date of the appearance of the star Sothis, or Sirius, they could then know when the floods would start. The team, led by Abdel-Halim Nur El-Din, a professor of Egyptology at Cairo University, then compared the modern Gregorian calendar, with the ancient Egyptian calendar (still used in farming in Egypt today) and the cycle of Sothis to get the pyramid's birthday. If they are right, then they have a margin of error of only a few days.

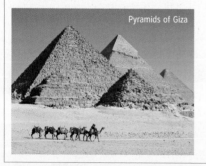
Pyramids of Giza

In actuality, little of Khufu's life is known, and the ancient Egyptian calendar is inexact. Most historians believe that Khufu's reign began earlier, around 2589 BC. Some believe that he ascended even earlier. It's safe to say, however, that the Great Pyramid is roughly 4,500 years old, was designed in advance of the king's reign, and took about 23 years to build.

A few theories have appeared to explain their construction. Some theories say that builders used an external ramp or hoisted the millions of blocks using pulleys. Another theory is that the Great Pyramid was built inside out. The architect designed the pyramid using a ramp that spirals around the pyramid's interior.

The sheer weight of the stone blocks, averaging 2.5 tons each, suggests that they must have been hauled to the site by water. Although buildings and the desert surround the pyramids today, the course of the Nile was different in antiquity, and it probably led directly to the base of the site.

Many people assume slaves did most of the construction work, but the sophistication of the pyramids' design and implementation suggests a great deal of skilled labor was employed in their building. Slaves may have been employed in the quarrying and transport of the estimated 2,300,000 stones used for the Great Pyramid, but even

Great Pyramid (Giza).

modern engineers cannot replicate the near-perfect symmetry of its base.

It has also become clear that participating in the construction of a pyramid would have been considered a great honor for many Egyptians, not one so easily bestowed upon slaves. Furthermore, a workers' village beside the pyramids complex supported perhaps 20,000 people and included copper workshops, bakeries, and other businesses. In 2002, archaeologists led by Mark Lehner uncovered sleeping quarters called galleries, capable of holding as many as 2,000 people at once in beds beneath half-open roofs supported by columns.

The workers also ate and drank well. Bones found suggest they consumed prime beef, fish, bread, and beer. They also had access to medical care, including the treatment of broken bones.

Lehner's studies at the workers' village could be considered part of a larger trend of "settlement archaeology." Egyptologists have mostly looked at the great temples and tombs of the pharaohs, rather than everyday Egyptians and their settlements. But the construction of the pyramids of Giza mobilized Egyptian society, creating a great project at the focal point of religious and civil life. The Great Pyramids were not simply monument to kings, but a driving force behind a great civilization. Today they stand as a testament to human ingenuity, a reminder of what was possible when a society mobilizes its efforts into accomplishing great endeavors.

Egypt's latest great project will be next to the pyramids. The new **Grand Egyptian Museum** down the road is slated to become the largest museum in the world (it may open in 2011 or 2012, but it is unclear at the time of this writing). Some estimate that 80% of the world's objects from antiquity are located in Egypt, but that only 20% of what lies beneath its sands has been excavated. And considering that the Egyptian Museum in Tahrir Square has more objects in storage than it does on display, it may take no less than a great mobilization of Egypt's efforts to fill the Grand Museum.

PYRAMIDS PLATEAU

If you take a taxi, you can reach the pyramids by two routes, the Ring Road (Tariq el-Da'airy), or the Pyramids Road (Sharia el-Haram). The former affords one of the rare places for a photograph of all three pyramids, but a good shot is possible only with a long-distance lens. The pyramid complex has two gates, one next to side streets filled with horse and camel stables, the other across from a luxurious colonial hotel, the Mena House hotel.

The Sound & Light Show

🕓 Site daily 8–6:30; pyramid and tomb interiors daily 9–4 (but the openings are staggered, so not all pyramid interiors are open every day); Sound and Light Show (in English) Oct.–Apr., Mon.–Wed. and Fri.–Sat. 6:30pm, Thurs. 7:30pm, Sun. 9.30pm; May–Sept., Mon.–Wed. and Fri.–Sat. 8.30pm, Thurs. 9.30pm, Sun. 11.30pm.

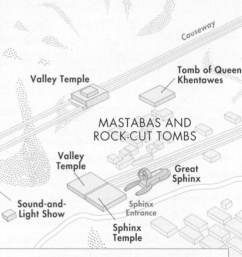

Causeway

Valley Temple

Tomb of Queen Khentawes

MASTABAS AND ROCK-CUT TOMBS

Valley Temple

Great Sphinx

Sound-and-Light Show

Sphinx Entrance

Sphinx Temple

✉ Pyramids Rd., Giza

☎ No phone

🎫 General admission £e60 (includes Sphinx, which has a separate entrance), Great Pyramid £e100, Khafre's Pyramid £e30, Mankaure's Pyramid £e25, Solar Boat Museum £e50, Sound & Light Show £e75

■ Only 300 tickets are sold for actual entry to the pyramids daily, 150 starting at 8 AM, and 150 staring at 1 PM.

■ To make sure you get a ticket, you must go early, especially during high season and especially if you are not part of a group. Friday is the most crowded.

■ Still and video cameras are not allowed into any of the pyramids. The parking lot above the complex offers good pictures.

■ Entrance tickets have set prices, but anything outside the walls of the complex can be negotiated. Aim to pay no more than 50% of the sellers' first offer.

■ For an adventure, rent horses at night, riding into the desert. At the top of a hill you'll find a man serving tea by fire as the light show illuminates the pyramids.

Entrance of mortuary temple in Giza

Menkaure's Pyramid and Pyramids of Queens

Giza pyramids

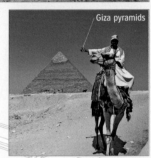

Pyramids of Queens

Menkaure's Pyramid

Mortuary Temple

Pyramid Entrance

Khafre's Pyramid

Mortuary Temple

MASTABAS (DYNASTIES IV & V)

Causeway

Boat Museum

Pyramids of Queens

Khufu's Pyramids

Ticket Office

MASTABAS (DYNASTIES IV & V)

Boat Pits

Causeway

→
TO CAIRO, MENA HOUSE OBEROI

The Solar Boat Museum

THE GREAT PYRAMIDS

Khufu's Pyramid, more than any other, is the focus of several fanciful beliefs that hold that the pyramids are either the site of initiation for a secret priesthood, an ancient observatory, a landing device for extraterrestrials, or even a way of projecting oneself into space. In a similar vein are ideas that, within the pyramid, dull razor blades are sharpened, food and drink are preserved, people are healed, and meditation is enhanced. Experiments with foods, blades, and the rest have shown no supporting evidence for these beliefs.

The stairs inside the pyramids are tight

MENKAURE'S PYRAMID

The smallest of the kings' pyramids at the Giza site, measuring 215 feet square and 215 feet tall. It is probable that **Menkaure** intended to cover his entire pyramid with a red granite casing, but only the bottom 16 courses of this were in place when he died. The completion of the casing in limestone may have been undertaken subsequently only to be plundered. His successor, **Shepseskaf**, was responsible for finishing his mortuary temple, a very pleasant place to tour, in mud brick. On the left side, as you climb the ladder to enter the pyramid, is a carved inscription concerning the restoration and care of the pyramid subsequent to its construction. The subterranean granite burial chamber contained a sarcophagus that was lost at sea in the 19th century as it was being shipped to Britain. The pyramid and mortuary temple were refurbished in the 26th Dynasty (664–525 BC), when the king's cult enjoyed a renaissance. There are two queen's pyramids and a subsidiary pyramid associated with Menkaure's pyramid complex.

KHAFRE'S PYRAMID

The second-largest pyramid on the Giza site measures 702 feet square and stands 470 feet tall. It still retains part of its fine limestone casing—brought from the quarries at Tura in the cliffs on the eastern bank of the Nile—at its summit. Like Khufu's complex, Khafre's includes five boat pits (empty of boats), together with mortuary and valley temples and a connecting causeway some 430 yards long carved out of the living rock. The underground burial chamber contains a red granite sarcophagus with its lid. Next to this is a square cavity that presumably once contained the canopic chest with the pharaoh's viscera. The pyramid has two entrances: one in the north face of the pyramid and another in the pavement on the north side. Before reaching the burial chamber, the two entrance passages connect beneath the pyramid. The pyramid was first entered in modern times by Giovanni Battista Belzoni in March 1818, an event he commemorated by scrawling his name in soot along the length of the burial chamber.

KHUFU'S PYRAMID

The oldest and largest monument at the Giza site, **Khufu's Pyramid** (the Great Pyramid) has a surprisingly modest north entrance dating to the 9th century, when the Caliph Ma'mun blasted his way inside searching for buried treasure. It leads through a curving passage and up to a long corridor that opens onto a small landing. From here, another passage leads to the so-called **Queen's Chamber,** which was probably used for the pharaoh's grave goods. The next stage from the landing is the magnificent **Grand Gallery** that soars up to the king's burial chamber. This contains a sarcophagus that was found empty because it had been robbed in antiquity. Narrow air passages lead out of the burial chamber. Remains of the mortuary temple are on the east side, with the Queens' pyramids beyond. The pyramid once had a low causeway leading to its gate, covered with reliefs decorated with scenes conveying the ideas of Egyptian kingship and festivals the king would enjoy in the afterlife.

THE GREAT SPHINX

The Sphinx

The enigmatic **Sphinx** is attached to Khafre's Pyramid complex, just north of his valley temple, with a building (now very much destroyed) in front of it. The Great Sphinx is thought to be Khafre in the guise of a manifestation of the sun god Ra.

The building in front of the sphinx with an open court is interpreted to be an early sun-temple. Khafre, as well as his son Menkaure took the title "son of Ra," after the former's predecessor Djedefra, who built the first known sphinx. In the New Kingdom Ra was combined with Horus, as Ra-Horakhty, or Ra-Horus of the Horizon. The Great Sphinx was then worshiped as the image of Horakhty. A stela stands between the Sphinx's paws, erected by the New Kingdom Pharaoh Tuthmose IV (1401–1391BC) who may have used the deified sphinx to legitimize his ascension after Amenhotep II.

The Sphinx was carved from bedrock, with additional details and the final casing made of limestone blocks. The monument used to sport a *uraeus* (the royal cobra) on its forehead and had a beard that has fallen off, bit by bit, through the ages. There has also been much speculation about the disappearance of its nose. The most common story is that Napoleon's troops used it for target practice, but it was likely gone before they arrived in 1799. The sphinx can be reached by the gate in front of it or down a road from the pyramids. And it is here, in front of the Sphinx (or in the open-air cafe at the complex entrance) that you watch the evening Sound & Light Show.

to combine Orientalist kitsch and elegance. ✉ *Off Shar'a Muhammad al-Saghir, Mari Girgis* ☎ *No phone* 🎫 *£E8* ☉ *Daily 9–4.*

RODAH ISLAND AND GARDEN CITY

Nilometer. At the southern end of Rodah Island, *al-miqyas* (the Nilometer) was used from pharaonic times until the completion of the Aswan Dam in the late 1950s to measure the height of the flood. If the Nile rose above 16 cubits (a cubit is about 2 feet), no flood tax would be levied that year. Needless to say, this was a ceremony that the populace followed with great interest—and if the floods were plentiful, with great celebration.

Built in 861 on the site of an earlier Nilometer, the present structure is considered to be the oldest extant Islamic building (the conical dome is an 1895 restoration). Inside is a shaft that houses the graduated column that served as the measuring device. Outside the structure is a model explaining how it worked. ✉ *Southern tip of Rodah Island, Rodah Island* 🎫 *£E15* ☉ *Daily 9–4.*

HELIOPOLIS

In 1905 the Belgian industrialist Édouard Louis Joseph, Baron Empain, bought a swath of land northwest of Cairo. His plan was to build a new self-sustaining community in the desert with housing, shops, and recreation facilities, which came complete with luxuries like street lighting, water, and drainage plus a tram link to the capital. The town he called Heliopolis became a hit with upper-class Egyptians and expat movers and shakers. It remained an oasis of well-manicured mansions, of weekends at the country clubs, and of cocktail parties with the social elite until the coup d'état of 1952.

By the 1990s, Heliopolis had been swallowed by the massive growth of Cairo and was decaying under decades of neglect. However, Suzanne Mubarak, wife of President Hosni Mubarak and a native of Heliopolis, pledged to save her home neighborhood, a campaign which has revived the heart of Heliopolis. It's now one of Cairo's most charming districts.

There are no particular attractions here. The early-20th-century palace, modeled on Angkor Wat Temple, that Empain built for himself now stands empty and isn't open to the public. The grand Heliopolis Palace Hotel is now the presidential palace, set behind well-guarded walls. However, the Downtown core—the Korba—a diminutive quarter of ornate colonnaded streets in neo-Renaissance style, is now gentrified with a smart coat of paint and is a lovely place to relax. The colonnades now house cafés, boutiques, and jewelry shops where the well-to-do families of the area stroll in the evenings.

GIZA

It used to be that you approached Giza through green fields. Cairo's expansion means that now you have to run a gauntlet of raucously noisy city streets clogged with buses, vans, taxis, and the odd donkey cart, not to mention a busy four-lane bypass. Unfortunately, the large concrete towers lining the road obscure the view of the Giza pyramids that loom at the desert's edge.

Although Giza is technically a suburb, it's one of the more popular places for tourists to stay when they visit Cairo. If you are staying in Central Cairo, you can get to the Pyramids by taking the Metro to Giza station (£E1), then the public bus that plies a route along Pyramids Road (£E0.50). To get to the Pyramids by bus from central Cairo, take a CTA bus from Abdel Meneim Riyadh Station on Tahrir Square for £E2; it will bring you to the foot of the Giza Plateau opposite the Mena House Hotel. Hiring a taxi for the day to take you to the Pyramids and other ancient sites is by far the most convenient way to get to and from the site. Your hotel can arrange a taxi, or you can hail one in the street. A reasonable daylong taxi hire should cost £E30–£E40 per hour—if you bargain well.

Fodor's Choice
★

Pyramid Plateau. Three 4th-Dynasty pyramids dominate the skyline of the desert plateau to the southwest of Cairo. The largest is that of Pharaoh Khufu (Greek name: Cheops) also known as "The Great Pyramid." The second was built by his son Khafre (Greek name: Chephren). The smallest of pyramids was built by Menkaure (Greek name: Mycerinus), the grandson of Khufu who reigned from 2490 to 2472 BC. These are surrounded by smaller pyramids belonging to their respective female dependents, as well as numerous *mastabas* (large trapezoidal tombs) of their lesser relatives and courtiers. The site is "guarded" by the monumental carved-limestone Sphinx. A small museum in the shadow of Khufu's Pyramid contains the Pharaoh's Royal Solar Boat, by tradition the boat used to transport the Pharaoh on his final journey to the afterlife after his mummy was entombed. The pyramid interiors are open on a rotating basis, and ticket numbers are limited to 150 per morning and another 150 per afternoon. A range of *mastabas* will be open to view on any given day. The ticket office will give you current information when you buy your ticket. Buses and cars are no longer allowed on the plateau; electric trams link the ticket office with the plateau, from where you'll be able to explore the site on foot. ⊠ *Pyramids Rd., Giza* 🕾 *No phone* 🖅 *General admission £E60 (includes both Pyramids and Sphinx), Great Pyramid £E100, Khafre's Pyramid £E30, Mankaure's Pyramid £E25, Solar Boat Museum £E50* ⊙ *Site daily 8–6:30, pyramid and tomb interiors daily 9–4 (but the openings are staggered, so not all pyramid interiors are open every day).*

Great Sphinx. Carved from the living rock of the pyramids plateau during the 4th Dynasty, the enigmatic limestone Sphinx is attached Pharaoh Khafre's funerary complex. The figure of a recumbent lion with a man's face wearing a *nemes* (traditional headdress of the pharaoh) was thought to be Khafre in the guise of Ra-Harakhte, a manifestation of the Sun God. The role of the Sphinx was to guard the vast royal necropolis that incorporated the pyramids and *mastabas* (large trapezoidal tombs) on the Giza plateau, and it's visited as part of the longer visit incorporating these other monuments at the site. It's possible to get close to the Sphinx along a wide viewing platform that has been built around it, but climbing is forbidden and there's no entry into the small interior chambers (most of the sphinx, however, is solid rock). ⊠ *Fayyum Rd., Giza* 🖅 *Sphinx £E60 (includes both Pyramids and Sphinx), Sound & Light Show £E75* ⊙ *Daily 8–6:30; Sound & Light Show (in English)*

Oct.–Apr., Mon.–Wed. and Fri.–Sat. 6:30 PM, Thurs. 7:30 PM, Sun. 9:30 PM; May–Sept., Mon.–Wed. and Fri.–Sat. 8:30 PM, Thurs. 9:30 PM, Sun. 11:30 PM.

OFF THE BEATEN PATH

Harraniyya. Intricate, handwoven carpets are the big draw in this small village, but you can see all kinds of textiles and pottery as well. The Ramses Wissa Wassef Art Centre—named after the family largely responsible for developing the town's crafts into an industry—is the best place to see them. Bring lunch and enjoy the lavish gardens between touring the workshops. Saturday through Wednesday are the best days to come. ⊠ *4 km (2½ mi) south of Giza on Saqqara Rd., Giza* 🕾 *02/3381–5746* ⊕ *www.wissawassef.com* ⊗ *Daily 10–5.*

WHERE TO EAT

Cairo's restaurant scene has really developed over the last decade, breaking out of the five-star hotels and onto the streets. Eating out is now a regular form of entertainment, affordable to the growing upper and middle classes in Egypt. Naturally, Egyptian food remains the local favorite, and Cairo is the place to find the best of the country's specialties. Restaurants compete mainly on quality of ingredients rather than refinement of preparations. However, the range of cuisine options has expanded dramatically to include Indian, Thai, French, Italian, and even Japanese.

Local beers (including Stella Premium, Luxor, and Sakara) are common, and you can usually find a range of drinkable, if unremarkable, local wines (the top-rate Grand Marquis label, then the passable Omar Khayyam, Sheherazade, and Obelisque, and a much less wonderful Rubis).

Egyptians eat late: lunch from 1 to 3 and dinner often starting at 9 or 10. Most restaurants are open daily for both lunch and dinner. Dress is generally smart casual. Local beers and wines are served in many restaurants, but expensive imported alcohol is limited to top-end establishments. Although fancier places levy a 12% service charge, it is customary to leave a tip in inverse relation to the size of the bill, ranging from, say, 8% at expensive places to 12% to 14% at cheaper places.

WHAT IT COSTS IN EGYPTIAN POUNDS				
	$	$$	$$$	$$$$
Restaurants	under £E50	£E50–£E100	£E100–£E150	over £E150

Restaurant prices are per person for a main course at dinner.

ISLAMIC CAIRO NORTH

$$

MIDDLE EASTERN

✕ **Naguib Mahfouz Café.** Named after Egypt's most famous novelist and run by the Oberoi Hotel Group, this is a haven of air-conditioned tranquility in the midst of the sometimes-chaotic Khan al-Khalili. The restaurant serves variations on the usual Egyptian dishes, dressed up in historically resonant names to justify what, by the standards of the area,

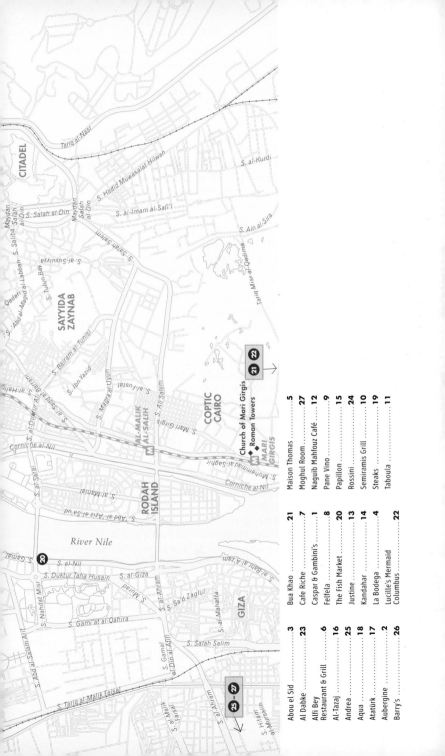

CITADEL

Tariq al-Nasr

S. al-Kurdi

S. Hadid Muwasalat Hilwan

S. al-Imam al-Safi'i

Maydan
Salah al-Din

Maydan
Salah al-Din

S. Salah al-Din

S. al-Suyuriyya

S. Saliba Salah al-Din

S. Salah Salim

S. Ain al-Sira

S. Qadari al-Magid al-Labbah

S. Abdal-Magid al-Labbah

S. Tulun Bay

Tariq Misr al-Qadima

SAYYIDA
ZAYNAB

S. Baram al-Tunisi

S. Ibn Yazid

S. al-Hafiz

S. al-Sadd al-Barani

S. Magra al-'Uyun

S. al-Fustat

COPTIC
CAIRO

S. Mari Girgis

S. Ali Salem

S. al-Duktur Aziz Ali

Corniche al-Nil

AL-MALIK
AL-SALIH

◆ Church of Mari Girgis
♦ Roman Towers
Ⓜ MARI
   GIRGIS

S. Muhammad al-Sadir

RODAH
ISLAND

S. al-Manial

Corniche al-Nil

S. Abd al-Aziz al-Sa'ud

River Nile

S. Gamal

S. el-Nil

S. Duktur Taha Husain

S. al-Giza

S. al-Bahr al-A'zam

S. Nahdat Misr

S. Murad

S. al-Ahram

S. Sa'd Zaglul

S. Gami'at al-Qahira

GIZA

S. Salah Salim

S. Mahatta

S. Abd al-Salam Arif

S. Gamal
al-Din al-Afifi

S. Tariq al-Malik Faisal

S. Malik
Faisal

S. Hisam
al-Mursain

constitute exorbitant prices. That being said, the food and service are also of higher quality than you'll find in most of the nearby restaurants. The adjoining café serves lighter fare, consisting mostly of sandwiches, at a fraction of the price of the main dishes. ⊠ *5 al-Badestan La., Khan al-Khalili, Islamic Cairo North* ☏ *02/2590–3788* ⊟ *AE, MC, V.*

MA'ADI

$$

THAI

✕ **Bua Khao.** Run by a Thai woman who uses ingredients flown in from Bangkok, this restaurant manages mouthwateringly authentic food that has saved many an expatriate longing for *massaman* or *Penang* curries. Start with a soup, perhaps *tom kar gai* (chicken in a coconut-milk broth), then move on to a delicious glass-noodle salad with shrimp, and end with a curry or two. ⊠ *9 Road 151, Ma'adi* ☏ *02/2358–0126* ⌕ *Reservations essential* ⊟ *MC, V.*

$$

AMERICAN–
CASUAL

★

✕ **Lucille's Mermaid Columbus.** Despite the arrival in Cairo of internationally recognized American fast-food chains, expats still flock to Lucille's for tasty authentic burgers—hand-crafted patties that are cooked to order—and Tex-Mex dishes. Lucille's also serves up great American breakfasts with all-day breakfasts Friday and Saturday. Fill up on fresh OJ, pancakes, and syrup. Authentic diner decor keeps homesick Americans happy. ⊠ *54 Shar'a 9, Ma'adi* ☏ *02/2359–2778* ⊟ *MC, V.*

DOWNTOWN AND BULAQ

$$

MIDDLE EASTERN

✕ **Alfi Bey Restaurant & Grill.** A mainstay of the old theater district since 1938, this restaurant, with its wood-paneled dining room, white tablecloths, and marble floors, is a step above the standard local eatery. Slow-cooked mutton and beef stews served with rice predominate, though the ribs (sold by the kilo) and grilled meats are especially good. No alcohol is served. ⊠ *3 Shar'a El Alfi, Downtown* ☏ *02/2577–1888* ⊟ *No credit cards.*

$–$$

MIDDLE EASTERN

✕ **Cafe Riche.** Founded in 1908, Cafe Riche was the social headquarters of much of Cairo's theater and literary communities and once had a cabaret where Umm Koulthum got her start in 1922. The food has not changed much since then and features such standard French-influenced Egyptian grill dishes as entrecôte in wine sauce with fries. The steak with pistachios is more innovative (and quite good), while there are all the usual local options, including *fatta* (a meat or vegetable casserole) and tahini. You can also get a good breakfast here. ⊠ *17 Shar'a Talaat Harb, Downtown* ☏ *02/2392–9793* ⊟ *AE, MC, V.*

$–$$

CAFÉ

✕ **Caspar & Gambini's.** This popular casual coffee bar and eatery is one of a chain around the Middle East. The Corniche branch opens out onto the mezzanine of the Towers Mall, and the clientele is a mixture of expats and young trendy Cairenes who work in the corporate office blocks around the area. The menu is a good mix of snacks (including sandwiches and wraps), salads, plus international entrées (including pastas and chili). The coffee is excellent, and there's Wi-Fi. ⊠ *Towers Mall at Nile City, Corniche al-Nil, Downtown* ☏ *02/2461–9201* ⊕ *www.casparandgambinis.com* ⊟ *AE, MC, V.*

$ ✕ **Felfela.** This Cairo institution is popular with both Egyptians and
MIDDLE EASTERN visitors for good Egyptian food at inexpensive prices. Felfela is a good
place to introduce yourself to such Egyptian staples as *shorbat 'ads*
(lentil soup), which is tasty with a squeeze of lemon in it; *taamiya* (the
local version of falafel); and *fuul* (stewed fava beans). Felfela serves beer.
There's also another Downtown branch on Maydan Ramses and others
around the city. ✉ *15 Shar'a Hoda Sharaawi, Downtown* ☎ *02/2392–
2833* ═ *No credit cards.*

$$$ ✕ **Pane Vino.** An ultracontemporary and fashionable open kitchen–style
ITALIAN Italian restaurant puts a modern twist on the traditional trattoria. Pane
Vino has Italian chefs who cook with authentic Italian ingredients. Sig-
nature dishes include crispy fried calamari or deep-fried carpaccio with
rocket salad and Parmesan cheese. You can eat light or enjoy a meal of
several courses, just as mama used to serve. ✉ *Semiramis InterConti-
nental, Corniche al-Nil, Downtown* ☎ *02/2795–7171* ⌲ *Reservations
essential* ═ *AE, MC, V.*

$$$$ ✕ **The Semiramis Grill.** This top-notch restaurant concentrates on simple,
CONTINENTAL classic Continental dishes. Starters include lightly cooked scallops. For
main courses, the menu divides evenly between seafood and meat; high-
lights include lobster with cheese ravioli and a delectable beef au poivre.
The extensive dessert menu is supplemented with a dozen or so daily spe-
cials, all of them enticing. Waiters in tails who are engaged in a sedate bus-
tle enhance the restaurant's contemporary gentleman's-club atmosphere.
✉ *Semiramis InterContinental, Corniche al-Nil, Downtown* ☎ *02/2795–
7171* ⌲ *Reservations essential* ═ *AE, DC, MC, V* ◷ *No lunch.*

ZAMALEK AND GEZIRA

$$ ✕ **Abou El Sid.** You'll feel as though you're walking into an Arabian
MIDDLE EASTERN palace when you pass through the portal of this restaurant—the decor
Fodor's Choice might be a touch kitschy, but the food definitely isn't. This is the place
★ to immerse yourself in the full works, Egyptian style, and it serves just
about the best Egyptian cuisine in Cairo. The choice of mezze—both
hot and cold—is impressive. For main courses you'll have a choice
of grilled meats, stuffed pigeon, and slow-cooked meat stews. There's
also a branch at City Stars Mall. ✉ *157 Shar'a 26th Yulyu, Zamalek* ☎ *02/2735–9640* ⊕ *www.abouelsid.com* ⌲ *Reservations essential*
═ *AE, MC, V.*

$$ ✕ **Aubergine.** This casual, mostly vegetarian, restaurant is a rare find,
VEGETARIAN with an airy Mediterranean-style ground floor and a darker, candlelit
upstairs. The always-innovative menu changes daily but usually consists
of a soup, a couple of salads, baked vegetable dishes, and pastas—as
well as meat and seafood specials. Favorites include green salad with
sautéed mushrooms and Parmesan shavings; baked avocado, mush-
room, and eggplant lasagna; pan-fried halloumi cheese with grilled
cherry tomatoes; and salmon ravioli in a creamy dill sauce. There's
Wi-Fi here. ✉ *5 Shar'a Sayed al-Bakry, Zamalek* ☎ *02/2738–0080*
⌲ *Reservations essential* ═ *AE, MC.*

$$$$ ✕ **Justine.** Established in the mid-1980s as Egypt's premier French restau-
FRENCH rant, Justine has only improved with age. The daily specials are always
★ great choices. Perhaps a shipment of fresh mussels from Alexandria is

given a light, delicious broth and placed over pasta; asparagus, harvested in the morning, is steamed and on your plate by evening; duck-and goose-liver pâté is transformed into an array of delights. The à la carte menu is equally inspired. At the end of your meal, prepare yourself for one last indulgence, because Justine is in a league of its own when it comes to dessert. Service is flawless. ☒ *4 Shar'a Hassan Sabri, Zamalek* ☎ *02/2736–2961* ⌂ *Reservations essential* ▭ *AE, MC, V.*

$$$
ECLECTIC

✗ **La Bodega.** This expansive restaurant, bar, and lounge is one of the hottest spots in town and one of the hardest reservations to get. The dining area is a series of elegant high-ceilinged rooms, which, with their dark wood and seductive lighting, evoke Casablanca as much as Europe. The see-and-be-seen crowd is as hip as Cairo gets. The kitchen produces a number of specialties hard to find anywhere else, including homemade focaccia with rosemary or olives, gazpacho, honey-glazed duck, and tuna carpaccio. The bar is at least as popular as the restaurant. Be prepared to eat early (by Cairo standards) if you want a shot at getting a table. ☒ *Balmoral Hotel, 157 Shar'a 26 Yulyu, Zamalek* ☎ *02/2735–0543* ⌂ *Reservations essential* ▭ *AE, MC, V.*

$
ITALIAN

✗ **Maison Thomas.** Famous among Cairenes for its pizza, Thomas also prepares smaller dishes to eat in or take out, including squid or mushroom salad, as well as various sandwiches based on local and imported cheeses and cold cuts available in the deli section. Most notably, it also sells pork products, a true rarity in Egypt. The real treat is dessert: the plain chocolate cake (ask to have it warmed) and chocolate mousse are heavenly. If you find yourself prowling around town at 4 AM, steer yourself here; Thomas never closes. Beer is sold to go only. ☒ *157 Shar'a 26 Yulyu, Zamalek* ☎ *02/2735–7057* ⌂ *Reservations not accepted* ▭ *No credit cards.*

RODAH ISLAND AND GARDEN CITY

$$$$
SEAFOOD

✗ **Aqua.** With a dining room lined by wall-size aquariums, this is the coolest and most expensive seafood restaurant in the city. The sushi and sashimi are incredibly fresh and varied, but the fusion-style menu moves from the simplest dishes such as panfried prawns, to unusual combinations like sea eel and foie gras, to great extravaganzas that include a terribly indulgent lobster served four ways. This is a grand dining opportunity with service to match. For surf and turf you can also order from the menu of neighboring Steaks restaurant. ☒ *Four Seasons Nile Plaza, Corniche al-Nil, Garden City* ☎ *02/2791–7000* ⌂ *Reservations essential* ▭ *AE, DC, MC, V* ☽ *No lunch.*

$$$$
STEAK

✗ **Steaks.** The sepia-toned photographs of proud owners and their cattle from around the world tell you what's on the menu, if the name of the restaurant isn't obvious enough. The steaks served here are not just any old slabs of flesh. Choice cuts from the finest beef-producing countries vie for attention, including Wagyu beef from Australia and prime or Black Angus meat from the United States. You can combine menus with Aqua, the hotel's seafood restaurant next door. ☒ *Four Seasons Nile Plaza, Corniche al-Nil, Garden City* ☎ *02/2791–7000* ⌂ *Reservations essential* ▭ *AE, DC, MC, V* ☽ *No lunch.*

$$ ╳**Taboula.** This cozy Lebanese restaurant with pale stucco walls deco-
LEBANESE rated with Lebanese crafts and a highly patterned tiled floor comes alive
in the evening with its warm atmosphere. Lebanese is somewhat different
from Egyptian cuisine, though some dishes have the same ingredients.
Grilled meats are a staple on the menu, or you can choose from a range
of excellent hot and cold mezze. Wines, spirits, and Lebanese *arak* (an
anise-based liqueur) are all available. ⊠ *1 Shar'a Latin America, Gar-
den City* ☎ *02/792–5261* ⊕ *www.taboula-eg.com* ▭ *AE, DC, MC, V.*

MOHANDISEEN

$ ╳**Al-Tazaj.** When it comes to speedy service, McDonald's could learn
MIDDLE EASTERN a thing or two from the Saudis who own Al-Tazaj. They claim to get
their produce from farm to grill in fewer than four hours, which is why
(despite the fast-food decor) this joint turns out some of Cairo's tasti-
est grilled chicken—and little else. The birds are small, so you might
want two; and while you're at it, ask for an extra container of the deli-
ciously garlicky tahini to use as a dip. ⊠ *13–14 Sour Nadi el-Zamalek,
Mohandiseen* ☎ *09018 in Egypt only* ⊠ *30 Talaat Harb, Downtown*
⌂ *Reservations not accepted* ▭ *No credit cards.*

$–$$ ╳**Atatürk.** More Levantine than Turkish—despite the name and kitsch
MIDDLE EASTERN Ottoman decor—this restaurant serves delicious food that is a bit of
a change from the routine. The *manakish* (flatbread) comes in a long
flat loaf covered in black cumin and sesame seeds rather than the usual
zaatar (sesame seeds mixed with powdered sumac and thyme); and
the *börek peynir* (phyllo pastries stuffed with cheese) are spiced with
a hint of nutmeg. You are likely to feel stuffed even before the heavy
main dishes arrive, but try to leave room for the *sharkassia* (half a
chicken in a mild walnut sauce). ⊠ *20 Shar'a Riyadh, Mohandiseen*
☎ *02/3347–5135* ▭ *No credit cards.*

$$$ ╳**Kandahar.** Overlooking Maydan Sphinx (Sphinx Square), Kanda-
INDIAN har serves superb North Indian food. Because all dishes are excellent,
consider ordering one of the set menus that include the highly sea-
soned mulligatawny soup, appetizers, a delicious stewed dal, a lamb
or chicken curry, and rice and bread, as well as dessert. This will give
you a chance to try a bit of everything. If you like your food heavily
spiced, make this known—the heat has been turned down for local
tastes. This is not a sign of a lack of authenticity—chili pepper is only
one of the spices in the Indian culinary palette. The service is some of
the best in town. ⊠ *3 Shar'a Gameat al-Dowal al-Arabiya, Mohandi-
seen* ☎ *02/3303–0615* ▭ *AE, MC, V.*

$$ ╳**Papillon.** Beautifully remodeled to resemble a stone mansion, complete
MIDDLE EASTERN with a grand staircase at the entrance and a dining area that feels like
a drawing room, Papillon serves superb Lebanese food. Although the
menu is inevitably biased toward meat, including delicious lamb kebabs
and *kofta* (ground meat shaped as kebabs), you can fashion a vegetarian
meal out of the substantial appetizers. Be sure to try *fattoush* (a salad
with fried-pita croutons) and the hummus, which comes with warm
'aish shami (a puffy bread). ⊠ *Tirsana Shopping Center (across from the
Zamalek Sporting Club), Shar'a 26 Yulyu, Mohandiseen* ☎ *02/3347–
1672* ⌂ *Reservations essential* ▭ *AE, MC, V.*

HELIOPOLIS

$$
MIDDLE EASTERN

✕ **Al Dabke.** The decor is pure Arabian and the cuisine authentic Middle Eastern, though you're in the heart of a modern five-star hotel. You can watch the bread being cooked in the open oven, so you know it's the genuine article. From soups and hot and cold mezze through the grilled meat and chicken and the stews, the food is delicious. ✉ *Fairmont Heliopolis, Shar'a Uruba, Heliopolis* ☎ *02/2267–7730* ⊟ *AE, DC, MC, V.*

$$$–$$$$
SEAFOOD

✕ **Rossini.** Rossini is in a renovated villa in Heliopolis, but you'll thank yourself if you forgo the pleasant (if generic) interior and sit in the garden for one of Cairo's few alfresco dining experiences, with tables scattered among spotlit palm trees. Rossini is best known for its Italian-influenced seafood, including tender stuffed crab and a delicious shrimp and linguine. For a more local touch, whole fish baked in a casing of salt is a Coptic favorite, especially during the holidays. For dessert, have an authentic tiramisu—Rossini is one of the few places in town that does this dessert right. Service is excellent. ✉ *66 Shar'a Omar Ibn al-Khattab, Heliopolis* ☎ *02/2291–8282* ⌂ *Reservations essential* ⊟ *AE, DC, MC, V.*

NILE DINNER CRUISES

For a different type of meal, try one of the many Nile cruise boats. Most offer a buffet dinner followed by a folk or belly-dancing show with live music. The Marriott-operated **Maxim** (✉ *Shar'a Saraya El Gezira, Zamalek* ☎ *02/2738–8888*) offers an à la carte menu as well as the buffet. The **Nile Peking** (✉ *Corniche al-Nil, Coptic Cairo* ☎ *02/2531–6388* ⊕ *www.peking-restaurants.com*) offers dinner cruises with a Chinese menu but no entertainment—though you may prefer to enjoy the views on deck to watching a show.

GIZA

$–$$
MIDDLE EASTERN

✕ **Andrea.** Out by the Pyramids and down an unmarked canal off Shar'a King Faisal, Andrea is hard to find—your taxi driver might know it, or ask pedestrians once you get out there—but it is absolutely worth the effort. Friday lunch in the gardens is an Egyptian family tradition. Chicken is grilled on beds of charcoal, and *warak einab* (stuffed grape leaves and chicken livers) are unequaled. At night, the Byzantine interior becomes Cairo's most sophisticated nightclub (only November through March)—and getting in is almost as hard as finding the place. ✉ *60 Maryotteya Canal, Shar'a Kerdessa, al-Haram, Giza* ☎ *02/383–1133* ⌂ *Reservations essential* ⊟ *AE, MC, V.*

$$
MIDDLE EASTERN
Fodor'sChoice
★

✕ **Barry's.** The magnificent views of the Pyramids would be reason enough to take the trip to Barry's, but this restaurant gilds the lily. You'll eat on a wide terrace furnished with local antiques—from the tables and chairs to the ornate lighting fixtures and eclectic mixture of grand oil paintings of pashas and belly dancers on the walls. The menu is typical local cuisine served in ample portions. Stay into the evening for the Sound & Light show—you'll be able to watch the full performance from your table. ✉ *2 Shar'a Abu Aziza, extension of Shar'a Abul Houl, Giza* *(close to the entrance to the Sound & Light Show)* ☎ 02/3388–9540 ⊕ *www.barry1.com* ⌘ *Reservations essential* ▭ *AE, MC, V.*

$$ ✕ **The Fish Market.** On the upper deck of a boat permanently moored on
SEAFOOD the west bank of the Nile, the scene here is decidedly simple: there's no
menu, just a display of unbelievably fresh fish, shrimp, crabs, calamari,
and shellfish on ice. Pick what appeals, pay by weight, and the kitchen
will prepare it however you like, with a slew of Middle Eastern salads
on the side. The delicious bread is baked on the premises in a *baladi*
(country) oven. ✉ *26 Shar'a al-Nil, Giza* ☎ *02/3570–9694* ⌘ *Reservations essential* ▭ *AE, MC, V.*

$$$$ ✕ **Moghul Room.** The Mohgul Room is a temple to the grandeur and
INDIAN refinement of Indian cuisine. The setting in the arches-and-romance
Fodor'sChoice splendor of the Mena House could hardly be more sublime, and Indian
★ musicians create a seductive aural backdrop. Try luscious, yogurt-
marinated tandoori; rich, buttery *masala* (a classic blend of spices); or
tender dal cooked slowly over a flame—all accompanied by delicious,
fresh-baked breads. The best of the desserts are *kulfi* (a slightly grainy
ice cream infused with pistachio and cardamom) and *gulab jamun*
(fried milk balls). ✉ *Mena House Oberoi Hotel, Shar'a al-Haram,
Giza* ☎ *02/3377–3222* ⌘ *Reservations essential* ▭ *AE, DC, MC, V*
⊘ *No lunch.*

WHERE TO STAY

Cairo has a growing number of five-star hotels (as rated by the Egyptian Hotel Association) scattered across the city, but many of Cairo's
big business hotels disappoint. This may be because they are too char-
acterless and modern (distinctive Egyptian atmosphere is lacking in
almost all cases) or because they simply fail to measure up to international standards, most often in terms of service. There are certainly
exceptions, and the general quality of the top hotels is on the rise at
this writing. Regardless, the top-end hotels will offer all the facilities
and modern conveniences you need to recuperate after a long day of
sightseeing and shopping. Outside the five-star range, Cairo's options
quickly grow limited, though there are still a few more budget-oriented
hotels that fit the bill.

Cairo's top hotels are all quite affordable by international standards,
but few have any sense of Old World charm. Expect to pay a substantial
premium for a Nile or Pyramids view. While government authorities
rate all hotels on a five-star scale, only a few really earn their stars.
Outside the five-star range, Cairo's options quickly grow more limited.
August and September are crowded with Gulf Arab arrivals, December
and January and Easter are peaks for Europeans, and the major Islamic
holidays see a lot of local and regional guests.

*All hotel reviews have been condensed for this book. Please go to
Fodors.com for full reviews of each property.*

WHAT IT COSTS IN U.S. DOLLARS AND EUROS			
	$	$$	$$$	$$$$
Hotels in Dollars	under $70	$70–$130	$130–$200	over $200
Hotels in Euros	under €45	€45–€80	€80–€130	over €130

Hotel prices are for a double room in high season, excluding 10% tax and service charges (usually 10%).

DOWNTOWN AND BULAQ

$$$$ **Conrad International.** A rather boxy-looking building, the Conrad rather disappoints when compared to other Corniche hotels, but it is a comfortable place to retreat at the end of a long day. **Pros:** The staff are friendly; the hotel offers the occasional homey touch, such as the apples in the giant glass vase that are available at check-in; no-smoking rooms. **Cons:** this is a big hotel and won't suit those who want a more personalized experience; three restaurants doesn't seem like much of a choice for such a large hotel; although all the rooms technically have Nile views, only the rooms in the front of the building on the high floors live up to the billing. ⊠ *1113 Corniche al-Nil, Downtown* ☎ *02/2580–8000* ⊕ *conradhotels1.hilton.com* ➪ *565 rooms, 56 suites* ♿ *In-room: a/c, safe, Internet, Wi-Fi. In-hotel: 3 restaurants, room service, bars, pool, gym, spa, laundry service* ▤ *AE, MC, V* ⅠⓄⅠ *EP.*

$$$$ **Fairmont Nile City.** Standing between two towering office blocks over-
Fodor's Choice looking the Nile, this luxury hotel will appeal to both business and
★   leisure travelers. **Pros:** most rooms have Nile views; shopping mall with cinema is part of the complex; the roof terrace is a great place to chill out. **Cons:** it's Downtown but not really within walking distance to the Downtown attractions. ⊠ *Nile City Tower, 2005 Corniche al-Nil, Bulaq* ☎ *02/2461–9494* ⊕ *www.fairmont.com* ➪ *567 rooms* ♿ *In-room: a/c, safe, Wi-Fi. In-hotel: 5 restaurants, room service, bars, pool, gym, spa, laundry service, parking (paid)* ▤ *AE, DC, MC, V* ⅠⓄⅠ *EP.*

$ **Pension Roma.** Hidden away above the Gattegno department store, this small, shoestring-budget pension is adored by students and backpackers. **Pros:** there's a real home-away-from-home feeling here. **Cons:** elevator is old and a little shaky; it's a long climb up the stairs; not all rooms have a private bathroom. ⊠ *169 Shar'a Muhammad Farid, Downtown* ☎ *02/391–1088* ➪ *32 rooms, 5 with bath* ♿ *In-room: a/c (some), no phone, no TV. In-hotel: laundry facilities* ▤ *No credit cards* ⅠⓄⅠ *BP.*

$$$$ **Ramses Hilton.** This large hotel is geared toward the needs of tour groups and business travelers (largely Japanese), and it's one of the most recognizable high-rises along the Corniche. **Pros:** A good choice of eateries on-site. **Cons:** the hotel is surrounded by major roads that make it difficult to wander around on foot; small pool and pool terrace, especially when many guests want to use it at the same time; balconies are small. ⊠ *1115 Corniche al-Nil, Downtown* ☎ *02/2577–7444* ⊕ *www.hilton. com* ➪ *900 rooms, 152 suites* ♿ *In-room: a/c, safe, Internet. In-hotel: 7 restaurants, room service, bars, pool, gym, laundry service, parking (paid), no-smoking rooms, some pets allowed* ▤ *AE, DC, MC, V* ⅠⓄⅠ *EP.*

A room in Fairmont Nile City

$$$–$$$$ **Semiramis InterContinental.** This modern high-rise was, for many years, the center of the city's hotel life. Today it's got more vigorous competition but stands up well when compared with newer properties. **Pros:** the hotel is a little less expensive than many of the same quality; it's in the heart of Downtown. **Cons:** could be a little too large and impersonal for some visitors. ⊠ *Corniche al-Nil, at Maydan Tahrir, Downtown* ☎ *02/2795–7171* ⊕ *www.ichotelsgroup.com* ⇨ *728 rooms, 79 suites* ♿ *In-room: a/c, safe, Internet. In-hotel: 6 restaurants, room service, bars, pool, gym, spa, laundry service, Wi-Fi hotspot, parking (paid), no-smoking rooms* ☰ *AE, DC, MC, V* ⊚ *EP.*

$$$ **Talisman Hotel de Charme.** The approach through dusty alleyways and the climb through floors of nondescript grey offices could be a little off-putting, but misgivings vanish as soon as you enter the Talisman's inviting reception area. **Pros:** Surrounding area has a range of inexpensive local cafés and bars, plus hundreds of shops; the design and decor are excellent; well-stocked library. **Cons:** a small, old, and creaky elevator serves the whole building; no restaurant on-site; no outside space. ⊠ *39 Shar'a Talaat Harb, Downtown* ☎ *02/2393–9431* ⊕ *www.talisman-hotel.com* ⇨ *24 rooms* ♿ *In-room: safe, refrigerator. In-hotel: laundry service, Internet terminal* ☰ *No credit cards* ⊚ *BP.*

Fodor's Choice
★

$ **The Windsor Hotel.** Opened in the early 1900s as the khedivial bathhouse and converted to a hotel in the 1930s, the Windsor oozes atmosphere. **Pros:** wonderful period history—the atmosphere is palpable; your fellow guests will be a cosmopolitan and interesting crowd of all ages. **Cons:** rooms are in need of some TLC; communal landings don't have modern soundproofing. ⊠ *19 Shar'a Alfi Bay, Downtown* ☎ *02/2591–5277* ⊕ *www.windsorcairo.com* ⇨ *55 rooms* ♿ *In-room:*

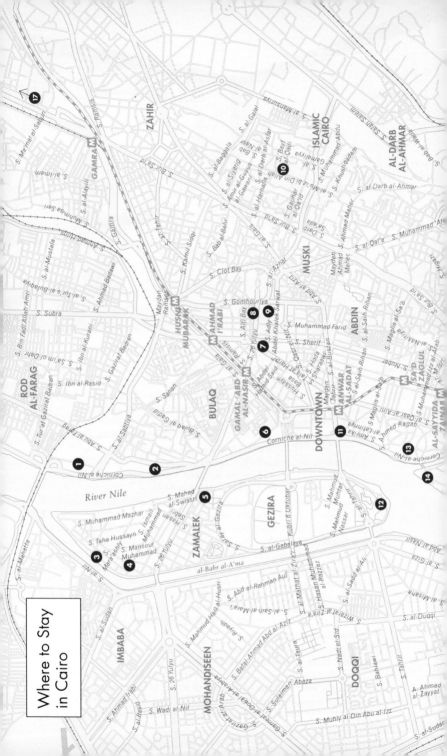

a/c, refrigerator. In-hotel: restaurant, bar, laundry service, Wi-Fi hot-spot, parking (free) ⊟ *AE, DC, MC, V* |⊙| *EP.*

ISLAMIC CAIRO NORTH

$$$$ **Le Riad Hotel—Hotel de Charme.** Founded and decorated by Madame Veronique, who also founded the Talisman, Le Riad is the first true luxury boutique hotel in Cairo. **Pros:** a very stylish property; suites are generous in size; the decor says Cairo. **Cons:** prices are as high as the large international hotels without the corresponding range of amenities. ⊠ *114 Shar'a Al Muizz, Khan El-Khalili* ☎ *02/2787–6074* ⊕ *www.leriad-hoteldecharme. com* ↩ *17 suites* ♨ *In-room: a/c, safe, kitchen, DVD, Wi-Fi. In-hotel: restaurant, bar, spa, laundry service* ⊟ *AE, D, DC, MC, V* |⊙| *BP.*

ZAMALEK AND GEZIRA

$$$$ **Cairo Marriott.** The centerpiece of this large hotel is a breathtaking
★ palace built by Khedive Isma'il to give French Empress Eugénie a suit-able place to stay on her visit for the opening of the Suez Canal in 1869. Unfortunately, you can't stay in the palace itself, because the Marri-ott's bright but comparatively indistinctive rooms are in two adjoining modern blocks. **Pros:** The gardens of the hotel make a peaceful retreat from the city; the restaurants at the Marriott attract lots of Cairenes and expats, so it's a great place to feel the authentic atmosphere of the modern city. **Cons:** it's the biggest hotel in Cairo, so not for those who want more personal service. ⊠ *16 Shar'a Saray al-Gezira, Zamalek* ☎ *02/2728–3000* ⊕ *www.marriott.com* ↩ *977 rooms, 111 suites* ♨ *In-room: a/c, safe, Internet. In-hotel: 17 restaurants, room service, bars, pool, gym, spa, laundry service, Wi-Fi hotspot, parking (paid), some pets allowed* ⊟ *AE, DC, MC, V* |⊙| *EP.*

$$$ **Golden Tulip Flamenco Hotel.** Cairo has very few hotels that bridge the gap between the luxury properties and the more basic budget options, but this one—part of a European chain—makes a good attempt. **Pros:** good value for the money. **Cons:** some rooms need a coat of paint; some staff are more helpful than others. ⊠ *Shar'a El Gezira El Wosta, Zamalek* ☎ *02/735–0815* ⊕ *www.goldentulipflamenco.com* ↩ *174 rooms* ♨ *In-room: safe (some), refrigerator, Wi-Fi (some). In-hotel: 2 restaurants, room service, bar, laundry service, Internet terminal* ⊟ *AE, MC, V* |⊙| *BP.*

$$ **Hotel Longchamps.** This lovely little bed-and-breakfast-style hotel is
★ on the upper floors of a medium-sized tower block, offering a quiet ref-uge from the city. **Pros:** excellent value for money; friendly, welcoming staff; Superior rooms have free tea and coffee. **Cons:** the old elevator is a touch creaky; lots of repeat guests means it can be difficult to get a room. ⊠ *Shar'a Ismail Mohammed, Zamalek* ☎ *02/2735–2311* ⊕ *www. hotellongchamps.com* ↩ *22 rooms* ♨ *In-room: a/c, refrigerator, Wi-Fi. In-hotel: restaurant, laundry facilities* ⊟ *MC, V* |⊙| *BP.*

$$$$ **Sofitel El-Gezirah Cairo.** The circular tower has been gracing the Cairo skyline for well over two decades, but the interiors here have been brought up to date after a takeover by Sofitel in 2006 (it was formerly a Sheraton), and the hotel has reemerged as a must-visit place for expats and visitors for its bars and restaurants. **Pros:** quiet (for Cairo) location surrounded

by greenery; all rooms have a view of the city and the Nile; cool Buddha Bar on-site. **Cons:** despite the central location, you're dependent on the hotel's taxi fleet to get anywhere because nothing is in easy walking distance. ⊠ *3 Shar'a El Thawra Council, Gezira* ⊙ *Box 732, al-Orman, Giza* ☎ *02/2737–3737* ⊕ *www.sofitel.com* ⤳ *383 rooms, 50 suites* ⟠ *In-room: a/c, safe, Internet, Wi-Fi. In-hotel: 6 restaurants, room service, bars, pools, gym, spa, laundry service, parking (paid)* ▭ *AE, DC, MC, V* ⧍∣*EP.*

RODAH ISLAND AND GARDEN CITY

$$$$ 🔲 **Four Seasons Hotel Cairo at Nile Plaza.** The most sophisticated address in the city, this Four Seasons is the top place to see and be seen. **Pros:** you'll be surrounded by the Cairo glitterati here; standard rooms have 500 square feet of space; the spa is excellent; no-smoking rooms. **Cons:** public spaces could be viewed as gaudy by some; atmosphere is more corporate than resortlike; not all rooms have terraces or balconies. ⊠ *1089 Corniche al-Nil, Maglis El Shaab, Garden City* ☎ *02/2791– 7000* ⊕ *www.fourseasons.com* ⤳ *288 rooms, 77 suites* ⟠ *In-room: a/c, DVD, safe, Internet. In-hotel: 6 restaurants, room service, bars, pool, gym, spa, laundry service, parking (paid)* ▭ *AE, DC, MC, V* ⧍∣*EP.*

$$$$ 🔲 **Grand Hyatt Cairo.** Occupying the very northern tip of Rodah Island, this high-rise hotel offers exceptional views of the river and the city from its business-regular rooms. **Pros:** Nile-side eateries offer lovely views by day and romantic views by night; the gym and spa facilities are excellent; no-smoking rooms. **Cons:** alcohol is not available in all bars and restaurants (only on the 41st-floor panorama restaurant and if ordered through room service). ⊠ *Corniche al-Nil, Rodah Island* ☎ *02/2356– 1234* ⊕ *www.cairo.grand.hyatt.com* ⤳ *633 rooms, 83 suites* ⟠ *In-room: a/c, safe, Internet. In-hotel: 12 restaurants, room service, bar, pool, gym, spa, laundry service, parking (paid)* ▭ *AE, DC, MC, V* ⧍∣*EP.*

HELIOPOLIS

$$$$ 🔲 **Fairmont Towers Heliopolis.** Cairo's most architecturally stunning hotel, the six-story building is designed to mimic the eye of Horus. **Pros:** only 10 minutes from the international airport, so it's excellent for onward travel and early morning flights; there's a wide range of amenities shared with the neighboring Fairmont Heliopolis; no-smoking rooms. **Cons:** it's a 45-minute drive to Downtown. ⊠ *Shar'a El Shaheed Sayed Zakaria, off Shar'a Uruba, Heliopolis Box 2466, Helipolis, Cairo* ☎ *02/2696–0000* ⊕ *www.fairmont.com* ⤳ *247 rooms* ⟠ *In-room: a/c, safe, Wi-Fi. In-hotel: 4 restaurants, room service, bar, pool, gym, spa, laundry service, Wi-Fi hotspot, parking (paid)* ▭ *AE, DC, MC, V* ⧍∣*EP.*

GIZA

$$$$ 🔲 **Four Seasons Hotel Cairo at The First Residence.** In a word, this hotel is
★ superb, offering luxury amenities and rooms in a serene setting. **Pros:** spacious rooms (Standard rooms start at 452 square feet); there's a shopping mall attached to the hotel; no-smoking rooms. **Cons:** the eastward Nile-view rooms face a residential tower; the swimming pool is in shade

for all but a few hours a day, so don't come here for a tan. ✉ *35 Giza St., Giza* ☎ *02/3568–1212* ⊕ *www.fourseasons.com* ⌑ *226 rooms, 43 suites* ⌂ *In-room: a/c, safe, Internet. In-hotel: 3 restaurants, room service, bars, pool, gym, spa, laundry service, Wi-Fi hotspot* ═ *AE, MC, V* ⊚ *EP.*

$$$$ ⊡ **Mena House Oberoi.** This is *the* great colonial-era hotel in Cairo and
★ has hosted almost every politician, celebrity, and member of royalty to visit Egypt, and it's both comfortable and convenient for the pyramids. **Pros:** proximity to the Pyramids cannot be beaten; the main building oozes period charm. **Cons:** it's at least 45 minutes from Downtown Cairo, so you might consider a one-night stay only for the day you visit the Pyramids; some rooms need to be renovated; only the suites in the main building have period furniture. ✉ *Shar'a al-Haram, Giza* ☎ *02/3377–3222* ⊕ *www.oberoihotels.com* ⌑ *498 rooms, 25 suites* ⌂ *In-room: a/c, DVD, safe, Internet. In-hotel: 5 restaurants, room service, bars, golf course, pool, gym, spa, laundry service, parking (free)* ═ *AE, DC, MC, V* ⊚ *EP.*

$$ ⊡ **Swiss Inn.** This modern but simple, 14-story hotel opened in 2008. **Pros:** equidistant between Downtown and the Pyramids (about 20 minutes to either by taxi); views of the city and of the Pyramids from the roof terrace; no-smoking rooms. **Cons:** music around the pool can be too loud; there's little around the hotel beyond the Pharaonic Village theme park, so it's a taxi ride to anywhere; beds are narrow and won't suit tall or wide travelers; only one dedicated no-smoking room per floor. ✉ *110 Shar'a El Bahr El Aazzam, Corniche al-Nil, Giza* ☎ *02/3776–6501* ⊕ *www.swissinn.net* ⌑ *90 rooms, 9 suites* ⌂ *In-room: a/c, safe, Internet. In-hotel: restaurant, room service, bars, pool, laundry service, Internet terminal, parking (paid)* ═ *AE, DC, MC, V* ⊚ *BP.*

NIGHTLIFE AND THE ARTS

The Cairo cultural scene defies preconceptions. You can go to a concert of classical Arabic music in a restored medieval house, watch dervishes whirl in an old palace, then take in a performance of *La Bohème* by the Cairo Opera Company, and end the night on a club's dance floor. Layered around this traditional cultural season is a thriving and hip nightlife scene that's one of the best in the Middle East, with bars and clubs that attract vacationing Gulf Arabs as well as Western visitors and expats. Occasionally the two meet in a fusion style—a jazz concert of trumpet and *oud* (an Arabic stringed instrument), for example—that is unique to this city. For the latest listings and movies, check the English-language *al-Ahram Weekly, Middle East Times,* the weekly *Cairo Times,* or the monthly *Egypt Today.* Always call ahead to double-check performances because arrangements can and do go awry.

THE ARTS

Multiscreen cinema complexes are springing up all over the city, usually linked to major malls. Foreign films are subtitled in Arabic and usually start 30 minutes after the scheduled time (arriving 15 minutes after that time is usually fine). All theaters have reserved seating. Also note

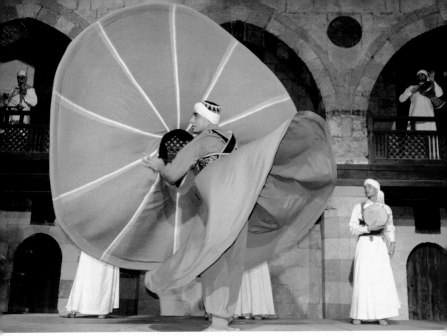

A whirling dervish Sufi dancer in motion at a performace in Cairo

that most embassies have cultural centers that show original-language (and uncensored) movies—these are well worth looking into if you're in the mood to see a film.

ABDIN

DANCE, OPERA, AND MUSIC

Gomhouriya Theater. This theater hosts many good visiting artists, who perform at this surprisingly elegant space near Abdin Palace. ⊠ *12 Shar'a Gomhouriya, Abdin* ☎ *02/2739–0114*.

DOWNTOWN

ART GALLERIES

Mashrabia Gallery. This gallery shows all the best contemporary artists in Egypt—including Adel al-Siwi, Muhammad Abla, Rehab al-Sadek, Hamdi Atteya, and Awad al-Shimy. The exhibits change monthly, and there is a small shop in the back. The gallery is generally open Saturday through Thursday from 11 to 8. ⊠ *8 Shar'a Champollion, Downtown* ☎ *02/2578–4494*.

The Townhouse Gallery. This eclectic space showcases the work of contemporary artists. Part of it is a converted factory space that hosts live performances, film screenings, and lectures in addition to art exhibitions. ⊠ *10 Shara'a Nawbawy, off Shar'a Champollion, Downtown* ☎ *02/2576–8086* ⊕ *www.thetownhousegallery.com*.

FILM

Metro Theatre. This theater is Downtown, streetside rather than in a shopping center or mall. ⊠ *35 Shar'a Talaat Harb, Downtown* ☎ *02/ 2393–7566*.

Ramses Hilton Annex. The top floor of this shopping mall next to the hotel has long been a popular choice for the latest English-language films. ✉ *1115 Corniche al-Nil, Downtown* ☎ *02/2574–7435.*

Renaissance Cinemas. This multiscreen complex shows the latest hits. ✉ *Nile Towers Mall at Nile City, Corniche al-Nil, Downtown* ☎ *02/2461–9101* ⊕ *www.nilecitytowers.com.*

GARDEN CITY

ART GALLERIES

Duroub Gallery. This gallery offers a variety of thematic exhibitions throughout the year. ✉ *4 Shar'a Latin America, Garden City* ☎ *02/2794–7951.*

GEZIRA

DANCE, OPERA, AND MUSIC

Al-Hanager. Part of the **Opera House** complex—but intended as a space for experimental performing arts—the Al-Hanager hosts some of Cairo's most interesting music and dance. The complex is currently undergoing a renovation, but some elements always remain open. There are also a café and gallery on-site. ✉ *Shar'a Tahrir, Gezira* ☎ *02/2735–6861.*

Opera House. Cairo's Opera House is the home hall for the Cairo Opera Company. Although not quite of international standard, the opera has an excellent soprano in Italian-trained Iman Mustafa. And the collection of performing arts companies housed here is unparalleled in Africa. There are also resident Western and Arabic orchestras in addition to a constant stream of visiting artists. Pick an event from the newspaper and go. Note that jacket and tie are compulsory in the Main Hall but not in the others. ✉ *Shar'a Tahrir, Gezira* ☎ *02/2739–0114 for ticket office* ⊕ *www.cairoopera.org.*

ISLAMIC CAIRO SOUTH

DANCE, OPERA, AND MUSIC

Wikala al-Ghuri. This venue offers regular whirling dervish and Arabic music performances in a medieval mansion setting. ✉ *Shar'a Mohammad 'Abdu, Islamic Cairo South* ☎ *02/2735–4234.*

RODAH ISLAND

FILM

Golden Stars Cinema. This multiscreen movie house shows Arabic- and English-language films. ✉ *Citystars Mall, Shar'a Ibn El Khattab, Heliopolis* ☎ *02/2480–1012* ⊕ *www.citystars.com.eg.*

MA'ADI

ART GALLERIES

The World of Art Gallery. This gallery offers a mixed program of exhibitions by local and regional artists. ✉ *6 Shar'a 77C, Gold Area, Ma'adi* ☎ *02/2351–4362.*

RODAH ISLAND

FILM

Good News Cinema. This small cinema offers a program of popular hits. ✉ *Galleria Mall, Grand Hyatt Hotel, Corniche al-Nil, Rodah Island* ☎ *02/2362–8400.*

ZAMALEK
ART GALLERIES
Centre des Arts. This state-run gallery is in an old villa that hosts the annual Youth Salon, which gives a good survey (the work can be of mixed quality) of what is happening in the local art scene. ⊠ *1 Mahad al-Swissri, Zamalek* ☎ *02/2340–8211.*

El Sakia. This name of this gallery, which can be translated as "The Waterwheel," is the legacy of writer and novelist Adel-Moneim El Sawy. It's a cultural center offering writing workshops, literary seminars, film screenings, musical performances, and art exhibitions. The programs cut across all genres. ⊠ *Shar'a 26 Yulyu, Zamalek* ☎ *02/2736–6178* ⊕ *www.culturewheel.com.*

NIGHTLIFE

Cairo's nightlife scene is certainly cool, but most locations defy easy definition, moving seamlessly from early evening cocktail lounge to midevening eatery to late-night dance venue. The clientele is a cosmopolitan mix of wealthy Egyptians, foreign residents and workers, and a grab bag of international visitors. In summer, Cairo is a great playground for visitors from Gulf countries, many of whom come to enjoy the city's clubs and bars. Popular clubs usually close around 2 AM, though some close earlier.

Bellydancing, which was once a favorite performing art, is falling out of favor with both Egyptians and visitors. Your best bet if you want to see tame versions of these once risqué performances is to visit one of the major hotels in the city. Belly dancers will normally gyrate for 15 or 30 minutes nightly at their signature Middle Eastern/Lebanese restaurants. At this writing, only a couple of hotels still offer dancers.

International coffee chains have arrived in Egypt, so there's no need to miss out on your favorite caffeine hit. However, Cairo has its own café culture, where you can be assured of a freshly brewed espresso or cappuccino, though you'll find that Egyptians will more often take tea.

DOKKI
BARS
Le Tabasco. This place is hard to find—look for the bouncer standing outside—but the seductively lit subterranean nightclub is easily Cairo's coolest bar scene. Look hip and go early if you want to eat dinner, because by 10 it starts to fill up with funky twentysomething Egyptians, and it doesn't empty until late. ⊠ *8 Amman Sq., Dokki* ☎ *02/3336–5583.*

DOWNTOWN
BARS
Odeon Palace Bar. The rooftop bar continues to attract crowds for its laid-back ambience despite the fact that the hotel has passed its prime. Relax on the low couches and enjoy shisha and views across the Downtown skyline. ⊠ *Odeon Palace Hotel, 6 Shar'a Abdel Hamid, Downtown* ☎ *02/2577–6637.*

Sangria. Part restaurant, part lounge, Sangria is definitely one of the "in" places in Cairo for its relaxed atmosphere. ⊠ *Casino El-Shagara, Corniche al-Nil, Downtown* ☎ *02/2579–6511.*

Windows on the World. This bar is on the top floor of the Ramses Hilton, drawing a forties-plus crowd for the late-night views and musicians playing softly in the background. ⊠ *Ramses Hilton, 1115 Corniche al-Nil, Downtown* ☎ *02/2577–7444.*

Windsor Hotel. The Downtown hotel has a quiet and comfortable bar with a prerevolutionary style that is better for a relaxing over an early-evening beer than for late-night reveling (it closes at 1 AM). ⊠ *19 Shar'a Alfi Bey, Downtown* ☎ *02/2591–5277.*

CAFÉS

Trianon. One of a chain of cafés with branches throughout Egypt, Trianon serves delicious coffee and mouthwatering pastries and cakes. ⊠ *Arkadia Mall, Corniche al-Nil, Downtown* ☎ *19020 (in Egypt only).*

DANCE CLUBS

After Eight. This nightspot has been on the scene for many years and gone through many reincarnations, but it still pulls in the crowds. There's a resident DJ as well as a program of live bands. ⊠ *6 Shar'a Qasr al-Nil, Downtown* ☎ *02/2574–0855.*

GIZA

BELLY DANCING

Abu Nawass Nightclub. This club has nightly belly dancing performances from 10 PM. ⊠ *Oberoi Mena House Hotel, Pyramids Rd., Giza* ☎ *02/3377–3222.*

ISLAMIC CAIRO NORTH

CAFÉS

Fodor's Choice
★

El Fishawy. This famous café is right in the heart of the medieval marketplace; this is *the* great café in Cairo, open around the clock and beloved by tourists and locals alike. The chairs spill out into the alley, and the walls are hung with thick, old-style mirrors decorated with elaborate woodwork. Tea with fresh mint is the house specialty. ⊠ *5 Sikkit Khan al-Khalili, Khan al-Khalili, Islamic Cairo North.*

MOHANDISEEN

BARS

Jazz Club. This club has dark, scruffy decor that isn't much to look at, but this is far and away the best place to hear live music in the city—not that there is much competition. Regular bands play a fusion of Western and Arab styles that always has the twentysomething crowd on its feet. ⊠ *197 Shar'a 26 Yulyu, next to 15th of May Bridge, Mohandiseen* ☎ *02/3345–9939* ⊕ *www.cairojazzclub.com.*

RODAH ISLAND

BARS

Hard Rock Café. Cairo's Hard Rock has a great staff, who do a creditable job with their dance routines, so the place is full of energy by 10 PM. It's no different than any other Hard Rock, but don't forget the souvenir T-shirt before you leave. ⊠ *Grand Hyatt, Corniche al-Nil, Rodah Island* ☎ *02/2532–1277.*

The famous El Fishawy café

ZAMALEK
BARS

★ **Buddha Bar.** One of the world's coolest international nightlife brands has found a home on the banks of the Nile, where its Asian-influenced decor gets a few pharaonic additions. There's a contemporary fusion menu, great cocktails, and chill-out sounds mixed under the Buddha Bar label. ⊠ *Sofitel El-Gezirah, 3 Shar'a El Thawra Council, Zamalek* ☎ *02/2737–3737.*

Deals. This regular expat haunt seems to have changed little in the last couple of decades. This basement bar has a rather down-at-the-heels appeal that draws seasoned pub goers. The large-screen TVs show mostly European sports. ⊠ *1 Shar'a Said el Bakry, Zamalek* ☎ *02/2736–0502.*

Pub 28. This bar is the perfect destination if you just want a few beers in a neighborhood bar with a friendly bunch of expats. ⊠ *Shar'a Shagaret El Dorr, Zamalek* ☎ *02/2735–9200.*

Fodor's Choice
★ **Sequoia.** An atmospheric tented venue on the banks of the Nile, Sequoia offers a contemporary menu that attracts as many people for dinner as for the laid-back ambience and great music. Come for a meal, and you can stay until the place closes. ⊠ *Shar'a Abdul Feda, Zamalek* ☎ *02/2735–0014.*

BELLY DANCING

Empress Lounge. The Empress has nightly belly dancing shows along with singing performances. ⊠ *Cairo Marriott Hotel, Shar'a Saray al-Gezira, Zamalek* ☎ *02/2728–3000.*

CAFÉS

The Promenade. In the gardens flanked by the restored palace that serves as the lobby of the Cairo Marriott, this is the best place to spend a summer night. The place is immensely popular with Gulf Arabs; it serves food and alcohol. It's open until 2 AM from May through October, until 6 PM from November through April. ⊠ *Cairo Marriott, Shar'a Saray al-Gezira, Zamalek* ☎ *02/2728–3000.*

CASINOS

Omar Khayyam. Most major five-star hotels have casinos that are open until sunrise, with all the usual games (roulette, blackjack, slot machines, and so forth), and horrifically poor odds. The best of them is the Omar Khayyam, which is open 24 hours and plies gamblers with free drinks as long as they're playing. ⊠ *Cairo Marriott, Shar'a Saray al-Gezira, Zamalek* ☎ *02/2728–3000.*

DANCE CLUBS

Bliss. Come here, and you will probably find either full-on house or techno music playing, but it's always right up to date with the current club music trends and attracts a predominately younger crowd. ⊠ *Imperial Boat, Shar'a Saray al-Gezira, Zamalek* ☎ *02/2736–5796.*

Morocco. This club occupies part of a stationary Nile cruise ship. Morocco has a resident DJ who flips between 1980s disco and contemporary dance, trance, and techno. For this reason it attracts cosmopolitan crowds that span the age range from teens to 40s. ⊠ *Blue Nile Boat, Shar'a Saray al-Gezira, Zamalek* ☎ *02/2735–3314.*

SHOPPING

Cairo has always been a great place to shop for traditional items because of its spectacular medieval marketplace, the Khan al-Khalili, where browsing and bargaining are half the fun. There is no tried-and-true bargaining strategy; just shop around, decide how much something is worth to you, and start bargaining lower than that in order to end up at that point. In the Khan, the opening price is *never* the final price.

In the last decade Cairo has embraced the shopping mall. These enclosed, air-conditioned spaces stacked with international brands have revolutionized shopping for residents. Most malls also have shops selling a range of the same kinds of souvenirs that you'd find in the Khan al-Khalili, though at higher, nonnegotiable prices.

Wealthy and upwardly mobile Cairenes not only have the wherewithal to fund their lifestyles, but they also have great taste, so you'll find a wide selection of art galleries, designer shops, and fashion boutiques to indulge your need for retail therapy.

Although most of what you see in tourist shops are reproductions of varying quality, there is a long local tradition in Egypt of connoisseurship in collectibles, which means that there is always the possibility of finding a real gem. Be prepared, however, for local tastes that favor ornate French-style furniture and antiques, not the Middle Eastern pieces you might be longing for. There are several nameless antiques shops in Downtown Cairo along Shar'a Hoda Sharaawi that are worth looking into. Lots are shown for several days in advance of a two-day auction, which usually operates on a cash-only basis. Check the *Egyptian Gazette* for the latest auction schedules.

BULAQ

SHOPPING MALLS

Towers Mall. Underpinning two vast office blocks (plus the new Fairmont Nile Towers hotel), this mall caters to upwardly mobile executives and office workers. There's also a multiscreen cinema on-site. ✉ *Nile City Towers, Corniche al-Nil, Bulaq* ☎ *02/2461–9000.*

DOKKI

JEWELRY

Azza Fahmy. Egypt's leading jewelry designer has become an international brand in the last five years with her traditional motif-inspired pieces. A purchase here is a genuine designed-in-Egypt souvenir. Another branch is at the Beyman Store at Four Seasons Hotel at Nile Plaza. ✉ *Mall at First Residence, 35 Shar'a Giza, Dokki* ☎ *02/3573–7687* ⊕ *www.azzafahmy.com.*

DOWNTOWN

ANTIQUES AND AUCTION HOUSES

Catsaros. One of the best auction houses in town is in an unmarked alley off Shar'a Qasr al-Nil. ✉ *22 Shar'a Gawad Hosni, Downtown* ☎ *02/2392–6123.*

Osiris. To get to this good auction house, look for a small blue sign on the building's second floor. ✉ *17 Shar'a Sherif, Downtown.*

ART GALLERIES

Mashrabia Gallery. This gallery is on the tree-lined Shar'a Champollion (the street named after the Frenchman who broke the hieroglyphic code), and it's Cairo's best contemporary-art gallery. The space itself is not much to look at, but the quality of work is sometimes exceptional. Be on the lookout for exhibitions by Adel al-Siwi, Muhammad Abla, Rehab al-Sadek, Hamdi Atteya, or Awad al-Shimy. The gallery is open Saturday through Thursday from 11 to 8. ✉ *8 Shar'a Champollion, Downtown* ☎ *02/2578–4494.*

BOOKSTORES AND NEWSSTANDS

Anglo-Egyptian Bookstore. With an excellent selection of books, especially nonfiction offerings, this is a good source for English-language book. It's open Monday through Saturday from 9 to 1:30 and 4:30 to 8. ✉ *165 Shar'a Muhammad Farid, Downtown* ☎ *02/2391–4237* ⊕ *www.anglo-egyptian.com.*

L'Orientaliste. L'Orientaliste is the best source in Cairo for old books, antique maps, and postcards. It's open Monday through Saturday from 10 to 7:30. ✉ *15 Shar'a Qasr al-Nil, Downtown* ☎ *02/2575–3418* ⊕ *www.orientalecairo.com.*

SHOPPING MALLS

Arkadia Mall. This is the largest Downtown mall, with more than 500 shops plus an arcade with games to keep the kids happy. ✉ *Corniche al-Nil, Downtown* ☎ *02/2579–2082.*

City Stars. Cairo's megamall is huge, with more than 500 stores. There are also three hotels and a variety of restaurants and cafés plus two food courts. ✉ *Shar'a Hashad, Heliopolis* ☎ *02/2480–0500* ⊕ *www.citystars.com.eg.*

GIZA

SHOPPING MALLS

Mall at First Residence. This series of upmarket boutiques sells jewelry, designer clothing, and elegant housewares in galleries around an open atrium. There's a café on the ground floor. ✉ *First Residence Complex, 35 Shar'a al-Giza, Giza* ☎ *02/3571–7806* ⊕ *ww.firstmallcairo.com.*

HELIOPOLIS

BOOKSTORES AND NEWSSTANDS

Virgin Megastore. This vast emporium offers a good choice of English-language reading from magazines to hardcover books, as well as music, films, and games. ✉ *City Stars Mall, Heliopolis* ☎ *02/2480–2240* ⊕ *www.virginmegastore.me.*

SHOPPING MALLS

City Stars. Cairo's megamall is huge, with more than 500 stores. There are also three hotels and a variety of restaurants and cafés plus two food courts. ✉ *Shar'a Hashad, Heliopolis* ☎ *02/2480–0500* ⊕ *www.citystars.com.eg.*

ISLAMIC CAIRO NORTH

BOOKSTORES AND NEWSSTANDS

Abd El-Zaher. This is the last working bookbinding company in Cairo. It's worth visiting to buy a beautifully leather-bound and gilt-decorated diary, sketchbook, or photo album. These skills are rare in the 21st century. What better place to buy a blank trip journal where you can record your thoughts? Abd El-Zahar will also bind your books or albums for you but require around 10 days turnaround. ✉ *31 Shar'a al-Sheikh Mohemmed Abdu, Islamic Cairo North* ☎ *02/2511–8041* ⊕ *www.abdelzaharbinding.com.*

MARKETS

Fodor's Choice
★

Khan al-Khalili. Cairo shopping starts at this great medieval souk. Although it has been on every tourist's itinerary for centuries, and some of its more visible wares can seem awfully tacky, the Khan is where everyone—newcomer and age-old Cairene alike—goes to find traditional items: jewelry, lamps, spices, clothes, textiles, handicrafts, water pipes, metalwork, you name it. Whatever it is, you can find it somewhere in this skein of alleys or the streets around them. Every Khan veteran has the shops he or she swears by—usually because of the fact (or illusion) she or he is known there personally and is thus less likely to be overcharged. Go, browse, and bargain hard. Once you buy something, don't ask how much it costs at the next shop; you'll be happier that way. Many shops close Sunday. ✉ *Islamic Cairo North.*

ISLAMIC CAIRO SOUTH

ARTS AND CRAFTS

Al Khatoun. This renovated yet still run-down workshop is an outlet for varied local artists and artisans including weavers, potters, and woodworkers. Styles vary from the traditional to the contemporary. ✉ *3*

Shar'a Mohamed Abdou (behind Al-Azhar Mosque), Old Cairo Islamic Cairo South ☎ *02/2514–7164* ⊕ *www.alkhatoun.net.*

MA'ADI
SHOPPING MALLS
Maadi City Centre. This small mall is a resource for the many families in this residential district; there are few designer names but lots of mainstream brands. The mall is anchored by a major supermarket. ⊠ *Maadi/Katyama Ring Road, Ma'adi* ☎ *02/2520–4000.*

RODAH ISLAND
SHOPPING MALLS
Galleria. The shopping center attached to the Grand Hyatt, has a small selection of individual boutiques, but it's anchored by a 12-screen cinema complex. ⊠ *Grand Hyatt, Corniche al-Nil, Rodah Island* ☎ *02/2356–1234.*

ZAMALEK
ARTS AND CRAFTS
Fair Trade Egypt. This shop sells an interesting selection of handmade items from more than 40 artisans and cooperatives around Egypt, including crafts from the Western desert oases, Fayyum, and Upper Egypt. Prices are fixed and, as the name suggests, fair for the producers. ⊠ *27 Shar' Yahia Ibrahim, First floor, Apt. 8, Zamalek* ☎ *02/2736–5123* ⊕ *www.fairtradeegypt.org.*

Nomad. Nomad offers relatively inexpensive, vaguely Bedouin-style jewelry, along with some interesting textiles from Siwa Oasis and the Sinai. ⊠ *Cairo Marriott, Shar'a Saray al-Gezira, Zamalek* ☎ *02/2736–2132* ⊕ *www.nomadgallery.net.*

FURNITURE
Mit Rehan. This is the best source for modern Egyptian furniture—which means Islamic or pharaonic motifs applied to traditional pieces, like mashrabiyya screens, or to Western-style pieces, like sofas. It's open Monday through Saturday from 10 to 8. ⊠ *13 Shar'a Mara'ashly, Zamalek* ☎ *02/2735–4578* ⊕ *www.mitrehan.com.*

GUIDED TOURS

Cairo is awash with companies offering tours and guides, but the quality varies greatly. Official tour guides have to be licensed by the Egyptian authorities and must undergo a strict program of training and examination before they receive their accreditation. This is your assurance of quality, so always make sure that any guide you engage is licensed. If you intend to visit the sites at Dahshur, Wadi Natrun, or Fayyum, booking a guided tour with a well-respected company or an accredited personal guide is your best option because you'll have travel and navigation taken care of, plus an expert on hand to answer questions you have during the tour. Booking through a company will also take care of any security issues with police escorts. If you are looking for a guided tour, your best bet is to try to set it up with a travel agent.

One well-respected American tour guide based in Cairo is Debbie Senters of Casual Cairo Detours. She organizes bespoke tours of any length and is happy to create a personal program for you. These tours are not cheap, but her guides are licensed, and tours include all transportation.

Contacts Casual Cairo Detours (☎ *02/2415–2726 or 010/568–2924 ⊕ www. casualcairotours.com).*

TRAVEL AGENCIES

Contacts American Express Travel (⊠ *15 Shar'a Qasr al-Nil, Downtown* ☎ *02/2574–7991).* **Misr Travel** (⊠ *1 Shar'a Tala'at Harb, Downtown* ☎ *02/2393–0010 ⊕ www.misrtravel.net).* **Thomas Cook** (⊠ *17 Shar'a Mahmoud Bassiouny, Downtown* ☎ *02/2576–6982, 16119 in Egypt only* ⊠ *Cairo International Airport* ☎ *02/2265–4447⊕ www.thomascookegypt.com).*

SIDE TRIPS FROM CAIRO

In order that the living could view the grandeur of the dead god-kings—and, in many cases, be buried alongside them—ancient Egyptians used the sites in the desert west of Memphis, one of the most enduring of ancient capitals, for their royal necropolises. These sites are filled with tombs from all periods of Egyptian history. Just beyond Cairo proper on the Nile's west bank, stand the monuments most closely identified with Egypt: the timeless Sphinx and the Pyramids of Giza. But slightly farther away lie the pyramids of Abu Sir, Saqqara, Dahshur, and the site of Memphis. Most of the visitable pharaonic sites in the environs of Cairo date from the Old Kingdom (2575–2134 BC), although these sites also contain monuments and statuary from the Middle and New Kingdoms and later.

Driving to the various Memphite cemeteries from central Cairo takes one to two hours, depending on which places you decide to visit. Part of the road to Abu Sir, Saqqara, Dahshur, and Memphis follows a canal and passes through small villages, fields, and palm orchards, which is soothing compared to the drive to Giza. Seeing Abu Sir should take a leisurely 1½ hours; Saqqara can take from four hours to an entire day. For Memphis an hour is more than enough, but allow two for Dahshur. Taking in a combination of sites in one day can be very pleasant—Giza and Saqqara; Abu Sir, Saqqara, and Memphis; Dahshur and Saqqara, and so forth. The Fayyum, Egypt's largest oasis, is farther south of Cairo, and the Wadi Natrun monasteries are northwest of Cairo; both require more travel time but can still be visited on day trips.

MEMPHIS

Memphis was the first capital of unified Egypt, founded in 3100 BC by King Narmer. Little is visible of the grandeur of ancient Memphis, save for what is found in the museum and some excavated areas (not open to the public as yet), that include the sites of temples to various gods and a curious embalming area used to mummify the sacred Apis bulls. Most of the monuments of Memphis were robbed throughout history for their stone. This stone, together with that stripped from the casings

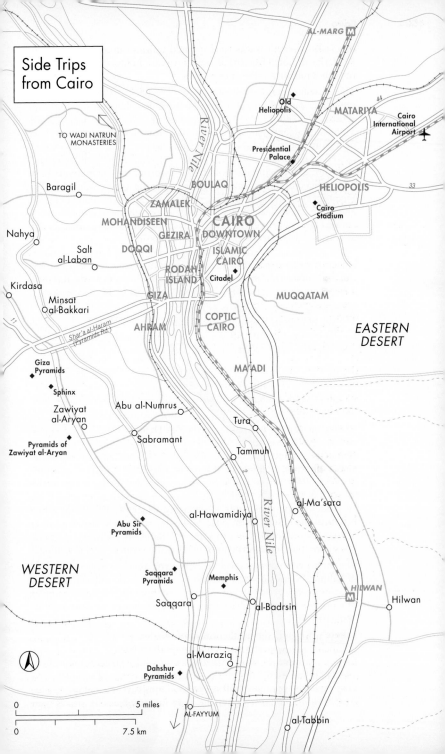

of various pyramids, was used to build Cairo. The modern village of Badrasheen, noted for its palm-rib furniture industry, covers most of the other remains of the ancient city.

The **museum** enclosure encompasses all of what is viewable in Memphis. The most dramatic object is the colossal limestone statue of Ramses II (1290–1224 BC) that lies within the museum proper. There is a viewing balcony that runs around the statue and provides good views of it from above. The statue shows fine details like a very elaborately carved dagger at the pharaoh's waist. Outside the museum building, a sculpture garden contains a scattered assortment of statuary, coffins, and architectural fragments recovered from the area of Memphis. The Egyptian alabaster sphinx is one of the larger sphinxes found in Egypt, and there are several statues of Ramses II in granite and limestone. A curious sarcophagus carved upside down also lies in the garden, as well as columns decorated with textile motifs, dating to the later periods of Egyptian history. A series of stalls selling replicas of Egyptian artifacts is set up on one side of the garden. Quality varies, but on the whole you can find some attractive items here. ⊠ *Mit Rahineh Rd., Mit Rahineh, 3 km (2 mi) west of Badrasheen* ☎ *No phone* ✑ *£E35* ☽ *Daily 8–4.*

GETTING THERE AND AROUND

The site of ancient Memphis is traversable by foot. The best way to get here is by hired car or with a tour. Combine it with Saqqara, or Giza and Saqqara—you needn't stop here for more than a half hour.

ABU SIR

23 km (14 mi) southwest of Cairo.

Abu Sir is the site of four pyramids—three of which are obvious, the fourth one less so—all dating to the 5th Dynasty (2465–2323 BC), as well as several mastabas and shaft tombs. The area has been the scene of much excitement because, in 1997–98, a Czech team of archaeologists came upon an intact shaft tomb of an official who lived sometime between 525 and 340 BC. This tomb is not open to the public at this writing; plans to make it visitable have been delayed. Abu Sir itself has been open to the public only sporadically, which means that the rather beautiful site nestled at the edge of the desert is rarely visited and free of tourists and touts. You can wander around the ruins, but the pyramids and other intact structures are closed to visitors at this writing.

The three pyramids that greet you when you arrive at Abu Sir are those of Sahure, Nyuserre, and Neferirkare. These—especially the pyramid of Sahure—are excellent pyramids to visit, because the whole complex of mortuary temples, valley temples, and a causeway are close together and easily visible.

Sahure's Pyramid, the northernmost of the three, is 257 feet square; its original height was 154 feet. This pyramid complex is typical of royal funerary complexes of the 5th Dynasty (Sahure ruled from 2458 to 2446 BC), and it contains all the elements of a pyramid complex, save boat pits. The pyramid itself is not too impressive, as its poor-quality core masonry collapsed after the Tura limestone casing stones were removed. Its interior has been closed to visitors since a 1992 earthquake rendered its internal structure unstable.

The mortuary temple is very pleasant to wander through, with its granite pillars, stairs leading to a now nonexistent second floor, and fine basalt pavement. It is one of the few mortuary temples found in Egypt that retains a sense of its ancient grandeur. The causeway was decorated with finely carved scenes (now removed from the site) showing archery and fighting. There is much less left of the valley temple: a pavement, some doorways, and a scattering of fallen blocks. The area of the valley temple is wet, because it is close to the water table.

Nyuserre's Pyramid is 265 feet square, and it was originally 169 feet tall. Not much is left of this pyramid because the casing stones and part of the limestone core were removed and burned for lime in the 19th century. The builder of this pyramid complex, Nyuserre (2416–2392 BC), usurped the valley temple and causeway of Neferirkare Kakai's Pyramid, which are therefore not directly aligned to the east of this pyramid but are at an angle out toward their original owner's pyramid.

Neferirkare's Pyramid is the largest on the Abu Sir site—344 feet square and originally 229 feet tall. The pyramid complex was meant to be larger than that of Sahure, but the pharaoh died prior to its completion. The pyramid itself, however, does dominate the site. Nyuserre usurped the causeway and valley temple, completed them, and appended them to his pyramid complex, leaving Neferirkare (2446–2426 BC) with only a pyramid and a mortuary temple that was completed after his death in cheap mud brick rather than limestone or granite.

The very large **Mastaba of Ptahshepses** lies between Sahure and Nyuserre's pyramids. The tomb is noted more for its size than for any remains of decoration. To the southwest is a double room that might have held boats, an unusual feature for a private tomb. The entire tomb is now completely inaccessible. ⊠ *Off the Abu Sir village road* ☎ *No phone* 🖃 *£E20* ⊗ *Daily 8–4.*

GETTING THERE AND AROUND

It is best to visit Abu Sir in conjunction with some combination of Giza, Memphis, Saqqara, and Dahshur. Either go with a tour or hire a taxi from your hotel or on the street (in the latter case, remember to bargain). To reach the site, go on the Saqqara Road, turn off for Saqqara, then turn right at the canal before reaching the Saqqara ticket booth, which is marked with a large blue-and-white sign. Continue down the road through the village, then follow the sign pointing left over a bridge that spans the canal. If you get lost, ask villagers for the Athar wa Haram Abu Sir. Walking is the best way to see the site itself.

SAQQARA

25 km (16 mi) southwest of Cairo.

Approached through orchards of waving palm trees, Saqqara is best known for being the site of the earliest stone pyramid constructed in Egypt, the Step Pyramid of Djoser. The site encompasses at least four other pyramid complexes of different dates, countless tombs from all

SAQQARA TOURING TIPS

■ **Watch for "no entry" signs.**
Saqqara is an active archaeological
zone, so expect that one or more
of the attractions may be off-limits
when you visit.

■ **It's reachable independently.** If
you're not taking an organized tour,
you can hire a taxi for the day from
your hotel or the street (bargain
hard, though).

■ **See what's nearby.** Combine
Saqqara with one or more sites, such

as Memphis and Abu Sir, or with
Giza. You might even combine a trip
to Saqqara with Dahshur.

■ **Try it on horseback.** One of the
more adventurous ways to combine
Saqqara and Giza is to join one of
the many horseback-riding tours
offered by the stables near the Giza
Pyramids.

■ **Look down.** Occasionally you'll
see the feet of statues that have
been broken at ground level.

eras of Egyptian history, as well as several animal necropolises, the
most notable of which is the Serapeum. Much active archaeological
work is being done at Saqqara by both Egyptian and foreign teams. In
the 1990s, a French team found the rock-cut Tomb of Maya, the wet
nurse of Tutankhamun, at the edge of the plateau. This find comple-
ments the earlier finds of the tombs of Maya (the treasurer), Horemheb,
and Aparel, all of whom were active during the reign of Tutankhamun.

Saqqara is large, sprawling, and best covered on foot and by car. A
suggested route, which depends somewhat on which tombs are open
to the public when you visit, is to start at the Step Pyramid complex
and the Imhotep Museum; from there visit the Pyramid of Unas, which
you can reach on foot. Then return to the car, drive to the Mastaba of
Mereruka and the Pyramid of Teti, then drive to the Serapeum if it is
open. If you have more time, visit the Tomb of Ti near the Serapeum.
There are other mastabas open near the Step Pyramid, as well as the
Mastaba of Ptahhotep near the Serapeum. See these if you have time,
energy, and interest. The ticket booth is at the main entrance to the
site, and a ticket covering the majority of the sites in Saqqara is £E60.

Imhotep Museum. One of the best places to really feel the energy of the
pyramid-building era, the Imhotep Museum brings together a collection
of artifacts and state-of-the-art educational aids to add background to
this pivotal era in the development of civilization. Highlights of the
seven-room museum, include a set of the blue and turquoise tiles that
decorated the interior of Djoser's Pyramid, remains of a seated Djoser,
and the feet of Imhotep on a monumental base. ⊠ *At the ticket office for
the Saqqara Monuments* 🕾 *No phone* 🖃 *£E60, as part of the Saqqara
general admission* ⊙ *Daily 9–4.*

★ **Kagemni's Mastaba.** This tomb adjoins the mastaba of Mereruka and
is also well decorated. Presumably the artist or atelier responsible for
decorating the mastabas in this area was the same, because certain
scenes keep reappearing, such as the force-feeding, the poultry yards,

Step Pyramid in Saqquara

and the tomb owner being carried about on a chair. ✉ *£E60, as part of the Saqqara general admission* ☉ *Daily 8–4.*

★ **Mereruka's Mastaba.** Shared by his son and his wife, this is the largest mastaba tomb in Saqqara. It dates to the 6th Dynasty (2323–2150 BC) and shows some of the finest scenes of fishing, hunting, metalworking (note the dwarfs), sailing, and force-feeding of animals, including a hyena in the statue chamber. A statue of Mereruka emerging from a niche marks the main offering spot for his cult. ✉ *£E60, as part of the Saqqara general admission* ☉ *Daily 8–4.*

★ **Niankhkhnum and Khnumhotep's Mastaba.** This tomb is considered one of the "new tombs" that have been excavated in Saqqara since the late 1990s and shares a separate admission with seven other tombs (the others are not terribly noteworthy but can be visited if you have extra time). This one dates from the 5th Dynasty and is also known as the Tomb of Two Brothers, or the Tomb of the Hairdressers. It's noted for its fine colors, as well as the unusually intimate poses of the two tomb owners. Niankhkhnum and Khnumhotep worked as the pharaoh's body servants, and they were buried together in this exquisitely decorated joint tomb. The scenes in the mastaba are fairly standard, showing everyday activities such as fishing, cooking, hunting, and the processing of foodstuffs. An unusual scene of the tomb owners on donkey back is carved on the second set of doorjambs. ✉ *£E30 as part of the New Tombs ticket* ☉ *Daily 8–4.*

Serapeum. This is site of the burials of the Apis Bulls. The Apis was a bull that was regarded as a manifestation of Ptah, a creator god. During its lifetime, the bull was worshiped, fed, washed, brushed, sung to, and generally made much of. When it died, it was elaborately mummi-fied and buried, with golden grave goods, in a large basalt or granite sarcophagus that was placed in a chamber of the Serapeum. Then the priests embarked on a quest for a new bull, which took up the position of Apis. The dusty and gloomy Serapeum galleries stretch for miles under the bedrock. The Serapeum is closed to the public but is due to reopen in December 2010, though no open hours or ticket prices are available at this writing.

★ **Step Pyramid.** The pyramid complex was built in the 3rd Dynasty (2649–2575 BC) for the pharaoh Djoser by his architect Imhotep, and it has been undergoing study and restoration since 1927. This monument has earned Djoser, and more importantly Imhotep, everlasting fame—Imho-tep was later deified and regarded as the patron god of architects and doctors. The base of the pyramid measures 459 feet by 386 feet, and the structure was originally 197 feet tall.

The pyramid complex is completely unlike those of the 4th and 5th Dynasties. It is the first stone pyramid (and complex) to have been built in Egypt, and its form imitates wood, papyrus, mud brick, and matting in limestone. The Step Pyramid itself was begun as a mastaba tomb, but its design was modified six times before the final, six-stepped pyramid emerged. The structure was enlarged by accreting vertical faces, visible on the east side as you walk around the pyramid rather than by stack-ing mastabas on top of one another.

You enter the complex from a small doorway that leads through a long passage flanked by columns that in turn leads to the vast open Heb-Sed court. The Heb-Sed was a race that the pharaoh had to run every 30 years, theoretically, in order to reaffirm his strength, power, and ability to rule—and to renew the favor of the gods. After he successfully com-pleted the race, the pharaoh would officiate and participate in religious rituals that emphasized the support of the gods for his reign and the fealty of his nobles and governors. These ceremonies took place in the adjoining courtyard, which is flanked by shrines.

The simple mortuary temple attached to the pyramid is to the north rather than to the east. Just before reaching it is a small structure, the *serdab* (a small room containing the statue of the deceased). It contains a statue of the pharaoh—a plaster cast, as the original is in the Egyptian Antiquities Museum—that was placed there to receive offerings. The substructure is closed to the public because it is unstable, but you can view it from a window that has been constructed.

The site of Djoser's Pyramid was a great attraction in antiquity: As the graffiti attests, people came here as tourists and seekers of blessings from as early as the Middle Kingdom (2040–1640 BC), if not earlier. Portions of the pyramid were restored in the 26th Dynasty. ⌦ *£E60, as part of the Saqqara general admission* ☉ *Daily 8–4.*

Teti's Pyramid. This pyramid measures 257 feet square and originally rose to 172 feet. Recognizing this as a pyramid is quite difficult, because the casing stones were stolen and the structure has been reduced to a pile of rubble. The site has two queens' pyramids to the east and north, which are virtually indistinguishable from the sand, and a mortuary temple to the east. The burial chamber, with its pointed roof, is decorated with pyramid texts and contains a basalt sarcophagus. Teti ruled from 2323–2291 BC. ☎ *£E60, as part of the Saqqara general admission* ☉ *Daily 8–4.*

Ti's Mastaba. This tomb is architecturally different from the mastabas of Mereruka and Kagemni in that it has a large courtyard that contains a stairway leading to Ti's burial chamber, which still contains his sarcophagus. The rest of the tomb is exquisitely decorated and painted, with the original roof preserved throughout much of the tomb. A statue—it is a reproduction—of Ti is visible in the serdab. ⊠ *Athar Saqqara* ☏ *No phone* ☎ *£E60, as part of the Saqqara general admission* ☉ *Daily 8–4.*

Unas's Pyramid. The last pyramid built in the 5th Dynasty was the first to contain a burial chamber decorated with the pyramid texts, a set of spells to ensure that the pharaoh had a successful afterlife. The pyramid occupies an area 188 feet square; its original height was 141 feet. The mortuary temple, on the east side, is ruined, save for the pavement, some column fragments, and a doorway leading to the causeway. The causeway is decorated in places with scenes of markets, transporting columns, wild animals, and so forth. To the south lie two empty boat pits. At the end of the causeway stand the remains of the valley temple. ☎ *£E60, as part of the Saqqara general admission* ☉ *Daily 8–4.*

GETTING THERE AND AROUND

Saqqara is 25 km (16 mi) southwest of Cairo and is easily reached by private taxi; it's also a popular stop on most guided tours (these often include Memphis and sometimes Dahshur). If you choose to visit on horseback, you'll be led around the Giza Plateau from the starting point by the Pyramids public ticket office, through the desert, on to Saqqara and back, for about the same price as taking a taxi. Saqqara is best seen via a combination of walking and driving or on horseback.

DAHSHUR

33 km (21 mi) southeast of Cairo.

★ Dahshur is one of the most tranquil and awe-inspiring pyramid sites. It contains five pyramids dating from the Old and Middle Kingdoms, of which three are obvious; only one—the Red Pyramid—can be entered. A suggested itinerary for the site is to drive to the first pyramid on the left of the entrance. After you take it in, drive over to the Bent Pyramid. You can walk around this, then over to the Black Pyramid (this is optional and takes about half an hour or so), and then return to the car.

At this writing, the site is undergoing active restoration supported by both the Egyptian government, the United Nations Development Program, the World Trade Organization, and UNESCO. At this writing, the plan is to have the Dahshur pyramids sufficiently supported so that their interiors can be reopened to the public. The Bent Pyramid could be open before the end of 2010, while the two Middle Kingdom pyramids could reopen by 2011. There is no information available at this writing regarding whether or not ticket prices will rise upon the completion of the restoration work.

Bent Pyramid in Dahshur

Named for the pinkish limestone of which it is made, the **North Pyramid** (Red Pyramid) belonged to the 4th-Dynasty pharaoh Sneferu (2575–2551 bc), father of Khufu. It is 721 square feet and was originally 341 feet tall—just a little smaller than Khufu's Great Pyramid. It marks the first successful attempt at building a true pyramid. This is the second of Sneferu's two pyramids. The other is the Bent Pyramid. Why he commissioned two pyramids is unknown; some scholars believe that Sneferu built this pyramid after the Bent Pyramid because he feared the latter would collapse. The North Pyramid contains three chambers with corbeled roofs and a plethora of 19th-century graffiti. Tomb robbers battered the floor of the topmost chamber in search of treasure they never found.

Built for Sneferu, the **Bent Pyramid** is obviously named for its unique shape, which seems to demonstrate the transition between the step and the true pyramid. It is 599 feet square, and its original height was 344 feet, although it was intended to be 421 feet. It retains much of its limestone cladding.

This was the first pyramid to have been planned as a true pyramid, as opposed to a step pyramid. Its unusual bent angle seems to have occurred because the builders felt that the initial angle was too steep, and that the pyramid would collapse if they did not adjust it. This pyramid is also unusual in that it has two entrances: the typical north-face entrance, and a second in the west face that is just visible above the change in the angle.

Although the pyramid itself was undecorated, its valley temple is among the earliest to be adorned. (None of the decorated portions are at the

DAHSHUR TOURING TIPS

■ **Choose drivers carefully.** It's easy to visit Dahshur on your own by taxi, but if you engage the services of a taxi in Cairo, make sure the driver knows his way around the sites. Many drivers in the capital don't. Dahshur can be combined with Saqqara and Memphis.

■ **Carry your passport.** You will travel through security checkpoints and may have to produce a passport, especially if you are not on a guided tour.

■ **Be prepared.** Dahshur is out in the desert, so remember sunglasses, hat, sunscreen, water, and clothing to cover arms and shoulders should you need to cover against the strong sun. Wear comfortable shoes if you wish to do any extensive walking.

■ **Allow enough time.** Dahshur is a very large site. You'll have to drive around to see everything.

site; the temple is a bit of a walk to the northeast, and it isn't very rewarding to visit.) The pyramid contains two chambers with corbeled ceilings. A passage from the north entrance leads to the chambers. To the south stands a subsidiary pyramid built of limestone, and on the east are the very ruined remains of a stone and mud-brick mortuary temple.

Built for Amenemhet III (1844–1797 BC), the **Black Pyramid** was constructed out of mud brick and faced with limestone. The limestone was plundered, leaving only the black mud brick that gives the pyramid its modern name. The pyramid measures 344 feet square and originally rose to 265 feet. The entrance to the burial chamber was not in the north face but outside the pyramid, in a courtyard opposite the southern corner of the east face. The top of the pyramid was crowned by a black basalt pyramidion, now in the Cairo Museum. Amenemhet, like Sneferu, had two pyramids; the other one is in Hawara in the Fayyum. The Black Pyramid is the southernmost of the Dahshur group of pyramids. ⊠ *Al-Haram Dahshur, Menshat Dahshur* ☎ *No phone* ⊡ *£E30* ⊙ *Daily 8–4.*

GETTING THERE AND AROUND

Drive down the Saqqara Road, past Saqqara and Memphis, and turn right at the sign for the Dahshur Antiquities. The road goes through the mainly mud-brick village of Dahshur straight into the site. You need to drive around the site, as it is very large. It is often convenient to combine a trip to Dahshur with a visit to Saqqara and Memphis.

THE FAYYUM

100 km (62 mi) southwest of Cairo.

The Fayyum is one of the largest and most fertile of all Egyptian oases, with an overall population of about 2 million people. Unlike the Western Desert oases, which are watered by artesian wells, the Fayyum is fed by a small river, the Bahr Yusuf (Joseph's River), which connects with the Nile. The rural Fayyum measures about 65 km (40 mi) from east to west, and the lake, Birket Qarun (which classical writers called Lake Moeris), is located in the northwest. The lake was much larger

FAYYUM TOURING TIPS

■ **You need transportation.** A vehicle of some kind is absolutely necessary to see the well-scattered attractions around Fayyum. If you hire a taxi from Cairo, make sure that the driver knows how to get from place to place. Most taxi drivers in the capital don't.

■ **Check the timing.** If you book an organized tour, find out how long you spend at each of the attractions so you can judge whether the tour will show you enough to meet your interests and needs.

■ **Verify that you can drive yourself.** Check with authorities before driving yourself to the area as security protocols can mean bans on foreign visitors traveling independently. If you are permitted to travel independently, you may be assigned a security detail during your trip.

■ **Be prepared.** Although relatively close to Cairo, this is still the desert. Carry a supply of water and sunscreen and dress for the dry heat and strong sunlight. Don't forget your passport since there may be security checkpoints along the way.

and richer in wildlife in antiquity, and it was the site of some of the earliest settlements (c. 6000 BC) in Egypt.

Sights in the Fayyum include the pyramids of al-Lahun and Hawara, the Greco-Roman site of Karanis, the large singing waterwheels, and some fine agricultural countryside that includes the lake, which is pleasant to visit on a warm day. The Fayyum was especially important during two periods of Egyptian history: the Middle Kingdom, when it began to be intensively exploited for agriculture, and the Greco-Roman Period (332 BC–AD 395), when it provided most of the grain for the Roman Empire.

EXPLORING FAYYUM

There are two centers of activity in the area: one is the very salty Birket Qarun, the other Medinet Fayyum, the major city. The site of old Karanis is on the way in from Cairo, as is the lake. Medinet Fayyum is 20 km (12 mi) south of the lake, and the Hawara and Lahun pyramids are south of the city. The Fayyum is a day trip on its own from Cairo, because there are several things to see here in addition to the pharaonic antiquities.

Kom Aushim. The Greco-Roman town site of Karanis is on the desert road on the way into the Fayyum, and it feels like a ghost town. It includes a temple dedicated to the local gods Petesuchs and Pnepheros, as well as the remains of houses, cooking installations, and bathrooms. Some of the latter are decorated with frescoes. A small **museum** at the entrance to the site contains two of the famed Fayyum Portraits, funerary masks laid over the faces of the linen-covered mummies. Some of the objects were unearthed here and others found elsewhere in the Fayyum and around Egypt. The collection also includes other mummies, statuary, relief fragments, a few objects of daily life, as well as Coptic and Islamic textiles and ceramics. It has a separate admission price. ⊠ *Fayyum Desert Rd.* ☎ *No phone* ⊡ *Site £E25, museum £E10* ⊙ *Daily 9–4.*

2

Medinet Fayyum. The center city of the oasis is built around **waterwheels.** They are an icon of the Fayyum, and you can hear them—the sound resembles the moaning of humpback whales—amid the honking of horns and the rush of traffic. There are four waterwheels in Medinet Fayyum, and many others are scattered throughout the oasis.

Al-Hawara Pyramid. At 393 feet square and originally 190 feet tall, this is one of Amenemhet III's two pyramids; the other is at Dahshur. Both are built of mud brick with a limestone casing. The interior structure, entered from the south, is full of dead ends and false passages and shafts, inaccessible now because of the high water table. In Classical times this pyramid was most famous for its **mortuary temple,** then known as the Labyrinth. It was located to the south rather than the east of the temple and was a very elaborate mazelike structure filled with riches, of which little remains. To the east lies a Greco-Roman cemetery, where many of the celebrated Fayyum mummy portraits were found. There was also a cemetery of sacred crocodiles revered in this area. ⊠ *Haram al-Hawara, about 12 km (8 mi) southeast of Medinet Fayyum* ☎ *No phone* 🎫 *£E35* ☉ *Daily 9–4.*

Al-Lahun Pyramid. Built by the Middle Kingdom pharaoh Senwosret II (1897–1878 BC, also called Sesostris II), this mud-brick pyramid's outer casing was stolen in antiquity. (The pyramid is 347 feet square, and the original height was 157 feet.) A natural knoll of rock was used as a central core for the pyramid, and stone walls were built radiating out from it; the interstices were filled with mud brick before finally being cased with fine limestone. This gives the illusion that this was a true pyramid completely built of stone. Lahun was the first pyramid to abandon a single northern entrance in favor of two entrances on the south side. Its underground chambers (inaccessible) contain dead ends and twists and turns to disguise the whereabouts of the granite burial chamber, which when discovered in modern times contained an empty red granite sarcophagus and an alabaster offering table. The devious layout of the substructure, along with the transfer of the entrance from north to south, was perhaps the result of a quest for greater security for the place of burial. ⊠ *On outskirts of al-Lahun village, about 21 km (13 mi) southeast of Medinet Fayyum* ☎ *No phone* 🎫 *£E35* ☉ *Daily 9–4.*

OFF THE BEATEN PATH

Nazla. The precariously perched kilns that dot the ravine at the edge of this village are a spectacular sight (note that some locals aggressively seek tips for pointing you in the right direction). Specialized pots, such as the *bukla,* a squat vessel with a skewed mouth, are made here, but all are sold at the Tuesday market in Medinet Fayyum. ✛ *From Medinet Fayyum take main road west about 20 km (12 mi) into Nazla; turn onto road next to mosque.*

WHERE TO EAT

$ ╳ **Cafeteria al-Medina.** The location is lovely: the restaurant was built in a green spot around the waterwheels at the center of town. The wheels' eerie whining and the cool splashing of water make a lovely accompaniment to a relatively unexceptional meal. The fare is basic: shish kebab, roast chicken, and the regular mezze. Service is not exactly speedy.

MIDDLE EASTERN

Beer is generally available, except during Ramadan. ⊠ *Off Shar'a al-Gomhurriya, Medinet Fayyum* ☏ *No phone* ⊟ *No credit cards*.

GETTING THERE AND AROUND

An organized tour might be your best bet for visiting The Fayyum because most Cairene taxi drivers don't know the geography of the area or its antiquities, and it can be difficult to navigate between sights. To get to the area, take Shar'a al-Haram and turn left just before the Mena House on the Alexandria road, which is marked for Alexandria and the Fayyum. Then follow signs to the Fayyum. The more adventurous can take a bus to Medinat Fayyum from Munib Station (every half hour, £E4). Once you get to the city, hire one of the ubiquitous pickup-truck taxis to take you to the various sites. ⚠ But before setting out to travel independently, you should always verify that independent travel by foreigners is being allowed. This can change on a day-to-day basis depending on the security level. A hotel concierge or the nearest tourist office should be able to do this.

THE WADI NATRUN MONASTERIES

100 km (62 mi) northwest of Cairo and 160 km (100 mi) southeast of Alexandria, just off the Desert Road near the dreary planned satellite town of Sadat City.

One of the many Egyptian contributions to Christianity was the idea of going off into the wilderness to subject yourself to all manner of deprivation as a means of devoting yourself to God. Monastic life began on the coast of the Red Sea with Saint Anthony in the 4th century. Some of his earliest disciples migrated to the desert just west of the Delta and established monasteries in Wadi Natrun. At its peak in the centuries after the death of Saint Anthony, the Natrun Valley hosted 50 monasteries and more than 5,000 monks. Afterward, however, it suffered almost uninterrupted decline until the 1970s, when the monasteries began to see something of a rebirth as educated, worldly Copts started taking their vows in record numbers.

Although the modern world encroaches on Wadi Natrun's earlier isolation, the monasteries still feel remote, huddled behind the high walls the monks built a millennium ago to protect themselves from Bedouin attacks. But make no mistake: these are some very hip monks. They speak countless foreign languages, run several successful businesses that include a large fruit and vegetable farm, and are more clued in to the ways of the world than most young Cairenes. They are, as well, profoundly devout, and the monasteries maintain an air of spiritual calm no matter how many pilgrims are visiting. And when the winds sweep off the desert, rustling the tall, graceful tamarind trees that shade the sand-hue domes and smooth walls of the churches, you feel a long, long way from Cairo.

Coptic Patriarchate of Cairo. There are now four active monasteries in Wadi Natrun: Deir Anba Bishoi, Deir al-Sourian, Deir Anba Baramus, and Deir Abu Maqar. Deir Abu Maqar has long been one of the most important Christian institutions in Egypt; as a result, permission to visit

Monks at St. Bishoy Coptic Orthodox monastery

is rarely granted without a very compelling devotional reason—even Copts find it almost impossible to get in. The monasteries are administered by the Coptic Patriarchate of Cairo. The first three are open to visitors—mostly Coptic pilgrims come here to pay their respects or to baptize children. It isn't necessary, as it has been in the past, to get advance permission from the patriarchate in Cairo; however, it is still worth calling ahead to verify opening hours, because they vary based on the fasting schedule (devout Copts fast the majority of the year). ⌂ *222 Shar'a Ramses, Abbasiya, Cairo ✛ Next to the Cathedral of St. Mark* ☎ *02/682–5374; 02/682–5375; 02/682–5376 for information from the patriarchate* ☉ *Roughly 9* AM *to 8* PM *(6* PM *in winter).*

THE MONASTERIES

Deir Anba Bishoi. If only by virtue of its accessibility, Deir Anba Bishoi has become the busiest monastery in Wadi Natrun, but it remains one of the most charming. The monastery dates from the 4th century, as does its oldest church (one of five), which was built with domes and irregular stone-and-silt-mortar walls covered in smooth sand-hue plaster. The interior consists of a high triple-vaulted main hall. Tiny apertures pierce the ceiling, admitting streams of brilliant sunlight that catch the plumes of incense that fill the air. To the left, through a spectacular 14th-century door, is the *haykal* (sanctuary), where contemporary frescoes depict John the Baptist, Saint Mark, and the 12 apostles, along with early monastic fathers. The carved wooden door (hidden behind a velvet curtain) was donated in the 7th century by the last Byzantine pope, just before the Arab invasion marked the emergence of Islam in Egypt. The coffin is that of Saint Bishoi.

CLOSE UP

Monastic Life

Copts may elect to join a monastery after they have fulfilled some surprisingly unspiritual requirements. They need to be at least 25 years old, and they have to have finished university and national military service and held a job, because professional skills are needed to run the monastery. The primary criterion for entry, of course, is devotion to God, and monks must take vows of poverty and obedience.

The monastic day begins at 4 AM, when the monks gather in the church to pray and chant. At 6 AM the liturgy is recited, although monks may elect to pray privately. Then the workday begins: on the farm, in construction, guiding tourists, and so forth, until 4 PM (in winter) or 8 PM (in summer), with a break at 1 PM to eat in the refectory. A half hour of prayer follows, and the monks are free to pray on their own until morning.

Fasting is an integral part of Coptic devotion, and it fills roughly two-thirds of the year. The comparison with Muslim fasting during Ramadan is interesting: Muslims do not eat, drink, smoke, or have sex during daylight hours, but Copts give up all animal products day and night for the duration of their fast. During fasts they eat nothing until early afternoon, when they eat a vegetarian meal. The fasting periods are usually broken with major holidays, such as Christmas or Easter.

Although Coptic monks may have retreated to the monasteries to forsake the world, they are very accustomed to having the world come to them. They run arguably the smoothest tour-guide systems in Egypt, with a knowledgeable *abuna* (father) to walk you through the compound and tell you genuinely useful information about what you are seeing—even if their claims about the age of the buildings or the achievements of the Coptic community at times sound a bit grandiose. They do not charge admission, and the baksheesh customary elsewhere in Egypt is inappropriate here. The monasteries do welcome donations, for which there is usually a box near the reception areas.

Dress modestly—no shorts, and the less skin showing the better—but you needn't expect any fanaticism on the part of the monks. Copts can seem remarkably casual in their devotion: pilgrims sleep on the floors of the church, and children run and play in the middle of Sunday mass (the same is true in mosques, except at prayer time). Of course, you would do well not to take similar license. Be sure to remove your shoes before entering any of the churches.

Elsewhere in the monastery, there is a workable (though unused) grain mill that looks every bit as old as the church itself. The monks live in cells known as *lauras*, and a cell is exactly what they are: small boxes with a single window and few comforts. Near the entrance gate is the keep, a defensive tower with a drawbridge into which the monks could retreat in the event of attack. The Coptic Pope Shenouda III maintains a residence within the monastery, but it is not open to the public.

If you exit the grounds by a small door in the back wall, you will see the rolling fields of farmland that the monks reclaimed from the desert and now use to grow dates, grapes, olives, and vegetables for sale in markets throughout the country. If that's not worldly enough, the monks even have their own gas station and car-repair shop. They employ impoverished Egyptians, mostly from the Upper Nile Valley, and teach them skills for use when they return to their home villages.

Deir al-Sourian. When you exit Deir Anba Bishoi, turn left, and a 10-minute walk brings you to Deir al-Sourian. Even if you have a car, it is worth walking: the approach gives you a powerful sense of the desert's small dunes with the lush foliage of the monastery just peeking over the high walls that shimmer in the haze of heat off the sands.

Deir al-Sourian was founded by a breakaway faction from Deir Anba Bishoi and dedicated to Theotokos (God's Mother). A later reconciliation made the new monastery redundant, so it was taken over by monks from Syria—hence its name al-Sourian, the Syrian. There is a tamarind tree in the rear of the monastery that supposedly grew out of the walking stick of the 4th-century Syrian Saint Ephraem. Challenged by younger monks, who thought he carried the staff to look authoritative, Ephraem announced: "Were it used due to weakness, it will bud out," and he stuck his staff in the ground.

Many sections of Deir al-Sourian, including the 9th-century Roman-style keep, are not open to the public, but the main church has a number of interesting sights. The most impressive is the ebony Door of Symbols, inlaid with ivory, in the haykal. Its seven panels represent what were thought of locally as the seven epochs of the Christian era. An inscription shows that it was installed in the church in the 10th century, when Gabriel I was the patriarch of Alexandria. On either side of the haykal are two half domes decorated with frescoes, one showing the Annunciation to the Virgin and the other the Virgin's Dormition. Many other frescoes have been discovered throughout the church including, most recently, several 7th-century renditions of as yet unknown Coptic martyrs. The monks are inordinately proud of these discoveries.

In the rear of the church is the refectory, with a kitschy display of monastic eating habits, complete with plaster figures dressed up like monks. If you duck through a narrow passage to the left of the refectory, you can find a stone cave that was Saint Bishoi's private laura. According to legend, Saint Bishoi tied his hair to a chain (now a rope) that hung from the ceiling to prevent himself from falling asleep during his marathon prayer sessions.

Deir Anba Baramus. This is thought to be the oldest monastic settlement in the wadi. Its Arabic name is derived from the Coptic word *Romeos* (meaning Roman), used in honor of Maximus and Domitius, sons of Emperor Valentinus who lived as monks in this area. It is impossible to access except by car and, despite its age, it is probably the least interesting of the three monasteries, because many of the buildings are of quite recent construction. The oldest church on the grounds is the restored 9th-century Church of al-'Adhra' (the Virgin). Work on the church in 1987 uncovered frescoes, in rather poor condition, long hidden by plaster. The coffins in the haykal are of Saint Isadore and Saint Moses the Black (a convert from Nubia). Adjacent to the coffins is a photograph of a T-shirt supposedly scrawled in blood during an exorcism. In the back corner of the church is a column, easily missed next to a wall, that is from the 4th century. It is the oldest part of the monastery, marking the spot where Saint Arsenius, the one-time tutor to the sons of Roman emperor Theodosius the Great, is said to have sat regularly in prayer.

WHERE TO STAY AND EAT

While the monastery complexes don't boast much in terms of food and drink, the area around them is building up so quickly that it might not be long before the golden arches rise up out of the sand. For now, you can find sandwiches, snacks, Continental dinners, and a full bar at the **Rest House,** 9 km (5½ mi) from Deir Anba Bishoi on the Desert Road. Just across from the Rest House, a service area catering to travelers on their way to Alexandria and the Mediterranean Coast features more refined and comfortable dining, serving everything from pizza to fast food to sit-down, Egyptian-style, full-course meals.

It's best to see Wadi Natrun as a day trip, but if you want to stay overnight, you can do so at the **El-Hammra Eco Lodge** (⊕ *www.elhammraecolodge.com*), a charming little rustic backwater. Permission to stay overnight at the monasteries is granted only in writing to theological students or groups traveling with their priest.

GETTING THERE AND AROUND

You have two options when traveling to the monastery. The most painless one is to book a tour with an approved travel agent and a guide. Altenatively, negotiate with a taxi driver from Ramses Square in Cairo to take you to each of the monasteries and back to the capital for around £E250–£E300, depending on your haggling skills and the number of people in your group. Be sure that the driver knows the way and understands the amount of waiting time involved—plan for an hour per monastery—and pay once you're safely back in Cairo. The ride should take 1½ to 2 hours each way.

Otherwise, West Delta air-conditioned buses leave every half hour between 6 AM and 8 PM from Cairo Gateway, behind the *al-Ahram* newspaper offices; one-way tickets cost £E5. The trip takes two hours to meander its way to the Wadi Natrun Rest House along the Desert Road, and from there on to the village. From the village, you can catch a service taxi with other people (50pt to £E1.25 per person) to Deir Anba Bishoi. It's an easy walk from there to Deir al-Sourian, but if you want to go on to Deir Anba Baramus, you have to rely on the kindness of those fellow pilgrims (with a vehicle), because there is no established transportation system between the monasteries. You can also hire a driver from the village to take you to the three monasteries, wait for you, and then bring you back to the village; depending on your bargaining skills, it should run no more than £E40 to £E50.

The last West Delta bus back to Cairo leaves at 6 PM from the village, but if you're feeling brave you can always flag down one of the frequent minibuses heading that way, from either the village or the Rest House. ⚠ But before setting out to travel independently, you should always verify that independent travel by foreigners is being allowed. This can change on a day-to-day basis depending on the security level. A hotel concierge or the nearest tourist office should be able to do this.

Alexandria

WORD OF MOUTH

"Explore the [Attarine Market] for interesting old shops selling antiques and reproductions. You can easily spend a good part of a day there. The library in Alex is worth seeing, and the museum is small and done easily in an hour."

—elmooloo

WELCOME TO ALEXANDRIA

Ras El-Tin · Fort Qayt Bay
Aquarium

Eastern Harbour

Mediterranean Sea

1 EL ANFUSHI

RAML **M** STATION
Chatby Beach

Roushdi Beach

San Stefano Beach

GOMROUK

2 EL MANISHIYA **4**

Tariq al-Geish

Four Seasons Hotel Alexandria

MISR TRAIN **M** STATION
3

Tariq Gamal Abdel Nasser

6 KARMOUZ

SIDI GABR STATION

GEBRIEL STATION **M**

TOP REASONS TO GO

★ **Café Culture.** Linger over coffee and pastry at the famous Grand Trianon Café.

★ **The Seaside Promenade.** Stroll or take a carriage ride along the seafront Corniche, taking in the faded glory of the turn-of-the-20th-century architecture.

★ **A Seafood Meal.** Order fresh seafood from the tantalizing choices on ice at Fish Market or Kadoura.

★ **The Remains of an Ancient Wonder.** Climb the parapet of Qayt Bay Fort, site of the famed ancient Pharos (lighthouse), for magnificent panoramas of the seafront.

★ **Antiquities on Display.** Visit the Greco-Roman Museum to explore artifacts excavated from ancient Alexandria.

1 **El Anfushi.** The westernmost tip of the main bay at the end of the Corniche, this colorful district is home of the fishermen, El Anfushi tombs, and Qayt Bay Fort. This was the city's core in ancient and medieval times. Some of the city's best seafood restaurants can be found here.

2 **Raml Station.** The heart of modern Alexandria has its main tram station on a square surrounded by early-20th-century buildings. Major shopping streets that are always bustling with people cut the district. Nowhere else in the city is its cosmopolitan past more alive. Most of the major sights are within a short taxi ride from Raml Station.

3 **El Manshiya.** The center of colonial Alexandria has fine squares and monumental buildings, colonnades, statues, and churches.

Raml Beach | Sidi Bishr Beach | Montazah Beach

Montazah Palace ◆ ◆ El-Salamlek Palace

MANDARA STATION

Renaissance Alexandria Hotel

ABU QIR | Abu Qir Bay

M **SIDI BISHR STATION**

M M 5 Ma'amoura Beach

MONTAZAH STATION

0 — 1 miles
0 — 1.5 km

4 **El Chatby.** Location of the iconic modern Bibliotheca Alexandrina and the closest public beach to Downtown.

5 **Montazah.** The once-royal domain has always been an upmarket district marking the traditional eastern limit of Alexandria. Visit the gardens and enjoy the facade of the old palace. Montazah marks the easternmost edge of the main tourist development in Alexandria.

6 **Karmouz.** Inland, and bounded by the canal El Mahmoudeya, this district has Alexandria's best known Roman-era ruins—the Catacombs of Koum Al Shukafa and Pompey's Pillar.

GETTING ORIENTED

As a rule, addresses are rarely used, and everyone navigates by names and landmarks, but with breezes almost always coming off the sea, orientation is fairly easy—when in doubt, head into the wind. Unfortunately, several of the city's best hotels are inconveniently located in or near Montazah. But it's a relatively painless drive into Downtown—about 15 minutes from Downtown to Montazah, less from other districts—past a string of neighborhoods with such evocative names as Chatby, Roushdi, and Sidi Gabr.

CAFÉ CULTURE

The *ahwa* (coffee shop) is where Egyptian males traditionally go to get their caffeine fix. Part café, part social club, it is an institution tracing back hundreds of years.

(above) Men playing backgammon at a tea shop. (opposite left) Taking time to taste the tea. (opposite right) It is custom to have a cool glass of water alongside your fresh cup of Turkish coffee.

A traditionally all-male preserve, the ahwa is an unpretentious place to while away the hours meeting friends, playing backgammon, or smoking *shisha* (the Egyptian water pipe). The tea and coffee drinking seem almost incidental. Egyptian ahwas can take many forms, from a cluttered hovel at the back of an alley to a spacious salon bathed in faded grandeur. All, however, share three basic ingredients: a drinks counter, a brazier of hot coals for the water pipes that line the walls, and small tin or wood tables that fill the indoor space or spill outside onto the pavement. While Alexandria's European-style cafés and patisseries exude a sense of sophistication, ahwas are unabashedly proletariat. They are animated yet restful cafés frequented mostly by older men sipping tea and puffing shisha over the sound of chatter, slapping dominoes, and Umm Kulthoum's haunting voice.

BLEND WITH THE LOCALS

Tea (*shai* in Arabic) ordered in coffeehouses is typically served koshary-style, that is, with the dregs. Ask for *shai libton* if you prefer the tea-bag variety. Either way, you'll be asked how sweet you want it. The four options are: *saada* (without sugar), *al-reeha* (lightly sweetened), *mazbout* (medium sweet), or *ziyada* (syrupy).

CAFÉ BEVERAGES

TEA

The gunpowder tea served in most cafés is not known for its subtle flavor. Egyptians drink it as strong and sweet as possible, avoiding the dregs at the bottom of the glass. Tea bags have caught on in upmarket cafés and may be offered first to foreigners. You can also request tea with milk (*shai bi laban*) or mint (*shai bi nanaa*)—the latter usually yielding a small glass of fresh-cut sprigs.

COFFEE

Thick *ahwa turki* (Turkish coffee) is brewed using the same Yemeni beans Egyptians have been importing since the Ottoman era. Finer establishments add cardamom to the blend. It is served in small glasses or cups, allowing the grounds to settle before drinking. Filtered coffee is served in some hotels, and espresso bars are becomingly increasingly popular in the cities.

HERBAL DRINKS

Karkaday, a bright red infusion made from boiled hibiscus flowers, has been popular since the days of the pharaohs. It's usually served chilled with ice and comes packed with Vitamin C. *Helba* is a yellow fenugreek tea said to reduce fever and ease congestion. *Yansoon,* an anise drink, has a medicinal taste but is purported to aid digestion. You can also ask for *irfa* (cinnamon) or *ganzabeel*

(ginger) tea, both of which can be served *bi-laban* (with milk).

SOFT DRINKS

Ask for *hagga sa'a* (literally "something cold"). Common offerings include *kakola* (Coke), *bibs* (Pepsi), and *seven* (7-Up). It's not likely you'll find beer, but you often come across *Birell,* a locally produced non-alcoholic malt beverage.

LEMON JUICE

Cafés pride themselves on being able to make a perfect *aseer laymoun* (lemon juice). Done right, it should be creamy, not too tart, not too sweet. Many stumble on the latter, so consider asking for it *sukkar aleel* (lightly sweetened).

CHICKPEA COCKTAIL

On chilly nights ask for *hummus al-sham,* a tummy-warming concoction of slow-cooked chickpeas, tomato sauce, lemon, and chili served in a tall glass. Eat the chickpeas and drink the soup.

MILK DRINKS

Unflavored *zabadi* (yoghurt drink) is surprisingly good, made better perhaps by requesting it *bil-asal* (with honey). *Rayeb,* however, is soured milk and something of an acquired taste.

SAHLEB

In winter, warm up with a hot glass of *sahleb,* a thick, creamy drink made from orchid root with milk, cinnamon, coconut flakes, raisins, and nuts. Every café has its own recipe.

Updated by
Lindsay and
Pete Bennett

There is a wonderful Italo Calvino story about a city so removed from its own history that it is as if the modern metropolis sits on the site of an unrelated ancient city that just happens to bear the same name.

At times Alexandria, which Alexander the Great founded in the 4th century BC, feels like that. Yet the fallen Alexandria of the ancient Greeks, of Ptolemy, Cleopatra, Julius Caesar, and the Romans, and of pagan cults and the Great Library is underfoot, quite literally, as all of modern Alexandria has been built on the ruins of the old, a city that was capital of Egypt from the 3rd century BC until AD 642, when the Arabs first arrived.

Overlay a map of the contemporary city with one from antiquity, and you see that many of the streets have remained the same: Shar'a al-Horreya runs along the route of the ancient Canopic Way, and Shar'a Nabi Daniel follows the route of the ancient Street of the Soma. Near their intersection once stood the Mouseion, a Greek philosophic and scientific center that had at its heart the collection of the Great Library. Yet only fleeting glimpses of this ancient city peak through the modern crust.

By the early 20th century, Alexandria was a wealthy trading port. The merchants were fantastically rich—cosmopolitan without being intellectual—and they enjoyed the sort of idle existence that is born of privilege, a privilege not of high birth but rather of colonial rule, which shielded foreigners from Egyptian law. They lived in villas with extravagant gardens, frequented luxurious shops, gossiped over tea in grand cafés, and lounged on the beach in private resorts along the coast. The population was a multicultural mix of Greeks and Arabs, Turks and Armenians, French and Levantines, Jews and Christians, and this spawned a unique atmosphere. It was this city that belonged to Constantine Cavafy, now regarded as the greatest Greek poet of his era. It was this city to which the novelist E.M. Forster, author of *A Passage to India,* was posted during World War I. And it was this city that gave birth to Lawrence Durrell's *Alexandria Quartet,* which captivated a generation of American readers when the books were published in the late 1950s.

Then quite suddenly everything changed. The intellectuals and merchants fled, driven out of Egypt by the nationalist revolution of the 1950s, the wars with Israel, and the nationalization of their businesses.

It's been five decades since most of the foreigners left—some Greeks and Armenians remained. But if you take the city as it is today and not as a faded version of what it once was, you will find that Alex (as it's affectionately known) remains an utterly charming place to visit. The Mediterranean laps at the seawall along the Corniche, and gentle sea breezes cool and refresh even in the dead of summer. Graceful old cafés continue to draw lovers and friends—Egyptians now, rather than foreigners—while the streets remain as lively and intriguing as ever. Alexandria is still a great city, even now, shorn of its many pasts.

PLANNING

WHEN TO GO
Alexandria's peak season is summer, when Egyptians flee here for the refreshing Mediterranean breezes. Hotels are also busy on weekends. Off-season, Alex is spectacular, as the city settles back into its natural, relaxed rhythm. It rains more here than anywhere in Egypt. Winter is chilly and sometimes windy, which can be a pleasant break from Cairo's annual 360 days of sunshine.

GETTING HERE AND AROUND
BY AIR
There is an airport in Alexandria, but flying to Alex from Cairo will end up taking longer than catching a train, which is why so few people do it. Taking into account ground transport to and from the airports, frequent delays of flights, and having to get to the airport an hour before your flight, the half-hour flight doesn't save any time. However, EgyptAir offers at least one flight per day to Alexandria Nozha Airport, and tickets currently cost around £E430 round-trip.

Contacts EgyptAir (☎ 03/486–5701).

BY BUS
If you want to travel between Cairo and Alexandria by bus, Super Jet and the West Delta Bus Company run air-conditioned deluxe buses every half hour from around 5 AM to midnight. Tickets cost £E35. Buses depart Cairo from Maydan Abdel Monem Riyad under the overpasses in front of the Ramses Hilton and take up to three hours, depending on traffic. Or you can depart from Almaza Station in Heliopolis or the station in Giza. They drop you off behind Sidi Gabr railway station in an Alexandria suburb, where they in turn depart for Cairo. The railway station is between Downtown and Montazah, so you need to take a taxi from the station to get to either place.

Contacts Go Bus (☎ 02/2342–5143 in Cairo; 03/420–5290 in Alexandria). **Super Jet** (☎ 02/2575–1313 in Cairo; 03/543–5222 in Alexandria). **West Delta Bus Company** (☎ 02/2575–9751 in Cairo; 03/480–9685 in Alexandria).

BY MINIBUS

Although most local bus routes are too convoluted to bother with, a constant stream of minibuses makes the Corniche run night and day. Flag them down anywhere, using a hand signal to point the direction you want to go, then pile in. They are shockingly cheap (£E1 to Stanley, say, and £E1.50 to Montazah) and, if anything, too fast. There are two catches to minibus travel: first, you have to know the name of the district to which you are traveling (Manshiya, Sporting, Montazah, and so forth), because you need to shout it in the window to the driver, who lets you know if he goes there. Second, you have to know what your destination looks like so you can tell the driver to stop. It's easier than it sounds, and your fellow passengers always help out.

BY CAR

Unless you plan to continue on to remote areas of the Mediterranean coast west of Alexandria, there is little reason to come by car. Taxis within the city are inexpensive, and parking is so difficult that a car is more trouble than it's worth. On top of that, the two highways connecting Cairo and Alexandria—the Delta and Desert roads—are both plagued by fatal car crashes. If you still want to come by car, the Desert Road, which starts near the Pyramids in Giza, is the faster route, taking roughly three hours. If you do come by car, avoid driving at night.

If you are brave enough to elect to drive to Alex, you'll find traffic relatively orderly compared to that of Cairo. Streets are less crowded, and drivers are better about obeying traffic regulations. The governor has even instituted a no-horns policy, complete with wooden cutout policemen at intersections to remind drivers. Although it's not totally effective, you'll notice far less horn noise than in Cairo.

The main road in Alexandria is the Corniche—technically 26th of July Street, but no one calls it that—which runs along the waterfront from Fort Qayt Bay all the way to Montazah. East of Eastern Harbor, the Corniche is mostly called Tariq al-Geish. Unless you park on a hill, be sure to leave your car in neutral, because people will push it around a bit to maximize parking space.

You can rent a car (without a driver) from Avis, Alex Car, or Target Limousine; the latter can also provide you a car with a driver.

Contacts Avis (⊠ *Cecil Hotel, Maydan Sa'd Zaghlul, Raml Station* ☎ *03/485-7400* ⊕ *www.avis.com*). **Target Limousine** (⊠ *Helnan Palestine Hotel, Montazah Gardens* ☎ *03/547-4033*). **San Stefano Company** (⊠ *186 Shar'a Abdel Salem Arefz St., San Stefano* ☎ *03/585-6963*).

BY TAXI

Taxis are the best way to get around Alexandria. They are very inexpensive, and you can flag them down almost anywhere. If you're alone and male, you're generally expected to sit in the front; women and couples can sit in the back. The reason for the men-in-front rule is that the driver might try to pick up another passenger en route—it's standard practice, so don't be surprised.

Drivers don't use their meters, so you have to guess at the appropriate fare. A ride within Downtown should be £E10 to £E15; from

Downtown to Montazah (15–30 minutes), roughly 6 km (10 mi), about £E30. If you look rich, expect to pay a bit more—this is a progressive system: elderly widows often pay little, whereas prices double, at a minimum, if a driver picks you up at a five-star hotel. There are no radio taxis in Alexandria, but major hotels always have taxis waiting.

BY TRAIN

Trains are by far the most comfortable and convenient option for getting to and from Alexandria, and

the travel time and ticket prices are the same in either direction. Turbo trains are the fastest (average journey time a little over two hours), and tickets for these services cost £E50 for first-class and £E35 for second-class. Tickets for the slower Express services (average journey times 3¼ hours) are £E35 for first class and £E19 for second class.

Currently Turbo trains depart Cairo at 8 AM, 9 AM, noon, 2 PM, 6 PM, and 7 PM. Returning Turbo trains depart Alexandria at 7 AM, 8 AM, 2 PM, and 7 PM.

Express trains depart Cairo at 6, 7, 8:15, 10, and 11:15 AM, 12:15, 1, 2:15, 3, 4, 4:15, 5:15, and 8:15 PM. Returning Express trains depart Alexandria at 6:15, 8:15, and 11:15 AM, 12, 12:30, 3, 3:30, 4, 5, 5:15, 6, 8, and 10:15 PM.

Be sure to confirm the scheduled departure times in advance. Seats are reserved, and tickets are best bought a day in advance—a laborious process that requires a trip to the station. If you take your chances, there are almost always seats available for same-day travel (except on the morning Turbo services), though summer Fridays out of Cairo and Sundays out of Alexandria can be booked up. When arriving in Alex, do not get off at the first station in the city, Sidi Gabr, as many of the passengers will; the main station is Misr Station, one stop farther, which is the end of the line.

BY TRAM

Picturesque and cheap, Alexandria's trams are likely to take four to five times longer to get where you're going than a taxi would. The main station is Raml, near Maydan Sa'd Zaghlul. Buy tickets onboard.

Blue trams (25 pt) run east: numbers 1, 2, 6, and 8 terminate at al-Nasser (formerly Victoria) College, Tram 3 at Sidi Gabr (by the sea; a two-hour trip), Tram 4 at Sidi Gabr Station, and Tram 5 at San Stefano. Yellow trams (25 pt) run west: Tram 16 goes to Pompey's Pillar (a 40-minute trip), Tram 11 to the Nouzha Gardens, and Tram 15 to Ras al-Tin. Numbers are marked—only in Arabic—on cards in the front windows, but the newer trams now have maps inside.

INTERNET

There's been a great expansion of Internet services in the city, but Internet cafés open and close with great regularity. Some hotels offer Wi-Fi in the lobby, and some cafés offer the same service.

Internet Cafés **Micro Media Center for Internet** (⊠ *8 Shar'a El Ghazaly, Al Laban* ☎ *03/393–9425*).

Wi-Fi Hot Spots **Caffé Cino** (⊠ *Bibliotheca Alexandrina Plaza* ☎ *03/483–9999*). **Starbucks** (⊠ *San Stefano Mall* ☎ *03/489–0216* ⊠ *Alexandria City Centre Mall, Cairo Desert Rd.* ☎ *03/397–0181*).

VISITOR INFORMATION

The maps and brochures at the Tourist Information Center are of poor quality, but the multilingual staff is easily one of the most helpful of any government office in the country.

Contacts **Tourist Information Center** (⊠ *Maydan Sa'd Zaghlul, Raml Station* ☎ *03/485–1556*).

TRAVEL AGENCIES

Contacts **Annie Travel** (⊠ *30 Shar'a Ahmed Orabi* ☎ *03/487–0007*). **Thomas Cook** (⊠ *15 Maydan Sa'd Zaghlul, Raml Station* ☎ *03/484–7830 or 16119 anywhere in Egypt*).

EXPLORING ALEXANDRIA

Alexandria has grown so rapidly in the last 50 years that it now runs along the coastline from the Western Harbor all the way to Montazah, a distance of more than 16 km (10 mi). It is, nonetheless, a great walking city because the historic Downtown occupies a compact area near the Eastern Harbor, while the ancient sights are a short taxi ride away.

PLANNING YOUR TIME

Three days in Alexandria is ample time to see the main sights. A visit to the Alexandria National Museum will give you some historical context; the ruins of the original Pharos were incorporated into Fort Qayt Bay; the great Library of Alexandria was destroyed, but its modern replacement is one of the world's most ambitious collections of printed and electronic media. Leave time to browse in the Attarine market and to walk along the Corniche. Be sure not to miss the wild European/Middle Eastern palace of the former khedive in Montazah; the gardens are also beautiful.

If you have any extra time, take a day trip and head west along the coast to explore the memorials on the El Alamein battlefields—reminding us of sacrifices made during World War II; you can do this by taxi or with a car and driver hired through your hotel.

DOWNTOWN AND RAML STATION

Nowhere is Alexandria's cosmopolitan past more evident than Downtown, where its Italianate buildings house French cafés, Armenian jewelers, and Greek restaurants. Because so few buildings survived the British bombardment in 1882, it is no surprise that what stands today

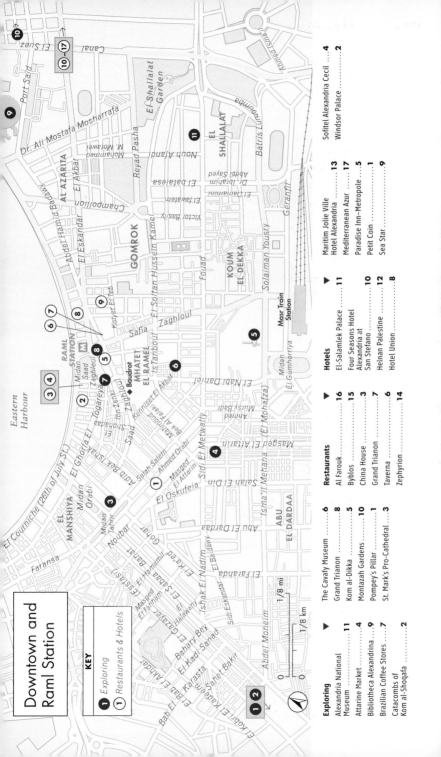

Downtown and Raml Station

KEY

1 Exploring

1 Restaurants & Hotels

0 ————— 1/8 km
0 ————— 1/8 mi

Exploring ▸

Alexandria National Museum **11**
Attarine Market **4**
Bibliotheca Alexandrina **9**
Brazilian Coffee Stores **7**
Catacombs of Kom al-Shoqafa **2**
The Cavalry Museum **6**
Grand Trianon **8**
Kom al-Dikka **5**
Montazah Gardens **10**
Pompey's Pillar **1**
St. Mark's Pro-Cathedral **3**

Restaurants ▸

Al Farouk **16**
Byblos **15**
China House **3**
Grand Trianon **7**
Taverna **6**
Zephyrion **14**

Hotels ▸

El-Salamlek Palace **11**
Four Seasons Hotel Alexandria at San Stefano **10**
Helnan Palestine **12**
Hotel Union **8**
Maritim Jolie Ville Hotel Alexandria **13**
Mediterranean Azur **17**
Paradise Inn-Metropole **5**
Petit Coin **1**
Sea Star **9**
Sofitel Alexandria Cecil **4**
Windsor Palace **2**

The Bibliotheca Alexandrina

reflects the late-19th-century European city that rose from the rubble of the city's past. There are a few historical and cultural sights Downtown, including the Roman Theater, the Greco-Roman Museum, and the resurrected Great Library and Montazah Gardens, which are a bit of a side trip from the heart of Downtown.

TOP ATTRACTIONS

4 **Attarine Market.** This area acquired its reputation in the 1960s as the place where the high-quality antiques sold by fleeing foreigners resurfaced. Those days are long gone. There are now only a few true antiques stores left in the area, but it's fascinating nonetheless to see the tiny workshops where the reproduction French-style furniture so popular in Egypt originates. Almost all the workshops will be happy to sell direct if you find a piece that appeals to you, but consider the challenge of shipping it back home before you give in to temptation. The market actually consists of a series of alleyways, the sum of which feels less established—and far less touristy—than Cairo's Khan al-Khalili. ✛ *To find the market, walk one block west of the Attarine Mosque and cross Shar'a al-Horreya to the alley between the café and the parts store, El Attarine.*

9 **Bibliotheca Alexandrina.** This monumental, $190 million, UNESCO-sponsored project began with an instinctively appealing idea: to resurrect the Great Library of ancient Alexandria, once one of the world's major centers of learning. Its location near the Silsileh Peninsula on the edge of the Eastern Harbor has tremendous symbolic resonance, having been the royal quarters in ancient times and one of several possible locations of the original library.

CLOSE UP

The Ancient Library of Alexandria

Relatively little is known about the ancient library itself, beyond its reputation for scholarship. It was founded by Ptolemy I in the 4th century BC and is said to have held a collection of 500,000 volumes—at a time when books were rare, costly commodities and all written by hand. Succeeding pharaohs gathered existing knowledge from around the Greek world but also invited scientists and scholars to contribute current research, ensuring that Alexandria was at the cutting edge of learning.

Theories about its destruction abound, but most assume it stood for roughly 500 years before being consumed by fire. What is known is that the Great Library—and the complex of lecture halls, laboratories, and observatories called the Mouseion, of which it was part—was a source of literary and scientific wisdom that changed the world. It was here, for example, that Euclid set forth the elements of geometry still taught in schools today, and Eratosthenes measured the circumference of the Earth. And it was here that the conqueror Julius Caesar had a new, more accurate calendar drawn up—the Julian calendar—that became the framework for the measurement of time throughout the Western world.

The modernist Norwegian-designed building is in the form of an enormous multitiered cylinder tilted to face the sea, with a roof of diamond-shaped windows that allow controlled light into the seven cascading interior floors. The most impressive feature, however, is the curving exterior wall covered in rough-hewn granite blocks from Aswan that have been engraved with letters from ancient languages.

With an aim to promote intellectual excellence, the library is a repository for the printed word—it holds millions of books including rare manuscripts—but is also a facility to store knowledge in all its forms, from tape recordings of the spoken word to electronic media. It is a robust academic organization with seven specialist research centers and has the Virtual Immersive Science and Technology Applications (VISTA) system, which transforms 2-D data into 3-D simulations so researchers can study the projected behavior of theoretical models. The library also acts as a forum for academic cross-cultural discussion and is home to more than 10 institutes. Membership allows you to explore the archive and use the Internet for research, but don't expect to be able to use the facility like an Internet café. Personal e-mails are not allowed.

Once you've enjoyed the view of the vast interior from the mezzanine gallery, there's little to hold you in the main hall, but the library has several small museums and exhibitions that are of more interest. The **Manuscripts Museum** has a large collection of rare documents, parchments, and early printed books. The **Impressions of Alexandria** exhibition features paintings and sketches of the city dating from the 15th to the 19th centuries and photographs taken in the late 19th and early 20th centuries. The **Antiquities Museum** on the basement level has a collection of finds from Pharaonic, Roman, and Islamic Alexandria. Examples of monumental Roman statuary include *Huge Forearm Holding a Ball* (nothing else remains of the immense piece), and a finely chiseled bust of the Emperor Octavian (Augustus). Egypto-Roman artifacts include the mummy of Anhk Hor, governor of Upper Egypt, and several 2nd-century funerary masks showing the prevalent cross-styling between the classical Egyptian and Roman Egyptian styles. A planetarium and IMAX theater are the latest additions to the complex, offering a range of science- and astronomy-based activities including stargazing and constellation identification and interactive museum displays. ⊠ *63 Shar'a Soter, Chatby* ☎ *03/483–9999* ⊕ *www.bibalex.org* 🖃 *Library £E10, Antiquities Museum £E20, Manuscripts Museum £E20 Planetarium and IMAX shows £E25* ⊙ *Sat.–Thurs. 11–7, Fri. 3–7.*

➋ **Catacombs of Kom al-Shoqafa.** This is the most impressive of Alexandria's
★ ancient remains, dating from the 2nd century AD. Excavation started in 1892, and the catacombs were discovered accidentally eight years later when a donkey fell through a chamber ceiling. A long spiral staircase leads to the main hall. The stairs run down the outside of a shaft, that excavators used to transport the bodies of the dead. The staircase leads to the rotunda, which, like all but the lowest chamber, is undecorated but striking for the sheer scale of the underground space, supported by giant columns carved out of the bedrock.

A few rooms branch off from the rotunda: the Triclinium was a banquet hall where relatives and friends toasted the deceased, and the Caracalla Hall has four lightly painted tombs and a case of bones. The next level down contains a labyrinth of smaller nooks for storing bodies and leads to the lowest excavated room, which is framed by columns and sculpted snakes. Casts of two statues stand here—the originals are in the Greco-Roman Museum—and three tombs are of interest for their mix of pharaonic and Greek imagery. ⊠ *Shar' El Shenity Abu Mandour, Karmouz* ☎ *03/482–5800* 🖃 *£E35* ⊙ *Daily 9–4:30.*

NEED A BREAK? Even if your body can't handle any more caffeine, it's worth stopping at Baudrot (⊠ *23 Shar'a Sa'd Zaghlul, Mahatet El Raml* ☎ *No phone*). A café of this name has been a major element in the social life of Alexandria for over 80 years, but it's been given a new breath of life at the end of the first decade of the new millennium. Walk through the period rooms to the peaceful vine-covered garden at the back to enjoy the sound of the birds chirping in the tress overhead as you sip on a cold soda.

➑ **Grand Trianon.** One of Alexandria's most stylish institutions since it
★ opened in the 1920s, the Grand Trianon remains a forum for courtship, gossip, and rediscovery. Its most popular area is the café, which has a certain old-world grandeur, despite being the least decorated part of the place. The adjacent restaurant is an extravagant art nouveau jewel, with colorful murals on the wall and a spectacular stained-glass window over the entrance to the kitchen. But the pièce de résistance is in the patisserie around the corner. There, behind elaborately carved wooden cabinets, a series of Venetian wood-panel paintings of sensual water nymphs will take your breath away. The colors are muted, but as your eyes adjust the images will start to shimmer like a Gustav Klimt

kiss. The café and restaurant close at midnight, the patisserie at 8 PM. ⊠ *Maydan Sa'd Zaghlul, Mahatet El Raml* ☏ *03/486–8539.*

❺ Kom al-Dikka *(Roman Theater).* The focal point of this excavated section of the ancient city is a well-preserved amphitheater—the only one of its kind in Egypt—originally constructed in the 4th century AD, then rebuilt in the 6th century, following an earthquake. At that time a large dome was added (only its supporting columns still stand), and the theater went from being a cultural venue to a forum for public meetings of the City Council—a change deduced from ancient graffiti promoting various political parties.

The other half of the site is the ancient baths and living quarters, although much of this area is, in fact, best seen through the fence from the side near Pastroudis Café, where the cisterns and walls are clearly visible. The red bricks mark the location of the heated baths—warmed by an elaborate underground system—which complemented the adjacent cold and steam baths. The whole area fell into disuse after the 7th-century Persian conquest of Egypt. One noteworthy site in the residential section is a Roman house known as the **Villa of the Birds**, so named for its colorful floor mosaics depicting birds in several forms. The colorful and detailed craftsmanship shows a high level of sophistication. The mosaics, now restored, are protected by a modern structure. ⊠ *Off Maydan El Shohada, opposite the Misr train station, Kon al-Dikka* ☏ *03/490–2904* 🖾 *£E20, £E15 for Villa of the Birds* ☽ *Daily 9–4:30.*

❿ Montazah Gardens. When the descendents of Mohammed Ali became *khedives* (princes) of Egypt in the mid-18th century, they began to surround themselves with the trappings of a royal lifestyle, and one of these rewards was the lavish El Montazah palace, built outside Alexandria in the 1890s by Khedive Abbas Hilmi Pasha. During the era of Egyptian Royalty (1922–1952) the palace, enlarged in ornate Italianate style by King Faoud and surrounded by acres of lush gardens, played host to lavish parties. It was from here that Faoud's son King Farouk made his last journey on Egyptian soil after his abdication in 1952. He went into exile in Rome, Italy, and died there in 1965. Today the palace (under renovation at this writing) is part of the presidential property portfolio. The formal gardens, with their flower beds, lawns, and beaches, offer a shady place to stroll or picnic and are very popular with local families. ⊠ *Corniche al-Nil, Montazah* ☏ *No phone* 🖾 *£E5 (unless you are checking into a hotel in the park)* ☽ *Daily 7 AM–11 PM.*

❶ Pompey's Pillar *(Serapium Oracle).* Despite being Alexandria's most famous tourist sight, Pompey's Pillar is a disappointment. After all, it's just a granite pillar—albeit at 88 feet, a very tall one—placed on a hill surrounded by ruins. Known in Arabic as *al-'Amud al-Sawiri* (Column of the Horseman), the pillar was misnamed after Pompeius (106–48 BC) by the Crusaders. In fact, it dates to the 3rd century AD, when it was erected in honor of the emperor Diocletian on the site of a Ptolemaic temple to Serapis.

Helpful signs on the ruins name each virtually empty spot as a "pool" or "bath," which to the untrained eye look like indistinguishable rocks.

The late-model sphinxes lying around on pedestals add a little character. The most interesting element, ironically, is that from the hill you can get a glimpse inside the walled cemetery next door, as well as a view of a long and busy market street. ⊠ *Corner of Amoud El Sawary and El Shenity Abou Mandour, Karmouz* ☎ *03/482–5800* ⊠ *£E20* ☉ *Daily 9–4.*

ALSO WORTH NOTING

⑪ **Alexandria National Museum.** A small but high-quality collection of artifacts includes items found under the waters of the Western Harbor during recent marine archaeological projects. The display galleries cover every era of the city's long history and include Christian pieces, Islamic arts and crafts, and more recent information about Alexandria's colonial era. The early-20th-century Italianate palace that houses the museum, designed by a French architect, is a prime example of this colonial past. ⊠ *110 Shar'a el Horreya, El Shallalat* ☎ *03/483–5519* ⊠ *£E30* ☉ *Daily 9–4.*

❸ **St. Mark's Pro-Cathedral.** After St. Mark visited Alexandria in AD 49, the city became an early Christian outpost, building its first cathedral by AD 282. This church, constructed in 1855, was one of the few buildings undamaged during the shelling of the city by British warships in 1882. It exhibits an odd mix of Western, Moorish, and Byzantine design elements that somehow manage to blend together harmoniously. The soft yellow stone and colorful stained-glass windows are particularly exquisite in the early morning sun. The walls are lined with plaques, some of which date back almost a century, commemorating members of the Anglican community for their years of long service to the church. ⊠ *Maydan Ahmed Orabi, Manshiya* ☎ *03/487–9927* ☉ *Daily 9–4 except during services.*

❼ **Brazilian Coffee Stores.** Little has changed since this stand-up espresso bar opened in 1929, as you can see from the foot-traffic patterns worn into the tile floor. The ancient roasters are visible to the right—if you're lucky they'll be roasting beans when you walk in, and the café will be filled with plumes of aromatic smoke. Lining the walls are the original stunningly painted mirrors showing a map of South America, along with population and coffee-production statistics for Brazil, now endearingly out of date. There's even an enormous Brazilian flag painted on the ceiling. ⊠ *44 Shar'a Sa'd Zaghlul, Mahatet El Raml* ☎ *03/482–5059* ☉ *Daily 7 AM–11 PM.*

❻ **The Cavafy Museum.** The writer Constantine Cavafy was ignored during his lifetime but has received international recognition since his death in 1933. His poetry, which focused on such themes as one's moral dilemmas and uncertainty about the future, spoke to the Greek-speaking community around the Eastern Mediterranean and has been translated into all major languages.

The small flat where Cavafy spent the last years of his life has been turned into a museum. Half of it is given over to a re-creation of his home, with a period-piece brass bed and a case of reputedly genuine Christian icons. On the walls is an endless collection of portraits and sketches of Cavafy that only the most vain of men could have hung in his own apartment. The other half of the museum houses newspaper

Constantine Cavafy

Constantine Cavafy (Konstantinos Kavafis) was born in Alexandria to Greek parents in 1863 and began writing poetry at age 19. It wasn't until much later, as a result of the exposure given to him in the novelist E. M. Forster's celebrated guidebook to Alexandria that Cavafy came to be regarded as the most accomplished Greek poet of our age. Cavafy's poems—including "God Abandons Antony," and, most famously, "The City"—are suffused with melancholy, and with a sense of his alienation from the society around him. Ironically, considering his rejection during his lifetime, they give such a strong evocation of place that they define the cultural memory of Alexandria in his time. Jacqueline Kennedy Onassis left a request that Cavafy's poem "Ithaka," which describes life's beauty being in the journey and not in the destination, be read at her funeral.

clippings about the poet's life and a library of his works, in the many languages and permutations in which they were published after his death—a remarkable legacy for a man who lived so quietly. There is, as well, a room dedicated to a student of Cavafy named Stratis Tsirkas, who lived in Upper Egypt and wrote a massive trilogy set in the Middle East. And there is one last curiosity: a cast of Cavafy's death mask, serene but disfigured, lying cushioned on a purple pillow. ⊠ *4 Shar'a CP Cavafy (formerly Shar'a Sharm El-Sheikh), Mahatet El Raml* ☎ *03/468–1598* 🖅 *£E20* ☉ *Tues.–Sun. 10–3.*

EL ANFUSHI

Somewhere—really, everywhere—under Alexandria lies a wealth of archaeological remains, but little of it has been excavated. As a result, the city's ancient and medieval remnants exist in scattered pockets. The most central sights are the Greco-Roman Museum and the Roman Theater *(⇨ Downtown and Raml Station, above)*, but none of the rest are more than a 15-minute taxi ride from Raml Station in the El Anfushi, Karmouz, Koum El Dakka, and El Shallalat districts.

TOP ATTRACTIONS

❷ **Anfushi Tombs.** You need to have a fairly serious death fetish to make the effort to see these 3rd century BC Ptolemaic tombs. Although built on a smaller scale than the Catacombs at Kom al-Shoqafa, this necropolis has more extant decoration, including paintings on the limestone walls that simulate marble and include various images from the pantheon of pharaonic gods. The tombs are on the spit of land (which at one time was an island) separating the Western and Eastern harbors, roughly a third of the way between the Palace of Ras al-Tin on the western point and Fort Qayt Bay on the eastern point. ⊠ *Shar'a Ras El Tin, El Anfushi* ☎ *No phone* 🖅 *£E20* ☉ *Daily 9–4:30.*

❶ **Fort Qayt Bay.** This sandstone fort lies on the very tip of the Corniche, dominating the view of the Eastern Harbor. It was built on the site of Alexandria's Pharos lighthouse, one of the seven wonders of the ancient

El Anfushi

Mediterranean Sea

EL ANFUSHI

Eastern Harbour

El Nadoury Pasha

El Couriniche (26th of July St.)

Sayed Mohammed Korayem

Sidi Taher Bey

Masged Taher Bey

El Saiyala

Yakout

El Haggery

Kasr Ras el Tin

El Mosafer
Khana Ga'far

Gouda

Ras el Tin

Safar Pasha Sidi Abu Warda

Isma'il Sabry

El Tarsana

Zawet El Arag

Faransa

Western Harbour

Masged
El Halwgy

El Shemerti

GOMROK

El Gomrok

El Maydan

Souk El Tabbakhin

El Bahareya

Wekalet El Laimoun

El Dakkakin

Faransa

Dwiko

El Nasr Sq.

El Nasr

El Sekka El Gadida

0   1/8 mi
0   1/8 km

Lawrence Durrell

Lawrence George Durrell was born in 1912 in northern India to expat parents of English and Irish descent. At the age of 11, Durrell was sent to England for his education, but he hated his time there and didn't complete his formal schooling. Instead, he resolved to make a living as a writer.

In 1935 he moved to Çorfu, an island off Greece, with his wife, mother, and brothers and sisters. He thrived there but was forced to leave when German troops invaded in 1941. He settled in Cairo with his wife and small daughter, then moved to Alexandria alone to take up a position as press attaché at the British Information Office.

After the war, Durrell returned to Greece for two years before taking up a post in Argentina, then in Yugoslavia. In 1952 he bought a cottage close to the coast in the north of Cyprus and took a job as an English teacher to fund his literary career. He wrote the first volume of *The Alexandria Quartet* in Cyprus. But peace was elusive, as Cyprus had become the focus of an independence struggle. Durrell moved one more time, to Sommières in the south of France, where he spent the final 35 years of his life, completing *The Alexandria Quartet* and two more cycles of novels. He died in 1990.

world and incorporates its remains—much of which are still visible—into the foundation. A Greek named Sostratus in the 3rd century BC constructed the lighthouse under the Ptolemies. Standing about 400 feet high and capable of projecting a light that could be seen 53 km (35 mi) out to sea, it was one of the most awesome structures created by ancients. The base of the four-tiered Pharos was thought to have contained some 300 rooms, as well as a hydraulic system for lifting fuel to the top of the tower.

In the centuries that followed, the Pharos was damaged and rebuilt several times, until it was finally destroyed in the great earthquake of 1307. It lay in ruins for two centuries until the Mamluk Sultan Qayt Bay had the current fortress constructed in 1479. Recently, a French team found what are thought to be parts of the Pharos in shallow waters just offshore, rekindling local interest in the ancient monument—there is even talk of an underwater museum, although that is unlikely to materialize anytime soon.

The outer walls of the fort enclose a large open space, and the ramparts' walk affords magnificent views of miles and miles of coastline. The fort also encourages romance—the arrow slits built into the ramparts that were once used to defend the fort now shelter Egyptian couples enjoying the chance to court each other in semiprivacy. The interior of the building within the fort, by comparison, is exceptionally dull, housing an undecorated mosque, a patriotic mural of President Jamal 'Abd al-Nasir (Nasser) reviewing a fantastically outfitted Egyptian navy, and a kitsch historical model of "the fleet of Senefroo." Upstairs are the iron bullets, swords, bombs, and shards of pottery recovered from Napoléon's ship *l'Orient,* which the British sank off Abu Qir, several

View of Fort Qayt Bay

miles east. ⊠ *Corniche (far western end), El Anfushi* ☎ *03/480–9144* ✈ *£E25* ⊘ *Daily 9–5:30.*

NEED A BREAK?

El Koubeze (⊠ *50 26th of July St., the Corniche, Gomrouk* ☎ *03/486–7860*), a small palace of marble decorated with piles of colorful fresh fruit, is one of the most incongruous places in Alexandria. Though a casual juice bar—the juice is pressed when you order, so it's mouth-wateringly fresh—El Koubeze's crisp uniformed staff look as if they could grace a fine-dining establishment. The only letdown is the cheap plastic seats and tables and the roadside setting. But it's great for a refreshing pit stop.

OFF THE BEATEN PATH

The Battlefield and Monuments of El Alamein. The desert west of Alexandria was the field of one of the decisive battles of World War II. In 1942, the British Eighth Army led by General Montgomery attacked the German Afrika Corps led by Field Marshal Rommel (the famous "Desert Fox") and sent them into a retreat, which would eventually clear Axis troops from the whole of North Africa.

Three carefully tended military grave sites hold the remains of Allied, Italian, and German soldiers—each with a suitably somber monument. The gardens of El Alamein museum display an array of military hardware used in the battle. Inside, the galleries offer background information on the forces involved and explain how the campaign in North Africa developed and how the decisive battle played out. However, the museum has collected a wealth of personal items, including letters and photographs from soldiers on all sides that layer a compelling human story on top of the military records. The sites are around an hour west

NEW FINDS

Active archaeology continues in the shallows of the Eastern Harbor, thought to be the location of Cleopatra's palace and the heart of Ptolemaic Alexandria. Since 1990, a team led by Franck Goddio has been mapping the harbor floor and discovering artifacts that include coins and many other artifacts both large and small. In January 2010, several cat statues brought to the surface indicate the site of a temple of Bastet, protector of Lower Egypt, who was depicted in feline form.

Given the importance of the site and the impossibility of raising the monumental structures, the Egyptian Government and UNESCO have reached an agreement to move forward with an imaginative project currently called the "Alexandria Underwater Museum," which will allow visitors to view the remains of the city where they lie.

Innovative architect Jacques Rougerie (⊕ www.rougerie.com) has produced a spellbinding design for the new structure incorporating an underwater tunnel that would allow tourists to come face to face with Cleopatra's city. However, the project is still at the embryonic stage.

of Alexandria along the coastal road. Renting a taxi for the morning would be the most convenient way to see the museum, monuments, and graveyards. Local tour companies also organize guides and transportation. ⊠ *El Alamein, 96 km (60 mi) west of Alexandria* ☎ *046/410–0031* ⌸ *£E10* ⊗ *May–Sept., daily 9:30–3:30; Oct.–Apr., daily 9:30–2:30.*

ALSO WORTH NOTING

❸ **Abu al-Abbas al-Mursi Mosque.** This attractive mosque was built during World War II over the tomb of a 13th-century holy man, who is the patron saint of the city's fishermen. The area surrounding it has been turned into Egypt's largest and most bizarre religious/retail complex, with a cluster of mosques sharing a terrace that hides an underground shopping center. Intruding on the space is a horrific modernism-on-the-cheap office building (with yet more shops) that is as pointed and angular as the mosques are smooth and curved. If you are dressed modestly and the mosque is open, you should be able to get inside. If so, remove your shoes and refrain from taking photos. ⊠ *Corniche, al-Anfushi, El Anfushi.*

WHERE TO EAT

Alexandria's culinary gift is extraordinary seafood, drawing on the best of the Mediterranean and the Red Sea. The preparation tends to be simple: grilled or fried, perhaps laced with garlic, herbs, or butter, and typically served with *tahini* (sesame paste) and a couple of salads on the side. The ingredients are so fresh that anything more elaborate would obscure their flavors. Most places display their offerings of fish, shrimp, crab, calamari, and mussels on ice, and you pay by weight or per serving. The price includes preparation and everything else—there are no hidden costs. If you need help choosing, there will always be someone on hand to guide your selection.

Because the focus is on fresh seafood, restaurants in Alexandria (especially the good ones) tend to be informal and quite inexpensive for the quality of what they serve. Naturally, many are near the water, some of them appropriately weathered, while others consist of no more than a few tables in an alley. A few places will levy a service charge, but most will not. In all places a tip of 10% is appropriate. Do not expect alcohol to be served in most restaurants.

Off-season, Alexandrians eat meals at standard times: 1 to 3 for lunch and 8 to 11 for dinner. But in summer dinner often begins much later. There is nothing more Mediterranean about Alexandria than the pace of dinner in the summer: after an evening siesta, have a *shisha* (water pipe) around 11, arrive at a waterfront restaurant after midnight, then wrap up the meal with an early morning espresso at an outdoor café nearby. You don't have to eat so late, of course, but you might be surprised how seductive it is.

WHAT IT COSTS IN EGYPTIAN POUNDS			
	$	$$	$$$	$$$$
Restaurants	under £E50	£E50–£E100	£E100–£E150	over £E150

Restaurant prices are per person for a main course at dinner.

DOWNTOWN AND RAML STATION

$
ASIAN
✕ **China House.** There are Indian, Chinese, and Thai chefs working here, so although the menu seems a little wide-ranging, you do get pretty authentic cuisine. Having said that, the choice in each cuisine type is limited, and chefs concentrate on what they can do easily given the limitation on some ingredients. The rooftop setting with views along the Corniche makes this one of the best places to enjoy the sunset and take a respite from the bustle of the city. ⊠ *Sofitel Cecil Hotel, Maydan Sa'd Zaghlul, Raml Station* ☎ *03/487–7173 Ext. 782* ⊟ *AE, MC, V.*

$$
CONTINENTAL
✕ **Grand Trianon.** This is Alexandria's most gorgeous restaurant, with high ceilings, elaborate carved wooden chandeliers, and swirling art nouveau murals decorating the walls. People have always said that some day the kitchen will be taken over by a chef equal to the decor, but for now the food remains enjoyable but unspectacular. If you stick close to the Egyptian or French basics, you'll play to their strengths. As appetizers the *sambousik* (phyllo pastries stuffed with cheese or meat) and French onion soup are quite good, and the entrecôte of beef makes an excellent main course. For dessert, you can linger at your table or relocate to the adjoining café. ⊠ *Maydan Sa'd Zaghlul, Raml Station* ☎ *03/482–0986* ⊟ *AE, MC, V.*

$
PIZZA
✕ **Taverna.** This is more a pizzeria than a real Greek taverna, but the pizza is delicious, assembled in front of you and baked in an oven to the left of the entrance. The baladi oven to the right is used for *fatir*, a kind of Egyptian pizza than can be sweet or savory; it's also often fairly oily—ask them to go light on the *ghee* (clarified butter). The menu also includes some fish and shrimp dishes. The proper seating

Dining at Fish Market

area is upstairs, but it's even cheaper if you eat at the informal area downstairs, where a *shawarma* (pressed lamb carved from a vertical rotisserie) sandwich makes a nice midday snack. ⊠ *1 Maydan Sa'd Zaghlul, Raml Station* ☎ *03/482–8189* ▭ *AE, MC, V.*

EL ANFUSHI

$$–$$$
SEAFOOD
★

✕ **Fish Market.** On the waterfront side of Alexandria Corniche, this is probably the biggest fish restaurant in the city and sees a regular crowd of locals who know they'll get excellent but simply cooked seafood plus a great view out across the harbor. The catch is priced by kilogram, and the rice and salads are included. Choose your fish and ask them to price it, so you know how much you'll be paying. There's also a decent wine list featuring local labels. ⊠ *Corniche (near the Abu al-Abbas al-Mursi Mosque), Gomrouk* ☎ *03/480–5114* ▭ *MC, V* ☽ *No lunch.*

$
MIDDLE EASTERN

✕ **Grand Café.** Adjacent to the Tikka Grill and under the same management, this outdoor restaurant is one of the coziest, most romantic places in Alexandria. Tables are scattered throughout a lush garden, amid palm fronds lit against the night sky and small wooden bridges leading to private corners. The menu offers the standard Egyptian dishes—kebabs, including *shish taouk* (chicken kebabs) and *kofta* (minced lamb on a skewer), and so forth—but it's the setting that should bring you here. ⊠ *Corniche (near the Abu al-Abbas al-Mursi Mosque), Gomrouk* ☎ *03/480–5114* ▭ *MC, V* ☽ *No lunch.*

$$
SEAFOOD

✕ **Kadoura.** Granted, it looks unpromising: not shabby enough to feel authentic, not stylish enough to feel elegant. So close your eyes. Kadoura is famous throughout Egypt, and it's every bit as good as its reputation. Fish is grilled with a delicious fresh tomato, garlic, and herb purée; calamari come lightly fried, tender, and tasty. Pick your seafood downstairs, grab a wood-block number, and sit upstairs. Everything else that comes to you—salads, tahini, drinks—is included in the price. It's very popular for lunch, especially on Fridays, when space is at a premium. ⊠ *47 26th of July St. (the Corniche), Gomrouk* ☎ *03/480–0967* ⌨ *Reservations not accepted* ▭ *No credit cards.*

$$ ✕ **Samakmak.** This seafood restaurant is located in a suitably rundown
SEAFOOD   area near the port where the fishing boats dock, and it is so close to the landing stage you could throw the fish straight from the dock to the restaurant grill. Inside, the place has a slightly more formal atmosphere than most and serves exquisitely fresh seafood that benefits from the short walk from boat to plate. The staff is friendly and helpful. ⊠ *42 Shar'a Ras al-Tin, El Anfushi* ☎ *03/481–1560* ⌨ *Reservations essential* ▭ *No credit cards.*

$ ✕ **Tikka Grill.** Alexandrians swear by this place, and it's packed with
ECLECTIC   families in the early evenings and an older crowd later on. It has surprisingly elegant decor and a magnificent setting next to the water—the only Eastern Harbor restaurant to have one, though the atmosphere can be a little manic as waiters rush around with trays full of food. The menu is wide-ranging, but you'd be best to stick with the Egyptian dishes. The roasted meats make good choices, as do the cold mezze. Try to get a table by the window for fantastic views across the harbor. ⊠ *Corniche (near Abu al-Abbas al-Mursi Mosque), Gomrouk* ☎ *03/480–5114* ▭ *MC, V.*

EASTERN SHORELINE

$$$$ ✕ **Al Farouk.** Named for King Farouk (who ruled from 1936 to 1952),
MEDITERRANEAN   this restaurant used to be his summer office. The decor is definitely fit for a king: alabaster columns, china, and stained-glass windows. The gorgeously printed menu mixes old photos of royal weddings and affairs of state with dishes on an internationally regal theme. Look for tender foie gras Louis XV (foie gras in a port-wine sauce) or decadent Caviar Raspoutine (caviar selection with blinis) served on a bed of ice. The best entrées are the *sharkesseya d'Istanbul* (chicken stewed in a subtle walnut sauce) and the *filet blanc et noir Ras el-Tin* (veal and beef steaks with foie gras and mushrooms). ⊠ *El-Salamlek Palace, Montazah Palace grounds, Montazah* ☎ *03/547–7999* ▭ *AE, DC, MC, V.*

$$$ ✕ **Byblos.** The signature restaurant of the Four Seasons, Byblos serves
MEDITERRANEAN   excellent Lebanese dishes and brasserie-style French cuisine—you can mix and match depending on your mood. Start with a selection of hot and cold *mezze*, then try *sheikh al manshee* (eggplant stuffed with minced beef and tomato sauce) or *kebbeh bel laban* (lamb meatballs smothered with yogurt sauce and mint). The French dishes steer clear of heavy sauces, concentrating instead on fine meat and fish, such as rack of lamb or roasted sea bass. ⊠ *Four Seasons Hotel, 399 El Geish Rd., San Stefano* ☎ *03/581–8000* ▭ *AE, DC, MC, V* ☉ *No lunch. Dec.– Apr., closed Mon.*

$$–$$$ ✕ **Zephyrion.** Established in 1929 in the dusty village of Abu Qir east
SEAFOOD   of Montazah, Zephyrion has been synonymous with good seafood for

three generations. The restaurant could seat 400 without effort—more in the summer when the veranda is open—so it never feels crowded, and the seafood is as fresh as it gets. The restaurant is at its most peaceful in the late afternoon sun. It has no address, but everyone in Abu Qir knows where it is, so just ask. Since it's 20 minutes from Montazah (and 40 minutes from Downtown), the big question is whether it's worth the trip. The answer: yes, if you see the trip itself as part of your adventure. ⊠ *Abu Qir* ☎ *03/562–1319* ⊟ *No credit cards.*

3

WHERE TO STAY

Hotels in Alexandria are located in two clusters that are roughly 30 minutes apart. Upscale resort hotels are all out along the eastern shoreline in Montazah, close to or even within the manicured khedivial palace gardens—but not convenient to the city or the historic sights. Lower-budget hotels are almost all Downtown, much more convenient but less tranquil.

In truth, with the exception of the Salamlek Palace and the Four Seasons, the luxury hotels in Alexandria are drab, generic places not worth what they charge. Fortunately, a couple of mid-range hotels, including the surprisingly elegant Metropole, make attractive alternatives in the city center. Summer is a busy season, when advance reservations are essential. In spring and fall you may find hotels fully booked on weekends (Friday through Sunday), when residents of Cairo head to Alexandria for some downtime. Outside peak summer season, most hotels discount their prices by 30% to 40%. Many hotels quote prices in U.S. dollars or euros, but if you pay with a credit card, your payment will be charged in the equivalent of Egyptian pounds.

All hotel reviews have been condensed for this book. Please go to Fodors.com for full reviews of each property.

WHAT IT COSTS IN U.S. DOLLARS AND EUROS				
	$	**$$**	**$$$**	**$$$$**
Hotels in Dollars	under $70	$70–$130	$130–$200	over $200
Hotels in Euros	under €45	€45–€80	€80–€130	over €130

Hotel prices are for a double room in high season, excluding 10% tax and service charges (usually 10%).

DOWNTOWN AND RAML STATION

$ 🖼 **Hotel Union.** Don't be misled by the dingy entrance and modest common area: this is the best inexpensive hotel in the city. **Pros:** excellent value for money, especially those rooms with sea views. **Cons:** some facilities in need of a little TLC; noise from the Corniche won't please light sleepers. ⊠ *164 Corniche, Raml Station* ☎ *03/480–7312* ⬎ *37 rooms, 26 with bath* ☐ *In-room: no a/c (some), safe (some), refrigerator, no TV (some)* ⊟ *No credit cards* ⦿ *EP.*

$$$ ★ **Paradise Inn–Metropole.** The best value in Alexandria, the turn-of-the-20th-century Metropole has an elegance few others can match. **Pros:** a delightful period atmosphere; friendly and helpful staff; excellent location for exploring Downtown on foot. **Cons:** rooms sizes can vary dramatically; some traffic noise in rooms overlooking the main street. ⊠ *52 Shar'a Sa'd Zaghlul, Raml Station* ☎ *03/486–1467* ⊕ *www. paradiseinnegypt.com* ↘ *66 rooms* ⑂ *In-room: a/c, safe, refrigerator. In-hotel: restaurant, room service, laundry service, Wi-Fi hotspot* ⊟ *AE, MC, V* †Ⓞ⧘ *BP.*

$ **Petit Coin.** The name ("Little Corner" in French) fits this cozy, simple hotel, just off Maydan Ahmed Orabi. **Pros:** views from the roof terrace, which is a good place to relax; friendly staff. **Cons:** street noise is a problem on lower floors; restaurant not recommendable. ⊠ *5 Shar'a Ahmed Orabi, Manshiya* ☎ *03/487–1503* ↘ *52 rooms* ⑂ *In-room: a/c, refrigerator. In-hotel: restaurant, laundry service* ⊟ *No credit cards.*

$ **Sea Star.** A rather basic hotel, Sea Star's greatest appeal is its location. If you are on a budget, it's a clean if uninspiring option that's close to the tram station and within walking distance of Downtown, the museum, and the library. **Pros:** clean option for the price; location means you're in the heart of the action but on a quieter side street. **Cons:** very ordinary decor; disinterested front desk staff; prices can change on a whim, so make sure to haggle. ⊠ *24 Shar'a Amin Fikhry, Raml Station* ☎ *03/487–1787* ↘ *49 rooms, 14 suites* ⑂ *In-room: no a/c (some). In-hotel: restaurant, room service* ⊟ *No credit cards* †Ⓞ⧘ *EP.*

$$$–$$$$ **Sofitel Alexandria Cecil.** With the Cecil, you're paying for history more than creature comforts, but if atmosphere is what you want you'll find it here in spades. **Pros:** excellent location for exploring Downtown on foot; cozy historic hotel; no-smoking rooms. **Cons:** rooms are overpriced for the size (hotel is priced partly because of its history); small bathrooms. ⊠ *16 Maydan Sa'd Zaghlul, Mahatet El Raml* ☎ *03/487–7173* ⊕ *www.sofitel.com* ↘ *83 rooms, 6 suites* ⑂ *In-room: a/c, safe, Internet. In-hotel: 2 restaurants, room service, bars, gym, laundry service, Wi-Fi hotspot* ⊟ *AE, DC, MC, V* †Ⓞ⧘ *BP.*

$$–$$$ **Windsor Palace.** Erected on the Alexandria Corniche in 1906, the Windsor Palace retains a period look and feel thanks to its furnishings, tapestries, and oil paintings. **Pros:** excellent location on the Downtown Corniche; period atmosphere harks back to the early-20th-century heyday of Alexandria. **Cons:** although grand in scale, the lobby has a soulless quality; on-site facilities are limited when compared to the competition. ⊠ *17 Shar'a al-Shohada, Raml Station* ☎ *03/480–8700* ⊕ *www.paradiseinnegypt.com* ↘ *71 rooms* ⑂ *In-room: a/c, Internet. In-hotel: restaurant, laundry service* ⊟ *AE, MC, V* †Ⓞ⧘ *BP.*

EASTERN SHORELINE

$$$$ ★ **El-Salamlek Palace.** Built in the late 19th century by the khedive as a lodge for his Austrian mistress, the Salamlek is Alexandria's most unusual luxurious hotel. **Pros:** small, intimate hotel with antique furnishings; exceptional restaurant on-site; no-smoking rooms. **Cons:** no resort-style facilities in the house, so in some ways it feels like a glorified bed-and-breakfast, albeit with a restaurant. ⊠ *Montazah Palace*

grounds, Montazah ☎ *03/547–7999* ⊕ *www.sangiovanni.com* ⤶ *14 suites, 4 rooms, 2 studios* ⟳ *In-room: a/c, safe (some), Wi-Fi. In-hotel: 3 restaurants, room service, bar, tennis courts, spa, beachfront, diving, water sports, bicycles, laundry service, Wi-Fi hotspot, parking (paid)* ⊟ *AE, DC, MC, V* ⦿|*BP.*

$$$$ 🏨 **Four Seasons Hotel Alexandria at San Stefano.** The opening of the Four Seasons in 2007 has at last given Alexandria a world-class five-star property. **Pros:** high-quality appointments throughout; a good choice of restaurants and cafés; spectacular two-story spa; no-smoking rooms. **Cons:** you must traverse a tunnel under the Corniche road to get to the beach; it's a 10-minute taxi ride to Downtown. ⊠ *399 El Geish Rd., San Stefano* ☎ *03/581–8000* ⊕ *www.fourseasons.com* ⤶ *118 rooms* ⟳ *In-room: a/c, safe, Internet. In-hotel: 6 restaurants, room service, bars, pool, gym, spa, diving, water sports, children's programs (ages 5–12), laundry service, Wi-Fi hotspot* ⊟ *AE, DC, MC, V* ⦿|*EP.*

$$$$ 🏨 **Helnan Palestine.** In a magnificent setting in the royal gardens between the old palace and a private cove, the fan-shaped concrete dreariness of the Palestine is an example of modernism gone very wrong. **Pros:** the hotel setting offers peace and tranquility. **Cons:** far from the energy of Downtown Alexandria; some staff members are indifferent. ⊠ *Montazah Palace grounds, Montazah* ☎ *03/547–3500* ⊕ *www.helnan.com* ⤶ *203 rooms, 27 suites* ⟳ *In-room: safe. In-hotel: 4 restaurants, room service, bars, pool, gym, spa, beachfront, water sports, laundry service, parking (free)* ⊟ *AE, DC, MC, V* ⦿|*EP.*

$$$–$$$$ 🏨 **Maritim Jolie Ville Hotel Alexandria.** The Renaissance will never win any design rewards; in fact, those with a love of period buildings or an eye for ultracontemporary architecture will find this late-20th-century tower rather dreary, but don't judge the hotel by its outer covering. **Pros:** good range of resort-style facilities on-site; sea-view rooms are the most recently renovated, so they offer the best value for money. **Cons:** service can be patchy for this caliber hotel. ⊠ *544 Tariq al-Geish, Sidi Bishr* ☎ *03/549–0935* ⊕ *www.maritim.com* ⤶ *116 rooms, 42 suites* ⟳ *In-room: a/c, safe, Internet (some). In-hotel: 3 restaurants, room service, bars, pool, gym, spa, diving, water sports, laundry service, Wi-Fi hotspot* ⊟ *AE, DC, MC, V* ⦿|*EP.*

$$$$ 🏨 **Mediterranean Azur.** On a delightful bay, this modern hotel offers international-style amenities in a resort setting, not often seen in Egypt. **Pros:** the closest beachfront hotel to Downtown; wide range of eateries on-site; no-smoking rooms. **Cons:** housekeeping can be lax; this is a popular wedding venue, and celebrations can go on well into the night. ⊠ *Shar'a el Corniche, Roshdy* ☎ *03/552–6001* ⊕ *www.azur.travel* ⤶ *148 rooms 13 suites* ⟳ *In-room: a/c, safe, Internet. In-hotel: 3 restaurants, room service, bars, pools, gym, spa, beachfront, laundry service, parking (free)* ⊟ *AE, D, DC, MC, V* ⦿|*EP.*

NIGHTLIFE AND THE ARTS

The arts scene in Alex lags way behind Cairo, but there are some beacons of interest to explore. Although Alexandria has a couple of annual and biennial festivals, none would warrant a special trip to Alexandria in itself; however, several events are worth attending if you're in town when they're on.

THE ARTS

ANNUAL FESTIVALS

Alexandria Biennial. This festival of international and local artists is held in October in even-numbered years at the Museum of Fine Arts, which has been renamed in honor of Husayn Sobhi. ☎ *02/3746–2142* ⊕ *www. alexbiennale.gov.eg.*

The **Alexandria International Film Festival.** Held every September at local theaters, this film festival tends to be chaotically organized, and it is regarded mainly as a chance for Egyptians to see fleeting nudity on screen (there's censorship the rest of the year). The festival occasionally brings interesting art films. ☎ *02/2570–0424* ⊕ *www.alexfilmfestival.com.*

The **Alexandria Song Festival** is a competition for international and local singers, songwriters, and composers held in late July.

MAJOR ARTS VENUES

In Alexandria, the main venues for music, theater, and exhibitions are the cultural centers attached to foreign consulates. Their programs are often very interesting, particularly those at the Cervantes Institute and the French Cultural Center, and they connect you with the cosmopolitan side of Alex that is often invisible in the city at large. To find out what's happening, call the individual consulates for their schedules; pick up *Egypt Today,* which occasionally lists events; or look for advertisements at expatriate hangouts.

Elite. This restaurant popular among expats is a good place to find out about local performances and other cultural events. ⊠ *43 Shar'a Safiya Zaghlul, Mahatet El Raml* ☎ *03/482–3592).*

FOREIGN CULTURAL CENTERS

American Cultural Center (⊠ *117 Shar'a Ahmed Shawky, Roushdy* ☎ *03/ 542–9617* ⊕ *www.aecc-egypt.com).*

British Council (⊠ *11 Shar'a Mahnoud Abou El Ela, Kafr Abdou* ☎ *02/ 19789 in Cairo* ⊕ *www.britishcouncil.org.eg).*

Cervantes Institute (⊠ *101 Shar'a al-Horreya,* ☎ *03/492–0214).*

French Cultural Center (⊠ *30 Shar'a Nabi Daniel, El Attarin* ☎ *03/492– 0804* ⊕ *www.cfcc-eg.org).*

German Cultural Center (⊠ *10 Shar'a Batalsa, El Azarita* ☎ *03/483–9870* ⊕ *www.goethe.de).*

Greek Cultural Center (⊠ *18 Shar'a Sidi al-Metwalli, El Attarin* ☎ *03/482– 1598* ⊕ *www.hfc.gr).*

Russian Cultural Center (⊠ *5 Shar'a Batalsa, El Azarita* ☎ *03/482–5645).*

Swedish Institute (⊠ *57 Shar'a 26 Yulyu, Manshiya* ☎ *03/485–5113* ⊕ *www.swedealex.org.)*

OTHER PERFORMANCE VENUES

Alexandria Creativity Centre. This performing arts center has a theater plus galleries and workshop space, running a varied program of arts performances, films, and exhibitions throughout the year. ⊠ *1 Shar'a al-Horreya* ☎ *03/495–6745.*

MUSIC AND OPERA

Alexandria Opera House. Alex's opera house is also known as the Sayed Darwish Theatre. The 1921 edifice reopened after a full renovation project early in the new millennium. It offers a season of eclectic performances plus the occasional visiting company. ⊠ *22 Shar'a al-Horreya* ☎ *03/486–5106.*

NIGHTLIFE

The joke among foreign residents in Alex is that if you want nightlife, go to Cairo. Things aren't quite that dire, but you'll still find that your nocturnal activities lean toward the wholesome rather than the iniquitous. Some top-end hotels have what pass for discos, and the Salamlek has a casino, but the city as a whole is definitely quieter than the capital.

BARS

Alexandria is a conservative town, so there's no bar scene to speak of, and most restaurants don't serve alcohol. If you want to enjoy a drink in convivial surroundings, head to the five-star hotels, which have a selection of international and local brands.

Bleu. This is Alexandria's coolest venue. You can enjoy the shisha along with your cocktail. With a contemporary decor and a marble-floored terrace overlooking the north coast beaches and Corniche (open May through November only), the bar offers a venue for the trendy in-crowd. ⊠ *Four Seasons Hotel, 399 El Geish Rd.* ☎ *03/581–8000.*

Cap d'Or (Sheikh 'Ali). A modest place, Cap d'Or is blessed with a gorgeous old art nouveau bar that serves a range of Stellas (the primary Egypt beer brand) along with some cognacs. Drinks will arrive with snacks that may be charged for—ask before you tuck in. The bar is on the small street that runs south from Sa'd Zaghlul; it is usually open until 2 AM. ⊠ *4 Shar'a Adib, Manshiya* ☎ *03/487–5177.*

Centro de Portugal. This bar has a more British Isles vibe than one from Iberia. No matter, it's a central element in the local expatriate life and a great source of information about what's happening in the city. It's more like a social club than a commercial bar, but you're sure to make friends. The bar is usually open from 1 PM to midnight, later on Thursday night. ⊠ *42 Shar'a Abdel Kader, next to Dr. Ragab's Papyrus Museum, Roushdi* ☎ *03/452–7599.*

Monty Bar. The Cecil's bar was named after General Montgomery, who commanded the Allied troops in the Battle of El Alamein. Monty Bar is a suitably conservative, wood-paneled venue. The clientele is a mixture of expat workers and sophisticated Cairenes. There's regular live music, but Monty's is too small to take the volume levels, so conversation can become impossible. ⊠ *Sofitel Cecil Hotel, Maydan Sa'd Zaghlul* ☎ *03/487–7173.*

Spitfire Bar. This is a real sailor's bar: banknotes and bumper stickers from all over the world cover the walls, and among the other decorations are a yellowing advertisement for the Marines by the cash register, a fairly tame poster of a woman in a wet T-shirt, and the inevitable dogs-playing-pool carpet. But the atmosphere couldn't be more congenial—it's almost sedate—and there isn't a hint of sleaze to be found anywhere. The Spitfire is just north of Shar'a Sa'd Zaghlul on Shar'a Ancienne Bourse. It's closed on Sunday, and open until midnight all other nights. ⊠ *7 Shar'a Ancienne Bourse, Manshiya* ☎ *03/480–6503.*

CASINOS

El Salamlek Casino. This small property, offers black jack, stud poker, and American roulette. It is also Alexandria's only casino. ⊠ *El Salamlek Palace Hotel, Montazah* ☎ *03/547–7999.*

FILM

Movies are a mixture of Arab-produced films in Arabic (Egypt has its own production facilities), as well as Hollywood and other English-language films—usually with original soundtrack with Arabic subtitles.

Alexandria City Centre. This move theater has six screens. ⊠ *City Centre Mall, Cairo Desert Rd.* ☎ *03/397–0157.*

San Stefano Cinema. This theater has ten screens and shows the latest blockbusters. ⊠ *San Stefano Mall, 388 Shar'a El Geish* ☎ *03/469–0057.*

SHOPPING

Alexandria isn't a shopping city. There's little to buy here that you can't do better finding in Cairo, where the selection is much greater. If you're looking for chain stores, try Shar'a Suriya in Roushdi, Alexandria's most upscale neighborhood (15 minutes east of Downtown by taxi), or one of the new shopping malls that have opened up in the past few years.

MARKETS

The **Attarine Market** is the best, if slightly informal, source for reproduction furniture and antiques *(⇨ Downtown Alexandria, in Exploring Alexandria, above).* Used books are sold at the street market on Nabi Daniel near al-Horreya, although mostly they are school textbooks. The other markets in Alexandria tend to be more basic and practical, selling kitchen items or cheap clothing and are aimed almost exclusively at locals. There's a **flea market** at the back end of the Attarine Market, and clothes are sold in the streets west of Maydan Orabi. Perhaps the most visually interesting market in Alexandria is the **produce market**, which begins at Maydan al-Gumhorreya in front of the Misr Train Station and runs west for a mile.

Souvenir pendants

MALLS

Alexandria City Centre. The city's largest mall is anchored by a huge Carrefour supermarket and includes such well-known names as Timberland, La Senza, and Sony stores. ⊠ *Alexandria International Park, Cairo Desert Rd.* ☏ *03/397–0009.*

Green Plaza Mall. This mall is just 10 minutes from Downtown by taxi, so it's convenient. A modern Hilton Green Plaza Hotel anchors it, and there are almost 400 shops on-site. ⊠ *Cairo Desert Rd.* ☏ *03/484–3264.*

San Stefano Mall. With Alexandria's most upscale shopping, this major mall sits underneath and around the new Four Seasons Hotel. You can buy designer sunglasses, jewelry, and formal and casual fashion clothing here. ⊠ *388 Shar'a El Geish* ☏ *03/582–3589.*

SHOES

Downtown has a large number of shoe stores, but most of the shoes are of poor quality. The best are on Falaki Street (try the Armenian-owned Gregoire or Fortis), where, given enough time, the *chaussuriers* can produce custom-made shoes at a fraction of the price they would be in Europe or the United States.

SPORTS AND THE OUTDOORS

BEACHES

The beaches along Egypt's Mediterranean coast differ greatly in character from those along the Red Sea and in the Sinai. Waves can be strong and persistent in fall, winter, and spring, helped by stiff offshore prevailing breezes. This wave action and water movement affects underwater visibility, making diving less enjoyable here than in the Red Sea.

The beaches along the Corniche in Alexandria are narrow but composed of fine sand. Many are formed from shallow coves interspersed with rocky outlets. The character of the public beaches in the city is much less cosmopolitan than at, say, Sharm El-Sheikh or Hurghada, and they are frequented far more by local and Cairene families than international visitors. For this reason you should dress modestly (no skimpy bikinis), though it must be stressed that the atmosphere is not oppressive. On hotel beaches, such as at the Four Seasons, there is no problem with beachwear, and you will be able to sunbathe without attention.

SPAS

Fours Seasons Hotel Spa and Wellness Center. This upscale spa is one of the biggest in Egypt; the facility has excellent fitness rooms and rooms for massage and body treatments in addition to separate sauna, Jacuzzi, and steam-room facilities for men and women. ⊠ *Four Seasons Hotel, 399 El Geish Rd., San Stefano* 🖀 *03/581–8000* ⊕ *www.fourseasons.com.*

The Nile Valley and Luxor

WORD OF MOUTH

"No amount of reading, even the pictures . . . does justice to the beauty, the variety, the thrill of experiencing the many sites in Luxor."
—PaoloCast

WELCOME TO
THE NILE VALLEY AND LUXOR

TOP REASONS TO GO

★ **The Valley of the Kings.** Follow the storyline of the pharaoh's journey into the afterlife in the images from the *Book of the Dead* on the walls of a royal tomb.

★ **The Temple of Karnak.** Stroll among the columns in the "petrified forest" of the hypostyle hall, which was built as a garden for the gods.

★ **Deir el-Bahri.** Step back and absorb the panorama of the multitiered facade at the mortuary temple of Queen Hatshepsut.

★ **A Trip on the Nile.** Make the Nile your home for a few days, either on the deck of a traditional wind-powered felucca or in the more comfortable cabin of a luxury river cruiser.

★ **The Temple of Edfu.** Admire the architectural perfection of the temple dedicated to Horus; it's the finest surviving Ptolemaic-era building in Egypt.

1 The Middle Nile Valley: Al Minya to Tel el Amarna. Tomb complexes from several dynasties lie around Al Minya. Farther south in Tel el Amarna, the Pharaoh Akhenaton's capital city, the epicenter of a move to monotheism, lasted just a single generation.

2 The Upper Nile Valley: Abydos to Luxor. Powerful pharaohs stamped their marks on the Nile with magnificent temple complexes. Seti I and Ramses II ordered the building at Abydos at the start of the New Kingdom, while the Ptolemies and Romans funded the Temple of Hathor, at Dendera.

3 Luxor. The capital of ancient Egypt in the late Middle Kingdom and New Kingdom eras—and home to two massive temple complexes—Luxor is now one of Egypt's busiest tourist centers and has the widest selection of hotels and restaurants in the Nile Valley.

4 The Theban Necropolis. The burial place of the pharaohs, the landscape on the Nile's West Bank is dotted with vast mortuary temples and extensive rock-cut tombs that constitute a high point in human art and architecture. The most famous of these mortuary temples are in the Valley of the Kings, but standing apart is the Deir el-Bahri, the mortuary temple for Queen Hatshepsut.

5 The Upper Nile Valley: South of Luxor. A rash of temples grace the Nile south of Luxor, including the finest Ptolemaic-era edifice at Edfu and Egypt's only dual-deity temple at Kom Ombo. Most can be visited on land excursions if you are not on a cruise.

GETTING ORIENTED

Most Upper Nile sights lie near the towns of Luxor and Aswan. Two of the more out-of-the-way monuments, at Abydos and Dendera, are both north of Luxor and can be seen on day trips. Luxor itself has two magnificent temples (the Karnak and Luxor temples) as well as a good museum. On the West Bank of the Nile is the Theban Necropolis, and many of the tombs can be visited in a single day if you organize your time well. South of Luxor, the Temple of Horus at Edfu can also be visited on a day trip. The Middle Nile Valley is actually closer to Cairo than to Luxor, so those sights are often visited as an overnight trip from Cairo.

4

Beni Mazar
al-Minya
Tuna al-Gebel · Beni Hassan
Hermopolis
Tel el Amarna
EASTERN DESERT
Assyut
WESTERN DESERT
Akhmim
Sohag
al-Balyana
Abydos
Nag Hammadi · Dendera · Qena
Deir el-Bahri · Qus
The Valley of the Kings · Temple of Karnak
Armant · Luxor
Esna · al-Kab
Temple of Edfu · Edfu

0 — 25 mi
0 — 25 km

Updated by
Toni Salama

The ultimate proof of Herodotus's claim that "Egypt is a gift of the Nile" is visible on a flight from Cairo to Upper Egypt. From the air the Nile is a thin blue line, fringed with green, wending its way through a limitless horizon of sand. You realize that this is the Sahara, and that here, on the edge of the world's harshest desert, Africa's greatest city and Egypt's 80 million souls rely on one river's undiminished bounty.

From antiquity until modern times, the Nile was a principal trade route between the interior and the Mediterranean. And Upper Egypt, the Nile Valley south of Abydos, was a gateway to Africa. Because of the ease of access it afforded, the river shaped destinies: Nubia, Sudan, and Ethiopia alternately benefited from trade and suffered the predations of pharaohs.

Luxor, originally called Thebes, was the capital of Egypt during the New Kingdom and the center of religion, which was focused on the enormous temple devoted to Amun-Ra at Karnak. The city's importance continued even into the Ptolemaic period and, later, the Roman period, interrupted only briefly during the reign of Akhenaton, who moved the capital to the Middle Egypt city of Akhetaten; when he died, his capital died with him.

Today, Luxor is one of the most-visited destinations in Egypt. With its range of archaeological sights and temples, it provides a wide, if not completely comprehensive, introduction to life in ancient Egypt. Many travelers either join or disembark from a Nile River cruise in Luxor. It's possible to visit the sights downriver (Abydos and Dendera) on a day trip, and the Temple of Horus at Edfu upriver on another day trip.

A more extensive trip is necessary to visit Al Minya, which is between Cairo and Luxor. Usually overlooked by tourists, this region offers a fascinating glimpse into Egypt's Middle Kingdom as well as the 18th-Dynasty ruler Akhenaton.

TOP REASONS TO GO

Temples. The Karnak Temples in Luxor are considered the "head-quarters" for the main triumvirate of deities, Amun, Mut, and Montu, and is renowned for the immense hypo-style hall in the main complex. But more than a dozen other temples vie for "finest" or "best," depending on the criteria—see the Temple of Seti I in Abydos for its excellent carvings and colors, or Edfu as an example of the "Greek style." Each temple has a story to tell—stories of battles won and gods worshipped and of how, whatever was going on here on earth, the gods were the one constant in the lives of the people.

Tombs. Life after death was an integral belief of the ancient Egyptians, and the complicated and ornate tombs carved for the ruling dynasty display the engineering prowess and the dazzling wealth of artistic talent found in Thebes (Luxor) during the New Kingdom era. These tombs were where the carefully prepared mummies would be interred, and from where the pharaoh would start his journey into the afterlife. Art in the royal tombs depicts scenes from the *Book of the Dead*, while those in the Valleys of the Nobles and tombs of the workers have scenes of home, family, and everyday life in pharaonic Egypt. And, of course, one mustn't forget the Tomb of Tutankhamun—the only tomb yet found with its royal treasure intact.

River Trips. The languorous waters of the Nile have an almost magnetic appeal. Spend several days aboard a Nile cruise and your floating hotel will carry you close to all the major monuments. Luxor has wonderful waterside landscapes to explore, plus, the sunset over the West Bank here is exceptional. Crossing the river by ferry (large or small) brings you face-to-face with a slice of everyday life in Egypt.

PLANNING

WHEN TO GO

Traditionally, high season begins at the end of September, peaks around Christmas, and lasts until the end of April. The heat kicks in as early as March in Upper Egypt—a dry, pollution-free heat that you can get used to. Evenings are always cool in the desert. And Luxor is typically cooler than Aswan, though the sun beats down on the Nile's West Bank, and the Valley of the Kings can seem like a furnace—which means early-morning starts are a must. A season of *mulids* (religious feasts) occurs about a month before Ramadan, the Islamic month of fasting. Life slows down (but never stops) during Ramadan.

PLANNING YOUR TIME

Are you taking a cruise? If yes, remember that some cruises may devote only a single day to Luxor, and this major city deserves more time. You'll need at least a day to visit the West Bank temples and tombs, another to visit Karnak and Luxor temples, and a third day if you want to explore Abydos or Dendera, which the majority of cruises omit. If you want to visit the Middle Nile Valley to see the sights around Al Minya, that trip alone requires two or three days, whether you are doing it as a side trip from Cairo or as a stopover on the trip between Cairo and Luxor.

GETTING HERE AND AROUND

AIR TRAVEL

Luxor is linked to Cairo by several EgyptAir flights a day, as well as to Alexandria, Aswan, and Sharm El-Sheikh. There are also many nonstop flights from European destinations.

Luxor Airport is approximately 7 mi (11 km) northeast of town; travel time from central Luxor is about 15 to 20 minutes.

EgyptAir flies daily to Luxor from Cairo, Alexandria, Aswan, and Sharm El-Sheikh, offering the only domestic air service. There are usually at least two 1-hour flights daily from Cairo; reconfirming tickets (in person or through your hotel) two days in advance is an absolute must. The Luxor office is open daily 8–8. EgyptAir also has scheduled international flights direct to Luxor from London, Brussels, Paris, and Rome. Many European discount carriers—including Transavia (from Paris and Amsterdam), Air Berlin (destinations in Germany and Austria), FlyThomasCook (from several cities in the United Kingdom), and Condor (from several cities in Germany)—have nonstop flights to Luxor; however, they don't support offices in town.

Contacts EgyptAir (⊠ *Corniche al-Nil, Sofitel Winter Palace Hotel Luxor* ☎ *095/238–0580, 095/238–0586* ⊕ *www.egyptair.com*). **Luxor Airport** (☎ *095/237–4655*).

BOAT TRAVEL

Nile cruises depart from Luxor to Aswan, as well as end here. You can also take a local felucca sailboat around the city.

You can still take the public pedestrian ferry in front of Luxor Museum for £E1. It plies back and forth every 15 minutes or so from 6 AM to 11 PM. Powerboats take you across the river a bit faster, for about £E5. They can be found all along Luxor's East Bank.

Feluccas have fixed rates that tend to be highly negotiable and start at around £E50 an hour. You can find out these rates at the Tourist Information Office, hotels, and Thomas Cook and American Express offices.

BUS TRAVEL

It's difficult for foreign travelers to travel by bus in Upper Egypt (authorities strongly discourage it). If you can get a ticket, it's definitely the cheapest way to move around, though not terribly comfortable.

Twelve-seater minibuses run services around town, and locals pay around £E1 to £E3 per trip, depending on the destination. However, drivers don't always stop for visitors and may try to charge more if they do stop. Know the fares (ask at the tourist office, as rates can change) and refuse to be intimidated into paying more.

Be aware that many intercity buses never leave Cairo unless a mechanic is aboard. There's a reason for that. Even if no mechanical problems

A felucca and a hot-air balloon touring the Nile Valley. –photo by bfalley, Fodors.com member

befall, buses to Upper Egypt can be a very rough ride, because of the condition of the seats, the sporadic functioning of the air-conditioning, and the blaring of the onboard videos. Egyptians who must travel overland from Cairo to Luxor almost always take the train. That being said, buses are by far the cheapest way to go—about £E90 one-way to Luxor. If you insist on spending the next 12 hours of your life on the bus to Luxor, purchase tickets from the Targoman Station in central Cairo.

Contacts Targoman Bus Station (⊠ *Shar'a Mahata Aboud, Downtown, Cairo* ☎ *02/2431–6723*).

CAR TRAVEL

A private car rental is less than ideal in Upper Egypt. It's easier, and usually no more expensive, to have someone drive you.

If you want to tour the Nile Valley on your own schedule, the best options are to hire a private car and driver—usually called limousine service—or take a taxi. Several of the better hotels publish set rates for popular destinations, and the taxis they work with will agree to the rate schedule. The limousine companies offer rates that are very competitive with, and sometimes even lower than, what you can haggle from a taxi driver; you'll be going in a nicer vehicle; and the company can help obtain the required police permission if you're going to sights farther afield. Traveling by car in Egypt is not the freewheeling experience found in Western countries. For security reasons, foreigners must obtain police permission, at least 24 hours in advance, if traveling by auto beyond the city's immediate tourist spots, and there are checkpoints along every route, with certain destinations requiring police escort.

Contacts El Sahaby Limousine Car (✉ *Shar'a Luxor-Karnak, Luxor* ☎ *095/235–7980; 010/522–6582*).

Far & Beyond Travel (✉ *1 Shar'a Salah el-Din, Luxor* ☎ *095/228–7990; 010/888–7666*).

CARRIAGE TRAVEL

In Luxor, take a Nile-side ramble in a horse-drawn carriage, called a calèche. The entire 45-minute Corniche promenade sets you back around £E30 to £E50, depending on your bargaining skills. Agree on the price up front, before you get into the rig: "That's 30 Egyptian, not 30 dollars, not 30 euros, right? And that's 30 for the ride, not 30 for each person, right?" If you care about animal rights, refuse to do business with any driver whose horse doesn't look healthy.

TAXI TRAVEL

Luxor is rife with taxis, usually six-seater Peugeot station wagons, but prices are the highest in Egypt. You can travel the length of the Corniche for about £E20; shorter trips cost £E10. Although prices can fluctuate from driver to driver, check with the tourist office or at your hotel to find out what the fixed rates are to all destinations. Several hotels publish set prices for the taxis they use, and drivers know they must adhere to the terms. But even around town, everyone knows the going rates, especially the taxi drivers; still, it's a good idea to agree to a price before you set out, especially if you are picking up a taxi on the street away from a major hotel. Tipping just a couple of extra pounds depending on the length of the journey is customary.

If you decide to take a taxi to the West Bank, the ride plus up to four hours of touring and waiting time on the West Bank costs about £E40 to £E50 per hour.

TRAIN TRAVEL

One easy and relatively cheap way to get to Luxor from Cairo is on the overnight trains operated by Abela. A compartment is fairly reasonably priced and allows you to travel overnight, arriving in Luxor early the next morning.

Regular seats are cheaper, and a more inexpensive way still is the first-class section of a regular train. The lights are always on and the air-conditioning functions sporadically, but the first-class trains otherwise are comfortable enough—at least until you need a bathroom break: Come prepared with your own tissue, seat covers, hand sanitizer, closed-toe shoes, and a strong constitution. From Cairo to Luxor, a one-way ticket is £E90 in first class. At this writing, foreigners traveling by train from Cairo were all but forbidden to take second-class trains and could only buy first-class tickets for travel at night; by day, Egyptian commuters are the priority passengers. You can also take the train from Luxor to Aswan, day or night; fares are £E41 first class.

Comfortable sleeper cars run by private company Abela make the daily trip to Luxor from the cavernous Ramses Station in central Cairo. Buy tickets at least 10 days in advance at the Abela office in the station, or arrange for tickets through a local travel agent. At this writing, there are four trains daily, two heading south and two heading north. Train

84 leaves Cairo at 8 PM, reaching Luxor at 5:05 AM; Train 86 departs Cairo at 9:10 PM, arriving in Luxor at 6:10 AM. For the return trip, Train 85 departs Luxor at 9:40 PM, reaching Cairo at 6:45 AM; Train 87 leaves Luxor at 12:40 AM and arrives in Cairo at 9:30 AM. The cost (per journey) of a single couchette with dinner and breakfast is $80; a double with dinner and breakfast costs $60 per person. These fares must be paid in a foreign currency, not Egyptian pounds.

Contacts Abela (✉ *Ramses Train Station* ☎ *02/2574-9474* ⊕ *www. sleepingtrains.com*).

RESTAURANTS

Luxor is a busy tourist destination and has a wide range of restaurants; outside of Luxor, your choices are more limited, particularly in Al Minya. Alcohol is not served everywhere.

The variable city tax on restaurants, combined with service charges, can total as much as 26%. Check menus to verify how each restaurant operates. Unless you are in a major hotel, consider tipping even if a service charge is included in the bill: waiters are not well paid, and the courtesy will be appreciated. If service is not charged, 10% to 15% is a reasonable tip. As a rule, most hotel restaurants are open to the general public. Reservations are recommended at all hotel restaurants.

HOTELS

Remember that rates are less expensive in summer—late April to the end of September—though Luxor has less dramatic variations than Aswan since tourism is strong year-round.

Almost all hotels include breakfast in their rates, and some offer meal plans. Most hotels arrange transportation from airport to hotel if requested.

If you choose to stay at a place that doesn't have a pool, be aware that many hotels open their pools to nonguests for a small fee (around £E50). In Luxor, the splendid Club Med includes a beverage in its pool fee, the Sheraton is on a peninsula extending into the Nile, and the Hilton has a peaceful Nile-side garden and pool.

All hotel reviews have been condensed for this book. Please go to Fodors.com for full reviews of each property.

WHAT IT COSTS IN EGYPTIAN POUNDS, U.S. DOLLARS, AND EUROS			
$	**$$**	**$$$**	**$$$$**
Restaurants	under £E50	£E50–£E100	£E100–£E150	over £E150
Hotels in Dollars	under $70	$70–$130	$130–$200	over $200
Hotels in Euros	under €45	€45–€80	€80–€130	over €130

Restaurant prices are per person for a main course at dinner. Hotel prices are for a double room in high season, excluding 10% tax and service charges (usually 10%).

VISITOR INFORMATION

Open daily 8 AM to 8 PM, the tourist office in Luxor has a good range of information about opening times, taxi and felucca fares, and train timetables. And with four locations—one in the airport, one at Luxor Museum, one inside the train station, and the main office just across from the train station—an office is never very far away.

Contacts Luxor Tourist Information (✉ *Across the street from the train station* ☎ *095/237–3294*).

THE MIDDLE NILE VALLEY: AL MINYA TO TEL EL AMARNA

Middle Egypt has a slew of extremely interesting monuments dating from all periods of Egyptian history. The major sites in the area that are easily accessible are the Middle Kingdom tombs of Beni Hasan, the New Kingdom town site and tombs at Tel al Amarna, the Greco-Roman tombs and catacombs at Tuna al-Gebel, and the Greco-Roman remains of al-Ashmunayn. Beni Hasan, Tel el Amarna, and Tuna al-Gebel are the most worthwhile sites, though al-Ashmunayn is intriguing if you are interested in more Classical-style remains.

GETTING HERE AND AROUND

Although a few tour operators offer an Al Minya itinerary as a day trip from Cairo, you can expect such a trip to depart in the wee hours, make cursory visits to Tel el Amarna and Beni Hasan, and return to Cairo well after sunset—about a 16-hour day. Realistically, you need at least two full days, starting from Al Minya, to hit the major Middle Valley sites. Tel el Amarna is best done on its own. Beni Hasan and Tuna al-Gebel are easily combined if you rent a taxi for the day. You could also combine Tel el Amarna and Beni Hasan in a day if pressed for time. Take plenty of food and water with you, as, for the most part, there is none at the sites.

AL MINYA

260 km (160 mi) south of Cairo; 450 km (280 mi) north of Luxor.

The best place for a base in Middle Egypt is the city of Al Minya, untouristed until now. Its name has varied only slightly through the millennia, and always with an interesting story attached. At one time, it was called Minat Khufu, meaning "Favorite of Khufu" (he who built the Great Pyramid of Giza). In more recent centuries, it got the nickname of Minya al-Fuli because of a Yemeni bean-trader who liked the city so well he decided to make it his home (*fuul* is Egyptian for "beans"). The town returned the honor by erecting a mosque that bears the al-Fuli name. Nowadays Al Minya calls itself the Bride of Upper Egypt and has named Egyptian First Lady Suzanne Mubarak the Nefertiti of Minya, because her family hails from these parts.

The city has a different feel to it from others on the Nile, perhaps because it is located on the river's West Bank. Several pleasant parks and tea gardens line its Downtown waterfront. Across the river, though, on the East Bank, the town's future is under construction. Housing developments are going up. A new museum for the Pharaoh Akhenaton is nearing completion. An international airport is on the drawing board. And local tourism officials are hoping that security and navigation improvements will soon allow Nile cruise boats to come this way again.

ESSENTIALS

Visitor Information Al Minya Tourist Authority (☎ *010/129–9479*).

WHERE TO STAY

There's not much choice of accommodation in Al Minya, and none of the hotels can be classed as luxurious. Just expect a basic room and bathroom and a restaurant on-site that serves such Egyptian staples as roasted chicken or kebabs with bread and salad, *fuul* (fava beans stewed with tomatoes), *ta'amiya* (falafel), and *koshary* (a meal of rice, lentils, and pasta served with browned onions and tomato sauce).

All hotel reviews have been condensed for this book. Please go to Fodors.com for full reviews of each property.

$$ ⊞ **Etap Hotel.** Al Minya has pretty much kept the same name for four thousand years. But in less than a decade, this hotel has gone by Nefertiti, Nefertiti and Aton, back to just Nefertiti, and now Etap, though the owner's haven't changed the sign outside. **Pros:** some balconies have river views. **Cons:** depressing atmosphere in public areas, particularly at night. ⊠ *Corniche al-Nil, Al Minya* ☎ *086/234–1515* ⟳ *54 rooms* ⌂ *In-room: refrigerator, Internet. In-hotel: restaurant, bars, pool, laundry service, parking (free)* ⊟ *No credit cards* ⫯◯ᵔ *BP*.

$ ⊞ **Horus Resort.** There's nothing but a few yards of landscaped plaza between you and the banks of the Nile at Al Minya's sorely needed newest hotel. **Pros:** at this writing, its Al Minya's best hotel; located right on the Nile. **Cons:** service is hit-and-miss; polished stone walkways are so slick as to be dangerous. ⊠ *Corniche al-Nil, Al Minya* ☎ *086/231–6660* ⊕ *www.horusresortmenia.com* ⟳ *57 rooms, 5 suites* ⌂ *In-room: refrigerator, Wi-Fi. In-hotel: 2 restaurants, room service, bars, pool, spa, laundry service* ⊟ *MC, V* ⫯◯ᵔ *BP*.

BENI HASAN

25 km (15 mi) south of Al Minya.

This magnificent cemetery site is on the East Bank of the Nile. Beni Hasan is generally approached from the West Bank by ferry, which shows the site to its best advantage: a narrow, vibrant strip of green bordering the river that suddenly ends in dramatically sloping limestone cliffs that stand out starkly against an intense blue sky. Tombs (39) of local rulers that date to the Middle Kingdom (c. 2040–1640 BC) pierce the cliffs. Generally only four or five are open to visitors at any time.

On the climb up the stairs, you pass shaft tombs (closed) for the less important people. The tombs of the wealthy and more important folk are in the upper portions of the cliff. There are three basic tomb types on the cliff, aside from the shaft tombs. The first has a plain facade and is single-chambered (11th Dynasty); the second (11th and 12th Dynasties) is plain on the outside, but its chamber is columned; and the third type (12th Dynasty) has a portico in front and a columned chamber.

You can never be sure of which tombs will be open, but the ones listed here usually are accessible. The lighting in the tombs varies greatly, so bring a flashlight. A café at the base of the cliff offers cold drinks, but you should bring your own packed lunch.

Tomb of Amenemhat (No. 2), 12th Dynasty. Not only was the tomb owner a nomarch, or governor, but he also was the military commander in chief of the area. This tomb has some entertaining scenes of musicians, knife makers, and leather workers, in addition to the usual daily-life scenes.

Tomb of Bakht III (No. 15), 11th Dynasty. Built for a governor of the Oryx Nome, this tomb contains seven shafts, which suggests that members of his family were buried with him. The wall paintings show hunting in the marshes and desert, weavers, counting livestock, potters, metalworkers, wrestlers, and offerings bearers. The desert hunt scenes are particularly interesting because they show some very bizarre mythological animals.

Tomb of Kheti (No. 17), 11th Dynasty. Kheti was the governor of the Oryx Nome. Scenes on the walls show hunting, offerings, daily activities, and the wrestlers that are typical of Beni Hasan. An attack on a fortress is also depicted.

Tomb of Khnumhotep (No. 3), 12th Dynasty. This large tomb, entered between two proto-Doric columns, belonged to Khnumhotep, a governor of the Oryx Nome as well as a prince. It is famous for its hunt scenes and depictions of foreign visitors to Egypt. Carved in the back wall is a statue of the deceased, and the color of the paintings is much better preserved in this tomb than in any of the others. ⊠ *Beni Hasan* ☏ *086/922–8362* ✆ *£E30* ☾ *Daily 7–5.*

GETTING HERE AND AROUND

Take a taxi from Al Minya to the ferry (be sure to agree on taxi fare before setting out); you may be assigned an armed security officer for the trip. This is a routine security procedure for travelers in this part of Egypt. If you are traveling as part of a prebooked tour, your guide or tour company will make any necessary arrangements. Then cross the Nile to the site. From the ferry landing proceed by microbus (note that service is erratic) or walk (a 10-minute walk at a slow pace) to the base of the cliffs and the ticket booth. From here it is a stiff climb up modern concrete stairs to the top of the cliff and the tombs. (Have your taxi wait while you visit the site and then take you on to other sites in the area.)

TEL EL AMARNA

40 km (25 mi) south of Beni Hasan.

Little remains of the magnificent town of Akhetaten, which was founded by the apparently monotheist pharaoh Akhenaton in the late 18th Dynasty. Akhetaten was quite an impressive city, with a population of 10,000 in its short heyday, but it has almost completely vanished. Indeed, it is hard to imagine this large expanse of barren desert as a bustling town busy with government workers, commerce, and artisans. The few visible remains include the foundations of the North Palace and the Small Aten Temple with its single restored pillar.

The northern tombs are more easily visited than their southern counterparts and are quite interesting, although somewhat ruined. Not all the tombs are open, but they are all relatively similar in design and decoration. Most of the tombs consist of an outer court, a long hall and a broad hall, sometimes columned, and a statue niche. The tombs are decorated in the typical "Amarna" style, with depictions of the town and architecture and scenes of the pharaoh and his family rather than the tomb's owner. (The tomb owner generally is shown only in the doorway, hands raised in praise of Aten.) People tend to be shown with sharp chins, slightly distended bellies, and large hips and thighs. Some tombs show evidence of being reused in the Coptic period, so watch for crosses, niches, and fonts (Tomb 6, for example). ⊠ *Tel el Amarna* ☎ *086/922–8362* ▩ *£E30* ☉ *Daily 8–5.*

GETTING HERE AND AROUND

To get here, hire a taxi and either cross the river at Al Minya and take the desert road to the site (not always easy), or drive down to Deir Mawass and cross over by ferry, which is the more traditional way to go. At the ferry, you can hire a hardy vehicle (a tractor or pickup) to get around the site, as walking would take all day. On the East Bank, purchase tickets for the site and pay for the vehicle. You may be assigned an armed security officer at the nearest police checkpoint to Al Minya, and this officer may accompany you to the site. This is a routine security procedure for travelers in this part of Egypt. If you are traveling as part of a prebooked tour, your guide or tour company will liaise with the police and make arrangements for your trip.

AL-ASHMUNAYN (HERMOPOLIS)

30 km (19 mi) south of Al Minya.

The site features a late-Roman basilica, the only surviving large building of its kind in Egypt, as well as a giant statue (one of a pair) of the god Thoth in the guise of a baboon. A large New Kingdom temple to Thoth, god of Ashmunayn, used to stand at the site but is pretty much invisible today. ☎ *No phone* ▩ *Free* ☉ *Daily 8–5.*

TUNA AL-GEBEL

10 km (6 mi) southwest of al-Ashmunayn.

Tuna al-Gebel was the necropolis of Hermopolis—a large and scattered site, its focal point being a cluster of Greco-Roman tombs. These tombs, built literally as houses for the dead, show an entertaining blending of Classical and Egyptian styles of art. The **Tomb of Petosiris** is one of the best preserved and is open to the public.

The **mummy of Isadora,** a woman drowned in the Nile in the second century AD, is on display in a nearby building; be sure to tip the guard. The other major attraction of the site is the elaborate **catacombs** containing burials of ibis and baboons, animals sacred to the god Thoth.

These date to the late Persian and Greco-Roman periods, and you can see some animal burials in situ. An embalming workshop is also visible at the entrance. Approaching the site, you can see on the right side, cut into the cliffs, the best surviving stela (now protected by glass) erected by Akhenaton; this one was to mark the western boundary of his capital, Akhetaten. ☎ 086/248–0556 🖃 £E20 ☉ Daily 8–5.

GETTING HERE AND AROUND

Al-Ashmunayn and Tuna al-Gebel are visited together because of their proximity. If you've only got one day in the area, save this duo for an afternoon stop, which can follow a morning at either Beni Hasan or Tell el Amarna. Otherwise, you can visit these sites on their own by hiring a taxi in Al Minya and heading due south; both monuments are on the West Bank. As with other overland excursions, you may be assigned an armed security officer at the nearest police checkpoint to Al Minya, and this officer may accompany you to the site. This is a routine security procedure for travelers in this part of Egypt. If you are traveling as part of a pre-booked tour, your guide or tour company will make the police arrangements for your trip.

THE UPPER NILE VALLEY: ABYDOS TO LUXOR

Traveling along the Nile takes you through both space and time. Ancient Egyptian civilization as we know it came alive around 3100 BC, when Narmer united Lower and Upper Egypt, and breathed its last breath in the 4th century AD during the simultaneous rise of Christianity and collapse of both paganism and the Roman empire. The monuments you see are the accretions of centuries of dynastic power, ritual practice, artistic expression, and foreign interference that continually adapted and renewed an inspiring system of beliefs.

You don't need to know any of this to appreciate the beauty and refinement of the paintings in Seti I's temple at Abydos or the majesty of the temples at Karnak. Just consider the high level of societal organization that it took to conceive and create what the ancient Egyptians left behind. Looking back at their civilization from the third millennium of the Christian era, we are gazing eye to eye with our equals in ambition, achievement, and, in many ways, technology.

ABYDOS

150 km (93 mi) north of Luxor.

The East Bank drive from Luxor to Abydos takes you north along the canals and farm roads that form the backbone of rural life in Upper Egypt. Sugarcane fields and vegetable plots bordered by date palms appear all the greener against the ochre of imposing eastern cliffs. Oxen, turbaned men, and the occasional tractor work the fields. Donkeys pull carts overburdened with the morning's harvest or speed their gait for impatient riders. Children and goats dodge tuk-tuks in the lanes of mud-brick villages. After the route crosses the Nile to the West Bank, the road winds through neighborhoods where bulls help themselves to the shade of porches and doorways. At the end of the trip, the temple

The Amarna Era

Akhenaton turned ancient Egypt upside down. When he came to the throne around 1353 BC, he took the name Amenhotep IV, but in the fifth year of his reign he underwent an epiphany. He declared that all the Egyptian gods—including Amun—were to be usurped by Aten (a minor God once worshipped in the Old Kingdom era), represented by a sun disk with rays emanating from it and an ankh symbol depicting the gift of life. The reason for this major religious change is unclear. The pharaoh was the only person allowed to have close contact with the god, a regulation that highlighted the pharaoh's divinity and reduced the power of the priesthood. Akhenaton moved the royal residence and capital of Egypt to the brand-new city Tel el Amarna (Akhetaten), thus effectively crippling the towns of Memphis and Thebes and putting distance between the seat of power and the priests at Karnak.

Ahkenaton revolutionized art in this era by introducing the so-called real style—with scenes of the royal family in very relaxed poses with the pharaoh kissing his children and sharing affection. Statues and carvings show the pharaoh as a long-skulled, long-chinned individual with an androgenous body form—wide hips, drooping belly, protruding breasts, and long fingers. Modern scientists have theorized that Ahkenaton suffered from Marfan syndrome (a genetic disorder of the connective tissue), but Dr. Zahi Hawass, head of Egyptian antiquities, put that speculation to rest in February 2010. Extensive DNA testing conducted to identify Tutankhamun's family showed that a previously unidentified—and perfectly normal—mummy from Tomb KV 55 in the

Valley of the Kings is most likely that of Akhenaton, and that Akhenaton was Tut's father. As initial evidence showed no genetic disorders that would explain the unusual depictions of the "heretic" king's face and body, Dr. Hawass concluded that Akhenaton may have chosen the distinctive artistic style for religious or political reasons.

As pharaoh, Ahkenaton had little concern for the well-being of his lands. Sensing weakness, Egypt's neighbors raided the borders, taking territory and instilling fear in the Egyptian people. Ahkenaton reigned for 18 years, and immediately upon his death the priests of Amun moved to reinstate Thebes and its temple to Amun as the true heart of Egypt. In addition, they systematically wiped Ahkenaton's reign from the history books. His capital was destroyed, and not only Akhenaton but also his successors, Smenkhkare, Tutankhamun, and Ay, were excised from the official records (this is one of the reasons the Tomb of Tutankhamun lay untouched throughout history, because there was so little evidence of his rule).

It wasn't until the 19th century that archaeologists began to piece together this missing segment in the Egyptian timeline, though many details are mysteries that still await answers. The last of the Amarna bloodline, Tutankhamun was christened Tutankhaten. His change of name indicates a final victory of Amun over Aten and a return to the old ways for the people of Egypt.

appears rather surprisingly amid a cluster of houses and shops, the desert stretching out behind them. In other words, Abydos is far enough off the beaten track to offer a break from whatever crowds there might be farther upriver.

Abydos was one of the most sacred sites in ancient Egypt, because it was the supposed burial place of Osiris, god of the netherworld. As a result, the most significant constructions here are named for or dedicated to Osiris, which can lead to some confusion. To simplify matters, it's easier to identify the largest temple here—the one of most interest to tourists—as the Temple of Seti I; and to identify a second and smaller temple as the Temple of Ramses II. A third and separate structure, believed to be the Tomb of Osiris, is called the Osireion.

The archeological complex here covers a large area and includes several temples, tombs, and sacred animal burials dating from the predynastic period onward. Now the only parts of the site accessible to visitors are the Temple of Seti I (19th Dynasty, 1290–1279 BC) and the one erected by his son, the Temple of Ramses II. At many times of the year, the roofless Osireion can only be viewed from above—it is below ground level—because rising ground water causes it to be submerged to one degree or another.

GETTING THERE AND AROUND

The drive up from Luxor takes about two hours and requires permission (at least 24 hours in advance) from the tourist police. You can arrange ahead of time for a private car and driver to ensure you have the most control over the time you'll spend at the sight, or you can join an organized tour through your hotel or one of several Luxor tour operators. Either way, the car company or the tour operator will obtain the police permit for you. If you have time, you can add a stop at Dendera on your return to Luxor.

Fodor's Choice
★

Temple of Seti I. This low-lying temple (1306–1290 BC), modestly stretching across the desert nestled amid a group of shops and houses, is one of the jewels of ancient Egypt. It is filled with exquisitely carved and colored reliefs that delight the eye and stir the soul. Seti I had initiated construction of the temple complex but died before its completion, which left Ramses II to finish it.

After passing the ticket booth, walk up to the ruined first pylon, which leads into the almost completely destroyed first courtyard built by Ramses II. This first court contains two wells, and only the lower level of the court's enclosure wall survives. These remaining walls are decorated with scenes of Ramses killing the enemies of Egypt and making offerings to the gods. A ramp leads to the second court, which is similarly decorated. Beyond this are a portico and the entrance to the temple proper. The portico is carved and painted with scenes of Ramses II making offerings to the gods and being granted a very long and prosperous reign in exchange.

From the portico, enter the **first hypostyle hall,** which was begun by Seti I and completed by Ramses II. (A hypostyle hall is one in which interior columns support a roof; in most temples the ancient roofs caved in long ago, but the ceiling is intact here.) The hall consists of 12 pairs

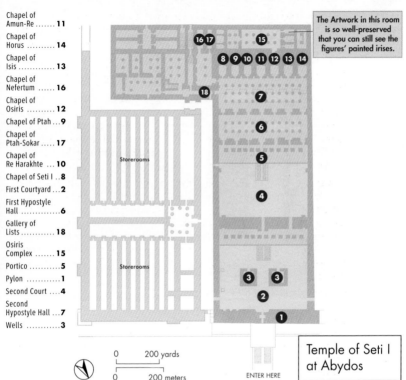

The Artwork in this room is so well-preserved that you can still see the figures' painted irises.

0   200 yards

0   200 meters

ENTER HERE

Temple of Seti I
at Abydos

of papyrus-style columns aligned to create seven aisles that lead to seven chapels set in the back wall of the second hypostyle hall. The walls are decorated with scenes showing the pharaoh offering to Amun-Ra (the sun god), preparing and dedicating the temple building and making offerings to Thoth (god of writing and knowledge).

The next room, the **second hypostyle hall,** was built and decorated—with its decoration scheme *almost* completed—by Seti I. The exquisite quality of the relief carvings here stands in stark contrast to the cruder work commissioned by Ramses II. Scenes include dedicatory texts of Seti I and show the pharaoh making offerings before various gods and receiving their blessings. A continuous row of fertility figures with *nome* (provinces of ancient Egypt) standards above their heads runs along below the main scenes.

The seven **chapels** off the rear wall are dedicated to various deities and are a rare feature in Egyptian temples. From left to right (east to west), they are dedicated to Seti I, Ptah (a creator god), Ra Harakhte, Amun-Ra, Osiris, Isis (goddess of magic), and Horus (the god associated with kingship). Each chapel is decorated with scenes showing the daily temple ritual, which involved offerings, libations, and censing. The Osiris chapel leads to the Osiris complex, which has depictions of Seti making offerings of wine, bread, incense, vases, and so forth to various

The Temple of Seti I

deities. The last rooms in the Osiris complex are mostly reconstructed. This is where the mysteries of Osiris were performed; their exact nature remains, of course, mysterious—in other words to modern scholarship.

Beyond the chapels, to the east, is a **hall** with two back rooms dedicated to Nefertum and Ptah-Sokar. The one on the right (west) is remarkable for its scenes showing the conception of Horus: as the story goes, Seth (who became the god of storms and deserts) had his brother Osiris, the king, killed and chopped up into pieces. Isis, Osiris's wife and a great magician, traveled throughout Egypt gathering the bits of her husband to remake him with magic. She found and reconstructed all of him, save his genitalia. These she fashioned out of mud, stuck them onto him, made them viable with magic, and, changing herself into a kite (a small hawk)—no one is absolutely certain why this bird is her animal counterpart—placed herself on his member and thus conceived Horus (who is often portrayed with the head of a falcon). Later, Horus avenged his father's death and became king, and Osiris became king of the netherworld. (Seth was exiled to distant places.)

The **Gallery of Lists** leads left from the portico before the seven chapels out to the Osireion. On its walls is a list of gods and kings that is one of the cornerstones of Egyptian history. This king list notes the divine and semidivine (i.e., pharaonic) Egyptian rulers in the order of their reigns. The list, though incomplete, has been of great importance in helping to retrace the chronology of the pharaohs. Other rooms (a sacrificial butchery court, a hall of ritual barques, or ships), all of which are closed, lead off this passage. Another corridor, known as the corridor of the bulls, was named for a scene showing Ramses II and one

ABYDOS TEMPLE TOURING TIPS

■ You really need to see this place. Imagine the grandeur of Karnak's hypostyle hall combined with the tomb colors found in the Valley of the Kings, and all under one roof. Add another day to your trip and make this an outing from Luxor. You won't be sorry.

■ If you have control of your schedule, concentrate your time on the Temple of Seti I. Set aside some alone time here to appreciate its mysterious appeal.

■ Go to the innermost part of the Temple of Seti I, all the way straight back to an area called the Osiris Complex. As you enter this chamber, look to your right and you'll see three smaller rooms. Be sure to enter the last, the farthest right, of these three. There, the paintings are so well preserved that you can still see the irises on the eyes of gods and kings.

■ The Osireion is a separate structure outside and behind the Temple of Seti I. Don't be disappointed if the Osireion is half-filled with water and is, therefore, inaccessible. The theory is that the ancients deliberately designed it to breach the water table; it's just that these days, the water table is a lot higher at many times of the year than it was in ancient times.

■ On the drive through the village to reach the temple, pay attention to the bovine population; cattle are indulged here. Inside the temple, find the scene of a young Ramses II roping a bull. Make the connection.

of his sons lassoing a bull before a god. A curious boat associated with Sokar, a god of the dead, is also carved on the wall.

Directly behind the Temple of Seti I lies the **Osireion.** Built of sandstone and granite, the monument was considered to be the Tomb of Osiris. The architectural style and massive quality of the building is reminiscent of Old Kingdom (2625–2134 BC) construction, and it was rebuilt during the reign of Seti I, who left the only decoration. The Osireion includes built-in pools of different shapes—an unusual feature—that might represent the primeval chaotic ocean of Nun. Most of the chambers off the central room are inaccessible because they are filled with water (a little poetic irony). At the far end of the central room is a transversal chamber, its ceiling adorned with a representation of the god Shu upholding the goddess Mut, the nocturnal journey of the sun, and a list of the constellations.

South of the Osireion is an extension, the **long passage,** added by Merneptah, Ramses II's successor. This is decorated with scenes from various books, such as the *Book of Gates,* the *Book of Caverns,* and the *Book of What Is in the Underworld,* containing spells to ensure a safe passage to the afterworld. ⊠ *Mabed Seti* ☎ *No phone* ⊴ *£E35 (includes Temple of Ramses II)* ⊙ *Daily 6 AM–5 PM.*

Temple of Ramses II. Some 300 yards northwest of the Seti I temple lies the Temple of Ramses II (1290–1224 BC). Its roof and most of the upper portions of its walls are missing, but enough of it remains to give you a feeling for its layout and decoration. What is left of the decoration

Seti I

Son of Ramses I, founder of the 19th Dynasty, Seti's main role during his rule (c. 1290 BC–1279 BC or c. 1294 BC–1279 BC) was to build up the cult of Amun and expunge the last memories of the Amarna era (i.e., the rule of Akhenaton and his successors), and also to strengthen the borders of an Egypt that was seen as vulnerable by its neighbors during the reign of Akhenaton. Seti opened a new quarry in Aswan and commissioned several monuments to aggrandize existing temples. He also started work at Abydos.

Militarily, Seti had several confrontations with the Hittites, the main threat to his empire, and regained lands lost under Akhenaton rule. He sent forces to Nubia and Libya, and his forces marched up the "Ways of Horus," the road that ran along the Mediterranean coast to what is now the Gaza Strip, pushing the Hittites back north. Seti's tomb is the longest in the Valley of the Kings, and his mummy rests in the Cairo Museum.

---

shows that this temple—unlike the inferior work that Ramses commissioned to complete Seti I's temple—is close in style and quality to what was done during the reign of Seti I. And the vibrant reds, yellows, and bright green here are a joy to behold.

The first pylon and court are no longer in existence; instead, the entrance is through the semipreserved second pylon, which leads to a court surrounded by pillars decorated with the figure of Ramses in an Osirid pose (as a mummy with arms crossed in front of his breast). The walls are carved and painted with scenes of Ramses making offerings to various deities, animals being taken for sacrifice, and prisoners of war.

From the court, walk up to the portico leading to two hypostyle halls with chapels off of them. Scenes of captives, religious processions, and offerings made by the king to the various gods adorn the walls. ⊠ *Mabed Seti* ☎ *No phone* 🖂 *£E35 (includes Temple of Seti I)* ☉ *Daily 6 AM–5 PM.*

DENDERA

65 km (40 mi) north of Luxor.

The prime point of interest in Dendera, a small village north of Luxor, is the Temple of Hathor. The countryside along the way is pleasantly green, and the ride provides an agreeable view of rural life in Egypt. The site of Dendera was occupied at least from the Old Kingdom onward, but it is the remains of the Late Period and Greco-Roman structures that are of interest here. The site includes the main temple, two *mammisis* (gods' birth houses), a Coptic church, a sanatorium, the remains of a sacred lake, and a small temple to Isis, as well as some other less visible monuments.

GETTING HERE AND AROUND

Dendera is an easy day trip from Luxor and can be combined with Abydos to make a full-day excursion. You can book a private taxi, sign up for a local motor coach tour, or join a day cruise with Dendera as its only destination.

Temple of Hathor. Hathor of Dendera was the goddess of love, beauty, music, and birth. She was often depicted as a cow, and in later periods of Egyptian history was synchronized with Isis. She was married to Horus of Edfu, and the two temples celebrated an annual festival, lasting about two weeks, when the statue of Hathor would sail upriver to Edfu to commemorate the divine marriage. This temple was built between the 4th century BC and 1st century AD.

As you enter the temple grounds through stone portals, there is a dramatic view of the temple facade fronted by a row of Hathor-head columns (their capitals carved with reliefs of the face of the goddess) and a decorated screen wall. The exterior of the temple is carved in relief with scenes of the pharaoh and divinities being suckled by goddesses and of the pharaoh making offerings to various gods.

The portal leads into the **outer hypostyle hall,** which consists of 24 tall columns (including the facade columns), all with Hathor-head capitals. The ceiling is carved and painted with a depiction of the night sky. The columns themselves are densely decorated with scenes of the pharaoh making offerings to the gods and receiving their blessings in return. This very crowded, *horror vacui* (fear of blank spaces) decoration is typical of the Greco-Roman period.

The next room is the **inner hypostyle hall,** with its six columns. Six small rooms open off this hall. These rooms are decorated with different scenes that supposedly illustrate what went on in them, or, more likely, what was stored in them. The first room on the left is the most interesting. Known as the **laboratory,** it is where ritual perfumes and essences were prepared. The other rooms include a **harvest room,** the **room of libations,** and the **treasury,** which is illustrated with carvings of jewelry and boxes containing precious metals.

The hall leads to the **first vestibule,** where many of the daily offerings to Hathor would have been placed. Gifts included all kinds of food and drink: breads, fresh vegetables, joints of meat and poultry, beer, and wine.

The **second vestibule** follows the first as a transitional area between the sanctuary and the rest of the temple. The **sanctuary** was the most sacred spot in the temple and in antiquity would have had an altar and a plinth supporting a *naos* (shrine) containing the sacred image of the goddess, probably either gilded or made entirely of gold. A corridor surrounds the sanctuary, and several chapels are off it. The best chapel is the one immediately behind the sanctuary, because it contains a raised shrine that is reached by a ladder.

Dendera also has at least 32 **crypts** built into the walls and under the floor of the temple—hiding places for temple plates, jewelry, and statues. Some of the wall crypts would have permitted priests to hide behind different images of the gods and act as oracles. One of these, behind

DENDERA TEMPLE TOURING TIPS

■ **Start with a picnic.** The landscaped grounds by the visitor center have large arbors with built-in benches shaded by bougainvilleas.

■ **Take it slow.** As you approach the entrance, notice the massive perimeter of mud brick enclosing the entire temple complex. It's every bit as old as the stone monuments it guards, and in some places it has better stood the test of time.

■ **Check out the sacred lake.** As you face the Temple of Hathor, make a detour off to the right, toward a thick grouping of trees. As you come closer, you'll see that the trees are growing from what used to be the sacred lake; only sand fills its bottom now. In each of the corners, you'll notice a staircase leading down. The interesting thing is that this very design has been produced in miniature replicas and can be found in museums. A fine example, about the size of a toaster, is on display at the Aswan Museum.

■ **Look up.** As you go inside the Temple of Hathor, stand still and look up at that gorgeous blue ceiling held in place by all those columns topped with Hathor-head capitals. Be sure to stand still while looking up (and look down when you walk—those uneven temple floors can trip you).

■ **Visit Cleopatra.** Don't leave before going out and around back to see Cleopatra and Caesarion, her son by Julius Caesar, etched into the walls.

and to the right of the sanctuary, is open to the public. It is beautifully carved with scenes showing divinities. Look for the exquisite relief showing the god Horus in his falcon form.

On the right side of the temple's ground floor is another small and beautifully carved **chapel,** called Wabet (the pure one). The ceiling shows the sky goddess, Nut, swallowing the sun and giving birth to it the next day, with Hathor emerging from the horizon.

The stairways that lead from both sides of the First Vestibule to the roof are carved with priestly processions wending their way up the sides. There are three chapels on the roof. The open chapel with Hathor-head columns was used for solar rituals; the two closed chapels were used for the cult of Osiris. The eastern one of these, on the right as you face the temple, contains the cast of a famous zodiac ceiling—the most complete early zodiac, the original of which is in the Louvre in Paris. A metal staircase leads to the highest part of the roof, which offers a wonderful panorama of the temple precincts and the surrounding landscape. Note the sacred-lake enclosure (now dry) on the west side of the temple.

The **temple exterior** is decorated with scenes of pharaohs and gods. The rear wall is particularly interesting, because it shows Queen Cleopatra VII—yes, the famous one, who was involved with Julius Caesar and Mark Antony and was Egypt's last pharaoh—presenting her son Caesarion to the gods as the next ruler of Egypt.

In the context of ancient Egyptian temples, mammisi (birth house) depict the birth of a god and are often concerned with the divinity of the king. The mammisi on the right side of the Temple of Hathor entrance

Temple of Hathor

is of the Roman period (built mainly by Trajan, who ruled from AD 98 to 117). It celebrates the birth of the god Ihi, son of Horus and Isis, as well as the divinity of the pharaoh. Ascend a short flight of stairs into a court; beyond it lies another courtyard with columns at the side. Two rooms then lead to the mammisi's **sanctuary,** which is illustrated with scenes of the divine birth and the suckling of the divine child by various divinities. The sanctuary is surrounded by an ambulatory, the outer portion of which is partially decorated.

Next to the Roman mammisi at the entrance to the Temple of Hathor lies a **Christian basilica** that probably dates from the 5th century AD, making it one of the earliest intact Coptic buildings in Egypt. There is no roof, but the trefoil apse and basilical hall and several shell niches are still visible.

Next to the Coptic basilica are the ruins of an earlier mammisi—founded by Nectanebo I (381–362 BC). Its decorative scheme is similar to that of the later, more intact mammisi.

Next in line stand the mud-brick remains of the temple's **sanatorium,** consisting of several small rooms and bathing areas for pilgrims. The pilgrims came to be healed by what today would be called dream therapy. They would sleep in the temple precincts and have dreams in which the gods came to them and cured them or told them what to do to be cured. The sanatorium contained several bathing areas lined with stones that were carved with spells and incantations. The water would run over the stones, taking the magic of the texts with it, and into the baths where pilgrims sat and received the magical waters' cures.

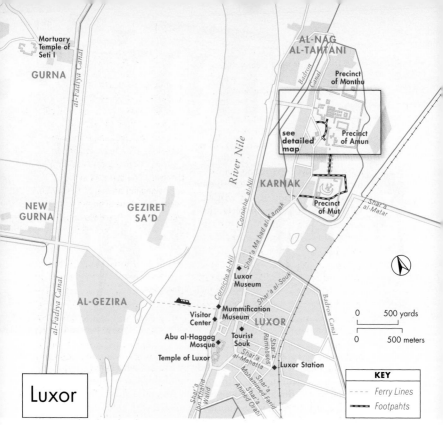

Luxor

Behind the main temple is a small **Temple of Isis,** which has a strange, dual orientation: east–west as well as north–south. It contains scenes of Isis's divine birth and consists of a court, a small hypostyle hall, another columned hall, two chapels, and the sanctuary. Here, as in the main temple, the pious Copts methodically defaced a number of the images of the ancient Egyptian gods. ⊠ *Mabed Dendera* 🕾 *No phone* 💷 *£E35* ⊘ *Daily 6 AM–5 PM.*

LUXOR

670 km (415 mi) south of Cairo; 210 km (130 mi) north of Aswan.

Known in antiquity as Thebes, Luxor takes its name from the Arabic al-Uqsur (the palaces). It is a town that merits both poetry and a grain of pragmatism. One of the world's most popular destinations, Luxor lives (or dies) from tourism. But if a well-worn path has been trod to every sight you see, Luxor's universal value in terms of art, natural beauty, and historic monuments is undeniable.

In December 2009, Luxor became its own governorate—it had been part of Qena Governorate—and has launched sweeping renovation and relocation projects that already are transforming the city proper, as well as its West Bank. Luxor's ambition is to be the world's largest outdoor museum. To that end, the slums that crowded Luxor and Karnak temples have been razed to make way for vast plazas, giving the antiquities some breathing room and Egyptian families a new place for evening picnics—not to mention space enough to receive more travelers. The famed Avenue of the Sphinxes, most of which lay buried for centuries beneath the modern town, is under excavation at this writing. When that project is complete, this 2.7-km-long (1.7-mi-long) processional way will again reunite Luxor and Karnak temples. Along the

DID YOU KNOW?

In ancient Egypt, settlements tended to be built on the East Bank of the Nile while tombs were located on the West Bank. This is because the sun rises, or is born, in the east. The sun gives life, so the east became associated with the living. The sun sets in the west signaling an end to the sun's energy, which became associated with death, so Egyptians buried their dead on the West Bank.

city's riverfront drive, the Corniche, shabby hotels, storefronts, and even some side streets are being demolished to make way for new ones. In fact, there's talk—Egyptians are not above a little friendly speculation—that the Corniche itself, now a good two stories above the river, will be lowered somehow or other, though they're hard pressed to say why. On the West Bank, the village of Abd el-Gurna has been scraped, in its entirety, from the Theban foothills, the better to protect the Tombs of the Nobles in that area. Many other changes are on the way, and judging by those that have taken place already, it's safe to say they will come quickly.

What won't change, can never change, is the spellbinding presence of Luxor itself.

Sunset in Luxor has a transcendent beauty. As the red orb returns to the Western Lands, setting the landscape ablaze, consider that this civilization was already ancient in antiquity. Egyptians who witnessed the erection of Karnak, for example, knew even then that the pyramids were at least 2,000 years old.

GETTING HERE AND AROUND

Luxor is the main airport for Upper Egypt and has frequent daily international flights from Europe as well as domestic flights to and from Cairo, Alexandria, Sharm El-Sheikh, and Aswan. It's also one of the endpoints for most Nile cruises (Aswan is the other). Luxor is also connected to Cairo by overnight train service.

ESSENTIALS
INTERNET

Much of Luxor is a Wi-Fi hotspot; for 7 km (4.3 mi) along the Nile, you can log on at the Karnak Temples, the Luxor Museum, or anyplace else where there's a concentration of hotels, cruise boats, and cafés. Buy scratch-off cards (£E50–£E150) from shops in any area that's "hot." Some independent businesses also offer Wi-Fi. Most major hotels offer some form of Internet connection, though not all have connectivity in the rooms. Internet cafés are around, too. One of the least expensive (£E10 per hour) is in the main Luxor Tourist Information Office, which has relocated across from the city's main train station.

EXPLORING LUXOR

On the East Bank of the Nile, the modern town thrives among the temples to the living. Across the river, the western Theban hills, with their tomb and temple openings gaping black in the beige stone, are dedicated to the dead. They are a constant presence in Luxor, as are the clip-clop and jangle of horse-drawn calèches and the twittering of birds. Along the tree-lined Corniche, clusters of tall felucca masts hem the shore, and the boat captains approach and ask: "Other side?" When you cross the Nile to the West Bank you enter another world, where beyond the narrow strip of lush farmland lie the Valley of the Kings and Valley of the Queens—awesome rock-hewn demonstrations of political muscle.

★ **Karnak Temples.** Karnak is, without a doubt, the most complex and impressive assemblage of ancient Egyptian religious monuments. The site is divided into three major precincts, dedicated respectively to the divinities Amun-Ra (the central complex), Mut (south of the central complex), and Montu (north). Inside the temple precinct, as in the Temple of Luxor, the Theban Triad of Amun-Ra, Mut, and Khonsu were the deities worshiped. The enclosure also includes smaller sanctuaries dedicated to Khonsu, Ptah, and Opet. The various temples were continuously enlarged and restored from at least the time of the Middle Kingdom down to the Roman period. We owe the most immense and enduring structures to the pharaohs of the New Kingdom.

The 660-yard-long **main axis** of Karnak proceeds from west to east, oriented toward the Nile. Another axis extends south toward Luxor from the midpoint of the main axis.

An **avenue of ram-headed sphinxes,** protecting statuettes of Pinudjem I between their front legs, opens the way to the entrance of the **first pylon.** This pylon was left unfinished by the kings of the 30th Dynasty. It is the most recent of all the pylons of Karnak, as well as being the most monumental on-site. Against the pylon, on the right side of Karnak's first **forecourt,** are the remains of ancient mud-brick scaffolding, used for the erection of the pylon. In the center of the court, a single open-papyrus column remains of what once was the 10-columned kiosk of Taharqa (690–664 BC), an Ethiopian pharaoh of the 25th Dynasty.

The small temple on the left side of the forecourt entrance is the **Shrine of Seti II** (19th Dynasty), some 1,000 years older than the first pylon. Seti II built this building, with its three small chapels, to receive the sacred barques of the Theban Triad (Amun-Ra in the center, Mut on the left, and Khonsu on the right) during the Opet processions. The barques are depicted on the walls of each chapel.

In the southeast portion of the forecourt, the **Temple of Ramses III** (20th Dynasty) is fronted by two colossi representing the king. It has the same structure as most New Kingdom temples: a pylon, a court with 20 Osirid statues of the king (Ramses III in the form of Osiris), and a hypostyle hall. Like others, the sanctuary is divided into three parts for the cult of the Theban Triad.

Next along the compound's main axis, the **second pylon** was built during the reign of Horemheb (18th Dynasty). Most of the pylon was filled with blocks dismantled from buildings of the heretic pharaoh Akhenaton.

The second pylon opens onto the **hypostyle hall.** Before you plunge into this fantastical court, the statue of Amun-Ra, in the company of a king, is on the left. Then wander into what seems like a stone forest—with its breathtaking 134 columns. Not only are the dimensions gigantic, but the colors and hieroglyphs are remarkable. The 12 columns alongside the processional way have open-papyrus capitals, while the remaining 122 columns have papyrus-bud capitals and are smaller. New Kingdom pharaohs built the elaborate hall: Ramses I began the decoration in the 19th Dynasty; Ramses III completed it some 120 years later in the 20th Dynasty.

Amenhotep III (18th Dynasty) constructed the **third pylon,** which leads to the **Obelisk of Thutmose I** (18th Dynasty), inside the **Court of Amenhotep III.**

The **fourth pylon,** erected by Thutmose I, gives access to the colonnade of Thutmose I, where an **Obelisk of Hatshepsut** (18th Dynasty), one of two, still stands. The lower part of the obelisk is well preserved because Thutmose III, Hatshepsut's successor, encased it with a brick wall—probably not to preserve it, however, because in other places he usurped her monuments and tried to erase her name from history. Perhaps the intention here was to mask its presence within the temple proper.

Pass through the fifth and sixth pylons. In the vestibule that follows, look for the two **Pillars of Thutmose III,** before the sanctuary, representing the union of Egypt. The papyrus (left) signifies Lower Egypt, and the lotus (right) represents Upper Egypt. There is also an elegant statue of the gods Amun-Ra and Amunet, carved during the reign of Tutankhamun. Philip III Arrhidaeus, brother and successor of Alexander the Great, built the **sanctuary of the sacred barques,** behind the vestibule. It is made of red granite.

At the end of the main axis rises, transversely, the **Festival Hall of Thutmose III,** also called the Akhmenu. This unusual building was erected to commemorate the king's military campaigns in Asia. The columns are exceptional—massive representations of tent poles used during those campaigns. On the main axis behind the hall is the famous **Botanic Garden of Thutmose III.** The reliefs on the walls show exotic plants and animals that the pharaoh brought back from his expeditions. The hall was later reused as a Christian church. At the end of the west–east axis is one of the eight monumental gates that gave access to the complex of the Temple of Karnak. Nectanebo I (30th Dynasty) erected this one.

Southeast of the temple lies the **sacred lake,** which is fed by the Nile. The morning rituals of the priests included purifying themselves in this lake. At the northwest corner of the lake, a large scarab dates from the reign of Amenhotep III and symbolizes the "newborn" sun. Legend has it that a woman who runs around it three times, clockwise, will become pregnant in the near future (at this writing, the southernmost sectors are not open to the public, so it's not possible to prove the theory). Farther on the left lie the remains of the other Obelisk of Hatshepsut (its partner is back between the fourth and fifth pylons).

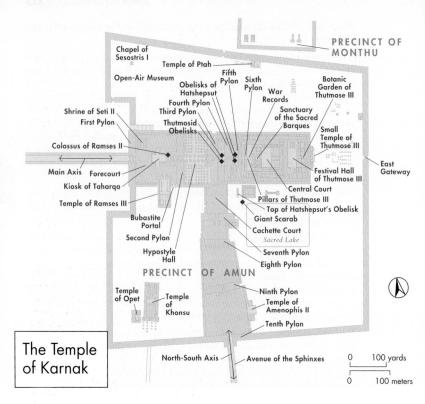

The **north–south axis** begins from an entrance between the third and fourth pylons and continues outside the Precinct of Amun with a south-bound avenue of sphinxes. The **Cachette Court,** at the top of the axis, was so named because thousands of statues were found in it in 1903. South lie the seventh through tenth pylons, each pair separated by a court. All elements of this axis date from the 18th Dynasty but many areas are not accessible at this writing due to active archaeological research work.

Besides fragments of temples and statues recovered from the Temple of Karnak itself, the **open-air museum** contains the small, white, well-preserved **Chapel of Senwosret I,** dating from the Middle Kingdom 12th Dynasty (1938–1759 BC). It was used during Senwosret I's reign to receive the sacred barques. Its new location and reconstructed state are due to the fact that Amenhotep III dismantled the chapel and used it to fill his Third Pylon. Two other small chapels lie beside it, also found inside the pylon. One of these is the Red Chapel of Hatshepsut. The museum is rather small, and its chapels and fragments are totally swallowed up in the gigantic complex of Karnak, which by its size detracts from the beauty of the museum's elements.

Karnak's **Sound & Light Show** includes a walk through the temple, with several monuments illuminated successively, and ends at the sacred

KARNAK TOURING TIPS

■ **Limit your exploring.** If you're pressed for time, or if you're worn out by temple hopping in the heat, just concentrate on the part of the complex that leads straight ahead, between the ram-headed sphinxes. If you only go as far as the hypostyle hall—and it's very near the front— you'll see what gives Karnak its power. Find a place to sit and feel the presence of these mighty pillars around you.

■ **Keep an eye on the path.** Resist the temptation to walk while looking up. The stone floors are uneven, and people trip on them all the time.

■ **Find the hidden church.** Continue on straight ahead, all the way to the Festival Hall of Thutmose III— it's a longer walk, past obelisks and pylons and the main sanctuary, and across a large, mostly vacant plaza. When you arrive at the Festival Hall, turn left to see what looks very much like a crucifix made from broken pieces of other statues. This area of Karnak served as a church during the early Christian era.

lake, where the second part begins. From stadium-like seating, the entire complex can be seen, with different temples lighted, music, and a narrated history of the site. On a rotating schedule throughout the week, shows are conducted in Arabic, English, French, German, Italian, Japanese, and Spanish. English shows run each night, the other languages less frequently.

It is best to visit the Temple of Karnak early in the morning for a few reasons: massive groups of people begin arriving around 9 AM; the slanting light calls relief carvings into better focus; and later in the day the heat can be overwhelming. ✛ *From the Temple of Luxor, follow the Corniche north 2 km (1 mi), New Karnak* ☎ *No phone* 🎟 *Temple £E65, Open-Air Museum £E25, Sound & Light Show £E75 (video camera £E35)* ⊗ *Temple daily 6 AM–5 PM. Sound & Light Show (in English) Oct.–May, Thurs.–Fri. and Mon. 6:30 PM, Tues.–Wed. and Sat.–Sun. 7:45 PM; June–Sept., Thurs.–Fri. and Mon. 8 PM, Tues.–Wed. and Sat.–Sun. 9:15 PM.*

★ **Luxor Museum.** The Luxor Museum contains, without a doubt, the crème de la crème of New Kingdom sculpture. On three floors, objects ranging from the Predynastic to Coptic periods are displayed in a soothing atmosphere. Each object has its own space, affording it the attention it deserves. Descriptions of artifacts are thorough and accurate.

The ground floor has several masterpieces. The statue of Thutmose III (18th Dynasty) in green schist of rare quality emits pharaonic inner peace and transcendence. The calcite statue of Sobek with Amenhotep III is also exceptional, both for its workmanship and its rather unusual subject—there are very few representations of the god Sobek offering life to a pharaoh. Colored reliefs, a sphinx, a scribe, and other royal statues are also superb.

On the first floor are Greco-Roman bronzes, a wooden maquette of a boat of Tutankhamun (18th Dynasty), papyri, royal statues, a sarcophagus, and other objects. At the end of the hall, in the first part of the first

Karnak Temples

floor, is a statue of the famous architect Amenhotep, son of Hapu, who served under Amenhotep III and had his own funerary temple in the West Bank. A little variation in style is offered with the two sculptures representing the head of the heretic pharaoh Akhenaton (18th Dynasty); they are a good example of the Amarna style (Akhenaton ruled from Tel el Amarna).

Back on the ground floor, a room to the left of the entrance is dedicated to the 16 New Kingdom statues found in 1989 in the cachette of the Solar Court of Amenhotep III in Luxor Temple. These were hidden to protect them from destruction by later rulers. ⊠ *Corniche al-Nil, 1 km (½ mi) north of the Luxor Temple, Corniche* ☎ *No phone* ✉ *£E80* ☻ *Daily 9–2 (last ticket at 1:30) and 4–9 (last ticket at 8:30).*

NEED A BREAK? **Tutti Fruitti Café.** Sometimes, all you need is a proper cup of tea—tout-free and no baksheesh—to set the world right again. At this casual café, an unhurried atmosphere prevails in the simple black-and-white interior. It's located in the Khaled Ibn El Waleed hotel zone, just down the street from the Hotel St. Joseph. Here, in what is part English tearoom, part dessert lounge, part bookish café, you can enjoy the air-conditioning and recharge with a panini or go for the best homemade scones outside of England. ⊠ *Shar'a St. Joseph* ☎ *016/627–4243.*

Mummification Museum. The Egyptian Antiquities Museum in Cairo has an entire section devoted to mummification, but a visit to this museum is worth the detour if you didn't have the opportunity to see the exhibits in Cairo. The exhibits here are intelligently designed and include the most important elements of the mummification rituals. And the slightly macabre atmosphere is perfect for the subject. The museum is divided into two parts: the first explains, with modern drawings based on ancient Egyptian reliefs and wall paintings, the stages the deceased goes through during mummification, as well as his journey toward heaven. To complement the scenes, a mummy is exposed at the end of the first section. After this introduction, the actual display of artifacts begins. There are tools, canopic jars, painted sarcophagi, and products used during the mummification process. There are also mummified animals, among them a baboon, a crocodile, a ram, a cat, and an ibis. The thrill here comes from the mummified animals—and the split human head, postmummification. The museum is 200 yards north of the Temple of Luxor, on the opposite side of the road, below street level. ⊠ *Corniche al-Nil, Corniche* ☎ *No phone* 🎫 *£E50* ☉ *Daily 9–2 and 4–9.*

NEED A BREAK? The venerable Victorian lounge at the Sofitel Old Winter Palace (⊠ *Corniche al-Nil, Corniche* ☎ *095/238–0422*), lined with richly upholstered divans and armchairs and hung with Oriental-style paintings of turbaned men wielding sabers, is a wonderful place to decompress with a spot of tea after a day of temple stomping. Afternoon light filters through tall windows, and birds twitter in the garden, while you nibble away at a plateful of sandwiches, pastries, and fresh-baked scones on the terrace. Tea is served (daily 4–6) in heavy silver pots and poured into porcelain cups. Note: Dress code is smart casual.

Temple of Luxor. Far easier to explore and digest than the sprawling Temple of Karnak just downriver, the Luxor Temple (built between 1390 and 323 BC) stands near the edge of the Nile in the city center. The temple was dedicated to the Theban Triad—the gods Amun-Ra, Mut (goddess of queenship), and Khonsu (moon god)—as well as to the cult of Ka (the royal spirit). The ancient name of the 285-yard-long temple was Ipet-Resyt (Southern Harem), the southern partner of Karnak, which was the starting point of the late-summer Opet festival. This feast involved a great procession of priests bringing the ceremonial barque of Amun-Ra from Karnak to Luxor, where the god would be united with the Mother of the King to allow her to give birth to the royal Ka.

It is likely that the largely 18th Dynasty (1539–1292 BC) temple was built over a Middle Kingdom predecessor. Amenhotep III (1390–1353 BC) started to develop the temple, and then Ramses II added to it a century later. Ruins from later periods also surround the main temple. The Avenue of Sphinxes was the creation of Nectanebo I (381–362 BC), almost 1,000 years later. The next considerable work was accomplished relatively soon thereafter, during the reign of Alexander the Great, who built, in the heart of the temple, a sanctuary for Amun-Ra's sacred barque.

During the Roman period, the temple was transformed into a fortified camp. Following the 4th-century AD (i.e., Christian) ban on pagan cults, several churches were built inside the temple. One of them, in the

Ramses II statues at the entrance of the Temple of Luxor

northeast corner of the court of Ramses II (19th Dynasty), was super-seded by the Abu al-Haggag Mosque during the 12th century AD, and locals refused to allow it to be torn down to complete the excavation of the Luxor temple.

Enter the temple compound from the east, across the polished stone pavement of a wide new plaza—part of the plan to turn all of Luxor into an outdoor museum. Beyond the ticket booth, you arrive in the temple esplanade at the south end of the 3-km (2-mi) **Avenue of Sphinxes,** which itself is on its way to complete restoration. The 6-yard-wide avenue at one time connected the Luxor and Karnak temples. At this writing, the Egyptian government has already excavated large sections of the avenue between here and the Karnak Temples—notwithstanding any mosques or churches that have been built in more modern times.

The Temple of Luxor's massive **first pylon** (58 yards wide) is the work of that tireless builder Ramses II—ample evidence of whom you can see in the scenes of the Battle of Qadesh (a campaign that Ramses II waged against the Hittites in Syria) that adorn the outer face of the pylon. Two obelisks and six colossi representing the king used to stand in front of the pylon. One of the obelisks was given to France as a present by Muhammed 'Ali Pasha; it graces the Place de la Concorde in Paris. Of the six colossi (two seated and four standing), only three are still on-site. France was also given two of these, and they are in the Louvre.

Beyond the pylon lies the **peristyle court of Ramses II,** a double row of papyrus-bud columns interspersed with a series of standing colossi representing the king. To the right of the entrance is a triple shrine, also called a way station, originally built by the queen Hatshepsut. Her

LUXOR TEMPLE TOURING TIPS

■ **Do go if you have time.** This small temple is often bypassed by tour groups, off in a hurry to see something bigger or more famous. But perhaps in part because of its smaller size, it's easier to "bond" with and feel a part of.

■ **Visit after dark.** Come at night; you'll fall in love with the place. There's no Sound & Light Show. There's no guided tour. You are simply free to explore this temple on your own, from the Avenue of the Sphinxes to a court of monumental statues of Ramses II.

■ **This temple evolved.** Luxor Temple is a living example of how an ancient sacred sight continues to be used into the present day. The Abu al-Haggag Mosque, where people still come to pray, is entered at what is now ground level, but is actually built over part of, and incorporated into, the ancient structure—with what is said to be the foundations of a Christian church sandwiched in a layer between.

4

successor, Thutmose III, usurped it—a relatively common practice by which a later ruler took credit for a monument by excising the original builder's cartouches and writing in his own. The shrines here are dedicated to the Theban triad: Amun-Ra in the middle, Mut on the left, and Khonsu on the right. The shrines' purpose was to receive their sacred barques during the Opet processions. To the left of the entrance to the court, and well above the temple's floor level, is the **Mosque of Abu al-Haggag,** built atop a Christian church. Al-Haggag was a holy man, originally from Baghdad, who died in Luxor in 1244 AD.

To the right of the entrance leading to the colonnade, on the western half of the southern wall, a relief scene shows the dedication of Ramses II's **second pylon.** It provides a view of what the pylon must have looked like after its construction. In front of the colonnade, two colossal statues represent Ramses II seated on a throne, with his wife Nefertari, as the goddess Hathor, standing at his side.

The **colonnade of Amenhotep III** consists of two rows of seven columns with papyrus-bud capitals. The wall decoration, completed by Amenhotep's successors, illustrates the voyage of the statue of the god Amun-Ra from Karnak to Luxor Temple during the Opet festival. On each side of the central walk are statues of Amun-Ra and Mut, carved during the reign of Tutankhamun, which Ramses II later usurped.

The Colonnade of Amenhotep III leads to the **solar court of Amenhotep III,** where 25 superbly executed 18th-Dynasty statues of gods and kings were found in 1989. This peristyle court is surrounded on three sides with a double row of columns with papyrus-bud capitals of remarkable elegance. At the far side of the solar court is a direct access to the **hypostyle hall of Amenhotep III,** which consisted of eight rows of four papyrus-bud columns. Between the last two columns on the left as you keep walking into the temple is a Roman altar dedicated to the Emperor Constantine.

South of the hypostyle hall are **three chapels**: one dedicated to Mut (directly on the east side of the central doorway) and two to Khonsu (on each side of the central doorway). The first antechamber originally had eight columns; they were removed during the 4th century AD to convert the chamber into a Christian church, with an apsidal recess flanked on both sides by granite columns in the Corinthian style. The ancient Egyptian scenes were covered with Christian paintings, which have been almost completely destroyed.

The second antechamber, known as the **offering chapel,** has four columns and leads to the inner sanctuary of the sacred barques. The chamber had the same divisions as the previous chapels, but Alexander the Great removed the four columns and replaced them with a chapel. This sanctuary received the sacred barque of Amun-Ra during the Opet celebrations.

On the east side of the Offering Chapel, a doorway leads to the **birth chamber,** dedicated to the divine conception of the pharaoh. The purpose of the scenes in the Birth Chamber was to prove that Amenhotep III was, indeed, the son of the god Amun-Ra, to strengthen the pharaoh's position as absolute ruler. On the left wall, birth scenes spread over three registers. In the first one, look for the goddess Selkis, the Queen Mutemwia (mother of Amenhotep III), and two goddesses suckling children, with two cows suckling children below it. In the second register, the third scene is the pharaoh's actual birth, in front of several divinities. In the fourth scene, Hathor presents the infant to Amun-Ra. The third register's fourth scene represents the conception of the royal child. The queen and Amun-Ra face each other, supported by Selkis and Neith. ⊠ *Corniche al-Nil, Luxor center, just north of the Winter Palace Hotel, Corniche* ☎ *No phone* ⊠ *£E50* ☉ *Daily 6* AM–*9* PM.

WHERE TO EAT

Use the coordinate (⚓ B2) at the end of each listing to locate a site on the corresponding "Where to Eat and Stay in Luxor" map.

Upper Egypt may not be an epicurean paradise, but the standard fare of soups, salads, *mezze* (hot and cold appetizers), grilled meats, and *tagines* (earthenware-baked vegetables, meat, or chicken in a tomato-based sauce, variously spiced) can be perfectly satisfying when well prepared.

Luxor is one of the most popular destinations in Egypt, so there are many restaurants that appeal particularly to the tourist trade. Most of the nicest establishments are in hotels, but you'll also find a wide range of restaurants (especially those serving Egyptian food) around town.

$$$
FRENCH
✕ **The 1886.** Play lord or lady of the manor beneath the Venetian crystal chandeliers of this dining room. Candlelight is reflected on the heavy silver plates and thick linens. Twenty-three-foot-tall windows open onto a garden. In massive gilt mirrors, you can observe yourself or the other diners struggling with a gigantic menu bearing complicated French names that sound terribly pedestrian in their English translations. White-gloved waiters are a bit over the top, but the food is fine, if overpriced. Dress and go for the ambience. ⊠ *Sofitel Old Winter*

Palace, Corniche al-Nil, Corniche ☎ *095/238–0422* ⌖ *Reservations essential* ⌖ *Jacket and tie* ▤ *AE, MC, V* ◷ *No lunch* ✛ *B4.*

$
MIDDLE EASTERN
✕ **El Hussein (The Diner).** One of the best values in Luxor caters to both Egyptians and foreigners. This no-frills restaurant is clean, the service is friendly, and the location—up a flight of stairs in a small shopping complex—is convenient for a break from shopping or sightseeing. Choose from grilled meats, vegetarian and meat tagines, soups, salads, pizzas, and sandwiches, all competently prepared and served in large portions for remarkably low prices. Air-conditioning, yes; atmosphere, no. No alcohol is served. ⊠ *Savoy Market, Corniche al-Nil, just south of El-Luxor Hotel, Corniche* ☎ *095/237–6166* ▤ *No credit cards* ✛ *C4..*

$$
MIDDLE EASTERN
✕ **El Hussein (Oriental).** Egyptians from as far as Al Minya, 426 km (265 mi) away, rave about the grilled meats at this large upper-story dining room framed by Oriental arches (no relation to the diner by the same name). Don't let the stained tablecloths deter you; eating from communal dishes can be a messy business. Standard mixed-grill items share the lineup with less common offerings such as turkey, duck, and rabbit. Set menus allow a choice of meat, fowl, or fish accompanied by a table laden with soups, salads, and vegetable dishes. If you're very lucky, they'll be serving the other reason locals flock here: molokheya (a type of greens). Chopped, boiled, spiced, and oiled, molokheya is unique to Egypt and considered a special-occasion treat in Egyptian homes. Finding it in a restaurant is a rarity. A second El Hussein location specializes in fish. ⊠ *New Karnak-Hilton St., about a block south of entrance to Hilton Hotel, New Karnak* ☎ *095/237–8355* ⊕ *elhussein.lxr.com.eg* ▤ *No credit cards* ✛ *D1.*

$$–$$$
SEAFOOD
★
✕ **El Hussein Sea-Food.** What El Hussein (Oriental) did for meats, it outdoes itself in fish and seafood cookery in this sister property a couple of blocks away. Here, a stairway leads to a softly lit room of green tabletops and creamy marble floors. The clatter of traffic from the street below fades away as you get down to the business of choosing among four set-menu combinations. Seafood bisque, shrimp *kofta* ("meat" balls), and squid are among the options. Or go for the mild, flaky, grilled sea bass, served whole; just watch out for the bones. Expect plenty of the usual Middle Eastern side dishes as well as dessert. ⊠ *New Karnak-Hilton St., about three blocks south of entrance to Hilton Hotel, New Karnak, Corniche* ☎ *095/236–2000* ⊕ *elhussein.lxr.com.eg* ▤ *No credit cards* ✛ *D1.*

$$ ✕ **El Tarboush.** This restaurant in the gardens of the Winter Palace Hotel
MIDDLE EASTERN sits under the canopy of mature palm fronds, serving excellent Egyptian
food in a lovely, quiet setting with views of the beautifully lit hotel.
There's a full range of hot and cold mezze for starters; main courses
include a decadent stuffed pigeon, *shish tawouk* (chicken kebab), or a
tender mixed grill. There's a full bar service and wine list. ⊠ *Sofitel Old
Winter Palace, Corniche al-Nil, Corniche* ☎ *095/238–0422* ▭ *AE, MC,
V* ⊘ *No lunch* ⊹ *B5.*

$–$$ ✕ **Jamboree.** A popular restaurant with visitors of all nationalities, Jam-
MIDDLE EASTERN boree has relocated to an upstairs perch in the heart of the pedestrian
souk, a mere five-minute walk from Luxor Temple. The menu concentrates on Egyptian staples of roast chicken, grilled meat, and stuffed
pigeon accompanied by rice and salad. But you can also opt for *shak-
shouka* (scrambled egg with green pepper and tomato), liver and onions
with green pepper, Red Sea shrimp in garlic butter, or just prowl the
salad bar. Seating indoors behind wide arched windows, or in the adjacent open-air terrace, offers slice-of-life people watching—merchants
hawking their wares in the street below, and housewives hanging out
the laundry on balconies across the lane. Egyptian beer and wine are
served. ⊠ *On Shari'a Souk, at Shar'a Abd el-Hamid Taha, Downtown*
☎ *012/781–3149* ▭ *No credit cards* ⊹ *C4.*

$$$ ✕ **Miyako.** Miyako is Luxor's finest Asian restaurant. The room is
JAPANESE sedately but luxuriously decorated in a Far Eastern style, with teals,
golds, and deep green marble. There is a formal tea area and a seques-
tered alcove for romance or business. A variety of Asian specialties
are available, including excellent sushi and sashimi, which is prepared
before your eyes at the sushi bar; however, the *teppanyaki* (Japanese
grill), prepared in flamboyant, percussive style, is a signature. ⊠ *Sonesta
St. George, Corniche al-Nil, Corniche* ☎ *095/238–2575* ▭ *AE, MC, V*
⊘ *No lunch* ⊹ *A6.*

$–$$ ✕ **Nubian Village.** This re-created Nubian village on the banks of the Nile
MIDDLE EASTERN has open-air, low-level seating, a *shisha* (hookah) area, an open grill, a
bread oven, and space enough to accommodate the ubiquitous motor
coach tours. The food is standard Egyptian, with mostly grilled meats
and mezze, but the setting is delightful—you are surrounded by trees
and away from the traffic in town. By day, a handcraft center is open.
You'll need a taxi to drop you off and pick you up after your meal.
⊠ *7 mi south of Luxor at the eastern end of the south bridge, Luxor
South* ☎ *010/355–2330* ▭ *No credit cards* ⊹ *B6.*

$ ✕ **Oasis Café.** In one of the few remaining 19th-century mansions in
CAFÉ town, this relaxed eatery decorated in period style lives up to its name.
American-owned, it's an informal place with soaring ceilings; color-
saturated walls hung with old photographs and works by contempo-
rary Egyptian artists; and a lively crowd of travelers around the globe.
Drop in for a coffee or light lunch of soups, sandwiches, or salads.
Main dishes feature fresh, organic ingredients and include pastas, cur-
ries, or mixed grills, and there's a wicked chocolate cake to finish. A
second location is in the works on Shar'a Joseph Hotel. ⊠ *Shar'a Lahib
Habashi, Corniche* ☎ *095/237–2914* ▭ *No credit cards* ⊹ *C4.*

$ ✕ **Snack Time.** One of a new generation of modern Egyptian fast-food
FAST FOOD   style cafés, this spot serves a combination of traditional street food
such as *shawarma* (thin-cut meat and salad wrapped in unleavened
bread—like a gyro), along with burgers, paninis, and salads. There's a
good choice of sodas, and the coffee is excellent. You'll find that tourists
in search of familiar fill-me-ups and teenage Egyptians out with their
friends frequent it. There is both an air-conditioned dining room and an
open-terrace eating area. There's also free Wi-Fi. ⊠ *Shar'a Mahata, facing Abu al-Haggag/Luxor Temple Plaza, Downtown* ☎ *095/237–5407*
▤ *No credit cards* ✛ *B4.*

$–$$ ✕ **Sofra.** Beyond the decorative tile steps to this former residence awaits
MIDDLE EASTERN   what has become a fast favorite among Anglo and European travelers, many testing the culinary mainstays of Egypt for the first time.
It's a good place to make acquaintance: far enough off the Corniche
as to be in a local neighborhood, decorated with just enough 1930s-
era antiques downstairs and Arabesque furnishings on the roof terrace
to capture that elusive "old-Cairo" style—without overdoing things.
Kofta, kebabs, lamb, and veal parade by on a menu that introduces all-
star dishes such as roasted rabbit with molokheya (a sort of greens)—all
prepared with an understanding of Western tastes. This is the place to
kick back with a fresh guava juice, smoke a shisha, and tell your friends
about once you return home. ⊠ *90 Shar'a Mohamed Farid, al-Manshiya*
☎ *095/235–9752* ⊕ *www.sofra.com* ▤ *No credit cards* ✛ *B5.*

$ ✕ **Tudor Rose.** This small dining room overlooks a tree-lined street, and
MIDDLE EASTERN   the standard Upper Egyptian and Western fare comes at reasonable
prices. Try the *kobbeba,* fried balls of crushed wheat stuffed with spiced
minced meat; ask for lime to squeeze on top. The moussaka is the same
tasty and filling eggplant-and-ground-meat dish smothered in béchamel
sauce you'll find in any Greek restaurant. ⊠ *Shar'a St. Joseph, adjacent
to St. Joseph Hotel, Khaled Ibn El Waleed* ☎ *095/238–1707* ▤ *AE,
MC, V* ✛ *B6.*

WHERE TO STAY

*Use the coordinate (✛ B2) at the end of each listing to locate a site on
the corresponding "Where to Eat and Stay in Luxor" map.*

In Luxor, hotel standards have little to do with the star rating you see
in the lobbies. They usually fall into three categories: the luxurious, the
mediocre, and the decrepit. The hotels of Upper Egypt give wonderful
clues to the local culture—when you know what to look for. In their
homes, Egyptians invest in floors first, the walls second. It's the same in
hotel lobbies. This is why marble is so prevalent, from the plain stone
squares in modest three-star accommodations to elaborate geometric
patterns in the five-star palaces. If there's enough money to extend the
marble up the walls, so much the better. You'll know the owners had
money left over if the lobby is topped off with crystal chandeliers.
Family-style lodgings not in the "star" system will be even homier, with
floors covered in the best-quality ceramic tile. Bedding in three-star
and family style accommodations also reveal Egyptian preference for
platform bed frames—usually twin-sized—topped with ultrafirm cotton

mattresses. If you want something larger, specify the bed size when making reservations, because many double rooms come with twin beds.

At properties with Nile views, rooms directly facing the river, or those with a partial river view, will cost more—just how much more depends on the season, the "fullness" of the view, and the property itself. If you feel that you'll be spending enough time in your hotel room to warrant the extra cost, then request a Nile view when making reservations. Otherwise, content yourself with the knowledge that you came to Egypt to see the sights beyond the hotel, and you'll have plenty of other chances to look at the Nile.

Most hotels in Luxor are located on the East Bank of the Nile, along or near the Corniche. A handful of others can be found on the West Bank. Prices at the large five-star hotels can be high, but you will rarely pay the rack rate if you book a package or tour or pay in advance online.

Hotels in Luxor can help you arrange tours and felucca cruises if you are traveling independently.

All hotel reviews have been condensed for this book. Please go to Fodors.com for full reviews of each property.

$ **El Nakhil Hotel and Restaurant.** The warmth of Egyptian hospitality and ★   exacting German housekeeping standards make this family-run West Bank hotel a standout lodging option on the bucolic side of the Nile. **Pros:** you're in the very heart of a rural Egyptian neighborhood, but with Western conveniences; food quality in the restaurant is very high. **Cons:** no pool. ⊠ *Gezira el-Bairat, Luxor West Bank* ☎ *095/231–3922* ⊕ *www.elnakhil.com* ↻ *17 rooms* ⌂ *In-room: a/c, no phone, no TV, Wi-Fi (some). In-hotel: Restaurant, laundry service, Internet terminal, Wi-Fi hotspot* ▭ *No credit cards* ⏐❍⏐ *BP* ✛ *A4.*

$ **Gezira Gardens Hotel.** Relaxed and welcoming, Gezira Gardens Hotel lives up to its name with rooms and housekeeping suites—all with balconies—that face tree-shaded patio tables and a small swimming pool. **Pros:** nice pool; outstanding restaurant. **Cons:** Standard rooms are small. ⊠ *Gezira el-Bairat, Luxor West Bank* ☎ *095/231–2505* ⊕ *www. el-gezira.com* ↻ *20 rooms, 8 suites* ⌂ *In-room: a/c, kitchen (some), Wi-Fi (some). In-hotel: 2 restaurants, bars, pools, laundry service, Internet terminal, Wi-Fi hotspot* ▭ *No credit cards* ⏐❍⏐ *BP* ✛ *B4.*

$$$$ **Hilton Luxor Resort and Spa.** The Hilton had me at hello. When this ★   Nile-front property returned from an extensive renovation, it brought a bit of high Dubai style with it, starting at the soaring, serene reception rotunda framed in lacy white Arabesque screens, a rosette design in its inlaid marble floor, a half-dozen chairs around the perimeter, and nothing else. **Pros:** Asian cooking classes; Arabic lessons; free shuttle service; some river views. **Cons:** because of its secluded location, the hotel can seem farther from the sights than it really is. ⊠ *New Karnak-Hilton St., New Karnak* ☎ *095/239–9999* ⊕ *www.hilton.com* ↻ *226 rooms, 10 suites* ⌂ *In-room: a/c, safe, minibar, Internet (some), Wi-Fi (some). In-hotel: 3 restaurants, room service, bars, pools, gym, spa, riverfront, laundry service, Internet terminal, Wi-Fi hotspot* ▭ *AE, MC, V* ⏐❍⏐ *BP* ✛ *D1.*

$$$$ 🏨 **Hotel Al Moudira.** A beautifully designed Arabian palace complete with
★ ornate Islamic arches and domes is set in 8 hectares of gardens. This
is a true oasis, where you can completely relax after sightseeing. **Pros:**
exceptional attention to detail; you'll think you've walked into a photo
shoot for a shelter magazine. **Cons:** the hotel is on the West Bank, quite
far from town and a 20-minute taxi ride from Downtown Luxor and its
restaurants. ⊠ *Al Moudira, Luxor West Bank* ✦ *From the ferry travel
inland and then turn left at the junction; the hotel is a 5-minute drive
along this road* ☎ *012/325–1307* ⊕ *www.moudira.com* ➲ *54 rooms*
△ *In-room: a/c. In-hotel: 2 restaurants, bars, pool, spa, parking (free),
no-smoking rooms* ▤ *AE, DC, MC, V* ⦿| *BP* ✦ *A2.*

$ 🏨 **Hotel St. Joseph.** This serviceable hotel is one of the preferred stop-
overs for demanding, budget-minded British travelers. Low-key decor,
a high standard of cleanliness, decent food, and a friendly staff are
among the advantages. **Pros:** clean and spacious rooms; pool on-site
(rare for a hotel in this price range). **Cons:** rooms are rather dated and
worn compared to newer budget options in Luxor. ⊠ *Shar'a Khaled
Ibn El Waleed, Khaled Ibn El Waleed* ☎ *095/238–1707* ➲ *75 rooms*
△ *In-room: a/c, refrigerator. In-hotel: restaurant, bar, pool* ▤ *AE, MC,
V* ⦿| *BP* ✦ *B6.*

$$ 🏨 **Iberotel.** Ideally situated at the southern end of the Luxor Corniche,
this rather uninspiring tower-block building combines a Nile-front
address and sufficient conveniences to keep European tour groups com-
ing back. There's just enough of the right stuff to maintain a four-star
rating, and not one frill more. **Pros:** Iberotel has the least expensive
direct Nile views in Luxor; good location for strolling along the Nile
to Luxor Temple and the Downtown area. **Cons:** dining and bar service
is slow; the pro-smoking crowd holds public areas, especially the bar,
hostage. ⊠ *Shar'a Khaled Ibn El Waleed, Corniche* ☎ *095/238–0925*
⊕ *www.iberotel-eg.com* ➲ *185 rooms* △ *In-room: a/c, safe, refrigera-
tor, Internet (some). In-hotel: 5 restaurants, bars, pool, laundry service*
▤ *AE, MC, V* ⦿| *BP* ✦ *B5.*

$$$–$$$$ 🏨 **Maritim Jolie Ville Kings Island Luxor.** Mother Nature reigns supreme at
☾ this garden-of-paradise resort, whose timeless, unsullied Nile vistas are
★ 4 km (2½ mi) from Luxor's bustling center (there's free shuttle service).
Pros: restful and natural surroundings; island location puts you at one
with the river; bank on-site. **Cons:** about 15 minutes by free shuttle bus
or taxi to reach the city center; some of the furnishings are showing a
little wear and tear. ⊠ *Luxor South* ☎ *095/227–4855* ⊕ *www.maritim.
de* ➲ *323 rooms, 4 suites* △ *In-room: a/c, safe, refrigerator, Internet.
In-hotel: 3 restaurants, room service, bars, tennis courts, pools, gym,
children's programs (ages 5–12), laundry service, parking (free)* ▤ *AE,
MC, V* ⦿| *BP* ✦ *B6.*

$ 🏨 **New Pola Hotel.** On the southern hotel strip—though not on the
river—this is a strong budget option, once you make it past the dim,
dreary lobby and disorganized reception desk. **Pros:** quite modern facili-
ties for the price; secure rooms; large enough that you can sometimes
find a room if you arrive without a reservation. **Cons:** just because a
hotel includes breakfast doesn't mean you want to eat it in a grim,
basement-like back room; just because your room has a phone doesn't

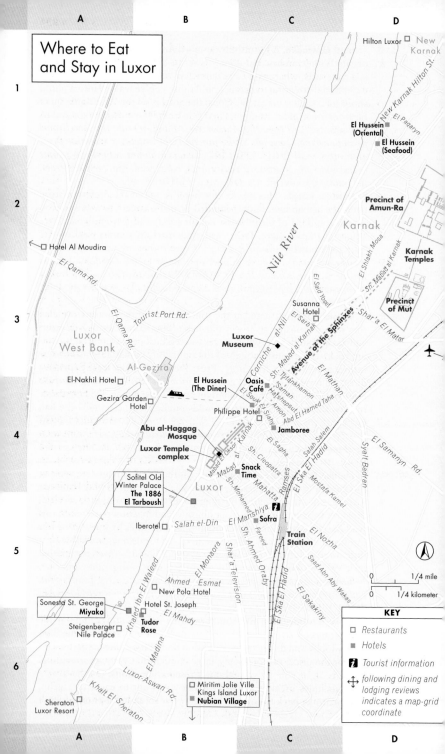

Where to Eat and Stay in Luxor

A   **B**   **C**   **D**

Hilton Luxor □   New Karnak

New Karnak Hilton St.

New El Paqaryn

El Hussein (Oriental) ■

El Hussein (Seafood) ■

Precinct of Amun-Ra

Karnak

El Shiakh Mosa

Sh. Mabad al Karnak

Karnak Temples

Precinct of Mut

Shar'a El Matar

El Mathan

Nile River

← □ Hotel Al Moudira

El Qama Rd.

El Qama Rd.

Tourist Port Rd.

Corniche al Nil

El Said Yosef

El Sarlak

Sh. Mabad al Karnak

Avenue of the Sphinxes

Luxor West Bank

Susanna Hotel

Luxor Museum ◆

Al-Gezira

El-Nakhil Hotel □

El Hussein (The Diner)

Oasis Café

Sh. Tutankhamon

Saman

Hatshepsut

El Souk El Slariy

Amon

Abd El Hamed Taha

Gezira Garden Hotel

Philippe Hotel ■

Jamboree ■

El Sagha

Salah Salem

Mostafa Kamel

El Samanyn Rd.

Syalt Badran

Abu al-Haggag Mosque ◆

Luxor Temple complex ◆

Mabad El Oksor

Mabad El Karnak

Sh. Cleopatra

Snack Time ■

Ramses

El Ska El Hadid

Luxor

Sofitel Old Winter Palace **The 1886 El Tarboush** ■

Iberotel □   Salah el-Din

Sh. Mohammed Farag

El Manshiya

Sofra ■

Mahatta

Fareed

Train Station 🛈

El Nozha

Saad Abn Aby Wakas

El Manshiya

Sh. Ahmed Oraby

Ahmed Esmat

New Pola Hotel

Shar'a Television

El Monaora

El Sha El Hadid

El Sakakiny

Sonesta St. George Miyako ■

Hotel St. Joseph □

Khaled Ibn El Waleed

Tudor Rose ■

El Mahdy

Steigenberger Nile Palace □

El Madina

Sheraton Luxor Resort

Khalt El Sheraton

Luxor-Aswan Rd.

□ Miritim Jolie Ville Kings Island Luxor

Nubian Village ■

0   1/4 mile

0   1/4 kilometer

KEY

□   *Restaurants*

■   *Hotels*

🛈   *Tourist information*

↔   *following dining and lodging reviews indicates a map-grid coordinate* mean calls will be transferred to you. ✉ *Shar'a Khaled Ibn El Waleed, Khaled Ibn El Waleed* ☎ *095/236–5081* ⊕ *www.newpolahotel.com* 🛏 *81 rooms* ♿ *In-room: a/c, refrigerator. In-hotel: 2 restaurants, bars, pool* ▭ *MC, V* ⭐| *BP* ✛ *B5.*

$ 🖼 **Philippe Hotel.** Leave the clamor of a shop-filled Downtown street and enter a cool, quiet retreat popular with budget tour groups—and fans of small marble lobbies. **Pros:** good location—halfway between Luxor and Karnak temples—and price; superior rooms are better furnished, with nicer bathrooms. **Cons:** bad location: at time of writing, right across from the smelly rest area for the calèche horses. Rooms vary in size; cheaper standard rooms aren't as nice and may have windows that open onto a common shaft. ✉ *Shar'a Dr. Labib Habashi, just off the Corniche al-Nil near the El-Luxor Hotel, Corniche* ☎ *095/237–2284* ⊕ *www.philippeluxorhotel.com* 🛏 *68 rooms* ♿ *In-room: a/c, refrigerator. In-hotel: restaurant, room service, bar, pool, laundry service, Internet terminal* ▭ *No credit cards* ⭐| *BP* ✛ *C4.*

$$$$ 🖼 **Sofitel Old Winter Palace.** This noble Victorian-style edifice, built in
★ 1886, exudes the heady scent of colonial luxury even as modern Luxor changes around it. **Pros:** one of Egypt's most iconic hotels; surroundings are luxurious yet still of their period; the gardens are a cool and quiet respite from the hubbub of the town. **Cons:** the dress code—tie and jacket in The 1886 restaurant, smart casual in the remaining venues— may be too restrictive for some travelers; the atmosphere may be too formal for families with young children. ✉ *Corniche al-Nil, Corniche* ☎ *095/238–0422 or 800/515–5679* ⊕ *www.sofitel.com* 🛏 *92 rooms* ♿ *In-room: a/c, safe, Internet (Pavilion). In-hotel: 4 restaurants, room service, bars, pool, laundry service, Internet terminal, Wi-Fi hotspot* ▭ *AE, MC, V* ⭐| *BP* ✛ *B5.*

$$$$ 🖼 **Sonesta St. George.** Neopharaonic ostentation squeezed into a small parcel of Nile real estate that has been developed to within an inch of its life—that's the St. George. The hotel is known throughout the region for its excellent cuisine and the profusion of colored marble in the lobby. **Pros:** excellent panoramas from Nile View rooms; activity programs include fishing trips; restaurants are uniformly good; bank on-site. **Cons:** there isn't much outside space for relaxation; service, especially at the reception desk, isn't up to five-star standards. ✉ *Corniche al-Nil South, Kahled Ibn El Waleed* ☎ *095/238–2575 or 800/700–3782* ⊕ *www.sonesta.com* 🛏 *224 rooms* ♿ *In-room: a/c, safe. In-hotel: 6 restaurants, room service, bars, pool, gym, spa, laundry service* ▭ *AE, DC, MC, V* ⭐| *BP* ✛ *A6.*

$$$$ 🖼 **Steigenberger Nile Palace.** The Nile Palace's sleek, art deco–inspired facade is easily the most visible hotel on the strip south of the Corniche. **Pros:** excellent design and decor throughout; good choice of eateries on-site; many rooms have Nile views; bank on-site. **Cons:** limited outside space; poolside can get crowded if the hotel is busy. ✉ *Shar'a Khaled Ibn El Waleed, Khaled Ibn El Waleed* ☎ *095/236–6999 or 866/991–1299* ⊕ *www.steigenberger.com* 🛏 *285 rooms, 19 suites* ♿ *In-room: a/c, safe, Internet. In-hotel: 6 restaurants, room service, bars, pools, gym, laundry facilities* ▭ *AE, MC, V* ⭐| *BP* ✛ *A6.*

$$ 🖼 **Susanna Hotel.** The best value in Luxor, the Susanna is one of the city's
★ newest stays, and it commands the only location in town that trumps

the Nile-front properties. **Pros:** inexpensive but well furnished; double-glazed windows cut down on outside noise; great location for access to Luxor temple, the souk, and the Corniche. **Cons:** rooms are small, but that is typical of hotels at this price point. ⊠ *52 Shar'a Mabed El Karnak, Downtown* ☎ *095/236–9915 or 095/236–9912* ↝ *45 rooms* ⟳ *In-room: a/c, refrigerator. In-hotel: restaurant, bar, pool, laundry service, Wi-Fi hotspot* ▭ *MC, V* ⦿| *BP* ⊹ *C3.*

SHOPPING

The variety of merchandise is wider in crowded Cairo, and you can get more for your money in less-visited Aswan. But shoppers who have the stamina for bargaining can leave Luxor with some satisfying finds. For atmosphere, you can't beat the souk, where a skillful haggler may pay no more than £E70 for a man's *galabeyya* (long cotton gowns) or no more than £E35 for a woman's scarf. If you feel you have only one good bargaining session in you, save it for the obligatory visit to a West Bank alabaster workshop.

Luxor Souk. Luxor's main souk is a long, narrow street running between concrete dwellings and lined with shops where turbaned men and black-robed women hawk their wares. Several restaurants and coffee shops have relocated here, having been moved out of their former locations by Luxor's new city-planning program. In fact, the souk itself has undergone a makeover, starting with new flagstone pavement, now that this is a pedestrian-only street. You'll find brass trays, alabaster vases and bowls, leather poufs, jewelry shops, and racks of brightly colored cotton scarves and *galabeyyas*—mixed with hardware stores and great piles of fruits and vegetables in hemp baskets. All is redolent of pungent spices, incense, tangy mint, and the aroma of something wonderful grilling in nearby kitchens. The souk is open daily from 7 AM until midnight. ⊠ *Shar'a al-Souk, off Abu al-Haggag Plaza, Downtown.*

The Queen Nefertari Museum. This museum has an extensive selection of fabulous fake antiquities. The small and midsize statuary crafted in the last century looks so real you must take a certificate to the airport so you won't be accused of smuggling artifacts. The shop's hours, however, are erratic. ⊠ *Corniche al-Nil, corner just north of El-Luxor Hotel, Corniche* ☎ *095/237–4702.*

NIGHTLIFE

Hotel St. Joseph. This hotel seems to draw everyone on this end of town to its rooftop restaurant, no matter which hotel they're staying in. ⊠ *Shar'a Khaled Ibn El Waleed, Khaled Ibn El Waleed* ☎ *095/238–1707.*

King's Head Pub. Like its logo—a portrait of English King Henry VIII with the face of the pharaoh Akhenaton—this pub is an anomaly, with an eclectic atmosphere and a mixed crowd. The bar is hung with coasters from around the world, pewter mugs, mosque lamps, and an Australian flag, and Bob Marley posters abound. A small blackboard announces the cocktail of the week. ⊠ *Shar'a Khalid Ibn el-Walid,*

Bring your haggling skills to the souks of Luxor.

*across the street from Sonesta St. George Hotel, then three flights up,
Khaled Ibn El Waleed* ☎ *095/228–0489.*

Susanna Hotel. This hotel's rooftop restaurant is ideally situated for
watching the sun set over the Theban Hills or the lights come on at
Luxor Temple. ⊠ *52 Shar'a Mabed El Karnak, Downtown* ☎ *095/236–
9915* ⊕ *www.susannahotelluxor.com.*

The Royal Bar. This bar is hardly a jumpin' joint, but it's worth a visit for
its colonial panache—burgundy walls, mahogany woodwork, beamed
ceilings, lavish drapery, and bookshelves stocked with such oddities
as *Who's Who of 1938* and a hardbound Tom Clancy novel. Enjoy
good mixed drinks in the lounge or at the semicircular brass-and-black-
granite bar. Complimentary canapés and nuts are available. ⊠ *Sofitel
Old Winter Palace, Corniche al-Nil, Corniche* ☎ *095/238–0422.*

ACTIVITIES

GUIDED TOURS

If you are not taking a cruise, you can arrange land-based tours to visit
the sights along the Nile between Luxor and Aswan, the most important
of which are Edfu and Kom Ombo *(for information on Kom Ombo,
see ⇨ North of Aswan: Kom Ombo and Daraw in Chapter 5, "Aswan
& Lake Nasser")*. You can also easily travel to the less-visited sights of
Abydos and Dendera, both north of Luxor, on a daylong guided tour,
either with a small group or a private guide and driver.

If you haven't prearranged tours, your hotel's concierge or tour desk
should be able to make recommendations or handle arrangements. If

The Scarab

One of the least expensive souvenirs you can bring back from your trip is a small scarab beetle carved from stone.

The scarab, or dung beetle, isn't the prettiest insect, but it had a special place in ancient Egyptian religion. The beetle pushes a ball of dung from east to west just as the god Khepri rolled the earth from east to west, so it's a symbol of a cycle of renewal that's central to ancient beliefs. In fact, Khepri is often portrayed as a man with a scarab head or simply as a scarab (in hieroglyphics).

The dung beetle also rises out of the earth when it hatches in the same way that ancient Egyptians hoped to emerge into the afterlife. That's why the image of this humble beetle is seen in royal tombs, and why tourists all across Egypt buy replicas every day. Indeed, even in ancient Egypt, the scarab was a common amulet, paperweight, or talisman given as a gift.

not, your best options for guided tours in Luxor are Thomas Cook and American Express. Both are particularly flexible in arranging tours to suit a variety of desires and budgets, even arranging last-minute Nile cruises, but any of the offices can arrange day trips. Just remember that the tourist police require at least 24 hours' notice of any intent to travel overland beyond Luxor and the West Bank. Most of the tour companies have conveniently located offices at hotels or along the Corniche and Shar'a Khaled Ibn el-Walid.

Contacts American Express (℡ 095/237-8333). **Noble Tours** (℡ 095/237-3155). **Karnak Tours** (℡ 095/237-2360). **Thomas Cook** (℡ 095/237-2620 ⊕ www.thomascookegypt.com).

HOT-AIR BALLOON RIDES

Balloon flights make for a very serene and peaceful way of viewing the Valley of the Kings and are a favorite activity among tourists. The balloons take off from the West Bank just after dawn and spend an hour or so gliding over the temples and tombs (exact route depends on the prevailing breezes). If you don't want to take to the air in a balloon, you can take off from the river in a seven-seater seaplane and take in the vistas of the East and West Bank of Luxor under powered flight.

Contacts Sindbad Balloons (℡ 095/227-2960 ⊕ www.sindbadballoons.com). **Viking Air** (℡ 095/227-7212 ⊕ www.vikingballoonsegypt.com). **Magic Horizons** (℡ 095/227-4060 ⊕ www.magichorizon.com).

THE THEBAN NECROPOLIS

4 km (2½ mi) west of Luxor.

At the edge of cultivated land across the Nile from what the ancients called Thebes—the City of 100 Gates—lies their City of the Dead, arguably the most extensive cemetery ever conceived. New Kingdom pharaohs built their tombs here, in the secrecy of the desert hills, with the goal of making them less accessible than the Old and Middle Kingdom

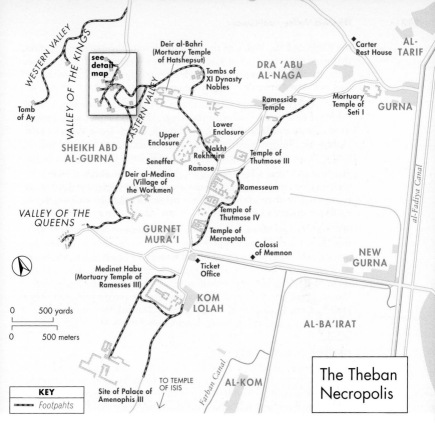

The Theban Necropolis

KEY
▬▬ Footpahts

royal tombs, which had been robbed even by the time of the New Kingdom. The pharaohs had their sepulchres hollowed out underground, and workers isolated from the East Bank decorated them. These artisans had their own village, temples, and cemetery at Deir al-Medina.

To celebrate their own greatness, as well as the magnificence of the god Amun-Ra, most New Kingdom rulers constructed huge mortuary temples surrounded by palace granaries. These monuments spread across the edge of the fields, as if to buffer the fertile land from the desert. The choice of the West Bank was based on its rugged landscape (which should have kept robbers away), but the overall rationale came from ancient Egyptian religious beliefs. Every night, the old sun set in the west and was reborn the next morning as Khepri, the young sun. By the same principle, the dead were buried in the west to prepare for their rebirth.

The West Bank is not only a royal necropolis, reserved for the sovereign and his family. A considerable number of tombs belonged to Egyptian nobles and other preeminent courtiers. Their sepulchres were of smaller dimensions, but the quality of their decoration was comparable to that found in the tombs of the kings.

Because the tombs of the nobles were dug into the limestone hills at the edge of an open plain, numerous objects were robbed over the centuries. The same destiny was reserved for most of the graves of the Valley of the Kings and the Valley of the Queens, despite the extreme measures that were taken to avoid it. The remarkable exception to this, of course, is the Tomb of Tutankhamun, which archaeologist Howard Carter discovered with its treasures nearly intact in 1922.

To do a full circuit of the various tombs, start making your way around the West Bank at the Valley of the Kings, then move on to the Temple of Hatshepsut at Deir al-Bahri, the Temple of Seti I, the Valleys of the Nobles, the Ramesseum, the Valley of the Queens, and Deir al-Medina. End with the splendid mortuary temple of Ramses III at Medinet Habu.

June through September are only for the brave—come then if you thrive on high heat and sweat. In these months, bringing a large bottle of water is even more essential than at other times. October, November, April, and May are the nicest months.

■TIP➔ The best times of day to see the monuments, especially in summer, are in the early morning or in late afternoon—to avoid the high heat of midday and, likewise the waves of sightseers who begin to arrive between 8:30 and 9 AM. In winter, the weather is perfectly bearable, and the main obstacle to seeing the monuments is other tourists. Again, early-morning and late-afternoon forays are best for avoiding crowds. After sunset, from December through March, you might want to carry a sweater around town with you; nights along the Nile can get chilly in winter.

GETTING HERE AND AROUND

There are several ways to cross the Nile from Luxor. The least expensive is by local ferry (£E1; tickets are available from the kiosk in front of the East Bank launch), which leaves from in front of the Luxor Temple. The ferry runs from early morning until about midnight, but the boat leaves only when it is fully occupied. For a quicker crossing, special boats can take you across the Nile for £E5. The most hassle-free way is to rent a private taxi in town £E50 per hour or better if you haggle hard, and this will take you across the bridge, which is 12 km (7½ mi) south of Luxor to reach the West Bank.

If you take the ferry, once on the West Bank, there are a few ways to get around. The easiest, fastest, and most expensive is by private taxi, but there are fewer taxis here than in Downtown on the East Bank. Service taxis (group taxis) are a very cheap way (£E1) to get to the middle of the tourist area, but they only take main roads and skirt the monuments. To get a service taxi to stop and let you out, knock on the little window in the front.

Alternatively, bicycles (rentals cost £E15) are always an option, as are donkeys. You can hire both at the West Bank docks. Cycling, or even walking, is definitely doable in winter, but either is exhausting in summer. As for the donkeys, they bring you through the local village to the sites, and they're an evocative form of transportation if time is not such a concern.

How to Make a Mummy

Mummification is indelibly linked with ancient Egypt, and mummies continue to fascinate us. However, the earliest mummies were likely made by accident, when bodies were placed in the dry desert sand. These mummies were probably accidentally found by the ancient Egyptians (after being disturbed by robbers or animals) and gave birth to the idea of mummification. The ancient Egyptian word for mummy was *saah*. The present-day word is derived from the Persian/Arabic word *mum*, which means pitch or bitumen, which was thought to have been used in making mummies. It was believed that the preserved body would provide a permanent house for the soul in the afterlife. The process of mummification changed throughout Egyptian history, reaching an acme in the 21st Dynasty.

The classic method of mummification was as follows: a slit was made in the left side of the body, and the lungs, liver, stomach, and intestines were removed. The heart, believed to be necessary for rebirth, was left in place. The viscera were mummified separately, wrapped, and placed either in canopic jars or back in the body cavity prior to burial, depending on the period. Then a chisel was inserted up the nose and through the ethmoid bone. A long, slim metal instrument was then used to poke, prod, and punch the brain before it was teased out of the nostril. The brain cavity was then filled with resin to purify it.

The body was first washed with palm wine, then packed with natron (a mixture of salt and carbonate found in the Wadi Natrun, northwest of Cairo), incense, and herbs. This process was repeated a few times over the course of 40 days. Then the body cavity was emptied, packed with resinous bandages and herbs, and sewn up.

After it was clean, the body was adorned with amulets and jewelry, wrapped elaborately in bandages while being prayed over by priests, anointed with oils, and enshrouded. The wrapping and anointing took another 30 days—a total of 70 days were required to make a good-quality mummy. During certain periods of Egyptian history a mask made of cartonnage (linen, papyrus, and plaster prepared like papier-mâché) or gold (like that of Tutankhamun) was placed over the head and shoulders of the mummy.

The body package was then put into a wooden coffin, which, in turn, was placed in a sarcophagus (like a coffin, but larger and generally of stone), before being placed in the tomb. The canopic jars with the viscera were buried next to the body. Sometimes a funerary text containing spells to help the deceased in the afterlife was written on papyrus and placed within the coffin.

DEIR AL-MEDINA

Take the main road from the ferry landing for 4 km (2½ mi).

Between the Valleys of the Nobles and the Valley of the Queens, in its own small valley, lies Deir al-Medina, the Village of the Workmen. Artisans who inhabited the village were in charge of building and decorating the royal tombs of the Valley of the Kings between the 18th and 20th Dynasties. The site includes their houses, the tombs of many of the workmen, and a small temple dedicated to several gods. The temple was founded during the reign of Amenhotep III (18th Dynasty) and was rebuilt more than 1,100 years later during the reign of Ptolemy IV. Coptic Christians later turned the temple into a monastery.

The village is made up of houses of small dimensions, built against each other. They have similar plans, consisting of three or four rooms, some of which are decorated. Some have basements, and all, probably, had second floors, or used their roof space. Hygiene in the village is believed to have been good—there was a village doctor—and the villagers likely lived much as local people do today.

Although the tombs are small, they are jewel-like, with vibrant colors and beautifully detailed images—in other words, the workers applied the technical and artistic skill that they used on their employers' projects to their own as well. On the outside of many tombs stood small pyramids, where offerings were brought for the deceased. Since the artisans worked on the royal tombs, it is natural that there would be certain similarities between the decoration of the tombs of the Valley of the Kings and the decoration of their own sepulchres.

One of the most astonishing workers' tombs is that of **Senedjem** (No. 1), who was an artist during the reigns of Seti I and Ramses II. The paintings on the walls of the burial chamber are extremely fresh looking. Notice on the opposite wall, left of the entrance, the god Anubis tending a mummy on a couch, surrounded with texts from the *Book of the Dead*. On the ceilings are several scenes showing the deceased kneeling in adoration before the gods. 🖼 *£E30 (access to two tombs)* ⊙ 6 AM–5 PM.

VALLEYS OF THE NOBLES

Abd al-Gurna, 4½ km (2 ¾ mi) from the ferry landing.

★ The Valleys of the Nobles are divided into several necropolises distributed over the West Bank at Luxor. More than 1,000 private tombs have been found and numbered. Most of them can be dated to the 18th through 20th Dynasties, although some were reused during the 25th and 26th Dynasties (760–525 BC). Because there are so many of these tombs scattered over a wide area, several ticket options exist. For example, some individual tombs have their own admission fees (usually around £E25–£E30). Other tombs are grouped together on a single ticket, sometimes combining one or two popular tombs with one or two lesser-known options.

As the name of the valley indicates, nobles mostly occupied the necropolises, but priests and officials were buried here as well. Funerary scenes appear in the tombs, but so do scenes of the daily life of the time; it is not unusual in these tombs to admire the joy of a banquet, discover the leisure-time activities, and analyze the professional lives of the deceased.

Sheikh Abd al-Gurna is the largest necropolis. A present-day village was built on top of the cemetery. To protect the site, the government tried to relocate the local population to another village, made espe-

TOMB NUMBERING

All tombs on the West Bank are numbered according to their positions in their respective valleys—the Valley of the Kings, the Valley of the Queens, and the Valleys of the Nobles—and the order in which they were discovered. The higher numbers indicate the most recent discoveries.

cially for them. The attempt was all in vain for many years. Finally, the government prevailed; at this writing, scarcely a trace of the village is left. Note that some tombs have their own separate admission fees.

Tomb of Nakht. The second tomb on the left opposite the Ramesseum, is somewhat small, and only the vestibule is decorated with vivid colors. Before the vestibule is a small display of the finds inside the tomb. Nakht was a royal scribe and astronomer of Amun (high priest) during the reign of Thutmose IV (18th Dynasty). Start with the first scene on the left of the entrance—which shows the deceased with his wife, who pours ointments on the offerings—and keep moving right scene by scene. Underneath the first is a butchery scene. Then three registers represent agricultural scenes in which Nakht himself supervises. The wall to the right of the agricultural scenes has a false door. The offerings bearers kneel, two tree goddesses carry a bouquet, and other offerings bearers stand before the gifts.

The wall opposite the harvest depictions presents a famous banquet scene with dancers and musicians—look for the blind harpist. The first scene on the right of the entrance represents, once again, the deceased and his wife pouring ointments on the offerings. To the right of the banquet scene, offerings bearers present gifts to Nakht and his wife. Farther right still, the wall shows hunting and fishing scenes in the delta with the deceased and his family. ⊠ *Tomb 52, Abd al-Gurna.*

Tomb of Ramose. This is one of the finest tombs of Abd al-Gurna. Ramose was a vizier during the reign of Akhenaton. His tomb is unusual for having both reliefs executed within the traditional norms of ancient Egyptian art, as well as reliefs done in the elongated Amarna style that the heretical pharaoh Akhenaton adopted. The tomb was left unfinished. It has a court with a central doorway that leads into a hypostyle hall with 32 papyrus-bud columns, most of which were destroyed, though others were reconstructed in modern times (full-height columns are all reconstructions). The inner hall that follows has eight columns and a shrine.

On the left side of the entrance to the hypostyle hall is a representation of the funerary banquet. The guests are seated in couples before the deceased. Their wigs are all different, and the eyes of the figures are accentuated with black contours. On the wall opposite, in an unfinished scene, Ramose presents the The-ban Triad and Ra-Harakhte to the king, Akhenaton, who is accompanied by Maat. To the right of this traditional scene, another scene bears the telltale Amarna influence: Ramose stands in front of Akhenaton and his wife, Nefertiti, adoring the sun disc Aten. From the parking area, the tomb is 100 yards ahead, on the right side. This is the only tomb that has a separate admission fee. ✉ *Tomb 55, Abd al-Gurna.*

Tomb of Rekhmire. The resting place of the governor of Thebes and vizier during the reigns of Thutmose III, Hatshepsut, and Amenhotep II (18th Dynasty) is well preserved, and the scenes are almost complete. The texts on the walls explain the installation, the duties, and the moral obligations of the vizier. The right wall of the hall to the left of the entrance shows the deceased inspecting and recording foreign tributes. Within this scene, you may recognize people of Punt bringing animals and incense trees; the Kheftiu with vases and heads of animals; the Nubians with animals; and Syrians bringing vases, a chariot, horses, a bear, an elephant, and human captives. The second scene, on the left inside the chapel, represents several stages of various crafts. The depictions of jewelry making and sculpting here helped archaeologists to understand the techniques used during the pharaonic period. The focus of the last group of scenes in the tomb is mainly on funerary rituals, such as the Opening of the Mouth Ceremony. To get to the tomb, you must make your way from the parking area to the top of the valley. ✉ *Tomb 100, Abd al-Gurna.*

Tomb of Sennefer. This tomb once held the body of the mayor of Thebes during the reign of Amenhotep II (c. 1439–1313 BC). He was the overseer of many daily activities in the city, responsible to the vizier for the smooth running of Nile commercial ports, collecting taxes on the grain harvest, and for the day-to-day maintenance of the temples. This was a position of great trust and responsibility.

In the antechamber are scenes of Sennefer receiving offerings presented by priests and family members. He sits under a fruit-laden vine—leading this tomb to be named Tomb of the Vineyards in earlier eras. The right-hand or eastern walls depict a funerary procession with Sennefer's possessions being carried into the tomb for his use in the afterlife. The burial chamber itself has colorful scenes of Sennefer's journey after death, the rituals he must perform during his journey and his rebirth into the afterlife, including a vivid image of Sennefer and his family making a pilgrimage to Abydos where the deceased has his heart

> **VALLEY OF THE NOBLES TOURING TIPS**
>
> ■ **Leave your camera back at the hotel.** Photos are forbidden in the tombs, and the bald slope of these foothills isn't photogenic.
>
> ■ **Bring a sketchbook and colored pencils.** If you're going to stray off the beaten track to see these tombs, you're either an artist or a scholar, and you'll want something personal to remember them by.
>
> ■ **A hiking stick could come in handy.** The steps down into some tombs are uneven, terribly steep, covered in sand, and have no hand railings.

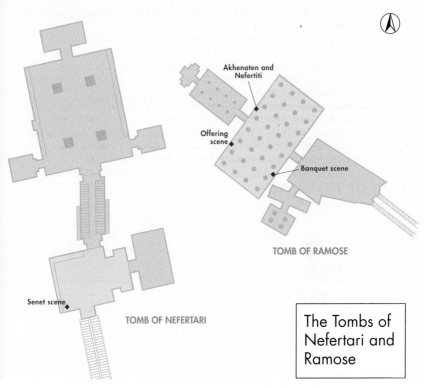

Akhenaten and Nefertiti

Offering scene

Banquet scene

TOMB OF RAMOSE

Senet scene

TOMB OF NEFERTARI

The Tombs of Nefertari and Ramose

weighed to ensure he is worthy of entrance to the afterlife. ⊠ *Tomb 96, Abd al-Gurna.*

Tomb of Userhat. Usherhat was a public servant during the reign of Amenhotep II, described as "the scribe who counts the bread in Upper and Lower Egypt." His tomb is a fine example of an inverted T-style, with a wide antechamber leading directly to a long, slender burial chamber. Scenes in the antechamber depict Userhat's earthly responsibilities—his counting boxes of grain and overseeing the distribution of bread rations to the Egyptian army. In the main chamber there are vivid scenes of Userhat hunting and fishing. ⊠ *Tomb 56, Abd al-Gurna.* 🖼 *Ramose-Userhat group of 3 tombs £E30; all other tombs £E25 per group* ☉ *Daily 6* AM–5 PM.

VALLEY OF THE KINGS

Valley of the Kings. While there's no experience quite like standing in the burial chamber of Egypt's short-lived "Boy King," the grave of Tutanhkamun is least—in size and splendor—of this valley's decorated tombs. Those of Ramses VI (KV 9) and Ay (KV 23) are known for their beauty and detail. And, like Tut's, theirs require an additional admission charge. Despite soaring temperatures in the valley and, surprisingly, even hotter conditions inside the tombs, the Valley of the Kings receives such a concentration of visitors that these precious monuments are endangered. Dr. Zahi Hawass, head of Egyptian antiquities, has plans: Re-create the most-visited or delicate tombs in a nearby location, starting with Tut's; light the valley and open the tombs for night viewing, thus spreading visitors throughout the day. Another project is already complete: The Carter Rest House, where Howard Carter lived, is open for tours (free, at this writing). ⊕ *10½ km (6½ mi) from the ferry landing: take the main road 3½ km (2 mi), then turn right. After 3 km (2 mi), turn left into the limestone hills. The valley is 4 km (2½ mi) farther* 🖀 *No phone* 🖃 *Ticket for three "regular" tombs £E80, Tutankhamun's Tomb £E100, Tomb of Ramses VI £E50, Tomb of Ay £E25* ⊙ *Daily 6* AM–5 PM.

VALLEY OF THE QUEENS

5½ km (3½ mi) from the ferry landing: take the main road 3½ km (2 mi), then turn left and climb into the limestone hills. The valley is 2 km (1¼ mi) farther.

The Valley of the Queens was also known as *Ta Set Neferu*, the Place of the Beautiful Ones. Although some 17th- and 18th-Dynasty members of the royal family were buried here, the valley was more widely used for royal burials during the Ramesside period of the following two dynasties.

About 100 tombs were cut into the valley rock. A great number are anonymous and uninscribed; others have extremely delicate and well-preserved paintings. The tombs of Nefertari, Amun-her-khepshef, Thyti, and Khaemwaset are at various points on the path through the valley, starting on the right side of the first fork to the right (Nefertari). That fork continues around a loop to Amun-her-khepshef, and then to Thyti's tombs. Another path leads right before the loop returns to the first fork; at the end of that path is Khaemwaset's tomb. ■ TIP➔ **Carry a penlight with you, as the lighting in some tombs is not good.**

★ **Tomb of Nefertari.** The tomb of the famous wife of Ramses II is generally closed to the public, which is regrettable since it has some of the most vivid surviving decorations of any tomb in the Theban Necropolis, as the postcards you will no doubt be offered will attest. Permission for a private viewing can be sought from the Egyptian Supreme Council for Antiquities for a substantial extra fee that is out of the reach of the typical traveler, though not of some highly expensive luxury tour groups. Like most tombs in the Valley of the Queens, Nefertari's consists of an antechamber, a corridor, various side chambers, and a tomb chapel. The walls of the antechamber are decorated with scenes showing Nefertari adoring several deities. One remarkable scene shows the queen herself seated playing *senet*, a popular backgammon-like game. ⊠ *Tomb 66.*

Tomb of Amun-her-khepeshef. This tomb was built for a prince who was a son of Ramses III (20th Dynasty). His tomb's wall paintings have very bright and lively colors and show scenes of the young prince, in the company of his father or alone, with a variety of gods. The anthropomorphic, uninscribed sarcophagus remains in the undecorated burial chamber. The tomb (it's the last one on the main road) contains an

Continued on page 257

VALLEY OF THE KINGS

Hoping to prevent tomb robberies, pharaohs from the zenith of Egypt's power chose to be interred in the remote Valley of the Kings, rather than in more elaborate pyramids, starting around 1550 BC.

Archaeologists have discovered 62 tombs in the royal necropolis, all from the New Kingdom. The last complete tomb found, that of Tutankhamun, was opened in 1923, but that hasn't stopped archaeologists from looking for more. Most of the tombs have a long, sloping corridor leading to a burial chamber, but the artwork varies greatly from one tomb to the next, depending on the artistic style of the time. Unlike private tombs, the burial places of pharaohs have exclusively religious texts aiding the king's journey through the underworld, instead of scenes from daily life.

As gods, the pharaohs were guaranteed a special place in the afterlife, using spells, most notably *The Book of the Dead*, to pass through the underworld.

⊹ 10½ km (6½ mi) from the ferry landing: take the main road 3½ km (2 mi), then turn right. After 3 km (2 mi), turn left into the limestone hills. The valley is 4 km (2½ mi) farther.

🎟 Ticket for three "regular" tombs £E80, Tutankhamun's Tomb £E100, Tomb of Ramesses VI £E50, Tomb of Ay £E25

🕑 Daily 6–5.

Tomb of Thutmose IV, Valley of the Kings

HISTORY

THE HISTORY OF THE VALLEY

Starting from the 11th dynasty, pharaohs ruled from Thebes, modern-day Luxor, building their mortuary temples in cities or at the edge of the desert. **Amenhotep I** (1525–1504 BC) was the son of and successor to Ahmose I, the founder of the 18th dynasty and the New Kingdom. Amenhotep founded the royal tomb-workers village of **Deir el-Medina**, on the west bank of the Nile at Thebes, to the south of the hill of **Sheikh Abd el-Qurna** (containing some of the most beautiful tombs in the Valley of the Nobles). Amenhotep and his mother Ahmose-Nefertari were the patrons of this village, and they were deified and worshiped there after their deaths. He is believed to be the first pharaoh to separate his mortuary temple from his actual tomb. Amenhotep's tomb sits not far from the summit of the range of cliffs rising behind Deir el-Medina, above the southern end of the Valley of Kings.

THE TOMB BUILDING BEGINS

Amenhotep inspired his powerful successor **Thutmose I** (1504–1492 BC), father of Queen Hatshepsut, to also separate his mortuary temple from the actual burial spot. Thutmose apparently took the advice of a noble named Anena (who is buried on the hillside of Sheikh Abd el-Qurna) for an even more remote spot than the one chosen by Amenhotep I—the area now known as the Valley of the Kings. Thutmose I established his tomb (KV 38) with great secrecy inside the desolate valley, away from tombs of most of his predecessors in Thebes, as well as Memphis (modern-day Giza).

THE VALLEY OF THE QUEENS

As a general rule in the 18th dynasty, only the pharaohs—or the queens who ruled as pharaohs—constructed tombs in the Valley of the Kings. Close relatives joined the king in the tomb, and sometimes a favorite vizier or noble was permitted a small rock chamber near his master. Ramses II (KV 7) buried his queen in a separate valley, which became the place of queens and princes for many generations. It is now known as the Valley of the Queens.

THE PROCESS OF BUILDING

The tombs in the Valley of the Kings probably began at the ascension of the king with the selection of fine, untouched rock. Tunneling proceeded with great speed, as shown by the size of tombs of even kings that reigned for relatively short periods. The early 20th-century archaeologist Arthur Weigall surmised

Valley of the Kings

Tomb of Ramses VI

Tomb of Amenhotep III

Tourist tram at Valley of the Kings

Tomb of Tutankhamun

Tomb of Ramses VI

MAJOR SIGHTS IN THE VALLEY OF THE KINGS

A Valley of the Kings Welcome Center. The visitor center has a fascinating 3-D scale model of the tombs cut into the hillside, which shows how the tombs sit and sometimes collide with one another. Take some time to explore the model to get a feel of how immense this whole complex is. The center also has videos about the Valley of the Kings. This room is quickly bypassed by most tour groups but offers interesting background information about discoveries and archaeological techniques.

B Tomb of Rameses IV. Rameses IV (20th Dynasty), the son and successor of Rameses III, is considered the first of a series of weak pharaohs whose declining power brought about the end of native kingship in Egypt. Rameses IV's tomb has graffiti from Ptolemaic and Coptic periods. The tomb's first striking scene is the sun disk with figures of the ram-headed god of the setting sun and the scarab deity of the rising sun, with Isis and Nephthys shown on either side. Much of the tomb contains spells divided into books relating to the king's identification with the gods and the journey through the underworld. The third corridor, for example, is dedicated to the *Book of Caverns*, which relates the journey of the sun god Ra through the 12 hours of night. These religious spells provided god-king with the means to pass into darkness. The sun god is later depicted in the burial chamber passing through the 12 gates of the underworld, each guarded by a dreadful serpent. In the third division of the underworld a

Tomb of Rameses IV

serpent divides 12 goddesses into two rows of six, representing the six hours before and after midnight. The goddess Nut is represented with the constellations of the heavens on her body. Rameses IV's sarcophagus is still inside the tomb. ✉ Tomb KV 2.

C Tomb of Rameses IX. This tomb held the body of one of the last great pharaohs of the 20th Dynasty and the New Kingdom. As with the tomb of Rameses IV, the outer lintel (here badly preserved) is decorated with a sun disk, inside of which is a scarab, adored by the king and surrounded by the goddesses Isis and Nephthys. Three corridors depict spells from several religious books. Most notably, the third corridor, on the left, contains passages of the *Am-duat* (*The Book of What Is in the Duat, duat* meaning netherworld) with images of rows of headless, kneeling captives. Three largely undecorated halls

Tombs are numbered according to their positions in their respective valleys—the Valley of the Kings (KV), the Valley of the Queens (QV), and the Valleys of the Nobles (NV)—and the order in which they were discovered. The higher numbers indicate the most recent discoveries.

↑ **A** TO WELCOME CENTER

Rameses VII ◆ 1

Rameses IV ◆ 2 **B**

3
46
4

D Merneptah ◆ 8

Rameses II ◆
7
5

E Tutankhamun
6 **C**
F
Tomb of Ramesses V/VI ◆ 9
62
55
Rameses IX

45
44

Amenhotep II ◆ 35
12
58 56
57
G
◆ Restrooms
28
27

43-58
11 10
16 ◆
17
Seti I
18
54
21

36
61
Rameses I
Rameses X

Hatshepsut & Thutmose I

13
29
60
20
19

14
40
38 ◆
mose I
47
26
59
30

43
Thutmose IV

Seti II ◆ 15
31
37
32

42
33
H
34
Thutmose III

---

follow, the last of which is the burial chamber. Nut is represented on the ceiling as part of the *Book of the Night*. The tomb does not contain a sarcophagus. ⊠ Tomb KV 6.

D **Tomb of Merneptah.** This tomb contained the successor of Rameses II and fourth king (1213–1204 BC) of the 19th Dynasty. His tomb comprises five corridors, three halls, and several side rooms. The wall on the left in the first corridor displays the king before the

god Ra-Harakhte. It is followed by three columns of the *Litany of Re*, and it ends with a disk surrounded by a crocodile and a serpent, adjoining the rest of the *Litany*. The wall opposite is completely devoted to the *Litany*. On both sides of the second corridor are figures of gods with texts from the *Book of the Gates* and the

Tomb of Merenptah

Am-duat. The jackal god Anubis is in the company of Isis on the left side, Nephthys on the right side. Most of the following chambers are decorated with passages from the Am-duat. The eight-pillared burial chamber contains the red granite inner lid of the sarcophagus, decorated with scenes from the *Book of the Gates*. ⊠ Tomb KV 8.

E **Tomb of Tutankhamun.** The world was thrilled when Howard Carter opened this tomb in 1923. While most other royal tombs had been robbed in antiquity, Tutankhamun's treasures were largely intact and have toured internationally for decades. Tut's body—minus its mummy

Tomb of Amenhotep II

wrappings—is now on display inside an air-conditioned glass case in the main chamber of his tomb and is the only mummy on display in the Valley of the Kings.

Little is known the life and death of Tut, the boy king. DNA tests show that Tut was probably a frail, sick boy beset with a bone disorder and malaria.

Significant efforts have been made to determine his familial lineage. DNA tests on two fragile fetus-mummies found in his tomb, for example, are being compared to other female mummies to try to identify Tut's mother—hopefully as one of the wives of the heretic Pharaoh Akhenaten: either Kiya or the powerful Queen Nefertiti.

The tomb (off the main path, on the west side of the court) has four small rooms, and only the burial chamber is decorated. One of the scenes, from the Am-duat,

represents the god Khepri in a sacred barque, followed by three registers each with four baboons, which among other functions "scream" to announce the sunrise. Inside the burial chamber is one of the gilded coffins where the mummy of Tutankhamun originally rested. ⊠ Tomb KV 62 Extra charge.

Ⓕ Tomb of Ramses V and Ramses VI. This beautiful, albeit unfinished, tomb was excavated during such a tumultuous time in ancient Egypt that Rameses VI may not have found time to finish it. The high priests simply replaced the cartouches of Rameses V with ones bearing the name of Ramses VI. The tomb was robbed shortly after Rameses' death, and it remained open in Greek times (Greek graffiti can be seen on the walls).

In the first corridor are scenes depicting a figure of the king with Harmachis and Osiris. Past that on the left,

a sun-boat is between the twelve hours of the night and the twelve hours of day. The second corridor has picture of Osiris enthroned with nine figures approaching him, with another sun boat above. The holy apes of Harmachis drive a pig, representing a wicked being, from the boat.

Past that is a third corridor, followed by a chamber, and then a four-pillared hall. The pillars are decorated with pictures of various gods, as is the ceiling. Above the door at the end of the chamber the king burns incense before Osiris. Next, two corridors precede an antechamber with a chapter from the *Book of the Dead*.

Tomb of Rameses VI

The unfinished burial chamber at the end has lovely astronomical figures on the ceiling. On the right wall a sun-boat has the sun god in the form of a beetle, representing the rising sun, and with the head of a ram, representing the setting sun. Two lions support the boat, drawn across the sky. Two birds with human heads, a typical depiction of the soul, worship the sun as he passes. ⊠ Tomb KV 9 🎟 Extra charge.

G Tomb of Amenhotep II. The impressive tomb was kept in a secret location known by high priests, who in the 9th century BC moved other mummies there for safeguarding. About 2,800 years later, in 1898, excavators found 15 royal mummies inside it. The entrance has a set of steps, followed by a sloping corridor. Another set of steps descends to a corridor containing a well, now covered with a bridge. The deep well was built to protect the tomb from floods and also to lead robbers

astray. The tomb builders cut a small chamber into it for deception. The entrance on the other side was also filled with plaster. On its other side an undecorated, two-pillared hall leads to another set of stairs to throw off robbers. At its end is the real tomb. A decorated, two-level hall that goes down to his sarcophagus. In the early 20th century, the custodians of the tomb often turned off all the lights except for one directly upon the mummy resting in its quartzite-sandstone sarcophagus beneath a ceiling covered with the stars of the heavens. The Egyptian Museum in Cairo has housed his mummy since 1928. ⊠ Tomb KV 2.

H Tomb of Thutmose III. Built for the 18th-Dynasty successor and stepson of the pharaoh queen Hatshepsut, who served as his co-regent while he was a child, this is the oldest tomb regularly open to the public. As one of the great warrior kings of Egypt, Thutmose III reestab-

lished Egypt's authority over Syria and Palestine. The beginning of the tomb is nearly identical to the tomb of his fierce son, Amenhotep II, until his two-pillared antechamber, which is decorated. The burial chamber's walls list divinities described in the Am-duat, scenes from which decorate the sarcophagus chamber. Note the curviness of the decorations—a remarkable feature of 18th-Dynasty royal burial chambers. The chamber is atypically shaped like a cartouche. The sarcophagus and lid, made of red sandstone, are still in the tomb. ⊠ Tomb KV 34.

Tomb of Thutmose III

TOMB ROBBING

Throughout Egypt's history, tomb robbing was commonplace, and even the pharaohs themselves quarried the tombs of their predecessors for their own burials. After all, the king was divine and as such was guaranteed a place in the afterlife. The rituals with the burial ensured this would happen, so ransacking their tombs would have little impact on their eternal lives. Tomb robbing, nonetheless, was severely frowned upon, and at times thieves went to trial for their crimes. A detailed account following a series of great robberies in the Valley of the Kings during the reign of Ramses X (1108–1099

BC) describes stories of disputes between officials, large round-ups of guilty and innocent persons, as well as confessions from robbers who burst into tombs, tore jewelry from the bodies of the kings, and burnt their coffins. It is obvious, then, why the pharaohs in the Valley of the Kings took great care to keep the locations of their tombs secret, although once they were known, they sometimes stood wide open. In the 21st Dynasty (1069–945 BC) robbery became so common that the priests moved at least 15 royal mummies to the secret tomb of Amenhotep II; the mummies were discovered only in 1898.

PLANNING YOUR VISIT

Valley of the Kings

Weather and Timing: The weather in the Valley of the Kings is hot year-round, scorching in the summer. The midday sun is particularly strong in the valley, so be sure to put on sunscreen, and bring a scarf or bandanna both to block the sun and to wipe off sweat. Plastic bottles with water are allowed. Ideally, arrive as close to sunrise as possible.

Crowds: Regardless of the time you travel, expect crowds. About 5,000 people visit the valley every day. Your best bet is simply to walk slowly and look around at the tombs that interest you most. Tour guides cannot give lectures inside the tombs, but they usually explain each tomb before you enter. If you read about the tombs in advance, you'll be able to target certain spots.

Photography: The valley is rather unimpressive, photographically speaking. Since photography inside the tombs is strictly forbidden (guards stand watch inside them and will stop you from taking photos), this is one place where you may want to leave your camera in the bus. You'll have ample opportunities to buy commercial postcards showing the interiors of the tombs.

Extra-charge Temples: Some people do not recommend buying the extra ticket to enter the tomb of Tutankhamun because it was probably not intended as a royal tomb, and is therefore sparsely decorated. However, it is the only tomb that contains an intact mummy. The tombs of Ramses V & VI and the tomb of Ay, Tut's trusted (albeit elderly) adviser, are more interesting.

PRESERVATION OF THE TOMBS

Not all tombs—even those that are generally open to the public—are open every day. Officials rotate open tombs every few months to protect the ancient stone and art from the most damaging effects of the air outside and the human breath of visitors: moisture and carbon dioxide. Some tombs—such as the tomb of Horemheb, the last pharaoh of the 18th Dynasty—have remained closed for extended periods. The government only reopened his tomb once it installed dehumidifiers in late 2009, after a 4-year closure.

unusual item inside a glass case: the mummified remains of a fetus (not the prince himself). ⊠ *Tomb No. 55.*

Tomb of Thyti. This cruciform tomb is well preserved. Thyti's sepulchre dates to the Ramesside period, but it is not known to whom she was married. The corridor is decorated on both sides with a kneeling, winged figure of the goddess Maat (who represented truth, justice, balance, and order) and the queen standing in front of different divinities. In the chamber on the right is a double representation of Hathor (goddess of love, music, beauty, and dancing), first depicted as a sacred cow coming out of the mountain to receive the queen, then as a woman, accepting offerings from Thyti. This tomb is on the main path, the second one on the left after the little resting place. ⊠ *Tomb No. 52.*

Tomb of Khaemwaset. Wall paintings in the tomb of this prince, who was the young son of Ramses III, are one example of the fine workmanship of the Valley of the Queens tombs. The scenes represent the prince, either with his father or alone, making offerings to the gods. Texts from the *Book of the Dead* accompany the paintings. To get to the tomb from the main path, take the left fork and continue left to the path's end. ⊠ *Tomb No. 44.* ✆ *Ticket for two tombs £E35* ⊙ *Daily 6–5.*

OTHER TOMBS AND MOMUMENTS

In addition to the four major clusters of tombs, there are other mortuary temples in the Theban Necropolis. Each pharaoh worked to assure his eternal life in the netherworld, as well as in the world of the living. One way of achieving it was to introduce a royal cult among the living. Offerings and rituals guaranteed the survival of the royal *ka* (the individual life force). For this purpose, several kings, from the 18th Dynasty to the 20th Dynasty, had mortuary temples built on the West Bank at Thebes. In these temples, deceased kings were adored as gods. Most of the mortuary temples are seriously damaged or utterly lost. Those that still stand demonstrate once again the ancient Egyptian mastery of architecture.

Colossi of Memnon. Standing (sitting, actually) over 50 feet tall, these seated statues of the great Amenhotep III are the most significant vestiges of his mortuary temple. The missing pieces were taken away for use in other buildings as early as the end of the New Kingdom. Alongside the legs of the colossi are standing figures of the king's mother and his queen, Tiyi. Relief carvings on the bases of the colossi depict the uniting of Upper and Lower Egypt. Ancient graffiti also covers the ruined giants.

The poetry of these colossi is the sound that the northern statue emitted in earlier days. After an earthquake fractured the colossus in 27 BC, it was said to sing softly at dawn. That sound recalled for Greeks the myth of Memnon, who was meeting his mother Eos (Dawn) outside the walls of Troy when Achilles slew him. In the 3rd century AD, Roman Emperor Septimus Severus had the statue mended. After this the colossus was silent. There is currently active archeological work taking place around the statues, but the viewing areas are still open to the public at this writing. ✢ *3 km (2 mi) west of the ferry landing, on the main road* ✉ *Free ☉ Dawn–dusk.*

★ **Deir al-Bahri.** The Mortuary Temple of Hatshepsut (1465–1458 BC), built by the architect Senenmut, is a sublime piece of architecture—some say the finest on the planet for its harmony with its surroundings. It consists of three double colonnades rising on terraces that melt into the foot of towering limestone cliffs.

Hatshepsut (18th Dynasty) was the most important woman ever to rule over Egypt as pharaoh. Instead of waging war to expand Egyptian territory like her predecessors, she chose to consolidate the country, build monuments, and organize expeditions to the land of Punt to bring myrrh, incense, and offerings for the gods. Prior to acting as pharaoh, she served as regent for her (then-young) successor, Thutmose III. As soon as Thutmose III came of age to rule over Egypt, he began a program of selectively eradicating her names and images from the monuments of Egypt. Curiously, he didn't erase all of her names, and in some cases the defaced and the intact cartouches are quite near each other.

The reliefs inside the first colonnade are damaged. They included a detailed scene of how the queen's granite obelisks were transported on boats from Aswan to Karnak. Take the large ramp that leads to the second court. The chapel on the left is dedicated to the goddess Hathor. The capitals of the columns are carved in the shape of the face of Hathor as a woman, with cow's ears surmounted by a sistrum. To the right of the chapel starts the second colonnade. Its first half is consecrated to the famous expeditions to Punt—modern scholars have yet to determine where Punt actually was—and shows the variety of products brought from Punt. The colonnade on the right of the second ramp is devoted to the divine birth of Hatshepsut, with Hatshepsut's mother seated with the god Amun-Ra, between the first and second columns. By showing that she was of divine origin, Hatshepsut proved she was able to rule over Egypt as pharaoh. The better-preserved chapel to the right is dedicated to Anubis.

The Third—upper—terrace is reached by a ramp flanked by twin representations of Horus. The hypostyle hall on the terrace has carvings depicting two different scenes. On the north side are celebrations for the "Beautiful Feast of the Valley," which observed the connection between the living and the dead. The carvings show priests carrying barques with statues of the gods and the Pharaohs followed by musicians and dancers. On the south side scenes of royal statues carried in barques with their associated coterie—depicting the mortuary cult of ancestor worship—in this instance for Hatshepsut. Beyond the wall and cut into the rock is the sanctuary of Amun, the Holy of Holies where the barque of Amun would rest in preparation for its next day of festivities.

The temple is not included on all guided tours, so be sure to verify its inclusion if you would like to see it. Otherwise, you can easily arrange private transportation. ✢ *From the ferry landing, take the main road; after 3½ km (2 mi), turn right; after 1½ km (1 mi), turn left; the temple lies ahead* ✉ *£E30 ☉ Daily 6 AM –5 PM.*

In the Valley of the Queens, also known as "the Place of the Beautiful Ones"

Medinet Habu. The mortuary temple of Ramses III (1550–332 BC) is an impressive complex that was successively enlarged from the New Kingdom down to the Ptolemaic period. Hatshepsut built the oldest chapel. Ramses III built the temple itself, which functioned as a temple to the deceased pharaoh.

The second king of the 20th Dynasty, Ramses III had a certain admiration for his ancestor Ramses II, so he copied the architectural style and decorative scheme of his predecessor. Following Ramses II's example a century before him, Ramses III consolidated the frontiers of Egypt. He also led successful campaigns against the Libyans and their allies, and against the Sea Peoples (the Phoenicians).

Enter the complex through the Migdol (Syrian Gate). Two statues of Sekhmet (goddess of plagues, revenge, and restitution) flank the entrance. The path leads directly to the first pylon of the mortuary temple. The reliefs on this building, as well as in the first court, relate the king's military campaigns. On the back of the pylon, on the right side, a scene shows how the hands and tongues of the enemies were cut off and thrown in front of the king. At the Window of Appearances, on the south side of the first court, the living pharaoh received visitors or gave rewards to his subordinates. The second court, through the second pylon, is dedicated to religious scenes, and the colors and reliefs in the court are well preserved. The remains of the hypostyle hall and the smaller chapels that surround the second court are less complete. On the left flank of the temple, inside the enclosure, are several mud-brick palaces that have been in need of restoration. ✛ *Take the main road*

VALLEY OF THE QUEENS TOURING TIPS

■ **Take the path less traveled.**
While others are packed into the Valley of the Kings, come here instead.

■ **So what if Nefertari's tomb is closed?** Go to that of Amun-her-khepeshef. It's better than King Tut's. It's more complex, with paintings on incised plaster, rather than flat surfaces. And it's just as sad. This son of Ramses III died in his teens—that's him on the walls, wearing that

strange prince's lock of hair—though it is said he may never have been buried here.

■ **Appreciate the artistry.** In the Tomb of Khaemwaset, look for a scene where this young prince is wearing a long, filmy garment. Notice how the painting shows the sheerness of the fabric, and the prince's arms and legs through it.

from the ferry landing for 4 km (2½ mi) and turn left; the temple is 500 yards ahead 🖂 *£E30 ⊘ Daily 6 AM–5 PM.*

The Ramesseum. The mortuary temple of Ramses II (19th Dynasty) is one of the many monuments built by the king who so prolifically used architecture to show his greatness and to celebrate his divinity. The temple is a typical New Kingdom construction, which means that it includes two pylons, two courtyards, and a hypostyle hall, followed by the usual chapels and a sanctuary. The numerous surrounding granaries are made of mud brick. A huge quantity of potsherds, from amphorae that contained food and offerings, was found in situ. It shows that the temple had religious—as well as economic—importance.

Note the 55½-foot-tall (when it stood) broken colossus of Ramses II, between the first and the second courts. It was brought here in one piece from quarries in Aswan. A Roman historian's flawed description of the colossus is supposed have inspired Percy Bysshe Shelley's poem "Ozymandias"—its title was the Hellenic name for Ramses:

I met a traveller from an antique land Who said: Two vast and trunkless legs of stone Stand in the desert. Near them, on the sand, Half sunk, a shattered visage lies, whose frown, And wrinkled lip, and sneer of cold command, Tell that its sculptor well those passions read Which yet survive, stamped on these lifeless things, The hand that mocked them, and the heart that fed. And on the pedestal these words appear: "My name is Ozymandias, king of kings; Look on my works, ye Mighty, and despair!" Nothing beside remains. Round the decay Of that colossal wreck, boundless and bare, The lone and level sands stretch far away.

Shelley got the facial expressions (if not the sculptors' talents), the fictitious inscription, and the desert location all wrong, but the poetic evocations of ancient political might and its wreck do have their power.
⊹ *From the ferry landing, take the main road; after 3½ km (2 mi), turn right, then turn right again after 700 yards* 🖂 *£E35 ⊘ Daily 6 AM–5 PM.*

Temple of Seti I. Seti I's 19th-Dynasty temple is the northernmost of the New Kingdom mortuary temples. Son of Ramses I and father of Ramses II, Seti I was one of the great kings who guaranteed safety inside

Kent Weeks and Tomb KV5

Recent archaeological work on the West Bank has concentrated on attempts by Dr. Kent Weeks to create a comprehensive database of tombs, temples, and archaeological sites across the Theban Necropolis. This venture, called the **Theban Mapping Project** (⊕ *www.thebanmappingproject.com*), was begun in 1978 and continues to this day. But something that happened in 1987 has overshadowed the progress of this worthy and necessary work.

While mapping the extant tombs in the Valley of the Kings, attention was turned to a small tomb at the very bottom of the valley, a tomb used as storage for the spoils unearthed by Howard Carter when he was excavating Tutankhamun's tomb. Kent and his team cleared this space and discovered a whole complex of tombs, the like of which had not been seen on the West Bank before. Long corridors leading off the initial antechamber revealed at least 150 separate carved rooms—a veritable underground palace. Weeks proposed that this tomb was built by Ramses II for his many children, and fragments of human bones found in one of the chambers proved to be those of Amun-her-khepeshef, eldest son of Ramses II, who died during his father's reign.

The tomb, called KV5, remains closed to the public as excavation work continues, partly because much of it lay under the old Valley of the Kings parking lot and the structure was weakened by the regular comings and goings of the tourist traffic above.

the country and repelled the attempts of enemies to upset the balance of Egyptian supremacy.

The temple, which is extremely damaged, is dedicated to Amun-Ra, Ramses I, Seti I, and Ramses II (who finished parts of it). Much restoration work has been accomplished, but the remains of the buildings are so poor that only lower parts of the walls were rebuilt. Nine impressive papyrus-bud columns of the peristyle hall, the hypostyle hall, and the sanctuary are the only massive parts of the temple still standing. ✛ *Take the main road from the ferry landing for 3½ km (2 mi), turn right and follow that road for 3 km (2 mi); turn left; the temple is 400 yards ahead* 🖼 *£E30* ☉ *Daily 6 AM–5 PM.*

THE UPPER NILE VALLEY: SOUTH OF LUXOR

There are three noteworthy stops south of Luxor: Esna, where two locks in the Nile require the cruise ships to line up and navigate their way; al-Kab, which has a little-visited temple; and Edfu, where the Temple of Horus is the most impressive and intact temple on the shores of the Nile. The Nile cruisers normally bypass Esna and al-Kab, though it's possible to book private tours from Luxor. Edfu is included on all Nile cruise itineraries, but the temple can also be seen on overland day trips from Luxor.

ESNA

54 km (33 mi) south of Luxor.

The town of Esna enjoyed some notoriety in the 19th century, when quite a number of singers, dancers, prostitutes, and other similar folk were exiled from Cairo and resettled here. French novelist Gustave Flaubert visited Esna expressly to see the performances of the artists and professionals. He wound up becoming somewhat obsessed with a prostitute–dancer, and he spent a good deal of time describing her (and his opium-induced visions) in letters to his long-suffering wife.

GETTING HERE AND AROUND

If you want to visit the site and your ship does not stop here, you'll need a security escort. Book a private taxi or inquire with a tour operator such as Thomas Cook in Luxor about current arrangements when you are there. Expect to pay a private taxi about £E200 for the three-hour round trip.

The **Temple of Khnum**, which is one of the most truncated and least attractively sited Egyptian temples that you are likely to see, was constructed between the 2nd century BC and the 2nd century AD. It sits in a 30-foot-deep pit in the middle of Esna, and to get to it, you have to run the gauntlet down a short street from the river that's lined with souvenir sellers anxious to peddle their wares. Resist all temptation to go into a shop here, because salespeople are known to be unpleasantly aggressive. The temple is in a pit because the level of the town has risen over time, sinking the partly excavated temple below the level of the modern houses. There is some fine stratigraphy, made visible from the excavations, in the soil behind the temple. The ticket booth is at the iron entrance gate that leads to a staircase descending into the pit.

Composed of 24 columns, only the hypostyle hall of this Ptolemaic/Roman temple dedicated to Khnum (the god associated with creating people) is visible. There is a question as to what happened to the rest of it—was it never built, or was it robbed for its stone in antiquity? The portion of the temple that remains is completely decorated and has some very unusual cryptographic inscriptions that are hymns to Khnum. One is written almost entirely with hieroglyphs of crocodiles, another with rams. The columns are also inscribed with significant texts that provide an outline of different festivals held at the temple throughout the year. The ceiling is decorated with zodiacal motifs, and fragments of paint are still visible. In the forecourt and around the temple lie picturesquely scattered fragments primarily of Roman and Coptic date, including a particularly charming lion-faced basin. At this writing, Esna is not a stop on most cruise-ship schedules (the ships usually just clear the locks and sail on into Luxor). ⊠ *Mabed Esna* ⛟ *£E20* ⊗ *Daily 6* AM–5 PM.

AL-KAB

32 km (20 mi) south of Esna.

Al-Kab, on the East Bank of the Nile, is the site of an impressive though imperfectly preserved town, temple area, and tombs. The site was first inhabited around 6,000 BC and occupied thereafter. It was sacred to the

ESNA TEMPLE TOURING TIPS

■ **Steel yourself.** A lot of tours, that is to say, Nile cruise boats, skip the Temple of Khnum—maybe because it's small, maybe because the trip through Esna Locks is more interesting, maybe because the walk from the river to the temple is choked with the most determined touts and shopkeepers on the Nile. You'd do better to do your shopping elsewhere.

■ **Will it move?** There's been talk that the temple might actually be relocated, in much the same way

the Nubian temples were, to a spot closer to the Nile.

■ **Dreary surroundings.** If you do come, you can see why it would be a good idea to relocate this monument. First, it's down in a hole; the town grew up, literally, around it. Second, guides point to evidence that increasing salt levels in the water table are leaching into the column bases, weakening them.

■ **Columns and more.** This temple is known for its variety of column capitals. See how many different ones you can identify.

vulture goddess of Upper Egypt, Nekhbet—the ancient name of al-Kab is Nekheb. Nekheb was allied with the town of Nekhen on the West Bank of the Nile (modern Kom al-Ahmar).

The town of Nekheb is enclosed by a massive mud-brick wall and includes houses, the principal **Temple of Nekhbet,** smaller temples, a **sacred lake,** and some early cemeteries, which are rather difficult to make out. About 400 yards north of the town are several **rock-cut tombs** that date primarily from the New Kingdom, although there are some earlier tombs as well. The most famous are those of **Ahmose Pennekhbet, Ahmose son of Ibana,** and **Paheri.** The first two are noted for their historical texts, which discuss the capture of the Hyksos capital Avaris and various military campaigns of the pharaohs of the early New Kingdom. The Tomb of Paheri is noted for its scenes, especially the small scene of a herd of pigs. Some distance into the wadis are the rock-cut **Sanctuary of Shesmetet,** a chapel, and a small **Temple of Hathor and Nekhbet** (these are not always open). ⊠ *Athar al-Kab* 🕾 *No phone* 🖾 *£E30* ⊙ *Not open on a regular basis; check with Luxor tourism office for status.*

GETTING HERE AND AROUND

The only way to get to the ancient site is by private taxi. You may need police permission and should visit the tourist office in Luxor before making the trip to find out what you need to do. Tour operators may also offer the trip, though it isn't a standard program. Service taxis go to the village but not to the antiquities, and they may be reluctant to carry tourists. Expect to pay a private taxi around £E300 (though perhaps more) for the half-day round-trip.

Temple of Horus at Edfu

EDFU

115 km (71 mi) south of Luxor; 105 km (665 mi) north of Aswan.

Although the town itself is somewhat dull, Edfu's temple, dedicated to Horus, would make even Cecil B. DeMille gasp. It is the most intact of Egyptian temples you are likely to see, and it is a most unexpected and breathtaking sight. Visiting Edfu's temple, set at the edge of the modern town of Edfu—portions of which peer over the temple enclosure wall—is the closest you can get to being an ancient Egyptian going on a pilgrimage. To get the full effect of this marvel, buy your tickets and walk along the exterior of the temple, around the pylon, to the end of the courtyard toward the birth house, without turning around. At the end of the courtyard, turn suddenly to face the great Temple of Horus at Edfu. A new feature at Edfu is the addition of a nightly Sound & Light Show.

GETTING HERE AND AROUND

Visit Edfu either on a Nile cruise (all cruises include tours to this temple), or by hiring a private taxi or limousine in Luxor or Aswan for a set price. If you plan on hiring a private taxi, be aware that you will need to obtain permission from the tourist police at least 24 hours or more in advance; and a permission fee may be involved. If you are coming from Aswan, you will probably also want to stop at Kom Ombo (⇨ *North of Aswan: Kom Ombo and Draw Camel Market, Chapter 5)*. Regular buses and service taxis also run from Luxor and Aswan, but they may be reluctant to carry tourists. If you can get a service taxi, be prepared to hire another taxi to get from the bus or service-taxi stop to the temple.

EDFU TOURING TIPS

■ **The temple astounds.** Before you get to Edfu, you'll have seen at least one or two temples in various states of ruin. That makes seeing Esna all the more thrilling. Its pylons, courts, and chambers are the most intact, period. It's still got its roof. When you see photos of a shaft of light filtering past a pharaonic column, illuminating a man wearing turban and galabeyya, that photo was taken here.

■ **Nighttime entertainment begins.** The Sound & Light Show

franchise has now expanded to Edfu. At this writing, the program was in final testing, making adjustments based on audience response. It offers the opportunity to see this old temple in a new light.

■ **Carriages.** If you are arriving in Edfu by Nilecruiser, the traditional way of reaching the temple is by horse carriage. If this bothers you, take a taxi, but make sure the driver waits for you.

★ The **Temple of Horus** is mainly from the Ptolemaic period. The temple does, however, rest on earlier foundations, which may date from the Old Kingdom (2625–2130 BC). The exterior walls are covered with texts that give details of the temple's construction. Ptolemy III started it in 237 BC, and the entire building was completely finished and decorated in 57 BC. Access to the temple originally would have been from the south, but because of the growth of the town, it is now entered from the north.

The enormous **pylon,** fronted by a pair of statues of Horus as a falcon, leads into a columned courtyard at the end of which stands another, better-preserved statue of Horus as a falcon. The doorway behind this leads to the **hypostyle hall.** The columns in this temple are typical of the Ptolemaic period, which means that they have varied capitals: palm-leaf capitals, lotus capitals, papyrus capitals, and a large variety of elaborate composite capitals. The bottoms of the column shafts, above the bases, are carved to show the leaves found at the bases of various plants.

Following the central axis, the hypostyle hall is succeeded by a series of rooms. The last in the series is the temple's sanctuary, which contains a finely polished monolithic *naos,* or shrine, of syenite (an igneous rock) that would have housed the statue of the god set in another smaller shrine made of gilded wood. An altar stands before the naos; originally gilded wooden doors, the sockets for which are visible in the jamb area, would have fronted the naos.

Rooms off the central axis are thought to have been storerooms for various ceremonial items, such as perfume, wine, incense, gold, and vessels made of precious metals. A series of rooms in the rear of the sanctuary contains access, now blocked for the most part, to crypts made to store the most precious of the temple's possessions. The central room at the back includes a model barque (a modern reproduction) that is very probably identical to the one used in antiquity to transport the golden statue of the god in religious processions around town and on boats north to Dendera.

The inner rooms of the temple are dark, lit by shafts of light entering from narrow slits at ceiling level. Originally the temple would have been lit thus, with additional light coming from flickering torches. The richly colored walls would have shone and glimmered like jewels in the half-light; it is easy to imagine priestly processions passing through the temple on sandaled feet, chanting and praying amid clouds of incense.

The interior of the temple is decorated with scenes of divinities and pharaohs making offerings to one another, as well as some scenes of the founding of the temple. Elements of a celestial ceiling are visible in the hypostyle hall. A **side chapel** to the east with its own tiny courtyard contains a beautiful ceiling showing the course of the sun as it is swallowed by the sky goddess, Nut, and then born from her the following morning.

The inside of the temple's stone enclosure wall shows scenes of Horus fighting with and defeating his enemy, the god Seth. This is one of the few places where an illustrated version of the Horus and Seth myth is visible. There are several variations on the tale in which Seth killed his brother Osiris and set himself up as ruler in his stead. Isis, Osiris's wife, used her magic to bring Osiris back to life and to become pregnant. The result was Horus, who sought to avenge his father's murder and to rule, as was his right. He and Seth engaged in a series of battles using both strength and magic. Ultimately Horus was the victor, and he was rewarded with rule over Egypt—hence the living pharaoh's identification with Horus—and Osiris ruled over the afterworld. Seth became god of deserts and distant lands.

The reliefs show Horus defeating Seth in his different guises (hippos, crocodiles, and so forth) and are quite entertaining. It is believed that a mystery play illustrating this struggle took place at a Horus–Seth festival at Edfu. Another amusing fact to note about this temple (and other Ptolemaic temples) is that many of the cartouches are left empty. This is because the Ptolemies overthrew one another so frequently and so speedily that the architects, contractors, and priests decided to leave blank cartouches that could be painted in with the ruling Ptolemy's name whenever the appropriate time arose.

On one side of the temple, between the outer and inner stone walls, is a **Nilometer**, a gauge used to measure the height of the Nile—and to calculate taxes. The expectation was that the higher the river, the better the harvest was going to be and, therefore, the higher the taxes.

At this writing, Edfu's Sound & Light Show is operating, but because the program is still new, there's a possibility that the temple closing time may vary. ⊠ *Mabed Edfu* ☎ *No phone* ✆ *Temple £E50, Sound & Light Show £E75* ◷ *Temple daily 7* AM–5 PM; *Sound & Light Show nightly (in English) at 8* PM, *9* PM, *and 10* PM.

Aswan and Lake Nasser

WORD OF MOUTH

"We sailed by Elephantine Island and the Aga Khan Mausoleum. It was so relaxing to just sit on the felucca and let the Nile and slight wind move us. . . . After a while, they decided that we had all had enough relaxation, and the three Nubians working the felucca started singing. . . . Soon after the song was over, we met the crocodile."

—Iowa_Redhead

WELCOME TO ASWAN AND LAKE NASSER

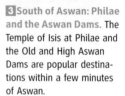

TOP REASONS TO GO

★ **Abu Simbel.** Study the powerful yet serene face of the pharaoh on the monumental statuary on the facade of the Temple of Ramses II.

★ **Philae.** Soak in the atmosphere at the island-bound temple dedicated to the goddess Isis, which still welcomed worshippers in the 5th century AD.

★ **A Felucca Sail.** Take to the Nile on a traditional sail around the Cataracts— the colossal mounds of granite that are scattered across the path of the river.

★ **A Nile Cruise.** Immerse yourself in Agatha Christie's novel *Death on the Nile* while relaxing on the upper deck of a luxury cruise boat.

★ **Nubian Culture.** Turn amateur anthropologist as you explore the long history of the Nubian people at the Nubia Museum or partake of their rich culture at a Nubian village.

1 **North of Aswan: Kom Ombo and Daraw.** Kom Ombo is a popular archaeological site that is on all Nile cruise itineraries and reachable overland from Aswan. Daraw's camel market is less visited and less tourist-oriented.

2 **Aswan.** A jumping-off point for Egypt's south, Aswan is a much more laid-back destination than either Luxor or Cairo. The center for felucca sails on the Nile and cruises on Lake Nasser, it's also a focus for exploration of Egyptian Nubian culture.

3 **South of Aswan: Philae and the Aswan Dams.** The Temple of Isis at Philae and the Old and High Aswan Dams are popular destinations within a few minutes of Aswan.

4 **Lake Nasser.** While New Kalabsha is reachable on a day trip from Aswan, other sights require either a flight (Abu Simbel) or a cruise (all other sights along the lake).

214

2

2

215

Abu Simbel

Abu Simbel

EGYPT
SUDAN

GETTING ORIENTED

For sights near Aswan, private taxis are by far the easiest way to get around. You can take a prebooked day trip to Kom Ombo and the camel market. The Aswan High Dam and the point of departure for Lake Nasser cruises is a short distance from town, as are the docks for boats going to the island temples of Philae and Kalabsha. Abu Simbel, south of Aswan on Lake Nasser, is a 30-minute flight from Aswan or a three-hour road trip.

5

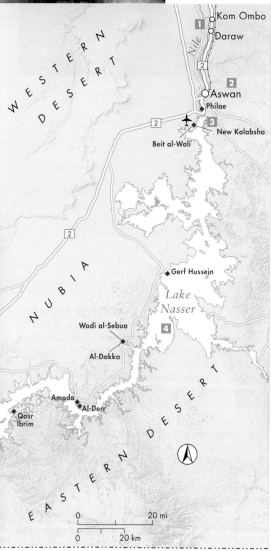

Kom Ombo
Daraw
Aswan
Philae
New Kalabsha
Beit al-Wali
Gerf Hussein
Lake Nasser
Wadi al-Sebua
Al-Dakka
Amada
Al-Derr
Qasr Ibrim

WESTERN DESERT
NUBIA
EASTERN DESERT
Nile

0   20 mi
0   20 km

Updated by
Toni Salama

Egyptians today take for granted modern control of the Nile: they open their faucets complacently, even if they don't always obtain the desired results. But in antiquity the river and its capricious annual floods were endowed with divinity and honored with all the force of the empire. The floodwaters acted as god and teacher, as the ancients learned the movements of the stars and devised calendars in order to predict the arrival of the inundation.

The Nile was the pharaohs' vehicle for empire building. It was the carriage road for troops, trade, and the massive granite blocks quarried in Aswan—the temples that line its banks from Al Minya to Abu Simbel glorify both the ancient gods and the Egyptians' ingenuity in putting the river's power and wealth to work. The river also made agriculture and the feeding of the population—the workforce—so easy: Herodotus noted in 460 BC that the Egyptians "gather in the fruits of the earth with less labor than any other people." Having mastered several straightforward irrigation techniques still in use today, farmers sowed their seeds and harvested two annual crops from the rich silt that the floods left behind.

No other river and no other ancient civilization have so fired the imagination of the modern West. But, aside from the works of ancient Greek, Roman, and Arab historians, and an antagonistic contact during the Crusades, the West remained essentially ignorant of Islamic culture and the marvels of the pharaohs until the late 1700s. And the people of the Upper Nile lived in relative isolation, working the land as they had for millennia.

In 1902 the British built the first Aswan dam to conserve late-summer floodwaters for the low-water season and increase agricultural output. As the population grew, these reserves became insufficient. The building of the Aswan High Dam in the 1960s altered the river's character dramatically, putting an end to the seemingly eternal and sometimes devastating annual floods. But the dams are just technological updates on what men have been doing for ages: tapping the river's power.

Today, the river remains the lifeblood of the country, but for most visitors it is first and foremost a leisure facility, the now benign waters allowing easy access to Egypt's most magnificent ancient monuments.

PLANNING

WHEN TO GO

Traditionally, high season begins at the end of September, peaks around Christmas, and lasts until April. To avoid crowds, stay away at these times. The heat kicks in as early as March in Upper Egypt—a dry, pollution-free heat that you can get used to. Evenings are always cooler in the desert. However, life slows down even more in Aswan in summer, when it is noticeably hotter here than in Luxor. Ramadan is much quieter still, especially in Upper Egypt.

PLANNING YOUR TIME

Most travelers spend only one night in Aswan to see the temple at Philae, maybe the Nubian Museum, and perhaps to take a short felucca sailing trip around the cataracts. If you are short on time, skip the High Dam; it looks no different than the ones you see at home. Add another day if you want to do the trip to Abu Simbel by air before joining a Nile cruise, which will take three or four nights. If you have more time, visit the Nubian village of Gharb Seheyl, or hike up to Saint Simeon's Monastery and the tombs of the nobles on Aswan's West Bank. Definitely reserve a day to see Kom Ombo if you are not taking a Nile cruise. You can also see the temples on New Kalabsha as a half-day excursion from Aswan.

GETTING HERE AND AROUND

AIR TRAVEL

EgyptAir, your only option for domestic flights, operates several flights a day from Cairo to Aswan and to Abu Simbel (usually direct). There are also regular flights linking Aswan with Alexandria, Luxor, and Hurghada. From Cairo to Aswan, the journey takes about two hours one way (often with a stop in Luxor); flights from Luxor to Aswan, or from Aswan to Abu Simbel, take 30 minutes one way.

Contacts EgyptAir (✉ *EgyptAir Building, 1 Shar'a Abtal al-Tahrir, Aswan* ☎ *097/231–5000* ⊕ *www.egyptair.com*).

AIRPORT TRANSFERS

The Aswan airport is about 15 to 20 minutes from town, a taxi ride of about £E50 from Aswan. An airport shuttle bus linking Abu Simbel airport with the temple is included in all EgyptAir tickets to Abu Simbel.

TOP REASONS TO GO

Temples. Beit al-Wali, located at New Kalabsha, is known for its vivid color; Abu Simbel for its monumental statues of Ramses II; and Philae for its Roman influences. Most of the Nubian temples are rarely visited, since they are visible only on a Lake Nasser cruise.

Tombs. Although much less visited than those in the Theban Necropolis, the Tombs of the Nobles on Aswan's West Bank can be visited on an easy day trip across the river and combined with Saint Simeon's Monastery via a short camel trek.

Nubian Culture. During ancient times, Egypt's southern neighbor, Nubia, was sometimes friend, sometimes foe. In modern times, the Nubian people who lived along the Nile Valley south of Aswan developed a culture independent of Arab Egypt, and it lives on in the households of 50,000 Nubians in and around Aswan. This culture is remembered at the Nubia Museum and kept alive in Aswan's Nubian villages.

River Trips. Popular Nile cruises begin or end in Aswan. For shorter trips in Aswan, the monumental rose-red granite boulders of the cataracts and their associated river islands make for wonderful late-afternoon felucca rides. Aswan is also the jumping-off point for the relaxing trip down Lake Nasser to Abu Simbel.

Birding. The Nile Valley offers a wealth of opportunities for bird-watching. Cattle egrets follow the farmers and herds, but they roost in the riverside trees at night. Heron species are abundant. Pied kingfishers and moorhens make a living on the water; various species of hirundines (swallows and martins) swoop for insects just above the surface, and black kites and ospreys—common raptors—circle the skies above. Along with endemic species, the Nile acts as a major pit stop during the spring and fall journeys of millions of migratory birds.

Relaxation. The pace in Aswan is simply slower than in the rest of the country, and the atmosphere less pushy. Part of Aswan's strong appeal is the chance to simply relax and explore at a less breakneck pace. The smart traveler uses his or her time in Aswan to enjoy the sunset with a drink, have a relaxing sail on a Nile felucca, or make a camel trip along the western bank.

BOAT TRAVEL

Aswan has no West Bank roads, so you have to travel by felucca to visit the sights across the river. Powerboats also run between sights, but they are less romantic and much more expensive, at about twice the cost to cut the already short travel time in half.

Public felucca ferries cross regularly to Elephantine Island for a couple of pounds from early morning to midnight. Catch them by the public park on the south end of the Corniche.

Individual feluccas have fixed rates that tend to be highly negotiable and start at around £E40 an hour. You can find out these rates at the Tourist Information Office, hotels, and the offices of local travel and tour agencies.

For longer felucca trips from Aswan, consult the Tourist Information Office for help in arranging tours to Kom Ombo (a full day and night); to Edfu (two days and nights); and to Esna (three days and nights). Prices for these trips are reasonable, from about £E50 per person per night (minimum six people, maximum eight, or you can rent the whole boat). Captains can be reluctant to sail all the way to Luxor, because the return trip upriver takes longer (and if you are going to end the trip south of Luxor, be sure to arrange to be picked up). You need a group of six people for one of these rustic, camp-out-style journeys. *(For information on arranging multiday felucca trips, see ⇨ Chapter 8, Nile and Lake Nasser Cruises.)*

Powerboats leave for New Kalabsha Island (its temples are Kalabsha and Beit al-Wali) from beside the entry to the High Dam; the £E45 fare allows for a visit of about an hour. Philae has its own dock about a 15-minute drive from town, on the east side of the basin between the Old Dam and the High Dam. Powerboats make the trip for about £E50—which can be shared among the passengers—but they may be willing to wait for only two hours, which is probably enough for most people. If you need more time to see Philae's Temple of Isis, mention this in advance; if you are traveling independently, make sure that the price you have agreed upon includes extra waiting time and the return journey. Expect a certain amount of chaos at the dock in Philae, and make sure you can recognize your boatman for the trip back.

BUS TRAVEL

Be aware that many buses never depart Cairo without a mechanic aboard; things can and do break down. Even Egyptians don't try to travel the full 879 km (546 mi) from Cairo to Aswan by bus. That's what the train is for. But if you will not be dissuaded, you can try to purchase tickets from Targoman Bus Station in Central Cairo.

Contacts Targoman Bus Station (⊠ *Shar'a Mahata Aboud, Downtown, Cairo* ☎ *02/2431–6723*).

CAR TRAVEL

Car rental isn't a practical option in Aswan since you can walk between downtown attractions, and most other sights (Philae Temple, Kalabsha Temple, Elephantine Island, West Bank attractions) involve a boat transfer. It's better to negotiate a taxi rate, or reserve a private car and driver, and ride with someone who knows their way around the town.

Individual foreigners traveling out of Aswan must travel in a convoy, if headed to Abu Simbel, or obtain police permission at least 24 hours in advance for destinations north, such as Kom Ombo or the Daraw camel market. These arrangements will be made for you if you are traveling with a tour company or a private car and driver. Convoys south to Abu Simbel depart at 3:45 AM and 11 AM, from a central location, which means your tour company or driver will pick you up at your hotel even earlier.

Contacts Limousine Safy (☎ *012/321–6347 or 012/233–1949*).

TAXI TRAVEL

You'll find plenty of taxis in Aswan, the same six-seater Peugeot station wagons as in Luxor. You can travel the length of the Corniche for about £E20; shorter trips cost about £E10.

You can also use taxis to travel outside Aswan; just remember that police permission must be requested at least 24 hours in advance. Approximate costs for Peugeot taxi service from Aswan—as quoted by the Tourist Information Office—and covering up to four passengers in the same vehicle are as follows: £E120–£E150 round-trip for the half-day, 90-km (56-mi) journey to Kom Ombo; £E300–£E350 one way for the full-day, 225-km (140-mi) trip to Luxor, including stops at the temples at Edfu and Kom Ombo. You should expect to pay about £E70 round-trip to Philae, including the driver's two-hour wait while you visit the temple (you'll also have to hire your own boatman if you go independently). But it may cost the same, about £E70, to add the High Dam and Unfinished Obelisk to the Philae route.

TRAIN TRAVEL

From Cairo to Aswan, the regular train costs £E109 for first class. At this writing, foreigners traveling by train from Cairo were all but forbidden to take second-class trains—they're probably doing you a favor, given the condition of bathrooms in second-class trains—and could only buy first-class tickets for travel at night; by day, Egyptian commuters are the priority passengers. You can also take the train from Luxor to Aswan, day or night; fares are £E41 first-class. Travel time between Luxor and Aswan is 3 to 3½ hours.

Most tourists traveling from Cairo to Aswan by train will prefer the comfortable sleeper cars run by Abela, which make the daily trip to Aswan from the cavernous Ramses Station in central Cairo. Tickets should be purchased at least 10 days in advance at the Abela office in the station, or you can arrange for tickets through a local travel agent. At this writing, there are two daily departures in each direction. Train 84 leaves Cairo at 8 PM, reaching Aswan at 8:15 AM; Train 86 departs Cairo at 9:10 PM, arriving in Aswan at 9:30 AM. For the return journey, Train 85 departs Aswan at 6:30 PM, arriving in Cairo at 6:45 AM; Train 87 leaves Aswan at 9:20 PM, arriving at Cairo 9:30 AM. A single couchette with meals costs $80 one way; a double couchette costs $60 per person. These fares must be paid in foreign currency, not Egyptian pounds.

Contacts Abela (⊠ *Ramses Station, Cairo* ☎ *02/2574–9474* ⊕ *www. sleepingtrains.com*).

RESTAURANTS

Aswan's independent eateries serve Egyptian food with a Nubian flair. Other cuisines are found in hotel restaurants. The variable city tax on restaurants, combined with service charges, can total as much as 26%. Check menus to verify how each restaurant operates. Unless you are in a major hotel, consider tipping even if a service charge is included in the bill: waiters are not well paid, and the courtesy will be appreciated. If service is not charged, 10%–15% is a reasonable tip. And one more thing: Bring cash; most local restaurants take nothing else. As a rule, most hotel restaurants are open to the general public. Reservations are recommended at all hotel restaurants.

HOTELS

Aswan has relatively few hotel choices, particularly in the midrange. You can expect rates to be higher here than for equivalent accommodations in Luxor or Cairo, except in summer. In Aswan, rates are less expensive in summer—late April to the end of September—sometimes dramatically so, and many hotels will offer discounted rates in times of low occupancy regardless of the season. Aswan in particular has a lot of large groups that stay only a night or two to see Philae and the local sights and then move on. The Aswan hotels that have island addresses automatically offer regular free ferry services to the town.

All hotel reviews have been condensed for this book. Please go to Fodors.com for full reviews of each property.

5

WHAT IT COSTS IN EGYPTIAN POUNDS, U.S. DOLLARS, AND EUROS			
	$	$$	$$$	$$$$
Restaurants	under £E50	£E50–£E100	£E100–£E150	over £E150
Hotels in Dollars	under $70	$70–$130	$130–$200	over $200
Hotels in Euros	under €45	€45–€80	€80–€130	over €130

Restaurant prices are per person for a main course at dinner. Hotel prices are for a double room in high season, excluding 10% tax and service charge (usually 10%).

VISITOR INFORMATION

The tourist information office is open daily. Winter hours are Saturday to Thursday, 8 to 3 and 6 to 8, Friday, 9 to 3 and 8 to 8. Summer hours are Saturday to Thursday, 8 to 3 and 7 to 9, Friday, 9 to 3 and 7 to 9. Ramadan hours are 10 to 2 and 6 to 8. The office has a very helpful, multilingual staff that can tell you about fixed taxi and felucca rates for short and long trips. The staff can also recommend guides and provide most any other information about Aswan.

Contacts Aswan Tourist Information Office (✉ *Next to train station* ☎ *097/231–2811*).

NORTH OF ASWAN: KOM OMBO AND DARAW CAMEL MARKET

The Temple of Sobek at Kom Ombo is the first stop on many Nile cruise itineraries; it's a widely visited and popular temple. For those not on Nile cruises, it's also possible to see it on a day trip from Aswan, or as a stopover on the way between Luxor and Aswan on the overland route.

KOM OMBO TEMPLE TOURING TIPS

■ **It's in the eyes.** In the first hypostyle hall, search the reliefs for the most important beings; you can identify them by their eyes, which originally would have been carved and inlaid.

■ **Listen to the stories.** Pick a spot where guides are explaining a particular scene. Wait there a while and see how many of the successive guides give different explanations, which is part of the fun.

■ **Look at the walls.** You found the depictions of surgical instruments. Now look for the birthing-chair illustrations.

■ **Relax.** If you are feeling the ennui of "temple fatigue," enjoy the view of this antiquity—it's on a low bluff beside the Nile—from the cool confines of your Nile cruise boat's swimming pool.

Lesser known is the camel market at Daraw, which remains a local institution, free of both tourist trappings and conveniences.

KOM OMBO

65 km (40 mi) south of Edfu; 40 km (25 mi) north of Aswan.

Kom Ombo, a fertile area, is interesting because it supports not only its original Egyptian inhabitants, but also a large Nubian community that was resettled here after the construction of the Aswan High Dam and the flooding of Lower Nubia. As a result, the town has grown considerably in the intervening years. Kom Ombo was an important town strategically because it was one of the places where the trade routes to the Nile Valley, the Red Sea, and Nubia converged. It is also the site of a very unusual double temple dedicated to the gods Sobek, depicted as a crocodile or a crocodile-headed man, and Haroeris, a manifestation of Horus represented as a falcon or a falcon-headed man.

GETTING HERE AND AROUND

You can visit Kom Ombo either as part of a Nile cruise, an organized tour, or by private taxi hired in Aswan for £E120–£E150 for the half-day round trip. Buses, minibuses, and service taxis also run from Aswan, but they may be reluctant to take foreigners.

WHAT TO SEE

★ **Temple of Haroeris and Sobek.** Built between the 2nd century BC and 1st century AD, the temple stands on a bend in the Nile. It is especially romantic to behold the temple in the moonlight, if you arrive on a cruise at the right time of the month. Virtually all the remains of the temple date to the Ptolemaic period and later, although evidence of earlier structures has been found, most notably an 18th-Dynasty gateway.

The temple is remarkable for its duality: it has two of almost everything, enabling its priests to conduct equal services for two deities simultaneously. The southern part of the temple, on the right when you face the entrance, is dedicated to Sobek, the northern part to Haroeris.

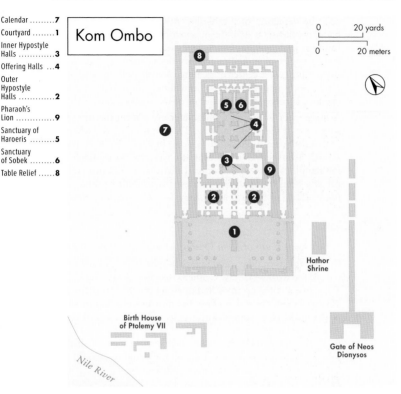

Kom Ombo

0   20 yards

0   20 meters

Hathor
Shrine

Birth House
of Ptolemy VII

Nile River

Gate of Neos
Dionysos

Immediately across the courtyard to the right after you enter the compound is a small shrine, dedicated to Hathor, which now houses some mummified crocodiles. Crocodiles, sacred to Sobek, were worshiped at Kom Ombo. The crocodiles were regarded as semidivine, and they were fed the finest foods, provided with golden earrings, and given elaborate manicures, which involved gilding their nails. Areas in the northwestern parts of the enclosure are thought to have been the place where the sacred crocodiles were kept when alive.

The double entrance to the temple proper is from the southwest, leading into a large courtyard—the structure was oriented with its entrance to the river, rather than having a true east–west axis. This courtyard is the only shared space in the temple proper; from here, the building is divided in two. There are two doorways that lead to **outer hypostyle halls, inner hypostyle halls,** a series of **offering halls,** and twin **sanctuaries.** The sanctuaries contain a set of crypts from which priests provided oracular advice and the respective god "spoke" whenever necessary. Behind the sanctuaries is a series of storerooms now inhabited by bats.

The decoration of the walls is the usual type found in temples: pharaohs making offerings to divinities and divinities blessing pharaohs. The different gods being honored show to whom the temple is dedicated. Look for a calendar on the southwest wall of the offering hall, and the depiction of a table laden with surgical implements on the back (northeast) wall of the outer stone enclosure. Surgical implements found at archaeological sites (and used worldwide until quite recently) can clearly be identified on the table as a clear reference to the fact that the temple was a center of healing. A rather charming relief of a pharaoh's pet lion nibbling on the unwillingly proffered hands of the king's enemies is carved on the exterior of the southeastern wall.

A large, deep well and a **Nilometer** are within the mud-brick enclosure west of the main building. This is also the area where the sacred crocodiles were supposed to have been kept. Fragmentary remains of a birth house stand at the temple's western corner (in front). Behind the temple is a yet-to-be-excavated area that was probably the site of priestly houses and a very modest town, built of mud bricks. ☎ *No phone* ✉ *£E30* ☽ *Oct.–May, daily 7–7; June–Sept., daily 7–9.*

DARAW CAMEL MARKET

5 km (3 mi) south of Kom Ombo; 35 km (22 mi) north of Aswan.

Known for its Sunday camel market—the largest camel market in this part of the world—Daraw is otherwise a hot, dusty, and flyblown place. The camels come up from Sudan along the 40 Days Road. Traditionally, they made the trek on foot, but now more and more of them arrive in the backs of Toyota pickup trucks, which the camel drivers rent at Abu Simbel for the final leg of their trip. Merchants from Cairo, mostly, make their way to Daraw to take the camels back to Cairo. The camels sold on Sundays are mostly destined for slaughter; rural Egyptians say camels make the best *kofta* (meatball) kebabs.

On Tuesdays, the Daraw market sells, in addition to camels, livestock: sheep, goats, cows, bulls, and poultry. Full of dust, tumult, and herders with whips, market days are nothing if not colorful and crowded with people and animals. However, while it's an exciting experience to push your way through the crowds, if you have a soft spot for four-legged creatures, you should brace yourself for the occasional upsetting sight. And it can be dangerous: Animals in crowded, unfamiliar surroundings can, and do, bolt. After you inspect the varieties of livestock and exchange views with Sudanese, Egyptians, and Beshari tribesmen about the animals, saunter over to the produce section before moving on to inspect the different sticks, staves, flyswatters, whips, and harness bits on sale here. Trading usually ends by 2 PM. In summer, the market is very hot and very odorous. ⚠ **Dress Code Alert: This market is not a vacation spot where immodest attire might be ignored. In fact, your guide may refuse to bring you if you are not dressed appropriately. This is rural Egypt, peasant Egypt, a rugged world where travelers of both genders had best wear long pants, long sleeves, and a headscarf—not just to be treated with respect by the *fellah* (farmers), but to avoid further distractions to the animals.**

GETTING HERE AND AROUND

The round-trip from Aswan by private taxi costs about £E50 per hour riding in a standard Peugeot cab. Depending on how long you stay at the market, the round-trip will take between two and three hours.

Continued on page 292

THE KINGDOMS OF EGYPT By Chip Rosetti

It may be a cliché, but there really is something eternal about Egypt. Today's Egyptians can justly claim to be heirs to one of the world's oldest civilizations, one that flows like the Nile itself across the expanse of human history. For millennia, Egypt has intrigued and attracted outsiders—from Alexander the Great to planeloads of tourists today—inevitably leaving its mark on each.

Egypt is nothing if not a bundle of contradictions that somehow seamlessly fit together: most of the country is desert, yet it has always been one of the most fertile places on earth, thanks to the Nile. Egyptians have a strong sense of their uniquely Egyptian identity, but their country was the prime champion of Arab nationalism in the 20th century. The achievements of ancient Egypt are still mind-boggling today, not least because their civilization is so ancient.

It's easy to forget that the Giza pyramids were already two millennia old by the time Antony and Cleopatra came along. But long after the pharaohs were gone, Egypt continued to play a decisive role in human civilization: from its formative role in early Christianity to its elegant Islamic architecture, down to its current position in the modern Middle East, as a vibrant 21st-century nation with a rich and varied history behind it.

Sarcophagus of Tutankhamun at the Egyptian Museum, Cairo

(top right) Saqqara pyramid;
(left) Cosmetic palette from the
Predynastic period, 3000 BC;
(bottom right) Narmer Palette

Predynastic Egypt

ca. 4500–3000 BC

There is evidence of a human presence in Egypt far back into the Paleo-lithic era, when much of north Africa was fertile, green, and wooded. As the Sahara expanded after 10,000 BC, sedentary communities developed closer to the Nile valley. Much of the culture we know as ancient Egyptian took shape in the formative Badarian (ca. 4500–4000 BC) and Naqada (ca. 4000–3000 BC) cultures, when Egyptians developed large-scale irrigation, complex social organizations, and, eventually, writing. Local kingdoms emerged, including one that ruled all of Upper Egypt from the capital of Abydos.

■ Abydos

The Early Dynasties and the Old Kingdom

3100–2055 BC

Around 3100 BC, Menes united both Upper and Lower Egypt for the first time: this union—which inaugurates Dynasty I, according to traditional chronologies—marks the beginning of the pharaonic era. The scene is recorded on the famous **Narmer Palette** in the Egyptian Museum, which depicts king Narmer (generally thought to be Menes) defeating his enemies. Menes/Narmer established his new capital at Memphis. Narmer's successors developed hieroglyphics, perfected the art of mummification, and built mud-brick burial mounds known as *mastabas*. The 3rd-

Dynasty pharaoh Djoser (ca. 2650 BC), along with his vizier Imhotep, constructed the **Step Pyramid of Saqqara**—Egypt's first pyramid and the world's oldest large stone structure. Djoser's innovation ushered in the great era of pyramid building, including the famous examples at Giza and Dahshur. Old Kingdom Egypt featured a strong central government, including a scribal bureaucracy and a sophisticated taxation system, headed by a god-pharaoh, who was tasked with regulating *maat* (divine justice and order) on earth.

■ Step Pyramid of Saqqara
■ Giza Pyramids
■ The Bent Pyramid of Dahshur

(left) Ancient statues in Karnak temple, Luxor; (top) Valley of the Kings, the tomb of Ramses II; (bottom) Abu Simbel Temple

2055–1550 BC

The Middle Kingdom and the Hyksos Invader

By the end of the Old Kingdom, regional governors grew more powerful and the country fragmented during the First Intermediate Period. Local kings from Thebes eventually re-extended their authority, and the Middle Kingdom witnessed a flourishing of literature and more lifelike statuary. As the fortunes of the Middle Kingdom waned, it succumbed to immigrants from southwest Asia, the Hyksos, whose superior technology (such as chariots) were unfamiliar to Egyptians.

- Karnak Temple
- Beni Hasan Tombs

1550–1069 BC

The New Kingdom

After 90 years of Hyksos domination, a unified Egyptian kingdom rose again with the 18th Dynasty. For many, the New Kingdom represents the apex of ancient Egypt: it extended Egypt's domain far into Nubia, down to the Fourth Cataract of the Nile, and as far as the Euphrates in Syria. Making Thebes their religious capital, the New Kingdom pharaohs added most of the impressive features to the already imposing Karnak and Luxor temples and venerated the new combined god Amun-Ra. They also began royal burials in the **Valley of Kings**. Some of the most familiar figures from Egyptian history date to this period: **Queen Hatshep-** sut (1479–1458 BC) became a powerful female pharaoh, sending a trade expedition to the distant land of Punt. **Akhenaten** (1352–1336 BC) launched his short-lived religious reformation, replacing traditional worship of the gods with a monotheistic devotion to the sun-disk Aten, only to have his policies reversed by his boy-king successor, Tutankhamun. **Ramses II** (1279–1213 BC) ruled for 66 years and left massive monuments dedicated to himself all over Egypt, including the colossal **Abu Simbel temple**.

- Abu Simbel
- Valley of the Kings
- Egyptian Museum

TIMELINE

747–656 BC Rule of
25th-Dynasty Nubian pharoahs

332 BC Alexandria
founded; Ptolemy I
becomes pharoah

| 1000 BC | 750 BC | 500 BC | 250 BC |

(above) Temple of the Oracle at Siwa Oasis; (far right) Temple in Edfu; (near right) The Greco-Roman Museum

The Late Period

1069–332 BC

The end of the 20th Dynasty marked the end of the unified New Kingdom. For the first time since the Hyksos, outsiders ruled Egypt, starting with a Libyan dynasty in the Delta and followed by the powerful **Nubian pharaohs** of the 25th Dynasty (ca. 747–656 BC), who saw themselves as heirs to the New Kingdom. The powerful **Assyrian Empire** played kingmaker in Egyptian dynastic struggles, and twice the world-conquering Persians occupied the country, generating much resentment.

■ Temple of the Oracle, Siwa Oasis
■ Nubian Museum, Aswan

The Ptolemies

332–30 BC

The return of Persian rule in 343 BC was so unpopular that the arrival of Alexander the Great in 332 BC was welcomed by many. In a shrewd display of public relations, the Macedonian conqueror visited the desert oracle in Siwa, where the priests declared him the son of Amun. Before leaving Egypt for good, Alexander founded the city of Alexandria, creating Egypt's first substantial link to the Mediterranean. After Alexander's death in 332 BC, his general Ptolemy claimed Egypt, eventually declaring himself pharaoh. Under Ptolemy and his heirs, Alexandria flourished, becoming a Greek-speaking capital of learning and culture. The Ptolemies built the Lighthouse, the fabled Library, and the Mouseion, a kind of ancient university. Many of the later Ptolemies—perhaps because of their tradition of inter-marriage—were irresponsible rulers, and Egypt's declining fortunes (and growing debts) soon brought it into the orbit of Rome. Cleopatra VII, daughter of Ptolemy XII, famously attempted to preserve her dynasty's diminished independence by forging relationships with first Julius Caesar and then Marc Antony, but with her suicide in 30 BC, all of Egypt became an imperial province of Rome.

■ Temple of Horus, Edfu
■ Greco-Roman Museum, Alexandria

| 30 BC Suicide of Cleopatra VII (end of Ptolemy period) | 391 Thephilus burns last remnants of the Library of Alexandria | 642 Muslims invade Egypt |

| 0 | AD 250 | 500 | 750 |

(top left) Pompey's Pillar, Alexandria; (bottom left) Philae Temple, Aswan; (right) Saint Catherine's Monastery

Roman Egypt

30 BC–AD 330

With the Ptolemies, Egypt had ceased to be ruled by native Egyptians, but it was at least independent. With the triumph of Octavian, Egypt became part of the Roman Empire. Alexandria continued to flourish under the Romans as a center for medicine, astronomy, and Neoplatonic philosophy. Rome also established lucrative mines in the Red Sea desert. According to Coptic tradition, Christianity arrived in Alexandria with St. Mark after AD 60, culminating in the horrific persecutions of the emperor Diocletian (AD 284–305).

■ Pompey's Pillar, Alexandria
■ Philae

Byzantium and the Copts

AD 330–642

The era of martyrs and Roman persecution came to an end when the emperor Constantine granted imperial support for Christians with the Edict of Milan in 313. Egypt had played a formative role in the growth of Christianity since the beginning. Christian monasticism was born in Egypt: desert hermits such as St. Antony (251–356) attracted numerous devotees and imitators. With the backing of the empire behind them, Christian leaders soon turned against local pagans. In 391, the bishop of Alexandria, Theophilus, led a mob against the city's remaining pagans, burning down the Serapeum temple and the last remnants of the Library of Alexandria. With the ascendancy of Christianity, Egypt cut its ties to its ancient pagan past. Egyptian Christians increasingly were at odds with the Greek-speaking hierarchy, now based in Constantinople, over whether Jesus had one nature (the "Monophysite" position), or two natures, human and divine (the "Melkite" position). Nearly two centuries of Egyptian resistance to Melkite orthodoxy meant that, by the time Islam arrived, Egypt had little reason to rue the departure of the Byzantines.

■ The Coptic Museum
■ Wadi Natrun Monasteries
■ Monastery of Saint Catherine

TIMELINE

868 Ahmad ibn Tulun
appointed governor
of Egypt

969 Cairo founded
by the Fatimids

800   900   1000   1100

(top) Mosque of 'Amr Ibn al-'As; (far right) Mosque of Ibn Tulun; (near right) View from inside Al-Azhar Mosque

The Early Islamic Period

642–969

In 641, the Arab general 'Amr ibn al-As led a Muslim army across Sinai into Egypt, where he laid siege to the Roman fortress of Babylon, now Coptic Cairo. For most Egyptians, Byzantine rule had long since come to be associated with an oppressive religious orthodoxy, and there was little resistance to the arrival of Islam. Muslims, in turn, considered Christians and Jews "people of the Book," and allowed them to practice their religions, provided they paid tax to the Muslim army. For several centuries, Egypt remained primarily a Christian populace ruled by a Muslim minority. Outside the walls of Babylon,

'Amr built the camp-city of Fustat, as well as his mosque, the first in Africa. In 868, a Turkish soldier named Ahmad ibn Tulun was appointed governor by the Abbasid caliph in Baghdad. But within months ibn Tulun shored up his position and declared Egypt independent from the Abbasids. He ordered the construction of al-Qata'i, a new city that was of legendary splendor. His successors were not as capable as he, however, and when the Abbasids reassumed control of Egypt in 905, they had the city razed, sparing only the magnificent Mosque of Ibn Tulun.

- Mosque of 'Amr Ibn al-'As
- Mosque of Ibn Tulun

The Fatimids

969–1171

Surprisingly, the city of Cairo proper was only founded in 969, when a Shi'ite dynasty known as the Fatimids conquered Egypt from their base in Tunisia. The Fatimids built the walled city of al-Qahira ("The Victorious"), which supplanted nearby settlements such as Fustat as Egypt's primary city. From their base in Egypt, the Fatimids controlled an empire stretching from North Africa to Syria and part of the Arabian Peninsula, and commanded trade between the Mediterranean and the Red Sea. Many of the city's most recognizable monuments date to the Fatimids, who, as patrons of science and learning, also founded Al-Azhar University and Mosque. The

(far left) Mosque of Sultan
Hasan; (top) The Citadel;
(near left) Bab Zuweila

5

early Fatimid rulers al-Mu'izz (969–975) and al-'Aziz (975–996) were tolerant and quick to establish good relations with local Jews, Christians, and Sunni Muslims—a necessary ingredient to economic stability. Subsequent caliphs, however, were less accommodating, in particular the possibly deranged al-Hakim (996–1021), known for his harsh edicts against non-Shi'ites. Internal power struggles weakened the Fatimid state, and the Crusaders looked toward Egypt as their next conquest.

- Al-Azhar Mosque and University
- Bab Zuweila
- Museum of Islamic Art

1171–1517

Saladin and the Mamluks

When the Crusaders attacked Egypt in 1168, the Fatimids requested assistance from the Seljuk Turks, who sent their effective military vassal Salah al-Din al-Ayyubi (1137–1193), known to Europeans as "Saladin." Salah al-Din assumed the post of vizier, and two years later, when the last Fatimid caliph died, declared himself sultan. Salah al-Din founded a citadel fortress above Cairo and began the tradition of building *madrasas* (religious schools), to reorient the populace to Sunni Islam after 200 years of Shi'ite rule. His relatives, known as the Ayyubids, ruled Egypt in his stead when he left to battle the Crusaders

in Syria, but by 1250, their slaves had usurped power and ushered in the era of Mamluk rule. The Mamluks, a term that means "owned," were a caste of professional slave-soldiers of Circassian or Turkish origin. Mamluks were bought as children, converted to Islam, and educated in the houses of the rich and powerful. They eventually acquired positions of considerable influence. While there was considerable infighting and fratricide in the struggle for ultimate power among the Mamluks, Egypt also enjoyed great economic prosperity. Art and architecture were very heavily funded during these years.

- The Citadel
- Khan al-Khalili
- Mosque of Sultan Hasan

(left) Men smoking hookahs in El Fishawy Coffee House; (top) Opening the Suez Canal 1869; (bottom) Muhammad Ali Mosque

The Ottoman Era

1517–1798

In 1517 the rapidly expanding Ottoman Empire defeated the last Mamluk sultan, and Egypt began three centuries as a dominion of the Ottomans, who declared themselves caliphs. The Ottomans appointed viceroys (*walis*) to run the country, and Egypt entered a period of decline: this period corresponded with the European age of discovery, when importance of the trade routes that Egypt straddled was eclipsed by the new Atlantic trade. Thus the province of Egypt came to resemble more and more a feudal backwater.

■ Bayt al-Suhaymi, Cairo
■ El-Fishawy, Cairo

An Egyptian Awakening

1798–1882

In a bid to disrupt British access to India, Napoléon Bonaparte launched an invasion of Egypt in 1798. Although Napoléon's conquest was short-lived, it served as Egypt's jarring introduction to modernity and to European technology. (Napoléon's decision to bring along hundreds of scholars on his campaign also ushered in a new fascination with Egyptian civilization in Europe.) When the rubble cleared, the new Ottoman viceroy to Egypt, an Albanian mercenary named Muhammad 'Ali Pasha, took the lessons of the invasion to heart. Realizing the need to modernize, he brought in

European advisors, reformed the military, and reorganized agricultural land, introducing cotton as a cash crop. Egypt under Muhammd 'Ali and his heirs (who later styled themselves *khedives*), became quasi-independent from the Ottoman Empire. The rush to modernize, however, had its costs, particularly with the heavy expenses involved in constructing the vital Suez Canal in 1869. As the holders of most of Egypt's debts, England and France began taking ever greater control of Egypt's finances. Finally, in 1882, the British occupied the country, having faced down a nationalist revolt headed by an army officer, Ahmed 'Urabi.

■ Muhammad 'Ali Mosque

(top) Bibliotheca Alexandrina; (far left) Gamal Abdel Nasser; (near left) Begin, Carter, and Sadat at Camp David 1978

1882–1952
A Modern Nation

Egypt chafed under British control. Nationalist feelings spilled over in 1919 during a series of demonstrations against the British. A formal independence came in 1923, but continued British meddling in Egyptian politics—and a foot-dragging royal family—hindered Egypt's political aspirations. Cairo was developing into a modern capital, and Alexandria remained a lively cosmopolitan enclave, but rural Egypt remained poor and underdeveloped, with a few powerful families controlling much of the country's arable land.

- Constantine Cavafy Museum, Alexandria
- Café Riche, Cairo

1952–Present
Revolution and Republic

Decades of frustrated nationalist hopes, followed by a military debacle in the 1948 war with Israel, set the stage for a surprise coup led by a group of young military men, calling themselves the "Free Officers," in July 1952. The bloodless coup sent Egypt's sybaritic King Farouq into exile, and the Arab Republic of Egypt was born. Egypt's dynamic new president, Gamal Abdel Nasser, nationalized the Suez Canal in 1956, facing down a triple invasion led by Britain, France, and Israel, and winning major credibility among newly independent Third World countries. A champion of Arab

nationalism who preached socialist ideals in public, but cultivated a growing police state to stifle opposition at home, Nasser's project foundered on the debacle of the Six Day War with Israel in 1967. He died three years later, only to have his successor, Anwar Sadat, make peace with Egypt's longtime adversary through the 1979 Camp David Treaty. Since Sadat's 1981 assassination, Hosni Mubarak has held the presidency of Egypt. Mubarak has continued Sadat's liberal economic policies, as well as his controversial Emergency Laws, while fending off both a growing political Islam and demands for greater political freedoms.

- Aswan High Dam
- Bibliotheca Alexandrina

Temple of Haroeris and Sobek

Make sure to tell the driver that you expect him to wait while you take in the sights. Some tour operators in Aswan have the market on their itineraries.

ASWAN

880 km (546 mi) south of Cairo; 210 km (130 mi) south of Luxor.

For thousands of years Aswan was the "Southern Gate," the last outpost of the Egyptian empire. Its name comes from the ancient Egyptian *swenet* ("making business"), and its reputation as a frontier emporium dates from the colonial era of the ivory trade and commerce in ebony, gold, slaves, spices, gum arabic, ostrich feathers, and, at least until 1929, panther skins. Today's souk may be tame by comparison but is no less interesting. Among the restaurants, juice stands, vegetable stalls—and yes, souvenir shops—people go about the business of Aswan knowing that this is a gateway to Africa, and that the Tropic of Cancer lies just a few miles to the south.

As seen in the climate-adapted architecture and gaily painted houses of the Nubian areas, Aswan town and its gracious inhabitants have an aesthetic sense rarely found in modern Egypt. This is a desert city, austerely clean, full of trees and gardens, the scents of baking sand and the Nile, oleander and frangipani.

It wasn't quite so shady when French troops arrived in 1799 on Napoléon's orders to capture or kill Mamluk leader Mourad Bey. By the time the exhausted regiment reached Aswan, the nimbler Mamluk cavalry had disappeared into the Nubian Desert. That gave the French

CLOSE UP

Gamel Abdel Nasser

Lake Nasser is named after Egypt's most important modern-day politician, Gamel Abdel Nasser (Gamal 'Abd al-Nasir), who broke the ties of colonialism during the 1950s, leading Egypt after independence and becoming a leading light in the pan-Arab movement.

Born in Alexandria in 1918, he graduated from the Military Academy in 1938 but had a deep desire for Egyptian autonomy and founded a group called the Free Officer's Movement. In 1952 the movement staged a military coup, ousting the Egyptian royal family. Nasser left the military and became prime minister in 1954.

Nasser tried to tread a middle path to avoid the tensions between the Communist bloc and the West by joining the nonaligned movement in 1955. But Egypt couldn't avoid making choices between the capitalists and the Soviets. The United States pulled out of a deal to fund the Aswan High Dam in 1956, so Nasser nationalized the Suez Canal to pay for the project, prompting military action by the Israelis, the British, and the French, which petered out after pressure from the United States. The Arab world saw this as a victory for Nasser, and he became a regional hero.

In 1956, Egypt officially became a socialist state. There was nationalization of key industries and land reform, but it never reached the amount of state control that it needed to truly live up to the title. But Nasser also announced Russian funding for the Aswan High Dam, and this further alienated the West. Pan-Arab relations took a step forward in 1958, when Egypt entered a political union with Syria under the banner United Arab Republic, but this wasn't a success and only lasted until 1961.

Throughout the 1960s, pressure in the region was building, and Nasser used his rhetoric against Israel in an attempt to drum up help from other Arab nations to crush the Jewish state. But the Israelis didn't wait and launched a preemptive action in 1967 that became known as the Six Day War. It brought a massive defeat for Egypt and a personal loss of face for its president. Nasser offered his resignation, but in a massive show of popular support his people took to the streets to call on him to reconsider. Although he remained president, the defeat had dampened his spirits. His health suffered, and he died of a heart attack in 1970 at the age of 52.

Nasser was not universally popular at home. After an assassination attempt in 1954, he clamped down on all domestic opposition, putting his main rival, Mohammed Naguib, under house arrest and replacing a judiciary that suggested rule of law ought to prevail. However, he is still viewed as a hero by many.

time to take stock of the pharaonic and Greco-Roman monuments that even now seem strangely remote.

Although Aswan was a winter resort popular with Greeks, Romans, and Egyptians in antiquity, Europeans didn't come until Thomas Cook sent down his luxuriously outfitted and provisioned *dahabiyyas* (large feluccas) in 1869. Credited by some as having created the travel industry in Egypt, Cook provided the means for wealthy Victorians to comfortably

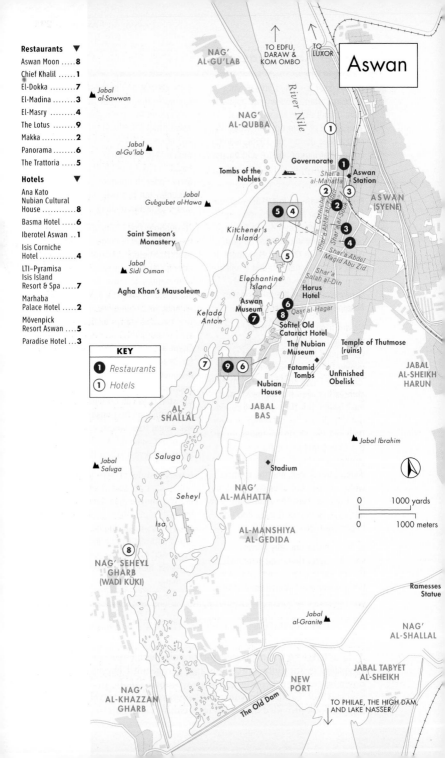

Aswan

Restaurants ▼

Aswan Moon 8
Chief Khalil 1
El-Dokka 7
El-Madina 3
El-Masry 4
The Lotus 9
Makka 2
Panorama 6
The Trattoria 5

Hotels ▼

Ana Kato
Nubian Cultural
House 8
Basma Hotel 6
Iberotel Aswan .. 1
Isis Corniche
Hotel 4
LTI–Pyramisa
Isis Island
Resort & Spa 7
Marhaba
Palace Hotel 2
Mövenpick
Resort Aswan 5
Paradise Hotel ... 3

KEY

1 *Restaurants*
① *Hotels*

TO EDFU,
DARAW &
KOM OMBO

TO LUXOR

River Nile

NAG'
AL-GU'LAB

*Jabal
al-Sawwan*

NAG'
AL-QUBBA

*Jabal
al-Gu'lab*

Governorate

Tombs of the
Nobles

*Jabal
Gubgubet al-Hawa*

Aswan Station

ASWAN
(SYENE)

Shar'a al-Mahatta

Shar'a Abdel el-Tahir

Shar'a al-Souk

*Shar'a Abdel
Magid Abu Zid*

Kitchener's
Island

Saint Simeon's
Monastery

*Jabal
Sidi Osman*

Elephantine
Island

*Shar'a
Salah al-Din*

Horus
Hotel

Agha Khan's Mausoleum

*Kelada
Anton*

Aswan
Museum

Qasr al-Hagar

Sofitel Old
Cataract Hotel

The Nubian
Museum

Temple of Thutmose
(ruins)

JABAL
AL-SHEIKH
HARUN

Fatamid
Tombs

Unfinished
Obelisk

Nubian
House

AL-
SHALLAL

JABAL
BAS

Jabal Ibrahim

*Jabal
Saluga*

Saluga

Stadium

NAG'
AL-MAHATTA

Seheyl

Isa

AL-MANSHIYA
AL-GEDIDA

0   1000 yards
0   1000 meters

NAG' SEHEYL
GHARB
(WADI KUKI)

Ramesses
Statue

*Jabal
al-Granite*

NAG'
AL-SHALLAL

NAG'
AL-KHAZZAN
GHARB

NEW
PORT

The Old Dam

JABAL TABYET
AL-SHEIKH

TO PHILAE, THE HIGH DAM,
AND LAKE NASSER

explore one of the outreaches of their realm while enjoying Aswan's excellent, dry climate.

Rich in granite, this area was quarried by Egyptians and Romans, the evidence of which stands in monuments up and down the Nile Valley. It continues to yield mineral wealth to this day—in addition to the distinctive pink-and-black-flecked Aswan granite, there are

iron foundries, aluminum mines, and important talc deposits that help fuel Egypt's development. South of Aswan, the High Dam testifies to Egypt's modern determination and its unparalleled ability to renew itself, even to the extent that Egypt no longer ends at Aswan. The use of Lake Nasser for tourism—and its open-air museum of salvaged monuments—extends the grand tour well into what is appropriately, and poignantly, called the New Nubia.

Aswan, like Luxor, is laid out along the Nile Corniche, but the West Bank here is undeveloped desert, accessible only by water. This means that you must make short river crossings by felucca—which are wonderful preludes to visiting Elephantine Island and Kitchener's Island, and the Tombs of the Nobles and Saint Simeon's Monastery on the West Bank.

GETTING HERE AND AROUND

Aswan is linked to Cairo by domestic air service (from EgyptAir) and overnight trains; flights and trains also connect Aswan to Luxor. Nile cruises either begin or end in Aswan, and the city is the jumping-off point for cruises on Lake Nasser, which begin a few miles south of town.

ESSENTIALS

INTERNET

Most major hotels offer some form of Internet connection, though not all have in-room service. Internet cafés are numerous but open and close with great regularity. Access is cheap (around £E10 per hour) but connections are not always fast. There is an increasing number of Wi-Fi hotspots for travelers with their own laptops, but Internet cafés are difficult to find.

THE EAST BANK

Aswan Souk. You won't find fresh elephant tusks here these days, as in the past, but this is still a lively, colorful marketplace filled with Nubian music—tourists by day, Egyptians by night.

From the Corniche, head a couple of blocks east, or start from the train station. Walking along the wide, traffic-free thoroughfare, you can find better cotton fabrics here than in Cairo—either plain white or printed with African or pharaonic designs (about £E11 per meter, which is a bit longer than a yard). Ready-made buys include *galabeyyas* (cotton shirts, £E120), tablecloths (£E100), and simple, fine white cotton scarves that come in handy in the heat of the day (£E25–£E40). If you really want to shop like the locals, watch for out-of-the-way staircases that lead to a lower level. Asking prices in these underground shops usually start at less than what hard bargaining will get you up on the street, not to mention better-quality merchandise. Antiquarians should be on the lookout for antique tribal items, such as daggers, jewelry, and household items. Carpets are also a good option, as many Bedouin and Nubian handmade carpets find their way to Aswan. Unfortunately, most vendors have their most kitschy patterns at the front of house (decorated with camels or village scenes), and you need to ask for the genuine article—giving away one of your bargaining chips by declaring an interest. Stop in a café for tea and watch the traffic flow. ⊠ *Souk St. (parallel to the Corniche), Downtown* ☉ *Daily 8* AM*–midnight.*

Nubia Museum. The Nubia Museum is the triumphant capstone of the effort to preserve Nubian culture and folk heritage in the wake of the building of the Aswan High Dam. The Egyptian government financed it with technical assistance from UNESCO. Arranged chronologically, it takes you through Nubia's prehistory; the pharaonic dynasties, including the Kingdom of Kush, when Nubian kings ruled Egypt; and onward through its Christian and Islamic periods. The selection of statuary is extraordinary for its range and eclecticism. There is also a diorama with scenes of Nubian village life. And that's just indoors. The museum's extensive grounds are a harmony of landscaping, water features, and artifacts, including a typical Nubian house. There is a lot to take in—allow about two hours for the well-curated displays.

The museum's harmonious architecture incorporates a Fatamid tomb. It comes from a group of poorly preserved monuments believed to date from the 8th to 12th centuries AD, located in the adjacent Fatamid Cemetery. The museum is a five-minute walk south of the Old Cataract Hotel. ⊠ *Shar'a el-Fanadek (across from the Basma Hotel), Aswan South* ☎ *097/231-9111* ⊕ *www.numibia.net* 🖃 *£E50* ☉ *Daily 9–9.*

Unfinished Obelisk. This site is an abandoned workshop, in which balls of greenish dolorite are still lying about. Dolorite is an extremely hard stone that was attached to rammers and used to pound and dress the surfaces of the quarried granite. Note the rows of slots where wooden wedges were driven in, then soaked in water to expand and split the rock. The ancient techniques were so precise that once a stone was hewn, it needed only finishing touches to ready it for its place in a temple wall.

In this case, a flaw was discovered in the massive obelisk-to-be, and it was left imprisoned in the bedrock. Had it been raised, it would have stood 137 feet tall—taller than any other obelisk—and weighed 1,162 tons. But the stone's supine potential makes it no less impressive and takes little away from the scale of the ambition of the builders of old. Note that the site is a 20-minute walk from the Nubia Museum. ⊠ *East of the Fatamid Cemetery, Aswan South* 🖃 *£E30* ☉ *Oct.–May, daily 7–4; June–Sept., daily 7–5.*

THE ISLANDS IN THE NILE

Unlike the stretch of the Nile that passes through Luxor, this section has several islands as it approaches the cataracts. Many of these are worth exploring.

ELEPHANTINE ISLAND

Sources attribute the name Elephantine to three possibilities: the elephant cult symbol of a predynastic Egyptian tribe; the ancient Greek name Abu (Elephant Land); and, more prosaically, to the presence of gargantuan granite boulders that resemble the animals' rumps. The island was the site of a sanctuary to the gods of the flood and the home of noblemen whose tombs lie farther north on the West Bank. These days Elephantine is, in large part, an open-air museum, brilliantly excavated and restored by German and Swiss archaeological institutes; the island also is home to a few Nubian villages and a five-star hotel.

Start with the **Aswan Museum,** built in 1912 to house the British engineer of the first dam. It is small and rather dingy, but you can pay your respects to the mummy of "the bearded man," whose horny toes peek out of the linen binding. A more modern **Museum Annex** is even smaller, but it is a revelation. Maps inside show the areas you are visiting as they appeared from 3000 BC to 300 AD, along with some unusual finds, such as a papyrus marriage contract—accompanied by its translation—and a hefty hoard of Ptolemaic coins.

The archaeological area is so jam-packed with debris of the island's ancient town that every time you move, you crunch pottery shards beneath your feet. Highlights include the **Temple of Satis** (the goddess who "let fly the current with the force of an arrow"), a fine example of modern restoration techniques. The **Temple of Khnum** (a ram-headed god of the flood and the whole locality) was the center of the ancient town and was cleared of rubble in the 1990s. On the southern tip of the island is a small Ptolemaic shrine dedicated to the Nubian god Mandolis. Beside it is a statue of an elephant. Back near the dock is the **Nilometer,** built by the Romans on the site of an older one and reused again in the 19th century to gauge the annual floods. Close by are a flight of metal stairs and a platform erected by the German archaeological team, from which you can take in a panoramic view of the island and its neighbors.

North of the archaeological area is a Nubian village, where you can go for a stroll and imbibe in the traditional rhythms of village life. Children are likely to approach you, and you might receive an invitation for a cup of tea. ☒ *Elephantine Island* ✛ *To get to the island, take a felucca from anywhere in Aswan, or the public ferry from the south end of the Corniche* ☒ *Island £E30, ferry £E1* ☉ *Oct.–May, daily 7–4; June–Sept., daily 7–5.*

KITCHENER'S ISLAND

Also known as the Island of Plants, Kitchener's Island is named after Lord Horatio Kitchener, famed for his campaigns in the Sudan at the start of the 20th century, his role as Consul General in Egypt, and his love of exotic trees and plants. The island's enchanting **botanical garden,** which he endowed, is proof of the latter, and the birds just love it. A public ferry will take you here for £E1, but you should also be able to hire a private felucca for about £E10—just be sure to negotiate a price in advance and make sure the felucca captain knows to come back and pick you up at an agreed-upon time. ⊠ *Kitchener's Island ✢ West of Elephantine Island, 15 min by felucca or public ferry* 🖃 *£E10* ☯ *Oct.– May, daily 7–4; June–Sept., daily 7–5.*

SEHEYL ISLAND

Seheyl Island is one of many islets (some of which are game preserves) in the cataract, or rapids, where the Nile narrows in the midst of dramatic outcroppings of pink-and-black granite—the trip here by felucca (£E60) through the cataract is half the reason to come. Seheyl was sacred to the goddess Anukis, who was entrusted with channeling the floodwaters upriver. A mountain of crumbling rock on Seheyl's southeast corner is covered with 250 inscriptions, the graffiti of several thousand years' worth of travelers. The **archaeological area** is gated, but the ticket kiosk is seldom manned. If the guardian isn't in, go to one of the nearby houses and someone will serve you tea (offer baksheesh in return for the courtesy) while you wait for him to return. ⊠ *Seheyl Island ✢ 40 min. south of Aswan by felucca. By taxi, it's 15 minutes south and over the Old Dam to Gharb Seheyl, where you can catch a public rowboat-ferry to the island* 🖃 *£E25* ☯ *Oct.–May, daily 7–4; June–Sept., daily 7–5.*

THE WEST BANK

You can take in the West Bank sights in a half-day trip. Just sail to the West Bank dock for nearby Gubgubet al-Hawa, also called Abu al-Hawa, and tell your felucca captain to pick you up at the Mausoleum of the Aga Khan (to the south) about four hours later. After visiting the Tombs of the Nobles, you can ride a camel through the desert (£E35 is the going rate) to the Monastery of Saint Simeon and onward, past the Aga Khan Mausoleum to the felucca landing at its feet. Bring a bottle of water with you (one per person) at all times of the year.

Mausoleum of the Aga Khan. The Fatimid-style Tomb of Sultan Muhammed Aga Khan III (d. 1957), leader of the Shi'a Isma'ili (Shi'ite) sect, stands sentry over Aswan on a cliff of the West Bank. The tomb is closed to the public, but you can pass the outer walls on your way to or from Saint Simeon's Monastery. ⊠ *Aswan West Bank.*

Saint Simeon's Monastery. This brooding mass dates from approximately the 7th century AD, and it is one of the largest and best-preserved Coptic monasteries in Egypt. Little is known of its origins, and although Saint Simeon is said to have lived here in the 5th century, findings suggest that the monastery may have been originally dedicated to someone else. The place feels like an abandoned town, full of vaulted passages and crumbling arches. Some poorly preserved frescoes remain in the basilica on the lower level. A stroll through this austere and mysterious romantic ruin, with its awesome desert vistas, is memorable.

The monastery is 4 km (2½ mi) through the desert from the Tombs of the Nobles; by camel the trip takes 40 minutes and costs £E35. From the Aga Khan Mausoleum, you can hike uphill to a footpath that leads from behind the mausoleum to the monastery, about a 30-minute walk.

Saint Simeon's Monastery on the West Bank

This is a strenuous and hot walk even in winter, so take plenty of water and wear sturdy shoes. ⊠ *Aswan West Bank* 🎫 *£E25* ⊙ *Oct.–May, daily 7–4; June–Sept., daily 7–5.*

Tombs of the Nobles and Gubgubet al-Hawa (Tomb of the Wind). The West Bank is the final resting place of the Keepers of the Southern Gate, the adventuresome ancient Egyptian noblemen of Elephantine who were entrusted with securing caravan routes, monitoring the granite quarries, and supervising trade shipments to the capital of Memphis. Take a camel or walk up the slope to the necropolis and enjoy a sense of discovery that you rarely achieve when perusing Egyptian antiquities. Many tombs are closed or undergoing excavation, but there is a great deal to see nevertheless. The view as you make your way south along the cliff is stunning.

Start with the north-end **Tomb of Serenput I** (No. 36, 12th Dynasty, 1938–1759 BC), which is noted for its lovely forecourt, with six columns inscribed with male figures, and its 28-yard-long inner passageway, forged through bedrock. (Ask the people at the kiosk if this tomb is open; if not, they can send someone who has a key with you). Move on to the **Tomb of Khounes** (No. 34, 6th Dynasty, 2323–2150 BC), located beneath the ruins of a Roman wall; traces remain of its conversion into a Coptic monastery. Look for the graffiti left by French soldiers in 1799. Continue south along the cliff to one of the best-preserved tombs of this era, that of **Serenput II** (No. 31, Middle Kingdom, 1980–1630 BC), grandson of Serenput I. Allow your eyes to adjust to the dim interior and watch the brilliantly colored reliefs (showing the deceased and his family) at the end of the 32-yard passage come to life. The last tombs are those of **Mekhu** and **Sabni** (No. 25 and No. 26, 6th Dynasty, 2350–2170 BC). These impressive rock-pillared chambers contain some frescoes—and the occasional bat. Mekhu died in equatorial Africa on an expedition. His son Sabni went to punish the tribe who killed him and to carry his father's body back home. Pharaoh Pepi II sent along mummification paraphernalia as a sign of appreciation for these exploits.

> **PHOTO OP**
>
> If you don't want to take a felucca ride, you'll find the best views of the Nile cataracts are from the landscaped waterside Fryal Gardens at the southern end of the Corniche. The entry fee is £E5, and you can sit and enjoy the vistas for hours.

On your way back from the Tombs of the Nobles take a short hike up to the domed **Gubgubet al-Hawa**—the tomb of a sheikh, though most locals just call it Abu al-Hawa (Father of the Wind)—for the best view in Aswan and a cooling breeze year-round. ⊠ *Aswan West Bank* ✆ *£E30* ⊙ *Oct.–May, daily 7–4; June–Sept., daily 7–5.*

WHERE TO EAT

Aswan is famed throughout Egypt for its fish, primarily from Lake Nasser. No Egyptian returns home from Aswan without bringing a gift of fish, salted and tinned on the spot. Some of the tastiest meals on the Nile—authentic Egyptian fare with a Nubian touch—are served in Aswan eateries to a devoted following of locals. The homespun fare of soups, salads, *mezze* (hot and cold appetizers), grilled meats, and *tagines* (earthenware-baked vegetables, meat, or chicken in a tomato-based sauce, variously spiced) can become heaven in the hands of Aswan's passionate chefs. If you want Continental or Asian cuisine or alcohol, try one of the five-star hotels or wait until you get back to Cairo. Right now, consider yourself divinely blessed: You're in Aswan; the bounties of a singular culture await behind many a restaurant door. You may not pass this way again. So yalla (let's go), let's eat!

$ × **Aswan Moon.** If all you do here is order the okra pot, you'll have
MIDDLE EASTERN learned why Egyptian cookery just can't be duplicated abroad. Fresh-
★ picked baby okra, scarcely more than an inch long, is baked in a tagine with an oniony tomato sauce and lamb. Because the okra is so small, it gets tender, never gummy. Main dishes here come with salads, rice, and sides; but you can also order à la carte. One to try: a soup called lisan asfour (bird's tongue), a stock-based broth with orzo. The something-for-everyone menu runs the gamut from omelets to calamari. This pontoon restaurant—one of five such floating eateries tethered to the Corniche—affords pleasantly shaded Nile-front dining and is best known among locals by its nickname: Amun. They wouldn't do that if they didn't love the place. ⊠ *Corniche al-Nil, Corniche* ☏ *097/231–6108* ▤ *No credit cards.*

$ × **Chief Khalil.** You know you're in a special place when a steady stream
SEAFOOD of Egyptians—a breed who believe mightily in home cooking—breeze in here to place the orders they'll later carry home to their families. Just

nine small tables, usually filled, sit among the nautical blues and yellows of decorative tiles inside; a couple of outside tables by the front door give onto the pedestrian souk. This is a fish place, where the subject at hand sits in small cases under ice. Take your pick of mullet, sole, or sea bream, for instance, and they'll tell you the price, cook it however you like, and serve it with rice and mezze. If you opt for tagine-style preparation—who knew a fish casserole could taste so rich?—just watch out for the bones. ⊠ *Shar'a Saad Zaghloul, next door to the Paradise Hotel, Downtown* ☎ *097/231–0142* ▭ No credit cards.

$$
MIDDLE EASTERN
★

✕ **El-Dokka.** This Nubian-style restaurant sits on one of the small islands around the cataracts of the Nile. Big picture windows, as well as patio seating, command scenes of river rapids, the gargantuan boulders of nearby Elephantine Island, and the desert beyond. Those views are upstaged only by what comes to your table, starting with fresh-baked brown flatbread cut in quarters, accompanied by a plate of mixed pickles, just like in Egyptian homes. Dishes of baba ghanoush, cucumber salad, and moussaka (just grilled eggplant) are decorated with carved vegetables. The quart-sized lamb tagine arrives still bubbling hot, topped with nicely browned onions. Live Nubian music adds extra spice to your dinner. Call to have the restaurant's boat pick you up, or just flag a felucca. ⊠ *On small island directly in front of the Sofitel Old Cataract Hotel, El-Dokka Island* ☎ *097/910–8000* ▭ No credit cards.

$
MIDDLE EASTERN

✕ **El-Madina.** In the heart of the souk, you can dine out on the small terrace and watch the world go, or revive yourself at one of the three (that's right, just three) tables in the exclusively small air-conditioned dining space. The menu holds no surprises; and the preliminary dishes are basic: correctly prepared, but no cause for excitement. The oomph arrives in the main courses: lamb kofta that's juicy and expertly spiced; grilled liver (somehow free of that bitter, metallic taste) with onions and green peppers; tender cuts of fried chicken or beef. Walls of bright white tiles and white tablecloths—soothing in Aswan's perpetual heat—are enlivened with touches of red on chairs and trim. ⊠ *Shar'a Saad Zaghloul, Downtown* ☎ *097/230–5696* ▭ No credit cards.

$
MIDDLE EASTERN

✕ **El-Masry.** Frequented by Egyptians and foreigners, the well-known El-Masry is a cool refuge from the rigors of the souk. The restaurant's been running since 1958 and has an American-diner-meets-French-café appeal. A broth of lamb and beef, a plate of rice, a dish of veggies, and a basket of whole-wheat flatbread precede the charcoal-grilled meats. Service is quick. No alcohol is served. ⊠ *Shar'a Matar, just off Shar'a al-Souk, Downtown* ☎ *097/230–2576* ▭ No credit cards.

$$–$$$
CONTINENTAL

✕ **The Lotus.** Whether you choose the apricot-color dining room, the outdoor terrace with its nighttime view of the lights of Aswan, or a table by the attractively lighted pool, the Lotus is nothing if not atmospheric. A pan-European menu includes a creamy veal Zurich, served with Swiss-style hash browns; grilled jumbo Red Sea shrimp in lemon butter; and lighter fare such as salad niçoise. Breakfast, lunch, and dinner buffets are also served. ⊠ *Basma Hotel, in front of the Nubia Museum, Aswan South* ☎ *097/231–0191* ▭ *AE, MC, V.*

$
MIDDLE EASTERN

✕ **Makka.** The pleasantest shortcut to learning about a culture is through its cuisine. And there's no better place in Aswan to begin your education that in this upmarket eatery floored in green marble and flooded with welcome air-conditioning. The menu offers staples like grilled meats accompanied by vegetable dishes—this is one of the few places that serves *loubia* (black-eyed peas)—salads, bread, and tahini. But go deeper. Order the stuffed pigeon (or a small stuffed chicken if pigeon's not available): If it's stuffed with rice, it's being served Nubian-style; Egyptian-style stuffing is made with *fereek* (cracked wheat). Don't be afraid to order whatever you see on someone else's table—chances are that your neighbors are Egyptian and will welcome your curiosity. There's no outdoor seating area, however. ⊠ *Shar'a Abtal el-Tahrir, Downtown* ☎ *010/464–6605* ▭ *No credit cards.*

$ ✕ **Panorama.** Part restaurant, part herbal pharmacy, part museum, Pan-
MIDDLE EASTERN orama is one of the city's Nile-front fab five of pontoon eateries. Dine
★ outside or in at this clean riverside spot where vegetarians, diabetics, and others with specific needs are served on the shady floating terrace or in the plant-filled, Nubian-decorated dining room. The walls are flush with beaded amulets, brass fetishes, basketry, and camel saddlebags. This is the place to order medicinal teas that promise to treat everything from coughs to weight problems. Oh, yes, about the menu: Egyptian tagines and charcoal-grilled *kofta* (ground-beef meatballs), kebabs, pigeon, and chicken. There is no alcohol, so instead try one of Aswan's ice-cold libations: *karkadey* (hibiscus tea), tamarind, carob, or *dom* (a drink made from the fruit of Sudanese palms). After the meal, don't miss the Bedouin coffee. ⊠ *Corniche al-Nil, just south of the EgyptAir office, Corniche* ☎ *097/230–6169* ▭ *No credit cards.*

$–$$ ✕ **The Trattoria.** The pasta and main dishes on the basic Italian menu
ITALIAN are appetizing alternatives to Aswan's ubiquitous kebabs and tagines. Tagliatelle served with a fresh tomato sauce and a remote relative of Parmesan cheese is fresh and surprisingly light. Although it's home-made, the lasagna is not always spinach-based, as advertised; this Upper Egyptian version is a hot, hearty tagine of spiced ground meat, pasta, and cheese topped with béchamel sauce. Breaded veal cutlets served in tomato sauce and cheese are tasty and substantial. ⊠ *Pyramisa Isis Corniche Hotel, Corniche al-Nil, Corniche* ☎ *097/231–5100* ▭ *AE, MC, V.*

WHERE TO STAY

At this writing, Aswan's grand dame, the Old Cataract Hotel, and its modern companion property, the New Cataract Hotel, were closed for massive renovation, both due to reopen at the dawn of 2011. But Aswan has several other five-star properties that cater to upscale tourists, the best of which is probably the Mövenpick on Elephantine Island. Like Luxor, Aswan has few good midrange hotels.

If you choose to stay at a place that doesn't have a pool, be aware that many hotels open their pools to nonguests for a small fee (around £E50). In Aswan, the Basma Hotel and the Isis have good pools.

You can consult hotel staff on taxi and felucca rates, which are fixed either by the hour or the length of your trip. Most hotels can also arrange sightseeing excursions.

All hotel reviews have been condensed for this book. Please go to Fodors.com for full reviews of each property.

$$
★
🏨 **Ana Kato Nubian Cultural House.** The best way to reach this exuberantly painted Nubian bed-and-breakfast is by motorboat from Aswan, slowly making your way against the current between hidden islands, through portions of the Nile few outsiders ever see. **Pros:** a cultural experience in a boutique setting; it's just plain fun; meal plans are available. **Cons:** if you want alcohol, you have to bring it with you; the village road is sandy and strewn with camel droppings. ⊠ *Gharb Seheyl, El-Noba* ☎ *097/345–1745* ⊕ *www.anakato.com* ⟿ *19 rooms* ☖ *In-room: a/c, no phone, no TV, safe, refrigerator, Wi-Fi (some). In-hotel: 3 restaurants, water sports, laundry service, Wi-Fi hotspot* ⊟ *No credit cards* ⃠ *BP.*

$$$
🏨 **Basma Hotel.** Occupying an airy promontory above Aswan, the Basma is itself a high point in Nubian-influenced contemporary architecture. **Pros:** large pool (heated in winter) and deck; there are no main thoroughfares passing close to the hotel, so it's relatively quiet. **Cons:** walking here uphill from town can be really tiring in the heat, so it's best to take a taxi from central Aswan (or the hourly hotel shuttle); a small number of rooms on the lower floors may pick up noise from the entry drive. ⊠ *In front of the Nubia Museum, Aswan South* ☎ *097/231–0901* ⊕ *www.basmahotel.com* ⟿ *188 rooms, 21 suites* ☖ *In-room: a/c, safe, refrigerator. In-hotel: 3 restaurants, room service, bars, pool, laundry service, Internet terminal, Wi-Fi* ⊟ *AE, MC, V* ⃠ *BP.*

$$$$
🏨 **Iberotel Aswan.** You don't have to go all the way to Hurghada or Sharm El-Sheikh to visit a Red Sea resort. The new Iberotel Aswan, part of the Jaz-Travco hotel empire, has brought one to town for you. **Pros:** all rooms are large and have balconies or terraces with direct Nile views; you'll find bowling and billiards right on-site if you get bored. **Cons:** it's not within walking distance of any Aswan attractions; rates, even on the Internet, seem high compared to other hotels in this category. ⊠ *Corniche al-Nil, Corniche* ☎ *097/232–8824* ⊕ *www.jaz.travel* ⟿ *179 rooms, 16 suites* ☖ *In-room: a/c, safe, refrigerator, Wi-Fi. In-hotel: 3 restaurants, room service, bars, tennis court, pool, gym, spa, laundry service, Internet terminal* ⊟ *AE, MC, V* ⃠ *BP.*

$$
🏨 **Isis Corniche Hotel.** All that work you put in on the Stairmaster is good preparation for a stay here. Not only does this hotel sit smack-dab on the waterfront, it's a quick two-block walk to the restaurants and shops of the souk, and a ferry ride away from Aswan's islands and West Bank—so long as several flights of stairs are no bother. **Pros:** location, location, and price, because Internet booking engines can make this hotel more affordable than so-called budget properties. **Cons:** rooms welcome smokers with matchbooks in the ash trays; Internet booking engines can fool you into thinking you've made reservations at the other Pyramisa in town, the one that's on an island. ⊠ *Corniche al-Nil, Corniche* ☎ *097/231–5100* ⊕ *www.pyramisaegypt.com* ⟿ *102 rooms, 2 suites* ☖ *In-room: a/c, refrigerator. In-hotel: 2 restaurants, room service, bars, pool, laundry service* ⊟ *AE, MC, V* ⃠ *BP.*

$$$–$$$$
🏨 **LTI-Pyramisa Isis Island Resort.** Sometime around New Year's 2006, a German couple checked in to this sprawling, low-rise retreat in the middle of the Nile. As of this writing, they haven't checked out yet.

5

The Old Cataract Hotel

The Old Cataract (⊕ www.sofitel.com), which opened in 1900, is a living monument to the age of imperialism. Rising out of a granite bluff overlooking the temples of Elephantine Island and the stark mountains of the West Bank, it belongs to the Nile. The orderly sprawl of the brick Victorian facade is dotted with wooden balconies and terraces where one could imagine Agatha Christie enjoying a gin and tonic while watching the sunset. This was the preferred winter resort of the blue bloods of the early 20th century. Howard Carter stayed here after his discovery of Tutankhamun's tomb downriver. Later, Winston Churchill passed through, and the late French president Mitterand was a frequent guest. The hotel's fame was revived in 1978 with the filming of Agatha Christie's *Death on the Nile*, starring Peter Ustinov, and modern visitors flocked to stay in this little piece of history. In 2008, this Sofitel affiliate closed to undertake a comprehensive renovation. At this writing, it is due to open its doors again around September 2011.

Pros: verdant surroundings with plenty of birdlife; the boat transfer to town operates 24 hours and takes you through the most beautiful part of the cataracts. **Cons:** room decor seems dated, compared to public spaces; large groups staying only one or two nights can give the lobby the atmosphere of an airport. ⊠ *Isis Island* ☎ *097/231–7400* ⊕ *www.pyramisaegypt.com* ⇆ *447 rooms* ⚏ *In-room: a/c, safe, refrigerator. In-hotel: 3 restaurants, room service, bars, tennis courts, pools, gym, spa, laundry service, Internet terminal, Wi-Fi* ⊟ *AE, MC, V* ¶◎¶ *BP.*

$$ 🖾 **Marhaba Palace Hotel.** Separated from the Nile and the Corniche by a small green space called Al Salaam Gardens, this hotel has Nile views from a few of its rooms on the upper floors. **Pros:** well positioned for visits to the Corniche and souk; a new-build in 2004 means things like air-conditioning and hot water usually operate problem-free. **Cons:** rates may not be competitive with properties that offer more facilities, so shop around; the pool loses sunlight in the afternoon, making it cool in winter. ⊠ *Corniche al-Nil, Corniche* ☎ *097/233–0102* ⊕ *www.marhaba-aswan.com* ⇆ *69 rooms, 8 suites* ⚏ *In-room: a/c, refrigerator, Internet. In-hotel: restaurant, room service, bar, pool, gym, laundry service, Internet terminal* ⊟ *MC, V* ¶◎¶ *BP.*

$$$–$$$$ 🖾 **Mövenpick Resort Aswan.** What's up with that broccoli stalk of a tower?
★   Take the free 24-hour shuttle boat from the Aswan Corniche, and in five minutes' time you can see for yourself: a tea buffet in the afternoon, a grand view of the changing pinks and oranges of an Aswan sunset, cocktails and an intimate dinner, maybe. The rooms down in the hotel aren't so bad, either. **Pros:** the pool is irresistible; Nubian wedding celebrations in the adjoining village start at midnight and end at sunrise. **Cons:** Nubian wedding celebrations in the adjoining village start at midnight and end at sunrise; new construction on the north end of the property may break the peace. ⊠ *Elephantine Island* ☎ *097/230–3455* ⊕ *www.moevenpick-aswan.com* ⇆ *180 rooms, 38 suites, 8 villas* ⚏ *In-room:*

a/c, safe, Internet (some). In-hotel: 3 restaurants, room service, bars, pool, spa, laundry service ☰ *AE, DC, MC, V* ⊧◐| *BP.*

$ 🔲 **Paradise Hotel.** Set on pedestrian-only Saad Zaghloul, this is a clean budget hotel with fixtures and fittings in good condition, though high-wear areas such as baseboards, door frames, and keyholes are rough around the edges. **Pros:** in the heart of the vibrant souk; little vehicular traffic noise. **Cons:** street noise can be an issue in rooms on lower floors, and there is some background train noise; some rooms are dimly lit by light shafts; some rooms have colored glass in the windows; elevator has no inner door. ✉ *373 Shar'a Saad Zaghloul, 50 yards from the train station, Downtown* ☎ *097/232–9690* ⊕ *www.paradisehotel-aswan.com* ⇆ *60 rooms* ⚴ *In-room: a/c, refrigerator. In-hotel: 3 restaurants, room service, laundry service, Internet terminal* ☰ *No credit cards* ⊧◐| *BP.*

NIGHTLIFE AND THE ARTS

Aswan doesn't have a buzzing nightlife scene. Most of the large hotels will have some kind of Nubian folk dance performance or can arrange for you to see one at a neighboring village. The most popular pastime in the town is finding somewhere to have a cocktail on a terrace while watching the sunset. Since the Old Cataract Hotel bar was closed for over two years since 2008, there are now a few more places to enjoy this Aswan ritual.

BARS

El Pasha Coffee Shop. This coffee shop has tables directly on the water's edge, which are at a premium in Aswan; therefore, this narrow café, with its coffee and *shisha* (hookah) services, is an increasingly popular place to relax in the evening. ✉ *Isis Corniche Hotel, Corniche* ☎ *097/231–5100.*

Panorama Bar. This bar offers the best panoramic views across the city from its full-length windows. It's a very contemporary bar that doesn't have the atmosphere of the Old Cataract but seats on four sides give you a choice of views—up- or downriver, out to the Tombs of the Nobles, or across to the Corniche. ✉ *Mövenpick Hotel, Elephantine Island* ☎ *097/230–3455.*

Roof Top Terrace. The Basma Hotel's rooftop terrace has a lovely setting with shaded tables, where you can sit and enjoy a drink with views of the cataracts, and the sunset. ✉ *Basma Hotel, across from the Nubia Museum, Aswan South* ☎ *097/231–0901.*

ACTIVITIES

GUIDED TOURS

Aswan has a wide range of tour companies that can help you arrange travel to all the surrounding tourist sights. Booking a tour is an easy, stress-free way of hitting the highlights. Or you can hire a taxi or private car and driver for independent sightseeing. If you don't book a tour through your hotel's tour desk, there are two major independent companies, American Express and Thomas Cook, that offer a full range of tours.

Contacts American Express (⊠ *Corniche al-Nil, near EgyptAir, Corniche* ☎ *097/230–6983*). **Thomas Cook** (⊠ *59 Abtal el-Tahrir, Corniche al-Nil, Corniche* ☎ *097/230–6839* ⊕ *www.thomascookegypt.com*).

SOUTH OF ASWAN: PHILAE AND THE ASWAN DAMS

Within a few miles of Aswan, between town and the northern shores of Lake Nasser, are a few popular sights, the most impressive of which are the High Dam or the Philae Temple, depending on how many pharaonic sights you've visited during your trip.

PHILAE: THE TEMPLE OF ISIS

Agilqiyya (Philae) Island, 8 km (5 mi) south of Aswan.

★ The oldest physical evidence, from blocks found on-site, of the worship of Isis dates back to the reign of the 25th-Dynasty Ethiopian pharaoh Taharqa (690–664 BC). During the 30th Dynasty, Nectanebo I built the temple's more imposing structures. The major part of the temple complex is the legacy of the pharaohs who ruled over Egypt between the reigns of Ptolemy II Philadelphus (285–246 BC) and the Roman emperor Diocletian (284–305 AD). The cult of Isis was upheld until the first half of the 6th century AD, when Justinian abolished the ancient Egyptian beliefs of the temple, by force.

The consequences of building the first dam on the Nile south of Aswan were alarming. In the case of Philae Island, water partially submerged the Temple of Isis when floods filled the dam as a result of seasonal rains upriver. Archaeologists feared that this periodic flooding would soften the monument's foundations, causing it to collapse. It was not until 1960, with the construction of the second dam, that UNESCO and the Egyptian Antiquities Service decided to preserve Philae and other important Upper Egyptian temples. The dismantling of the Philae complex started in the early 1970s, when a huge cofferdam was erected around the island. Then nearby Agilqiyya Island was carved so that the Temple of Isis would stand just as it had on Philae, and the whole complex was moved and meticulously reinstalled on Agilqiyya. The process took until 1980, when authorities reopened the site to the public.

The first sight that strikes you, once on the island, is the long **first court,** surrounded by a series of refined columns, all unique. The first building on the left is the **Kiosk of Nectanebo I.** The **west colonnade,** built during the Roman period, leads up the west side of the island. In the first court, turn east to admire, from right to left, the **Temple of Arensnuphis,** the **Chapel of Mandulis** (both are Nubian gods), the first **east colonnade** (Roman period), and Ptolemy V Epiphanes's small **Temple of Imhotep.**

The first court leads to the **first pylon of Ptolemy XIII Neos Dionysos.** Both of the obelisks erected in front of the pylon are now at Kingston Lacy, in Dorset, England, taken there by Giovanni Battista Belzoni in 1819. Belzoni (1778–1823) was an Italian explorer, adventurer, and excavator.

PHILAE TEMPLE TOURING TIPS

■ **This is a must-see.** On Nile tours, the temples are the highlights, one of the main reasons you came to Egypt. But it's easy to get tired of seeing so many in a short three- or four-day Nile tour. If you feel you need to skip a temple visit, don't let it be this one. Seeing Philae's columns and pylons reflected in the Nile will stay with you long after you've forgotten the heat and fatigue.

■ **Take a tour.** Philae is one place that's easier to see on a guided tour. The process of hiring a boat to get you out to the island is chaotic, as is the approach to the island. On a tour, your guide will hire the boat and will help steer you back to the correct driver for the ride back to land.

■ **See it both ways.** Tour the entire complex by day, then come back at night for the Sound & Light Show.

His methods destroyed a lot of valuable material, but considering the techniques used in his day, he was no worse than other archaeologists.

The small *mammisi* (chapel) on the left side of the **second court** was erected in honor of the birth of Horus. Earlier New Kingdom (1539–1075 BC) counterparts of Greco-Roman mammisi are reliefs depicting the divine birth of the king, as in Hatshepsut's temple at Deir al-Bahri (Luxor West Bank) and Thutmose III's shrine in the Temple of Luxor (East Bank).

At the north end of the second court, through the **second pylon**, the **hypostyle hall** is the actual entrance to the Temple of Isis. It consists of 10 columns and is mainly the work of Ptolemy VIII (Euergetes II). The majority of the reliefs on the walls are offering scenes: the king, by himself or accompanied by his wife, donates incense, vases, and wine to the gods to please them.

It is not uncommon to hear scholars call the art of the Greco-Roman period decadent and coarse. Although it is less classically Egyptian than the art of preceding periods, it nevertheless is an interesting mixture of Hellenistic and Egyptian traditions. At the same time, the religious beliefs—the most important part of the functioning of the temples—remained the same throughout the centuries, because the temples gained a degree of independence inside Egypt.

As with every temple, the **sanctuary** is the focal point in the complex. The **pronaos**, behind the hypostyle hall, was converted into a Coptic church, with an altar visible on the right—which also explains the crosses on the walls. To the east of the Temple of Isis, close to the riverbank, the unfinished **Kiosk of Trajan** is a small open temple with supporting columns. Inside are offering scenes.

The **Sound & Light Show,** like the one at the Temple of Karnak, has two parts. The first is a walk through the partly illuminated temple, and the second delivers a brief history of the site combined with music and the light show. It is a pleasant spectacle, less showy than that at Karnak.

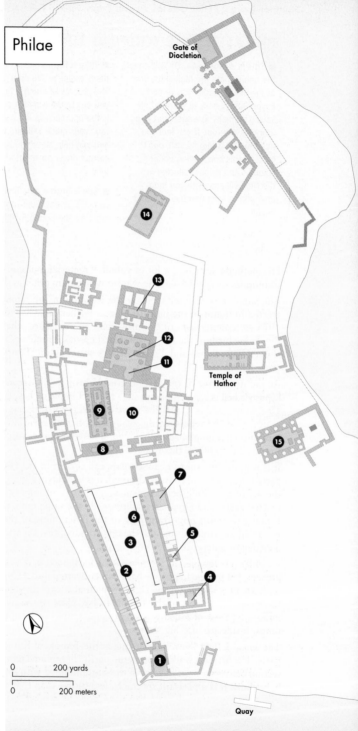

Philae

Gate of
Diocletion

Temple of
Hathor

Quay

0   200 yards

0   200 meters

Temple of Isis

Agilqiyya Island is in the basin between the Old Dam and the High Dam. Boats leave for Philae from the docks of Shellal, south of the Old Aswan Dam. ☎ No phone ✉ Temple £E50, boat (cost is divided among passengers) £E50, Sound & Light Show £E75 ☺ Temple Oct.–May, daily 7–4; June–Sept., daily 7–5. Sound & Light Show (in English) Oct.–May, Mon. and Fri.–Sat. at 6:30 PM, Tues.–Wed. at 7:30 PM, Thurs. and Sun. at 8:30 PM; June–Sept., Mon. and Fri.–Sat. at 8 PM, Tues.–Wed. at 9:15 PM, Thurs. and Sun. at 10:30 PM.

GETTING HERE AND AROUND

Whereas most ancient temples are surrounded by modern habitations, the temple of Philae stands alone on an island a few miles south of Aswan. The easiest but also the most expensive way to get to the docks is by private taxi or with a group tour, which you can arrange at your hotel. If you visit as part of a group, your guide will negotiate for the boat passage out to the island; if you go on your own, you'll have to negotiate with the boatman yourself. Buy tickets for the temple before you board the boat at Shellal. The boat to the monument takes you past islands of rock, among which rises, as an image of order amid the natural randomness, the magnificent Temple of Isis. The approach can be chaotic, as many boats jostle for space; expect that you may have to climb over other boats to get onto the dock.

THE ASWAN DAMS

Two large dams have been built in Egypt to control the flow of the Nile and to preserve its flow for later irrigation of crops. One dates to the turn of the 20th century; the other (a much more massive undertaking)

CLOSE UP

The Cult of Isis

Isis is a central figure in the Egyptian pantheon. Wife of Osiris, she was responsible for bringing her husband back to life after his jealous brother Seth killed him. After his reincarnation, Osiris impregnated Isis who gave birth to Horus. Through these activities Isis is identified as "life giver" and "nourisher"; she was a protective force for the pharaoh in life and in death—often seen on temple carvings carrying the *ankh* (which symbolizes the life force). The role of Isis in the resurrection of her husband also imbued her with power over magic, healing, and miracles.

In the Hellenic and Roman eras, worship of Isis spread far beyond the boundaries of Egypt. Temples to the goddess were built in Delos and Delphi in Greece, Pompeii and Rome in Italy, and also in Spain, Germany, and along the Black Sea coast. The Cult of Isis was even an early rival to Christianity. Worship of the goddess died out when Emperor Constantine outlawed pagan cults throughout the Roman Empire in the early 4th century; however, the core temple at Philae remained active into the 5th century because many of its worshippers came from Nubia, well beyond the reach of Rome.

was built in the 1960s. The latter dam created Lake Nasser, the largest man-made lake in the world.

GETTING HERE AND AROUND

The Old Dam is five minutes south of town, on the way in from the airport. The High Dam is 15 minutes south of town. You can get to both by taxi or on a guided tour (these tours often stop at the Unfinished Obelisk as well). Allow 1 to 1½ hours to take in the spectacle.

WHAT TO SEE

The Old Dam. The British built the first Aswan Dam between 1898 and 1902 using blocks of local granite. The structure stands more than 130 feet tall, some 8,000 feet long, and has a capacity of 7 billion cubic yards of water. In its day, it was one of the world's largest dams, and one of the sights to see in Aswan. Over the years it was heightened, but eventually was deemed inadequate. These days the High Dam dwarfs it, and you can only drive over the Old Dam, because no stopping is allowed. The Old Dam is five minutes south of town, on the way in from the airport.

The Fisherman's Port. Just before you get to the High Dam, on the way out from Aswan, turn left down the road to the water to get to this ramshackle port, with its jumble of *African Queen*–style fishing boats and launches for the **Temple of Kalabsha.** The launch to New Kalabsha Island costs £E50.

Aswan High Dam. Gamel Abdel Nasser's vision of a modern Egypt rose and fell on the construction of the dam, which began in 1960. It took Soviet financing, plus the sweat of 30,000 Egyptians working around the clock, to complete the work by 1971. The volume of the dam itself is 17 times that of the Great Pyramid.

Aswan High Dam

Lake Nasser is the world's largest man-made lake, 500 km (310 mi) long—150 km (93 mi) of which is in Sudan—and it has a storage capacity of 210,000 billion cubic yards of water. The dam doubled Egypt's power-generating capabilities, and it ensures a net surplus of 26 billion cubic yards of water as a reserve against low annual floods upriver.

The disadvantages of damming the Nile included the loss of fertile silt that the floods brought, which has made the use of chemical fertilizers a necessity. An incalculable loss is Nubia, which now lies beneath so many cubic yards of water that its 100,000 inhabitants relocated along the river valley. As one Nubian elder put it, "we cut off the arm to save the body."

Visit the stylized lotus monument commemorating the Russian–Egyptian collaboration, and try to convince the guard to take you up the tiny elevator for a view of unsurpassed splendor. The lake and Nubian Desert stretch out to one side; on the other stretches the now-tamed Nile. 🖃 *£E20* 🕙 *Oct.–May, daily 7–4; June–Sept., daily 7–5.*

LAKE NASSER

Until a few decades ago, Lower Nubia, the area south of Aswan above the First Cataract, was much like the Nile Valley north of Aswan—save for the fact that the primary inhabitants were Nubian Egyptians, rather than Egyptians of other descent. As in Upper Egypt, Nubia's thin ribbon of green, fed by the Nile, was hemmed in by desert. Nubians cultivated their fields, and massive pharaonic monuments lined the riverbanks.

The Aswan High Dam and Lake Nasser put an end to that, of course, forcing the Egyptian Nubian population inhabiting the flooded areas to move downriver to areas around, and to the north of, Aswan. Many of the monuments from antediluvian Nubia were also relocated to higher ground, or salvaged and removed to foreign countries—all after a hasty excavation effort. Unfortunately, others could not be saved, and the waters of Lake Nasser swallowed them up.

Except for Abu Simbel and Philae, the temples along the shores of Lake Nasser are less visited than those along the lower reaches of the Nile. It's possible to take a cruise on Lake Nasser to see many of these, and Kalabsha is reachable by boat from Aswan. *For information on Lake Nasser cruises, see* ⇨ *Chapter 8.*

NEW KALABSHA

30 minutes south of Aswan by taxi (or bus) and ferry.

The temples from the sites of Kalabsha and Beit al-Wali were moved to the island of New Kalabsha near Aswan. This rocky island, redolent of fish, is uninhabited save for a few dogs, foxes, and the antiquities guards that care for the temple and monitor the ticket booth. The view of the lake and the dam is very fine from the island, and especially charming from the landing dock.

The largest freestanding Egyptian temple in Nubia, **Kalabsha** was built by Augustus Caesar (who reigned from 27 BC to AD 14) and dedicated to Osiris, Isis, and Mandulis, the latter a Nubian fertility god with a very elaborate headdress. Although the temple building was almost completed in antiquity, its decoration was never finished. Only three inner rooms, as well as portions of the exterior, are completely decorated with reliefs. Kalabsha's half-finished column capitals and fragments of relief decoration do, however, provide a great deal of information about ancient construction and carving techniques.

The temple complex includes a birth house, in the southwest corner, and a small chapel in the northeast corner, dating to the Ptolemaic period. A large rock stela dating to the reign of Seti I has also been erected at this site. Its original location was Qasr Ibrim.

Several large boulders covered with petroglyphs of uncertain date stand along a walkway on the south side of the temple. The petroglyphs, which resemble those of the southern African San (Bushmen), include carvings of people and animals, such as elephants and antelopes.

Behind the Temple of Kalabsha, a walkway rounds a bend and arrives at the small, rock-cut temple of **Beit al-Wali**. This diminutive but colorful monument was removed from its cliff-side home—the ancients carved it out of the cliff, like the temples at Abu Simbel—and moved to New Kalabsha in the 1960s. Ramses II commissioned Beit al-Wali and dedicated it to Amun-Ra and other deities.

Originally, the temple was fronted by a mud-brick pylon, which was not moved, and consisted of an entrance hall, a hypostyle hall, and a sanctuary. This small, jewel-like temple is a delight, because its painted decorations—its reds, blues, and greens—still look very fresh. The entrance

Lake Nasser

WESTERN DESERT

LIMESTONE PLATEAU

Nile

Aswan Dam (Old Dam)
Aswan
Philae
High Dam
New Kalabsha
Beit al-Wali

Kurkur

Kalabsha (original location)

SINN EL KADDÂB

Dungul

Gerf Hussein
Al-Dakka (original location)

NUBIA

Lake Nasser

Maharraka (original location)

Wadi al-Sebua
Al-Dakka

Maharraka

Al-Derr (original location)
Amada
al-Sibû
Al-Derr
Aniba
Amada (original location)
Qasr Ibrim

EASTERN DESERT

Abu Simbel
Abu Simbel
Nefertari Temple

EGYPT
SUDAN

SAHARA DESERT

0 — 15 mi
0 — 15 km

Kiosk of Kertassi (Qertassi) at Kalabsha Temple site

hall contains scenes of Ramses II quelling various enemies of Egypt, often accompanied by a pet lion. The columned hall shows the pharaoh interacting with different deities, chief among them being Amun-Ra. The sanctuary contains carved seated statues of Ramses II and deities, such as Horus, Isis, and Khnum. ☎ *No phone* ✉ *£E35* ☺ *Oct.–May, daily 7–4; June–Sept., daily 7–5.*

GETTING HERE AND AROUND
The site is a stop on Lake Nasser cruises, and it is accessible from Aswan—by taxi to the fisherman's port east of the High Dam, then by boat (£E50) to the island.

INTERIOR LAKE NASSER MONUMENTS

All of Lake Nasser's interior monuments—those located apart from Aswan and Abu Simbel—can only be visited on a multiday lake cruise. They are set in rather bleak landscapes relieved only by the odd reed and bird. You don't need entry tickets, because admission is included with your cruise. *(For more information on Lake Nasser cruises, see ➪ Chapter 8.)*

Wadi al-Sebua. Famous for being the site of two New Kingdom temples, the island's earlier temple, which had both freestanding and rock-cut elements, was constructed by Amenhotep III and added to by Ramses II. It consists of a sanctuary, a court, a hall, and pylons. The temple was originally dedicated to a Nubian form of Horus but was later rededicated to the god Amun-Ra.

The more dramatic and larger site at al-Sebua is the Temple of Ramses II, Ra-Harakhte (a sun god), and Amun-Ra. It is yet another of Ramses II's projects, and it once stood about 150 yards northeast of the Amenhotep III Temple; it was moved about 3 km (2 mi) to the west. This temple has both freestanding and rock-cut sections.

Al-Dakka. The Ptolemaic and Roman Temple of al-Dakka has been moved from its original site to a new one not far from Wadi al-Sebua. Dakka was originally built by reusing fragments of an older temple dating from the 18th Dynasty.

Amada. The main part of the Temple of Amada, dedicated to Amun-Ra and Ra-Harakhte, was constructed in the 18th Dynasty. Various 19th-Dynasty pharaohs repaired it and added to it. Between 1964 and 1975 it was moved to its current spot, about 2 km (1 mi) away from its original location.

Amada is noted for two important historical inscriptions. One dates to the reign of Amenhotep II; it appears on a round-topped stela on the eastern wall of the sanctuary. The inscription describes a definitive military victory over rebellious chiefs in Syria. The other is on a stela carved from the northern thickness of the entryway and dates to the reign of King Merneptah (1212–1202 BC). It describes how the king successfully repelled a Libyan invasion of Egypt in the early years of his reign.

Al-Derr. The Temple of al-Derr was moved near the site of Amada in 1964. It is a rock-cut temple built by Ramses II and dedicated to himself, Amun-Ra, Ra-Harakhte, and Ptah. The temple is well decorated, and its bright colors are still visible—particularly in the area before the sanctuary.

Qasr Ibrim. This is a large site on what is now an island. Not too many years ago the area was attached to the mainland by a spit of land. Because of the rise in the level of water in the lake, it is now impossible to land and walk around Qasr Ibrim, although archaeological work here continues. The fortress is interesting because it encompasses several periods of history: pharaonic, Roman, Christian, and Arab/Nubian, up to the mid-20th century.

The island houses the remains of temples from the 18th and 25th dynasties, as well as rock-cut shrines dedicated to different pharaohs and assorted gods dating to the 18th and 19th dynasties. Remains of a sizable fortress of the Augustan period are also visible, as are portions of a large basilica and foundations and standing sections of dwellings. Archaeologists working at the site have found much well-preserved evidence—leather, manuscripts, pottery, and animal and botanical remains—that sheds light on daily life during the various periods of occupation at Qasr Ibrim.

ABU SIMBEL: THE TEMPLES OF RAMSES II AND NEFERTARI

280 km (174 mi) south of Aswan.

★ Abu Simbel began as a small village of a few houses clustered at some distance from the temples of Abu Simbel. Now it is a lush oasis with hotels and a sizable settlement. Arriving by plane or bus steals some of the drama that is so much a part of Ramses II's monument of monuments. The lake approach, on the other hand, fulfills every fantasy you might have about the grandeur of ancient Egypt.

Ramses II's two enormous temples at Abu Simbel are among the most awe-inspiring monuments in Egypt. The pharaoh had his artisans carve the temples out of a rock cliff to display his might as the Egyptian god-king and to strike dread into the Nubians—and the temples are most effective as such. They originally stood at the bottom of the cliff that they now crown (they're some 200 feet above the water level and 1/3 mi back from the lake shore).

The first of the two temples of Abu Simbel, the **Great Temple**, was dedicated to Ramses II (as a god) and to Ra-Harakhte, Amun-Ra, and Ptah. The second was dedicated to the goddess Hathor and Nefertari, Ramses II's wife and chief queen. The Great Temple is fronted by four seated colossi, about 65 feet tall, of Ramses II wearing the double crown of Upper and Lower Egypt. (One of the four heads fell to the ground in antiquity and was kept in that position when the temple was moved). Around the legs of the statues stand smaller figures of Ramses II's wives and offspring. The top of the temple facade is covered by a row of rampant baboons praising the sun as it rises. Between the two pairs of statues is a carved figure of Ra-Harakhte that stands over the door to the temple.

The doorway between the colossi leads to the **first hall**, which contains columns decorated with figures of Ramses II. The hall itself is carved on the right (north) with reliefs showing events from Ramses II's reign, most notably his self-proclaimed victory at the Battle of Kadesh in Syria (his opponent might beg to differ). It shows the besieged city, the attack, and the counting of body parts of the defeated enemies. The left (south) side shows Ramses' battles with Syrians, Libyans, and Nubians, and it has some fine scenes showing Ramses on a chariot. Vultures with outstretched wings decorate the ceiling. Several side chambers are accessible from this hall. These were probably used as storerooms for the temple furniture, vessels, linen, and priestly costumes.

The **second hall** contains four square columns and is decorated with scenes of Ramses II and Queen Nefertari making offerings to various deities, including the deified Ramses himself. This hall leads into a narrow room that was probably where the pharoah made offerings to the gods of the temple.

Three chapels branch off the narrow offering room. The two side chapels are undecorated, but the central chapel, the **main sanctuary**, is decorated not only with scenes of the pharaoh making offerings and conducting temple rituals, but also with four rock-carved statues of the deities to whom the temple is dedicated. They are, from left to right, Ptah, Amun-Ra, Ramses II, and Ra-Horakhte. These were originally painted and gilded, but the paint and the gold have long since gone. The temple was originally constructed so that twice each year the first rays of the rising sun would pierce the dark interior of the temple and strike these four statues, bathing them in light. When the temple was

ABU SIMBEL TOURING TIPS

■ **Don't miss this.** These two temples are truly unique in all of Egypt. For many visitors, they are better than the Pyramids. But they occupy a relatively small footprint, so they don't demand the time or the stamina required to tackle Karnak, or Edfu, or the Valley of the Kings.

■ **Good but fast.** Don't feel distressed about what appears to be a short amount of time at the temples. Remember that Abu Simbel is a tiny village, the temples are close to the airport, and most people who come here are on the same tight schedule. When all is said and done, a couple of hours here is more than enough.

■ **Stay over.** If you want to a significant amount of time at the temples, or you want to see the Sound & Light Show, arrange to spend a night in Abu Simbel, perhaps in connection with a Lake Nasser cruise. This is a pleasant place to explore the simple life of a rural village, and you may find the village more intriguing than the antiquities.

moved, this was taken into consideration and still happens, albeit a day late, on February 21 and October 21.

The smaller temple at Abu Simbel is the **Temple of Queen Nefertari,** dedicated to Hathor. Six colossal standing rock-cut statues of Queen Nefertari and Ramses II front the temple. Each statue is flanked by some of their children. The temple doorway opens into a **pillared hall** that contains six Hathor-head columns much larger than those in Deir al-Bahri. The ceiling contains a dedicatory inscription from Ramses II to Queen Nefertari. The hall itself is decorated with scenes of the royal couple, either together or singly, making offerings to or worshiping the gods. A narrow vestibule, decorated with scenes of offerings, follows the pillared hall, and the **main sanctuary** leads off this vestibule. The sanctuary contains a niche with a statue of Hathor as a cow, protecting Ramses. ⊠ *Mabed Abu Simbel* ☎ *No phone* 🖃 *Site £E90, Sound & Light Show £E75* ⊙ *Temple Oct.–May, daily 7–4; June–Sept., daily 7–5. Sound & Light Show Apr.–Sept., nightly at 8* PM, *9* PM, *and 10* PM; *Oct.–Mar., nightly at 7* PM, *8* PM, *and 9* PM *(show will only go on if at least 30 people have made a booking).*

GETTING HERE AND AROUND

EgyptAir flies to Abu Simbel from Cairo (2½ hours) and makes the journey from Aswan (½ hour) several times a day. The flight is structured to allow you only two hours on the ground, including the transfer between Abu Simbel and the airport; these flights book up far in advance, and independent travelers would be well advised to work with a travel agent or tour operator to book this portion of their trip. If you want more time to explore, it's possible to arrange your return on a different day (but making this arrangement is out of the norm, so it's best to use a travel agent to book your ticket). It's also possible to visit Abu Simbel in the daily convoy via the desert road.

Overland Convoys to Abu Simbel

As is the case throughout Upper Egypt, foreign tourists are not allowed to travel independently. All taxis and private cars carrying foreign tourists—as well as larger tour groups—must travel in regularly scheduled convoys. You can book an overland trip to Abu Simbel through a tour company in Aswan (at a cost of around $90 per person) or by contracting a private taxi in Aswan to transport you to the temple and back. If you use a private taxi, haggle hard to get a day rate;

note that you should offer to pay for the driver's lunch while you are in Abu Simbel, which will cost you an extra £E10–£E20. These arrangements should be made at least one day in advance, as tour operators may need to take your passport details to the police so that they know you are traveling in the convoy on a given date. The convoy for Abu Simbel departs from behind the Nubia Museum in Aswan at 4 AM and 11 AM daily. The journey takes around 3½ hours.

WHERE TO EAT AND STAY

Abu Simbel is a small, rural town. There are no international-style restaurants in the town; however, small street stalls and basic cafés offer a seemingly never-ending supply of grilled meats and chicken, rice, and soup to keep hunger pangs at bay. Look for roadside stalls selling seasonal fresh fruits. Alternatively, if you travel by land convoy or are staying over, you can carry supplies with you from Aswan and have a picnic. Even if you fly in, you may have time for a snack, coffee, or cold drink at the small café next to the monument entrance.

If you can make the time, it's well worth staying overnight at Abu Simbel. You can visit the temples when the hoards of day-trippers have departed, take in the Sound & Light Show, and enjoy the bucolic atmosphere of the town.

$–$$ **Eskaleh Nubian Cultural House.** Fikry Kachif can remember what Nubia was like before it was swallowed up by Lake Nasser. He decided to keep that memory alive through this bed-and-breakfast. The best reason to stay here may be to admire the architecture and construction methods; you can see exactly how the mud bricks fit together to make the characteristic Nubian domes and barrel vaults. In the rooms, authenticity goes to the beds—wood frames lashed to carved legs—and to recessed cupboards in thick walls. Take a hint: The mosquito netting isn't just for show. Open stairways lead to rooftop terraces. And there's a small library. The dining room, hung with personal mementos, serves vegetables grown in the hotel's garden, and is large enough to welcome bus tours making the day trip from Aswan. **Pros:** an authentic architectural experience; domestic beer and wine are available. **Cons:** if the nearby airport doesn't break the spell, the bus-tour dining might. ⊠ *Abu Simbel* ☎ *097/340–1288* ⊕ *www.eskaleh.net* ⟿ *5 rooms* ⅏ *In-room: a/c, no phone, no TV. In-hotel: restaurant, laundry service, Internet terminal, parking (free)* ⊟ *No credit cards* ⧖ *BP.*

$$$$ **Seti Abu Simbel Lake Resort.** The most comfortable hotel in the town is right on the shore of Lake Nasser. Nubian-style bungalows are scattered

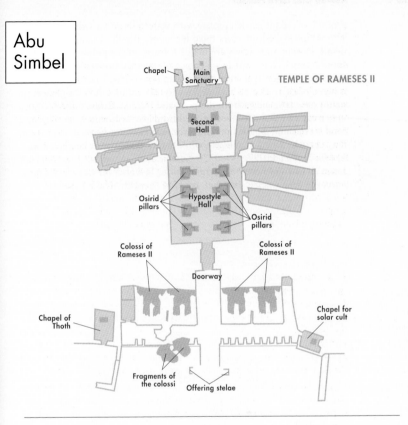

Abu Simbel

TEMPLE OF RAMESES II

Chapel

Main Sanctuary

Second Hall

Osirid pillars

Hypostyle Hall

Osirid pillars

Colossi of Rameses II

Colossi of Rameses II

Doorway

Chapel of Thoth

Chapel for solar cult

Fragments of the colossi

Offering stelae

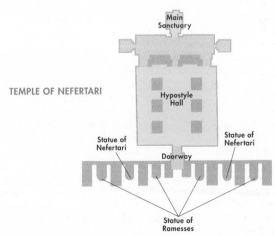

TEMPLE OF NEFERTARI

Main Sanctuary

Hypostyle Hall

Statue of Nefertari

Statue of Nefertari

Doorway

Statue of Ramesses

around a verdant garden replete with waterfalls and a swimming pool. The whitewashed interiors have terracotta-tile floors and faux-stone detail. Domes and arches are major features of the public areas and in some rooms. The resort has a choice of eateries, but some may not be open to hotel guests if a bus-tour group (on convoy to or from Aswan) is given priority. **Pros:** a stylish place to relax after a day of sightseeing; panoramic lake views from the pool and terrace. **Cons:** some facilities may not be available off-season or during low-occupancy (laundry and food service may not be operating, for example); the lights in your room may cease to function at night, while the air-conditioner keeps running. ⊠ *Abu Simbel* ☎ *097/340–0720* ⊕ *www.setifirst.com* ⇱ *136 rooms, 6 suites* ⚲ *In-room: a/c, refrigerator, safe. In-hotel: 3 restaurants, bars, pool, laundry service, Internet, parking (free)* ▭ *MC, V* ⦿ *MAP*.

The Sinai Peninsula and the Red Sea Coast

WORD OF MOUTH

"If your hotel [in Sharm El-Sheikh] has a dive center, definitely book your trip through them. That way you don't have to take a bus or anything, you just go direct. I think it's worth it even if it's more expensive."

—LMcDowell

WELCOME TO THE SINAI PENINSULA AND THE RED SEA COAST

TOP REASONS TO GO

★ **Saint Catherine's Monastery.** See the chapel that purports to hold the burning bush that appeared to Moses.

★ **Scuba Diving.** Dive to the wreck of the *Thistlegorm* in the protected waters of Ras Mohammed National Park.

★ **Climbing Mount Sinai.** Rise before dawn and climb up the mountainside to welcome the sunrise over the Sinai mountain range.

★ **Kite Surfing.** The tides and winds are perfect along the Red Sea Coast; catch some air while kite surfing off Mangroovy Beach at El Gouna.

★ **Dancing the Night Away.** Sinai resorts are magnets for young club goers from all over Europe; strut your stuff on the dance floor in one of the top spots—Pacha Club in Sharm El-Sheikh.

1 The Sinai Peninsula. Come here for spectacular desert mountainscapes, the natural home of the Bedouin peoples, and Saint Catherine's Monastery. Around the fringes, the growing resorts of the coast offer excellent rest and relaxation, including some of the world's best diving and Egypt's best beaches, especially near Sharm El-Sheikh. From Taba it's possible to take a day trip to fabled Petra in Jordan.

2 The Red Sea Coast. Excellent diving, great beaches, and a wealth of water sports are the major draws of this coast, which is popular with European vacationers for its year-round sunshine. The main destination is Hurghada. Beaches here are not quite as good as those on the Sinai Peninsula, but the diving is even better.

3 The Suez Canal. Visit the canal region if you like 19th-century architecture and an authentic small-town Egyptian atmosphere. Don't visit if you're seeking ancient monuments or great beach resorts. Most people visit on a day trip from Cairo, but those who appreciate a slower pace may wish to spend the night.

GETTING ORIENTED

Because the Sinai Peninsula and Red Sea Coast both have seaside activities and ancient monasteries—the most impressive mountain scenery is in the Sinai—you don't need to go to both areas. Air connections are limited and unreliable. To avoid long desert drives, you can fly from Cairo, Luxor, or Alexandria to your beach resort of choice. The resorts on the Red Sea Coast are also best reached by plane (or by road from Luxor). Bur Sa'id is best seen as a day trip from Cairo or as a stopover on the way to the Sinai if you are going by road.

6

DIVING IN EGYPT

Always featured among the top dive destinations in the world, the Red Sea seems to have it all: magnificent corals, shoals of playful fish, large pelagic species to add thrills, and eerie shipwrecks to add drama.

(above) Hanging coral reef in the Red Sea. (opposite left) Blue Hole diving site in Dahab. (opposite right) The reefs of Sharm El Sheikh.

The Red Sea is a premier diving location for everyone from beginners to experts. Almost a backwater and cut off from the oceans, its water is warm year-round—usually between 75°F (November through March) and 82°F (April through October)—which is ideal for coral formation. Warm temperatures also means that divers don't get too cold, making it a great spot for beginners.

Coral reefs run close to land along much of the Egyptian coast and support a rich ecosystem of over 1,000 marine species. Whichever town you choose as your dive base, you'll have a quality experience with few time-consuming boat transfers to dive sites and great dives, whether you explore the shallows or the depths. Visibility is good, on average 49 feet (15 meters), so you get great views while you're on your submarine explorations.

RED SEA ENVIRONMENTAL CENTRE

The Red Sea Environmental Centre (⊕ *www.redsea-ec.org*) in Masbat, Dahab, is a private conservation institute dedicated to the study of the Red Sea marine environment. In collaboration with the Egyptian Environmental Affairs Agency and educational institutions worldwide, the center offers training to dive instructors as well as tourists.

EGYPT'S BEST DIVE SITES

DAHAB

The Blue Hole. Internationally famed, this narrow natural chimney at 100 feet below the surface leads to drop-off of over 1,000 feet. The water's hue gives the dive its name. Marine life abounds in the upper levels.

Eel Garden. The sandy bottom at around 100 feet makes the perfect habitat for hundreds of eels that stick their heads out of their holes in unison to feed. You also see a wide variety of hard and soft corals.

HURGHADA

Abu Hashish. Named after the acres of sea grass that blanket the seafloor, the landscape of Abu Hashish is characterized by coral bommies (individual towers of coral) erupting from the sea floor through the swaying fronds. It rewards divers with the chance to glimpse some of the more secretive sea life including octopus, seahorses, and cuttlefish.

El Minya. Meaning "the harbor," this Soviet-built minesweeper was bombed and sunk by the Israelis in Hurghada harbor in the late 1960s. It's bristling with antiaircraft guns, and you can enter the interior, home to a large moray eel.

Small Giftun Island. A mixture of drifting ergs (underwater sand dunes), chimney caves, and a deep drop-off add up to the variety here, with soft and fan corals,

glass fish, lionfish, and groupers among the more colorful inhabitants. Erg Somaya has a deep drop where hammerheads and barracuda gather.

MARSA ALAM

Elphinstone. A short but spectacular section of reef has precipitous walls dropping on both flanks, plus natural arches and pinnacles. The soft corals are noteworthy, and the sea life includes groupers and morays, with visiting hammerhead sharks a regular sight.

SAFAGA

Arba Erg. Also known as Tobia Arba, this site has a group of seven rocky peaks rising from the seafloor to just under the water surface with good coral growth and marine life including lionfish, puffers, and groupers.

SHARM EL-SHEIKH

Jackson Reed, Tiran Strait. A favorite hunting ground of hammerhead and tiger sharks, dolphins, and turtles, the reef has impressive gardens of both soft and hard corals and varieties of colorful fish that always make your trip worthwhile.

SS *Thistlegorm*, Ras Muhammed National Park. This 400-foot cargo steamer was sent 100 feet to the bottom by a German bomb in 1941. The explosion ripped the superstructure apart, spreading its contents of vital war supplies across the seabed.

EGYPT'S BEST BEACHES

The beaches of the northern Sinai are made unforgettable by their backdrop of sheer, jagged mountain peaks. Farther south, along the mainland Red Sea Coast, the allure is in just the right combination of pale golden sand and shimmering azure waters.

(above) Mahmya Beach on Giftun Island. (opposite left) Beach at El Gouna. (opposite right) Beach at Naama Bay, Sharm El Sheikh.

The long coral reef running the length of Egypt's Red Sea Coast is the source of these superb beaches; over thousands of years, dead coral has eroded into fine grains of golden sand. The lack of tides and strong currents—or extreme weather events such as hurricanes—means the sand is pretty stable.

The best beaches, an almost unbroken stretch of sand, are found down the west coast of the Sinai, with the more easterly Hurghada region having only a handful of sandy bays. Until the latter part of the 20th century, these strands were almost untouched by human development, but even today, despite the popularity of the Red Sea Riviera as a tourist destination, it's possible to escape the crowds, especially in the Sinai.

TURTLES IN THE SINAI

Green, hawksbill, leatherhead, and loggerhead turtles nest in the region, coming ashore on beaches in early summer to lay their eggs. Immediately after hatching, the young make their way to the water and out into the open sea. The males never come ashore again, but the females will return to their birthplace at around the age of 20, to lay their eggs and begin another life cycle.

EGYPT'S BEST BEACHES

Generally, the best beaches in Egypt are located on the Sinai Peninsula; diving is generally better on the Red Sea coast.

EL GOUNA

Hotel beaches in El Gouna are private, reserved solely for the guests of the resorts; however, the region does have a couple of public beaches.

Mangroovy Beach. The sand is plentiful and golden, but the main draw here is the kite surfing in the seemingly endless offshore shallows. As the name suggests, the groove here is cool throughout the day and wild at night, when the beach parties kick off.

Zeytouna Beach. El Gouna's main and only public-access beach is set around an offshore island with gently lapping waters and a whole raft of facilities from salsa lessons to a genuine coral reef just offshore.

HURGHADA

On the whole, Hurghada's beaches are just not as good as those on the Sinai coast. Since there are no good public options, it's important to pick a resort with one of the better stretches of sand.

Makadi Bay. A house reef just a few feet offshore mirrors this long, sinuous golden beach. A series of luxury resorts have sprung up here since the late 1990s, each looking to cater to your every whim.

Giftun Island. Great swaths of pale sand surround this small island 45 minutes offshore, leading into iridescent shallows that are perfect for snorkeling. This is a picture-perfect beach, and the marine life is amazing.

NUWEIBA

With both good beaches and good offshore reefs, Nuweiba offers some of the best of both worlds to divers and resort goers looking for a more laidback destination.

Basata Beach. This unspoiled ribbon of sand washed by cerulean sea with a rustic eco-resort of tropical shacks, nestled against the serrated treeless peaks of the Sinai Mountains is the perfect place to escape from the world.

SHARM EL-SHEIKH

Sharm has some of Egypt's best beaches and most lavish resorts.

Main Beach, Ras Muhammed National Park. This relatively short strand at the heart of the protected area offers options for sunning, snorkeling, and diving around the corals just offshore. The sea life is incredible, even in the shallows.

Na'ama Bay. A beautiful arc of fine golden sand fronted by azure shallows and backed by excellent restaurants, bars, and water sports shops couldn't be better. But you must love company because this beach draws crowds.

6

Updated by
Lindsay and
Pete Bennett

For centuries, European traders and Arab merchants had to sail around the Cape of Good Hope to travel east to Asia from Europe and the Mediterranean. However, 2,000 years earlier, ancient Egyptians had that problem licked. The records of the Greek historian Herodotus speak of a canal begun around 600 BC that connected the Nile to the Gulf of Suez.

The canal was used during the time of Alexander the Great, left to ruin, then reopened during the Arab domination that began around AD 645. The canal was the primary route between the Nile Valley and the Arab world's trading center in Mecca, on the west coast of Saudi Arabia. Then the ancient canal was abandoned, and traders returned to the desert, risking their goods and their camels. Aside from the accounts of historians, all traces of that canal have vanished. The Suez Canal—an effort of thousands of Egyptian men who manually shoveled tons of sand between 1859 and 1869 to create a 110-km (66-mi) trench through the desert—follows a different course.

Since the dawn of human culture in Africa and the Middle East, the Sinai and Red Sea region has been an important crossroads—then a land bridge, now a sea bridge—connecting East and West, North and South. Enormous container ships and fancy ocean liners line up to pass through the Suez Canal. Canal towns such as Ismailiya and Bur Sa'id (Port Said) make interesting day trips from Cairo, if you have the time. But the novelty of passing ships can wear off rather quickly, leaving little else to do.

Not so the Sinai Peninsula and the Red Sea Coast, where relaxing on the beach, trekking through the desert, and diving amidst a wealth of marine life are probably the opposite of what you'd expect from a trip to Egypt. The desert itself, inland Sinai, has changed little since the times when Bedouins moved from one watering hole to the next. It remains awe inspiring, especially if you get up for sunrise and catch the mountains changing from purple to red, then orange to yellow. The Red Sea continues to be an underwater haven, a living aquarium, in spite of the impact that a rush of divers has had on the reefs. Since the mid-1990s this coastline has undergone a multimillion-dollar makeover and has been transformed into the so-called Red Sea Riviera and marketed successfully to vacationers across northern Europe and the newly emerging countries of the old Soviet bloc. If you want resort amenities and the option of escaping to virgin desert spotted with shady acacia trees and lazy camels, this is the place for you. If you want to see ancient monasteries and biblical sites, or follow Moses' path from Egypt to Jordan, you can do that here, too.

Although Egypt is conservative when it comes to everyday attire, guests in the resort areas of the Sinai and the Red Sea often walk around in shorts and tank tops. Some people choose to dress up for dinner, although it is not mandatory. If you plan to visit any of the monasteries, dress modestly. The Suez is not a resort area, so don't walk around in shorts, women especially; long, loose clothing is a better idea. If you are driving around the area, and definitely if you are taking buses, wear long pants and short sleeves (nothing sleeveless).

Remember that you will be in a desert, and prices will necessarily be higher than elsewhere in the country because so many things have to be imported. If you plan to shop, plan to haggle. Always carry identification as you may be stopped for security checks, and if you visit a Bedouin village, take along some candy, pens, or notebooks to give to Bedouin children.

If you are a woman traveling alone or in a group of women, be alert and street smart. You are likely to be heckled—just ignore it—or hit on in the coastal resorts.

PLANNING

WHEN TO GO

April through October are the hot months, when temperatures climb as high as 113°F. It's a great time to come for diving, because the visibility is at its best. November through March is cooler, with temperatures as low as 46°F. The desert gets very cold at night, and temperatures may even drop below freezing, so bring warm layers in winter. The Sinai's high season is during the hotter months, but July and August are considered low season, as the heat is oppressive during this time. The Red Sea, on the other hand, is great in winter, which is its most popular time. Except in March, during the *khamaseen* (sandstorm) season, the sun shines here almost every day of the year.

PLANNING YOUR TIME

If time is short, the Sinai is a better choice; Saint Catherine's Monastery, with its proximity to Mount Sinai, is a greater draw than the monasteries of Saint Anthony and Saint Paul. Sharm's golf course is one of the best in Egypt. Diving and kite surfing are better on Egypt's mainland Red Sea Coast, but the beaches are inferior to those in the Sinai. The Suez Canal is best seen on a day trip from Cairo, but you can also stay overnight in Bur Sa'id or Ismailiya and continue the next day to Sharm El-Sheikh or the Red Sea Coast if you are traveling overland.

GETTING THERE AND AROUND

AIR TRAVEL

Regularly scheduled EgyptAir flights connect Sharm El-Sheikh to Cairo (a bit over an hour), Alexandria, Luxor, and Hurghada. Hurghada also has regularly scheduled EgyptAir flights from Cairo (less than an hour), Alexandria, and Aswan. Both Sharm and Hurghada have frequent service from many different European destinations on low-cost European airlines as well as on EgyptAir; some of this service is seasonal. You can also fly to the privately operated Marsa Alam airport from Cairo (three times weekly) or from Europe, and to the airport at Taba once weekly from Cairo with EgyptAir Express or from Europe. *For information on international flights, see* ⇨ *Air Travel in Egypt Essentials.*

Hurghada International Airport is in the desert, 4 km (2½ mi) west of the Sheraton at the southern end of town. Most hotels offer airport transfers, but these will need to be prebooked; the taxi fare from the airport to the Sheraton Road, Sakalla, is around £E30. Marsa Alam Airport is 20 km (12 mi) north of Marsa Alam town and 2½ km (1 mi) west of Port Ghalib. Taxi fare into Marsa Alam town is approx £E100. In Sharm El-Sheikh, it's a £E55 fare into Na'ama Bay and a £E70 to £E80 taxi fare to downtown Sharm; however, if you are light on luggage you could take the public minibus service that costs £E2 one way to Na'ama Bay or downtown (though these don't drop you directly at your hotel).

Airline Contacts EgyptAir (☏ 02/2267–7010 in Cairo, 069/366–1058 in Sharm El-Sheikh, 065/364–3034 in Hurghada, 065/364–3034 in Marsa Alam, 0900/7000 for National Call Center ⊕ www.egyptair.com).

Airport Contacts Hurghada International Airport (✉ Sheraton Rd., 4 km [2½ mi] west of the Sheraton, Hurghada ☏ 065/446–772 ⊕ www.eac-airports.com). **Marsa Alam Airport** (✉ Marsa Alam ☏ 065/370–0021 ⊕ www.marsa-alam-airport.com). **Sharm El-Sheikh Airport** (✉ Airport Rd., Sharm El-Sheikh ☏ 069/360–1140 ⊕ www.eac-airports.com). **Taba International Airport** (✉ Airport Rd., Taba ☏ 68/500–432 ⊕ www.eac-airports.com).

BUS TRAVEL

The best way to get to the Suez Canal Zone is by bus from Cairo. You can take one early in the morning from Cairo to Bur Sa'id, walk around for a couple of hours, then hop on another bus to Ismailiya. Have lunch there, explore a bit, then head back to Cairo in the evening. Travel time on the buses will total around five hours.

However, long-distance bus travel to the Sinai or Red Sea Coast takes time and patience; obnoxious dramatic movies play for the duration, and despite NO SMOKING signs everywhere, even the driver lights up. El Gouna Bus Company offers frequent service between Cairo and Hurghada and El Gouna. Frequent East Delta Bus Company buses run daily from Sinai Station in Abbasia to Sharm El-Sheikh, Nuweiba, and Taba. Go Bus Company operates services to various destinations in the Sinai and Red Sea. Super Jet has buses to Sharm El-Sheikh and

Hurghada from Cairo's Maydan Tahrir station. The Upper Egypt Bus Company has several buses a day between Cairo and Hurghada, al-Quseir, and Marsa Alam; their company also operates routes to Luxor.

Super Jet and East Delta Bus Company buses run frequently from two stations in Cairo—from the Cairo Gateway Bus Station (formerly Turgoman) in Bulaq's Cairo Gateway complex, and from Almaza Station in Heliopolis to Bur Sa'id, from where you can catch connecting services direct to St Catherine's. Buses also connect Bur Sa'id to Ismailiya. These buses vary in cleanliness. Be sure to book front seats, and get to the station ahead of time to book your ticket. And be aware that the ticket salespeople are not always helpful.

Contacts El Gouna Bus Company (☏ 065/355–6188, within Egypt the call center number is 19567). **East Delta Bus Company** (☏ 02/2405–3482 in Cairo; 069/366–0660 in Sharm El-Sheikh; 069/364–0250 in Taba; 069/352–0371 in Nuweiba; 069/364–0250 in Dahab; 064/366–5885 in Ismailiya; 066/364–9617 in Bur Sa'id). **Go Bus Company** (☏ 02/2578–5548 in Cairo; 065/354–1561 in Hurghada; 069/336–4953 in Sharm El-Sheikh). **Super Jet** (☏ 02/2579–8181 in Cairo; 065/355–3499 in Hurghada; 069/366–1622 in Sharm El-Sheikh; 02/2579–8181 in Bur Sa'id). **Upper Egypt Bus Company** (☏ 02/2260–9279 in Cairo; 065/354–4582 in Hurghada; 065/325–1253 in Safaga; 065/333–0033 in al-Quseir; 062/366–4258 in Suez).

CAR TRAVEL

To cross the Suez Canal, you should take the Ahmed Hamdy Tunnel from the city of Suez on the southern end into the Sinai Peninsula; expect to pay tolls. Foreign travelers in vehicles who don't have a resident's permit will be expected to join a traveler's convoy. The times for these cars can vary, so if your hotel has a concierge, ask them to confirm times and the meeting place. If you employ a driver, he will organize your departure time to take into account convoy times, so you don't need to worry.

Roads in the Sinai are mostly single lane, though a two-lane highway is partly built along the west coast. Though the main roads are in fine condition, you might want to take a taxi instead. Getting to remote sights requires some skill, and negotiating winding roads through the mountains requires extreme caution because local drivers usually don't stay in their own lanes.

The advantage of renting a car and driving to the Red Sea Coast is flexibility, but that might not outweigh the dangers posed by other drivers, including many trucks, and the hairpin turns before Ain Sukhna. If you don't have nerves of steel, fly to Hurghada or hire a taxi to take you to the monasteries. If you plan to stay in Hurghada or El Gouna, you will not need a car. If you are going to travel south as far as al-Quseir or Marsa Alam, having a car will be helpful. The road there is well-marked and easy to drive.

Renting a car in Egypt is no different than it is in the United States. You will need to bring both your domestic license and an international driver's license. Prices for a compact car are around $60 per day, hiring a driver is about $25 extra per day (with further charges if you want to keep the driver overnight). Cars in Egypt do not usually have unlimited mileage, so there may be a per-km charge if you exceed the daily allotment.

You do not need a car if you are staying in either Bur Sa'id or Ismailiya.

Car Rental Contacts Avis (✉ *Morgana Mall, off Peace Rd., Na'ama Bay, Sharm El-Sheikh* ☎ *069/360–2400* ⊕ *www.avisegypt.com* ✉ *Shar'a Sheraton, Hurghada* ☎ *065/344–7400*). **El Gouna Limousine** (✉ *Tamr Henna, El Gouna* ☎ *065/358–0061* ⊕ *www.elgouna-limousine.com* ✉ *Taba Heights* ☎ *069/358–0234*). **Europcar** (✉ *Sharm El-Sheikh International Airport, Sharm El-Sheikh* ☎ *016/554–4313*) (✉ *Hurghada International Airport, Hurghada* ☎ *016/661–1025* ⊕ *www.europcar.com*).

FERRY TRAVEL

The easiest way to get to Sharm El-Sheikh from the Red Sea Coast is by ferry. Sharm El-Sheikh–Hurghada ferries operate daily with an alternating slow and fast ferry service. The trip takes two to three hours by fast ferry and six hours by slow ferry, depending on sea conditions, and costs are $50 per sector for fast ferries, $40 for slow ferries. Prices for foreign nationals are quoted (and payable) in U.S. dollars, but if you pay by credit card, you will be charged in the equivalent price in Egyptian pounds. Payment can be made directly in U.S. dollars. At this writing, fast ferries operate Monday, Thursday, and Saturday; slow ferries operate on Monday, Wednesday, and Friday, although these timetables are subject to regular changes.

Contacts Red Sea Jet Company (☎ *02/257–61798 in Cairo; 012/822–9877 in Sharm El-Sheikh; 065/344–9481 in Hurghada*).

TAXI TRAVEL

Within Sharm El-Sheikh, Dahab, and Nuweiba, a taxi ride will cost about £E10. There are no meters, so be sure to agree on a price with your driver before you get into the car. You can also take a taxi between towns; here are some fare estimates: £E200 between Sharm El-Sheikh and Dahab; £E300 between Sharm and Saint Catherine's Monastery; £E220 between Sharm and Nuweiba; and £E130 between Nuweiba and Taba. Taking the microbus in Sharm will be much cheaper.

In Hurghada, taxis are only available on the street (not by phoning a dispatcher). Taxis will cost at least £E15 for the shortest distance in Hurghada. A better, if more communal, option would be to flag down a microbus, which will cost only £E2 to £E5 per person. To travel between El Gouna and Hurghada, a taxi will cost around £E90. Within El Gouna, taxis are unnecessary since free microbuses and boats stop at all key hotels and hot spots.

In the Suez Canal Zone, taxis are everywhere. Just flag one down, and agree with the driver on a price before you get in. In Bur Sa'id, you should pay no more than £E5 for any local trip. In Ismailiya, you might pay up to £E10. The drivers are usually pleasant, and they will turn down the music if you ask them to. But brace yourself: they drive very fast.

Shark Bay near Sharm El-Sheikh

⚠ At this writing, tourists were being targeted by a note-switching scam in Hurghada. When you give a taxi driver, perhaps, a £E50 note for a fare, he quickly switches it for a 50pt note and tells you you've given him the wrong amount. Always look at your cash before handing it over.

INTERNET

Internet cafés are popular and numerous, but they come and go with surprising regularity, especially in the resort towns. Wi-Fi is growing in availability, with most major hotels and some bars and cafés offering services; however, free Wi-Fi is not common. Costs run around £E20 for 30 minutes but are cheaper per hour if you pay for blocks of time (more than five hours).

RESTAURANTS

The Sinai and the Red Sea Coast resorts cater primarily to European tastes, so resort food tends to be Continental and Italian fare and buffet breakfasts. Fresh seafood can be very good. Typical Egyptian food is most readily available in the cities of Bur Sa'id and Ismailiya along the Suez Canal. A few words of caution: Water is not always potable, so stick to bottled water to be safe. Likewise, vegetables are not always washed properly, so stay away from uncooked greens, especially lettuce and cucumbers. Oil, ghee, and butter, along with anything fatty, iare very popular. A dish that you would expect to be light, like sautéed vegetables, may come dripping with oil.

HOTELS

Around the Sinai and the Red Sea you'll find everything from luxury resorts to motels and seedy camping areas. Prices are considerably higher in peak seasons (September through November and April through June). European tour operators generally buy these rooms in bulk and sell them only as part of holiday packages; therefore, independent travelers may find it difficult to book upscale resort rooms. Hotel rates are almost always charged in either U.S. dollars or euros. In Suez, lodging options are much more limited; the Resta in Bur Sa'id and the Mercure Hotel in Ismailiya are the best hotels, and both are comfortable and have waterfront views. Bear in mind that, as elsewhere in Egypt, there is a precipitous drop in quality between high- and low-end hotels, with very few options in the middle.

All hotel reviews have been condensed for this book. Please go to Fodors.com for full reviews of each property.

WHAT IT COSTS IN EGYPTIAN POUNDS, U.S. DOLLARS, AND EUROS			
$	$$	$$$	$$$$
Restaurants	under £E50	£E50–£E100	£E100–£E150	over £E150
Hotels in Dollars	under $70	$70–$130	$130–$200	over $200
Hotels in Euros	under €45	€45–€80	€80–€130	over €130

Restaurant prices are per person for a main course at dinner. Hotel prices are for a double room in high season, excluding 10% tax and service charges (usually 10%).

THE SINAI PENINSULA

The Sinai Peninsula is a bridge between continents, and for ages, travelers from Europe, Africa, and Asia have crossed and recrossed it. It's also one of history's hotbeds of conflict, where time and the elements have weighed in on the harsh terrain, leaving behind majestic landscapes cradled by the crystal blue waters of the Red Sea and the gulfs of Aqaba to the east and Suez to the west. On its desert sands more than 4,000 years ago, ancient Egyptian expeditions set out in search of copper and turquoise. Here, Moses led the Israelites across arid wastes before moving north to their promised land. Christian Europe's crusaders marched through the Sinai from the 11th through the 13th centuries, trying to take the Holy Land from the Muslims who ruled it. During the 20th century, Egypt and Israel traded the land back and forth in war as they fought for it in 1967 and 1973, launching the desert once again onto the world's strategic stage.

Forty million years ago, the Sinai was part of the African-Asian landmass. Then seismic activity began a process that split the landmass into two separate plates—Saudi Arabia and Yemen on one side and Egypt and Sudan on the other—each plate pulling equally in opposite directions. Further plate motion tore at and wrinkled the region, creating a protected underwater ecology, and leaving vast uninhabited areas of rugged mountain terrain and arid desert.

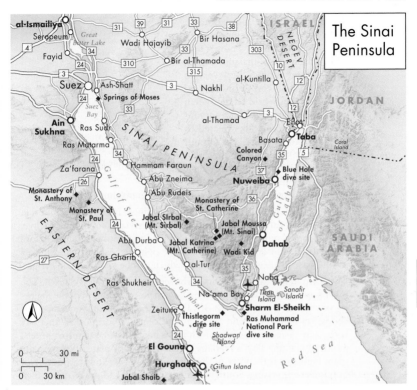

Three geological areas make up the Sinai. The first lies to the north and consists mainly of pure, shifting, soft-sand dunes. Herein lie ancient *wadis* (dried-up riverbeds), where you can find fossils from the Mediterranean. The second area is in the central part of the peninsula, a flat elevated plateau broken occasionally by limestone outcroppings and water sources. Toward the south of the central massif, the landscape begins to change to a granite and volcanic rocky region—the beginnings of the third area, which forms a natural barrier between desert and sea. If you are driving into southern Sinai through the mountains, look out for that breathtaking view of the blue sea peeking out from behind the mountains.

SHARM EL-SHEIKH

510 km (320 mi) southeast of Cairo.

In the mid-1980s, Sharm El-Sheikh, at the Sinai's southern tip, had one hotel, two dive centers, and a snack bar. Today this bustling little town has more than 160 hotels, with respective dive centers, malls, casinos, and restaurants, and more Europeans than Egyptians. This exponential expansion marks the town as Egypt's key resort in what marketers call the Red Sea Riviera. Indeed, Sharm, as it is fondly called, is known for having some of Egypt's most lavish hotels, world-renowned dive centers, and nightlife galore. In many ways the town is more than a little schizophrenic. It's now a firm favorite for fun-in-the-sun singles, couples, and families, but every so often this small corner of the Sinai takes to the world stage when political leaders gather for summit meetings or peace talks related to Middle East issues. The summit of May 2008 saw more than 150 world leaders—including President George W. Bush—and their associated entourages transform the town into a giant think tank.

> **DID YOU KNOW?**
>
> There are two theories regarding the origin of the name *Sinai*. The ancient inhabitants of this desert worshipped Sin, a moon goddess, therefore naming the land in her honor—perhaps. Or it could be that the Semitic word *sin* (tooth) gets the credit; the peninsula indeed has the shape of a tooth.

Get rid of any preconceived notions of visiting a barren wasteland rich in archaeological sites and a simple desert lifestyle. If your aim is to dive, snorkel, enjoy outdoor and water activities, or simply to lounge before you hit the nightlife scene, you're in the right place. Sharm also makes a solid base for nearby desert sites, which can be visited on day trips.

There are four main areas within the vicinity of Sharm El-Sheikh. The most popular is known as Na'ama Bay, the central hub with the majority of the hotels, restaurants of various culinary merit, souvenir-filled shops, key nightspots, and excellent dive centers. North of Na'ama Bay is the new district of Nabq, which has a handful of large resort hotels. South of Na'ama Bay is Hadaba (the name means plateau), where the main highlight is the view of the surrounding area, and the number of hotels has been rising. South of Hadaba, Sharm al-Maya is often called downtown Sharm El-Sheikh. It's set on the more down-to-earth Sharm El-Sheikh harbor, where the dive boats dock at night. Here are more hotels, as well as typically Egyptian *ahwas* (cafés) where men smoke *shisha* (water pipes) and play backgammon.

Sharm isn't the place for sightseeing: the resorts don't have any sights to see, though a National Museum complete with some ancient artifacts is expected to open in 2011. It's the seaside activities—windsurfing, parasailing, waterskiing, and diving and snorkeling—and side trips to the desert that make boredom an unknown quantity here.

GETTING HERE AND AROUND

At the very tip of the Sinai Peninsula, Sharm has regular flights from Cairo and also from Alexandria, Hurghada, and Luxor. Air-conditioned bus services from Cairo are numerous and inexpensive. Foreign travelers in rental vehicles traveling from the capital may need to join a security convoy. Bus services also link Sharm with the other towns on the Sinai coast. A ferry service links Sharm with Hurghada on the mainland Red Sea Coast. Taxis are the best way to get around town, but agree fares before you set off on your journey.

NEED A BREAK?

We know you don't need a full review of Starbucks (⊠ *King of Bahrain St., Old Market Area, Na'ama Bay* ☎ *069/360–2238*), but we have decided to make an exception for this branch, whose ever-willing staff happily takes nonstandard orders and serves the best coffee we've had at the chain. Plus the apple pie with cinnamon is delicious. A prime location means the whole gamut of visitors passes your table in the evenings.

WHERE TO EAT

The Na'ama Bay boardwalk is restaurant central. Grilled sea bass marinated in lemon juice, pepper, onions, and fresh garlic, served with french fries, is a local favorite. If you'd rather not bother with fish bones, look for flounder grilled or fried, served with lemon juice and a tasty garnish.

$$
MIDDLE EASTERN
★
✕ **Abou el Sid.** The best traditional Egyptian cuisine in the area is served here in an air-conditioned dining room or on an ample terrace. The number of Middle Eastern clients here tells you the food is authentic. Try a selection of mezze, which include excellent stuffed vine leaves and tabbouleh, or opt for an entrée of roast quail or slow-cooked lamb shank served with rice. Be prepared for massive portions; it's easy to order too much food and find yourself overwhelmed. The restaurant serves alcohol and has a good, if expensive, selection of Egyptian wines. Stay after your meal to enjoy a shisha and some mint tea. ⊠ *Sultan Qabous St., Na'ama Bay* ☎ *069/352–0320* ⊟ *AE, MC, V* ☉ *No lunch.*

$
FAST FOOD
✕ **Don Panino.** Mouth-watering wraps, pizza slices, and sandwiches are the backbone of this modern eatery with a terrace made for people-watching on one of Na'ama Bay's busiest pedestrian thoroughfares. The freshest, crispest salad ingredients combine with Cajun beef or barbecue chicken in the wraps; these and the sandwiches are made to order in a clean, open kitchen. Unlike many fast-food joints in town, you can get chilled beer here, plus a selection of sodas. Don Panino's makes a great pit stop any time of the day, but it's very popular for post-clubbing refreshments since it stays open until 4 AM. ⊠ *King of Bahrain St., Old Market Area, Na'ama Bay* ☎ *069/360–0700* ⊟ *AE, MC, V.*

$$$$
SEAFOOD
✕ **Fish Restaurant.** One of the most upscale restaurants in Sharm, Fish Restaurant serves a short menu of nouvelle-style seafood, and your food is like a picture on a plate. Popular choices include expertly prepared fillets, calamari, and lobster. The silver service and outdoor terrace out in the mature garden just off the beachfront boulevard let you know that this restaurant is all about image and special occasions, and accordingly, the dress code is casual-elegant. A splurge here is rewarded with a better wine list and more attentive service than you'll find at the more mainstream restaurants. ⊠ *Hilton Sharm El-Sheikh Fayrouz Resort, Peace Rd., Na'ama Bay* ☎ *069/360–1043* ⌂ *Reservations essential* ⊟ *AE, DC, MC, V* ☉ *No lunch.*

NATIONAL MUSEUM

As part of a grand plan to showcase Egyptian history across the country, a state-of-the-art Sharm El Sheikh National Museum will have several major ancient pharaonic artifacts, including the ornate 21st-Dynasty sarcophagus of nobleman Imesy, which was repatriated to Egypt by U.S. authorities in April 2010. The museum is also benefiting from donations by Egyptian benefactors, including a collection of eleven pieces of Coptic art currently under conservation. At best, the museum will open in 2011.

6

Sharm El-Sheikh

NAAMA BAY
TO AIRPORT

Na'ama Bay

Red Sea

OLD TOWN

TO RAS
MOHAMMED
NATL. PARK

RAS UM-SID

Peace Rd.

City Council St.

El Fanar St.

Motels St.

0   1 mi
0   1 km

KEY
❶ *Restaurants*
① *Hotels*

$$ **✕ Mexican Bar.** The decor and name suggest Tex-Mex, but the menu
ECLECTIC runs from Italy to the Alamo via the Far East. Despite the geographi-
cal stretch, the kitchen does a good job whether you order the spicy
fajitas or the pasta carbonara, and there's a large terrace where you can
enjoy your food in relative calm, somewhat removed from the throng
of the Old Market area. Mexican Bar has a full range of international
liquor brands including a selection of tequilas, and it's a popular preclub
meeting place as evening turns to night. ⊠ *Tropitel Na'ama Bay Hotel,
Corner of Sultan Qabous St. and King of Bahrain St., Old Market Area,
Na'ama Bay* ☎ *069/360–0570* ▤ *AE, MC, V.*

WHERE TO STAY

*All hotel reviews have been condensed for this book. Please go to
Fodors.com for full reviews of each property.*

$$$ 🛏 **Hilton Sharm El-Sheikh Fayrouz Resort.** Sitting across the boardwalk
from the largest section of beachfront on Na'ama Bay, this hotel is a
low-rise series of whitewashed bungalows within mature gardens. **Pros:**
within walking distance of downtown Na'ama Bay and all its attractions; a good range of sports and activities available on-site; family
rooms (limited number) mean kids aren't hidden behind a connecting door; no smoking rooms. **Cons:** rooms at the very front of the

property look out over the Na'ama Bay boardwalk and lack privacy; family atmosphere may not appeal to singles. ⊠ *Peace Rd., Na'ama Bay* ☎ *069/360–1043* ⊕ *www.hilton.com* ⤳ *206 rooms, 4 suites* ⏚ *In-room: a/c, safe, Internet. In-hotel: 3 restaurants, room service, bars, tennis court, pools, beachfront, diving, water sports, children's programs (ages 4–11), laundry service, Wi-Fi hotspot, parking (free), some pets allowed* ▭ *AE, DC, MC, V* ⏸◐| *BP.*

$$$$ ▦ **Ritz-Carlton.** Combining the sensuality of ancient Egypt and the breezy
★   hush of a desert oasis, the Ritz offers its guests the definitive Red Sea resort experience. **Pros:** excellent spa on-site; expansive, lush gardens and grounds. **Cons:** away from the buzz of downtown. ⊠ *Om El-Sid, Hadaba* ⌂ *Box 72, South Sinai* ☎ *069/366–1919* ⊕ *www.ritzcarlton. com* ⤳ *286 rooms, 35 suites* ⏚ *In-room: a/c safe, Internet. In-hotel: 6 restaurants, room service, bars, tennis courts, pools, gym, spa, beachfront, diving, water sports, laundry service, parking (free)* ▭ *AE, DC, MC, V* ⏸◐| *BP.*

$$–$$$ ▦ **St. George Three Corners Resort.** High on the escarpment between Na'ama Bay and downtown Sharm El-Sheikh, this family-friendly hotel is highly regarded by the British visitors who frequent it. **Pros:** excellent range of amenities for the price point; very much a family hotel, so children will feel at home; no-smoking rooms. **Cons:** sun beds around the pool are rather cheek by jowl; it's not on the beach; it's a taxi ride to restaurants and nightlife. ⊠ *Magless El Madina St., Um El Sid* ☎ *069/366–0888* ⊕ *www.threecorners.com* ⤳ *262 rooms* ⏚ *In-room: a/c, safe, refrigerator. In-hotel: 2 restaurants, room service, bars, gym, spa, diving, water sports, laundry service, Internet terminal, parking (free)* ▭ *MC, V.*

$$ ▦ **Tropicana Rosetta.** This large hotel is on the mountainside off Peace Road, offering comfortable accommodation and good facilities without the frills—or price tag—of the typical four- or five-star Sharm resort. **Pros:** excellent pool facilities for a hotel in this price range; within easy access of Na'ama Bay's downtown but away from the hubbub. **Cons:** lack of a beach won't suit families with young children; the dining room has not been expanded as new rooms have been added, so breakfast can be very busy during prime hours. ⊠ *Peace Rd., Na'ama Bay* ☎ *069/360–1888* ⊕ *www.tropicanahotels.com* ⤳ *358 rooms* ⏚ *In-room: a/c, safe, refrigerator. In-hotel: 3 restaurants, bars, pools, diving, laundry service, Internet terminal, parking (free)* ▭ *AE, DC, MC, V* ⏸◐| *BP.*

$$–$$$ ▦ **Tropitel Na'ama Bay Hotel.** Contributing to the heartbeat of Na'ama Bay with its restaurants and clubs, this hotel puts you where it all happens. **Pros:** downtown location is great for fun lovers; rooms on the upper floors have private balconies; hotel not directly on the beach. **Cons:** can be some noise from Na'ama Bay's clubs, which remain open until 3 or 4 AM; not a lot of room around the pool if the hotel is full. ⊠ *Corner of Sultan Qabous St. and King of Bahrain St., Old Market Area, Na'ama Bay* ☎ *069/360–0570* ⊕ *www.tropitelhotels.com* ⤳ *327 rooms, 10 suites* ⏚ *In-room: a/c, safe, Wi-Fi. In-hotel: 5 restaurants, room service, bars, tennis court, gym, spa, diving, water sports, children's programs (ages 6–14), laundry service, Wi-Fi hotspot, parking (paid), no-smoking rooms* ▭ *AE, DC, MC, V* ⏸◐| *AI, BP, FAP, MAP.*

6

SPORTS AND THE OUTDOORS

DIVING

Almost every hotel rents space to independent dive shops, most of which provide the same services for the same prices: PADI, NAUI, and CMAS courses from beginner to instructor levels; three- to seven-day safaris; and daily trips to Ras Muhammad, Tiran, and other local sites. What sets the dive centers apart is their degree of professionalism, quality of guides and boats, and levels of hospitality. Supervised introductory dives, local boat dives, and shore dives cost about €40 for two dives, weights included. Longer boat dives cost about €60; daily equipment rental costs €25; and a five-day, open-water certificate course costs about €350.

Tiran, one of Sharm's most-visited sites, is a one-hour drive east off the coast. It can be rough as you cross the Straits of Tiran, but it is well worth the trip. On a day of diving, you cover two of the four reefs in this area; north to south they are Jackson, Woodhouse, Thomas, and Gordon. It is popular for its strong fly currents—there are drift dives only—and rich coral walls, and you may spot some big fish.

The *Thistlegorm* wreck is a diving-safari favorite, and some companies in Sharm will organize a day of diving that begins at 4 AM and returns you to Sharm, exhausted, at 5 PM. Strong currents and low visibility make this a hard dive, but it's a fantastic site.

Jackfish Alley is a great drift dive, with ergs swarming with shoals of glassfish and basking stingrays, a coral garden, and a gully where you should see large jackfish.

Ras Nasrani is a favorite shore dive 18 km (11 mi) northeast of Na'ama Bay that is also often done by boat. From the shore you may get lucky and get a private tour of the reef with the resident napoleon fish, which will take you around and bring you right back to the entry point. Remember *not* to feed him, or any other fish.

★ **Ras Muhammad National Park,** at the southernmost tip of the Sinai Peninsula, is considered one of the world's top dive sites. With great beaches and more than ten reefs to choose from, the park is a great place for shore and boat diving. The yellow starkness of the desert contrasts wonderfully with the explosion of life and color under the water. The most popular boat-dive plan includes Shark's Reef and Jolanda Reef, where you can see hordes of great fish, beautiful coral, and some toilets and sinks deposited by the Cypriot freighter *Jolanda,* which sank here in 1980. ⊠ *30 km (15 mi) south of Sharm El-Sheikh*.

DIVE OPERATORS

International Divers. If you want to be pampered, check in with one of the oldest centers in the area, which has other centers in the Sofitel Hotel and in two hotels in Hurghada. Managed by a team of professional divers who have been here for almost 20 years, International Divers owns its own boats, which means that even if you are the only diver booked, your excursion will not be canceled. The company also picks you up from your hotel and drops you off there at the end of the day. Or you can return to the dive center for a comfortable chat and coffee with the

Underwater diving with a humphead wrasse fish in Sharm al-Sheikh

dive guides and instructors. ✉ *White House, Peace Rd., Na'ama Bay* ☎ *069/360–0865* ⊕ *www.diversintl.com.*

Ocean College Dive Centre. This company offers excellent instruction but also offers a live-aboard diving option if you'd rather concentrate on enjoying the ocean depths than hit the bars in downtown Sharm. Other Ocean College centers can be found at the Ocean Club Hotel and the Na'ama Bay Hotel. ✉ *Hilton Waterfalls Hotel, Ras Um El-Sid, Hadaba* ☎ *069/366–4305* ⊕ *www.ocean-college.com.*

Red Sea Waterworld. This five-star PADI dive center works in collaboration with the National Geographic dive educator program. In addition to individual courses, it offers family dive training, including kid-friendly hours and supervision on boats so that parents don't have to worry if their children don't dive or don't stay down as long as they do. ✉ *Hyatt Regency Hotel, Gardens Bay, Na'ama Bay* ☎ *069/362–0315* ⊕ *www.redseawaterworld.com.*

SUBEX. The Swiss-run company has an international reputation for being tightly run (if a bit stringent) and well-equipped with staff, facilities, and gear. Guided dives go out with a maximum of four people, you must take a guide with you if you have fewer than 30 dives, and all divers have to go on an orientation dive to determine experience levels. There are good programs for junior divers. ✉ *Maritim Jolie Ville Resort and Casino, Na'ama Bay* ☎ *069/360–0122* ⊕ *www.subex.org.*

GUIDED TOURS

Abanoub Travel Agency. The company runs camel, jeep, and trekking tours of varying durations to all parts of the Sinai and also offers overnight trips to Petra and Cairo. ✉ *Aida Villas, Hadbet Om El-Sa'id, Sharm El-Sheikh* ☎ *069/366–5731* ⊕ *www.abanoub.com.*

Thomas Cook. Thomas Cook, the original travel agency for Egypt, is an all-around source for tours in a wide variety of price ranges. ✉ *8 Shar'a El Sheraton* ☎ *065/344–3338, or 16119 in India only* ⊕ *www. thomascookegypt.com.*

SNORKELING

Snorkeling is quite popular on the Sinai Coast. All dive centers rent snorkeling equipment, and some run specific snorkeling trips, though there's also good snorkeling from shore at most resorts. In addition, you can join diving trips as a nondiver with snorkeling gear; the downside is that you will be left to your own devices, snorkeling by yourself as the guide takes the divers into deeper waters. This could be disconcerting at best, dangerous at worst, especially if you are unfamiliar with the water conditions.

Unlike scuba diving, you do not need certification to rent and use snorkeling equipment. ■ TIP→ Wherever you snorkel, wear a T-shirt or even a wet suit to protect your back from the sun. Sunscreen alone absolutely does not provide enough protection.

Divers International. This dive operation has a one-day snorkeling excursion aboard one of three dive boats. You visit some of the area's most pristine locations, have lunch, and bask in the sun. The price including lunch and equipment is €38 to €43 per person. The company also offers a two-day introductory course with training sessions and several dives included in the price. ✉ *Sofitel, Na'ama Bay* ☎ *062/600–276.*

Sun 'n Fun. This all-around sports outfitter offers snorkeling trips that last from one hour to a full day. ✉ *Beach Boardwalk, Hilton Sharm El-Sheikh Fayrouz Resort, Peace Rd., Na'ama Bay* ☎ *069/360–0136 Ext. 170* ⊕ *www.sunnfunsinai.com.*

GOLF

Sharm El-Sheikh Golf Resort. What do California fan palms, Jerusalem thorns, Hong Kong orchids, and sand dunes have in common? They can all be found at Egypt's top golf course. Set along the Red Sea between Sharm El-Sheikh International Airport and the center of Na'ama Bay, this Sanford Associates–designed expanse of green is a well-watered oasis. The 18-hole course has 17 lakes, and PGA-qualified professionals are on hand to give lessons. Call ahead for tee times and to schedule lessons. ✉ *Maritim Jolie Ville Golf & Resort Sharm El-Sheikh, Um Marikha Bay, Na'ama Bay* ☎ *069/360–3200 for the hotel; 069/360–0635 for tee-time reservations* ⊕ *www.jolieville-hotels.com.*

WATER SPORTS

There are so many water sports to choose from here—waterskiing (you can take lessons or barefoot ski), windsurfing, parasailing, and paddleboating. Another favorite, banana boating, is great fun, with a hint of danger: five or six people straddle a yellow, banana-shaped boat and

Taba Heights Golf Resort

hold on for dear life as a speedboat pulls them around the bay. The driver will try to throw you off by taking sharp turns. Just hope you don't fall onto any fire coral.

Be prepared to pay for whatever you choose to do: about $15 for a 15-minute round of waterskiing; $15 for an hour of windsurfing; $36 for 10 minutes of parasailing for a single ($60 for two). Ask your hotel what activities it offers, or head to the beach at Na'ama Bay where several water-sports companies operate right from the beach, offering a wide array of activities for hotel guests and nonguests.

Sun 'n Fun. One of the Sinai's biggest water-sports outfitters offers a wide selection of activities from its water-sports center. ⊠ *Beach Boardwalk, Hilton Sharm El-Sheikh Fayrouz Resort, Peace Rd., Na'ama Bay* ☎ *069/360–0136 Ext. 170* ⊕ *www.sunnfunsinai.com.*

SHOPPING

For quality Egyptian-produced souvenirs, Sharm is disappointing, but it's brimming with shops selling mass-produced goods. Most hotels have their own shopping arcades, but their prices will be at least double what you would pay in Cairo. The only thing you might have an easier time finding in Sharm would be Red Sea or Sinai T-shirts. So if you plan to spend any time in Cairo at all, save your shopping for there.

Aladin. This is the best place for genuine Egyptian handicrafts from small collectibles to fashion accessories to furniture. There are four branches in Sharm. ⊠ *King of Bahrain St., Na'ama Bay* ☎ *069/360–0305* ⊕ *www.aladinsinai.com.*

Mercato. This is a smart, open-air Italian Renaissance–style mall that opened in early 2008. Stores sell recognizable brand names, and cafés include Starbucks and Costa. Familiar names in the mall include Virgin Megastore, Timberland, and The Body Shop. ⊠ *Hadabet Um El Seed, Hadaba* ☎ *069/366–2204.*

Sharm El-Sheikh Marketplace. This shopping center across from Pacha nightclub has more than 20 stores that sell everything from carpets to expensive jewelry, from water pipes to T-shirts. ⊠ *Na'ama Bay.*

Sharm Old Market. The largest traditional shopping area in the Sharm El-Sheikh region offers some genuine handmade Bedouin carpets and leather goods in addition to the usual kitsch souvenirs. Some of the carpets and leather goods are fabricated in small family-owned workshops. ⊠ *Sharm el Maya.*

NIGHTLIFE

Sharm El-Sheikh may be hot, but the nightlife is supercool. The resort is one of the must-play gigs on the international celebrity DJ circuit, and the clubs are thronged by the young and beautiful from around Europe. The town buzzes into the early hours of the morning; after a night of dancing, you can seek out one of the many shisha cafés, where you simply sink into a carpeted lounger and reflect on whatever comes to mind. If you feel lucky, head to the casino for slots or the gaming tables.

BARS

Camel Bar. Sharm's original "anything goes" dive bar continues its run though it was fully refurbished in 2010. Regulars love the relaxed atmosphere of the main bar, with its scattering of ground peanut shells on the floor, but if you head to the rooftop bar, you'll find a more comfortable area with plump cushions and rugs—ringside seats for the Na'ama Bay evening bustle. ⊠ *Camel Hotel, King of Bahrain St., Na'ama Bay* ☎ *069/360–0700.*

Ghazala Beach Bar. This is where almost everyone makes their way at some point during a Sharm vacation. Big-screen sports, a three-hour happy hour, and the vocal talents of Zaki (who covers 1970s to '90s chart music) every evening between 9 PM and midnight, mean there's always something going on. It's fun and lighthearted enough for all ages. ⊠ *Beach Boardwalk, Ghazala Hotel, Na'ama Bay* ☎ *065/346–0150.*

Little Buddha. A sibling of the ultrasophisticated Buddha Bar in Paris, this cool lounge offers great music and a laid-back vibe from the resident DJ (or the occasional special guest) along with a sushi bar and restaurant. The atmosphere suits couples and singles over 25. ⊠ *Tropitel Na'ama Bay Hotel, Corner of Sultan Qabous St. and King of Bahrain St., Old Market Area, Na'ama Bay* ☎ *069/360–1030* ⊕ *www. littlebuddha-sharm.com.*

CLUBS

El Fanar. It's possible to turn day into night at this beach club with an Italian restaurant that transforms itself into a buzzing, open-air dance club by night. The setting is particularly dramatic, with fantastic coastal vistas that can distract from the dance floor. Chill out away from the beat in various private, carpeted corners and on the rocks, which are

ST. CATHERINE'S TOURING TIPS

■ **Do it the easy way.** Myriad companies offer well-priced organized tours leaving from Sharm El-Sheikh, Nuweiba, Dahab, and Taba, ensuring a stress-free visit.

■ **Stay over.** Stay overnight at Saint Catherine's to give you maximum time at the monastery. If you stay overnight at the village, make sure you have warm clothing for the evenings, even during the summer.

■ **Have your papers in order.** If you travel independently from the coastal resorts, you'll pass several security checkpoints so carry your vehicle rental papers and passport.

■ **Tone down.** Dress conservatively to gain entry to the monastery (long pants/skirt and long-sleeved shirt are sensible choices). Also maintain conservative behavior: no loud mobile phones or MP3 players.

stunningly lit by the varying hues of the disco floor. ⊠ *Ras Umm Sid, Hadaba* ☎ *069/366–2218* ⊕ *www.elfanarsharm.com.*

Kamanga. This ultracontemporary restaurant, club, and lounge has a long cocktail list and innovative menu that aims to appeal to a more sophisticated clientele. It's one of the town's smaller open-air venues and just out of earshot of the clubs of central Na'ama Bay. ⊠ *Peace Rd., Na'ama Bay* ☎ *012/777–3003.*

★ **Pacha.** The queen of Sharm clubs—because of its association with the famed Ministry of Sound London (the club that introduced house and trance music to Europe) and HedKandi (the house-music production label)—is an open-air venue that hosts weekend sessions by alumni from the DJ Hall of Fame. When the house DJs are in residence, there's a rotating program of funk, house, or trance with regular chill-out sessions. It's a must-visit location for under-25s from around Europe. ⊠ *King of Bahrain St., Na'ama Bay* ☎ *069/360–0197* ⊕ *www.pachasharm.com.*

CASINOS

Casino Royale. This casino offers American roulette, blackjack, stud poker, and 77 slot machines, all set in a hall designed in Ancient Egyptian–style. ⊠ *Maritim Jolie Ville Resort, Na'ama Bay* ☎ *069/360–1731* ⊕ *www.casinoroyale.com.eg.*

Sinai Grand Casino. The Middle East's largest casino opened in 2008, and it's a veritable palace for the gaming tables. Blackjack and several styles of poker keep gamblers happy, plus there are hundreds of slots. Vegas-style shows and a restaurant put the icing on the cake. ⊠ *Peace Rd., Na'ama Bay* ☎ *069/360–1050* ⊕ *www.sinaigrandcasino.com.*

SAINT CATHERINE'S MONASTERY

240 km (150 mi) northwest of Sharm El-Sheikh.

★ The very image of the walled monasteries pictured in luxurious medieval tapestries, Saint Catherine's rests at the foot of Mount Sinai, nestled in a valley between jagged granite mountains. The monastery-cum-fortress was commissioned by the Byzantine emperor Justinian in AD 530 to protect those of Greek Orthodox faith. It also served as a strategic post on a bandit-ridden caravan route connecting Africa to Asia.

About 12 Greek Orthodox monks live and work here; the archbishop, who resides in Cairo, visits at Easter and other important holidays. Outside and around the monastery live the Christian Bedouins of the Jabaliyeh tribe, who have long served the monks by working in the gardens and orchards.

Buildings within the monastery have been erected and expanded upon throughout the centuries. The most important of these are the basilica, the Chapel of the Burning Bush, the monks' quarters, the Skull House, and the library, with its treasury of rare books that includes a 4th-century translation of the Hebrew Bible commissioned by Constantine the Great (the library is closed to the public). All buildings are enclosed by the fortress wall, which ranges in height and thickness as it adapts to the shape of the encompassing mountains.

Stepping through the modern-day north-side entrance, you see the fountain of Moses to your left. It serves as the main source of fresh water. To the right, a minaret of a mosque was built in the 10th century in order to protect the church from the Fatimid Caliph's order to destroy all churches and monasteries. After passing the fountain, step through to the **basilica**, also known as the Church of the Transfiguration, in which the apse is adorned with an ancient mosaic of the Transfiguration of Jesus. Chandeliers and decorated ostrich eggs hang from the ceiling, and gilded icons from Crete decorate the walls. Take your time in here—there are treasured works of art all around. The basilica doors date to the 6th century.

The **Chapel of the Burning Bush**, behind the basilica, is the most sacred of the buildings in the monastery. Unfortunately, it's not always open to the public. Dating from the 4th century AD, the chapel is the oldest part of the church, and its walls are covered with icons, of which the monastery itself has 2,000. (You can see yet more icons in the hall next to the library; the rest are kept in secured rooms, closed to the public.) Outside the chapel, you can see the bush where it is believed that God spoke to Moses. Many attempts to transplant branches of the bush have failed.

The **Skull House** is a chamber to which the bones of deceased monks are transferred from the cemetery after five years of interment. (The burial plot is very small and must be constantly reused.) The skulls number around 1,500 and are lined up in neat rows. ☏ *02/2482–8513 in Cairo* ⌨ *Free* ⊕ *www.sinaimonastery.com* ☽ *Mon.–Thurs. and Sat. 9–noon.*

GETTING HERE AND AROUND

There is good road access to the monastery from the tourist towns of the Sinai coast. It's a three-hour journey from Sharm El-Sheikh. There is regular bus service from these towns and also from Cairo. If you arrive in St. Catherine's village by public transportation, you'll need to take a taxi to the monastery site.

WHERE TO STAY

Better roads and improved journey times between Saint Catherine's and the coastal resorts—not to mention the easy availability of day trips to the interior—have combined to cause accommodation close to the monastery (and Mount Sinai) to suffer in quality. If you want a luxurious stay, book a hotel in Sharm El-Sheikh and make an early morning start to reach the monastery.

All hotel reviews have been condensed for this book. Please go to Fodors.com for full reviews of each property.

$$ ⊞ **Morgenland Village.** The stunning setting of this hotel is awe-inspiring—the peaks of the Sinai range that are reflected throughout the day in the waters of the on-site swimming pool surround it. **Pros:** Proximity to the start of the Mount Sinai hike and Saint Catherine's Monastery; excellent pool with stunning vistas. **Cons:** Careworn rooms; little atmosphere as most guests pass through on a one-night stay. ⊠ *3 km (2 mi) from St. Catherine's Monastery, just east of St. Catherine Rd., near the Zeituna area* ☎ *069/347–0700; 02/795–6856 in Cairo for reservations* ⌖ *248 rooms* ⌂ *In-hotel: a/c, restaurant, pool, parking (free)* ⊟ *No credit cards* ⧄ *MAP.*

GUIDED TOURS

Desert Fox Safari. Desert Fox Safari offers exceptional Bedouin guides for multiday trips throughout the Saint Catherine's Protectorate. Based in Saint Catherine's Village, Fox guides also can arrange trips all over Sinai. ⊠ *St. Catherine's Village* ☎ *069/347–0344* ⊕ *www.desertfoxsafari.com.*

JABAL MOUSSA (MOUNT SINAI)

240 km (149 mi) northeast of Sharm El-Sheikh.

From the base of Mount Sinai, any fellow hikers who have preceded you look like dots 7,504 feet ahead of you, and the prospect of reaching the top begins to assume biblical proportions. As you step up to the mountain, only passersby and the odd camel driver seeking your patronage disturb the serenity of the surrounding hills. Stop every now and then to notice how the clean desert mountain air awakens your senses. The dusty-rose tone of the granite mountains and the absolute peace make it no surprise that this land has fostered so many religious expeditions and revelations. New Age advocates also believe there are ley lines of gravitational energy running through the landscape here. Whatever you believe, it's truly a humbling place.

Mount Sinai rises above Saint Catherine's Monastery to the spot where Moses is supposed to have received the Ten Commandments. Scholars have debated the legitimacy of this claim for millennia now and have resolved nothing. Other locations have been suggested for the biblical Mount Sinai, but the mountain's position on the chief ancient trade route and the accounts in the journals of pilgrims do seem to substantiate the claim for this mountain.

In 1934, a small chapel dedicated to the Trinity was built on the summit of Jabal Moussa, covering the ruins of a previous Justinian temple.

Continued on page 355

THE COPTS: EGYPT'S

Stepping into a Coptic church or monastery feels like walking back into the early centuries of Christianity. Bypassed by most non-Egyptian visitors, Coptic sights have a sanctity and stillness that make them a refuge from more crowded tourist venues. Even those travelers who aren't religiously inclined will find in Egypt's rich Coptic heritage a fascinating perspective on the country's past and present.

CHRISTIANS By Chip Rosetti

Most tourists come to Egypt to see the splendors of the pharaohs and the allure of Cairo's Islamic and Arabic heritage, all too often overlooking the country's numerous Christian sites. While exact numbers are elusive, it is likely that 10% of Egypt's current population are Copts, the term for Egyptian Christians. Egypt's contributions to Christianity are many, from the key points of Christian doctrine hammered out in Alexandria, to monasti-cism and the first compilation of the New Testament. Today, the Coptic Church is undergoing a revival and maintains a large diaspora outside of Egypt. Whether you are visiting the ancient churches of Coptic Cairo, strolling through a desert monastery, or tracing the path of the Holy Family during their time in Egypt, you will encounter an unforgettable facet of Egyptian life, offering a window into its deep spiritual and religious roots.

DEEP ROOTS

The Coptic Orthodox Church traces the origin of Christianity in Egypt to St. Mark, who is said to have come to Alexandria around AD 60 and begun making converts. At the time, Alexandria was a thriving intellectual center, where dogma on the nature of Christ was worked out in debates during the 2nd and 3rd centuries AD. Other early Egyptian Christians turned to the mystical philosophy known as "Gnosticism," as shown by the revealing "Gnostic Gospels," an eye-opening cache of papyrus texts found in Nag Hammadi in Upper Egypt in 1945.

Some scholars think that Christianity took hold so firmly in Egypt because it melded easily with pagan concepts and symbols: for Egyptians familiar with the divine triads such as Osiris, Isis, and Horus, the leap to the Christian trinity was not difficult. Likewise, the common motif of Isis nursing Horus was easily transferable to the image of Virgin and Child. Others have pointed to the similar shapes of the *ankh* and the cross.

MONASTICISM

Roman persecutions of Christians fell hard on Egypt's growing Christian population, most notably under the emperor Diocletian. Even earlier, persecutions had often led Christians to seek refuge in desert places, far from imperial authorities. Their experiences in desert places almost certainly contributed to the emergence of monasticism in Egypt: one early desert hermit was St. Antony (251–356), whose anchoritic life inspired numerous followers. But it was the communal religious life, according to rules laid out by St. Pachomius (290–346) that became the model for monasteries across the Christian world. By the early 4th century, monasteries were springing up all over Egypt, includ-

Religious art in the St George Greek Orthodox Church in Cairo

ing the much-visited monasteries at **Wadi Natrun**, and the **Red Sea monasteries** of St. Antony and St. Paul. Interest in Coptic monasteries has seen a revival in recent decades.

RIFTS

The early debates over the nature of Jesus' divinity took on national and ethnic dimensions in the 5th century, when a debate over whether Jesus had one divine nature, or two natures— both human and divine. Adherents of the one-nature belief (known as "Monophysites") tended to be Egyptian Christians, while the dual-nature advocates had the backing of Constantinople and its Greek-speaking hierarchy. Following the divisive Council of Chalcedon in 451, the resistance of Egyptian Monophysites to Constantinople's imposed orthodoxy became the basis for the separate Coptic Orthodox Church. Although Copts rarely describe themselves as Monophysites today, they remain a separate religious church, with their own Pope,

Brother Nicodeme. Saint Bishoy coptic
monastery in Wadi Natrun

6

IN FOCUS THE COPTS: EGYPT'S CHRISTIANS

known formally as the "Pope of Alexandria and the Patriarch of the See of St. Mark." The Coptic language, a late derivation of ancient Egyptian, is no longer spoken today but continues to be the primary ecclesiastical language of the Coptic Church.

THE COPTS TODAY

The word "Copt" comes from an Arabic alteration of the Greek *Aiguptos*, which is also the source of our word "Egypt." *Aiguptos* was the Greek rendering of the ancient Egyptian name for the capital Memphis, known as *Ha-ka-Ptah*, or "The Abode of the Soul of Ptah." So while "Copt" once referred to Egyptians in general, it now refers specifically to those Egyptians who have remained Christian. Copts are well-represented in the ranks of Egypt's business elite and in public life. Boutros-Boutros Ghali, for example, served as Egypt's foreign minister before becoming the United Nations Secretary General. While they are a religious minority today, and there are occasional flare-ups of Muslim–Copt tension, Egyptians' strong sense of a shared Egyptian identity that transcends religious affiliation has ensured Copts a place in the modern nation.

THE HOLY FAMILY IN EGYPT

The Gospel of St. Matthew relates that an angel appeared to Joseph in a dream, warning him of Herod's plans to have the infant Jesus killed: "Arise, take the young Child and His mother, flee to Egypt, and stay there until I bring you word" (Matthew, 2:13). Drawing on this brief scriptural reference, Egyptian Christians early on embraced the tradition of the Holy Family's flight to Egypt.

In the Coptic tradition, the Holy Family stayed three and a half years in Egypt, passing through various locations from the Delta all the way to Asyut in Upper Egypt, and performing miracles en route. In all, the Coptic Church recognizes around two dozen sites as part of the Holy Family's route, which are often revered by both local Copts and Muslims alike as holy places.

THE HOLY FAMILY ROUTE

Since 2000, Egypt has officially promoted Holy Family tourism encouraging religiously inclined tourists to visit the sites traditionally visited only by the Copts themselves. The Coptic Church officially celebrates the Holy Family's sojourn on June 1 each year, when these sites are likely to be crowded. Other times they are not. Except in greater Cairo, many of these places are well off the beaten tourist path. The full Holy Family route is circuitous and includes a number of places practically inaccessible to tourists. The following are some of the more accessible ones; with the right planning, it is possible to visit them all.

1 FARMA: Fleeing from Herod, the Holy Family crossed northern Sinai, arriving in Pelusium (now Farma) in what is now the east side of the Suez Canal. From Qantara, take the main highway 20 miles in the direction of Al-Arish. The Farma site, including the ruins of an early church, is north of Balloza village.

2 BUBASTIS: The first city in the Delta they came to was the cult center of the cat goddess Bastet. Although the locals were unwelcoming, the infant Jesus created a spring here that is believed to have healing properties (although as punishment for the townsfolk's ill treatment, the well has no effect on locals). The well is still in use and is located just outside the modern city of Zagazig, accessible by train, bus, or long-distance taxi from Cairo.

Church of Our Lady of El-Zeitoun

Lake Burullus

Dumyat

THE DELTA

Mansura

Bur Said

Alexandria

Sakha
120km(75mi)
north of Cairo) **3**

Damanhur

Tanta

al-Ismailiya

Farr

Wadi Natrun

2 Bubastis
80km(50mi)
northeast of Cairo

Cairo
4-7

Giza

Suez

al-Fayyum

River Nile

Bahariyya Oasis

Gebel el-Teir
8 32km(20mi)
north of al-Minya

al-Minya

ARABIAN DESERT

al-Ashmunein
48km(30mi)
south of al-Minya **9**

River Nile

GHURD ABU MUHARIK

Dayr
al-Muharraq 10
60km(37mi)
north of Asyut

Asyut

Church of Saint Sergius

Church of the Holy Virgin, Ma'adi

Al-Ashmunein

Mediterranean Sea

al-Arish

Apporox 75km(47mi)
from Bur Said
by Service taxi

❸ SAKHA: Two miles outside the northern city of Kafr el-Sheikh lies Sakha, another stop on the route. The town is famous for a stone purporting to show the mark of Jesus' footprint. The stone, known as "Bikha Isus" (Jesus' Footprint), was buried for centuries, but unearthed during excavations of an ancient church in the 1980s. Kafr el-Sheikh is accessible by bus from Cairo or by private taxi.

❹ THE VIRGIN'S TREE AT MATARIYA: This site, near the Ain Shams district of northeast Cairo, is accessible by Cairo subway (the EL MATARIYA stop). The site is a sycamore tree under which the Virgin Mary rested, and where Jesus again brought forth a spring. The tree and spring are now in a sizeable walled enclosure, along with an open-air shrine, and are an easy afternoon visit from downtown Cairo.

❺ CHURCH OF OUR LADY OF EL-ZEITOUN: While this church was not on the original Holy Family route, it was the site of a yearlong apparition of the Virgin in 1968, where she appeared at the top of the church spires. Thousands came to see it (including Egyptian president Gamal Abdul Nasser), and it has since become a popular pilgrimage site. The El-Zeitoun neighborhood is just southeast of Matariya, one stop away on the Cairo metro, at HELMIYET EL-ZEITOUN.

❻ CHURCH OF ST. SERGIUS: The church in Coptic Cairo is built over a cave where the Holy Family spent the night. The cave, now a crypt below the altar, is unfortunately flooded.

❼ CHURCH OF THE HOLY VIRGIN AT MA'ADI: Located on the waterfront corniche in Ma'adi, south of the Maadi Yacht Club, this church was built at the site where the Holy Family boarded a boat to take them to Upper Egypt. The stone stairs leading down to the water are believed to be the same ones the Holy Family used.

❽ GEBEL EL-TEIR: Its name means "Bird Mountain," and fittingly enough it sits high on a high on the east side of the Nile and is home to plenty of birds. The site itself is a 4th-century monastery called Deir al-'Adhra (Monastery of the Virgin), built on a site where the Holy Family spent the night. The monastery is a few miles' drive from al-Minya on the opposite bank.

❾ AL-ASHMUNEIN: Located about 30 miles south of al-Minya, this was a further stop on the itinerary and the site of a major ancient city called Hermopolis Magna. The extensive ruins still visible (including an early Coptic basilica) testify to its importance then as a pagan center. Taxis can be hired in al-Minya for a round-trip visit.

❿ DAYR AL-MUHARRAQ: Literally meaning "The Burnt Monastery," this working monastery is built over a cave where the Holy Family lived for six months—their longest single stay during their time in Egypt. Coptic tradition calls the church here the oldest in Egypt.

TIPS FOR THE HOLY FAMILY ROUTE

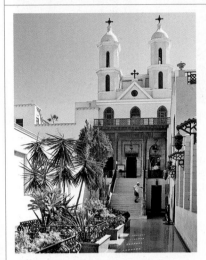

The Hanging Church in Cairo's Coptic Quarter

GETTING AROUND

Seeing Egypt's Coptic sites independently involves some careful planning, since bus schedules are not always convenient, and access to taxis may be hit or miss (unless you've negotiated a round-trip with a driver beforehand to take you there and back). In addition, overly cautious local police in al-Minya and Asyut may require that you be accompanied by a police escort to out-of-the-way places. If you plan to visit sites in Upper Egypt, you may want to use al-Minya as your base of operations, and make taxi trips from there. Sites in the Delta are best done as day trips from Cairo.

TOUR COMPANIES

As Holy Family tourism has grown in the last decade, a number of specialized travel companies have appeared to facilitate tours. Many cater to groups, rather than to individual travelers, although they may be able to arrange something for you or put you in touch with one of their tour guides. Highly recommended is the Cairo-based Biblical Vacations (⊕ *www.biblevacations.com*), which offers a variety of tours, although primarily for church groups. Dr. Cornelis (Kees) Hulsman, a Dutch authority on Coptic life, runs Holy Family Egypt (⊕ *www.holyfamilyegypt.com*), which may be able to integrate individual travelers into one of their group tours.

ADVICE FOR VISITORS

All of the Holy Family sites are places of worship for Egyptian Copts, so appropriate dress is a must. That means no shorts, short skirts, or sleeveless tops, for both genders. In many monasteries and churches, you should remove your shoes and leave them outside the door before entering a chapel. Often a monk or priest at the site will be happy to show you around the site; due to the extensive Coptic diaspora, don't be surprised to find a monk who speaks fluent English in even the most remote location. There is no cost, but donations are always welcome.

PRACTICAL TIPS

■ Remember that weekends tend to be busy, as many Copts make family visits to these sites on Saturdays.

■ A number of monasteries, such as at Wadi Natrun, also own farmland and sell their produce to visitors. If you're so inclined, pick up a bag of fruit for the ride back to Cairo, or a bottle of olive oil.

■ A visit to the Virgin Tree in Matariyya is a surprisingly serene experience; although the city is just outside the walls, the water and the ancient tree make for a peaceful experience.

■ Gebel El-Teir is best visited in the morning, so the sun is behind you when you look west across the river. Also, without much shade at the top of the hill, the monastery gets quite warm in the afternoon.

Looking southeast from the peak, you'll have a crystal-clear view of the top of Mount Catherine, which is the highest point on the Sinai Peninsula at 8,652 feet. With granite mountains in all directions, it may feel as if you're at the center of the earth.

There are two routes up the mountain, and two essential times of day at which to start. The climb takes between 2½ and 3 hours. For a very steep climb, take the 3,750 steps that begin behind the monastery and lead directly to the summit. Please note that this is not exactly a proper staircase, and if you have knee problems, this will only exacerbate them. There is another route that is also a camel track; its last 230 feet consist of 700 steps. If you take this route, you can bet that drivers will ask—repeatedly—if you want a ride. If you opt for the camel, ask around for the going rate, then haggle. Expect to pay around £E70. ⚠ The camel ride isn't the easy option it might first appear. Riding a camel can be somewhat strenuous and put pressure on your knees, especially on the descent. And some people get motion sickness because the camel does sway like a ship as it moves.

The climb is strenuous, and you'll need to take along water and a snack to eat at the top (bring a backpack if you can). Many visitors begin this climb around 2 AM to arrive at the summit at sunrise. If you are here during January, February, or March, it won't be too hot for a midday trip (which is much less crowded); at other times, it will be. If you're going to do the night hike, take long pants, because it gets cold, and a good flashlight, and wear layers that you can take off and put back on as you warm up and cool down. A solid pair of shoes (preferably hiking boots) is also essential.

GETTING HERE AND AROUND

The typical dawn hike up Mount Sinai begins after an overnight stay at Saint Catherine's Monastery. Some organized tours will leave Sharm El-Sheikh in the wee hours of the morning and arrive at the base of the mountain shortly before dawn.

DAHAB

100 km (55 mi) northeast of Na'ama Bay.

The drive from Sharm to Dahab snakes through the mountains of south Sinai offering you a peek at the precipitous peaks of the interior. Dahab itself is another world, still half stuck in the 1960s, with New Age believers carrying on the original laid-back hippie philosophy that put this place on the international map. It's also a legendary location in the world of scuba. A new generation of dive students from Northern and Eastern Europe mix with seasoned veterans who return here year after year for the excellent conditions and unpretentious dive community. Many Bedouins have taken up the government's offer of permanent homes in the town, and they've brought along their goats and camels, which roam the streets blissfully uncaring of the 21st-century trucks and buses zipping by. All this adds to the slightly surreal but relaxed atmosphere. There's little more to do here than hang out and snorkel and dive.

St. Catherine

Born in Alexandria to a ruling family in the 4th century, Catherine was a highly educated and erudite woman for her time. She presented herself at the court of Roman Emperor Maximinus to plead for the lives of Christians who were routinely put to death by his regime. Maximinus organized a caucus of learned men to refute and confound Catherine's arguments, but in fact the caucus was won over by her arguments. When they converted to Christianity, Maximinus had them put to death while Catherine was whipped and thrown into a cell. The Emperor's wife paid a visit, chaperoned by the head of the Roman army. They, too, heard Catherine's message and were converted—and were soon added to the list of Christian martyrs. After the conversion and martyrdom of the Emperor's wife, Catherine was put under sentence of death on the breaking (spiked) wheel. However, when she approached it, the apparatus fell to pieces under her touch. Undeterred, the Emperor had Catherine beheaded, but after her death it was said that angels carried her bones to the flanks of Mount Sinai where the monastery now sits.

In the centuries that followed, Catherine became a mainstream female saint, and virtuous maidens where especially devoted to her. She was included on the list of the "Fourteen Holy Helpers"; Joan of Arc said at her trial that she had been visited by the saint and was inspired to take on her crusade.

The spiked wheel that should have been the original means of her martyrdom—a popular form of torture in medieval times—became known as the Catherine wheel, and this name later transferred to the round firework that whirls at celebrations in modern times.

Saint Catherine is still very much revered by Christians in the Orthodox and Catholic communities, but there is very little incontrovertible evidence that she actually existed. Some scholars have pondered whether Catherine had been a fictitious character whose story—the embodiment of maidenly Christian virtue—was meant to inspire medieval worshippers.

Dahab stretches around a headland and now encompasses two flanking bays. Its four main areas are the **Assala**, where you find camps and independent dive resorts; the **Masbat**, a stretch of restaurants, shops, and Bedouin-style cafés that all look the same but blast different music, resulting in a strange cacophony; **Mashrab**, a combination of both the Assala and the Masbat; and **Dahab City**, the modern municipal district with a handful of larger hotels.

If the promise of resort holidays brought you to the Sinai, then Dahab probably isn't for you. Stray cats and dogs might snuggle up to you as you eat dinner. The resort seems to have eschewed large-scale tourist development, though, and it's working well in its own eclectic way.

Diving is the lifeblood of tourism in Dahab, and the waters here provide a top-flight training location. Water entry in Dahab is all done from the shore rather than from dive boats offshore, so entry does require balance and good footing but is much more convenient than it might otherwise be. The town is also known for windsurfing. And Dahab has easy access to some superb inland sights, including the Colored Canyon (see ⇨ Nuweiba, below). As with any off-the-beaten-path desert excursion, it is a good idea to go with a guide. ⚠ Marijuana is easily available in Dahab (as it has been since the 1960s), but it is illegal to possess under Egyptian law, which imposes stiff penalties for those found guilty of possession or use of any illicit drugs, including marijuana. The Egyptian police are not routinely rigorous in checking for drugs, but there are occasional clampdowns, which can result in visitors being charged and jailed.

Wadi Kid. The trip to to Wadi Kid is a gorgeous trek that leads to Ain Kid. *Ain* in Arabic means "spring." As is often the case in the Sinai, the wadis lead to springs, where the fresh water gives life to luscious green trees and grazing areas. Your hotel can arrange a trip to the wadi. On the way you drive through a Bedouin village. Stop off for a tea in the shade of an acacia tree. This is a great photo op. ⊠ *Approximately 20 km (12 mi) south of Dahab*.

GETTING HERE AND AROUND

There is no direct air service to Dahab, which is linked by road to Sharm El-Sheikh; the trip takes about two hours. You can also drive easily to Taba and Nuweiba to the north. There is regular bus service running along this coastal route as well. Some buses also run west to Cairo. Once in town there are inexpensive minibus services or numerous taxis to get you around.

WHERE TO EAT

Restaurants and cafés in the Masbat all offer the same thing—pizza, pasta, fish, and chicken. The resorts offer typical breakfast and dinner buffets and have beach bars that serve sandwiches and salads; you might even find a theme lunch.

$ ✕ **Al Capone Restaurant.** Al Capone's is one of a dozen Bedouin-style
ECLECTIC cushion-and-carpet outdoor restaurants in the Masbat. If you're not in the mood for pizza or fish, order a vegetable salad, tomatoes with Bulgarian cheese, and *shakshuka* (a spicy Middle Eastern omelet) with pita bread and play a game of backgammon while you wait. There's regular live music served up by a resident DJ. ⊠ *Beachfront Blvd., Masbat* ☎ *069/364–0181* ⊟ *No credit cards*.

WHERE TO STAY

If you don't mind roughing it, you can find inexpensive rooms at any of the camps in the Assala area. Be prudent about what you choose because cheap doesn't imply clean, and rarely does it include private bathrooms. If you must stay at any such establishments, wear flip-flops when you shower. At the hotels, although they are far from the mellow center of town, you can count on a higher quality of comfort and services.

All hotel reviews have been condensed for this book. Please go to Fodors.com for full reviews of each property.

$$ ▦ **Bedouin Moon Hotel.** At this simple but clean hotel, you'll find the headquarters of Reef 2000, one of the best dive centers in Dahab.

Pros: spacious, modern pool and sun terrace on the property; English-speaking management; lively atmosphere for divers. **Cons:** a taxi ride or 30-minute walk from the restaurants and cafés of Masbat; some rooms don't have balconies or air-conditioning; hotel's beach is narrow and rocky. ⊠ *Blue Hole Rd., Assala* ☎ *069/364–0087* ⊕ *www.reef2000. com* ⇆ *29 rooms, 3 dorm rooms* ♿ *In-room: no a/c (some), no phone (some), refrigerator (some), no TV (some). In-hotel: restaurant, bar, pool, diving, water sports, Internet terminal* ▭ *AE, MC, V* ⦅◯⦆ *BP.*

$$–$$$ 🏨 **Hilton Dahab.** The largest resort in Dahab, this Nubian-style, white-washed adobe village is set dramatically against the reddish hues of the Sinai Mountains. **Pros:** styling is sympathetic to the local area; direct access to a private beach. **Cons:** a taxi ride away from the Masbat. ⊠ *Dahab City* ⟐ *Box 25, Dahab City 46617* ☎ *069/364–0310* ⊕ *www. hilton.com* ⇆ *141 rooms* ♿ *In-room: a/c, safe, Internet. In-hotel: 4 restaurants, room service, bars, tennis court, pools, beachfront, diving, water sports, laundry facilities, laundry service, parking (free)* ▭ *AE, D, MC, V* ⦅◯⦆ *BP.*

$$$–$$$$ 🏨 **Le Méridien Dahab Resort.** This luxury resort designed by French architect and designer Alain Jaouen offers a 21st-century oasis in the Sinai. **Pros:** visually stunning property that's appeared in style magazines; sea views from all rooms; excellent cuisine at three on-site restaurants; no-smoking rooms. **Cons:** a taxi ride away from the fun and nightlife scene of the Masbat area; there's nothing else in the immediate vicinity; expansion planned for 2010 may mean some disruption on-site. ⊠ *Al Tahrir St., Dahab City* ⟐ *Box 2, Dahab* ☎ *069/364–0425* ⊕ *www.lemeridien. com* ⇆ *178 rooms, 4 suites* ♿ *In-room: a/c, safe, DVD, Internet, Wi-Fi. In-hotel: 3 restaurants, room service, bars, pools, gym, spa, beachfront, diving, water sports, children's programs (ages 4–12), laundry service, Wi-Fi hotspot, parking (paid)* ▭ *AE, DC, MC, V* ⦅◯⦆ *BP.*

NIGHTLIFE

Dahab has a reputation as a laid-back resort once known for its pot-smoking hippies. Things have changed, and today easygoing divers have replaced the hippies, while the nightlife scene, which is centered in Masbat, has evolved to include a line of bars and some nightclubs.

Black Prince. This is Dahab's major late-night clubbing venue, which attracts a varied mix of nationalities from Brits to Italians to Russians. The retro "Hits" parties are extra popular. ⊠ *Beachfront Blvd., Masbat* ☎ *012/412–9578.*

The Furry Cup. For a decade this bar has been a favorite postdive evening hangout for a relaxed drink. There are live events throughout the summer. ⊠ *Blue Beach Club, Assala* ☎ *069/364–0411* ⊕ *www. furrycupdahab.com.*

SPORTS AND THE OUTDOORS

DIVING

Three popular dive sites are about 30 minutes north of Dahab, so you might want to dive with one of the hotel dive centers, which can arrange transportation. Bring water with you, and plan to pass some time relaxing under the awning of a Bedouin cafeteria that provides basic refresh-

The clear water at Ras Mohammed National Park

ments. No toilet facilities are available, so follow the cardinal rule of the desert: women to the left, men to the right.

The **Blue Hole** is among the best dives in the Red Sea (*see* ⇨ *Egypt's Best Dive Sites at the beginning of this chapter*). **The Canyon,** right around the corner from the Blue Hole, is another great dive. You feel as if you're sky diving as you descend through 100 feet of coral cliffs on either side of you. The **Lighthouse** close to Masbat is the perfect dive for beginners, offering masses of sea life along the sloping reef at 25 meters that include wrasse, triggerfish, and moray eels, but it also offers good experiences at deeper levels and is a particularly popular night dive.

DIVE OPERATORS

Poseidon Divers. One of Dahab's major dive outfitters offers the PADI/National Geographic Open Water Course and diving Career Development Courses along with other programs, dive safaris, and live-aboards. They also have an office at the Le Méridien Hotel. ✉ *Crazy Camel Camp, Mashraba* ☎ *069/364–0091* ⊕ *www.poseidondivers.com.*

Reef 2000. A PADI Gold Palm center close to the famed Blue Hole dive site, the company offers dive training and technical courses, plus guided dives for those already qualified. Their yoga/dive programs are certainly unique. You can also book camel/diving safaris (where the camels carry your equipment and you trek to the dive site, overnighting in a camp) and boat trips. ✉ *Blue Hole Rd., Assala* ☎ *069/364–0087* ⊕ *www.reef2000.com.*

GUIDED TOURS

Crazy Camel Desert Safaris. In Dahab, Crazy Camel Desert Safaris organizes two- to six-day four-wheel-drive or camel excursions suited to your interests, be it Bedouin culture or bird-watching. ⊠ *Masbat, Dahab* ☎ *0105–575161* ⊕ *www.crazy-camel.de.*

Embah. Embah offers a full range of adventure activities, plus interesting options like a "Desert Dweller" tour to visit the Bedouins, and herb-gathering trips. ⊠ *Beachfront Blvd., Masbat, Dahab* ☎ *069/364–1690* ⊕ *www.embah.com.*

WATER SPORTS

Dahab is building a reputation as a windsurfing and kite-surfing center with ideal water and wind conditions. Most hotels have boards to rent, and there's an excellent school for both sports.

Harry Nass Surf & Action Center. Dahab Bay glistens with the colorful sails of windsurfers, which rent for €40 per half-day (minimum) or €190 to €210 per week from the Harry Nass Surf & Action Center. ⊠ *Novotel Coralia Dahab, Dahab City* ☎ *069/364–0559* ⊕ *www.harry-nass.com.*

> **MAN'S BEST FRIEND?**
>
> In the late 1990s a solitary dolphin, soon named Holly, made a home in the bay off Nuweiba el Muzeina. Though she was a sociable animal who became an international celebrity, she formed a special bond with Abdallah, a deaf fisherman. Over the years, Abdallah succeeded in developing limited language skills, his confidence swelled by this unusual relationship across the species divide. Holly stayed in the area until her death in 2006, and she's much missed by locals and visitors alike.

NUWEIBA

70 km (44 mi) north of Dahab.

Nuweiba serves as both a crucial Gulf of Aqaba port and a resort with a couple of hotel areas and a quaint town center. Its name means "bubbling springs," and Nuweiba has long been an important oasis for Muslim pilgrims en route to Mecca. Sandy beaches and colorful coral reefs accessible from the shore have earned it a reputation as a dive center, though it hasn't thrived in the last decade in the same way as the rest of the Red Sea Riviera.

Maagana Bay, the main port area, sees constant traffic from trucks full of goods and equipment and travelers making their way to Mecca or Jordan. This is where you'll find a post office, telephone office, bus station, and beckoning taxi drivers. About 6 km (4 mi) north of the port lies the touristy city center, its simple stores filled with cheap local clothing, trinkets, souvenirs, and household goods. Inexpensive restaurants serve basic food, and supermarkets carry an adequate range of supplies. But you'll probably spend most of your time enjoying the beach, its coffeehouses, and the Sinai scenery.

Nuweiba, which has a population of about 3,000, is the center for two tribes. Their members, once the outstanding fishermen of the Sinai Coast, still inhabit the area in two communities: Nuweiba el Muzeina, south of Nuweiba's city center, and Nuweiba Tarabin, to the north.

Because of its central position on the Sinai Coast, Nuweiba makes a good base for trekking into the Sinai interior to the Colored Canyon. Getting a glimpse of the Colored Canyon's red, yellow, rose, brown, and purple hues deep within the mountains northwest of Nuweiba is something that you can do only by camel or four-wheel-drive vehicle. The Abanoub Travel Agency *(see ⇨ Tour Options in Sinai Peninsula Essentials, below)* or your hotel can arrange a trip to the canyon; you can also take tours from Sharm El-Sheikh or Dahab.

> ## A CANINE COUSTEAU
>
> The latest Sinai celebrity is Moka, the chocolate Labrador at Castle Zaman who may have been a dolphin in a previous life. She dives to the bottom of the swimming pool at any opportunity to retrieve items thrown in by admiring fans.

GETTING HERE AND AROUND

Nuweiba is linked by road to Sharm El-Sheikh and Dahab to the south, and Taba to the north. Regular bus service runs along this coastal route. Some buses also run west to Cairo. Once in town there are inexpensive minibus services or numerous taxis to get you around.

WHERE TO EAT

$$$$
MIDDLE EASTERN
✕ **Castle Zaman.** Probably the most unusual restaurant in the northern Sinai, this is to the eye a ruined medieval castle on a bluff above the Sinai Coast; however, it was built from scratch starting in the late 1990s by architect Hany Roshdy. Eat in the stone-and-wood interior or on the terraces, which have magnificent views. The menu focuses on traditional slow-cooked dishes, including melt-in-your-mouth lamb shank or skirt steak. Since these dishes take a while to prepare, it's best to book at least a day in advance—to ensure the food is perfect. There's a pool on-site, and the set price includes time for lounging and swimming. ✚ *On the coast, 25 km (14 mi) north of Nuweiba* ☏ *012/214–0591* ⊕ *www.castlezaman.com* ⬧ *Reservations essential* ⊟ *MC, V.*

WHERE TO STAY

All hotel reviews have been condensed for this book. Please go to Fodors.com for full reviews of each property.

$$$
🏨 **Hilton Nuweiba Coral Resort.** This Hilton is only a five-minute taxi ride from Nuweiba's port, so it's ideally situated for trips into the Sinai interior as well as to Jordan, which stands directly across the Gulf of Aqaba. **Pros:** well-maintained resort with mature, shady gardens; a comfortable base not far from most Sinai attractions, almost equidistant from Taba to the north or Sharm to the south; large balconies offer a great space for taking in cooling sea breezes. **Cons:** there's little to do in the immediate area, so it's a taxi ride if you want to eat out or browse for souvenirs. ✉ *Maagana Bay* ☏ *069/352–0320* ⊕ *www.hilton.com* ⇆ *200 rooms* ⬧ *In-room: a/c, safe. In-hotel: 3 restaurants, room service, bar, tennis court, pools, gym, beachfront, diving, water sports, laundry service, Internet terminal, parking (free)* ⊟ *AE, DC, MC, V* ⦿*BP.*

6

$ ★ ⊡ **Nakhil Inn.** This small, laid-back dive resort is on a wonderful, sandy stretch of beach. Older rooms are spacious, while the newest wing (Nakhil Dreams) is made up of cute wooden bungalows, each with a mezzanine bedroom area. **Pros:** neatly kept rooms offer excellent value for money; there's a broad sandy beach on-site; Wi-Fi works even on the beach, so you can surf by the surf. **Cons:** it's a 30-minute walk or a short taxi ride to what passes for downtown Nuweiba. ⊠ *Tarabeen Beach, 2 km (1 mi) north of downtown* ☎ *069/350–0879* ⊕ *www.nakhil-inn.com* ⏎ *28 rooms, 2 suites* ⚒ *In-room: a/c, no phone, refrigerator. In-hotel: restaurant, bar, beachfront, diving, Wi-Fi hotspot* ⊟ *AE, MC, V* ⏐⊘⏐ *BP.*

SPORTS AND THE OUTDOORS
CAMEL TREKKING
Habiba Camel Training School. For a real Gertrude Bell or William The-siger experience, head to the Habiba Camel Training School, where you can learn about stewardship of this feisty ship of the desert during a three-day course that teaches you about camel characteristics, diet, riding techniques, and day-to-day care. After going through the training and receiving your license, you can choose to embark on a 3- to 10-day safari through the Sinai during which a Bedouin guide shows you the way, but you are responsible for your designated animal. You'll live as the Bedouin did, finding kindling for the campfire and sleeping under the stars. Camel School prices are €355 with half board at Habiba Camp (though you can stay in other accommodation and still attend the course). A three-day trek to the Colored Canyon is €210 with meals, guide, and camel included. ⊠ *Downtown Nuweiba* ☎ *069/350–0770* ✐ *habiba@sinai4you.com.*

TABA

48 km (30 mi) north of Nuweiba.

Taba borders Israel and is a sister city of the Israeli resort town of Eilat. It has been important since biblical times as a stopover for travelers entering or leaving Egypt.

Pharaoh's Island, so-called because it was first used during the reign of Ramses III (1194–1163 BC), is a long, rocky island surrounded by reefs and the turquoise waters of the gulf. The dramatic remains visible from shore mark the best-known period in the island's occupation. These are the ruined walls of the Crusader outpost created here in 1115 by Baldwin I. For 55 years, the Crusaders controlled both the trade and pil-grimage routes that passed this way from the safety of the island. But in AD 1171, shortly after coming to power in Egypt, Salah al-Din attacked the fortress by surprise, having transported his dismantled ships secretly through the Sinai on camelback. Despite repeated attempts, the Cru-saders never again regained control of the island. Most of what now remains dates from the Mamluk period (14th century).

Diving or snorkeling is good around the excellent reefs off the north end of the island (though currents are strong). With its ruined Crusader castle and Ottoman additions, Pharaoh's Island (also known as Coral Island) attracts many a roadside photographer. Boats to the island run

CLOSE UP

A Day Trip to Petra

One of the most popular excursions from all Sinai resorts is a day trip to the rose-red city of Petra, in Jordan at the northern tip of the Red Sea. It's a long journey from Sharm El-Sheikh, but only a couple of hours' travel from Nuweiba or Taba.

The capital of the Nabataean Empire, which grew rich on trade after the 4th century BC, the city thrived until the 4th century AD and is famed for its excellent collection of rock-cut buildings. The facade of the Treasury will be familiar to you if you have seen *Indiana Jones and the Last Crusade.*

While the trip into Petra is best done at dawn, it's still worth it to enter later in the day if this is likely to be your only chance to visit. Of course, some people simply choose to visit Petra for a two-day trip before their return home. Before you travel, find out from your travel agent if a day trip to a neighboring country is allowable with your Egyptian visa.

from the Salah El-Deen Hotel; in high season the island can get quite crowded with travelers from Eilat and Aqaba. ⊠ *250 yards offshore* 🏰 *Castle $10, ferry $5* ⊙ *Daily 9–5 (boats run every 15 minutes).*

Taba Heights, the northern Sinai's largest new tourist venture, aims to develop into a self-contained settlement anchored by excellent tourist facilities including high-class accommodations, sports outfitters, shopping, and entertainment. This is a project that's still evolving, but already there are five hotels, an excellent dive center, an 18-hole golf course, a wide range of water sports, and a program of excursions, all set against the dramatic backdrop of the Sinai peaks and fronted by 5 km (3 mi) of golden, sandy beaches. A village-style Old Town, with independent shops and eateries and served by shuttle buses from the hotels, adds interest and dining variety. ⊠ *20 km (12½ mi) south of Taba.*

GETTING HERE AND AROUND

At the very northeastern corner of the Sinai, abutting the border with Israel, Taba has a small airport with a weekly flight to Cairo. Road links are good, with direct buses to the capital and down the coast to Sharm El-Sheikh through Nuweiba and Dahab. Central Taba is walkable, but to reach Taba Heights you'll need to take a taxi or have a rental vehicle.

WHERE TO EAT

$$$

SEAFOOD

✕ **El Mare.** The InterContinental's à la carte seafood restaurant has a quiet beachfront location. You can eat under a canopy of fairy lights or in the circular templelike dining room. The entrées span the expected (an enticing seafood platter) to the imaginative (flaky grouper baked in a sea-salt crust or served in Provençale sauce), while the appetizers and desserts, including a formidable tiramisu, borrow influences from world cuisine. ⊠ *InterContinental Taba Heights Resort, Taba Heights* ☎ *069/358–0300* ✍ *Reservations essential* ▭ *AE, DC, MC, V* ⊙ *No lunch.*

WHERE TO STAY

All hotel reviews have been condensed for this book. Please go to Fodors.com for full reviews of each property.

$$ ⊡ **El Wekala**. Designed along the lines of a grand Arabian family living complex, the shady courtyard with its cooling fountain that greets your arrival at El Wekala draws you into its Moorish appeal while the decorated domes, curved arches, wooden fretwork, and traditional Cairene tiled floors in the rooms add to the atmosphere. **Pros:** village-like setting gives hotel a more authentic feel rather than a resort feel; excellent sports facilities of Taba Heights available to guests; all-inclusive but offers a dine-around option with other hotels in Taba Heights. **Cons:** the private beach area is remote from the hotel (access by shuttle bus only); corridors resonate sound if you have noisy fellow guests. ✉ *Taba Heights* ☎ *069/358–0150* ⊕ *www.threecorners. com* ⤵ *178 rooms, 14 duplexes, 23 suites* △ *In-room: a/c, safe, refrigerator, Wi-Fi. In-hotel: 2 restaurants, room service, bars, golf course, pools, diving, water sports, bicycles, children's programs (ages 4–12), laundry facilities, laundry service, Internet terminal* ▭ *MC, V* ⦿ *AI.*

$$$$ ⊡ **Hyatt Regency Taba Heights**. Looking as if Dr. Seuss had designed it, the strong colors and off-the-wall lines and curves that characterize the neo-Nubian architecture of this resort do set the scene for vacation fun. **Pros:** dramatic architecture; excellent sports programs; access to the other hotels and downtown Taba Heights means you have ample off-resort dining opportunities. **Cons:** Taba Heights is a new tourism complex, so there's no old Sinai feel nearby. ✉ *Taba Heights* ☎ *069/358–0234* ⊕ *www.hyatt.com* ⤵ *426 rooms, 10 suites* △ *In-room: a/c, safe, Internet. In-hotel: 3 restaurants, room service, bars, golf course, tennis courts, pools, gym, spa, beachfront, diving, water sports, children's programs (ages 4–10), laundry service, Wi-Fi hotspot, parking (free)* ▭ *AE, DC, MC, V* ⦿ *BP.*

> ### NATIONAL GEOGRAPHIC DIVER
>
> National Geographic wanted to take dive training to a new level and got together with PADI to formulate its own diving certification program. In addition to the standard requirements for PADI open-water certification, the National Geographic course includes instruction on the marine environment and a module on marine conservation. Only dive centers with a proven track record and a commitment to sustainable diving are chosen by PADI/ National Geographic to run these courses, so you can be guaranteed the highest-quality (and most environmentally sensitive) training.

SPORTS AND THE OUTDOORS

DIVING AND WINDSURFING

The area has the coolest waters in the Egyptian Red Sea, but this does not mean that the diving is disappointing. On the contrary, there are protected reefs running all along the shelf just offshore. Conditions are also ideal for both sailing and windsurfing, and most of the dive centers offer these activities as well.

★ **Red Sea Waterworld.** This PADI five-star Gold Palm Resort and National Geographic Dive Center has a professional team of managers and a multilingual staff with great modern equipment. It's also a recognized catamaran sailing school and windsurfing school. ✉ *Taba Heights* ☎ *069/358–0099* ⊕ *www.redseawaterworld.com.*

GOLF

Taba Heights Golf Resort. Warm winter temperatures and an excellent selection of resorts draw Northern European golfers to Taba Heights Golf Resort for an easily organized golf break with prearranged tee times. John Sanford designed the undulating 18-hole, par-72 course with dramatic mountain- and seascapes. There's PGA tuition, a driving range, and short practice area, plus a well-stocked golf shop. ✉ *Taba Heights* ☎ *069/358–0073* ⊕ *www.tabaheights.com.*

THE RED SEA COAST

The Red Sea is one of the few seas on earth that is virtually closed, surrounded in this case by arid land: the Sinai to the north, the Eastern Sahara on the west, and the Arabian Peninsula to the east. The sea pours into the gulfs of Aqaba and Suez to the north; to the south, its mouth narrows into the strait of Bab al-Mandeb—The Gate of Tears. The Red Sea is 1,800 km (1,100 mi) long and 350 km (215 mi) wide. Along its central axis, depths reach 10,000 feet. The combination of minimal tidal changes, currents and wind, and almost year-round sunshine fosters the growth of a unique underwater ecology.

The Red Sea has been an important conduit for trade throughout human history. Along its coasts, archaeological sites currently being excavated date as far back as the earliest ancient Egyptian gold and turquoise expeditions, made more than 4,000 years ago. Ottoman outposts are being renovated and will reopen another chapter of life on the edge of the Eastern Sahara. Deeper in the mountains, Christian monastic life began at the Monastery of Saint Paul, founded by the Eastern church's first known hermit-priest.

Meanwhile the 21st century is very much in evidence as tourism increases in economic importance. Diving started the trend, and though this remains the paramount reason for spending a few days here, new resorts and activities are attracting visitors in ever-increasing numbers.

AIN SUKHNA

120 km (75 mi) southeast of Cairo; 45 km (29 mi) south of Suez.

The waters of Ain Sukhna (the name means "hot spring") originate at Jabal Ataka, a mountain on the Red Sea Coast. The turquoise water is clear and warm year-round. There is little to do here in the way of sightseeing, but it's a convenient day trip from Cairo or the Suez Canal zone if, like picnicking Cairenes, you're looking for a seaside day in the sun. The development along the coastline here has grown rapidly in the last decade, with villas and apartments bought up by wealthy residents of the capital.

GETTING HERE AND AROUND

It's a two-hour drive from Cairo to Ain Sukhna. The roads through the town of Suez are good and continue south along the coast to Hurghada. There is regular bus service in both directions offering inexpensive connections. Service taxis are the best way to get around the town.

WHERE TO STAY

All hotel reviews have been condensed for this book. Please go to Fodors.com for full reviews of each property.

$$ ⌂ **Palmera Resort.** On the sea with a beautiful private beach, the Palmera sprawls out into lush gardens. **Pros:** wide, sandy beach; generous main pool; good choice of resort facilities for the price point. **Cons:** mosquitoes can be a problem; some fixtures and fittings are a little careworn. ⌂ *30 km (20 mi) south of Suez, on the way to Ain Sukhna* ☏ *062/410–8124* ⊕ *www.palmerabeachresort.com* ⟿ *282 rooms, 18 suites* ⌂ *In-room: safe, refrigerator. In-hotel: 6 restaurants, bars, pools, gym, beachfront, water sports, laundry service, Internet terminal, parking (free)* ⊟ *AE, MC, V* ⏏ *BP.*

THE MONASTERIES OF SAINT ANTHONY AND SAINT PAUL

Egypt's oldest monasteries stand at the forefront of Christian monastic history. Isolated in the mountains near the Red Sea, they have spectacular settings and views of the coast. Getting to the monasteries isn't exactly a picnic, but their remoteness was the reason the saints chose these caves as their hermitages. The saints' endurance in the desert—against Bedouin raids, changing religious tides, and physical privation—give them an allure augmented by paintings and icons that add color to their otherwise stark appeal.

GETTING THERE AND AROUND

To get to the monasteries you will need to rent a car or, preferably (because driving in Egypt is such a harrowing experience), hire a private taxi from Cairo (about £E500) or Hurghada (£E225). Note that Copts fast for 43 days in advance of Christmas, during which time most monasteries are closed to visitors. Call before you set out to confirm that the gates will be open.

Thomas Cook (⌂ *8 Shar'a al-Sheraton, Hurghada* ☏ *065/344–3338, or national number throughout Egypt 16119* ⌂ *17 Mahmoud Bassiouny St., Cairo* ☏ *02/2574–5191* ⊕ *www.thomascookegypt.com*) runs tours to the monasteries from Cairo and Hurghada.

THE MONASTERY OF SAINT ANTHONY

110 km (69 mi) southwest of Ain Sukhna.

Saint Anthony is a prominent figure in Coptic Christianity because of his influence on the monastic movement. And even though his contemporary Paul was the first hermit, Anthony was the more popular. He was born in the middle of the 3rd century AD to wealthy parents who left him with a hefty inheritance upon their death, when he was 18. Instead of reveling in his riches, he sold all his possessions, distributed the proceeds to the poor, sent his sister to a convent, and fled to dedicate his life to God as a hermit in the mountains overlooking the Red Sea.

The Monastery of Saint Anthony

Disciples flocked to Anthony, hoping to hear his preaching and to be healed. But the monk sought absolute solitude and retreated to a cave in the mountain range of South Qabala. After his death in the 4th century—the hermit lived to age 104—admirers built a chapel and refectory in his memory. Saint Anthony's grew. In the 7th, 8th, and 11th centuries, periodic Bedouin predations severely damaged the structure. It was restored in the 12th century.

Saint Anthony's is deep in the mountains. Its walls reach some 40 feet in height. Several watchtowers, as well as the bulky walls' catwalk, provide for sentries. The **Church of Saint Anthony** was built over his grave, and it is renowned for its exquisite 13th-century wall paintings of Saint George on horseback and the three Desert Fathers, restored in the 1990s.

Four other churches were built on the grounds of the monastery over the years. The most important of them is the 1766 **Church of Saint Mark**, which is adorned with 12 domes and contains significant relics.

A 2-km (1-mi) trek—be sure to bring plenty of drinking water along—leads you to **Saint Anthony's Cave**, 2,230 feet above sea level, where he spent his last days. Views of the Red Sea and the surrounding mountains are superb, and you're likely to encounter interesting local bird life on the hike to the cave. Inside the cave, among the rocks, pilgrims have left pieces of paper asking the saint for intervention. ☎ *02/419–8560 monastery residence in Cairo* ⊕ *www.stanthonymonastery.org.*

The Monastery of Saint Paul

THE MONASTERY OF SAINT PAUL
112 km (70 mi) south of Ain Sukhna.

Saint Paul of Thebes (also known as Saint Paul the Anchorite) made his way into the desert to live as a hermit in the 4th century, after a wealthy upbringing in Alexandria. It was his fellow penitent Anthony who revealed his sainthood to him. The monastery was built in the 5th century, after the saint's death. Following several raids about a thousand years later, the monastery was abandoned. Again Anthony came to Paul's aid: monks from the Monastery of Saint Anthony eventually reopened Saint Paul's.

A 7-km (4-mi) drive west from the Red Sea Coast highway twists through the rugged mountains and deposits you near the entrance of Saint Paul's Monastery. The high walls of the monastery are surrounded by a village, which has a bakery, mills, and a few surrounding fields. The buildings of the monastery are believed to encompass the cave in which Saint Paul lived for nearly 80 years. In the **Church of Saint Paul**, paintings of the Holy Virgin cover the walls.

To experience the ascetic life of the monastery, you can overnight in guesthouses here; women lodge outside the walls, men inside. For permission to lodge here, and for information on open days and hours, contact the monastery residence in Cairo. ☎ *02/419–8560 monastery residence in Cairo.*

HURGHADA

410 km (255 mi) south of Ain Suhkna; 530 km (331 mi) south of Cairo.

Hurghada is an old fishing town that became a popular base for diving in the 1960s. As a result of the 1967 war between Egypt and Israel, Hurghada was closed to tourism and did not reopen until 1976. By this time, Sharm El-Sheikh, which was under Israeli occupation, was flourishing as a diving town. Hurghada had a lot of catching up to do.

Now, with a population of about 50,000, and some 75 hotels in and around town, Hurghada is definitely a Red Sea hot spot. Vacationers flock here in fall and winter specifically for its mild climate. But if it's sun, sand, and sea that you're after, other areas along Egypt's Red Sea Coast have more appealing beaches and desert diversions. Come to Hurghada if you're into scuba diving, however.

Hurghada has grown inexorably in the last decade, and almost all the development is tourism-related. The first hotels took the town beachfront. The oldest hotel here is the Sheraton (closed at this writing), and it is often used as a landmark. The main boulevard, with its 15 car-splitting speed bumps, is called Shar'a Sheraton in the Sakalla district. Newer development stretches north along the road to Cairo and south through the newly gentrified Old Vic Village district, the 20 km (12 mi) to Sahl Hasheesh Bay where vast all-inclusive resort hotels are set in ample grounds.

This town is known for its strong north-northwesterly winds, so if you plan to lounge about, find a spot with a protective windbreak. From April to October, the hotter months, be prepared to battle the bugs: mosquitoes, light-brown desert flies, and other flying insects have nasty bites. Bring bug repellent and spend your time in the sea.

GETTING HERE AND AROUND

Hurghada Airport has regular flights from Cairo, as well as less frequent flights to Alexandria, Aswan, and Sharm El-Sheikh. Road connections are good along the north coast to Cairo, west to Luxor, and south to Marsa Alam with frequent bus service running all three of these routes. There is a ferry connection to Sharm El-Sheikh. There are some minibus services in Hurghada town, but taxis are numerous are the most practical way to get around.

WHERE TO EAT

Downtown Hurghada caters primarily to a European and Eastern European/Russian package-tour clientele, who are drawn to the abundance of Italian and fast-food eateries featuring kitsch decor. The town's newer hotels are often all-inclusive featuring international buffets of varying levels of quality. However, a few notable restaurants are worth seeking out.

$–$$

MIDDLE EASTERN

✕ **Felfela.** A sister of the Cairo-based Felfela, this is the best place in town for a traditional Egyptian meal. The restaurant's four levels all have great harbor views. Sit down to a fresh lemonade and start choosing appetizers from the menu—tasty *fuul* (the classic fava-bean dish) and *koshary* (like a vegetarian chili). From the grill dig into kebabs or wheat-stuffed pigeon. The grilled catch of the day is another delicious choice. Specialties here are the mezze: tahini, humus, *baba ghanouj* (eggplant dip), cumin-spiced tomatoes, *labne* (a yogurt-and-mint dip), and stuffed grape leaves. ⊠ *Shar'a Sheraton, 2 km (1 mi) north of the Sheraton Hotel* ☎ *065/344–2410* ▭ *No credit cards* ⊘ *No lunch.*

$ ✗ **Heaven Bistro.** Funky modern eatery full of bright colors, Heaven's
FAST FOOD a step beyond the standard Egyptian fast-food joint. You can make a pit stop here on the way back from the beach or before heading to a club for anything from a crisp salad to a burger, a bowl of chili, or beef Stroganoff. It's just a shame there isn't any outside space where you could enjoy your meal alfresco. ⊠ *Off El Arosa Square on the way to Ministry of Sound, Sekalla* ☎ *012/104–2766* ⊕ *www.heavenbistro.com* ▭ *No credit cards.*

$$$–$$$$ ✗ **Zaafran.** With only 40 seats, Zaafran offers an intimate meal of fine
INDIAN Indian cuisine in a cozy room full of rich reds and golds and the dulcet
★ tones of live Egyptian guitar. The varied cuisine of the subcontinent is reflected in the menu with succulent *tandoori* chicken (roasted with a mint and spice marinade), a rich *rogan josh* (meat in a spiced tomato sauce), and fragrant *biryani* (saffron rice with meat and vegetables) as just some of the options. Top off your meal with a refreshing *kulfi* (dense Indian-style ice cream) for dessert. ⊠ *Oberoi Sahl Hasheesh, Sahl Hasheesh Bay* ☎ *065/344–0777* ⊛ *Reservations essential* ▭ *AE, DC, MC, V* ⊘ *No lunch.*

WHERE TO STAY

All hotel reviews have been condensed for this book. Please go to Fodors.com for full reviews of each property.

$ ⊡ **Hotel White Albatros.** If you're looking for cheap, clean no-frills accommodation in the heart of Hurghada, then this is the best option. **Pros:** no price hike for foreigners, this is as inexpensive as it gets; near all the nightlife; balconies offer great bird's-eye views of downtown Hurghada. **Cons:** traffic on the main thoroughfare can be noisy day and night. ⊠ *Sheraton Rd., Sakalla* ☎ *065/344–2519* ⊕ *www.walbatros.com* ⤳ *45 rooms, 1 suite* ⚘ *In-room: a/c, refrigerator. In-hotel: restaurant, pool, Internet terminal* ▭ *No credit cards* ⦿ *CP.*

$$$$ ⊡ **Oberoi Sahl Hasheesh.** The first boutique all-suites hotel along the Red
★ Sea Coast, the Oberoi is still the tops. **Pros:** this is a genuine five-star luxury hotel, not a package-tour resort; 24-hour butler service; boutique size means you are never subjected to crowds of other guests. **Cons:** it's a 17-km (10-mi) journey to downtown Hurghada, though there is a strip mall within a mile of the hotel. ⊠ *Sahl Hasheesh Bay* ☎ *065/344–0777* ⊕ *www.oberoisahlhasheesh.com* ⤳ *100 suites* ⚘ *In-room: a/c, safe, Internet. In-hotel: 3 restaurants, room service, bars, pool, gym, spa, diving, laundry service, parking (free)* ▭ *AE, DC, MC, V* ⦿ *BP.*

$$$–$$$$ ⊡ **Steigenberger Al Dau Beach Hotel.** Close enough to town that you can enjoy the delights of Hurghada, yet offering a luxury retreat for relaxation, this resort offers the best of both worlds. **Pros:** amenities are excellent, with a large 10-room Thalasso Spa, dive center, and golf course; close to the bars and nightlife of the town; no-smoking rooms. **Cons:** rooms are in one vast building rather than being scattered around

the resort; atrium design could lead to possible noise if reception area is busy. ⊠ *Yossif Afifi Rd., Old Vic Village* ☎ *065/346–5400* ⊕ *www. steigenbergeraldaubeach.com* ⌐ *364 rooms, 16 suites* ⌂ *In-room: a/c, safe, refrigerator. In-hotel: 4 restaurants, room service, bars, golf course, pools, gym, spa, beachfront, diving, water sports, bicycles, children's programs (ages 4–12), laundry service, Wi-Fi hotspot, parking (free)* ⊟ *AE, DC, MC, V* ⦿| *BP.*

$$ ⚏ **Steigenberger Al Dau Club.** This good midsize Hurghada option is one block back from the waterfront, which means more reasonable prices. The hotel has its own private beach with dive center and beach bar. **Pros:** you can take advantage of the golf course and gym facilities at the five-star sister hotel; good-size free-form pool; desert garden with hammocks offers a place to escape your fellow guests. **Cons:** all-inclusive pricing doesn't tempt you to try other options; Standard rooms are too small and have no balconies, so we recommend only Superior rooms. ⊠ *Youssif Alifi Rd., Old Vic Village* ☎ *065/346–5200* ⊕ *www. steigenbergeraldauclub.com* ⌐ *237 rooms, 9 suites* ⌂ *In-room: a/c, refrigerator. In-hotel: 2 restaurants, room service, bars, tennis courts, diving, bicycles, children's programs (ages 4–12), laundry service, Internet terminal, parking (free)* ⊟ *AE, DC, MC, V* ⦿| *AI.*

SPORTS AND THE OUTDOORS

BEACHES

Hurghada's beaches are simply not as good as those on the Sinai Coast. Because public beach access is virtually nonexistent—and public beaches are not worth going to—it's best to stick with your hotel's beachfront. The newer hotel developments south of the downtown area have much better beaches but no public access at all.

DIVING

Giftun Drift, on Small Giftun Island (*see* ⇨ *Diving in Egypt for more information*), is a beautiful, deep-wall dive that is one hour offshore east of Hurghada; this is one of the deepest sites in the area, and the marine life here is beautiful. **Abu Ramada,** south of Small Giftun Island, has remarkable multicolored corals. **Shu'ab al-Erg** looks like a large crescent with big ergs (shifting dunes) at its tips. The site, two hours from Hurghada, has a gorgeous coral garden. You may also see dolphins here.

Expect to pay about €50 for a day of diving, including two tanks; full gear rental per day is usually around €24. Inquire about diving packages of up to 10 days, which include 20 dives. An open-water course costs €315.

DIVE   **SUBEX.** Specializing in underwater safaris south of Hurghada, SUBEX
OPERATORS   is always in search of virgin reefs unpopulated by divers and boats; the guides offer weeklong live-aboard trips to the kinds of sites that make a splash in *National Geographic.* ⊠ *Aldahar* ☎ *065/354–3261* ⊕ *www. subex.org.*

Divers' Lodge. Pioneers of technical diving in the Red Sea, Divers' Lodge has its own jetty, fully equipped live-aboard boat, and several contracted daily boats. The company runs PADI courses from beginner to

Mahmya beach on Giftun Island

instructor levels and has night diving, technical diving, and NITROX and rebreather courses. The staff is warm and professional and includes divers from around the world. Divers' Lodge also has the only courses in Egypt in sign language for the hearing impaired, conducted by a hearing-impaired instructor. ⊠ *Continental Resort Hurghada, Hurghada–Safaga Rd., Km 17* ☎ *065/346–5100* ⊕ *www.divers-lodge.com.*

KITE SURFING

Kite surfing is a growing sport in the Red Sea region, where the wind and water conditions are almost perfect year-round, offering tranquil shallows just offshore. You must take a tutorial in order to learn how to kite surf. Prices for an introductory course are around €120; it helps to have some windsurfing experience, but these are very different sports.

Colona Watersports. This is the leading kite-surfing training center in Hurghada, with introductory courses for beginners and equipment rental for experienced riders (full day €80, half day €55). ⊠ *Magawish Resort, Youssif Alifi Rd., Old Vic Village* ☎ *010/344–1810* ⊕ *www. colonawatersports.com.*

WATER SPORTS

Waterskiing, windsurfing, parasailing, kayaking, and paddleboating are among the aquatic possibilities in Hurghada. Wave runners, however, have been banned from the area. Inquire at your hotel about what activities it offers; the staff can point you in the right direction if your hotel doesn't offer the activity you're looking for.

NIGHTLIFE

With the arrival of the iconic Ministry of Sound club, Hurghada has been transformed into one of the clubbing hot spots for younger (teens to early twenties) European party goers. This, in turn, has attracted branches of other well-known clubs and bars that keep the place rocking into the early hours.

BARS

Orange Café and Dutch Bar. This Dutch/Egyptian–owned bar offers a pub-style menu, great beer, music (from the 1970s to now), billiards, big-screen TV, karaoke, and occasional live bands. There's always a fun atmosphere. ⊠ *Opposite the Royal Palace Hotel, Old Vic Village Rd.* ☎ *012/247–3492.*

CLUBS

Little Buddha. A sibling of the famed Paris Buddha Bar, this cool sushi bar and lounge early in the evening transforms into a progressive music club with resident and guest DJs after 11:30 PM. ⊠ *Sinbad Resort, Old Vic Village Rd.* ☎ *065/345–0120* ⊕ *www.littlebuddha-hurghada.com.*

★ **Ministry of Sound.** Having launched house and trance music across Europe, the club empire's celebrity DJs run regular sessions in conjunction with the HedKandi house record label at this iconic beach bar and club. Come to groove or to chill—but do make sure you come to feel the pulse of the current international nightlife scene. ⊠ *Papas Beach Club, next to the public beach, Sakalla* ☎ *016/883–3551* ⊕ *www. ministryofsoundegypt.com.*

EL GOUNA

20 km (12 mi) north of Hurghada; 510 km (319 mi) south of Cairo.

El Gouna is the dream of an Egyptian businessman who has utterly transformed a secluded bay and its surrounding resources. In 10 years, this virgin seacoast has been transformed into an established resort town and also a settlement for more than 10,000 full-time residents. Equipped with its own wells in the mountains, a hospital with a hyperbaric chamber for dealing with divers' decompression problems, four power plants, a school, a department of the American University in Egypt, and an impressive array of services, this environmentally friendly resort town is practically self-sustaining. El Gouna caters to wealthy Egyptians and expat workers who come to unwind from the hustle and bustle of Cairo, plus year-round tourist arrivals.

Designed around a series of seawater lagoons, the heart of El Gouna is **al-Qafr,** also known as Downtown, a modern rendition of a traditional Egyptian settlement. To the north is **Abu Tig,** a majestic marina filled with multimillion-dollar yachts designed to re-create the atmosphere of the French or Italian Riviera. A second, larger marina with accompanying hotels, apartments, and golf course was rolled out in 2010. South of al-Qafr is El Gouna's original golf course, which is surrounded with lagoon-side villas and apartments. Visitors have the choice of 16 hotels and an excellent range of water-sports activities.

GETTING HERE AND AROUND

Hurghada is a 20-minute drive to the south, and its airport offers direct air links to Alexandria, Aswan, Cairo, and Sharm El-Sheikh. Regular buses connect the town with Hurghada and continue north through Suez to Cairo.

There's an excellent free public transport system within the town connecting all the hotels with the central districts. The downtown and the marina area are walkeable.

> **DID YOU KNOW?**
>
> El Gouna recycles 97% of its waste by using gray water on the golf course, composting what's natural, selling what's valuable, and transforming plastics into solid paving and Tetra Pak containers into heavy-duty paper bags.

WHERE TO EAT

El Gouna has a wide range of international eateries spread across the village center and in the hotels. You'll find everything from snacks to silver-service dining.

$$
SEAFOOD

✕ **El Sayadin.** What better place than a rustic waterfront shack to enjoy a lazy lunch or dinner? The weathered wooden deck of El Sayadin, overlooking the resort's main inlet, is the ideal place to take in the fantastic beaches and seascapes of El Gouna. The menu combines excellent seafood with Egyptian specialties. Start with a mezze plate and then tuck into the grilled catch of the day, salmon served three ways, or *fritto misto* (crispy fried seafood). The restaurant's about 10 minutes by foot from downtown. ⊠ *Mövenpick Resort & Spa El Gouna, El Gouna, southeast of downtown, about 10 minutes by foot* ☎ *065/354–4501* ⊟ *AE, DC, MC, V.*

$–$$
ITALIAN

✕ **Kiki's.** Not only is this a great Italian restaurant, serving arguably the best food in El Gouna, but it's also a hip hangout. Kiki's opens at 8 PM to serve great plates of pasta plus grilled meats and seafood, but it really comes alive around 11—and keeps kickin' through the night until the last person leaves. ⊠ *Museum Square, Downtown* ☎ *065/354–9701* 🍴 *Reservations essential* ⊟ *No credit cards* ⊗ *No lunch.*

$$–$$$
SEAFOOD

✕ **Hedra.** A good-value option in the heart of El Gouna, this restaurant serves a wide range of seafood as well as steaks in the evening. But it offers a menu of sandwiches and light snacks during the day, including a delicious *shawarma* (thin-cut meat and salad wrapped in unleavened bread—like a gyro), if you want to grab a bite to eat while you are out and about in town. There's a terrace overlooking the square, so you can watch the world stroll by. ⊠ *Tamr Hedr Food Court, Downtown* ☎ *065/354–9702* ⊟ *MC, V.*

WHERE TO STAY

All hotel reviews have been condensed for this book. Please go to Fodors.com for full reviews of each property.

$$

🏨 **Dawar El Omda.** The name of this hotel within the Qafr means "the mayor's house," and that is its theme, with decorative touches depicting 19th-century Cairene styling. The rooms are cozy, and each has a balcony overlooking the canal and pool. ⊠ *al-Qafr* ☎ *065/358–0063* ⊕ *www.*

dawarelomda-elgouna.com ⤴ *66 rooms, 3 suites* ⚓ *In-room: a/c, safe, refrigerator, Wi-Fi. In-hotel: 2 restaurants, bar, pool, Internet terminal, Wi-Fi hotspot* ⊟ *AE, DC, MC, V* ⫟◉*BP.*

$$$ 🏨 **Mövenpick Resort and Spa El Gouna.** El Gouna's oldest resort— it opened in 1995—has its longest beachfront, plus such a range of added features that it might be tempting not to leave the resort and explore the rest of El Gouna. **Pros:** excellent selection of eateries and activities on-site; the extended facilities of El Gouna are just a shuttle-bus ride away; all no-smoking rooms. **Cons:** a rolling program of refurbishment through early 2012 may mean temporary closure of some facilities. ✉ *El Gouna (southeast of downtown, about 10 minutes by foot)* ☎ *065/354–4501* ⊕ *www.moevenpick-elgouna.com* ⤴ *535 rooms, 19 suites* ⚓ *In-room: a/c, safe, Internet, Wi-Fi. In-hotel: 7 restaurants, room service, pools, gym, spa, beachfront, diving, water sports, bicycles, children's programs (ages 5–12), laundry service, Wi-Fi hotspot, parking (free)* ⊟ *AE, DC, MC, V* ⫟◉*BP.*

$$$ 🏨 **Steigenberger Golf Resort.** In designing this resort, the innovative architect Michael Graves took cues from Egyptian and Bedouin influences, creating a style now known as neo-Nubian. **Pros:** beautiful setting surrounded by lagoons and a golf course; lagoon beaches on-site offer a quiet place to relax; it's the closest El Gouna hotel to the golf course; no-smoking rooms. **Cons:** the sea and water sports are a shuttle-bus ride away; farthest hotel from downtown El Gouna and the marina (about a 10-minute bus ride); no free bottled water in room. ✉ *El Gouna (southeast of downtown, about 10 minutes by bus)* ☎ *065/358–0140* ⊕ *www.steigenberger.com* ⤴ *209 rooms, 59 suites* ⚓ *In-room: a/c, safe, Internet, Wi-Fi. In-hotel: 3 restaurants, room service, bars, golf course, pools, gym, spa, bicycles, children's programs (ages 5–12), Wi-Fi hotspot, parking (free)* ⊟ *AE, DC, MC, V* ⫟◉*BP.*

$$ 🏨 **Turtles Inn.** Usually booked up by the diving and kite-surfing crowd, Turtles Inn offers unpretentious accommodation in the heart of El Gouna marina. **Pros:** location in the heart of the marina with direct access to restaurants, bars, and shops; Orca Dive Center on-site; energetic, young vibe. **Cons:** lack of on-site amenities won't suit families with young children; not on the beach (a shuttle takes you to Zeytouna Beach). ✉ *Abu Tig Marina* ☎ *065/358–0171* ⊕ *www.turtles-inn.com* ⤴ *28 rooms* ⚓ *In-room: a/c, safe, Wi-Fi. In-hotel: restaurant, bar, diving, Wi-Fi hotspot* ⊟ *AE, DC, MC, V* ⫟◉*EP.*

SPORTS AND THE OUTDOORS

Info-center. Water sports, desert excursions, and golf are available in El Gouna. If you can't arrange these at your hotel, stop by the local information center to find out more. ✉ *al-Qaf* ☎ *2100 from any phone within El Gouna* ⊕ *www.elgouna.com.*

BEACHES

Hotel beaches in El Gouna are private and are reserved for the use of hotel guests only. **Zeytouna Beach** (*see ⇨ Best Beaches in Egypt*) is an island; to get here, hop on one of the boat buses that moor along the canals. **Mangroovy Beach** (*see ⇨ Best Beaches in Egypt*) is a dedicated kite-surfing and water-sports beach with some great action. Both of these beaches are open to the public and guests of any of the resorts in El Gouna.

DIVING

Um Gamar means "mother of the moon." Roughly 90 minutes offshore by speedboat, this is truly an amazing dive, with great walls and caves. The current here is light, making this one of the area's easier dives. **Abu Nahas** is a wreck diver's haven, with four large freighters sunk at reachable depths. About 25 years ago a ship carrying copper (*nahas* in Arabic) hit the reef and sank, hence the name of the site. The Tile Wreck carried Spanish tiles and sank in the same vicinity. And the Lentil Wreck became a smorgasbord for fish. You will encounter huge napoleons, groupers, schools of snappers, and catfish. *Giannis D.* hit the reef in 1983 and is a favorite; at 82 feet underwater you will find a large air pocket where you can speak to your buddy. Remember not to breathe the air, though, because it is stale and probably poisonous.

DIVE OPERATORS

★ **Emperor Divers.** El Gouna's major dive operator is right on the beach at the Mövenpick Hotel. The young, international staff is passionate about diving and water sports. The impressive selection of dive courses includes all levels of PADI courses and technical diving, including the "Scubility" diving course. ✉ *Mövenpick Resort and Spa, El Gouna (southeast of downtown, about 10 minutes by foot)* ☎ *012/325–8277* ⊕ *www.emperordivers.com.*

GOLF

El Gouna Golf Course. El Gouna's golf course was designed by professional golfer Fred Couples and Gene Bates. The course has a sinuous design among the lagoons of El Gouna. The par-74 course caters to many skill levels; there are an aqua driving range and a practice putting green. ✉ *South of Downtown, El Gouna* ☎ *012/746–4712* ⊕ *www.elgouna.com.*

GUIDED TOURS

Pro Tours. This company can arrange anything from day outings, to golf trips, to a Nile cruise. ✉ *Abu Tig Marina, El Gouna* ☎ *065/358–0085* ⊕ *www.protourstravel.com.*

SCUBILITY

Scubility is a revolutionary dive program specifically designed to allow divers with mobility issues to try diving and to undertake open-water certification. Scubility is designed to take into account and work around the varied challenges faced by divers with disabilities. The training also extends to the able-bodied with buddy training, which allows the dive buddy to understand what is happening to the diver in the water and how they can offer the most appropriate assistance. Dive instructors can upgrade their expertise by undertaking a Scubility Instructor upgrade program.

KITE SURFING

The wide stretches of coastal shallows of El Gouna offer ideal conditions for the sport, and several international competitions have been held here. Training courses for beginners cost €245, private lessons €55 per hour.

★ **Kitepower El Gouna.** With its own private expanse of El Gouna shallows, this operation has a great location and offers expert training. ⊠ *Mangroovy Beach* ☎ *012/265–9596* ⊕ *www.kitepower-elgouna.com.*

SPAS AND WELLNESS

★ **Angsana Spa.** Wellness is a mantra for the third millennium, and El Gouna has a large facility run by one of the most respected names in the business. Angsana Spa has 14 treatment rooms, a sauna, steam room, and Jacuzzi. The spa offers Asian-inspired treatments in a tranquil setting to ease tension or sooth the muscles you've strained on the golf course or under the kite board. There are also smaller Angsana Spa outlets at El Gouna Golf Club and Steigenberger Golf Resort. ⊠ *Mövenpick Resort and Spa El Gouna, El Gouna (southeast of downtown, about 10 minutes by foot)* ☎ *065/354–4501* ⊕ *www.angsanaspa.com.*

WATER SPORTS

The Orange Concept. This outfitter offers professional training in wakeboarding and has a talented, multilingual staff; the company also offers such water sports as waterskiing, parasailing, and banana boat rides. Parasailing is €30 per single flight; wakeboard training sessions cost €30 each; banana boat rides are €8 per person. ⊠ *Ocean View Hotel, Abu Tig Marina* ☎ *065/354–9702 Ext. 77976* ⊕ *www.theorangeconcept. com.*

NIGHTLIFE

The cream of Cairo society has second homes in El Gouna (and often a yacht in the harbor); they visit on weekends and holidays, adding a touch of glamour to the nightlife venues.

BARS

Moods Bar. At the mouth of Abu Tig Marina and flanked by motor cruisers and yachts, this is the place to watch day turn to evening over a sunset cocktail. Everyone gathers here for aperitifs before moving on to dinner and then, perhaps, a club. It's a great location with beautiful people. ⊠ *Abu Tig Marina* ☎ *010/555–6493* ⊕ *www.moods-elgouna.com.*

Peanuts Bar. A contemporary beer and ground-nuts bar, Peanuts offers unpretentious fun with a mixed crowd of visitors and expats. ⊠ *Ocean View Hotel, Abu Tig Marina* ☎ *065/358–0350.*

Roof Bar. After finishing the day's activities, the dive crowd gathers to chat over beer at Roof Bar, which has a popular happy hour—but the divers tend to stay long after the cheap drinks dry up for the great conversation and convivial atmosphere. ⊠ *Turtles Inn, Abu Tig Marina* ☎ *065/358–0171.*

CLUBS

DuPort Pool Club. By night, the classical temple-like interior of the DuPort Lido is transformed into a cool lounge with views out across the marina. ⊠ *Ocean View Hotel, Abu Tig Marina* ☎ *065/358–0350.*

6

BUR SAFAGA (PORT SAFAGA)

40 km (25 mi) south of Hurghada, approximately 200 km (124 mi) northeast of Luxor.

Like other cities on the Red Sea, this commercial town has been undergoing a transformation, slowly metamorphosing into a holiday resort. Like other cities on the Red Sea, the commercial port town sits close to great offshore dive sites. Unlike others, however, tourist development hasn't taken off in a meaningful way. But if the mass tourism in Hurghada is a turnoff, Safaga offers a small-scale and much more low-key alternative, though the best dive sites can still be seen on a day trip from Hurghada. Safaga is also the closest beach resort to Luxor and the Valley of the Kings, which lies 200 km (124 mi) to the southwest; when cruise ships offer land excursions to Luxor, they often do so through Safaga.

GETTING HERE AND AROUND

Bur Safaga is a 30-minute drive south of Hurghada, and there is regular bus service between Hurghada to Bur Safaga, continuing through Suez to Cairo. There is also a good road heading west to the Nile River and Luxor, though check that there are no restrictions on foreigners using public transport on this route before you book tickets. Once in Bur Safaga, taxis are the best way to get around town.

WHERE TO EAT

$$ GREEK ★ **Taverna Barba Kiriakos.** The owner of the InterContinental Abu Soma Resort was born in Greece, and this genuine taverna with its blue-and-white decor and fishing boat outside is a little reminder of his homeland. Start with a crisp Greek salad or *dolmades* (stuffed vine leaves). Excellent slow-cooked *stifado* (beef stew in tomato sauce) and *moussaka* (a dish of eggplant, ground beef, and tomato sauce) make delicious entrées. Plate throwing is optional. ✉ *InterContinental Abu Soma Resort, Abu Soma Bay, Hurghada–Safaga Hwy.* ☎ *065/326–0700* ▭ *AE, DC, MC, V* ⊙ *No lunch.*

WHERE TO STAY

All hotel reviews have been condensed for this book. Please go to Fodors.com for full reviews of each property.

$$$ **InterContinental Abu Soma Resort.** Set on the finest stretch of beach along the entire Red Sea Coast, the InterContinental is the most imposing edifice in this low-key town. **Pros:** excellent water sports offerings; lovely stretch of sand separate from the water sports area; extensive organized programs make it an excellent choice for families; no-smoking rooms. **Cons:** there's little to do outside the hotel complex; prevailing winds may suit sports-minded guests but can get strong enough to disrupt sunbathing; children's programs must be booked separately through the Mark Warner Company (⊕ *www.markwarner.co.uk*). ✉ *Abu Soma Bay, Hurghada–Safaga Hwy.* ☎ *065/326–0700* ⊕ *www.ichotelsgroup.com* *445 rooms, 63 suites* *In-room: a/c, safe, refrigerator, Internet. In-hotel: 5 restaurants, room service, bars, tennis courts, pools, gym, spa, beachfront, diving, water sports, children's programs (ages 2–17), laundry service, Wi-Fi hotspot, parking (free)* ▭ *AE, DC, MC, V* *EP.*

EL-QUSEIR

85 km (53 mi) south of Bur Safaga.

Until the completion of the Suez Canal, el-Quseir was a crucial port, principally because of the *hajj* (pilgrimage to Mecca) and Middle East trade. With the canal in place, the port of el-Quseir was no longer needed as a stop for ships, laden with goods, passing from the Nile Valley across the Red Sea and beyond, and so it fell into decline. A development boom along the entire Red Sea Coast has started to transform el-Quseir into a resort town. Modern construction aims to be environmentally conscious, not only of marine life but also of land that is thought to be rich in artifacts, from bits of Roman-era glass to Mamluk archways.

Quseir Fort was one of many strategically located military posts that the Ottoman Turks built along the Red Sea Coast, and it was one of the chief posts that the Napoleonic Expedition in 1799 thoroughly bombed and then rebuilt. It is estimated that the fort was commissioned in the early 16th century during Ottoman rule by the sharifs of Mecca and Medina. They wanted to protect the hajj route and to maintain control of the passage of goods against the threat posed by the Portuguese fleet: the area around el-Quseir was a profitable granary for wheat and coffee from Yemen, and the most valuable spices of India and Persia were reloaded here. A small museum displays find uncovered during excavation work at the site. ⊠ *el-Quseir* ☎ *No phone* 💲 *£E15* ☉ *Daily 9–5.*

GETTING HERE AND AROUND

El-Quseir is approximately 70 minutes south of Hurghada by road. Regular bus service connects the town with Hurghada, continuing north through Suez to Cairo. There is also a good road heading west to the Nile River and Luxor, though check that there are no restrictions on foreigners using public transport on this route before you book tickets. Taxis are the best way to get around town.

WHERE TO STAY

All hotel reviews have been condensed for this book. Please go to Fodors.com for full reviews of each property.

$$$ ★ **Mövenpick Resort El Quseir.** This is one of the more tranquil settings on the Red Sea Coast—even the buildings blend with the surrounding environment. **Pros:** environmentally aware; traditional styling; extensive range of on-site activities; no-smoking rooms. **Cons:** isolated location. ⊠ *Sirena Beach, al-Quadim Bay, 7 km (4½ mi) north of el-Quseir* ☎ *065/333–2100* ⊕ *www.moevenpick.com* 🛏 *250 rooms* ⬩ *In-room: a/c, Internet, Wi-Fi. In-hotel: 3 restaurants, room service, bars, tennis courts, pools, gym, spa, beachfront, diving, water sports, laundry service, parking (free)* 🟰 *AE, DC, MC, V* ⦿ *BP.*

DIVING

SUBEX. The tightly run Swiss dive outfitter is well equipped with staff, facilities, and gear. Guided dives go out with a maximum of four people; you must take a guide with you if you have fewer than 30 dives under your belt, and all divers must go on an orientation dive to ascertain experience levels. ⊠ *Mövenpick Resort El Quseir, al-Quadim Bay* ☎ *065/333–2100.*

MARSA ALAM

132 km (82 mi) south of al-Quseir.

The far southern enclave of the Egyptian Red Sea Coast, Marsa Alam, has flourished since the opening of an international airport in 2001. The **Port Ghalib** project plans a living community of nine Arabian- and Nubian-style villages along with beach resorts and a 1,000-vessel marina. The first villa owners took possession of their new homes in 2007 and four hotels managed by InterContinental hotel group are now operating along with the marina, but the project is still very much a work in progress at this writing.

THE SUEZ CANAL

The construction of the Suez Canal changed the nature of European trade by connecting the Red Sea to the Mediterranean. Ismailiya and Bur Sa'id were home to workers and leaders of the engineering team. Unfortunately, only a little of the colonial feel lingers in the old buildings that remain, raised on high wooden beams and decorated with French windows. National museums with small halls and a limited but interesting collection suffice as sources of historical information.

The Suez Canal was by no means the first attempt to bridge the short distance between the Mediterranean and the Red Sea. It is, however, the only canal that has bypassed the Nile. In 1855, after years of lobbying with Sa'id, the Egyptian khedive, French consul to Egypt Ferdinand de Lesseps received approval to incorporate the Suez Canal Company. After the sale of shares to raise the necessary cash, a contract was signed by the company and Sa'id, namesake of Bur Sa'id, that granted the French a 99-year concession to operate the canal. Construction began in 1859. And pressure was on, as the international demand for Egyptian cotton grew exponentially; the canal would facilitate the transfer of cotton to Europe and America.

Ten years later, on November 17, 1869, the world celebrated the inauguration of the Suez Canal. These weeks of lavish celebration nearly broke Khedive Isma'il, Sa'id's successor. No expense was spared to make this grand affair run as smoothly and elaborately as possible. To pay for his debts, Isma'il sold most of his shares in the Suez Canal Company to the British. From this point on, a French and British consortium managed the canal, ushering in the British influence that lasted until 1956, when President Gamal Abdel Nasser expelled them from the country.

> **DID YOU KNOW?**
>
> In the 2009 fiscal year, the Suez Canal earned Egypt US$4.3 billion in income. That's the third-largest source of revenue for the country after tourism and money sent home by Egyptians working abroad.

The Suez Canal

In principle, the British agreed to let any nation at war or during peace-time use the canal. But in practice, during the two world wars, they strategically positioned soldiers along the canal and permitted only Allied nations to pass. In 1950, because of the Arab-Israeli war, Egypt banned all Israeli vessels from the canal. After the British were expelled from the Canal Zone—and later the entire nation—they joined the United States in refusing to lend Egypt the funds with which to build the Aswan High Dam. In response, Nasser nationalized the canal and combined the income from the canal with loans from the former Soviet Union to construct the dam.

On October 29, 1956, after several border clashes, Israel invaded Egypt. Great Britain and France then attacked Egypt a week later in an attempt to restore international control over the canal. After United Nations interventions, the canal was reopened in 1957 under Egyptian manage-ment and was policed by the United Nations. It was closed again in 1967 during the Arab-Israeli war by sunken ships, and it didn't reopen again until 1975. Three years later Egypt lifted the ban on Israeli ships, and in 1980, a 16-km-long (10-mi-long) tunnel was built under the canal to facilitate the passage of motor vehicles into and out of the Sinai.

ISMAILIYA

120 km (75 mi) east of Cairo; 87 km (54 mi) north of Suez.

Halfway between Bur Sa'id and Suez, this quaint city on Lake Timsah was founded by and named after Khedive Isma'il for those working on the canal. The director of the Suez Canal Company, Ferdinand de

Lesseps, lived here until the completion of the canal, and his home still stands—off-limits, alas—to the public. Ismailiya's population is close to 700,000, and the city is known for its wide streets, expansive public gardens, and cleanliness.

There is a distinct colonial feel in the area known as Hay al-Afrangi (the foreign district), because of the French colonial architecture of the remaining buildings. A stroll down Shar'a Muhammad 'Ali leads you along the Sweetwater Canal and eventually to the house of Ferdinand de Lesseps.

Perpendicular to Shar'a Muhammad 'Ali, running away from the Sweetwater Canal, Shar'a Sultan Hussayn has a number of restaurants, stores, banks, and a Thomas Cook office. From here, if you turn left (southwest) onto Shar'a Saad Zaghloul and walk to Maydan al-Gummhurriya, you'll get a feel for the wide streets and calm pace.

> ## A TOWN IN LIMBO
>
> The 19th-century governor of Ismailiya, Limbo Bey, was so unpopular during his tenure that after his death the townsfolk burned an effigy of the man. This one-off political statement developed into the annual Limbo Festival, but in modern times it's expanded scope beyond the hated Bey. A week after Coptic Easter, likenesses of almost any unpopular public figure, from a local soccer player going through a dry period to a soap opera character dishing the dirt, will be set alight after dark on the streets of Ismailiya.

The small **Ismailiya Regional Museum** has a modest collection of pharaonic and Greco-Roman artifacts. The majority of its collection consists of coins, pottery shards, and jewelry. The most impressive piece is a 4th-century Roman mosaic that has been cleverly laid in the floor of the hall. The picture shows Phaedra sending a love letter to her son Hippolyte. Other exhibits cover the ancient canals from the Nile to the Red Sea and contemporary canal history. ⊠ *Shar'a Muhammad 'Ali, across from the Mallaha Gardens* ☎ *064/291–2749* ⌨ *£E15* ☉ *Daily 9–5.*

GETTING HERE AND AROUND

Ismailiya is linked by fast highway to Cairo, and the journey time from the capital is around 90 minutes. Air-conditioned bus services ply the route between the two destinations, or you can hire a taxi or car with driver if you plan to take a day-trip from Cairo. Once in town, taxis are the most practical way to get around unless you already have a car and driver.

WHERE TO EAT

$ ╳ **George's Restaurant.** This small, dark restaurant, with its English pub–
MIDDLE EASTERN like feel, seats no more than 30 people. Its full bar, an unusual facility in Ismailiya, is decorated with old signs for beer and liquor. The menu combines Egyptian and Greek staples. Dishes such as baba ghanouj and lightly sautéed calamari are hardly extravagant, but they are tasty. Beer and wine are available—or toss back a glass of ouzo. ⊠ *11 Shar'a El Thawra* ☎ *064/391–8327* ⊟ *No credit cards.*

WHERE TO STAY

All hotel reviews have been condensed for this book. Please go to Fodors.com for full reviews of each property.

$$ ⊞ **Mercure Forsan Island Ismailiya.** On the shores of Lake Timsah, the Mercure has a peaceful setting and a solid list of amenities. **Pros:** spacious gardens; lake views from most rooms; the closest thing you'll find to an international-standard hotel in the region; no-smoking rooms. **Cons:** hotel often draws large gatherings, which can disrupt the laid-back ambience; fixtures and fittings are dated and worn. ⊠ *Forsan Island* ☎ *064/391–6316* ⊕ *www.accorhotels.com* ⇨ *137 rooms, 5 suites* ⚲ *In-room: a/c, refrigerator. In-hotel: 2 restaurants, room service, bars, tennis court, pool, beachfront, water sports, laundry service, parking (free)* ⊟ *AE, MC, V* ☉*BP.*

> ### THE HORUS ROAD
>
> Egyptologists have pretty much ignored the northern Sinai in the rush to excavate the rich sites in the Nile Valley. The region was not well settled in ancient times, but it was the location of an arterial transport route, the Horus Road, that linked Egypt to the lands of the Levant and the Hittite Empire, which was a major power player at this time. Both Seti I and Ramses II led armies up this route to do battle with the Hittites. In 2007, digs led by Dr. Mohamed Abdel-Maqsoud uncovered a large fort believed to be used as a staging ground for troops on these campaigns.

6

BUR SA'ID (PORT SAID)

88 km (55 mi) north of Ismailiya.

Seaside Bur Sa'id is a charming and lively town with a decidedly European feel—and fading glamour from the era of the big ocean liners. Much of the architecture is French colonial in style, giving the city a slight resemblance to the New Orleans French Quarter. It is a pleasant town to roam around in and to enjoy the seafront and canal-side promenades—think of it as a less-crowded, more tranquil alternative to Alexandria—but it isn't the kind of place that screams for a stop if you're in Egypt to see antiquities.

The city was founded in 1859 by Khedive Sa'id, in time for the start of excavation. Much of the area is built on sand fills from the digging of the canal. During the Arab-Israeli wars, most of the city was bombed, and parts of it still haven't been restored. At the north end of town, Bur Sa'id's Mediterranean beach has limited appeal, in part because of its unswimmable, polluted waters.

Port Said National Museum. This small museum has an exquisite collection of artifacts spanning the history of Egypt from predynastic times until the 19th-century reign of Muhammed Ali. It's also the only place in Egypt to see finds from the Mamluk port of Teinis. The ground floor is dedicated to pharaonic history, the top floor to Roman, Coptic, and Islamic periods, including artifacts of the Khedival family. ⊠ *3 Shar'a 23 Julio, next to the Sonesta Hotel* ☎ *066/223–7419* ⌷ *£E15* ☉ *Daily 9–5.*

GETTING HERE AND AROUND

Bur Sa'id is linked by fast highway via Ismailiya to Cairo, and the journey time from the capital is around two hours. Air-conditioned bus services ply the route between the three destinations. Once in town, taxis are the most practical way to get around.

OFF THE BEATEN PATH

Port Fouad. Bur Sa'id's sister city is on the other side of the canal, which you can cross by free ferry. You can see large vessels and pretty homes from the slightly malodorous and rundown ferry. Port Fouad was built for the employees of the Suez Canal administration. With its English colonial-style houses and front gardens, it is a stark contrast to Bur Sa'id's bustling port-city/bazaar atmosphere.

WHERE TO EAT

$$$

MIDDLE EASTERN

✕ **Canal Cruise Floating Restaurant.** The perfect way to combine sightseeing and dining, the glass-sided cruise launch glides along sections of the canal, offering arguably the best views of the historical buildings on both banks. You can get either soft drinks or a full buffet meal featuring a mix of Egyptian and international items. Cruises take two hours; call ahead for exact departure times. ⊠ *Port Said, in the port area* ☎ *066/334–5222* ⊕ *www.canalcruiseportsaid.com* ▭ No *credit cards.*

WHERE TO STAY

All hotel reviews have been condensed for this book. Please go to Fodors.com for full reviews of each property.

$$$$

🏨 **Resta Hotel.** The modern decor lacks charm, and the boxy form fails to win any plaudits despite its jaunty yellow accents; nevertheless, this hotel is pleasant, and the sea, the canal, and the city center are all a stone's throw away. **Pros:** canal-view rooms allow you to watch the passage of ships from your window; you can enjoy the city on foot from the hotel; a range of eateries on-site means you don't have to venture into the city in the evening unless you want to. **Cons:** swimming in the sea is not possible because of water quality; you don't get much for your money here. ⊠ *Shar'a Sultan Hussayn* ☎ *066/332–5511* ⊕ *www.restaresorts.com* ◄ *100 rooms 10 suites* ⚙ *In-room: a/c, safe, refrigerator. In-hotel: 4 restaurants, room service, bar, beachfront, water sports, laundry service, Internet terminal, parking (free)* ▭ *AE, MC, V* ⦿ *BP.*

The Western Desert Oases

WORD OF MOUTH

"I did the Bahariya Oasis . . . and I tell you I felt like I was the only tourist there. Particularly the white desert—outstanding, and not another person for miles, just me, my guide and driver. Wonderful experience."

—scotsgirl

WELCOME TO THE WESTERN DESERT OASES

TOP REASONS TO GO

★ **Dune Bashing in Siwa.** Set out in a four-wheel-drive vehicle to explore the towering golden dunes of the Great Sand Sea.

★ **Sunsets in the White Desert.** Watch the color of the chalk columns change and mellow as the sun drops over the desert.

★ **The Bagawat Necropolis.** Peer into early Christian history at this sprawling ancient burial site in Kharga.

★ **The Golden Mummies.** Examine one of the famous gilded faces on display at the Antiquities Inspectorate in Bahariya.

★ **Explore Al-Qasr.** Wander the well-preserved streets of this abandoned medieval town in Dakhla renowned for its Islamic mud-brick architecture.

1 Bahariya Oasis. Rich in history, Bahariya is the location of the Valley of the Golden Mummies. It's a friendly, laid-back place that serves as a staging post for desert safaris.

2 Farafra Oasis. Most travelers breeze through its sleepy main town on their way to the White Desert, an ancient sea floor with fascinating geological formations and fossils.

3 Dakhla Oasis. Dotted with fortified Islamic towns built on Roman foundations, Dakhla is one of the less-visited oases, but travelers may be drawn to the relaxed pace of traditional village life.

4 Kharga Oasis. Although more modernized than other oases, Kharga is justifiably famous for its Christian burial ground at Bagawat, as well as a string of crumbling fortresses that once guarded ancient caravan routes.

5 Siwa Oasis. Isolation has helped Siwa retain its traditional Berber culture. This is the place to go if you want to buy authentic desert crafts and jewelry.

GETTING ORIENTED

Most oasis trips begin in Cairo. If you're driving to Siwa, head toward Alexandria. For the other oases, head toward the Pyramids in Giza. Check that your car is up to the trip, and make sure you have spare parts (especially a working jack), extra gasoline, water for you and the car, maps, guidebooks, and—if available—a good GPS. Always top off your tank when you come across a gas station because they're few and far between.

7

Mediterranean Sea

Marsa Matruh

THE DELTA

Alexandria

Damanhur   al Kubra   5

Tanta

PLATEAU   106

106   Shibin al Kom   11

11

Giza   CAIRO

22

FAIYUM OASIS

al Faiyum   25

Beni Suef

QATTARA DEPRESSION

10

21

Beni Mazar

1

Bawiti

BAHARIYYA OASIS

al Minya

Black Desert

21

10   White Desert

25   Asyut

Qasr al-Farafra

FARAFRA OASIS

GHURD ABU MUHARIK

2

Nile

Abu Minqar

25

10   3   Bashindi (Tomb of Ketinus & Tomb of Sheikh Bashindi)

Qasr al-Dakhla

DAKHLA OASIS   Mut   Qasr al-Kharga

10   KHARGA OASIS

218

Baris   4

25   Qasr al-Dush

WHAT IS AN OASIS?

(above and opposite page) Agriculture at work at the Oasis of Dakhla

You're all familiar with the image—a group of travelers crawling across an infinite desert expanse suddenly encounter a sparkling patch of fertile land—trees! water! All too often their senses have deceived them; it's only a mirage. But here in Egypt, oases are a reality.

An oasis is an isolated stretch of fertile ground and vegetation surrounded by desert. The elevation of this fertile area is low enough that the water table comes close to the surface, causing a natural spring. Because oases offer the only available water, vegetation, and shade in vast expanses of uninhabitable desert, these areas have played a vital role for trade and transportation routes. Caravans traveling across the desert depend on oases for food and water, making them extremely critical and sought-after territories. Historically, once a particular group claimed political or military control over an oasis, they also gained control of trade along that route. So oases have long figured as crossroads or gateways between distant lands. They allowed travelers crossing from Africa into Asia a chance to restock their water and food supplies.

WORD ORIGIN: OASIS

The word *oasis* actually comes from the Greek word όασις, which may have been adopted from the ancient Egyptian, or Demotic. The geographic origin is probably linked to North Africa. The word is also believed to be borrowed from the Coptic word *ouahe*, which means "dwelling area." This makes sense because fertile spots in the desert are natural centers for habitation.

WHAT CAUSES OASES?

On average the Sahara receives only about three inches of rain annually. Since the sand is so porous, much of it seeps right down to the bedrock, which rests a couple hundred feet below the desert surface. Where the elevation is so low from erosion that the water table lays directly below the surface, a spring can ooze water onto the surface. Any seeds that land on that territory are able to sprout and grow roots into the land. What results is an oasis.

The only force capable of radically transforming the desert landscape is the wind. Hence, the larger oases were formed when severe storms, which can carry up to 100 million tons of sand and dust, swept away an even more massive expanse of desert. For example, the Kharga Oasis, located in southern Egypt in the Libyan Desert, stretches for over 100 mi. This oasis was formed when erosion caused the perimeters of a deep depression, about the size of Connecticut, to drop down to the water table.

OASES IN ANCIENT EGYPT

Egypt has six major oases. Five of them were controlled by the ancient Egyptians and exploited for various purposes. Kharga and Bahariyya were used for making wine. Wadi Natrun was crucial because it contained the salt *natron*, a central ingredient in Egyptian embalming. The only oasis not under ancient Egyptian control (not until the 26th Dynasty: 600–500 BC) was Siwa, an isolated settlement in Western Egypt in the Libyan Desert. It was here that Alexander the Great came, as legend has it, by following birds across the desert, confirming his divine personage and legitimizing him as king of Egypt. Many oases, including Siwa, were used as places of exile for political prisoners or criminals during pharaonic and Roman rule. Surrounded by arid desert, these "prisons without bars" needed very little to keep their prisoners from running away.

THE OASES TODAY: THE RISE OF ECOTOURISM

Traveling to oases has become much easier. A journey that once took days or weeks traversing the desert on camelback now requires half a day in a bus. To get off the beaten path of Egypt's annual 10 million tourists who move in bus herds along the predictable course (primarily along the Nile), some visitors prefer to slip away to the desert oases with a small group. There, visitors enjoy meeting the local Bedouins and other tribespeople, dipping into the steaming hot spring waters, camping in the desert under the stars, and sleeping in eco-lodges or traditional huts. This kind of tourism offers a more authentic experience of the natural Egyptian landscape and local people.

Updated by
Cam McGrath

A few hundred years ago the only outsiders interested in Egypt's oases were occasional desert raiders bent on stealing the fruits from the orchards, destroying water supplies, and abducting women. Generation after generation, life followed the seasons with little change. The most exciting events of the year were the autumn date harvest and the subsequent caravans that would assemble and trek to the Nile Valley to take the fruit to market.

In the 1970s, the government built an asphalt ring road joining Bahariya, Farafra, Dakhla, and Kharga—the four southern oases—to the Nile Valley, and the tranquility of thousands of years of isolation met the hustle of 20th-century Egypt. Over the next few years, telephones, electricity, televisions, and elements of the modern world as we know it began to enter the traditional lives of the oases. Since the building of the road, increasing numbers of migrants from other parts of Egypt have settled with the native inhabitants, bringing new working practices and technologies.

Egypt's Western Desert covers over 1 million square miles of southwestern Egypt, half of which is sand. Edged by the fertile soil of the Nile Valley, this desert is part of the vast Sahara belt that runs across northern Africa as far as the Atlantic Ocean. In some places the desert has faulted and dropped, bringing subterranean water nearer the surface. This ancient water has slowly made its way north from central Africa, traveling downhill for centuries as it follows the African continental slope into the Mediterranean Sea. It bubbles to the surface in the depressions, creating the famed oases. Just as it sustains life today, it provided the necessary water for human beings at the dawn of history, but beyond the reassuring verdant and fertile oases lie inhospitable lands that beckon the human spirit.

For millennia the oases accommodated the permanent settlements of farmers and passing traders and nomads. The strict boundaries of today's nation states have all but ended nomadic desert life, and

Bedouins and farmers mostly live together. Oasis dwellers possess qualities that seem to be vanishing from the societies of the modern world: honesty, integrity, respect for tradition and the law, and a high moral code.

There's always something interesting happening the minute you step into the desert. The setting changes constantly as you move from place to place—from mighty golden dunes, to high rocky escarpments, to chalk pillars, to dusty scrubland. You could discover that you're in a field of nummalites (small, coin-like fossils of sea creatures) and desert diamonds (small pieces of quartz that look like diamonds when polished). Man has also left a mark with huge ruins: Roman forts in Kharga, fortified Islamic towns in Dakhla and Siwa, mysterious underground aqueducts, desert monasteries, and Roman watering stations. There are also a handful of pharaonic monuments in the Western Desert, most of which were built during the 26th Dynasty (c. 664–525 BC), when the oases served as an artery to Libya.

PLANNING

WHEN TO GO

The Western Desert is not always as hot as you'd expect, and during the winter months (December–February) the nights can be downright cold. Avoid traveling in March and April, when the *khamaseen* (cyclonic wind) whips up frequent sandstorms, and during the summer months (June–August), when the intense heat can be unbearable. The desert's finest days fall between mid-September and March, with October marking the end of the all-important date harvest.

PLANNING YOUR TIME

Bahariya and Farafra, some 365 km (226 mi) southwest of Cairo, make a good two-day trip. Plan to spend at least one night in Bahariya so you have a full day for the Black Desert and to camp in the White Desert. With another two days, you could add a trip to Siwa or Kharga (and Dakhla). If you choose to go to Siwa, do that first and then drive east across the desert to Bahariya. Allow at least a week to visit all of the Western Desert oases; more time if you intend to fully explore them.

GETTING THERE AND AROUND

AIR TRAVEL

EgyptAir has no scheduled service to any of the oases. However, tourists in a hurry may be able to book a seat on Petroleum Air Services (PAS), which flies prop planes from Cairo every Sunday to Kharga, and every Tuesday to Dakhla. The one-hour flight from Cairo to El-Kharga costs about £E1,000.

Contacts Petroleum Air Services (☎ *02/2392–1674*).

TOP REASONS TO GO

Natural Beauty. The Great Sand Sea to the south and west of the oases is a mass of golden dunes, while the forest of chalk columns in the White Desert (north of Farafra) and the dramatic black and terra-cotta hills of the Black Desert (around Bahariya) are remnants of an ancient seafloor.

Mummies. The vast cache of well-preserved and intricately decorated Greco-Roman era mummies discovered in Bahariya is a major find for Egyptologists.

Hot and Cold Springs. Artesian springs have given the oases their fertility. Cleopatra's Pool in Siwa is the most famous of the springs. However, the most beautiful—and normally less crowded because it's only reachable by a four-wheel drive vehicle—is Bir Wahed.

Camping. Pitch a tent in a dune field or sleep out in the open under a starry sky. Bedouin guides can take you deep into the desert and set up camp while you explore. Bahariya is known for its rugged beauty, Farafra is famous for its surreal landscape, while Siwa has towering dunes.

Desert Forts. The immense Roman fortresses of Nadura, Deir al-Ghanayim, and Qasr al-Labeka north of Al-Kharga protected ancient trade routes. The fortified Islamic settlement of Al-Qasr in Dakhla protected the local population inside its walls.

Off-Roading. Historically, trade caravans plied set routes, but today's desert trips are purely for adventure. Off-road excursions can last a morning, a day, or weeks, and you can travel on foot, by camel, or by four-wheel-drive vehicle. You can easily arrange a desert safari from abroad or Cairo, but you'll save significantly if you make your own way to the desert and make all your plans there. Whatever you do, don't go into the desert unescorted; always have a knowledgeable guide.

BUS TRAVEL

Buses to all oases except Siwa leave Cairo from the Targoman Station (Cairo Gateway) off Shar'a Galaa in Boulaq, and from Moneib Terminal, about 400 meters north of Moneib metro station in Giza. At least four buses travel each day from Moneib Terminal to Bahariya (4½ hours), one of which continues on to Farafra (7 hours) and Dakhla (12 hours). Overnight buses to Kharga (8–10 hours) leave the Targoman Station and travel via the Desert Road that runs parallel to the Nile Valley as far south as Asyut before cutting inland to the oasis. At least one bus a day continues on to Dakhla, about three hours farther on. There is also a morning bus from the Targoman Station to Bahariya.

For Siwa, you must travel first to Alexandria (3 hours) or Marsa Matruh (7 hours) then change. Buses leave Sidi Gabr Station in Alexandria for Siwa (9 hours) several times a day, stopping briefly at Moharrem Bey Terminal and taking on new passengers in Marsa Matruh. Alternatively, you could travel by bus to Marsa Matruh then take a local service taxi to Siwa, a 4-hour trip.

Ticket prices are quite cheap: from Cairo it's about £E30 for Bahariya, £E55 for Farafra, £E75 for Dakhla, and £E70 for Kharga, while from Alexandria it's £E60 for Siwa. Tickets can only be booked one way.

It is advisable to book bus seats a day in advance when traveling from Cairo, while tickets can be purchased on the bus when traveling within or leaving the oases. Super Jet buses are generally more luxurious than those of the other companies and come equipped with air-conditioning and toilets. All buses are subject to frequent breakdowns and delays.

Microbuses also serve the oases and cost about the same as regular buses. They depart from different stops throughout Cairo—such as the Bahariya Café (Shar'a Qadri, off Shar'a Bur Sa'id in Sayida Zaynab), Moneib Terminal, and Ramses Station—typically as soon as they fill up. There are seats for 12, but you can buy two or three seats to give yourself some extra room.

Contacts East Delta Bus Company (☎ 02/2577–8347). **Super Jet** (☎ 02/2579–8181). **Upper Egyptian Bus Company** (☎ 02/2431–6723).

CAR TRAVEL

If you can manage the chaotic streets of Cairo, driving the quiet asphalt roads that connect the Western Desert oases is a breeze. Off-road driving, however, requires a different skill set. Using a guide with local knowledge and desert driving experience is strongly recommended. It is also advisable to avoid driving at night; some drivers don't use their headlights, and those who do will blink them on and off at you as you approach, which is blinding. It's illogical and dangerous, but it's the local custom.

There are gas stations within the oases, but always, always top off your gas tank whenever you see one—the next gas station you encounter may be out of fuel.

CAR RENTAL

Good car-rental agencies in Cairo offer a variety of vehicles. These rental companies have offices in all major hotels throughout Egypt and outlets in major cities, but have no representation in the oases. To rent a car, you must have an International Driver's License. Note that driving off-road may violate the terms of your rental car contract.

OFF-ROAD EXPLORING

If you want to do some off-road exploration, you can rent a four-wheel-drive vehicle to drive to the desert, or come by bus or car and book a four-wheel-drive tour through many of the hotels or restaurants in the oases. If you do travel into the desert with your own four-wheel-drive vehicle, don't go off-road without a second vehicle and a guide. Between getting stuck and getting lost, the opportunities for fatal errors are abundant. If you're determined to sit behind the wheel yourself, you'll need to take some instruction and prove yourself competent before a desert tour agency will agree to put a guide in your vehicle or let your vehicle tag along on its tours. If in doubt, hire a driver and enjoy the adventure from the passenger seat.

Police permission is required to visit some of the more isolated destinations or to camp overnight in the desert (though this rule is often overlooked in the White Desert). Some destinations are off-limits because they are controlled by the Egyptian military. Tourist information offices can advise on the situation, but you'll either have to visit local authorities yourself or enlist a tour operator to carry out the paperwork ahead of your trip. Most permits can be obtained in less than a day, but permits to remote areas such as Gilf Kebir and Jebel Uwaynat can take up to six weeks.

TAXI TRAVEL

There are no taxis in Bahariya, Farafra, or Siwa, though Siwa has small, canopied donkey carts driven by teenage boys. Taxis ply the roads of Kharga's capital, and you may spot a few in Dakhla. Most are available for hire by the day.

ESSENTIALS

INTERNET

Internet access is still rare in the oases, even in hotels. You may find a couple of small Internet cafés in each town, but most are one-machine affairs in the backs of coffee shops. Many connections are still dial-up, so systems are slow and unreliable. Prices are around £E10 to £E15 for one hour.

MONEY MATTERS

Cash is king in the oases. There is at least one bank with an ATM in every oasis except Farafra, though the ATMs may refuse foreign cards or simply be out of order. Exchange services are nonexistent outside hotels, which may be willing to change your money or accept foreign currency in payment. The best advice is to change money in Cairo and bring plenty of Egyptian pounds with you.

RESTAURANTS

You can expect to dine on wholesome fare—mostly grilled chicken, vegetable stews, rice, and *shorbet lisan al-asfour* ("bird-tongue" pasta soup). Dining is generally alfresco, because the few restaurants that do exist are street-side affairs. Alcohol isn't usually available except at hotel restaurants. Finish off with tea made the Bedouin way.

Fresh fruit and vegetables from the local stands are perfectly safe, though you should wash everything in bottled water. Don't miss out on oasis dates or Siwa's olive oil, which is rich and heady—gourmet without trying to be. Dates come in a number of varieties: sweet, firm, and yellow; sweet, mushy, and dark brown; or bitter, crunchy, and red. Try them all.

HOTELS

There is a range of accommodations in the desert, from simple chalets and eco-camps to traditionally styled mud-brick hotels. Prices are generally lower than in the Nile Valley. Some hotels have air-conditioning, but you'll pay a premium for it. For much of the year a fan is sufficient to cool your room at night. In winter you may need blankets.

Your hotel experience will depend heavily on how fully booked the property is. Facilities are better maintained and restaurant service tends to improve when a large tour group checks in. On the other hand, you may enjoy the tranquility of having the grounds to yourself once they've gone. Although most hotels stay open throughout the year, May through September is the summer low season and a time for renovations and maintenance. Since restaurants are not numerous, most hotels offer a meal plan; some require it.

All hotel reviews have been condensed for this book. Please go to Fodors.com for full reviews of each property.

WHAT IT COSTS IN EGYPTIAN POUNDS, U.S. DOLLARS, AND EUROS			
$	**$$**	**$$$**	**$$$$**
Restaurants	under £E50	£E50–£E100	£E100–£E150	over £E150
Hotels in Dollars	under $70	$70–$130	$130–$200	over $200
Hotels in Euros	under €45	€45–€80	€80–€130	over €130

Restaurant prices are per person for a main course at dinner. Hotel prices are for a double room in high season, excluding 10% tax and service charges (usually 10%).

TOUR OPTIONS

It's possible to arrange multiday sightseeing tours to the oases that include transportation, accommodation, meals, and desert tours. Expect to pay about $100 to $150 per person a day when booking from Cairo or abroad. Tours organized locally in the oases cost much less—about $50 per person a day—but then you have to make your own way out to the oases.

Contacts Aegyptus Intertravel (✉ 3 Shar'a Lotfy al-Sayed, 'Abbasiya, Cairo ☎ 02/2682–4747 ⊕ www.aegyptus.com). **Cairo International Tours** (✉ 21 Shar'a Mokhtar Said, Heliopolis, Cairo ☎ 02/2291–1491 ⊕ www.cit-eg.com). **Marzouk Desert Cruiser** (✉ 1 Maydan Ibn Sandar, Heliopolis, Cairo ☎ 02/258–8083 ⊕ www.marzouk-dc.com). **Memphis Tours** (✉ Qorh Ibn Sherik, Shar'a Morad, Giza, Cairo ☎ 02/3571–6050 ⊕ www.memphistours.com). **Minamar Hotels and Tours** (✉ Building 28, Shar'a 269, Ma'adi, Cairo ☎ 02/2517–3803 ⊕ www.minamar.com). **Oasis Expeditions** (✉ 6 Shar'a 231, Ma'adi, Cairo ☎ 02/2516–5706 ⊕ www.oasisexpeditions.com). **Pan Arab Tours** (✉ Saudi Egyptian Building 5, Shar'a al-Nozha, Heliopolis, Cairo ☎ 02/2418–4409 ⊕ www.panarabtours.com). **Suneast Tours** (✉ Shar'a al-Nasr, Nasr City, Cairo ☎ 02/2415–3687 ⊕ www.suneasttours.com).

VISITOR INFORMATION

Apart from tiny Farafra, all oases have tourist information offices. All are usually open Saturday through Thursday from 8 to 2, often with additional evening hours; sometimes they're open Friday. They can help with hotels, tours, transportation, emergencies, and most anything else. You may need to ask around to find someone who speaks English.

BAHARIYA OASIS

Ancient travelers had to cross a dune belt several miles wide (and hundreds of miles long) to reach the Bahariya Oasis from the Nile Valley. These days you glide easily along the asphalt road at high speed, only slowing down to enjoy the descent that cuts through the cliffs and leads into the oasis. At this point, you must slow down in other ways, too, as you adjust to the rural way of life. Here, donkeys outnumber cars, and time is related not by the clock but according to the five daily prayers. The local inhabitants, while accustomed to seeing tourists, maintain strong traditional values that emphasize loyalty, integrity and hospitality.

Bahariya is the smallest of the four southern oases, covering about 1,200 square km (460 square mi). Its northern end, where most people live, is replete with springs, orchards, and ancient ruins—as well as a rich collection of fossils dating back to the Late Cretaceous Era. Heading south from the oasis capital, Bawiti, the relatively abundant greenery yields to the dramatic scorched earth vistas of the Black Desert.

Bahariya is deceptively rich in history. Pharaonic, Greek, Roman, and Coptic antiquities are spread across the oasis. Until recently, however, many of these sights were off-limits to the public. The situation started to change in the late 1990s after the discovery of the Valley of the Golden Mummies, one of the largest caches of mummies ever found in Egypt. Renewed interest in the archaeological heritage of the oasis has resulted in further discoveries, including the tombs that had been lost beneath sand and houses.

BAWITI

About 365 km (226 mi) southwest of Giza, 180 km (112 mi) northeast of Qasr al-Farafra.

In Bawiti, anybody's business is everybody's business. Donkeys, vegetables, and trucks are inspected and haggled over passionately in this small, bustling village while spectators sitting at the local cafés throw in their opinions for the crowd's entertainment. The town is the capital of Bahariya, having usurped the position of the older capital, Al-Qasr, a few generations ago. These days the two communities are blended together. The older village sections go back hundreds of years and are now being abandoned for newer homes.

Don't be discouraged by Bawiti's dusty main drag; the town's back streets still maintain their charm. Here you will find crumbling old houses, dozens of vintage jeeps, pharaonic and Islamic tombs, and the remains of an ancient *manafis* (underground aqueduct) that fell into disuse with the arrival of motorized water pumps.

WHAT TO SEE

★ **Antiquities Office.** The local antiquities office sells a combination ticket that includes admission to the five major sights—the Mummy Exhibit, the Tombs of Zed Amun Ef Ankh and Bannentiu, the Tomb of Amenhotep Huy, the Temple of Alexander the Great, and the Temple of Ain al-Muftillah.

The **Mummy Exhibit** at the Antiquities Office displays some of the finds from the Valley of the Golden Mummies including several gilded mummies. In a typically provincial style, the Greco-Roman mummies are plastered, gilded, and decorated with scenes from the underworld. These mummies were not prepared in the same way as those in the Valley of the Kings, resulting in some degradation. The heat and humidity

The Golden Mummies

In 1996, an Egyptian antiquities guard on a donkey stumbled into a hole in the ground, accidentally discovering the first of a series of important Greco-Roman era mummies (from the 4th century BC to early 4th century AD). The uncovered mummies were in excellent condition, providing archaeologists with a rich seam of evidence and information about life in the waning days of ancient Egyptian religious beliefs and practices. Particularly striking are the funerary masks of the mummies. Many have gilded faces—which inspired the popular name of the site, Valley of the Golden Mummies—with gold paint covering their face. Others have flesh-color stucco masks, but all were sculpted to show an image of the person during life, with painted hair and differing facial expressions. Some masks were made from casts of the individuals. The finest examples have gilded fingernails and toenails added to the bodies after mummification. They are encased in highly ornate sycamore-wood sarcophagi, usually depicting scenes from the Egyptian *Book of the Dead*. Archaeologists are particularly excited about studying the details of the mummification process and funerary rituals and how they differ from those used in earlier periods.

in the rather makeshift museum is also not helping to preserve them either. ⊠ *Up the hill from the main street, near the hospital, Bawiti* ☎ *02/3847–1900* ✒ *Combination ticket for Mummy Exhibit, the Tombs of Zed Amun Ef Ankh and Bannentiu, the Tomb of Amenhotep Huy, the Temple of Alexander the Great, and the Temple of Ain al-Muftillah £E45* ☉ *Antiquities Office Sat.–Thurs. 8–5; Mummies Exhibit Sat.–Thurs. 9–4.*

★ **Black Desert.** South of Bawiti lies the Black Desert, a Martian landscape of orange sand and black peaks formed by a string of ancient volcanoes. Off-road travel is possible for short distances in a regular car, but a four-wheel-drive vehicle is required to climb the sand dunes and explore at length; so is a guide, who can direct you to the desert's less obvious sights. Visitors can climb one of the scorched peaks, or arrange a trip to dunes where some outfitters offer sand surfing.

Toward the southern end of the oasis, the Black Desert yields to a series of springs that provide enough water for small-scale agriculture projects, including an experimental cactus farm, and tiny frontier settlements. ⊠ *About 25 km (16 mi) south of Bawiti, on road to Farafra Oasis.*

Oasis Heritage Museum. Local artist Mahmoud Eid opened the museum to display his interesting and extensive works of art, which depict scenes of traditional oasis life. The large castlelike mud-brick structure is filled with clay sculptures, sand paintings, and traditional objects of rural life. Village scenes, including a barber performing a circumcision, are expressed in clay. Most of the works have been relocated from Mahmoud's old studio and museum in Bawiti, which can also be visited upon request. The museum is usually locked, so call for an appointment or check with Camel Camp next door. ⊠ *On the Cairo road, 1 km*

7

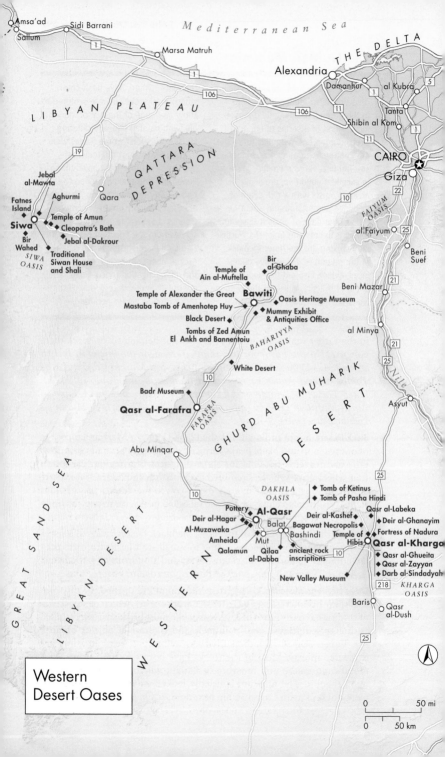

Western
Desert Oases

Black Desert near Bahariya

(¾ mi) east of Bawiti ☎ 012/710–7965 ✉ Free; donations welcome
🕑 Hours vary.

Temple of Ain al-Muftillah. Once thought to be four separate chapels, this temple was built during the 26th Dynasty by the governor of the oasis (his tomb was among those uncovered in the Valley of the Golden Mummies); it was expanded over the centuries. The sandstone complex has well-preserved colorful bas-reliefs and four sanctuaries dedicated to, among others, Horus and Bes. One panel depicts 12 of the panoply of Egyptian gods, a who's who of the ancient deities. The surrounding extensive mud-brick ruins are storerooms and living quarters. The high ground behind the temple provides a panoramic view of the oasis.
✉ 3 km (2 mi) west of Bawiti, reached from a turnoff on the Siwa Rd.
☎ No phone ✉ £E45, combination ticket for all local archaeological sites 🕑 Daily 8–5.

Temple of Alexander the Great. Surrounding this desolate ruin made of sandstone are more ruins of mud-brick storerooms and living quarters. The sanctuary contains the eroded reliefs of Alexander the Great depicted in pharaonic garb. His face and cartouche have, unfortunately, been obliterated by the elements. ✉ 5 km (3 mi) southwest of Bawiti ✛ Drive west on the Siwa road, turn left onto a dirt track after Ahmed Safari Camp ☎ No phone ✉ £E45, combination ticket for all local archaeological sites 🕑 Daily 8–5.

Tomb of Amenhotep Huy. If you've seen the tombs of Saqqara or Luxor, this one is likely to disappoint; the few reliefs are in very poor condition, and you will need a car (preferably a guide) to find the tomb. Still, if you have come all the way to the oasis, it is usually included on guided tours. ⊠ *3 km (2 mi) west of Bawiti* 🕾 *No phone* 🎫 *£E45, combination ticket for all local archaeological sites* ☉ *Daily 8–5.*

★ **Tombs of Zed Amun Ef Ankh and Bannentiu.** These 26th-Dynasty tombs are proof that in ancient Egypt if you had enough wealth you could buy eternity. The wealthy merchant and his son, who appear to have made their fortunes in the wine trade, are interred in tombs with all the hallmarks of royal burials. The style is charming and informal, and the colors are vivid. The Tomb of Zed Amun Ef Ankh has the unique feature of painted papyrus columns, an element normally found only in temples. The grander tomb of his son, Bannentiu, elaborately depicts scenes from the *Book of the Dead* including the solar barque traveling to the underworld. ⚠ **The descent to the tombs is difficult because of the steep, narrow stairs.** ⊠ *Qarat Qasr Selim, down the hill from the Antiquities Office, Bawiti* 🕾 *No phone* 🎫 *£E45, combination ticket for all local archaeological sites* ☉ *Sat.–Thurs. 8–5.*

WHERE TO EAT

Locals rarely eat out, so apart from the hotel restaurants, the few options are thinly spread along the main road. Don't wait too late for dinner either, as you might find all kitchens closed.

$ ✕ **Popular Restaurant.** Something of an institution, this street-side café
MIDDLE EASTERN has been serving traditional food to locals and foreigners for nearly 30 years. Its galabiyya-clad owner, the irascible Bayoumi, spills wrath onto locals and sweet talks the foreigners, all in the same breath. Don't expect to walk past without him at least cooing or blasting a whistle. His charm compensates for the basic and dirty surroundings. You can dine alfresco at a long table exposed to the safari touts, or semiprivately indoors behind a blue lattice. There's no menu, so ask for the price in advance to avoid surprises. One special is prepared each day. A typical meal includes boiled meat or grilled chicken, rice, potatoes or vegetable stew, soup, bread, and tea. ⊠ *Center of town, near the tourist office, Bawiti* 🕾 *No phone* 🖃 *No credit cards.*

$ ✕ **Rashed Restaurant.** A popular lunch stop for safari groups by day, this
MIDDLE EASTERN restaurant is often transformed into a shisha (hookah) café packed with locals watching football matches by night. There's seating indoors, but the shaded, ceramic-tiled terrace is really the place to be. The grilled chicken here is possibly the best in town and comes with the usual side dishes as well as some tasty local olives. It sometimes has dessert, too. ⊠ *On the main road, opposite the old Oasis Heritage Museum, Bawiti* 🕾 *02/384–7237* 🖃 *No credit cards.*

WHERE TO STAY

Bawiti offers a decent choice of lodging options, with new properties opening all the time. Apart from the hotels, there are also a number of "safari camps" just outside town with huts or rooms around a courtyard. Their basic facilities might suffice for a night in a pinch, but they are really little more than holding pens for those signed up for desert safaris.

All hotel reviews have been condensed for this book. Please go to Fodors.com for full reviews of each property.

$ 🏠 **El-Beshmo Lodge.** Occupying a peaceful spot at the mouth of a gorge and overlooking the palm groves, this hotel is named after Bawiti's central hot spring, which feeds its tiny pool. **Pros:** the courtyard is a great place for conversations with fellow travelers, as it is cool in summer and sheltered from the wind in winter; the restaurant serves simple but delicious local cuisine; the hotel's (murky, but therapeutic) plunge pool is very private. **Cons:** room furnishings and paint need some attention (everything is clean but worn); cracks in some walls at the back of the property. ⊠ *Al-Beshmo Springs, Al Qasr* ☎ *02/3847–3500* ⊕ *www. beshmolodge.com* ⊅ *25 rooms*

> **FLIES AND MOZZIES**
>
> Egypt's oases have a reputation for the most aggressive flies and mosquitoes in the country. Any outdoor location will attract flies during the day, and this can make dining alfresco or sunbathing by a pool a lot less appealing than it sounds. Once the sun sets, the mosquitoes come out in force. And unlike their Nile Valley brethren, oasis mosquitoes prefer biting over buzzing. Watch out for rooms adjacent to palm groves or springs, or with high, dark ceilings that make the mozzies hard to spot or swat.

⚐ *In-room: a/c (some), no phone, refrigerator (some), no TV. In-hotel: restaurant, pool, parking (free)* ⊙ *CP* ⊟ *No credit cards.*

$$ 🏠 **Palm Village Hotel.** The tranquil desert setting and spacious interior spaces have made this midpriced hotel a favorite of visiting groups of archaeologists and paleontologists. **Pros:** new rooms are spacious with big bathrooms and modern styling; tranquil desert setting. **Cons:** frequent power cuts; no alcohol or shisha available; too far out of town to walk. ⊠ *Agouz village, 6 km (4 mi) northeast of Bawiti and reached by taking a left turn off the Cairo road just after the Oasis Heritage Museum* ☎ *02/3849–6272* ⊅ *40 rooms* ⚐ *In-room: a/c, phone, refrigerator (some). In-hotel: restaurant, parking (free)* ⊟ *No credit cards* ⊙ *MAP.*

$$$ 🏠 **Qasr El Bawity Hotel.** This stone complex makes a dramatic impression,
★ rising up the hillside like an Islamic citadel. **Pros:** traditional styling that's well crafted; the restaurant serves excellent *tagines* (traditional stews); there's a small children's play area. **Cons:** no a/c in the standard rooms, though fans and domed ceilings help to keep the air cool; expensive compared to other area accommodations. ⊠ *Bawiti* ☎ *012/258–2586; 02/2516–8407 Cairo booking office* ⊕ *www.qasrelbawity.com* ⊅ *24 rooms, 4 suites* ⚐ *In-room: no a/c (some), no phone, no TV* ⊟ *No credit cards* ⊙ *MAP.*

$$ 🏠 **Sands Baharia.** Spacious grounds and a remote location make this
★ beautifully designed property a treat for couples or small groups who want to experience the silence and solitude of the desert. **Pros:** natural surroundings and (usually) unearthly silence; the indoor restaurant serves up delicious and varied meals using organic produce from the hotel's gardens; the scent of jasmine from the surrounding fields perfumes the night air. **Cons:** the silence can be deafening during low occupancy; far from town and sights. ⊠ *6 km (4 mi) west of town, Bawiti* ☎ *02/3749–0167* ⊕ *www.sandslodges.com* ⊅ *11 rooms, 3 suites*

7

Qasr El Bawity Hotel

⚴ *In-room: a/c (some), no phone, no TV. In-hotel: restaurant, bar, pool, parking (free)* ⏁❙ *MAP* ⊟ *No credit cards.*

$ 🏨 **Western Desert Hotel.** Smack-dab in the middle of Bawiti, this hotel is an obvious choice for anyone who might be arriving late at night or who doesn't like to feel too far removed from civilization. **Pros:** convenient location; a relaxing rooftop garden catches evening breezes and offers interesting views of the rooftops below and the desert beyond. **Cons:** soulless lobby and restaurant; touts wait near entrance. ✉ *Center of town, near the tourist office, Bawiti* ☎ *02/3847–1600* ⊕ *www.westerndeserthotel.com* 🛏 *52 rooms, 3 suites* ⚴ *In-room: a/c (some), no phone, refrigerator. In-hotel: restaurant, Internet terminal* ⏁❙ *CP* ⊟ *No credit cards.*

NIGHTLIFE AND THE ARTS

Tour leaders often arrange evening entertainment, but if you're traveling on your own, nightlife options can look pretty bleak in the desert. Apart from joining the locals watching TV in the cafés, there's really not much to do. One thing you should not miss, however, is a live Bedouin music performance. The intense emotions and romantic longings of the desert dwellers are expressed nowhere better than in their music. The song of the *simsimeya* (Egyptian lyre), the quick beat of the *tabla* (drum), and the drone of the *mizmar* (double-reed flute) will transport you.

★ **Bedouin Rock Tent.** Opposite the Qasr El Bawity Hotel, you'll find nightly performances of Bedouin music in this tent starting around 9 PM. Most of the hotels can arrange transport here, or they can book one of a dozen or so freelance musicians to come perform at your hotel or campsite. ✉ *Opposite the Qasr El Bawity Hotel, Bawiti* ☎ *012/255–6854.*

CLOSE UP

Hot and Cold Springs

Springs provide the water for drinking and to irrigate fields in this otherwise arid environment. They are also a pleasure to enjoy for bathing or therapeutic care. There are hundreds of springs in the Western Desert, but don't get any romantic notions—most are simply pipes that gush water into a cement tank in the open air. That said, in some parts of the world people pay small fortunes for the medicinal effects of hot and cold springs. Here, they're free.

Each spring has its own properties: some are hot, some are cold, some have a sulfurous odor, and others leave a rusty residue that stains clothes. Before going to any spring, ask locals what to expect. Women should swim with their arms and legs covered if local people are around. ⚠ People with high blood pressure or heart conditions, and pregnant women, should avoid the hotter springs.

SPORTS AND THE OUTDOORS
DESERT TOURS

Bawiti is teeming with desert safari operators, so you won't have to go far to find them; more likely, they'll find you. Touts and guides await arriving buses and service taxis from Cairo, funneling passengers into four-wheel-drive vehicles that spirit them off to the desert or "safari camps" on the edge of town. The competition is fierce and prices negotiable.

A good starting point is Bawiti's Tourist Information Office, where Mohamed 'Abd al-Qader (☏ *012/373–6567*) can explain your tour options and help with pricing. Expect him to plug his own crew, who run vanilla half-day tours to the desert sites near Bawiti for £E100 per vehicle. A standard overnight trip to the White Desert (including stops in the Black Desert, Al-Hayez, Crystal Mountain, and Al-Agabat) runs £E700 a vehicle (maximum four people) plus park fees. For an extra £E100, the driver will drop you off in Qasr al-Farafra the following morning.

Of course, you're free to choose from the dozens of other operators. The most reliable are those attached to established hotels and safari companies. While eager freelancers might beat them on price, their competence and accountability become increasingly important the further off the beaten path you go. An overnight trip to the White Desert is easily managed, but inexperience will become obvious—and possibly dangerous—on longer excursions.

Whichever outfit you select, ensure that the four-wheel-drive vehicles are in good condition and that you have adequate water in case of a breakdown. All off-road trips should include at least one extra support vehicle to carry fuel, supplies, and spares.

Another way to experience the desert is to travel on foot or by camel. Overnight and multiday treks can be organized independently, or in conjunction with jeep safaris. The going rate on camel safaris at press was £E100 to £E120 per person per day.

Desert Ship Safari. This company is a small outfit run by desert guru Yahia Kandil, who arranges everything from one-day camel safaris to weeks-long jeep trips to the Gilf Kibeer. His prices are hard to beat, and the quality is tops. ⊠ *Agouz village, Bawiti* ☎ *02/3849–6754 or 012/321–6790* ⊕ *www.desertshipsafari.com.*

El Beshmo Lodge. This lodge is the home of veteran guide Lotfi 'Abd al-Seed, whose son Ahmed now leads excursions as far afield as the Gilf Kibeer with consistently good reviews. ⊠ *Al-Beshmo Springs, Al Qasr* ☎ *02/3847–3500* ⊕ *www.beshmolodge.com.*

Western Desert Hotel. The hotel has a fleet of off-road vehicles and arranges budget-oriented trips to the Black and White deserts. It also has sandboards, which you can use to surf the towering dunes once there. ⊠ *Center of town, just off main street, Bawiti* ☎ *02/3847–1600* ⊕ *www.westerndeserthotel.com.*

White Desert Tours. This tour company is run by German transplant Peter Wirth, who uses reputable local guides for everything from laid-back day trips to adrenalin-filled desert excursions. His reputation is sterling. ⊠ *International Hot Spring Hotel, entrance just outside town on the road to Cairo, Bawiti* ☎ *02/3847–3014* ⊕ *www.whitedeserttours.com.*

HORSEBACK RIDING

Palm Village Hotel. This hotel has stables with about a dozen horses to rent at £E80 per hour (Oct.–Apr. only), but you need to be an experienced rider since there's no instruction for beginners. There are no riding helmets available, either. ⊠ *Agouz village, 6 km (4 mi) northeast of Bawiti and reached by taking a left turn off the Cairo road just after the Oasis Heritage Museum* ☎ *02/3849–6272.*

BIR AL-GHABA

15 km (9 mi) west of Bawiti.

The "forest spring" is a hot spring traditionally reserved for visitors. It lies in a small forest of eucalyptus trees, reached by a picturesque drive—or hike—from Bawiti. The rough track passes oasis gardens where farmers plant, grow, and harvest a variety of crops interspersed with fruit trees.

On the way to Bir al-Ghaba, about 7 km (4½ mi) from Bahariya is Bir al-Mattar, a tepid spring with a slightly sulfurous odor; it's on the left of the road and is a great place for a quick dip. After covering more desert, you enter a garden and, suddenly, Bir al-Ghaba appears. Camping is welcome here, and several primitive "camps" offer basic accommodation in thatched huts with no electricity. Bring your own food and plenty of bug repellant if you intend to overnight here.

FARAFRA OASIS

Farafra is the least populated of the four southern oasis, but perhaps the most geologically diverse, combining elements of Bahariya to the north, and Dakhla to the south—plus a few of its own. Its most celebrated attraction, the White Desert, is a plain of surreal, wind-scoured chalk monoliths that capture the imagination. The oasis also boasts several hot springs, dune fields, and a small lake that attracts migratory birds.

In pharaonic times Farafra was known as ta-iht, the "Land of the Cow." Today, agriculture still dominates the local economy and only a handful of people are involved in tourism. As a result, there are few touts, and few tourist facilities, but plenty of genuine smiles.

QASR AL-FARAFRA

About 180 km (112 mi) southwest of Bawiti; 310 km (192 mi) north-east of Mut.

Two decades ago Qasr al-Farafra had a frontier atmosphere, and only a few timid one-story buildings spilled down from the fortress hill to meet the sparse traffic on the Cairo road. These days, the village has spread to both sides of the road. The discovery of water has been changing the area's demographics, with scores of Egyptians from the Nile Valley homesteading in the oasis (20,000 at the last count). The increase in population has helped to bring some measure of prosperity—enough to expand Qasr al-Farafra—but despite this rapid growth, it remains one of the most enchanting places in the desert. Sitting in the village is an experience in itself because the locals enjoy mingling with the travelers who come through (rarely are there more than 20 travelers here at a time).

The best way to savor the village and the surrounding desert is by walking. A meander through the maze of alleys in Qasr al-Farafra still gives you a sense of oasis life before the road linked Farafra to the rest of Egypt: old men gather and debate in front of the mosque, children play in the street, families leave their doors open and welcome in passersby for tea. The palm groves behind the town are replete with date palms, as well as olive and fruit trees. Visitors are welcome to wander the paths, but should not enter fenced areas uninvited.

★ **Badr Museum.** The small, constantly evolving museum, which was built from mud-bricks by the local artist Badr 'Abd al-Moghny, is a multi-level castle of the imagination, where exterior and interior staircases and bridges connect terraces and courtyards to exhibition rooms. Badr's clay sculptures and paintings of the Farafra people, the desert, and his surreal dreams are displayed here. Carvings of Arabic calligraphy and desert scenes also adorn the walls. Around the building Badr is creating an almost grotesque-looking minidesert, with tree trunks that resemble camels and stones fashioned to resemble old women. The museum doesn't have set hours; if it's closed, you can ask about the artist's whereabouts at the nearby Nice Time Coffee Shop. ⊠ *Next to the school, between the main road and El Waha Hotel, Qasr al-Farafra* ☎ *092/751–0091* 🖙 *Free; donations welcome* ☉ *Hours vary.*

WHERE TO EAT AND STAY

Tiny Qasr al-Farafra is not a place known for its options, but you can be assured of finding a filling meal and comfortable night's sleep. Aside from the hotel restaurant at the Badawiya Hotel, a string of flyblown eateries lines the road running from the main road to the old mosque.

The lower batch caters mainly to truck drivers, while farther up the hill you'll find a few more accustomed to tourists. They're not much to look at, but the food is inexpensive and filling.

All hotel reviews have been condensed for this book. Please go to Fodors.com for full reviews of each property.

$–$$
MIDDLE EASTERN

✕ **Badawiya Restaurant.** Offering a welcome change from the usual grilled chicken, this large, air-conditioned dining hall prepares delicious and varied meals. There's a set menu each night with meat or chicken, as well as traditional dishes and fresh bread. Ingredients are sourced in the oasis and the surrounding area. Dinner guests can eat on the terrace during the warmer months, and the chef sometimes fires up the barbeque. ✉ *Shar'a Jamal 'Abd al-Nasir, at the northern entrance to town, Qasr al-Farafra* ☎ *092/751–1060* ⊕ *www.badawiya.com* ▭ *No credit cards.*

$
★

🏨 **Badawiya Hotel.** Travelers often arrive in Qasr al-Farafra with low expectations, which makes this attractive and comfortable locally owned hotel just north of town a pleasant surprise. **Pros:** nice styling throughout; suites are particularly well appointed and a good value for the money; great pool. **Cons:** only the suites are air-conditioned. ✉ *Shar'a Jamal 'Abd al-Nasir, at northern entrance to town, Qasr al-Farafra* ☎ *092/751–1060; 02/2526–0994 Cairo booking office* ⊕ *www. badawiya.com* ⤴ *20 rooms, 13 suites* ⚲ *In-room: a/c (some), refrigerator (some), no TV. In-hotel: restaurant, pool, parking (free)* ▭ *No credit cards* ⑩ *BP.*

WHITE DESERT

35 km (22 mi) north of Qasr al-Farafra.

★   The magical scenery of the White Desert in the northern portion of the Farafra depression enchants travelers and stirs the imagination. The desert here appears dusted in a layer of snow with a forest of chalk monoliths rising from the ground, their wind-sculpted forms resembling mushrooms, camels, birds, whales, and elephants. The outcroppings are all that is left of an ancient seafloor, its thick layer of calcified deposits scoured and shaped by the elements.

The desert extends from the west of the oasis, where a forest of inselbergs (chalk monoliths) rise up from the ground, across the highway to the so-called "Old" and "New" White Desert, where safari operators prefer to camp. The surreal landscape is best viewed at sunset when the monoliths turn shades of orange, pink, and violet in the dimming light. The show continues into the night as the entire desert shimmers in the pale light of the moon, its chalk columns rising above a snowy field.

For this reason, many travelers enjoy camping in the White Desert, which was declared a national park in 2002. Tours can be arranged easily in Cairo, Qasr al-Farafra, or Bawiti—the latter offering the best prices. If you do it on your own, you'll need to get permission from the police in either Farafra or Baharia. All visitors must pay $5 park entry fee and £E10 to camp overnight.

White Desert

Much of the White Desert is accessible by car or motorcycle, though a four-wheel-drive vehicle is required to reach the more remote sections. Be sure to bring food, fuel, sleeping bags, and water, and then just pick a spot. Supplies, including warm camel-hair blankets, are available in Bawiti or Qasr al-Farafra.

DESERT TOURS

There is less competition among safari operators in Farafra than in Bahariya, so it is fortunate that the two main outfitters offer rock-solid service.

TOUR OPERATORS

Aquasun. Owned by desert rally driver Hisham Nessim, the company arranges tours and has its own lodging at Bir Sitta, 6 km (4 mi) west of town. It definitely has the upper hand on longer excursions to the Great Sand Sea and Gilf Kebir, though these should be arranged well in advance to give them time to secure the necessary permits. ⊠ *Bir Sitta* ☎ *010/667–8099.*

Badawiya Expedition Travel. The tour-operator arm of the Badawiya Hotel offers pricey day trips to the local sites, including Bir Sitta, Lake Abu Nos, and a camel farm for about £E1,500 per vehicle (maximum four passengers). Sunset trips to the White Desert cost £E700 per vehicle including park fees, while an overnight stay can run up a £E1,500 tab. ⊠ *Shar'a Jamal 'Abd al-Nasir, next to the post office, Qasr al-Farafra* ☎ *092/751–1163* ⊕ *www.badawiya.com.*

DAKHLA OASIS

Dakhla's rich patchwork of shifting yellow dunes, red earth, green
farmland, and ancient mud-brick
villages is like a mirage against the
backdrop of pink and white cliffs
that rise up sharply to shelter the
oasis. This was once a breadbas-
ket for the Roman Empire, and its
fields and orchards still flourish on
the iron-rich soil.

DAKHLA HATS

Look out for the hats worn by
farmers in the countryside around
Dakhla. These round, narrow-
brimmed caps made of soft, handwoven straw with a colored cotton
trim are unique to the oasis.

A number of significant sites from antiquity are spread across the oasis,
including the restored Roman-era Temple of Deir al-Hagar, the ruins
of a large Roman settlement called Amheida, and the tombs of several Old Kingdom governors. Yet Dakhla is better known for its fortified Islamic towns, most notably Al-Qasr and Balat, which are built
on Roman foundations and probably sit atop pharaonic settlements.
There's strong evidence that the oasis has been inhabited continually
since Neolithic times.

MUT

*About 310 km (192 mi) southeast of Qasr al-Farafra; 205 km (127 mi)
west of Al-Kharga.*

Mut (pronounced *moot*), Dakhla's capital, is a likeable place if you get
beyond the ugly rows of low-rise residential tenements that line its main
streets. The town's old Islamic quarter, partially obscured by modern
buildings, is a fascinating warren of dark alleyways and crumbling
mud-brick houses. At least 1,500 people still live in the district, going
about their daily routine.

Mut is comprised of only a half-dozen main streets, but its lack of public
transport means that without a car you could be doing a lot of walking.
The wide avenues and "countdown" traffic lights suggest a chronic traffic problem, but for most of the day the town's streets are eerily empty.

For travel within the oasis there are service taxi stations at Maydan Tahrir and—less conveniently—about 1½ km (1 mi) east near the hospital.
Buses and service taxis also pick up passengers at Maydan Jama'a, the
sleepy square that was once the town's center.

Mut al-Kharab. A red mound beyond the cemetery at the southwest corner of town marks the remains of an ancient city dedicated to the goddess Mut, consort of Amun. There's not much to see, but if you climb
up to the top at sunset, you'll be rewarded with views of verdant fields,
golden dunes, and farmers racing home on their donkey carts. ⊠ *Just
west of Shar'a al-Jomhuriya, Mut.*

**NEED A
BREAK?**

El Forsan Hotel. If you're looking for a place to eat in the center of town, a
former cruise-boat chef whips up decent, hearty meals here. ⊠ *Near Maydan Jama'a, Mut* ☎ *092/782–1343.* Service can be slow.

The old Islamic quarter of the desert town of Mut in Dakhla

WHERE TO EAT

The best of Mut's restaurants are spread out along the road to Al-Qasr, just west of Maydan Tahrir. That's good news if you're staying on this strip, but it could mean a fair hike across town if you're not and don't have a car. The handful of places with English signs and small gardens target tourists, but the quality is often better at the simple roast chicken shacks, whose signs are only in Arabic. Meals are invariably served with soup, rice, salad, and flatbread.

$ ✕ **Abu Muhammed Restaurant.** The reputation of Abu Muhammed is as
MIDDLE EASTERN big as the portions. The food is simple and delicious—primarily rice, slow-cooked stews, and grilled meats—served indoors or on the tiny, leafy terrace. Beer is available. This is also a good place to rent bicycles, and it's one of the only places in Mut with an Internet terminal. ⊠ *Shar'a al-Thauwra al-Khadra, Mut* ☏ *092/782–1431* ▭ *No credit cards.*

$ ✕ **Ahmed Hamdi Restaurant.** Restaurants run in Ahmed Hamdi's fam-
MIDDLE EASTERN ily. Originally, his father operated a restaurant. His brother—they're friendly rivals—runs a restaurant on the same street; both are clean and friendly, practically side by side near the Mebarez Tourist Hotel. The food is good, and the prices modest. (A third brother runs tours that you can book at either restaurant.) You can dine inside or out. For breakfast, try the tomato omelet along with fuul, which is made from mashed fava beans and is the national dish of Egypt, and ta'amiya (Egyptian falafel, also made from fava beans. ⊠ *Shar'a al-Thauwra al-Khadra, Mut* ☏ *092/794–0767* ▭ *No credit cards.*

WHERE TO STAY

There are no international-standard hotels in Mut; most new development in the oasis is geared toward eco-themed hotels sited 15 to 30 km (9 to 18 mi) away near the village of Al-Qasr.

All hotel reviews have been condensed for this book. Please go to Fodors.com for full reviews of each property.

$ ⛰ **Bedouin Oasis Village & Spa.** This kooky hilltop spot is part laid-back hippie village and part architectural experiment—a borderline kitsch mud-brick complex that takes "Bedouin-fication" to a whole new level. **Pros:** management style is laid-back; possibility of a cold beer after a day exploring in the heat. **Cons:** management style can be too laid-back; rooms are very compact and over-priced; a long walk into town. ⊠ *Shar'a al-Thauwra al-Khadra, 2 km (1½ mi) northwest of Maydan Tahrir, Mut* ☎ *092/782–0070* ⤴ *30 rooms* ⚬ *In-room: no a/c, no phone, no TV. In-hotel: 2 restaurants, bar, pool, parking (free)* ⬛ *No credit cards* ⫶⊙⫶ *MAP.*

$ ⛰ **Mebarez Tourist Hotel.** What makes this four-story hotel noteworthy is that it brings the standard of midrange interchangeable international hotels to the desert—where a nondescript hotel is in fact unique. **Pros:** well-maintained three-star property; inviting spring-fed plunge pool at the back of the hotel (to be upgraded soon, according to management). **Cons:** not all rooms have private bathrooms; it's a long walk into town and hard to flag down passing service taxis. ⊠ *Shar'a al-Thauwra al-Khadra, ¾ km (½ mi) northwest of Maydan Tahrir, Mut* ☎ *092/782–1524* ⤴ *30 rooms* ⚬ *In-room: a/c, refrigerator (some). In-hotel: restaurant, pool* ⬛ *No credit cards* ⫶⊙⫶ *CP.*

$$ ⛰ **Sol Y Mar Mut Inn.** This curious two-part motel-style property makes a good overnight stop but is less inviting for a longer stay. **Pros:** restaurant serves exceptional Egyptian fare; hot springs on-site are soothing, especially on chilly winter evenings; alcohol is available. **Cons:** rooms around the pool are small; beds in twin-bed rooms are very narrow. ⊠ *3 km (2 mi) north of Mut, Mut Talata* ☎ *092/782–1530, 02/3854–2058 in Cairo for reservations only* ⤴ *21 rooms* ⚬ *In-room: a/c (some), no TV. In-hotel: restaurant, bar, pool, parking (free)* ⬛ *No credit cards* ⫶⊙⫶ *MAP.*

DESERT TOURS

Tours of the oasis and surrounding desert are not as numerous as in Farafra or Bahariya, though most hotels and tourist restaurants offer packages. The most popular package is a tour of Dakhla's medieval Islamic villages, but you can also visit the escarpment and various dune belts. Travel farther afield to places such as the Gilf Kebir or Jebel 'Uwaynat must be arranged well in advance through tour operators in Cairo.

Oasis tours are usually divided into half-day sections: one for sights in the east of the oasis, and another for sights in the west. A typical eastern tour will include Asmant al-Khorab, Balat, Bashendi, and the rock art near Teneida; while western tours usually incorporate Qalamoun, Muzawaka Tombs, Deir al-Hagar, Al-Qasr, and a short trip to a dune field. Either way, the current going price is about £E150 to £E250 per car, or £E300 to £E400 to combine both trips. Off-road adventures can be arranged through hotels and restaurants, or by visiting the tourist office. Police permission is required for all overnight trips from Dakhla, and rarely given, though many outfitters operate on the sly.

TOUR OPERATORS

Dohous Bedouin Camp. This company specializes in camel treks and can have you viewing the sunset from the top of a dune for about £E80 per person. Haj Saleh, a human GPS, often guides longer expeditions. ⊠ *El-Dohous Village, 7 km (4½ mi) north of Mut* ☎ *092/785–0480 or 010/622–1359* ⊕ *www.dakhlabedouins.com.*

EN ROUTE There are two paved routes from Mut to Al-Qasr. The main road runs north past the Islamic settlement of Budkhulu, while the longer, more scenic secondary road heads west from an intersection 5 km (3 mi) north of Mut, passing the Mamluk fortress-town of **Qalamoun** and its ancient Islamic cemetery against a dramatic background of palm trees and distant cliffs. Several kilometers to the north, the ruined arches and towers of **Amheida**, an ancient Roman town scattered over a large area close to the road, are impressive even today.

AL-QASR

32 km (20 mi) west of Mut on Farafra Road.

★ Of the many fortified Islamic settlements that dot the oasis, Al-Qasr is by far the most impressive. Seen from the main road, its mud-brick houses and minarets peer above lush palm groves and a small lake, and sit beneath the breathtaking backdrop of the Dakhla escarpment. The approach to Al-Qasr leads past the faceless modern village to a square with a new mosque.

The old town, which dates back over 1,000 years and sits atop Roman foundations, appears as if it was abandoned in a hurry centuries ago. Its twisting, covered alleys, multistory mud-brick houses, and heavy wooden gates are in mint condition—all that is missing are the people. In reality, the town's abandonment is quite recent, with most residents having relocated in the past few decades. It is still inhabited in some parts, and you may be invited for tea by one of its remaining elderly occupants. Most visitors will stop by the **Mosque of Nasr al-Din**, a mud-brick structure whose 60-foot-high minaret has stood since the 12th century (though rebuilt in the 19th century). Its thorny crown of wooden planks once held a balcony, where a muezzin would sound the call to prayer. Inside the mosque is the mausoleum of its patron, Sheikh Nasr al-Din.

Other important stops in the village include ingenious medieval air-cooling towers, a restored olive press, and a **madrassa** (Islamic school) that once doubled as a town hall and courthouse. Wander long enough and you may also find the donkey-driven grain mill and a working blacksmith's forge.

Many of the houses in Al-Qasr incorporate stone blocks from earlier structures, some containing hieroglyphic inscriptions. Equally fascinating are the beautiful acacia-wood lintels on houses that provide clues about their origin. Their carved Kufic and cursive Arabic inscriptions usually name the carpenter, home owner, construction date, as well as verse from the Qu'ran. The earliest dates to 1518.

Ethnographic Museum. Old Al-Qasr is a protected historical site and conservation work is currently underway. The small, privately run museum near the tour center displays cultural artifacts from all of the oases in the Western Desert. It also sells local crafts. ⊠ *Al-Qasr* 🕾 *No phone* 🎟 *£E5* ☉ *Daily 10–5.*

Tour Center. While there is no admission fee, staff at the village's spartan tour center will record your nationality and offer you a free tour. Should you accept, a village custodian will lead you through the labyrinth of alleys, unlock doors, and point out sites of interest—though he may not speak much English. Tip him as you see fit. ⊠ *Al-Qasr* 🕾 *No phone* 🎟 *Free* ☉ *Daily 9–5.*

OFF THE BEATEN PATH

Al-Muzawaka. While the two vividly painted Roman-era tombs that made this windswept necropolis famous have been closed for many years, it is still an interesting place to explore. For a little baksheesh, the caretaker will direct you to a collection of mummies recovered from the tomb-riddled knoll. ✛ *Take the road to Farafra west from Al-Qasr for about 5 km (3 mi), then take the left (south) turnoff and continue for about 1 km (½ mi) to the tombs* 🕾 *No phone* 🎟 *Free (baksheesh expected)* ☉ *Daily 9–5.*

Deir al-Hagar. Shifting sands played no small role in preserving this small sandstone temple, which was commissioned by the Roman emperor Nero and continued under Vespasian, Domitian, and Titus. A sand dune consumed the temple in antiquity, collapsing its roof but preserving its hypostyle hall and sanctuary for posterity. The temple is dedicated to the Theban triad of Amun, Mut, and Khonsu. Its interior shows images of Roman rulers in pharaonic guise making offerings to the gods. The inscriptions are in good condition, and some still retain their color. The mud-brick ruins of an early Christian monastery surrounding the temple have remains of frescoes. ✛ *Take the road to Farafra west from Al-Qasr for about 9 km (5 mi), then take the marked turnoff on the left (there are no signs in English) and follow this road until it ends (about 4 km [2½ mi]), then drive 2 km (1 mi) east across the desert to the temple* 🕾 *No phone* 🎟 *£E25* ☉ *Sat.–Thurs. 9–5, Fri. 9–noon.*

WHERE TO STAY

All hotel reviews have been condensed for this book. Please go to Fodors.com for full reviews of each property.

$$ **★** 🏨 **Badawiya Hotel.** Owned by the same trio behind the popular Badawiya Hotel in Farafra, this property is grander and more luxurious, yet still with down-to-earth room rates. **Pros:** private balconies with cushioned sitting areas; large bathrooms with separate shower stalls; good restaurant with a set menu that changes nightly or switches to a buffet if there are enough guests. **Cons:** no bar or alcohol; could do with a little more greenery; not as close to Al-Qasr as they'd have you believe. ⊠ *Al-Qasr Road, about 29 km (17 mi) from Mut, Al-Qasr* 🕾 *092/772–7451; 02/2526–0994 in Cairo for reservations only* ⊕ *www.badawiya.com* 🛏 *44 rooms, 2 suites* ⌂ *In-room: a/c, Wi-Fi. In-hotel: restaurant, pool, parking (free)* ¶⚫¶ *MAP* ▭ *No credit cards.*

$$$ 🖫 **Desert Lodge.** Perched on a hill overlooking Al-Qasr, this luxurious
Fodor's Choice   eco-lodge commands stunning views of the town and the surround-
★   ing desert. **Pros:** an active eco policy, with filtered water that's suit-
able for drinking (to avoid use of plastic bottles) as well as a recycling
program; the restaurant serves organic vegetables that are grown on
the property's own nearby farm. **Cons:** no air-conditioning in rooms;
Internet access costs $12 an hour. ✉ *On a hill above the town, Al-Qasr*
☎ *092/772–7062; 02/2690–5240 in Cairo for reservations only* ⊕ *www.
desertlodge.net* ⤴ *32 rooms* ♿ *In-room: no a/c, no TV. In-hotel: res-
taurant, bar, pool, laundry service, Internet terminal, parking (free)*
▭ *AE, MC, V* ⧖*MAP.*

BALAT

22 km (14 mi) east of Mut.

Straddling a low hill, Balat retains much of its medieval Islamic char-
acter. The fortified village's covered alleys and wooden gates once pro-
tected its inhabitants from fierce sandstorms and desert raiders. Many
of the mud-brick houses are still inhabited and display carved acacia-
wood lintels similar to those found in Al-Qasr.

Qilaa al-Dabba. These small mastaba tombs are significant in that their
discovery provided the first evidence that Dakhla was known to the Old
Kingdom. Archaeologists have uncovered seven mud-brick mastabas,
including one containing the mummy of a 6th-Dynasty governor. The
site is believed to have been the necropolis for an ancient settlement at
Ain 'Asil, about 1½ km (1 mi) farther east. You can enter the restored
burial chamber of governor Khentika, which sits at the bottom of a
huge pit and has painted reliefs dating back to around 2250 BC. The
desert around the site is full of mud-brick ruins. ⟁ *From the road to
Al-Kharga, turn left onto the track on the eastern edge of Balat, and
follow it into the desert for about 1 km (½ mi)* ☎ *No phone* ▭ *£E25*
☾ *Daily dawn–dusk.*

BASHINDI

25 km (16 mi) east of Mut.

Sometimes referred to as a *real* pharaonic village, Bashindi does have an
unusual architectural style. Everything seems to be softly curving and
undulating in this tidy little place. Many houses are built over Roman
tombs and decorated with pastel colors and Hajj scenes. The cemetery
behind the village contains the domed **Tomb of Pasha Hindi,** a medieval
sheikh, and is littered with empty sarcophagi.

Ancient Rock Inscriptions. A collection of inscriptions on a sandstone out-
crop just off the highway near Teneida, some 45 km (28 mi) east of Mut,
attests to Dakhla's earliest inhabitants and its position on the ancient
caravan routes. The carvings include naïve depictions of giraffes, fish,
camels, antelopes, and hunters. There are also Arabic inscriptions, as
well as graffiti carved by passing Bedouins and early European explor-
ers. Although prehistoric rock art is common in North Africa, this is one

of the most accessible sites for viewing. ⚠ To preserve the inscriptions, do not add to them or take rubbings.

Tomb of Ketinus. Only one tomb in Bashindi's ancient cemetery is still intact, despite being occupied by soldiers and villagers for many years. Pharaonic reliefs show scenes of mummification and the deceased Roman-era official in front of the gods. Ask in the village for the caretaker who can open the tomb. ✛ *From the main road to Al-Kharga, turn left about 3 km (2 mi) east of Balat and follow road to the end of Bashindi village* ☎ *No phone* 🖃 *£E25* ⊙ *Daily dawn–dusk.*

KHARGA OASIS

Although it has impressive ruins, dunes, and cultural sights, tourists rarely spend more than a night in Kharga. And that's a shame. Beyond the concrete and pavement of its modern capital, the oasis's oft-overlooked sights warrant further investigation.

From Al-Kharga, the charmless capital, a spur road heads south past a string of crumbling fortresses that once guarded Egypt's southern frontier and taxed caravans arriving from what is now Sudan. Many of these forts are of pharaonic origin, though the surviving structures are typically of Roman construction. All can be visited with police permission on a daytrip, or as part of a tour that begins or ends in Luxor.

North of Al-Kharga lies the 2600-year-old **Temple of Hibis**, the early Christian burial ground at **Bagawat**, and the ruins of various monasteries and fortresses. You may also catch a glimpse of an abandoned railway built by the British in 1906, its tracks now mostly buried beneath golden dunes.

Security is heavier in Kharga than in the other oases, and tourists will receive an armed police escort unless they sign a waiver. Even then they will be expected to inform police of their movements, and can expect officers to radio headquarters for permission. The precautions are more a symptom of police paranoia than due to any genuine safety threat, but the overbearing security presence can dampen tourists' experience.

AL-KHARGA

About 205 km (127 mi) east of Mut; 575 km (357 mi) south of Cairo.

Kharga's purpose-built capital is the administrative headquarters of the New Valley Governorate and home to over 70,000 Egyptians, many having relocated here from the crowded Nile Valley. At first glance it appears as a tidy but uninspiring congregation of ugly buildings, low-rise apartments, and ramshackle shops. With a little exploring, however, the streets of Al-Kharga reveal the strong rural flavor of the city's tight-knit agrarian community.

Orientation is simple: Al-Kharga's three main streets form a triangle whose base roughly marks the boundary between the modern city and its original mud-brick settlement. Government offices, banks, and police stations line Shar'a Jamal 'Abd al-Nasir; small shops and food stands

Early Christian necropolis in Bagawat, Oasis of Kharga

cluster around Maydan Basateen; and service taxis and cheap eats can be found at Maydan Showla.

The old town, west of Maydan Showla is behind the bustling market that leads to the **Darb al-Sindadyah**, a dark and sinuous medieval passage that once ran 4 km (2½ mi), but is now reduced to ruins. Houses in this area are wonderfully decorated with Hajj paintings depicting their owners' journeys to Mecca. If you stop to chat, you will inevitably be invited in for tea.

Al-Kharga's city transport is fairly extensive, and buses and service taxis cover all the main routes. Unmetered taxis are also plentiful. The intercity bus station is located about 100 yards south of Maydan Basateen, while its tiny airport lies just north of town on the road to Asyut. A once-weekly train used to run from a station 5 km (3 mi) south of the city to Luxor, but was not in service at the time of writing. Should it resume, the trip usually takes 7–12 hours depending on how much sand must be cleared from the track. Alternatively, a private taxi can be hired for about £E400–£E500 to drive the newly built direct road to Luxor. The trip takes just two hours and requires prior police clearance.

The **Tourist Friends Association** (☎ 092/792–1451) organizes free guided tours of the city's sights, including visits to local carpet-making, pottery, and date processing factories.

★ **Bagawat Necropolis.** Hundreds of mud-brick chapels spill over the crest of a hill at this early Christian cemetery. They date from a time between the 4th and 7th centuries AD, when Christians wrestled among themselves over the concept of God the Father, God the Son, and the Holy Spirit—was God one, or three in one?

Bagawat is probably the oldest Christian cemetery of such magnitude in the world. Most of the 263 chapels, which served as individual tombs and family mausoleums, are unadorned. Two tombs have Biblical scenes painted on their ceilings. The Chapel of Peace is the best preserved, with depictions of Adam and Eve, Noah's Ark, and St. Paul dating from the late 5th century AD. The Chapel of the Exodus at the summit of the complex dates from the 4th century AD, and the Biblical scenes and characters here are depicted in an earlier, more naive artistic style. Pharaonic elements and Byzantine allegorical symbols can be seen on the walls, which are littered with centuries of graffiti.

The necropolis was arranged in a series of streets as a "city of the dead." The remains of an early mud-brick basilica occupy the middle of the complex, and hundreds of unexcavated graves cover a nearby hill. ⊠ *3 km (2 mi) north of Al-Kharga* ⊹ *Drive north on the road to Asyut, turnoff is on the left past Hibis Temple* ⌛ *£E30, combined ticket with Deir al-Kashef* ☉ *Daily 8–5.*

Deir al-Kashef *(Monastery of the Tax Collector).* The mud-brick monastery overlooks one of the most important caravan crossroads in the Western Desert. The imposing ruin contains a honeycomb of hermit cells and once stood five stories tall. Below it are the ruins of a small church. ⊠ *4 km (2½ mi) north of Al-Kharga* ⊹ *Reached by a track from the Bagawat Necropolis* ⌛ *£E30, combined ticket with Bagawat Necropolis* ☉ *Daily dawn–dusk.*

Deir al-Ghanayim. Also known simply as Al-Deir (which means "the monastery"), this Roman mud-brick fortress with 12 towers once guarded the main caravan route to the Nile. Reached only by a four-wheel-drive vehicle, its sand-swept ruins are littered with the graffiti of disgruntled British soldiers stationed here during WWI. ⊠ *About 20 km (12 mi) northeast of Al-Kharga* ⊹ *Drive north on the road to Asyut, turn right onto marked dirt track that ends about 2 km (1 mi) before site* ☏ *No phone* ⌛ *Free* ☉ *Daily dawn–dusk.*

New Valley Museum. The small, well-organized museum is a perfect finale to a trip to the Western Desert oases. The collection spans more than 15,000 years of New Valley history. Finds are displayed from the Neolithic, pharaonic, Greco-Roman, Coptic, and Mamluk to Ottoman periods. The displays are presented in rather staid wood-and-glass cases, but the information in English is well put together. The ground floor concentrates on ancient finds, and pride of place must go to a small selection of Greco-Roman era mummies just beyond the entrance, including a gilt-faced "Golden Mummy" from Baharia. The most rare objects are the nondescript Old Kingdom terra-cotta jars displayed in the hall to the right of the mummies, which are unique to the oases region. The second floor displays items from the Islamic era, including blue tiles, cut glass, and Mamluk clothing from Al-Qasr. ⊠ *Shar'a Jamal 'Abd al-Nasir, at corner of Shar'a al-Keneesa, Al-Kharga* ☏ *No phone* ⌛ *£E30* ☉ *Sun.–Thurs. 9–5, Fri. 9–noon and 3–5.*

Qasr al-Ghueita *(Palace of the Beautiful One).* A Persian temple built on an earlier pharaonic site and continued under the Ptolemies, this sandstone temple was dedicated to the Theban triad of Amun, Mut, and Khonsu. The fortress was later used by a Roman garrison, who beefed up its mud-brick enclosure wall. ✉ *20 km (12 mi) south of Al-Kharga* ✛ *Drive south on the road to Baris for 18 km (11 mi), turn left and follow road for 2 km (1 mi)* ☎ *No phone* 💰 *£E30* ⊙ *Daily 8–5.*

Qasr al-Labeka. The Roman mud-brick fortress, which was built between the 3rd and 5th centuries AD, occupies a sand-choked wadi at the base of the northern escarpment. Its 12-meter (40-foot) walls protected a garrison that monitored passing caravans, and there was a large settlement here supported by a nearby spring. In ancient times, several *manafis* (underground aqueducts) brought water from the spring. One has been cleared and is now used to cultivate fields. ✉ *35 km (22 mi) north of Al-Kharga* ✛ *Drive north 23 km (14 mi) on the road to Asyut, turnoff is on the left; continue on dirt track about 10 km (6 mi) into the desert* ☎ *No phone* 💰 *Free* ⊙ *Daily dawn–dusk.*

Qasr al-Zayyan. The temple at Qasr al-Zayyan is dedicated to the local deity Amenibis (Amun of Hibis), protector of the oasis. The temple's sandstone gate is well preserved, but its walls are swamped in sand. Next to the temple is a small Roman fortress. ✉ *25 km (16 mi) south of Al-Kharga* ✛ *Drive south on the road to Baris for 18 km (11 mi), turn left and follow road for 7 km (4½ mi)* ☎ *No phone* 💰 *£E30* ⊙ *Daily 8–5.*

Fortress of Nadura. On a desert hill east of the main road to Asyut is this Roman mud-brick fort and temple that once guarded the caravan routes. The site is in ruins, but the view of the oasis from the top is worth the short ascent. ✉ *2 km (1 mi) north of Al-Kharga* ✛ *Drive north on the road to Asyut, turnoff is on the right opposite Hibis Temple* ☎ *No phone* 💰 *Free.*

Temple of Hibis. This temple is one of only a handful of surviving Persian monuments in Egypt. It was built during the reign of the emperor Darius I (510–490 BC) on the site of an earlier temple dedicated to Amun. Later rulers surrounded the temple with a series of stone enclosures, and built an avenue of sphinxes. The reliefs are in good shape, and you can still see the garish colors on the bas-reliefs. Unfortunately, attempts by conservationists to protect the temple from rising groundwater have accelerated its destruction. The temple was closed at writing, but expected to reopen soon. ✉ *2 km (1 mi) north of Al-Kharga* ✛ *Drive north on the road to Asyut, temple is on the left* ☎ *No phone* 💰 *£E30* ⊙ *Daily 8–5.*

OFF THE
BEATEN
PATH

Qasr al-Dush. The legend that the temple here was covered in gold conveys the strategic importance of this hilltop fortress. As well as ruling over Darb al-Arba'in—the southern gateway to Egypt on the ancient caravan trail to sub-Saharan Africa—the mud-brick Roman fortress probably controlled the Darb al-Dush route to Edfu and Esna in the Nile Valley. The crumbling fortress walls tower 10 meters high in some areas, while underground chambers go down five levels. A temple built of sandstone by Domitian in the 1st century AD and dedicated to Osiris and Seraphis, abuts the eastern flank of the fortress. The remains of the Roman garrison town of Kysis are scattered over the hillside below. ✉ *115 km (75 mi) southeast of Al-Kharga* ✛ *Drive south for 90 km*

(56 mi) to Baris, continue south about 15 km (9 mi) to turnoff, then east to temple ☎ *No phone* 🎫 *£E30* ⊙ *Daily 8–5.*

WHERE TO EAT

Al-Kharga may be the largest town in the oasis, but that doesn't translate into a very large range of fine-dining options. You could well find yourself eating at the same place for the duration of your stay. Grilled fish and roast chicken restaurants cluster around Maydan al-Basateen, but you'll also find a *fiteer* (sweet or savory pastry) shop by the service taxi stand at Maydan Showla.

$ ✕ **Wemby al-Basateen Restaurant.** With its polished granite walls and
MIDDLE EASTERN floors, and a small outdoor terrace, this restaurant is the best of a cluster of cheap eateries around the square. It even has a "family section," really just an alcove separated by a wooden panel. There is no menu, but you can choose from grilled chicken, meat kebabs, or a rather chewy steak. All are served with the usual soup, salad, and rice. Check prices before ordering. ⊠ *Maydan al-Basateen, Al-Kharga* ☎ *092/793–7105* ▬ *No credit cards* ⊙ *No lunch Fri.*

WHERE TO STAY

With the exception of the properties listed below, most hotels in Al-Kharga are dark, dilapidated piles. A high-end traditional-style property, the Qasr El Bagawat Hotel, is currently under construction and due to open in 2011, which should improve competition.

All hotel reviews have been condensed for this book. Please go to Fodors.com for full reviews of each property.

$ 🏨 **El Kharga Oasis Hotel.** The dreary main building is a museum of 1970s hotel design, but the cheerful white chalets in the palm garden out back are welcoming and clean. **Pros:** pleasant and peaceful courtyard; clean chalets; quiet in the evening. **Cons:** too bad there's no pool; sliding glass doors tend to stick; deadbeat restaurant. ⊠ *Shar'a Aref, facing Maydan Nasir, Al-Kharga* ☎ *092/792–4940* 🛏 *48 rooms* ⌂ *In-room: a/c, no phone (some), refrigerator (some), In-hotel: restaurant, Wi-Fi hotspot, parking (free)* ⑩ *CP* ▬ *No credit cards.*

$$ 🏨 **Sol Y Mar Pioneers Hotel.** The salmon-colored Pioneers is the only truly international-style hotel in the oasis, offering amenities such as a comfortable lounge-bar where you can enjoy a drink, and a pool where it takes more than five strokes to get from one end to the other. **Pros:** facilities here are truly up to international standards; a good-size pool (£E50 for nonguest day use) surrounded by manicured lawns. **Cons:** the hotel design and decor don't convey any sense of location; bathrooms often dirty; avoid the pool area after dark if you're afraid of bats. ⊠ *1 km (¾ mi) north of Maydan Nasir on the road to Asyut, Al-Kharga* ☎ *092/792–9751* ⊕ *www.solymar.com* 🛏 *96 rooms, 6 suites* ⌂ *In-room: safe. In-hotel: restaurant, bar, pool, laundry service, parking (free), no-smoking rooms* ▬ *AE, MC, V* ⑩ *BP.*

DESERT TOURS

Despite the great number of sights around Al-Kharga, the paucity of tourists means arranging tours here isn't as easy as it is in the other oases—and much-needed all-terrain vehicles are difficult to come by.

Moreover, the local police are reluctant to grant permission for camping in the desert and may insist on accompanying you wherever you decide to go. Expect to pay £E50 for a private taxi to the cluster of sites just north of town, including waiting time, and £E200–£E 300 for the trip to Dush. Tour prices skyrocket if a four-wheel-drive vehicle is involved.

TOUR OPERATORS

Sol Y Mar Pioneers Hotel. This hotel can arrange tours of sites around the oasis. ⊠ *1 km (¾ mi) north of Maydan Nasir on the road to Asyut, Al-Kharga* ☎ *092/792–9751* ⊕ *www.solymar.com.*

Tourist Information Office. A good starting point for any excursion is to seek the advice of a local. Emad Mahmoud, who works at the tourist office, speaks English and can assist in arranging tours to the antiquities near Al-Kharga city as well as to destinations further afield. Other employees at the tourist office are helpful and may even agree to take you in their own vehicle—though discreetly and for a price. ⊠ *Al-Kharga* ☎ *010/431–1931.*

> ### THE TOSHKA PROJECT
>
> Egypt's most ambitious civil engineering project since the building of the Aswan High Dam, the Toshka Project (or New Valley Project) aims to cultivate 1.4 million acres of desert land in southern Egypt by 2020. The $70-billion megaproject involves the construction of a network of canals, including a 310-km-long (193-mi-long) canal that will bring water from Lake Nasser to irrigate Kharga Oasis. A giant pumping station the size of 10 football stadiums has been constructed to pump 25 million cubic meters of water a day into the canal.

SIWA OASIS

Siwa deserves some time. The most isolated of the five Western Desert oases, it is also the most unique. Located near the Libyan border, and surrounded by a sea of sand, its influences have come from Berber North Africa rather than the Nile Valley. Its native inhabitants maintain their own culture, traditions, and language (a Berber dialect called Siwi).

The main town, Siwa, dates back to the 13th century AD, but the oasis was well known in antiquity. By 500 BC the oasis was famed throughout the ancient world for its oracle at Aghurmi, the ruins of which are still visible today. Pharaonic ruins and Roman settlements can be found throughout the oasis, which appears to have been an important agricultural center in antiquity.

While Siwa was formally incorporated into Egypt in 1819, assimilation didn't really begin until the road to Marsa Matruh opened in 1986. Even today, it's clear from the moment you arrive in Siwa that there's something special about the place.

Siwan culture has endured the influx of foreign influences and a flood of settlers from the Nile Valley. Television and cell phones are omnipresent, but families remain tight, and traditions are still honored. This is a conservative society, in which women rarely venture out alone, and even then are usually covered from head to toe. Visitors are welcome, but families here are generally more guarded about their domestic life than in other areas of Egypt.

Water is plentiful in the oasis, and most of its 25,000 inhabitants are engaged in agriculture. But water is also problematic, as the water table lies just a foot below the surface, so groundwater swells up through porous rocks across the depression. Unused, it collects and evaporates under the baking sun, leaving behind salts that render fields infertile. Projects to create drainage catchment areas or to pump water out of the depression (which lies below sea level) have proven costly, but the growing demand for bottled water may offer a solution. To date, four companies have established water-bottling plants that are exploiting Siwa's excess groundwater while pumping money back into the oasis.

SIWA

About 305 km (190 mi) southwest of Marsa Matruh; 783 km (485 mi) west of Cairo, via Marsa Matruh.

Most Siwans live within sight of their ancestral home, the hilltop fortress of Shali. Its *karshif* (salt-impregnated mud) walls and heavy wooden gates protected its inhabitants for centuries until three days of heavy rains in 1926 melted their mud homes and forced them to relocate to the plain below.

Aesthetically, modern breeze-block houses are no match for their former homes, but Siwans seem content with the extra room and creature comforts. They have also enjoyed the perceived benefits of development, including new schools, television service, and better health care.

Early visitors were treated with suspicion, and at times hostility. Today, Siwans welcome visitors, and tourism fuels a small economy focused on the town's main square. Most hotels, shops, and restaurants are located here, and kid-driven donkey taxis offer cheap and fun rides around the square or to the outskirts of town.

Despite rapid changes, Siwa town still retains a village feel. Women sheathed in fabric scurry from door to door, double-parked donkeys get into mischief, and village elders gossip over strong tea. You'll quickly recognize all the main characters and plots, and after a few days here you're bound to feel as if you're part of a soap opera.

Siwa town is small enough to get around on foot, though a bicycle is handy for trips to other parts of the oasis. Nearly all visitors arrive by road from Marsa Matruh, but intrepid travelers can arrange permission to leave by the desert route to Bahariya. The track is partially paved, but should only be attempted by experienced off-road drivers in high-clearance vehicles equipped with extra fuel, spare parts, and plenty of water in case of a breakdown.

Before leaving, be sure to peruse the shops and stalls around town, as Siwa is the best place in the Western Desert to buy traditional crafts and jewelry. ⚠ There's only one bank in Siwa, so bring plenty of Egyptian cash with you.

★ **Aghurmi.** This was the first fortified settlement in the oasis, built on the site of the ancient Oracle of Amun, which lies ruined within its

DID YOU KNOW?

Shali was a fully functional town dating back to the 13th century. In 1926 heavy rain destroyed much of it; and the town continues to fall into ruins because of its construction of salt, mud, rock, and plaster.

walls. While archaeologists disagree on the original date of the oracle's construction, it is clear that by the 26th Dynasty (664–525 BC) it was known throughout the ancient world.

In 524 BC the Persian king Cambyses dispatched an army of 50,000 men to destroy the oracle after he heard that it had been badmouthing his occupation of Egypt, but according to the Greek historian Herodotus, the soldiers marched into the desert never to be seen again. The oracle's anti-Persian tendencies may be what prompted Alexander the Great to consult it in 331 BC before marching against the Persian Empire.

A staircase ascends to the covered entrance of the ruined fortress, which sits atop a limestone outcropping. Portions of the original structure have been restored, including the sanctum that housed the oracle. There are stunning views of the palm groves and dunes beyond from several vantage points.

Nearby are the remains of the **Temple of Amun**, a 30th-Dynasty shrine that was blasted to pieces in the late 19th century by an overzealous treasure hunter. ⊠ *4 km (2½ mi) east of the town of Siwa* 🎟 *£E25, Temple of Amun free* ⊙ *Daily 9–5; Temple of Amun daily dawn–dusk.*

★ **Bir Wahed.** This hot spring and picturesque lake amid dunes were created accidentally by exploratory drilling for oil in the late 1980s. The firm found water instead. A cement tank filled with the spring's hot, slightly sulfurous water is relaxing and therapeutic. The nearby reed-lined lake appears like a mirage at the end of a hot day of dune bashing and is perfect for a cool swim. A permit to visit this desert site is easily arranged through the tourist office or safari operators. Most visitors arrive by jeep around sunset. ⊠ *15 km (9 mi) southwest of the town of Siwa.*

Cleopatra's Bath. It's rumored that Cleopatra once swam in this fresh-water spring east of town. Nowadays local men frequent the deep circular pool, while women may feel more comfortable using the nearby Tamusi Bath, which is less exposed. ⊠ *3 km (2 mi) east of the town of Siwa* ✛ *Take the road to Jebal al-Dakrour and follow signs* 🎟 *Free* ⊙ *Daily dawn–dusk.*

Fatnes Island. Dubbed "Fantasy Island," it is a popular outing on the shimmering salt lake of Birket Siwa. The lush island is an ideal picnic spot and best visited at sunset when the colors of the distant hills are most striking. There's a deep, circular spring-fed pool of cool water for swimming, and a small kiosk in the grove that offers tea and soft drinks. Its owner also fires up a grill when there are enough people around. ⊠ *5 km (3 mi) west of the town of Siwa.*

Jebal al-Dakrour. This spot is known for its traditional rheumatism treatments, which include being buried up to your neck in the hot sand that pours off the mountain's slopes. It is also the site of the ancient Siyaha (Tourism) festival, which marks the end of the date harvest and involves three days of feasting, dancing, and matchmaking. The event is held during the first full moon in October, and everyone is welcome. ⊠ *5 km (3 mi) southeast of the town of Siwa.*

Jebal al-Mawta *(Mountain of the Dead).* The conical hill just north of town is honeycombed with tombs. The finest, the Tomb of Si-Amun, depicts a wealthy merchant with curly hair and a beard and his family worshipping Egyptian gods. You will need to find the site caretaker to open it. More than 1,600 individual tombs have been identified dating from the 26th Dynasty to the Roman period, though only a handful have any decoration. ✉ *About 1 km (½ mi) north of the town of Siwa* 💲 *£E25* 🕙 *Daily 9–5.*

Shali. Siwans once inhabited a fortified settlement at Aghurmi, just east of Siwa town, but by the 13th century AD their numbers had been reduced to just seven families as a result of bloody feuding and incessant attacks by desert raiders. A decision was made to build and relocate to a new stronghold they called Shali ("The Town" in Siwi language), and the original 40 menfolk who moved here are still honored to this day.

> ## AN EGYPTIAN WEST SIDE STORY
>
> All is peaceful in Siwa these days, but much of its history was consumed by a blood feud between the two rival clans that cohabited the fortified town of Shali. Enmity between the original inhabitants, the "Easterners," and a group of newcomers from Libya, the "Westerners," often erupted into violence. Although the two sides appear to have sorted out their differences, even today the new town is largely divided along these lines. Siwans still proudly acknowledge from which side they are descended.

Shali was constructed out of *karshif* (salt-impregnated mud) in the saddle of a limestone knoll. It was a medieval walled town with a labyrinth of narrow alleys and three gated entrances that could easily be defended. As Shali's population grew, the Siwans added extra stories to their homes rather than live outside its protective walls.

The walls proved no match for cannons, and the fiercely independent Siwans quickly capitulated to an artillery force dispatched by Egyptian ruler Muhammad Ali in 1819. The final blow came in 1926, when a rare torrential downpour dissolved Shali's walls and houses, forcing most of the town's inhabitants to relocate to the plain below.

Paths from Siwa's main square lead up to the peak of the limestone outcrop, from where there are fantastic views over the modern town, palm groves, and a pair of glittering salt lakes. You can also peer down into the ruins, as well as the remaining occupied houses on its fringe. Don't miss Shali's 800-year-old mosque, whose undulating karshif facade still bears the handprints of its original builders.

Traditional Siwan House. This house serves as a museum of Siwan domestic life, with a good collection of pottery, tools, jewelry, and clothing used until very recently in the houses of the oasis. ✉ *Behind the main mosque, Siwa* 📞 *No phone* 💲 *£E5* 🕙 *Sun.–Thurs. 9–noon.*

WHERE TO EAT

Siwa's restaurants serve up typical oasis fare, as well as a few local specialties. Most restaurants are located near the town's main square or in hotels, but a few cafés lie tucked inside the lush palm groves. They make an ideal place to spend a few hours sipping fresh juice (try the date milkshakes), playing backgammon, or smoking a shisha. Alcohol

The Curse of Qara

The oasis village of Qara, northeast of Siwa, traditionally had no more than 300 residents. The number was precise because, after being refused the hospitality normally given to travelers, a local sheikh put a curse on the village, vowing that its population would never exceed 300. Qarawis relate that if the population reached 301, someone in the village would die (in an accident or of natural causes) to bring the number down again.

Villagers lived in fear of the curse for many years, going so far as to expel a resident every time a baby was born in order to avert the dire consequences. Today the population has well exceeded 300, proof some say that the curse has been lifted. But lessons have been learned, and Qara has earned a reputation for its effusive generosity to travelers.

is only available at a few high-end hotels outside the main town, and is not for sale anywhere in the oasis—though you may find some locals willing to share their illicit date wine.

$
MIDDLE EASTERN

✕ **Abdou's.** The longest running of Siwa's restaurants offers tasty food, friendly service, and a central location that have made it a hub of activity. Just about everybody eats here at least once, and its cheerful owner has a devoted following. Traditional dishes, roast chicken, slow-cooked stews and couscous are served on plastic plates at reasonable prices. It's a good place to meet people, or watch them go by. ⊠ *On the main square, Siwa* ☎ *046/460–1243* ▭ *No credit cards.*

$
MIDDLE EASTERN
★

✕ **Albabenshal Restaurant.** The terrace of this roof-top hotel restaurant commands a view over Siwa's central square and catches the cool evening breeze beneath the floodlit ruins of Shali. The well-executed menu is primarily typical oasis cuisine but also includes a few unusual dishes, such as tagines (slow-cooked stews served with couscous), *moza begui* (braised lamb shank), and a delicious *khodar masani* (grilled vegetable platter). Backlit gypsum softly illuminates the outdoor dining area, and a niche in the karshif walls serves as a romantic indoor dining room. ⊠ *On the main square, Siwa* ☎ *046/460–2299* ▭ *No credit cards* ☽ *No lunch.*

$
MIDDLE EASTERN

✕ **Kenooz.** One of the best restaurants in town allows you to go on the rooftop terrace, shaded by date palms that rise up through the floor, or to recline on pillows in the downstairs den by the fireplace. Either way, you'll enjoy traditional fare served up piping hot. The eclectic menu also includes delicious crepes, lamb casserole, and a chicken curry that would pass muster in Mumbai. The staff are friendly and attentive. Give them enough notice and they'll prepare a stuffed lamb for your party. ⊠ *Shali Lodge, Shar'a al-Seboukha, Siwa* ☎ *046/460–1299* ▭ *No credit cards.*

$
MIDDLE EASTERN

✕ **Tanta Waa.** Built of mud and palm trunks, this simple and cheery café nestled under lush palm trees beside Cleopatra's Pool is a popular lunch stop. Staff fire up *kofta* (ground meat on skewers) and barbecued chicken, while locals and tourists lounge in hammocks and palm-frond chaises while enjoying a postswim tea or fruit juice. Come in the evening, and you may find a glowing campfire with lamb, goat, or camel meat on the grill—definitely a memorable experience. ⊠ *At Cleopatra's Pool, 3 km (2 mi) east of town, Siwa* ☎ *010/472–9539* ▭ *No credit cards* ☾ *May–Sept. opening times can be erratic.*

WHERE TO STAY

Hotel rooms in Siwa are scarce around Christmas and New Year, and during Ramadan. Reserve a room well in advance if you plan to come at these times.

All hotel reviews have been condensed for this book. Please go to Fodors.com for full reviews of each property.

HOT SAND DETOX

The hot-sand bath has been a traditional remedy for rheumatism and many other ailments, but it has recently gained popularity as a detox treatment. It's not for the faint of heart: you'll be immersed in hot sand and left in the desert heat so that the toxins in the body leach out as you sweat. Some patients undertake several daily treatments to completely cleanse the system, ingesting only fruit, vegetables, and water during this time. The **Natural Hospital** (☎ *010/128-7642*) on the slopes of Jebal al-Dakrour offers hot-sand treatments for around £E150 and rents bungalows if you'd like to take residential treatments.

$$$$ ▤ **Adrere Amellal Eco-Lodge.** Cer-
★ tainly the most expensive hotel in the oases—and the most unusual—it has been watched by eco-travelers with great interest. **Pros:** you'll be staying in one of world's top eco-resorts; the rustic oasis design is impressive; complete privacy; desert sightseeing trips are included in the nightly rate. **Cons:** no electricity at all at this lodge; lighting levels are low at night, which means you may have difficulty reading the book you brought; location is remote, so it's difficult to explore on your own; unless you're a heavy drinker, hard to justify the stratospheric all-inclusive price. ⊠ *At Sidi al-Ja'afar, 17 km (11 mi) west of town, Siwa* ☎ *046/460–1395; 02/2736–7879 in Cairo for reservations only* ⊕ *www.adrereamellal.net* ⇆ *35 rooms, 2 suites* ⚿ *In-room: no a/c, no phone, no TV. In-hotel: restaurant, pool, spa, laundry service, parking (free)* ▭ *AE, MC, V* ⍚ *FAP.*

$–$$ ▤ **Albabenshal Heritage Lodge.** Nestled below the jagged ruins of Shali,
★ this eco-lodge has been designed to blend with the architecture of the 13th-century fortress. **Pros:** traditional styling and architecture blend in with the surroundings; prime location right in the heart of town. **Cons:** no air-conditioning; there's no outdoor space except the roof terrace and the small, high-sided courtyards, which can be a little stifling. ⊠ *On the main square, Siwa* ☎ *046/460–2299* ⇆ *11 rooms, 1 suite* ⚿ *In-room: no phone, no a/c, no TV. In-hotel: restaurant* ▭ *No credit cards* ⍚ *BP.*

$ ▤ **Palm Trees Hotel.** This three-story concrete building's best assets are its beautiful, lush palm garden, friendly atmosphere, and central location. **Pros:** a no-frills hotel offering good value for money for budget travelers; the hotel's leafy palm garden is a good place to meet other travelers. **Cons:** rooms in the main building are worn and often dirty; tours booked through the hotel are hit-and-miss. ⊠ *Off the main square, on the road to Jebal al-Dakrour, Siwa* ☎ *046/460–1703* ⇆ *25*

rooms ☐ *In-room: no a/c (some), no phone, no TV. In-hotel: restaurant, bicycles, laundry facilities, Internet terminal* ☐ *No credit cards* ⊙| *BP.*

$-$$ ☐ **Shali Lodge.** This traditionally styled hotel made from red stone, kar-shif, and palm trunks has rooms leading off an internal courtyard. **Pros:** traditional building and styling is in keeping with the location; the ter-race café is a great place to while away an evening over cups of Bedouin tea. **Cons:** no air-conditioning; there are few amenities on-site; most rooms lack private patios or balconies. ☒ *Shar'a al-Seboukha, Siwa* ☎ *046/460–1299; 02/2736–7879 in Cairo for reservations only* ⬌ *16 rooms, 4 suites* ☐ *In-room: no a/c, no TV (some). In-hotel: restaurant* ☐ *No credit cards* ⊙| *BP.*

$$-$$$ ☐ **Siwa Safari Paradise.** The owner of one of the longest-established hotels in the oases continues to expand and improve the choice of rooms. **Pros:** choice of rooms in several price ranges; with 140 rooms there's always room, even in high season; refreshing pool. **Cons:** new buildings have taken over some of the garden's space, so when it's busy there's not much space to relax. ☒ *Shar'a Aghurmi, about ½ km (¼ mi) northeast of town, Siwa* ☎ *046/460–1290* ⊕ *www.siwaparadise. com* ⬌ *140 rooms* ☐ *In-room: no a/c (some), no phone (some), no TV (some). In-hotel: 2 restaurants, pool, bicycles, laundry service, parking (free)* ☐ *V* ⊙| *MAP.*

$$$ ☐ **Siwa Shali Resort.** One of the prettiest and best-equipped hotels in the
★ oases, the traditional styling of these single-story mud-brick bungalows surrounded by maturing gardens helps make the resort a relaxing place to stay. **Pros:** rooms are spacious and have an oasis ambience in the decor; well-regarded spa and beauty center; classy air-conditioned res-taurant, catering to special diets as well as alfresco dining. **Cons:** it's a long way from town and staff can be surly about you not using their overpriced transport. ☒ *5 km (3 mi) southeast of town on the south side of Jebal al-Dakrour, Siwa* ☎ *010/111–9730* ⊕ *www.siwashaliresort. com* ⬌ *30 rooms, 21 suites* ☐ *In-room: a/c, refrigerator. In-hotel: 2 restaurants, pool, gym, spa, laundry service, parking (free)* ☐ *AE, MC, V* ⊙| *MAP.*

DESERT TOURS

Strangely for an oasis on the edge of the Sahara, Siwa has almost no camels. Instead, excursions to the desert are conducted by four-wheel-drive vehicles, which can take you to springs, sand-covered ruins, and some of the most impressive dunes you're likely to see in Egypt. Local safari operators can have you dune bashing in the Great Sand Sea in no time, and a few outfits even offer sand surfing.

Most of the hotels, restaurants, and souvenir shops in Siwa can organize trips, so pricing is competitive. At the time of this writing, the going rate for an afternoon of dune bashing ending with a refreshing dip in the spring-fed lake at Bir Wahed is £E80–£E100 per person. The trip requires a permit (about $5 per person), which can be arranged by your safari operator or the tourist office.

Popular day trips and overnight excursions include visits to Bedouin settlements, Zeitun Lake, and Qara Oasis. A shared pickup truck or jeep to Bahariya Oasis costs £E1,200–£E1,600 and can be arranged through the tourist office or safari operators. All desert trips require permits, which may not be included in the cost.

The top-end resorts tend to offer more luxurious and professional tours, but if you're looking for a decent tour on a budget, you might try some of the smaller or more specialized operators.

TOUR OPERATORS

Tourist Information Office. At the Siwa tourist office, Mahdi Hweiti is a mine of information about Siwa and local tour options. ⊠ *Siwa* ☎ *010/546–1992.*

Sahara Adventure Shop. This is the place to go for sand-boarding safaris. 'Abdullah Baghri rents boards for £E30–£E50 and can have you surfing 100-foot dunes till sunset then camping under the stars for about £E400 per person. ⊠ *On the main street, near Banque du Caire, Siwa* ☎ *010/203–0215.*

Siwa Safari Tours. This company organizes trips to sites around the oasis or further afield. ⊠ *On the main square, Siwa* ☎ *046/460–1904.*

Tala Ranch. This company offers camel trips within the oasis and to the Great Sand Sea. Overnight trips start at £E300 per person. ⊠ *Jebal al-Dakrour, Siwa* ☎ *010/588–6003.*

SHOPPING

Siwa's handicrafts and silver jewelry are highly prized by tourists, and Siwan fashion has found its way to the runways of Europe. Not surprisingly, Siwans eager to get a piece of the lucrative tourist trade have set up shops around town to plug "traditional" handicrafts and designs. Original pieces are rare, but replicas of Siwan silver jewelry, carpets, and stunningly beautiful embroidered wedding dresses are available for purchase. You will also find attractive handwoven baskets, woolen shawls, and pottery.

Siwa's estimated 300,000 palm trees and 80,000 olive trees produce some of the tastiest dates and olives in Egypt. Arrive in the fall after the harvest and you can be the judge. Several shops in town sell packaged dates and olives of innumerable varieties, as well as local honey and medicinal herbs.

Cruising the Nile and Lake Nasser

WORD OF MOUTH

"[W]hat is there to say [about cruising down the Nile]? The boat floated and we sat around and watched it all go by. Yet, sitting here a week after we have returned home, I notice that whenever my mind drifts off into dreaming of the trip, the images I most often return to are those from that day of cruising."

—Abby97

Updated by
Toni Salama

In 1979, only a half-dozen cruise boats plied the Nile. They took a lazy week or more to make the 540-mi trip between Cairo and Aswan. Since then, the number of boats has burgeoned and the route has shrunk. The fleet now stands between 300 and 350 vessels, most of them motor ships, though only some 260 to 280 are in operation at a time. The hottest trend right now is the increasing presence of luxury sailboats called dahabiyyas—about 50 at last count.

With only a handful of exceptions, the entire Egyptian cruise industry sails along one relatively limited stretch of the Nile, just the 130 mi between Luxor and Aswan. Until now, security concerns and navigational problems made the truncated route a necessity. But things are changing north of Luxor. Some ships already venture to Dendera, a few on day trips and a few more as part of four- and seven-night itineraries that begin or end in Luxor. One ship is going a bit farther, putting its passengers within reach of Abydos. Down the river, communities have high hopes that the cruise boats will return, and soon. They could use the business, yes, but they also have worthy sights to see. Beyond Luxor—past Dendera and Abydos—lie the Red and White Monasteries, Tel al-Amarna, Beni Hasan, the Fraser Tombs, Dahshur, and a lot of other places most people have never heard of.

South of Aswan, Lake Nasser cruises cover a distance of some 200 mi in the strange, empty world created by the building of the Aswan High Dam. Boats here stop at Nubian temples and tombs that were relocated to higher ground as the waters of Lake Nasser rose. They don't stop at Nubian villages because there aren't any; the Nubian people, about 100,000 strong, were moved either to Kom Ombo or Sudan.

But make no mistake, the Nile at Luxor, at Aswan, and in between possesses some of the most famed and significant antiquities the world has ever known—and some of the planet's most memorable landscapes. A Nile cruise is the most comfortable—and certainly the most scenic—way to get from point to point. Between Aswan and Abu Simbel on Lake Nasser, the cruise stops at monuments that are impossible to reach any other way.

Note: Most of the ancient temples and tombs of Upper Egypt are all within a few miles of where your boat will dock. At some locations, both on the Nile and on Lake Nasser, you can actually see some of the temples from the ship. At Kom Ombo and Qasr Ibrim, the boat pulls right up to the base of the temple. (*The monuments themselves are covered at length in ⇨ chapters 4 and 5.*)

CHOOSING A CRUISE

The traditional Nile cruise is recommended for first-time visitors to Egypt, not only because of the great diversity of monuments that you can view, but also because of the opportunity to see rural Egyptians, their villages, and, in places, local crafts. The Lake Nasser cruise is recommended if you have an archaeological bent, or if you simply want to get away from it all in the wide-open space of the lake.

You can travel the Nile on three-, four-, and seven-night cruises. From north to south, the major sights included in all Nile cruises are Karnak Temple, the Colossi of Memnon and the Valley of the Kings at Luxor; the locks at Esna; the Temple of Horus at Edfu; the Temple of Haoerus and Sobek at Kom Ombo; and the Unfinished Obelisk, High Dam, and Philae Temple in Aswan. Most cruises will add other notable monuments to the lineup of inclusions. Three-night itineraries depart from Aswan and go no farther than Luxor. Four-night itineraries depart Luxor and head to Aswan, though a rare few will loop north far enough to make a stop at Dendera. Depending on the ship, seven-night cruises may simply make a round trip of a combined three- and four-night itinerary, or it may head in one direction only, allowing more time for sightseeing.

Lake Nasser cruises embarking in Aswan last four nights; those embarking in Abu Simbel last three nights. From north to south, sights viewed include the relocated temples of Kalabsha, Beit al-Wali, and Kertassi on the island of New Kalabsha near the High Dam; the temples of Sebua, Dakka, and Meharakka, which have been reconstructed at Wadi al-Sebua; the temples of Amada, Derr, and the tomb of Penout reconstructed at Amada; Qasr Ibrim on its original site; and at Abu Simbel the famous temples of Ramses II and his wife, Nefertari—hallmarks of the UNESCO-funded Nubian salvage operations. One decided advantage to visiting Abu Simbel as part of a Lake Nasser cruise itinerary is that you will have the opportunity to visit the site before or after the tourist hordes depart, or buy a ticket to see it illuminated during the nightly Sound & Light Show.

If you are taking a Nile cruise and don't want to miss Abu Simbel, a flight can take you there and return you to Aswan the same day; flights are timed so that you have about 2 or 3 hours on the ground, which is sufficient time to see the monument. Likewise, if you are taking a lake cruise, you can fly to Luxor for a day to see its famous East and West Bank monuments. The Aswan–Luxor flight lasts 30 minutes.

8

Continued on page 440

THE NILE: EGYPT'S LIFELINE

Sure, Egypt wouldn't exist without the Nile. But the Egyptians have more than returned the favor. For 6,000 years Egyptian culture has blessed the riverbanks with many of the world's most inspiring monuments.

Egyptians are quick to report that the world's longest river flows through 3,172 miles and ever so many other cultures before it ever reaches Egypt. If the Nile has become synonymous with Egyptian civilization, it is because the ancient Egyptians took faith, resurrection, and eternity seriously—so much so that they built their most sacred and enduring places on the very shores of the Nile, the bringer of life. Temples and tombs were built to last, and they run the length of the country, 960 mi (1,545 km) from the deepest outpost at Abu Simbel all the way to the Mediterranean.

For millennia, Egyptians themselves—peasants, priests, monarchs—and even their gods, got about on the river, conducting the affairs of everyday life and making pilgrimages. Boats, sacred and ordinary, figured prominently in temple reliefs and in festive processions. Consequently, the Nile remains the time-honored avenue for proceeding from one complex to the next. After a hot and sweaty morning of temple and tomb visits, few comforts are more refreshing to modern travelers than the glass of lemonade, the chilled washcloth, the private bath, and the bountiful buffet that await aboard most Nile and Lake Nasser cruisers.

By Toni Salama

(opposite) Feluccas on the Nile river in Aswan; (top) Kalabsha temple, Lake Nasser

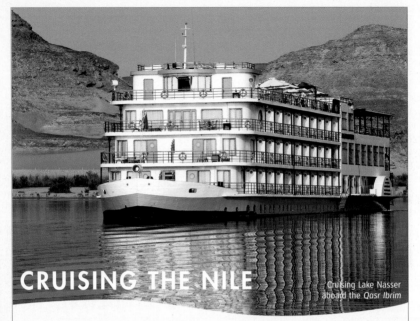

CRUISING THE NILE

Cruising Lake Nasser
aboard the *Qasr Ibrim*

There is nothing like a trip up or down the Nile. In three, four, or seven nights, a cruise combines the convenience of unpacking only once, the bucolic scenery of rural landscapes while the ship is underway, and port calls at some of the world's most significant monuments.

On a Nile cruise between Luxor and Aswan, there's a timeless, almost biblical quality to the palm-fringed farms and rustic villages that unfold as you follow the river. The classic Nile cruise usually includes a photo-op at the Colossi of Memnon; tomb visits in the Valley of the Kings; tours of the temples at Karnak, Hatshepsut, Edfu, Kom Ombo, and Philae; and stops at Aswan High Dam and the Unfinished Obelisk.

On the Lake Nasser cruise between Aswan and Abu Simbel, you are, quite literally, sailing the desert. There's an otherworldly quality to the barren hills and sand dunes that break its surface. They're the mountaintops of ancient Nubia, which now lies in a watery grave

hundreds of feet below. Temples and tombs have been relocated above the water line, mostly grouped in threes for easier access. Expect stops at Kalabsha Temple, incuding Beit al-Wali and Kertassi; Wadi el-Seboua, with Dakka and Meharraqa; Amada, with Derr and the Tomb of Penout; a view of Kasr Ibrim from your ship; and both temples at Abu Simbel.

CRUISE FAST FACTS

- 4-night Nile cruises go south from Luxor
- 3-night Nile cruises go north from Aswan
- 7-night cruises might do a round-trip from Luxor or Aswan (or simply travel slower)
- Only 1 Nile cruiser, Abercrombie & Kent's MS *Sunboat III*, visits Abydos
- 4-night Lake Nasser cruises go south from Aswan
- 3-night Lake Nasser cruises go north from Abu Simbel

FROM ABYDOS TO EDFU TEMPLE

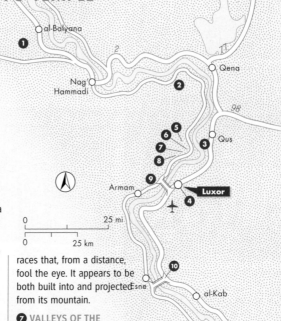

al-Balyana

Qena

Nag Hammadi

Qus

Armant

Luxor

Esne

al-Kab

Edfu

TO ASWAN ↓

0   25 mi
0   25 km

1 ABYDOS

Don't let the plain-Jane façade fool you. The inner recesses of the Temple of Seti I preserve a peerless combination of strong colors painted on gracefully detailed reliefs.

2 DENDERA

The late-Ptolemaic Temple of Hathor is a knockout: a hypostyle hall of Hathor-headed columns; ceiling frescoes on a faience-blue background; and Cleopatra VII and Caesarion carved into the exterior walls.

3 KARNAK TEMPLES

It's adored for its procession of ram-headed sphinxes, famed for its expansive Hypostyle Hall, but few comers have the time or the stamina to cover the rest of this 247-acre multi-temple behemoth.

4 LUXOR TEMPLE

Bypassed by most tour groups, this jewel is best discovered on your own against the velvet backdrop of night, when Ramses II and Tutankhamen are bathed in golden light.

5 VALLEY OF THE KINGS

Tutankhamen may "pack the house," but several less-visited tombs in this steep-walled canyon offer a more rewarding experience.

6 DEIR EL-BAHRI

The Mortuary Temple of Queen Hatshepsut—make that *Pharaoh* Hatshepsut—is a cascade of colonnaded terraces that, from a distance, fool the eye. It appears to be both built into and projected from its mountain.

7 VALLEYS OF THE NOBLES

Too lowly for Valley of the Kings, too lofty for Workmen's Village, at least a thousand of Thebes's ranking nobles were buried in a scattering of West Bank necropoli.

8 RAMESSEUM

Ramses II's Mortuary Temple, adrift in colossal broken statues, was a favorite of "Ozymandias" buffs in earlier generations. Never mind that Percy Bysshe Shelley's cryptic verses defamed Ramses's strong, serene face.

9 COLOSSI OF MEMNON

Worn by time, ravaged by scavengers, and assaulted by earthquakes, Amenhotep III's pair of truly colossal seated statues still has the power to stop tour buses in their tracks.

10 ESNA LOCKS

With the addition of a second lock, Esna is no longer the cruise bottleneck it once was. But coming out on deck to watch the process, no matter the hour, remains a popular activity and one of the Nile's best shows.

11 EDFU TEMPLE

Just because it was built by the Ptolemies doesn't mean that the Temple of Horus isn't authentic. In fact, its relative youth makes it the most intact Egyptian temple around.

8

TOP SIGHTS

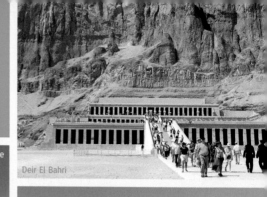

Deir El Bahri

Luxor Temple

Temple of Edfu

Abu Simbel

Temple of Kom Ombo

Valley of the Kings

The key to the Sun Temple of Abu Simbel

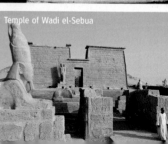

Temple of Wadi el-Sebua

FROM KOM OMBO TO ABU SIMBEL

Portrait of a colossus, Abu Simbel

① KOM OMBO

There's much ado here about the "double-ness" of the Temples of Haroeris and Sobek. But what's really interesting are the medical hieroglyphs: depictions of surgical tools and a birthing chair.

② UNFINISHED OBELISK

This would have been the largest obelisk ever hewn from a single block of granite: 1,162 tons, 138 feet high. Carvers abandoned the project when they detected flaws.

③ PHILAE TEMPLE OF ISIS

Rescued at the eleventh hour from Lake Nasser's rising waters and 12 feet of silt, the last pagan temple to close still honors Isis nightly during the Philae Sound & Light Show.

④ ASWAN HIGH DAM

It's not much to look at, but its numbers impress: 2.4 miles long, 364 feet high, 0.6 miles wide at its base.

⑤ KALABSHA, BEIT EL-WALI, KERTASSI

With Cleopatra and Marc Antony out of the way, Octavian Caesar Augustus, depicted himself as heir to Egypt's crown at Kalabsha. Beit el-Wali and the Temple of Kertassi are part of the visit.

⑥ WADI EL-SEBOUA, DAKKA, MAHARRAQA

A courtyard of sphinxes leads to the Temple of Wadi el-Seboua. At the Temple of Dakka, the soaring pylon stands out. The small Temple of Maharraqa sports an ancient spiral staircase.

⑦ AMADA, DERR, TOMB OF PENOUT

The painting-filled Temple of Amada and the bright colors in the Temple of Derr are worth the desert trek. The Tomb of Penout, viceroy of Nubia, completes the stop.

⑧ QASR IBRIM

It has survived Pharaonic, Greco-Roman, Coptic, and Islamic eras, but tramping tourists may be more than it can take. It must be admired only from the deck of your cruiser.

⑨ ABU SIMBEL

These two temples are twice a marvel: first, that such serene and massive constructs could have been hewn from solid rock; second, that they were moved to their current location.

TO EDFU

Daraw

Aswan

Beit al-Wali

Gerf Hussein

Lake Nasser

al-Derr

al-Dakka

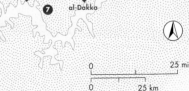

Abu Simbel

0 — 25 mi

0 — 25 km

8

BUILDING LAKE NASSER

(left) The Aswan High Dam; (right) Nikita Khrushchev with Nasser during contractions of Aswan High Dam.

With 56 million cubic yards of material, the volume of the **Aswan High Dam** is more than 17 times that of the Great Pyramid. It holds back the waters of the world's largest man-made lake: almost 137 million acre-feet, at capacity.

The High Dam was President **Gamal Abd el-Nasser**'s legacy project, funded by Soviet Russia, thanks to Cold War politics. Construction began in 1960. Even before its completion 11 years later, the High Dam obliterated ancient Nubia. The fate of the Nubian antiquities that lay in harm's way, not to mention the future of the Nubian population, seemed almost an afterthought.

Only a few antiquities could be saved, as archeologists and engineers worked frantically against a tight deadline and rising waters. The logistics were staggering: how to dismantle and reassemble monumental carvings in fragile sandstone; how to move painted plaster over many miles without damaging priceless frescoes. Fifty nations in all, as

well as UNESCO, helped rescue a score of monuments.

The Temples at Abu Simbel were the flagship project. Ramses's carved head being separated from his body and hoisted away to storage captured the world's attention. Meanwhile, the greater part of the Nubian population was moved to homes in Aswan and Kom Ombo, the rest to Sudan.

Egypt needed to tame the Nile to support its growing population, but the attendant loss of silt brought the use of chemical fertilizers, which now pollute the river. Farms and cities below the dam face another growing problem: increasing salt levels in the soil.

On the positive side, the High Dam brought electricity to many Egyptian villages for the first time in history and made way for factories and jobs. Cropland increased from 9.3 million to 14 million acres. Lake Nasser feeds Egyptians with 40,000 tons of fish annually. And Nile navigation is at last manageable.

NILE MYTHOLOGY

Seti I Worships Isis (second from left), Osiris (second from right) and Horus (left) at Abydos

Just as the daily life of Egyptians played out along the river, so, too, did that of their gods. Ancient Egyptians believed that the Nile's annual inundation arose in the vicinity of present-day Aswan from an underground source near the First Cataract. This was home to the male fertility god **Hapy**—depicted as blue- or green-skinned, heavy-breasted, full-bellied, and sporting a false beard.

Hapy was not the god of the Nile, exactly, but of the inundation and, by extension, the god of the resulting abundance the rising waters brought with them. Ancient Egyptians attributed the distribution of silt to a trio of gods: Khnemu, Anqet, and Satet.

The Nile also was deeply associated with **Osiris**, the murdered king—and later god of the afterlife—whose body was dispatched into the currents by his assassin and brother, Set. The dead Osiris nevertheless sired a son, **Horus**, who avenged his father and himself became a god whose greatest temple still stands at Edfu, a lonely 107 mi from the temple of his wife, **Hathor**, at Dendera. Only the Nile could bring them together. Every summer, the statue of Hathor was taken from her temple at Dendera and sailed upriver with great pomp by barge to Edfu Temple, where Horus resided.

Hapy, the ancient Egyptian god of the Nile and its flood, ties together the symbols of upper Egypt (the lotus, left) and lower Egypt (the papyrus, right).

Hathor-headed Column

Aswan–Abu Simbel takes 30 minutes; Luxor–Abu Simbel takes 90 minutes. Cruise costs do not include these flights.

If a week or more on the water is your goal, some travel agencies are now offering combined river and lake cruises.

TYPES OF SHIPS

FLOATING HOTELS

The so-called floating hotel is the standard Nile and Lake Nasser cruiser. These tiered boats look like boxes with windows stacked on low-slung hulls—the waters are calm enough not to require seagoing vessels—and these ships are essentially the same, differing only in size, decor, and facilities. The craft are air-conditioned and have pools, hot tubs, dining rooms, lounge bars, and panoramic halls for viewing the passing scenery. Many of the larger ships also have exercise equipment, saunas, steam rooms, and massage services. Most cruise ships have between 50 and 60 cabins. The newer luxury boats are of a smaller class and are more intimate.

Given the sheer number of vessels on the Nile, we recommend that you book only those boats with solid reputations, for safety's sake. For example, it's important to travel on a ship that meets high standards of water filtration, especially in the kitchen. But such measures don't necessarily mean traveling on a wildly expensive ship. You can expect the standards of all five-star superior and five-star deluxe boats to exceed acceptable standards, and there's a huge price range within this category. These also most closely meet American and British standards for hygiene and sanitation. Lake Nasser currently has five boats, and all these vessels are of a high standard.

DAHABIYYAS

During the early 20th century, Nile travelers often journeyed aboard luxurious double-masted vessels called dahabiyyas. These elegant wooden houseboats with sails at bow and stern offered comfortable cabins for up to 12 people and a full kitchen with the indulgences to which rich travelers of the era had become accustomed.

This style of travel is making a comeback. These modern re-creations have six to eight individually decorated cabins plus a dining room/lounge and a small shaded deck. They are generally designed in a retro style, with lots of polished wood and brass in addition to modern comforts like electric lighting, toilets, showers, and air-conditioning. They offer a more intimate approach to cruising—and most require a small-group charter—but don't offer amenities such as a pool or long, gourmet menus. Think of them as floating villas as opposed to the floating hotel that is the large Nile cruiser. Itineraries often can be customized, as these ships are able to moor where larger motor ships cannot.

The current dispute among dahabiyya fans is whether a craft can be truly authentic if it has an engine on board. Purists insist that a dahabiyya is not worthy of the name if it has an onboard engine. However, it's rather a moot point: Nile navigation isn't always smooth sailing; friendly currents and prevailing breezes aren't guaranteed. So, even the ships that forego an onboard engine may be accompanied by a motorized tug to keep them on schedule.

SANDALS

The traditional working boat of the Nile, the *sandal* has almost disappeared from the river, but a few of these double-masted craft have been converted into sailing cruisers with three or four cabins and a staff

to captain, cook, and clean the vessel. Yes, there are toilets and showers, but these craft are more practical than luxurious.

FELUCCAS

Felucca is the name given to those single-masted boats that are the romantic symbol of Nile sailing. They have cushioned benches along the sides, sometimes a table at the center, and provide a pleasant way to spend an hour or two sailing along the Nile, especially at sunset. They are decidedly *not* the standard vessels for taking multiday cruises.

For adventurers, nature lovers, and those who want to sample a simpler life, larger feluccas can be hired for three or four days (depending on your interests) between Aswan and Edfu, or perhaps as far as Esna. Most won't go all the way to Luxor because they would have to traverse the locks at Esna, so you will need to make arrangements for ground transportation to Luxor from your disembarkation point.

When carrying overnight passengers, these vessels always sail from south to north, with the flow of the river, and on such trips you sleep in the open, on deck, wrapped in blankets. This trip is recommended only for travelers who come well supplied with mosquito repellent and are prepared to go without cabin, mattress, toilet, or shower. Also keep in mind that food is bought locally, cooked by the sailors, and may not meet your normal standards of hygiene. Depending on the size and comfort of the felucca, the average cost is around £E70 to £E125 per person per day, inclusive of food and sightseeing. These prices are for a minimum of six people and a maximum of eight people. If you want to hire a felucca with fewer people, you'll need to haggle to achieve a suitable price.

The felucca captain usually is responsible for obtaining the necessary police clearance to take a group on the Nile, and that requires time to arrange. Be mindful that feluccas are subject to the wind and the current; they aren't the kind of vessel that follows the clock. It's best to allow a day or two of "wiggle room" in your schedule. Let your captain know if you have a plane to catch, and agree that if you are not at your intended destination by an agreed-upon time, he will drop you off along the way and arrange for overland pickup.

FELUCCA CONTACTS

You can arrange for a felucca locally, but there are also now a few companies to help facilitate making your arrangements in advance. Sandal and dahabiyya charters should be made in advance since there are fewer of these sailing on the Nile.

Abd El Hakeem Hussein. The general manager of the Tourist Office in Aswan is happy to put you in contact with reliable felucca captains if you want to organize your own trip. ⊠ *Outside the Railway Station, Aswan* ☎ *097/231–2811 or 010/576–7594.*

Responsible Travel. This British-based company and Internet portal offers felucca cruises as part of its range of socially and environmentally aware tours. ⊠ *3rd floor, Pavilion House, 6 Old Steine, Brighton UK* ☎ *01273/600030* ⊕ *www.responsibletravel.com.*

Sail the Nile. An English-Egyptian company, Sail the Nile offers felucca, sandal, and dahabiyya trips of varying lengths for groups of two to 12 people. ⊠ *Al Gezera Village, West Bank, Luxor* ☎ *010/356–4540* ⊕ *www.sailthenile.com.*

THE CRUISE EXPERIENCE

Nothing is more relaxing than spending an afternoon on a boat's partially shaded upper deck sipping a beverage. Lie back on a chaise longue and take in the wide valley of the Nile—its belts of palm groves and clusters of dun- and multicolored stucco houses passing in the foreground, its long ranges of limestone mountains stretching across the horizon. On a lake cruise, you'll look out on pristine deserts' tender, pale violet shadows patching ocher landscapes, the water turning to liquid gold from the reflection of the sunset.

Sailing, on river or lake, combines relaxation with sightseeing. Itineraries are structured around the time of the year and the hours that your boat reaches towns and monuments. In summer, shore excursions start before breakfast to avoid the heat and resume in the late afternoon, when a fair breeze often picks up and cools the heat of the day. In cooler winter months, tours start after breakfast and continue after the midday meal. Shore tours, admission to the monuments, and English-speaking guides are almost always included, but verify that when you make your cruise arrangements.

CHECKING IN

Check-in usually takes place before lunch, checkout after breakfast. Passports are registered at the reception area but may not be returned to you until you settle your onboard charges at checkout. After checkout, and before you head to the airport, you may very well do some sightseeing either in Aswan or Luxor.

ENTERTAINMENT

Entertainment is an important part of Nile cruises, and there is usually something different offered each evening: a cocktail party, a belly dancer, Nubian dancers (either a troupe from Aswan or the Nubian staff on board). One evening, guests arrange their own entertainment: a treasure hunt, a fancy dress party, a play, or a folkloric party in a tent-like setting where you sit on cushions and rugs, eat traditional food, smoke a *shisha* (water pipe) if you like, and men are encouraged to don *galabiyyas*, traditional full-length robes that *fellahin* (rural people) still wear. (It's kitschy, but more fun in context than it sounds.) Group photographs are taken as souvenirs. A candlelight dinner overlooking

Abu Simbel temples is a highlight of some Lake Nasser cruises.

The lounge is the best place to read or to enjoy a drink. The larger vessels generally afford a panoramic view, the smaller provide a cozy, drawing room–like atmosphere. Most boats have small libraries with a selection of books about Egypt, largely in English, as well as novels, magazines, newspapers, and board games. Many boats have TVs in the cabins and offer Internet access and Wi-Fi (for an extra charge). Actually receiving a signal is a different matter: TV and Wi-Fi reception is available only when the ships are docked.

MEALS

Most meals on most boats are buffet style, with a wide variety of hot and cold food, as well as a selection of international, Egyptian, and vegetarian dishes. (There is plenty of choice if you follow a special diet.) The staff takes professional pride in these buffets, and each is more like an excessive dinner celebration than an ordinary meal. However, the new generation of five-star boutique-style boats offers à la carte restaurant service at dinner. All three daily meals are served in a dining room unless a barbecue is set up on the sundeck; afternoon tea or coffee is generally served in the open air.

PRECAUTIONS

Water onboard is safe for bathing, because boats have their own purification systems built with the latest technology. However, tap water is not recommended for drinking, and bottled water is available.

The "gippy tummy" has its place in Nile cruise lore. Locals attribute it to excessive consumption of iced drinks immediately after touring in the hot sun, or sitting in direct sunlight for an extended time. The symptoms are diarrhea, sometimes severe, combined with feeling slightly queasy. It is almost certainly attributable to contaminated water, which makes drinking bottled water and not taking ice in drinks strongly advisable. *(For food-related and other health precautions, see ⇨ the Health section in Egypt Essentials.)*

SECURITY

The security issues of the late 1990s caused the Egyptian government to stop all cruises between Cairo and Upper Egypt (Luxor and Aswan). Travel in Upper Egypt and Nubia is relatively safe, but the Egyptian government put in place a series of security measures in the aftermath of these problems that are still current. This security includes armed police strategically placed at popular tourist sites along the Nile, vessels manned by Egyptian security forces accompanying tourist vessels between Luxor and Qena on a Luxor–Dendera cruise, and armed Bedouins on the hills overlooking the monuments of Nubia. (Armed guards are not an uncommon sight in Egypt and should not cause alarm. They are also evident at the ancient sites, and outside embassies, museums, and the residences of foreign diplomats.)

TOUR GUIDES

When you book a Nile or Lake Nasser cruise, an English-speaking guide is almost always part of the package. Boats may have a resident guide or they may hire them temporarily as needed. If you happened to be on a boat with different nationalities, there will be a guide for every language group. If you are traveling individually, rather than as part of a group tour, you probably will be assigned your own guide.

Gone are the days when *dragomen* (a 19th-century term given to locally hired tour managers) conducted tourists to the monuments telling them tall tales of ancient kings. Today's guides are bi- or trilingual professionals who are granted official licenses only after successfully passing an examination that covers pharaonic, Greco-Roman, Islamic, and modern history. They are personable young men and women with a sound knowledge of political and social events in Egypt, and they are informed about environmental matters and the flora and fauna of their country. Traveling with a cruise is a sought-after job, and cruise operators choose only top performers, whose professionalism is evaluated by the travelers themselves. That being said, not all guides are created equal. In general, the better the cruise line, the better the guide.

WORD OF MOUTH

"As we were going through the [Esna] locks, there were lots of sellers [on the banks] throwing rugs and towels up to the boat and bargaining with folks onboard. It was lots of fun to watch, and our friend who bargained and bought a table covering said it was the most fun she has had shopping in a long time. Plus, she got a very good deal."

—jcasale

WHAT TO PACK

Travel light, and remember that Egypt is a conservative country. Egyptians dress modestly and respect those who observe their customs. When walking around Luxor and Aswan, it is wise to wear T-shirts with short sleeves rather than sleeveless tops, and trousers or skirts that come to the knee. (Sleeveless tops for women are entirely acceptable onboard a Nile cruiser, however.) Swimwear should only be seen around the pool, and topless sunbathing is forbidden. Although the weather is sunny in winter, the evenings can be very cool, so bring clothing that you can layer, with at least one medium-weight woolen sweater for the nighttime chill of the after-dark Sound & Light performance at Karnak or Abu Simbel. You'll need a windbreaker in winter for the daytime. Proper walking shoes are a must—sandals are uncomfortable when walking in sand and gravel—and take hats, sunglasses, sunblock, tissues, and a small bottle of water on shore excursions. It doesn't rain, so rain gear is unnecessary.

Although casual wear is acceptable at meals during the day, four- and five-star vessels have a casual-but-elegant standard at night. This does not necessarily mean jackets for men, merely long trousers and a collared shirt. Laundry service on boats is excellent; laundry bags are picked up in the morning and returned by the evening of the same day.

Behind the Scenes on Your Nile Cruiser

CLOSE UP

The Nile cruise industry is continuously developing, but there is one aspect that remains constant: every boat must have a crew. Starting on the bridge, the floating hotels will usually have three captains, two on board working 12-hour shifts each, and the third on vacation. They'll all have come from a family of river captains, commonly bringing their sons along to learn by their sides. They wear the traditional long robe called a galabiyya and perhaps a turban as well; and they usually sit cross-legged in the captain's chair. But they do rely on 21st-century technology and are in constant radio contact with captains of other ships. The larger boats will have perhaps 10 sailors and a crew of between 70 and 90 men—just

men—who work a 45-day schedule before taking 15 days off. They may have jobs in the engine room, housekeeping, laundry, kitchen, dining room, bar, gift shop, or reception, but they all bunk together, by department, in quarters below the guest decks. A perk for management staff is a private cabin. All meals are prepared onboard in the ship's kitchen, which has its own supply of filtered water, separate refrigerators for vegetables and eggs, a separate meat freezer and butchery area, and ovens where they bake bread made from scratch. Dahabiyyas, on the other hand, operate on a much smaller scale. They may have a total crew of just 11, also working a 45-day schedule.

There is a great deal to photograph, so be sure to bring enough battery power for your camera, as well as film or electronic storage for the images you take.

ITINERARIES

Daily itineraries are structured around visits to monuments. Bear in mind that because cruises run back-to-back, visits can seem hurried around Luxor and Aswan, the two cities with the heaviest concentration of ancient sights.

On Nile cruises, for example, Luxor itineraries are necessarily rushed because there is enough to occupy even casual sightseers for several days. The monuments lie on both sides of the Nile and spread over a wide area—the two major Luxor and Karnak temples are on the East Bank, and the Theban Necropolis on the West Bank includes the mortuary temples (such as Deir al-Bahri and Madinet Habu), the Valley of the Kings, the Valley of the Queens, and Tombs of the Nobles. Guides are obliged to keep to schedules and might not give you as much time at sights as you would like. Consider spending one or two nights at a hotel in Luxor or Aswan at either the beginning or end of your cruise to give yourself time to see sights not included on the boat's itinerary, or to revisit monuments that you want to see in greater depth.

On Lake Nasser cruises, the boat docks beside the High Dam near Aswan, but these itineraries include none of Aswan's top sights. The only thing near Aswan that the Lake Nasser cruise includes is a visit to see Nubian monuments reconstructed at New Kalabsha. You should stay an additional night or two in Aswan to see the Nubia Museum, the Temple of Isis at Philae, the famous granite quarries, the Tombs of the Nobles, Elephantine Island, and the 5th-century Saint Simeon's Monastery.

> **TOP TIP**
>
> Most short-duration Nile cruises sail during the night, which means you miss a lot of that wonderful river landscape. If you want to enjoy the river voyage as well as the ancient temples and tombs, book a longer tour.

CRUISE COSTS

Each season, cruise companies determine their prices based on what they expect upcoming demand will be. Prices listed below are therefore guidelines. At this writing, prices per person per night, double occupancy, ranged from $103 to $845 in high season (October through April), for five-star deluxe accommodations, depending on the boat. Note that prices increase 25% to 40% during Christmas, New Year's, and Easter, and they drop by 50% or more during the hotter summer months.

If you are not on a group tour combined with a Nile cruise, transfers from airport to boat are not always included; round-trip transfers should cost no more than $20 to $40 per person, depending on how you book them. On board, a special gratuity box might be displayed at the reception area for the boat crew; theoretically funds thus collected are shared equally. But it is always correct to reward directly those who provide exceptional service. For groups, tour guides might take it upon themselves to pass a separate envelope among members of their party, with a suggestion that $5 to $10 per passenger per day is appropriate, depending on the number of fellow passengers in your group. This is what the guide hopes to receive; tip whatever you feel is appropriate based on the service provided. The same applies for gratuities to the boat crew.

At booking, it's best to ask whether beverages are included in the cruise package. Some lines may include water, some may include alcohol. Others may offer an optional beverage package. Otherwise, payment for beverages and other services, such as laundry and outside phone calls, will be due at check-out. The charge for laundry is usually a pittance, but for alcoholic drinks it can be substantial. You sign bills when drinks are presented and services rendered, and you pay these at trip's end, just as on an ocean cruise. Egyptian and some foreign currencies are accepted, and most boats accept credit cards. Most boats are reluctant to play banker, however, and may refuse to break large bills—which is another good reason to add some time to your trip in Luxor, Aswan, or Cairo and stock up on cash.

8

WHAT IT COSTS IN U.S. DOLLARS AND EUROS			
$	$$	$$$	$$$$
Cruises in Dollars	under $250	$250–$475	$475–$700	over $700
Cruises in Euros	under €207	€207–€394	€394–€580	over €580

Average per diem per cabin, based on double occupancy, in high season (prices are 30% to 50% lower May–Sept.), excluding tips.

WHEN TO GO

The best time of year for a cruise is from the beginning of the winter season in October to the first half of April. Low water levels between late April and September may affect sailings north to Qena for the visit to Dendera, but very few boats make this trip. Sailings between Luxor and Aswan are not generally affected by water level. May is not recommended because of the likelihood of the *khamaseen,* sand-laden storms accompanied by scorching winds that make sightseeing all but impossible. Summer weather, especially in July and August, is dry. Temperatures in Upper Egypt and Nubia can soar to 108°F. Weather is ideal from November through February, when the mercury hovers between 75°F and 80°F. Temperatures drop at night, in both summer and winter.

BOOKING A CRUISE

USING A TRAVEL AGENT

If you intend to take a Nile cruise, make your bookings through a recognized international travel agency, preferably one that is a member of the American Society of Travel Agents (ASTA) or the Society of Incentive and Travel Executives (SITE). With more than 350 vessels in operation, the majority owned by small businesses, the choice of boats is vast, and standards among them vary considerably. The use of an established travel agent as a go-between is the best insurance that you will get what you think you are paying for.

Checklist: Get a printed itinerary with full details of communications, excursions, meals (whether included or not included), and availability of an English-speaking guide when you book your cruise. ⚠ Most Nile cruise boats are not designed or equipped to safely welcome small children. Typical age limits are 6 or 8 years. Check with the cruise line about age limits before you book.

RECOMMENDED AGENCIES IN EGYPT

There are hundreds of travel agencies in Egypt that can book Nile cruises. The following are among the most reliable.

Abercrombie & Kent. Apart from having good connections with many cruise companies, Abercrombie & Kent operates its own fleet five-star vessels on the Nile. The company also can combine Nile cruises with other sights throughout Egypt and the Middle East and Africa. ⊠ *18 Shar'a Youssef al-Guindy, El-Boustan Centre, 10th floor, Cairo* ☎ *02/2393–6255* ⊕ *www.abercrombiekent.com.*

CLOSE UP

Multiple Moorings

With so many cruise vessels on the river, most ships have to dock side by side at Luxor, Aswan, and at temples along the route so that passengers can disembark. This means that you very likely will pass through the lobby of one or more other boats to get to shore or return to your own vessel. It also means that at times all you can see out of your cabin window is the flank of the vessel moored alongside—a disappointment if you specifically booked a vessel with picture windows so you could enjoy the views. Understand that this practice is common to river cruising; the same thing happens on European rivers, though not to the extent it does in Egypt. It also helps to understand that this is the way Egyptians have solved the problem of too few docks.

Many passengers find it fascinating to watch the crew maneuver the boats into position. Of course, this isn't just a practice among the floating hotels. Feluccas and ferries line themselves up this same way, with similar "commuting" demands placed upon their passengers. Some cruise companies have private moorings, but this is not necessarily a guarantee that each of their ships moor individually. It may simply mean that only the boats of that company are tied together. In Luxor, new docks are on the drawing board to address this situation. In the mean time, it helps to keep some perspective. If a boat is docked, it is either because you are out seeing the sights or the day is over, it's time for bed. Enjoy the view from your cabin while it is under sail; that's the beauty of balconies and picture windows. Or just go up on deck. You'll see a lot more from up there anyway.

8

American Express. Amex is a major agency in Egypt and offers a wide variety of mostly five-star Nile cruises. ⊠ *Shar'a Abtel El Tahrir, El Corniche, Aswan* ☎ *097/230–6983* ⊠ *15 Qasr al-Nil, Cairo* ☎ *02/5747–9912* ⊠ *33 Shar'a Nabil El Wakkad, Heliopolis, Cairo* ☎ *02/2413–0375* ⊠ *Winter Palace Hotel, Luxor* ☎ *095/237–8333.*

Egypt Panorama Tours (Ted Cookson). This company has a good reputation among expatriates for efficiency and reliability. ☐ *Box 222, Ma'adi, Cairo 11728* ☎ *02/2359–0200 or 02/2358–1301* ⊕ *www.eptours.com.*

Emeco Travel. This is a well-established Egyptian company. ⊠ *2 Shar'a Tala'at Harb, Cairo* ☎ *02/2577–4646 or 02/2574–9360* ⊕ *www.emeco.com.*

Memphis Tours. This Egyptian company, established in 1955, specializes in custom private itineraries and now takes all of its bookings over the Internet, even if you stop by in person at the home office. It can book tours aboard the SS *Misr,* a historic Nile cruiser. ⊠ *1 Shar'a Qorh Ibn Sherik-Morad, Giza Square,Giza, Cairo* ☎ *800/282–3615 in the USA; 0800/098–8548 in the UK* ⊕ *www.memphistours.com.*

South Sinai Travel. South Sinai Travel is partnered with many U.S. travel agencies because of the company's expertise, efficiency, and reliability; it owns only one ship of its own but works with many others. ⊠ *79 Shar'a Merghany, Heliopolis, Cairo* ☎ *02/2418–7310* ⊕ *www.southsinai.com.*

Feluccas on the Nile. –photo by vacationwhipple, Fodors.com member

Thomas Cook. Thomas Cook was the first company to run Nile cruises. The Thomas Cook Offices at Luxor and Aswan offer a last-minute service that allows you to book and start your Nile cruise within one or two days. Visit their offices and let them know the level of luxury you want, and they will contact Nile cruise companies in that range to find out which boats have last-minute vacancies. Last-minute prices are discounted at all times of year, but you can't guarantee a particular vessel. *See ⇨ Guided Tours in Sports and Activities in the respective chapters for contact information for local offices in Aswan and Luxor.* ✉ *17 Shar'a Mahmoud Bassiouny, Cairo* ☎ *02/2576–6982.*

Travcotels. Among the largest Nile cruise operators, Travcotels owns a fleet of 22 boats (some bear the Iberotel or Jaz flags): 18 Nile cruisers, two Lake Nasser cruisers, and two dahabiyyas on the way, at this writing. ✉ *26th July Corridor, Sheikh Zayed City, Giza, Cairo* ☎ *02/3854–3222* ⊕ *www.travcotels.com.*

Voyageurs du Monde. This travel company, actually headquartered in France, manages bookings for the SS *Sudan*, the historic Nile steamer that appeared in the 1978 film *Death on the Nile.* ✉ *55 rue Sainte-Anne, Paris* ☎ *33/142–861–716* ⊕ *www.steam-ship-sudan.com.*

RECOMMENDED AGENCIES IN THE UNITED STATES

A number of travel agents arrange special-interest and tailor-made cruises.

Abercrombie & Kent. High-end tours range from family holidays to custom itineraries for couples and individuals. As part of the Splendors of the Nile tour, you take a four-day cruise between Aswan and Luxor that includes a flight to Abu Simbel and stops at Kom Ombo, Edfu,

Thomas Cook and the Birth of Mass Tourism

Born in 1808 in Derbyshire, England, Thomas Cook was a cabinetmaker, but he was also a Baptist and member of the Temperance Society. He began organizing day trips to local beauty spots for his fellow members, and in 1841 arranged for a local railway company to run a special train for his group, for which they charged a fixed fee that included passage and food—the first holiday package tour. By 1844 this had become an annual operation.

Cook quickly expanded this sideline. He organized trips for 165,000 people to attend the Great Exhibition in London in 1851, and four years later arranged his first tour outside Britain, when he sold packages to the Exposition Universelle in Paris. By the end of the decade, he was offering a European Grand Tour with travel, meals,

and hotels included. In the 1860s he added Egypt to his portfolio.

Cook went into partnership with his son, John Mason Cook, who had better business acumen than his father. John invested in the first Nile cruisers that were said to be the most luxurious seen on the river since Cleopatra's royal barge. When the British took control of Egypt in the 1880s, Thomas Cook Inc. became involved in military transport and postal services, and John became one of the most powerful men in Egypt.

Thomas Cook died in 1892 and John in 1898. The business stayed in the family until 1928, when Cook's grandsons sold it to Companie Internationale des Wagons-lits. However, the Thomas Cook name lives on in Egypt as the foremost tour operator.

---

and Dendera. ✉ *1411 Opus Place, Executive Towers West II, Suite 300, Downers Grove, IL* ☎ *630/954–2944 or 800/554–7016* ⊕ *www. abercrombiekent.com.*

African Travel. This company offers nine-day tours that hit major sights from Cairo to Aswan and include either seven or four days cruising the Nile. The average tour group has 10 people. The company also offers an Egypt and Kenya itinerary of 15 days including four days on the Nile. ✉ *1100 E. Broadway, Glendale, CA* ☎ *818/507–7893 or 800/421–8907* ⊕ *www.africantravelinc.com.*

American Express Travel Service. Many Amex agents are Egypt specialists and can book a wide range of tours. ✉ *822 Lexington Ave., New York, NY* ☎ *212/758–6510* ✉ *605 N. Michigan Ave., Suite 105, Chicago, IL* ☎ *312/943–7840* ✉ *327 N. Beverly Dr., Beverly Hills, CA* ☎ *310/274–8277.*

Destinations & Adventures International. This tour operator offers an 11-day excursion through Egypt that includes a four-day cruise between Luxor and Aswan. ✉ *8820 Wilshire Blvd., Suite 240, Beverly Hills, CA* ☎ *310/854–6060 or 800/659–4599* ⊕ *www.daitravel.com.*

Geographic Expeditions. The company offers tours of Egypt—as well as trips that combine Egypt and Jordan—that include a four-night Luxor–Aswan cruise. ✉ *1008 General Kennedy Ave., San Francisco, CA* ☎ *415/922–0448 or 800/777–8183* ⊕ *www.geoex.com.*

Rediscovering the Golden Age of Nile Cruising

People have been cruising the Nile for thousands of years, but thanks to archeological novels like those by Elizabeth Peters and mysteries like those by Agatha Christie, perhaps no mode of Nile navigation carries such emotional currency as steam-powered paddle-wheelers. The bygone mystique of the "Golden Era" of Nile cruising, which dates back to late 19th and earlier 20th centuries, lives on aboard three historic ships that now provide modern comforts amid their highly polished timbers. These three—the SS *Sudan,* the SS *Karim,* and the SS *Misr*—were, in fact, worthy of royalty. And there's still nothing like them. The 1885 SS *Sudan* (23 cabins, 5 suites) was a gift to King Fuad I, and decades later it served as the set for much of the action in 1978's *Death on the Nile.* The 1917 SS *Karim* (15 cabins) was yet another gift to Fuad I and sports

a small pool. The 1918 SS *Misr* (16 cabins, 8 suites) was originally built for the British Royal Navy but later was converted to a pleasure steamer for King Farouk, who was fond of celebrating his birthday on board. While each ship has its own profile and personality, they all possess certain traits in common. On each boat, every cabin is individually decorated to the period, but no two are alike. Public areas—a proper dining room and a lounge-bar—are dignified with dark woods and gleaming brass; cane chairs grace the sun decks. Booking passage on one of these ships is to partake of its proud history. The Sudan is managed by Voyageurs du Monde, the Misr by Memphis Tours (*see* ⇨ *Recommended Agencies in Egypt*), and the Karim by Voyages Jules Verne (*see* ⇨ *Recommended Agencies in the United Kingdom*).

Grand Circle Tours. Once owned by the AARP, Grand Circle specializes in tours for travelers over-50 and has a robust program of Egyptian tours virtually year-round; all these tours include a three- or four-night Nile cruise, but the cruise cannot be booked separately. The company's ship, the MS *River Anuket* (70 cabins), is privately owned. ☎ *800/959–0405* ⊕ *www.gct.com.*

Journeys of the Mind. Journeys of the Mind specializes in educational adventures, well off the beaten path, that promote cultural understanding. Cruises are part of varied programs led by Egyptologist guides (who are professors) to archaeological digs, dinners in Egyptian homes, and cruises between Luxor and Aswan. ✉ *221 N. Kenilworth Ave., No. 413, Oak Park, IL* ☎ *708/383–8739* ⊕ *www.journeysofthemind.com.*

Lindblad Expeditions. This upscale adventure-oriented travel company has a good reputation and also owns it own boat. Tours may include talks with preservation specialists. ✉ *96 Morton St., 9th Fl, New York, NY* ☎ *212/765–7740 or 800/397–3348* ⊕ *www.expeditions.com.*

Misr Travel. This Egyptian company specializes in Middle East tours and has been in business since 1934; it is based in Cairo and has a solid reputation in Egypt. ✉ *1270 Ave. of the Americas, Ste. 604, New York, NY* ☎ *212/332–2600 or 800/223–4978* ⊕ *misrtravel.org.*

Tarot Tours Garranah. This operator offers a choice of cruises and itineraries in many different price ranges. ✉ *378 Columbia Ave., Cliffside Park, NJ* ☎ *201/606–2255 or 866/646–4602* ⊕ *www.tarottoursusa.net.*

RECOMMENDED AGENCIES IN THE UNITED KINGDOM

Abercrombie & Kent. ✉ *St. George's House, Ambrose St., Cheltenham, Gloucestershire UK* ☎ *0124/254–7700 or 0845/618–2200* ⊕ *www.abercrombiekent.co.uk.*

Bales Worldwide. This company offers a range of cruises and is a booking agent for a fleet of dahabiyyas. ✉ *Bales House, Junction Rd., Dorking, UK* ☎ *0845/057–1819* ⊕ *www.balesworldwide.com.*

Imaginative Traveller. This budget-oriented tour operator offers overnight and multinight felucca trips as part of some of its itineraries and arranges small-group tours and custom itineraries. ☎ *0845/077–8802 in the UK or 800/241–2137 in the U.S.* ⊕ *www.imaginative-traveller.com.*

Thomas Cook. ✉ *Thomas Cook Business Park, Bretton Way, Peterborough, Cambridgeshire, UK* ☎ *0871/895–0055* ⊕ *www.thomascook.co.uk.*

Voyages Jules Verne. This is a well-established company that offers luxury Egypt voyages and owns a classic Nile cruiser, the SS *Karim.* ✉ *21 Dorset Sq., London, UK* ☎ *0845/166–7003 in the UK only or 0207/616–1000* ⊕ *www.vjv.com.*

PAYMENT

You must pay the full cost of the cruise up front. If you have booked through a tour operator in Egypt, you may be asked to send payment via wire transfer; this is a common situation (and one reason why people often choose to book through a tour operator in their own country). However, you may save considerably if you make your arrangements directly through the Egyptian operator of your cruise. At long last, Egyptian-based travel companies are increasingly doing business online. On the whole, travelers are more than satisfied with their cruise experience, lauding it in glowing terms as a trip of a lifetime, an experience never to be forgotten. Of course, some customers go away more than dissatisfied. If that turns out to be you, and you feel that your experience was beyond atrocious, consider requesting a refund.

MAJOR NILE CRUISE LINES

$$$$ ⊞ **Abercrombie & Kent.** Since its founding as an African safari company in 1962, Abercrombie & Kent, or simply A&K, has grown into a worldwide luxury travel leader with headquarters in the United States and Great Britain, and three-score offices around the globe, including a major operation in Egypt. It consistently earns top ratings from every English-language travel magazine out there. On the Nile, A&K conducts three-, four-, and seven-night cruises, usually as part of a larger itinerary that includes Cairo and Abu Simbel, though cruises be booked separately. Its ships moor at private docks in Luxor and Aswan. The company has an unimpeachable reputation for refined, intelligent comfort on all fronts. A&K's reputation is such that its guests are sometimes allowed access to sights that are off-limits to other groups. In fact, MS *Sunboat III* (16 cabins, 2 suites) became the first Nile cruiser in recent years to reinstate port calls at Nag Hammadi to visit Abydos, and it is one of the few to include a stop at Dendera. MS *Sunboat IV* (36 cabins, 4 suites) also visits Dendera as part of its four-night itinerary. The new *Zein Nil Chateau* (4 cabins, 2 suites) is one of six dahabiyyas that can be booked through A&K; it sails seven-night itineraries that make rare calls at El-Kab and Gebel Silsileh, though guests who charter the entire ship can customize the trip to their liking. **Pros:** elegant decor, studious service, fine dining, and some of the most gifted Egyptologist guides in the country set the line apart. **Cons:** some guests may find traveling primarily with other English speakers a bit too insular; prices are very high. ☎ *800/554–7016 in the U.S. and Canada; 0845/618–2200 in the UK; 02/2393–6255 in Egypt* ⊕ *www.abercrombiekent.com, www.abercronbiekent.co.uk* ▭ *AE, DC, MC, V.*

$$$–$$$$ **Belle Epoque Travel Bureau.** Since the mid-1980s, Cairo-based Belle Epoque has been crafting custom tour programs for small groups and one-of-a-kind journeys for individual travelers. Its artisan approach to travel—every detail is lovingly thought out—translates into that rarest of delights in Egypt: the complete boutique travel experience. Of its six dahabiyyas, two are available for weeklong charters between Luxor and Aswan. Booking on the other four are through Bales Worldwide (*see* ⇨ *Recommended Agencies in the United Kingdom, above*). Each of Belle Epoque's wooden dahabiyyas (six cabins each) are new but built by hand in the traditional way, furnished with Cairo antiques that re-create the 1930s, and finished with Egyptian-made handicrafts: needlework tapestries that shade the sundecks, earthenware dishes used at mealtimes, locally made olive-oil soap in cabin bathrooms. Moorings are close to nature at private spots along the Nile's pastoral West Bank in both Luxor and Aswan, or on islands en route—a plan that adds garden walks and riverside picnics to temple and tomb visits. Meals are generally served on deck or in the salon—buffet lunches and a set-menu dinner—and often feature organic ingredients grown in the company's riverside vegetable patches. The company's two motor ships, the MS *Eugenie* and the MS *Kasr Ibrim*, were the first launched on Lake Nasser; they follow three- and four-night itineraries. On Lake Nasser, the MS *Eugenie* (52 cabins, 2 suites) takes the guise of a turn-of-the-century paddle wheeler. The MS *Kasr Ibrim* (55 cabins, 10 whirlpool suites) recalls the art deco era. Both count bars, steam rooms, exercise equipment, and swimming pools among their assets. **Pros:** the nearest you can get to experiencing the era of the monarchy, without giving up air-conditioning. **Cons:** the dahabiyyas have no bar and do not serve alcohol, but guests are welcome to bring their own provisions. ☎ *02/2516–9649 in Egypt* ⊕ *www.dahabiya.com* ▭ *AE, MC, V only on the Lake Nasser boats.*

$$$–$$$$ **Mövenpick.** Before this Swiss-based company became a resort empire, it was already an established name in the food sector. (Many Europeans swoon at the very mention of Mövenpick ice cream.) Speaking of names, "Mövenpick" came when the founder was inspired by the graceful flight of a seagull. Its hotels went international with the launching of Mövenpick's first Nile cruiser, MS *Radamis I*. The company operates four Nile cruise boats on classic three- and four-night sailings between Luxor and Aswan. A fifth ship makes three- and four-night cruises between Aswan and Abu Simbel on Lake Nasser. In the Nile, the MS *Radamis I* (61 cabins, 4 family cabins, 4 suites), MS *Radamis II* (69 cabins, 6 suites), MS *Royal Lotus* (60 cabins, 2 suites), and the MS *Royal Lily* (56 cabins, 4 whirlpool suites) exhibit the design virtues that have become a hallmark of the company's land-based resorts: clean lines, rich woods, a scattering of warm-colored fabrics, and no froufrou. That holds whether the ship follows a more European-modern aesthetic, as in the MS *Radamis I* and *II*, a decidedly Asian bent aboard the MS *Royal Lily*, or a Euro-Saharan blend aboard the MS *Royal Lotus*. As befitting a company that started in food service, meals aboard take the Swiss approach toward healthy lifestyles. On Lake Nasser, the MS *Price Abbas* (42 cabins, 18 junior suites, 4 royal suites) takes the form of an old-time steamer, where cabins are entered from wooden walkways that run around the decks. **Pros:** you can book directly online with the ship of your choosing, and the cabin category you want, just as you would a hotel room. **Cons:** Nile ships in this price range ought to add the stop at Dendera. ☎ *800/344–6825 in the US; 0800/441–1111 toll-free in the UK, 02/2418–2282 in Egypt* ⊕ *www.moevenpick-hotels. com* ⊟ *AE, DC, MC, V.*

\$\$\$–\$\$\$\$ ☷ **Nour El Nil.** At the dawn of the 21st century, one small company decided it was time to make sailing the Nile a more comfortable experience than that offered by feluccas, at a more relaxed pace than that of the motor ships. That company was Nour El Nil, and it takes credit for reintroducing dahabiyya tourism to Egypt. On the Nile, it operates in one direction only from Esna to Aswan, on five-night voyages that visit the temples of Edfu, Al-Kab, Gebel Silsileh, and Kom Ombo. Because its itinerary lays claim to the longest actual navigation (sailing) times of any boats between Luxor and Aswan, there is plenty of time for other activities such as desert walks, island stops, encounters with the locals, and, best of all, the joy of being on the river among the passing scenery. True to the era that inspired their birth, the boats of Nour El Nil are not motorized, though they do generate electricity. And they are not air-conditioned; sailing conditions make it unnecessary most of the year. The idea is to offer not just the dahabiyya style of ship, but the authentic dahabiyya lifestyle along with it. That doesn't mean they are void of luxury, though. The *Meroe* (eight cabins, two suites) is the company's largest craft, and its pair of signature red-and-white striped sails recalls the days when all such vessels were known by their own unique colors. Beneath those sails, guest accommodations in the *Meroe*, the *El Nil* (eight cabins, two suites), the *Malouka* (six cabins, two suites), and the company's smallest vessel, the *Assouan* (six cabins, two suites), all share the same striking design features. Here, brilliant white walls, ceilings, and bedding, accented with boldly colored throw pillows, bring an oh-so-photogenic Parisian aesthetic to the Nile. Even the shaded decks are hung with crystal chandeliers. **Pros:** individuals can book a cabin without having to charter the entire boat. **Cons:** lack of air-conditioning may discourage some travelers; you must bring your own mosquito netting. ☎ *33/142–257–716 in France; 010/657–8322 in Egypt ⊕ www.nourelnil.com ▤ No credit cards.*

$$$$ ⬚ **Oberoi.** This India-based hotel empire got its start in the 1930s and is one of the world's top luxury-travel brands. In addition to hotels and cruises, the company has launched a corporate-travel agency and charters private jets. It has reputation for exclusivity—and the prices to match. On the Nile, it includes Dendera on four- and six-night classic motor-ship cruises aboard boats that are, quite simply, the most prestigious on the river. You can't talk about Nile cruises without oohing and aahing over the Oberoi boats. The MS *Philae* (54 cabins, 4 suites) assumes the look of a turn-of-the-century paddle wheeler on the outside, while interiors bring the décor of an English manor house to the Nile. Every cabin has private balcony. The yachtlike MS *Zahra* (25 cabins, 2 suites with private whirlpool terrace), which may well be the Nile's most expensive stay afloat, takes the minimalist gallery-space approach to decor and counts an à la carte restaurant and a full-service spa among its assets. Both ships dock at private moorings in Aswan and Luxor. **Pros:** top-of-the-line service, luxury touches, and attention to detail are Oberoi hallmarks. **Cons:** en suite balconies are a great idea, but they're not exactly private; curious Nile fisherman and souvenir touts sometimes follow cruise ships in their own boats. ☎ *800/562–3764 in the U.S., 866/377–5241 in Canada; 00–800/1234–0101 toll-free in the UK ⊕ www.oberoihotels.com ▤ AE, DC, MC, V.*

$–$$ ⬚ **Overseas Adventure Travel.** This tour company, whose parent is Grand Circle Travel, a company that markets exclusively to older (over 50) travelers and was once the travel arm of the AARP, includes three or four nights aboard its privately owned ship the MS *River Hathor* (16 cabins) on all its Egypt tours. Because the company has a regional office in Egypt, it's a major player in Egyptian tours, operating them nearly year-round. The small-group tours are limited to 16 people, but two tour groups ordinarily sail on the cruise together, with separate guides that remain with the group throughout the entire tour that includes the cruise portion. The company aims primarily at the over-50 market, but some group members are almost always younger. The MS *River Hathor* is a small but comfortable cruiser, with all the basic features including Internet and a small pool on the sundeck. However, cabins are fairly small and basic (there are no TVs, for instance). Lunches and breakfasts are generally buffets, but some dinners are served à la carte; however, this is not luxury touring by any means. OAT's parent Grand Circle Travel also operates tours and cruises on the Nile, but their groups tend to be much larger. **Pros:** Reasonable single supplements that are sometimes waived; a small ship is a more intimate experience. **Cons:** The ship is comfortable but basic; the cruise cannot be booked separately from a longer tour of Egypt. ☎ *800/493–6824 ⊕ www.oattravel.com ▤ AE, DC, MC, V.*

$$$–$$$$ ⬚ **Sonesta.** The company that would eventually become Sonesta started in the 1940s with a beach hotel in Massachusetts. Four decades later it set forth upon the world's longest river with the MS *Nile Goddess*. The line runs between Luxor and Aswan on three- four- and seven-night Nile Cruises—in ships that are so grand, they may actually upstage the very monuments that people come to Egypt to see. Take the MS *Star Goddess* (33 suites). The balconied curves of its lobby lead to suites where the bathrooms have glass sinks and marble tub surrounds. The MS *St. George I* (47 cabins, 10 suites) enjoys ceilings higher than most Nile cruisers, and its baroque-style decor says, "Napoleon was here." The MS *Moon Goddess* (49 cabins, 4 suites) blesses every cabin with a balcony, and the sports-minded with a jogging track. In comparison, the newly refitted MS *Nile Goddess* (47 cabins, 6 suites) is decidedly understated, in a cigar-bar-meets-desert-sheikh sort of way. The *Sonesta Amirat Dahabeya* (6 cabins, 2 suites) is also now under sail. **Pros:** cabins and public spaces are a delight for interior-design fans. **Cons:** the MS *Sun Goddess* is currently in dry dock, leaving one less Sonesta to choose from; some guests may find the exuberant ship decor too much of a contrast to life along the riverbanks. ☎ *800/766–3782 in the U.S. and Canada; 02/2262–8111 in Egypt for the Goddess fleet; 02/2418–3540 in Egypt for St. George I* ⊕ *www.sonesta.com* ▬ *AE, MC, V.*

$–$$ 🖥 **Travcotels.** In the early 1980s, an Egyptian started out with one Nile cruiser and an entrepreneurial spirit. That venture has since grown into a travel empire—Travco Group—that has a hand, one way or another, in serving over a million travelers a year, and that's just in Egypt. The company's acquisition of Steigenberger Hotels in 2009 put Travco at the head of 124 properties in Egypt, Europe, and the Middle East. On the Nile, it conducts three-, four-, and seven-night classic motor-ship cruises under the Iberotel, Jaz, and Travcotel brands. Many of its ships dock right downtown in Luxor and Aswan, within walking distance to points of interest. At this writing two dahabiyyas are in various stages of completion. On Lake Nasser, it operates three- and four-night voyages between Aswan and Abu Simbel. Travco builds and manages its own vessels, most of which are rated five-star superior and five-star deluxe. Its largest Nile cruiser, perhaps the largest on the river, is the Iberotel MS *Crown Empress* (120 cabins, 8 suites with balcony), with a steam room, sauna, and massage services aboard. Its most plush ship, the Jaz MS *Omar El Khyam* (68 cabins, 8 grand suites, 4 royal suites), navigates Lake Nasser dressed in dark woods, crisp black-and-white brocades in the dining room, and silky bedcovers in the cabins—all of which have private balconies. The MS *Nile Empress* (29 cabins), with only five-star status, is an older ship with small cabins furnished much like American budget hotel chains. Guest hail from Britain, Western Europe, and Asia—where Travco has offices—and most are on a Travco package tour that includes Cairo and its sights. Now that Travco ships can be booked online just like hotels, it's easy for individuals from anywhere to plan a trip. **Pros:** high-standard accommodations, meals, and service at prices that put a once-in-a-lifetime Nile cruise within reach of budget travelers. **Cons:** most ships are large and may lack an intimate feel. ☎ *02/3854–3222 in Egypt* ⊕ *www.travcotels.com* ▬ *MC, V.*

$$$$ 🖥 **Uniworld.** From its beginnings in the 1970s, Los Angeles–based Uniworld has become a top river-cruise operator in Europe, and it's gotten the awards to prove it. In 2009, Uniworld introduced its special brand of boutique river cruising to the Nile with its very own boat, the MS *River Tosca*. On the Nile, Uniworld follows three-, four, and seven-night

The main lobby of a Uniworld Nile cruiser

classic motor ship cruises, with the four- and seven-night sailings stopping at Dendera. Its cruises may only be booked as part Uniworld's 7- and 11-night cruise tours that also include Cairo. The MS *River Tosca* (41 suites, 2 owners' suites) is distinguished by dark, polished woods in public areas—the coffered ceilings come as a pleasant surprise—and classic furnishings that would not be out of place in Vienna. At this writing, the *River Tosca*'s one-room suites are reputed to be the largest on the Nile, decorated in restful country-white finishes; picture-frame trim adds to the luxurious statement. All cabins feature Juliette balconies, custom beds, and large bathrooms with bidets and separate marble tubs and showers. Egyptian-made toiletries are supplied in-cabin and in the small spa that provides massage services. Uniworld's solid reputation for fine service and customer satisfaction attracts English-speaking guests; predominantly Americans and British, but Australians and South Africans sometimes may be along for the ride. Dinner most evenings is à la carte, rather than a buffet. **Pros:** possibly the only Nile cruiser with 24-hour self-serve coffee and tea bar, where guests also can help themselves to a snack. **Cons:** although the company is known worldwide for its European river cruises, it is new to Egypt and has yet to establish its cachet there. ☎ 800/773–7820 ⊕ *www.uniworld.com* ▭ *AE, MC, V.*

EGYPTIAN ARABIC VOCABULARY

It's easier to think of Arabic not as one language but two. The first is the written language, which is taught in schools and is understood by educated individuals throughout the Arabic-speaking world. This is the language of publications and official situations; the more formal the occasion, the higher the likelihood that standard Arabic will be spoken. But that's not what you'll hear on the streets. The other Arabic is the spoken form, which varies greatly in vocabulary, accent, and pronunciation from country to country, and locality to locality. To envision this, think of standard Arabic as equivalent to Shakespearean English; then realize how different that is from English as it is really spoken by California surfers, Edinburgh presbyters, Harrod's department store clerks, New Orleans jazz musicians, Bronx auto mechanics, Irish shepherds, or Melbourne vintners.

Although Arabic is the official language of Egypt, most Egyptians that cross paths with the tourism industry speak English at least at the introductory level (with the possible exception of drivers). Many also may speak French, German, Italian, Spanish, or Japanese. It is not necessary to learn Egyptian Arabic to enjoy a trip to Egypt, but mastering a word or two will greatly enrich your experience. Even a feeble attempt on your part to speak Egyptian Arabic will be met with enthusiasm, delight, perhaps a little extra in the way of service, and sometimes an invitation to dinner with the family.

Egyptian Arabic is a good dialect to acquire because it is understood throughout most of the Arab-speaking world. This is because Cairo for decades has been the epicenter of the film, television, music, and advertising industries throughout North Africa and the Middle East. That being said, it's worth knowing that Upper Egypt, Middle Egypt, and Lower Egypt have their own customs of pronunciation and appropriate (and taboo) vocabulary. Don't worry: as a tourist you won't be held to such standards.

THE DIFFICULTIES OF ARABIC

One of the problems of translating Arabic into English is that, if the standard form is translated, you'll have a tough time trying to connect the words you study with the ones you hear, because some of the vocabulary is different. Another challenge is that the Arabic alphabet doesn't just look different from Roman-based ones, its letters represent sounds that do not occur in English. To further complicate matters, scholars have never agreed upon a uniform set of symbols—an extended English alphabet, as it were—to correspond to those sounds. Individual translators (and would-be students) are on their own in deciding how to proceed.

PRONUNCIATION

In the accompanying chart, we address some of those challenges as follows: When you see *gh* in this vocabulary, pronounce it like a French *r*, lightly gargled at the back of the throat. If unsure, stick to a *g* sound. When you see *ch* in this vocabulary, pronounce it as you would the German *ch*, as in *achtung*. If you are having trouble, use a breathy *k* sound. The *j* sound common to the rest of the Arabic-speaking world is most often pronounced *g* in Egypt, so that's what we've used here.

Egyptian Arabic also employs glottal stops (the brief pause in "ah oh," for example); and in Cairo especially there's a habit of dropping the *q* sound and substituting a glottal stop in certain words. In both cases we indicate that with a ', though we've kept such use to a minimum.

EGYPTIAN ARABIC

ENGLISH	ARABIC TRANSLITERATION	PRONUNCIATION

GREETINGS AND BASICS

ENGLISH	ARABIC TRANSLITERATION	PRONUNCIATION
Hello: Peace upon you.	al-salaam alaikum	as-sa-**lahm** alla-**ay**-koom
(Reply)		
Hello: And peace upon you.	w alaikum al-salaam	wi alla-**ay**-koom as-sa-**lahm**
Hello: Welcome.	ahlan w sahlan	**a**-hlan wa **sa**-hlan
(Reply to a man)	ahlan bik	**a**-hlan **beek**
(Reply to a woman)	ahlan biki	**a**-hlan **beek**-ee
Goodbye.	ma al-salaama	maa' sa-**lah**-ma
Mr., Sir	ya fandim, beh, hadritak; ustaaz	ya **fan**-dim; bey, ha-**drit**-ak; oo-**staz**
Mrs., Madam	hadritik; madam	ha-**drit**-ik; ma-**dam**
Miss	anissa	aa-**nis**-sa
How are you? *(to a man)*	izzayak?	iz-**zay**-ak?
How are you? *(to a woman)*	izzayik?	iz-**zay**-ik?
(Reply)	al-hamdu lillaah	al-**ham**-du li-laah
Pleased to meet you.	tasharafna	ta sha-**raf**-na
Yes	aywa; naam	**aye**-wa; nahm
No	la	**la'**
Please *(to a man)*.	min fadlak	men **fad**-lak
Please *(to a woman)*.	min fadlik	men **fad**-lik
Thank you.	shukran	**shoo**-kran
(Response)	afwan	**af**-wahn
God willing.	insh'Allah	in-**shah**-ahl-lah
I'm sorry *(from a man)*.	ana aassaf	**an**-a **aa**-saf

EGYPTIAN ARABIC

ENGLISH	ARABIC TRANSLITERATION	PRONUNCIATION
I'm sorry *(from a woman)*.	ana aasfa	**an**-a **aas**-fah

DAYS

Today	al-yum	al-youm
Yesterday	imbarah	im-**berr**-eh
Tomorrow	bukra	**book**-rah
Sunday	il-had	ih-**had**
Monday	il-itneen	'lit-**neen**
Tuesday	il-talatt	it-ta-**latt**
Wednesday	il-arbaa	'lar-**bah**
Thursday	il-khamis	il-kha-**mees**
Friday	il-gumae	ig-**goum**-mah
Saturday	il-sabt	is-**sab**-t

NUMBERS

1	wahid	**wa**-hid
2	itneen	it-**neen**
3	talata	ta-**lat**-ta
4	arbaa	ar-**bah**
5	khamsa	**kham**-sah
6	sitta	**sit**-tah
7	sabaa	**sa**-bah
8	tamanya	ta-**man**-ya
9	tisa'	**tis**-sah
10	aashara	**aa**-she-rah
11	hidasher	**hid-ash**-er
12	itnasher	it-**nash**-er
20	aashreen	ash-**reen**
50	khamseen	kham-**seen**
100	miya	**mee**-yah

EGYPTIAN ARABIC

ENGLISH	ARABIC TRANSLITERATION	PRONUNCIATION
200	miyateen	mee-ya-**teen**

USEFUL PHRASES

Do you speak English?	tatkelem englisi?	tet **kel**-em **in-gleez-ee**?
I don't understand.	ana mish afham.	**an**-a **mish af**-ham
I'm lost.	ana khasyrt.	**an**-a kha-**sert**
I'm American (man).	ana amriqui	**an**-a am-**ree-kee**
I'm American (woman).	ana amriqiya	**an**-a am-**ree-kee**-yah
I'm British (man).	ana inglisi	**an**-a in-**glee**-zee
I'm British (woman).	ana inglisiya	**an**-a in-**glee**-zee-ya
What is this?	eh da?	'**eh** dah?
Where is?	fin?	feen?
the airport	al-matayyar	al-ma-**tayy**-ar
the train station	al-maatr	al-ma-**at**-'r
the hotel	al-fundu'	al-**foon-doo**'
the museum	al-mathaf	al-**mat-haf**
the coffee shop	al-'ahwa	al-**ah**-wah
the restaurant	al-mataam	al-**ma-taa**-am
the telephone	al-tilifoon	it-**til-lee**-foon
the hospital	al-mustashfa	al-moo-**stash**-fah
the post office	al-bosta	al-**bost-a**
the rest room	al-hamam	al-**hamm**-aam
the pharmacy	al-farmacia	al-**far-ma-see**-ya
the bank	al-banq	al-baynk
the embassy	al-sifara	as-**see**-far-**ra**
I (man) want to buy . . .	ana ayz ishtary . . .	**an**-a ayeez **ish**-ta-ree . . .
I (woman) want to buy . . .	ana ayza ishtary . . .	**an**-a **aye**-zah **ish**-ta-ree . . .

EGYPTIAN ARABIC

ENGLISH	ARABIC TRANSLITERATION	PRONUNCIATION
a city map	khareta al-medina	kha-**ree**-ta al-me-**dee**-nah
two tickets	itneen tazkara	it-**neen taz**-kar-ah
How much is it?	bi kam?	bee kaam?
It is expensive (he, she).	ghali; ghaliya	**gha**-lee; **gha**-lee-ya
A little	shwaya	**shway**-ya
A lot	kitir	kit-**teer**
Enough (Stop).	kifaiya	key-**fay**-ya
I (man) am ill.	ana ayaan	**an**-a aye-**yaan**
I (woman) am ill.	ana ayaana	**an**-a aye-**yaan**-ah
I (man) want a doctor.	ana ayz doctor.	**an**-a ayeez dok-**tohr**
I (woman) want a doctor.	ana ayza doctor.	**an**-a **aye**-zah dok-**tohr**
I have a problem.	aandi mushkila.	**aan**-dee moosh-**kill**-la
Left	shimal	she-**mal**
Right	yamin	ya-**meen**
Help!	al-ha'ony!	al-ha'-**oo**-nay!
Fire!	haree'a!	ha-**ree**-'ah!
Caution!/ Look out!	chaly b'aelek!	**cha**-lee **b'aal**-ek!

DINING

I (man) want . . .	ana ayz . . .	**an**-a ayeez . . .
I (woman) want . . .	ana ayza . . .	**an**-a **aye**-zah . . .
Water	mayya	**may**-yah
Bread	aysh	**ay**-eesh
Vegetables	khudaar	**khu**-dar
Meat	lahma	**la'h**-mah
Fruit	fawakeh	fah-**wah**-kuh
Tea	shay	shay

EGYPTIAN ARABIC

ENGLISH	ARABIC TRANSLITERATION	PRONUNCIATION
Coffee	'ahwa	**'ah**-wa
Fork	shoka	**show**-kah
Spoon	maala	**mahl**-a
Knife	sikeena	sik-**keen**-ah
Plate *(Dish)*	tabaq	**ta**-bak

Travel Smart Egypt

WORD OF MOUTH

"Drink water. Drink Water. DRINK WATER. This can NOT be said enough! Dehydration will make you feel like you've been poisoned if you let yourself get there."

—Casual_Cairo

GETTING HERE AND AROUND

Egypt has always been ruled by the close relationship between the Nile and the desert. Nile waters make the land fertile and even today the vast majority of Egyptians live within a mile or so of the river. The river was also the major conduit for transport until the arrival of the railways just over 100 years ago. The country's major rail line follows the river, as does a modern highway.

Since ancient times, the country has geographically been divided into two regions, Upper Egypt and Lower Egypt. Lower Egypt is the northernmost section of the Nile Valley (closest to the Mediterranean Sea), incorporating the oldest Egyptian capital of Memphis, the modern capital Cairo, and the Nile Delta. It's called Lower Egypt because it refers to the lower reaches of the river. Upper Egypt covers the southern stretches of the country and the ancient capital of Thebes (modern Luxor). The name refers to the fact that this part of the country lies around the most upstream sections of the Nile that lay within the boundaries of Egypt.

Cairo, the capital since the end of the first millennium AD, is still the country's main hub for transport connections. Domestic air flights will offer the fastest connections anywhere, and a 2-hour flight will get you almost anywhere in the country. Overland, the train trip from Cairo to Luxor takes around 12 hours, 15 hours to Aswan, and 2 or 3 hours to Alexandria.

The Red Sea and the Sinai Peninsula are east of Cairo. The two main towns, Hurghada on the Red Sea and Sharm El-Sheikh in the Sinai, can both be reached by road and by air from Cairo. Road surfaces are generally good. Flights take around 1 hour with the overland journey being around 7 hours to Hurghada and 6 hours to Sharm.

Until the 1970s, the only way to reach the Western Desert oases was by camel train. Today, there are paved highways, dropping the journey time from Cairo to Bahariyya from many days to a half day. The road is in good condition. Siwa is considerably more remote, a 15-hour nonstop journey from Cairo on a circuitous route with road conditions that vary from excellent to poor (though it's certainly passable with a standard vehicle). You'll need permission and a four-wheel-drive vehicle to use the cross-country route from Siwa to Bahariyya. Sand has swallowed up much of the old asphalt road, making navigation difficult. The journey takes around 6 hours. Bear in mind that although road surfaces are generally in good condition, signage is poor, and there are numerous hazards, from slow-moving animal carts to people walking on the highway. You may prefer not to undertake long journeys by public bus.

TRAVEL TIMES FROM CAIRO	BY AIR	BY BUS	BY TRAIN
To			
Alexandria	½ hour	2½ hours	2–3 hours
Sharm El-Sheikh	1 hour	6 hours	N/A
Hurghada	1 hour	7 hours	N/A
Luxor	1½ hours	N/A	9½ hours
Aswan	2 hours	N/A	12½ hours
Baharriya	N/A	5–6 hours	N/A

▌ AIR TRAVEL

Flying time to Cairo from New York is 10 hours on a nonstop flight; from the West Coast, the minimum flying time is 17 hours (you'll need to make at least one stop). Cairo is 4 hours from Paris, Amsterdam, and Frankfurt, and 5 hours from London.

If you need to book domestic flights after you have arrived in Egypt, you'll need to visit an EgyptAir office (or book online) or a reputable travel agent at least one day before you fly—but don't expect there to be seats available that late, especially in peak season. Book flights to Abu Simbel as early as possible as these flights fill up fast at all times of year.

AIRPORTS

Cairo International Airport is the country's primary international airport and the only one that has nonstop flights from the United States. Terminal 3, which opened in late 2008, is devoted to EgyptAir, both international and domestic flights, and EgyptAir's Star Alliance partner airlines that fly to Egypt (at this writing, Austrian Airlines, BMI, Lufthansa, Singapore Airlines, and Turkish Airlines). Small numbers of scheduled flights from Europe also land at Sharm El-Sheikh, Hurghada, and Luxor.

If you book a package through a travel agent or have prearranged a tour, your airport transfers will almost certainly be included in the price. Look for your company's sign as you exit baggage claim. If you book independently, then you may have to take a taxi. Ask your hotel if it has a limo transfer service; most hotels do, and though the vehicle is not a true limousine, it will be a vehicle in good condition. You will be charged more than the normal taxi fare for this service (some hotels include transfers if you book an executive-floor room), but after a long flight, the stress-free transfer may be worth the extra money.

Cairo Airport also offers fixed-rate car service (called a limo, although it is generally an average sedan) to all hotels. Private taxis try to charge the same, but with the limo there's no need to haggle a fee, and the vehicles are in good condition.

Be sure to give yourself a full two hours for international check-in, and allow an hour to travel to the airport from Downtown/Zamalek unless you are flying late at night or early morning, when it can take a little more than half an hour.

Information Cairo International Airport (*CAI ⊠ Cairo* ☎ *022/265–5000*). **Hurghada** (*HRG ⊠ Hurghada* ☎ *065/344–2592*). **Luxor International Airport** (*LXR ⊠ Luxor* ☎ *095/237–4655*). **Sharm El-Sheikh International Airport** (*SSH ⊠ Sharm El-Sheikh* ☎ *069/362–3304*).

FLIGHTS TO AND FROM EGYPT

Only EgyptAir and Delta Airlines offer nonstop flights to Egypt from the United States. Both fly from New York's JFK into Cairo. Most European airlines offer flights to Egypt, and the majority of Americans must connect in Europe to reach Cairo. Some European budget airlines also fly to Egypt, though few of these airlines have telephone numbers in the country, relying instead on their Web sites.

Nonstops to Egypt Delta (☎ *02/2735–9770 in Cairo, 800/241–4141 in the U.S.* ⊕ *www. delta.com*). **EgyptAir** (☎ *0900/70000 (national call center) in Egypt, 212/581–5600 in New York, 310/215–3900 in Los Angeles* ⊕ *www. egyptair.com*).

Major European Airlines Air France (☎ *02/2770–6250 in Cairo, 800/237–2747* ⊕ *www.airfrance.us*). **Alitalia** (☎ *02/3333–0618 in Cairo, 800/223–5730* ⊕ *www. alitaliausa.com*). **Austrian Airlines** (☎ *02/2735–2777 in Cairo, 800/843–0002* ⊕ *www.aua.com*). **British Airways** (☎ *02/2480–0380 in Cairo, 800/247–9297* ⊕ *www.britishairways.com*). **Finnair** (☎ *02/2579–8601 in Cairo, 800/950–5000* ⊕ *www.finnair.com*). **KLM Royal Dutch Airlines** (☎ *02/277–0625 in Cairo, 800/225–2525* ⊕ *www.nwa.com*). **Lufthansa** (☎ *19380 in Cairo, 800/399–5838* ⊕ *www.lufthansa.com*). **SAS Scandinavian Airlines** (☎ *800/221–2350* ⊕ *www.flysas.com*). **Swiss International Airlines** (☎ *02/2737–7738 in Cairo, 877/359–7947* ⊕ *www.swiss.com*).

European Budget Airlines Air Berlin (⊕ *www.airberlin.com*). **Astreaus** (⊕ *www. flystar.com*). **Condor Airlines** (⊕ *www. condor.com*). **Easyjet** (⊕ *www.easyjet.com*).

Jet Air Fly (⊕ www.jetairfly.com). **Thomas Cook Belgium** (⊕ www.thomascookairlines. com). **Thomsonfly** (⊕ www.thomsonfly.com). **Transavia** (⊕ www.transavia.com). **XL Airways** (⊕ www.xl.com).

FLIGHTS WITHIN EGYPT

EgyptAir is the only provider of scheduled domestic flights in Egypt. In addition to Cairo, Aswan, Luxor, Hurghada, and Sharm El-Sheikh, EgyptAir flies to Abu Simbel, Alexandria, Assuit, and Marsa Alam.

Domestic Egyptian Airlines EgyptAir (☎ 0900/70000 [national call center] in Egypt, 212/581–5600 in New York, 310/215–3900 in Los Angeles ⊕ www.egyptair.com).

▌ BUS TRAVEL

Privately owned buses are the cheapest way to get around Egypt, but because of security concerns, the Egyptian authorities dissuade independent travelers from using them on certain routes, specifically from Cairo down the Nile to Luxor and from Luxor east to Hurghada.

Bus transport in Egypt is divided geographically, usually with one major company providing services in each region, except in the Sinai and Red Sea coastal areas, where there is some competition. Fares are cheap, and buses are generally modern and in good condition, though the stream of video entertainment played at high volume and overzealous air-conditioning can make the journey slightly unpleasant. Driving standards are poor.

Cairo has a new bus terminal, called Turgomon, for all of its bus service around the country. The station is located near Downtown and all the ticket windows are labeled with the geographic region. There are a handful of bus companies. The East Delta Travel Company runs from Cairo to the Suez Canal and the Sinai; El Gouna Transportation runs from Cairo down the Red Sea Coast; Super Jet offers services from Cairo to the Sinai and the Red Sea; the Upper Egyptian Bus Company

has service from Cairo down the Nile to Luxor and Aswan and east from Luxor to Hurghada; the West and Middle Delta Company covers routes to Alexandria, and along the Mediterranean Coast to the Libyan border and Siwa Oasis.

Bus Information East Delta Travel Company (☎ 02/2577–9347 or 02/262–3128 ⊕ www. eastdeltatravel.com). **El Gouna Transportation** (☎ 19567 [in Egypt only] or 02/2201–9941). **Superjet** (☎ 809/682–9670). **Upper Egypt Company** (☎ 809/682–9670 ⊕ www.bus. com.eg). **West and Middle Delta Company** (☎ 809/682–9670 ⊕ www.bus.com.eg).

▌ CAR TRAVEL

Driving in Egypt can be a stressful and harrowing experience. Egyptian drivers usually ignore speed limits on open roads and drive vehicles that are dangerous from a structural and mechanical point of view. Out in the countryside, there are no pedestrian walkways, and the road shoulders are not well defined. You'll need to watch out for little children, goats, camels, and oxen—constant vigilance is required. At night these same animals can still be problems, but worse is the fact that few Egyptian drivers use their headlights after dark, so it's not always easy to see oncoming traffic.

In the city, you'll need to watch constantly for other traffic and for pedestrians who cross the street anywhere. They can and do appear from behind stationary vehicles, and they cross in the gaps between moving traffic.

Wherever you travel by road in Egypt, you meet police checkpoints. The authorities control all traffic but particularly vehicles carrying foreign tourists. If you are traveling along the Nile Valley in Upper Egypt by car, you should travel with a guarded traffic convoy. Visit the tourist office to find out where the convoy meets and at what time; if you don't join the convoy, you'll be stopped at the first checkpoint out of town and either turned back or told to wait for the next convoy or for a guard to be assigned to your vehicle. Waiting for a guard can take well over an hour and could ruin any carefully prepared itinerary.

GASOLINE
Gas stations and rest areas are plentiful on major highways, and credit cards are widely accepted. In areas that see fewer travelers, such as the Western Desert, they are less so. Carrying cash is a good idea, and always be sure to take extra gas with you when traveling in the Western Desert. Most gas stations in Egypt are full-service, and it's customary to tip the attendant who fills up your car a pound or two. All gas is unleaded and is sold by the liter. Plain unleaded is called *tamanin*, or 80, denoting the level of purity. Higher-quality gasoline is available as *tisa'in*, or 90, and occasionally *khamsa wa tisa'in*, or 95.

Prices are reasonable by U.S. standards—£E1.50–£E1.80 per liter (the equivalent of $1.02–$1.22 per gallon) depending on the grade of gasoline. Most pumps show amounts in Roman numerals but you still may find some in Arabic. Watch as the attendant starts the pump to see that it reads 000. You should give the attendant a tip of a few Egyptian pounds.

ROAD CONDITIONS
Road conditions are generally good, especially in the Sinai and along the Red Sea Coast. There are very few maps available, and signposting—although in Arabic and English—is generally poor.

ROADSIDE EMERGENCIES
Make sure that your car-rental company provides you with the contact details or a 24-hour emergency number to call in case of any problems.

Any traffic accidents will be dealt with by police.

Always take extra water when traveling long distances, especially on the desert roads. If at all possible, carry a cell phone with you as well as the telephone numbers of police stations and hotels along your route. If you have car trouble on the highway, get your car off the road as soon as possible, then wait and flag down any passing vehicle. Daily buses serve even remote areas, and they will stop for you if they see you. More worrisome are accidents. Many Egyptian car owners don't carry insurance, and disputes tend to be resolved on the scene with more or less fanfare depending on the seriousness of the accident. Insist on getting a policeman who speaks English, and take down the license number of the other driver. For serious accidents in which people have been injured, get emergency help first and then immediately contact or drive to your embassy. In all situations, insist on having present a senior police officer who speaks English.

Emergency Services Police (☎ 122).

RULES OF THE ROAD
Speed limits are 60 KPH in built-up areas and 90 KPH on the open road (these should be posted at regular intervals at the side of the highway), but most local drivers ignore these and drive as fast as they can. Lane discipline is nonexistent, and drivers will try to pass even on bends and up hills when they cannot see if there's traffic coming in the other direction. There are restrictions against using cell phones while driving, and seat belts are compulsory. However, drivers regularly flout these laws. There are numerous traffic officers in the main towns, but enforcement is patchy. Fines of £E100 are the norm, but officers can confiscate your license if they feel you have been driving dangerously.

Drunk driving is a serious offense, and perpetrators can be arrested, fined (around £E500), and have their vehicles confiscated. The legal blood alcohol level above which it is an offense to drive is 0.05%. However, breath tests are not common because most Egyptians don't drink alcohol. There is no legislation relating to children. Car-rental companies do not supply car seats for infants; if you have small children, consider bringing a car seat from home.

Around Egypt, there are police checkpoints every 30 km or so along every highway, and also at all major intersections and river crossings. You should show your passport to the officers manning the barrier. Foreigners are sometimes stopped for no reason in an attempt by the officer to squeeze money from them. If you smile and insist you did not break the law, they will usually let you go.

Right turns are permitted on red at some intersections—indicated by a flashing light above or to the side of the traffic lane. But not all drivers waiting in this lane want to turn right.

You are not allowed to take cars rented in Egypt out of the country.

In Cairo many traffic lights at intersections do not work, and traffic officers who control traffic with hand movements man these areas. ⚠ Authorities have recently installed cameras at intersections in parts of downtown Cairo to catch drivers who cross intersections.

If you are traveling in one direction on a main highway but want to turn around—or if you merge onto a highway but cannot initially travel in the direction you want, you need to look ahead for a midstream turning area on the left-hand side of the highway. You should see a sign on the overhead gantry, but these are not always well signposted. Be very careful as these feeder lanes lead you directly into the flow of the fastest traffic.

In Upper Egypt, tourist traffic is organized into guarded convoys that follow set routes at set times each day. Whether you self-drive, have a driver, book a day tour, or travel in an organized itinerary, you'll have to work within the convoy system and travel at prescribed times.

CAR RENTAL

Egypt is one destination where renting a car is not generally recommended. There are several reasons for this. First, the level of driving skill in Egypt is generally erratic; there's little adherence to laws and safety guidelines, and driving at dangerous speeds for the conditions is the norm. Second, major towns and cities have poor signage, making navigation next to impossible; parking is almost nonexistent. Finally, for security reasons, the government organizes all tourist traffic along the Nile Valley into convoys, which run a certain fixed hours. Even if you self-drive, you must join a convoy, making it impossible to travel on your own timetable.

Because of all these difficulties, you'll find numerous tour operators on the ground, all of which provide inexpensive, reliable tours to all major sights, making the need to rent a car redundant. In addition, you may be able to book private tours and guides for little more than the cost of renting a car.

The one area where it may be sensible to rent a vehicle is in the Sinai or for trips along the Red Sea Coast from a base in Hurghada or El Gouna—roads here are less busy.

Since the late 1990s the number of international car-rental companies in Egypt has dropped dramatically. You cannot rent a car in Luxor or Aswan, for instance, though you can rent in Cairo or Alexandria, on the Red Sea Coast, and in the Sinai, though even those offices with an international brand name will be franchises.

Most companies have minimum age limits (normally 21 or 23). ⚠ You'll also need an international driving license. Unlimited mileage is generally not offered in Egypt; most car-rental deals only offer 100 km per day in the basic rental price. The average rate for each kilometer (0.62 mi) after that is around $0.25. This can add greatly to your bill when you return the vehicle. Most car-rental agency agreements prohibit off-road driving, so avoid dirt roads in the Sinai or desert tracks away from the Nile Valley.

Make sure that the car you receive is in good condition; it is wise to specify that you want a new car. Many vehicles are at least two years old and most have dents and scrapes. Make sure you receive an emergency number you can call 24 hours a day in case of mechanical problems or accident.

With so little demand you should have no problem finding car rentals at any time of the year. If you decide to rent in a resort, visit the rental office a couple of days before you need the car. If you want to rent from the time of your arrival, book from home.

If you rent and intend to park at your hotel between journeys, you'll be asked to hand in the car registration document and your driving license at the security gate during your time in the hotel complex. The documents will be returned when you leave. Don't forget the registration card because if you don't return it with the car at the end of your rental period, there's a huge penalty of $300 to $500 to cover the time and cost for the rental company to get a replacement.

If you intend to return your rental car to Cairo airport during the day (except on Friday), add an extra 60 minutes to your travel time in case of traffic delays.

Major Agencies Avis (☎ 800/331–1084 in the U.S., 02/265–2429 in Cairo ⊕ www.avis.com). **Budget** (✉ Cairo International Airport, Heliopolis, Cairo ☎ 02/265–2395 ☎ 800/472–3325 in the U.S. ⊕ www.budget.com). **Europcar** (✉ 6m Misr Lel Taamir Bldgs., Masaken Sheraton Buildings, Heliopolis, Cairo ☎ 02/2267–2439 ✉ Cairo International Airport, Heliopolis, Cairo ☎ 02/2267–2439 ⊕ www.europcar.com). **Hertz** (✉ Ramses Hilton, 1115 Corniche al-Nil, Cairo ☎ 02/575–8914 ✉ Cairo International Airport, Heliopolis, Cairo ☎ 02/265–2430 ✉ Le Méridien Pyramids Hotel, Giza, Cairo ☎ 02/3377–3388 ☎ 800/654–3001 or 02/347–2238 for central reservations office in Egypt ⊕ www.hertz.com).

Local Agencies Smart Rental (✉ Corniche al-Nil, Ma'adi, Cairo ☎ 02/524–3006 ⊕ www.smartlimo.com).

CAR INSURANCE

Most rental companies in Egypt include full insurance in the quoted rental price, but do check the fine print to make sure you're getting on paper what was agreed to verbally. Insurance does not cover the loss of the car registration document; if you don't return this with the car, you'll be liable for at least $300 for a replacement (including loss of income as the vehicle stands idle while the rental agency waits for the replacement document).

■ TAXI TRAVEL

Taxis are the backbone of transport in Egypt. Fares are cheap and, in theory, regulated, but if you take a black taxi, you'll need to haggle. Ask your guide or hotel concierge what are realistic fares between destinations before you depart. Taking a taxi to or from any hotel will always be more expensive than taking one from the street. And always make sure you agree to a fare with the driver before you enter the taxi.

In Cairo, white and yellow taxis have meters. Make sure the driver turns on the meter when you enter. White taxis start at £E2.50 and yellows at £E3.50. They typically charge £E0.50 by the kilometer and the same for one minute of waiting. Yellow taxis charge less for the wait, so if you take one to a tourist site, it is not a bad idea to ask the driver to wait for you outside.

In Sharm El-Sheikh, taxi fares are posted at major taxi stands, but visitors rarely make it to these places to check out the prices. Hikes in fuel prices in 2008 have also played havoc with well-established fares.

Information City Cab (yellow) (☎ 16516 or 19195) in Cairo only, especially for airport transport.

▌ TRAIN TRAVEL

Between Alexandria and Cairo, Turbo trains are the fastest form of transport (average journey time is two to three hours), and tickets for these services cost £E52 for first class and £E29 for second class. There are three types of trains: Turbini, Spanish, and French. The Turbini takes two hours and 10 minutes, the Spanish two hours and 20 minutes, and the French takes three hours, although trains often run late.

Currently, Turbini trains depart from Cairo at 8 AM, 2 PM, and 5 PM; Spanish trains at 9 AM, noon, 5 PM, and 10:30 PM; and the French trains at 6 AM, 8:30 AM, 11 AM, 3:10 PM, 4 PM, and 8 PM. From Alexandria Turbini at 8 AM, 2 PM, and 5 PM; Spanish trains at 7 AM, 3 PM, 7:30 PM, and 10:15 PM; and French trains at 6 AM, 8:15 AM, 11 AM, 3:30 PM, 5 PM, and 8 PM.

Trains also travel between Cairo and Upper Egypt. From Cairo to Luxor, a one-way ticket is £E90 in first class and £E46 in second class; from Cairo to Aswan it's £E109 in first class and £E55 in second. First class offers you more space, and you have a choice of traveling during the day or at night. For night trains, foreigners sometimes only have the option of riding first class, so if the train is fully booked, you might not find a seat. Buy your tickets one day in advance. Considerably more comfortable sleeper cars run by private company Abela make the daily trip to and from Luxor and Aswan. Buy your tickets far in advance (at least one week). Fares are in U.S. dollars, and the price is $60 per person each way in a double compartment.

For exact schedules and ticket prices, inquire and purchase tickets a few days before departing at the main Ramses train station in Cairo.

Information Abela (✉ *Ramses Train Station, Cairo* ☎ *02/2574–9474* ⊕ *www.sleepingtrains. com*).

ESSENTIALS

ACCOMMODATIONS

The Egyptian government awards star ratings to all hotels, with five stars being the highest rating. The star rating of a hotel or cruise ship also dictates the price range the management can charge. However, Egyptian star ratings don't quite equate to international standards. You may notice a difference in service and standards of fixtures and fitting when compared to an equivalent hotel at home.

Egypt has a huge range of choice in the five-star and one- or two-star categories, but relatively little choice in the middle range. Under three stars, properties are basic but usually clean. Most will have a small basic en-suite shower-only bathroom.

Five-star hotels have a wide range of facilities. Those in Cairo also cater to business clients, so they tend to have smaller pools and fewer or no sports facilities, whereas hotels on the Red Sea Coast and in the Sinai have large pools and more expansive leisure facilities. More expensive hotels generally have Web sites that allow you to book online, but large tour operators often book huge blocks of rooms far in advance, so don't be surprised if you don't initially find a vacancy even in the off-season. It's sometimes easier to book upscale hotels through travel agents and tour operators for this reason.

Smaller and more inexpensive hotels don't always accept credit cards. Enquire before you book. It's not uncommon for cheaper properties to require an electronic wire transfer for payment, which they will usually ask for in advance.

All hotel reviews have been condensed for this book. Please go to Fodors.com for full reviews of each property.

TIP→ Assume that hotels operate on the European Plan (**EP**, no meals) unless we specify that they use the Breakfast Plan (**BP**, with full breakfast), Continental Plan (**CP**, Continental breakfast), Full American Plan (**FAP**, all meals), Modified American Plan (**MAP**, breakfast and dinner) or are all-inclusive (**AI**, all meals and most activities).

CATEGORY	COST IN U.S. DOLLARS	COST IN EUROS
$	Under $70	Under €45
$$	$71—$130	€46—€80
$$$	$131—200	€81—€130
$$$$	Over $200	Over €130

All prices in dollars or euros for a standard double room in high season, based on the European Plan (EP) and excluding 10% tax and service charges (usually 10%).

COMMUNICATIONS

INTERNET

Paid Internet access of some kind is available in almost every hotel. Most of the five-star hotels in Cairo have paid access in the rooms, though free Internet access is usually one of the privileges of booking an executive-floor room. In remote areas of the country, Internet access is typically only at Internet cafés.

Wi-Fi is becoming more prevalent in the better hotels, particularly in Cairo; it is usually free but generally exists only in the lobby and some public areas, rather than in your room. Most modern coffeehouses use Internet through a service provided by one of the mobile phone operators in Egypt. If you make a purchase, most places will give you a free scratch card for access, but you will need to input a local mobile phone number. There are dozens of Internet cafés in Cairo, and usually one or two in each of the major towns and resorts. Access prices vary from £E5 per hour in Internet cafés in the capital to £E30 per 30 minutes in hotels.

PHONES

To call Egypt from the United States, dial 00, then the country code 20 and the local number.

CALLING WITHIN

To make a local call, you must dial the regional code plus the seven-digit or eight-digit number (Greater Cairo has eight-digit numbers). Directory assistance for calls within Egypt is 140; its operators are known to speak English well.

City codes within Egypt include: Cairo 02; Alexandria 03; Luxor 095; Aswan 097; Sharm El-Sheikh 069; and Hurghada 065.

Rates for calling within Egypt vary by the hotel, but local calls are sometimes only a few piastres per minute, unless you are calling from a five-star hotel, which charges significantly more, varying from one hotel to the next.

CALLING OUTSIDE EGYPT

From Egypt, just dial 00–1 plus the area code and number to call the United States or Canada. For the international operator, dial 120. It's cheaper to call after 8 PM in the evening.

The AT&T USA Direct and MCI calling cards can be used in Egypt. Simply dial the access number and follow the instructions. If you use a pay phone to call, you may require a coin or card deposit. Some hotels block the use of these numbers. If this is the case, try contacting the telephone company operator for a connection.

Phone cards, which are sold at gift shops and supermarkets, can usually give you considerable savings if you're calling the United States or Canada.

Access Codes AT&T (☎ 02/2510–0200). **MCI** (☎ 02/279–5570).

MOBILE PHONES

The mobile phone network is well established in Egypt. Vodafone, Mobinil, and Etisalat are the three major companies in Egypt, and they have offices all across the country. If you have a quad-band GSM phone, it will probably work in Egypt, but you can also bring an old phone from home (get the phone company to unlock the phone for you) and buy a SIM card once you get to Egypt so that you can receive calls and texts on a local number. Phones start at £E180, SIM cards cost around £E25, and you can buy top-up minutes from £E10 to £E200 at one time. To call internationally, the cost is £E1.99 per minute, but you might have to contact the provider first to get this price.

Contacts Cellular Abroad (☎ 800/287–5072 ⊕ www.cellularabroad.com) rents and sells GMS phones and sells SIM cards that work in many countries. **Mobal** (☎ 888/888–9162 ⊕ www.mobalrental.com) rents mobiles and sells GSM phones (starting at $49) that will operate in 140 countries. Per-call rates vary throughout the world. **Planet Fone** (☎ 888/988–4777 ⊕ www.planetfone.com) rents cell phones, but the per-minute rates are expensive.

■ CUSTOMS AND DUTIES

When entering Egypt, there are few restricted items, beyond the normal prohibited goods, such as firearms, narcotics, etc. Customs officers will be concerned if you bring in goods in large amounts to sell for a profit—for instance, large numbers of cameras or mobile phones—but most visitors have no problems.

The Egyptian authorities are very keen to keep control of their historical heritage, so you'll need official paperwork to allow you to export anything regarded as an antique or antiquity.

If you want to bring your pet, you'll need a certificate of origin and a health certificate. The certificate of origin should be from the breeder or store where you bought your pet. The certificate of health needs to be dated and stamped by your vet.

When you arrive in Egypt you can bring in alcohol and tobacco duty-free. You can also buy further supplies at accredited duty-free shops during the first 48 hours after you arrive. In Cairo, you'll find shops at the airport, City Stars Mall, and in the Mohandiseen district. There are also shops in El Gouna and Sharm El-Sheikh.

U.S. Information U.S. Customs and Border Protection (⊕ *www.cbp.gov*).

▌EATING OUT

Local eateries are no more than street kitchens with a couple of tables, though you can find better restaurants serving local food in Cairo and the major tourist towns.

Cairo and Alexandria are both well known for their *ahwas* (coffee shops). Today U.S.–style joints offering caffeine in a range of flavors and styles are joining these traditional cafés.

In all major towns you'll find a range of international cuisines including Thai, Chinese, and Italian. The best restaurants are usually found in upscale hotels. Vegetarians will always be able to find local salads, hummus, and rice to sustain them; however, finding variety during a trip may be a problem (pizza is available in most tourist destinations, as are delicious soups, just be aware that some of these soups are made with meat-based stocks).

For information on food-related health issues, see ⇨ *Health below.*

MEALS AND MEALTIMES

Unless otherwise noted, the restaurants listed in this guide are open daily for lunch and dinner.

The main meal of the day is lunch (*ghada*). It starts with a soup, such as *shorbat'ads* (lentil), for which Egypt is famous throughout the Middle East, or *molukhiyya,* a thick green-leaf soup. A wide range of *mezze* (appetizers) follows, and this can make a meal in itself. You'll taste dips like *tahini* (sesame-seed paste) or *baba ghanouj* (mashed roasted eggplant), *wara einab* (stuffed grape leaves), a crispy local *ta'ameya* (Egyptian felafel),

and *fuul* (stewed fava beans). The main course is invariably grilled chicken, often roasted whole in a rotisserie oven, lamb or beef shish kebab (skewered in chunks), or *kofta* (minced lamb on skewers). *Hamam mahshi* (stuffed pigeon) is popular. Fresh vegetables are hard to come by, except in the rather generic cucumber salad, but stewed vegetables such as *bamia* (okra) are common. Every meal comes with round loaves of pita-style bread, either *'aish baladi* (coarse-grain wheat) or *'aish shami* (white). *'Asha,* or dinner, is composed of a similar menu, although many Egyptian families partake in only a light meal at night, consisting of fruit and sandwiches.

For *fitar* (breakfast), you can do as Egyptians do and indulge in a steaming plate of ful, accompanied by fried eggs, bread, and pickles. Lighter fare includes croissants and other savory pastries, bought fresh from the local bakery and topped with cheese or jam. In Cairo, there are a few American-style breakfast restaurants, but these are by no means widespread. Certain places like El Fishawy Café in the Khan al-Khalili stay open for 24 hours.

In the countryside, few Egyptians eat out and so restaurants there tend to be rudimentary affairs. In cities and resorts you'll find a range of restaurants, from street kitchens to gourmet spots with silver service. Most restaurants stay open throughout the day, so you'll always be able to find something when you get hungry.

PAYING

Credit cards are widely accepted in hotel restaurants; less so in private establishments. More private establishments in Cairo and the Red Sea resorts accept cards than in the rest of the country.

For guidelines on tipping see ⇨ *Tipping below.*

CATEGORY	COST IN EGYPTIAN POUNDS
$	Under £E50
$$	£E 51–£E100
$$$	£E 101–£E150
$$$$	Over £E150

All prices are per person in Egyptian pounds for a main course at dinner.

RESERVATIONS AND DRESS

Make reservations when planning to dine in upscale hotel restaurants, particularly if you are not a guest. Restaurants requiring a jacket and tie for men are rare, with the notable exception of several restaurants in the Sofitel Winter Garden Hotel in Luxor. Diners in upscale Cairo restaurants tend to dress up, however.

WINE, BEER, AND SPIRITS

Although Egypt is an Islamic country and many Egyptians do not drink alcohol, the country does produce its own beer and wine. Local beers are very thirst quenching, especially if drunk cold. Look for the trade names Luxor, Saqqara, and Heineken (brewed under license in Egypt). The wine industry isn't competition for the French or Californian vineyards but does supply acceptable table wine—look for the labels Grand Marquis, Cape Bay, or Jardin du Nil.

Many local restaurants don't serve alcohol, so ask before you order your food if this is important to you. Any hotel above two stars should by law serve alcohol, but outside the tourist hot spots there may not be enough demand for hotels to hold a stock. Imported alcohol and wine are very expensive, so expect to pay a premium for these when they are available. On religious holidays and during the month of Ramadan, many restaurants do not serve alcohol.

▌ ELECTRICITY

The electrical current in Egypt is 220 volts, 50 cycles alternating current (AC). Most wall outlets take rounded plugs, so North American travelers will need both a converter and an adapter.

If your appliances are dual-voltage, you'll need only an adapter. Don't use 110-volt outlets marked FOR SHAVERS ONLY for high-wattage appliances such as blow-dryers. Most laptops operate equally well on 110 and 220 volts and so require only an adapter.

▌ EMERGENCIES

Violence against foreign tourists is very rare in Egypt; pick-pocketing and theft can sometimes be a problem in busy markets and at popular tourist sights. Tourist police patrol all main tourist areas and have brown uniforms with TOURIST POLICE on their armbands. They are helpful, but not all the street officers speak English well.

If you are a victim of theft, you'll need to report it to the regular police and get a case number in order to make a claim on your insurance policy. This can be a time-consuming exercise (two or three hours).

If you are ever threatened on the street or in a public place, do not hesitate to scream for help or make a scene—it will not go unheard, and you'll find more than one person coming to your defense. Whatever the emergency, expect Egyptians to go out of their way to help.

Medical personal generally speak some English, and almost all doctors are English speakers. Medical facilities are not as good as at home, particularly throughout the Western Desert oases. Pharmacists are well qualified and able to give advice on common low-risk ailments; they can also prescribe many medications (including antibiotics and even Viagra) that are available only by prescription in the United States. Each town or district has at least one late-night pharmacy but these open in rotation—so ask your hotel concierge to find out which one is open when you need it. Pharmacies normally stay open until 10 PM. In major cities you'll also find 24-hour pharmacies; ask at your hotel's registration desk if you need to find a nearby pharmcy.

If you are the victim of a serious crime or accident, contact the U.S. Embassy in Cairo for assistance.

Emergencies Ambulance (☎ 123). **Fire Brigade** (☎ 125). **Police** (☎ 122). **Tourist Police** (☎ 126).

U.S. Embassy United States Embassy (✉ 8 Shar'a Kamel El Din Salah, Garden City, Cairo ☎ 02/2797–3300).

▮ ETIQUETTE AND BEHAVIOR

Dress is a very important part of respect in Egypt. Wearing shorts, short skirts, and halter tops in the streets is considered inappropriate, despite the fact that many tourists persist in being inappropriately attired. Cover shoulders and knees when you enter mosques and churches.

Beyond this, the relationship between the sexes is very different compared to a non-Muslim country. Public displays of affection such as kisses on the lips between couples are frowned upon in Egypt. This is a country where kissing and cuddling is considered private behavior. Public drunkenness is also discouraged.

Sexuality is not widely discussed in Egypt, and homosexuality remains taboo. Therefore an open gay population is hard to come by, and a general acceptance also isn't prevalent. However, there is a large gay and lesbian population that remains underground. While there's no law against homosexuality, gay men in particular can be jailed and/or prosecuted under Egypt's wide-ranging and ill-defined indecency laws. With discretion, gay travelers can expect to get along fine, as most Egyptians will assume that the relationship is simply a friendship, and public shows of affection amongst men (holding hands and walking arm in arm) is a normal show of masculine brotherhood in Egypt and many other Muslim countries.

▮ HEALTH

There are several minor hazards in Egypt that you need to bear in mind. First, never underestimate the power of the sun. Even in the coolest months, there's a risk of sunburn and sunstroke. Stay out of the sun as much as possible, wear a hat when you are out and about, apply high-SPF sun cream regularly (international brands are available in pharmacies and supermarkets), and keep hydrated by drinking plenty of fluids (not alcohol).

Water quality is a concern. Never drink water from the tap water or from public fountains. Local people drink this water but it may contain microbes that your body isn't used to. Ice in five-star hotels should be produced using purified water, but if in doubt ask for drinks without ice (*min gheir talg*). Bottled water (*mayya ma'daniya*) is inexpensive and readily available. Remember to check that the seal on the bottle is intact before you open it.

If you are traveling with children, all this advice goes double. Children may not be aware that they are beginning to suffer from dehydration or sunstroke. Give them plenty to drink even if they don't complain of being thirsty, and keep their heads and skin covered.

Most people get some form of intestinal disturbance in Egypt. This can be a minor change in regularity put down to a change in water supply or the hot weather, but it's sometimes more serious and may be related to the ingestion of contaminated food or water. To minimize your risk, make sure the meat you eat is well cooked, avoid unpeeled fruits and vegetables, and avoid dairy products, unless the packaging looks as if it comes from a legitimate factory and is stored in a functional refrigerator. Ask about whether the salad in your hotel has been washed in purified water. Antinal is a locally produced remedy for traveler's diarrhea that's inexpensive and effective, but if symptoms become severe call a doctor immediately. The main danger here is dehydration, so if you cannot keep down liquids, don't hesitate to call for a doctor immediately.

Do not swim in the Nile, and don't drink the river water because of the risk of picking up waterborne parasites. Avoid all standing freshwater, as there is the risk of bilharzia (schistosomiasis).

There's little risk of malaria in Egypt—so there's no need to take antimalarial tablets—but it's worth protecting yourself from insect bites as some of these little critters do carry dengue fever or West Nile virus. You can buy anti-insect skin creams and sprays in pharmacies and tourist shops. It's easy to buy the antimosquito coils that burn to give off fumes that repel the insects.

MEDICAL INSURANCE AND ASSISTANCE

Consider buying trip insurance with medical-only coverage. Neither Medicare nor some private insurers cover medical expenses anywhere outside the United States. Medical-only policies typically reimburse you for medical care (excluding that related to preexisting conditions) and hospitalization abroad, and provide for evacuation. You still have to pay the bills and await reimbursement from the insurer, though.

Another option is to sign up with a medical-evacuation assistance company. A membership in one of these companies gets you doctor referrals, emergency evacuation or repatriation, 24-hour hotlines for medical consultation, and other assistance. International SOS Assistance Emergency and AirMed International provide evacuation services and medical referrals. MedjetAssist offers medical evacuation.

Medical Assistance Companies AirMed International (⊕ www.airmed.com). **International SOS Assistance Emergency** (⊕ www.internationalsos.com). **MedjetAssist** (⊕ www.medjetassist.com).

Medical-Only Insurers International Medical Group (☎ 800/628–4664 ⊕ www.imglobal.com). **International SOS** (⊕ www.internationalsos.com). **Wallach & Company** (☎ 800/237–6615 or 540/687–3166 ⊕ www.wallach.com).

SHOTS AND VACCINATIONS

The CDC recommends routine vaccinations as well as a vaccination against hepatitis A; it's also wise to have a vaccination against hepatitis B. The risk of typhoid is generally low, but if you plan to visit the Western Desert oases or stay in the countryside you should discuss this risk with your doctor; get a typhoid vaccination if you intend to take a multiday felucca trip on the Nile. Rabies is recommended for travelers spending a lot of time outdoors, especially in rural areas.

Health Information National Centers for Disease Control & Prevention (CDC ☎ 877/394–8747 international travelers' health line ⊕ www.cdc.gov/travel). **World Health Organization** (WHO ⊕ www.who.int).

OVER-THE-COUNTER REMEDIES

Pharmacies in Egypt are well stocked—you can even buy antibiotics over the counter—and medications are quite inexpensive by U.S. standards, but not all product names will be the same as in the United States. Pharmacists are trained to help and will be able to offer you the generic drug you need or one that will deal with your symptoms. For headaches, Panadol (more generally known as acetaminophen in the United States) is the most common remedy.

■ HOURS OF OPERATION

Banks are open for business 9 to 2 Sunday through Thursday, although certain branches stay open until 5 PM. In addition, you can withdraw money from your home bank using ATMs found outside major banks and inside hotels. Businesses are usually open by 8 AM and close by 4 or 5 PM Sunday through Thursday.

Egypt's postal offices are open from 8:30 to 3. The larger post offices in Cairo—Muhammad Farid (Downtown), Ataba Square (next to the Postal Museum), and the Ma'adi offices—are open until 6 PM daily.

Shops are generally open 9 AM until 10 PM, although they may open and close later. Many close for at least an hour for Friday prayers and some close on Sundays, though in the tourist towns, souvenir shops are open daily. In the coastal resorts, shops sometimes close during the afternoons.

HOLIDAYS

Egypt's fixed national holidays include New Year's Day (January 1) Sinai Liberation Day (April 25), Labor Day (May 1), Evacuation Day (June 18), and Revolution Day (July 23).

The Muslim lunar calendar is normally 10 to 11 days earlier than the Gregorian year. The month of Ramadan lasts for anywhere from 28 to 30 days and entails fasting—no food, water, or smoking—from dawn to sunset. It's followed by Ead al-Fetr, known as the "small feast" in English. The "big feast" is Eid al-Adha, which occurs at the end of the Pilgrimage Period. The other two main Muslim holidays are the Muslim New Year (in late March or early April), and the Prophet Muhammad's birthday (falling anywhere

between late May and late June). Coptic holidays are observed by Coptic citizens only. They are Christmas (January 7), Baptism (January 20), Palm Sunday (the Sunday before Easter), and Easter.

■ MAIL

Egypt Post maintains post offices in all large villages and towns and in every city district. Postcards to countries outside the Middle East cost £E1.50 and take a minimum of seven days to reach their destination. A more costly express-mail service is also available with arrival within 48 hours. Note that these are expected delivery times, as advised by the postal service; they don't reflect how long mail actually takes to arrive. If in doubt, double these times. If you need to send a package home, it's more reliable to use FedEx or DHL, which are very expensive.

■ MONEY

It's fine to tip tour guides in U.S. dollars, but for small tips (restroom attendants especially) local currency is better since £E1 is worth far less than US$1. Few stores accept U.S. dollars, so you should plan to exchange currency. ATMs (*makinat al-flus*) are plentiful in major tourist areas, and you can rely on them to restock your wallet with Egyptian pounds, but they may be difficult to find (or broken) in smaller, more out-of-the-way places. Most large tourist hotels have banks right in the hotel that can do currency exchange; some of these will also have ATMs.

You'll need cash to purchase locally produced souvenirs in markets, cheap snacks and beverages in small stores, and for taxi, felucca, and carriage rides. All restrooms in Egypt are attended, and the staff expect a small tip of £E1 or at least 50 piastres. Be prepared to tip a few pounds for all kinds of service; £E5 and £E10 are the most useful notes for short taxi rides, small purchases, and for tipping. All major hotels, cruise ships, and leading restaurants take payment by credit cards.

In shops and *souks*, cash is still king. Far fewer establishments outside hotels take credit cards, and paying by credit card can incur 2% to 3% surcharges.

Prices throughout this guide are given for adults. Substantially reduced fees are almost always available for children, students, and senior citizens.

ITEM	AVERAGE COST
Cup of coffee	£E25 for American coffee
Glass of wine	£E30–£E60
Glass of beer	£E22–£E30
Sandwich	£E20
One-mile taxi ride in capital city	£E10
Museum admission	£E30–£E80

ATMS AND BANKS

Your own bank will probably charge a fee for using ATMs abroad; the foreign bank you use may also charge a fee. Nevertheless, you'll usually get a better rate of exchange at an ATM than you will at a currency-exchange office or even when changing money in a bank. And extracting funds as you need them is a safer option than carrying around a large amount of cash.

ATMs that accept international cards (Cirrus and PLUS) are numerous in Cairo, Luxor, Aswan, and in the coastal resorts of Hurghada, El Gouna, and Sharm El-Sheikh. You can find them at bank branches, in shopping malls, post offices, and in the lobbies of major hotels. Major providers include the National Bank of Egypt, HSBC, Credit Agricole Egypt, and National Societe General Bank (NSGB). Screen commands are in Arabic, English, and sometimes French.

In the oases of the Western Desert, the banking system still lags behind the rest of Egypt. Bring enough cash with you to fully fund your trip.

CREDIT CARDS

Throughout this guide, the following abbreviations are used: **AE**, American Express; **DC**, Diners Club; **MC**, MasterCard; and **V**, Visa.

It's a good idea to inform your credit-card company before you travel, especially if you're going abroad and don't travel internationally very often. Otherwise, the credit-card company might put a hold on your card owing to unusual activity—not a good thing halfway through your trip. Record all your credit-card numbers—as well as the phone numbers to call if your cards are lost or stolen—in a safe place, so you're prepared should something go wrong. Both MasterCard and Visa have general numbers you can call (collect if you're abroad) if your card is lost, but you're better off calling the number of your issuing bank, since MasterCard and Visa usually just transfer you to your bank; your bank's number is usually printed on your card.

Major credit cards (American Express not as often) are accepted at most hotels, large stores, and restaurants.

Reporting Lost Cards American Express (☎ 202/5672–404 in Cairo, or 336/393–1111 collect from abroad ⊕ www.americanexpress. com). **Diners Club** (☎ 800/234–6377 in the U.S. or 303/799–1504 collect from abroad ⊕ www.dinersclub.com). **MasterCard** (☎ 800/627–8372 in the U.S. or 636/722–7111 collect from abroad ⊕ www.mastercard. com). **Visa** (☎ 800/847–2911 in the U.S. or 410/581–9994 collect from abroad ⊕ www. visa.com).

CURRENCY AND EXCHANGE

The Egyptian pound (£E) is divided into 100 piastres (pt). Bank notes currently in circulation are the following: 10pt, 25pt, and 50pt notes; £E1, £E5, £E10, £E20, £E50, and £E100 notes. There are also 5pt, 10pt, 20pt, 25pt, 50pt, and £E1 coins, the latter two being the most common. Don't accept any dog-eared bills, as many vendors will refuse to take them.

Just politely give it back and ask for a replacement.

You should change money into Egyptian pounds, as most places do not accept foreign currency, with the exception of crowded tourist areas. Beware that when vendors do accept foreign currency, you will probably not get a fair rate of exchange. At this writing, the exchange rate was approximately £E5.6 to US$1.

You can find currency-exchange offices at all airports and most major hotels, as well as on the street, and in major shopping areas throughout the island. A passport is usually required to cash traveler's checks. Save some of the official receipts you are given with your transaction. If you end up with too many Egyptian pounds when you are ready to leave the country, you may need to show the receipts when you exchange the pounds for dollars since they are not convertible outside of Egypt. Hotels provide exchange services, but, as a rule, offer less favorable exchange rates.

Google does currency conversion. Just type in the amount you want to convert and an explanation of how you want it converted (e.g., "14 Swiss francs in dollars"), and then voilà. **Oanda.com** also allows you to print out a handy table with the current day's conversion rates. **XE.com** is another good currency conversion Web site.

Conversion sites Google (⊕ *www.google. com*). **Oanda.com** (⊕ *www.oanda.com*). **XE.com** (⊕ *www.xe.com*).

TRAVELER'S CHECKS

Traveler's checks can still be converted into local currency and in Egypt (unlike some other destinations) can still provide a reliable back-up. Since American Express is one of the world's largest providers of traveler's checks and has offices in all major tourist destinations, it is the company of choice for most travelers. It can be difficult to exchange traveler's checks in banks, and traveler's checks are rarely accepted as payment by even major hotels.

Contacts American Express (☎ *888/412–6945 in the U.S., 801/945–9450 collect outside of the U.S. to add value or speak to customer service* ⊕ *www.americanexpress.com*).

▌PACKING

The key to packing for a trip to Egypt is to focus on lightweight and practical items for daytime sightseeing. Cottons, linens, and moisture-wicking fabrics make the most sensible choices for the heat. Egypt is an Islamic country, albeit a more open society than some in the Middle East, but attitudes toward dress are still more conservative than in the United States, particularly with regard to women's attire. The clientele in Cairo's upmarket hotels and nightclubs tend to dress up. Resort towns on the Red Sea are the exception; foreign women are more or less free to dress how they want.

It's important that all travelers—but particularly women—not expose too much flesh. Pack T-shirts with sleeves that end between shoulder and elbow rather than tank tops or those with spaghetti straps. Many women wear light scarves to cover their necks and shoulders; these can be bought cheaply on the street or in bazaars. Long shorts and Capri pants are fine for women, but full-length pants are better. Skirts should be at least knee length. Short shorts and short skirts will cause stares; moreover, to visit churches and mosques in Egypt women must have shoulders and knees covered. In mosques you'll also need to cover your hair, so if you don't want to use a scarf supplied by the mosque, carry your own lightweight scarf.

For men, long shorts are acceptable when you're traveling on tours, but full-length lightweight pants are preferable and are especially recommended in Cairo and in the desert, where they offer more protection from the sun. Regular T-shirts are fine, but lightweight collared shirts help protect your neck and arms from the sun better. Only a few hotels require a jacket and tie (most notably the Sofitel Winter

Palace in Luxor), but men will be expected to wear long pants, collared shirts, and shoes (not sandals) in the evenings.

If you travel in winter, pack a fleece or a jacket for the cold evening air. This is especially true if you intend to overnight in the desert.

Beachwear is appropriate only around the pool or at upscale beaches. You may find visitors of other nationalities scantily dressed in hotel lobbies and even around town, but this is against local sensibilities.

Must packs: comfortable shoes, because you'll be walking a lot and climbing up and down rickety or badly set stairs into tombs; a hat, because the sun is hot at all times of year; sunglasses, because temple facades and rock faces are extremely bright in the daylight; and sunscreen to protect any exposed skin. Pharmacies in Egypt are well stocked. ■TIP→ Don't bother bringing expensive prescription medicine for intestinal upsets. Instead, buy Antinal, a locally available intestinal antibiotic that is commonly used to treat diarrhea, when you arrive in Egypt, and take a couple the moment you feel any problems. It's cheap (about $1.50), available in every pharmacy, and very effective. In more serious cases, a doctor or pharmacist can prescribe a stronger antibiotic, which will cost much less than at home.

Extra stuff that will be helpful includes: a small flashlight for visiting dimly lit tombs and temples; lightweight binoculars, to allow you a clearer view of monumental temple facades, and for bird-watching on the Nile; antibacterial gel, so that you can clean your hands before eating no matter where you are.

Except in the Western Desert, you can buy almost anything you need in the cities and main towns, from baby formula to feminine hygiene products and contact lens supplies, but prices may be more expensive than at home.

■ PASSPORTS AND VISAS

U.S. and EU citizens can buy tourist visas on arrival in Egypt at any Egyptian international airport; the process takes only a few minutes, and the windows selling visas are immediately before immigration (look to the left in Cairo). The current cost of a single-entry visa is $15 (payable in U.S. dollars, euros, or pounds sterling), and it is valid for two weeks. If you plan to stay longer you will have to apply at the Mogamma, a building that serves as the bureaucratic center of the country, located in Cairo across from the Egyptian Museum. The visa is often more expensive if you buy it in advance in your home country. You'll find a kiosk immediately before immigration in every major airport. All visitors must have at least six months validity on their passports to enter Egypt.

If you have booked through a tour operator or have arranged a transfer with your hotel, the representative will be waiting for you in the arrivals hall and will help with this process, but it's not complicated.

If you arrive in Egypt via Israel at Taba you will not be able to buy a full tourist visa at the border crossing. They will only issue a visa limiting you to the Sinai region; to get a tourist visa that allows you to travel to other parts of Egypt, you must visit the Egyptian Consulate in Eilat.

U.S. Passport Information U.S. Department of State (☎ 877/487–2778 ⊕ travel.state.gov/ passport).

■ RESTROOMS

Outside of five-star hotels, finding a clean restroom can be quite a challenge. For a safe bet go to a chain or fast-food restaurant, although some require that you make a purchase to use the restroom. Many women avoid public restrooms altogether, which is frustrating because the hot weather requires drinking plenty of water. Women should keep wipes on them to be safe. For men, finding a urinal is not so difficult, although the stench is sometimes unbearable. Public restrooms are rarely clean and often do not have toilet paper. There is also a problem with flushing toilet paper, so you will usually find a wastebasket for used paper. Most restaurants, bars, and hotels have a restroom attendant who should receive at least £E1, even if the area is not adequately clean. Tips are often their only source of income. Highway rest stops usually charge £E1 to use their facilities.

▌ SAFETY

Egypt has suffered a number of terrorist attacks in the past two decades; a spate of attacks in Luxor and Cairo in the mid-1990s, as well as bombings in the Sinai and in Cairo in 2004 and 2005. These attacks appear to have been undertaken by domestic terrorists whose purpose is to unsettle the government by hitting the tourist market (the country's biggest money earner) rather than part of a wider terrorist network.

The U.S. State Department advisory on Egypt gives clear advice on travel to these regions.

Security measures are in place to protect foreign travelers in Egypt. These include providing armed officers to travel with tourists, arranging visitors traveling by road into convoys, and ensuring that all hotels have guards and X-ray machines to check all incoming bags.

That said, the atmosphere in the streets and at attractions, cafés, and hotels is generally relaxed, with no threatening overtones. Most Egyptians are very welcoming of foreign visitors, and if you get a chance to chat with any Egyptians, they are usually very interested in finding out about you.

Violent crime against tourists in Egypt is very rare and even petty theft is at a low level compared to other international destinations. While robbery is unlikely, you are more likely to be ripped off by a taxi driver or a vendor who makes easy money from tourists who are poor hagglers. However, in Red Sea and Sinai resort areas where there are a lot of tourists, crime (particularly theft) is rising, and you should exhibit the same caution you would in any unfamiliar destination. Never leave items on the beach when you go for a swim. If you have a safe in your hotel room, use it.

You'll be approached for *baksheesh* (tip money) for almost anything (⇨ *Tipping*). Young kids will feel happy to say hello as you pass, then as you reply immediately open their hands for money. At major attractions, men may engage you in conversation as you cross a road then stop the traffic to ease your crossing—then demand a cash reward. One should always be mindful of the poverty of many households, but on the other hand, should you pay out for services that you did not specifically demand or even want? Don't feel obliged to hand over money if you don't feel that it has been earned.

Beware a young Egyptian male who attaches himself to your party as you explore the markets. He'll notice your interest and produce samples of bread or dates for you to try, then eventually will ask for "guiding" money. Another scam is to encourage you into a local shop in the pretence that it's only for tea and a chat, only to press a sale once you're seated and relaxed. But, remember too that these individuals are mixed in with hundreds of very genuine Egyptians who are willing to help for no reward except a chance to chat with a visitor and practice their English, so don't treat everyone with suspicion, just be aware that these approaches do happen.

Women may find themselves on the receiving end of attention from teenage boys and men. This attention is mainly blatant staring and some kind of opening gambit to engage you in conversation, but it can also include very inappropriate comments. This sort of behavior is best ignored. Assault is not common, but occasionally men will attempt to touch women. If this happens to you, do not stay silent. Shout, "Leave me alone" or "Stop that" loudly, and this should result in a chastened offender. Make it very clear you find this behavior offensive.

GOVERNMENT INFORMATION AND ADVISORIES

Advisories U.S. Department of State (⊕ *travel.state.gov*).

▌TAXES

There is no departure tax when you leave the country. On services such as hotel rooms, group travel, and car rental, a 10% tax is levied. Imported goods are highly taxed, but this is included in the ticketed sale price.

▌TIME

Egypt is two hours ahead of GMT. The country alters its daylight saving time each year so it is best to check the local time upon arrival.

▌TIPPING

Tipping, or *baksheesh,* is a way of life in Egypt. Everyone who performs some kind of service for you will expect some kind of monetary reward. This has become so engrained into Egyptian society that small children may come up and simply ask for money. Adults may engage you in conversation and then ask for a little *baksheesh* as you part company. Another ploy is to offer you a free gift, a small piece of alabaster or a scarab, then ask for a monetary "gift" in return. The amounts are small—£E1 is sufficient for restroom attendants, £E2 or £E3 is sufficient for most other small services—but it is up to you whether you feel obliged to hand over cash for such "services." Lots of households live very close to the poverty line in Egypt, and the dollar you hand over will have far more spending power in Luxor than in Los Angeles.

A 12% service charge is included in almost all restaurant bills. When in doubt, ask. Even then it's still expected that you will tip an extra 5% to 10% in cash (especially if you are using a credit card) if the service was to your liking. In hotels, it's customary to leave at least a dollar per day for the hotel maid. Taxi drivers don't expect a tip for short journeys around town, but you should tip if you engage a driver to take you to several attractions with waiting time, or book a driver for a day (add 10% to the agreed fee). Hotel porters expect at least $1.

▌TRIP INSURANCE

Comprehensive trip insurance is valuable if you're booking a very expensive or complicated trip (particularly to an isolated region) or if you're booking far in advance. Comprehensive policies typically cover trip cancellation and interruption, letting you cancel or cut your trip short because of illness, or, in some cases, acts of terrorism in your destination. Such policies might also cover evacuation and medical care. (For trips abroad you should have at least medical-only coverage. *See* ⇨ *Medical Insurance and Assistance under Health.*) Some also cover you for trip delays because of bad weather or mechanical problems as well as for lost or delayed luggage.

Another type of coverage to consider is financial default—that is, when your trip is disrupted because a tour operator, airline, or cruise line goes out of business. Generally you must buy this when you book your trip or shortly thereafter, and it's available to you only if your operator isn't on a list of excluded companies.

Always read the fine print of your policy to make sure that you're covered for the risks that most concern you. Compare several policies to be sure you're getting the best price and range of coverage available.

Insurance Comparison Info Insure My Trip (☏ *800/487–4722* ⊕ *www.insuremytrip.com*).

Square Mouth (☎ *800/240-0369* ⊕ *www. squaremouth.com*).

Comprehensive Insurers Access America (☎ *800/284-8300* ⊕ *www.accessamerica.com*). **AIG Travel Guard** (☎ *800/826-4919* ⊕ *www. travelguard.com*). **CSA Travel Protection** (☎ *800/873-9855* ⊕ *www.csatravelprotection. com*). **Travelex Insurance** (☎ *888/228-9792* ⊕ *www.travelex-insurance.com*). **Travel Insured International** (☎ *800/243-3174* ⊕ *www.travelinsured.com*).

▌ VISITOR INFORMATION

Before You Leave Egyptian Tourist Author-ity (☎ *212/332-2570 in New York City, 323/653-8961 in Los Angeles, 312/280-4666 in Chicago* ⊕ *www.egypt.travel*).

In Egypt Ministry of Tourism (✉ *Misr Travel Tower, Maydan Abbassiya, Downtown, Cairo* ☎ *02/285-4509*).

ONLINE RESOURCES

Egypt Today (⊕ *www.egypttoday.com*) is an English-language current affairs and culture magazine covering a range of issues. **Go Red Sea** (⊕ *www.goredsea.com*) has useful back-ground information about the main Red Sea resorts and a booking engine for hotels and travel packages.

Guardian's Egypt (⊕ *www.guardians.net*) brings together information and news about Egypt and Egyptology. **History for Kids** (⊕ *www.historyforkids.org*) has helpful, simple information to help your kids understand what they'll see on their trip. **State Information Service** (⊕ *www.sis.gov.eg*) has information about a range of issues from politics to travel to culture, issued by the Egyptian govern-ment. **TourEgypt** (⊕ *www.touregypt.net*) is the official site of the Egyptian Ministry of Tourism, which provides lots of information about the country, as well as comprehensive history of pharaonic Egypt.

INDEX

PHOTO CREDITS

NOTES

ABOUT OUR WRITERS

Lindsay Bennett has written or contributed to more than 40 travel guides on destinations aruond, from the little-explored wilderness destination to the fashionable urban metropolis, and her passion for setting out to far horizons is as fresh as ever. She often works in tandem with her husband, **Pete Bennett**, who is also a renowned destination and lifestyle photographer. Egypt is an enduring favorite. Though still entranced by the majesty of the ancient monuments, the couple are also happy relaxing over a glass of tea or two at a street-side café in Cairo, Alexandria, or Siwa and soaking up the rich atmosphere of 21st-century Egyptian life. Lindsay and Pete divide their time between their homes in the UK and France, hotel rooms around the world, and journeys in their 34-foot-long Winnebago.

Andrew Bossone is a journalist in the Middle East. He has been a contributor for National Geographic News and the Economist Intelligence Unit, and a video producer for Reuters VCSS. While based in Cairo he worked for several local Egyptian publications including *Al-Masry Al-Youm, ICT Business,* and *Business Today.* He has a master's degree from the Medill School of Journalism at Northwestern University and a bachelor's degree from the School of Communications and Theater at Temple University.

Sara Lafleur-Vetter grew up in small towns outside of Philadelphia, PA rifling through old *National Geographic* magazines and dreaming of far-away places. Since then she has graduated from Reed College with a degree in Russian and Anthropology and traveled to Europe, Central Asia, Russia, and Africa in search of poignant photographs and stories. For more information, check our her Web site: ⊕ *www. saralafleur.com.*

Cam McGrath is a Canadian journalist and travel writer based in Cairo. He is the Egypt correspondent of IPS News and a regular contributor to CNN Traveller and The Middle East.

A native of Boston, **Chip Rossetti** worked for a number of years as an editor in New York, while learning Arabic in the evenings. He first visited Egypt in 2003, and moved there in 2005 to work at the American University in Cairo Press. He is a translator of Arabic fiction, and has written for *Saudi Aramco World* magazine and *National Geographic.* He holds a BA in Classics from Harvard and is currently a doctoral candidate in modern Arabic literature at the University of Pennsylvania.

Texan by birth, Egyptian by marriage, and Chicagoan by way of a story that's too long to unravel here, **Toni Salama** is an award-winning travel journalist of national distinction. During her many trips to Egypt, the former staff travel writer, photographer, and online videographer for the *Chicago Tribune* has developed an enduring passion for the county's rich contemporary culture that equals her admiration for Egypt's matchless antiquities.